T0202633

Lecture Notes in Computer Science 13790

Advanced Research in Computing and Software Science
Subline of Lecture Notes in Computer Science

More information about this series at https://link.springer.com/bookseries/558

Gagandeep Singh · Caterina Urban (Eds.)

Static Analysis

29th International Symposium, SAS 2022
Auckland, New Zealand, December 5–7, 2022
Proceedings

 Springer

Editors
Gagandeep Singh
VMware Research and University of Illinois
Urbana-Champaign
Urbana, IL, USA

Caterina Urban
Inria and ENS/PSL
Paris, France

ISSN 0302-9743   ISSN 1611-3349 (electronic)
Lecture Notes in Computer Science
ISBN 978-3-031-22307-5   ISBN 978-3-031-22308-2 (eBook)
https://doi.org/10.1007/978-3-031-22308-2

Preface

This volume contains the proceedings of the 29th edition of the International Static Analysis Symposium, SAS 2022, held during December 5–7, 2022, in Auckland, New Zealand. The conference was a co-located event of SPLASH, the ACM SIGPLAN conference on Systems, Programming, Languages, and Applications: Software for Humanity. Travel restrictions as a result of the COVID-19 pandemic forced us to organize the conference in a hybrid form.

Static analysis is widely recognized as a fundamental tool for program verification, bug detection, compiler optimization, program understanding, and software maintenance. The series of Static Analysis Symposia has served as the primary venue for the presentation of theoretical, practical, and application advances in the area. Previous symposia were held in Chicago, Porto, Freiburg, New York, Edinburgh, Saint-Malo, Munich, Seattle, Deauville, Venice, Perpignan, Los Angeles, Valencia, Kongens Lyngby, Seoul, London, Verona, San Diego, Madrid, Paris, Santa Barbara, Venice, Pisa, Paris, Aachen, Glasgow, and Namur.

SAS 2022 called for papers on topics including, but not limited to, abstract interpretation, automated deduction, data flow analysis, debugging techniques, deductive methods, emerging applications, model checking, data science, program optimizations and transformations, program synthesis, program verification, machine learning and verification, security analysis, tool environments and architectures, theoretical frameworks, type checking, and distributed or networked systems. Besides the regular papers, the authors were encouraged to submit short submissions in the NEAT category to discuss experiences with static analysis tools, industrial reports, and case studies, along with tool papers, brief announcements of work in progress, well-motivated discussions of new questions or new areas, etc. Authors were encouraged to submit artifacts accompanying their papers to strengthen evaluations and the reproducibility of results.

The conference employed a double-blind reviewing process with an author response period, supported on EasyChair. This year, SAS had 48 submitted papers (43 regular and five NEAT). Of these, five were desk rejected due to not being in scope for SAS. The Program Committee used a two-round review process, where each remaining submission received at least three first-round reviews, which the authors could then respond to. The author response period was followed by a two-week Program Committee discussion where consensus was reached on the papers to be accepted, after a thorough assessment of the relevance and the quality of the work. Overall, 18 papers were accepted for publication (16 regular and two NEAT) and appear in this volume. The submitted papers were authored by researchers around the world: Canada, China, France, Germany, India, Israel, Italy, Singapore, the UK, the USA, and several other countries.

We view the artifacts as being equally important for the success and development of static analysis as the written papers. It is important for researchers to be able to independently reproduce experiments, which is greatly facilitated by having the original artifacts available. Marc Chevalier, the artifact committee chair, set up the artifact committee. In line with SAS 2021, the authors could submit either the Docker or Virtual Machine images as artifacts. A public archival repository for the artifacts is available on Zenodo, hosted at https://zenodo.org/communities/sas-2022. The artifacts have badges awarded at three levels: Validated (correct functionality), Extensible (with source code), and Available (on the Zenodo repository). The artwork for the badges is by Arpita Biswas (Harvard University) and Suvam Mukherjee (Microsoft). SAS 2022 had 16 valid artifact submissions, of which one was desk rejected as the authors did not submit a valid artifact. The review process for the artifacts was similar to those for the papers. Each artifact was evaluated by three members of the artifact evaluation committee, and eight out of 15 valid artifacts were accepted.

In addition to the contributed papers, SAS 2022 also featured three invited talks by distinguished researchers: Suguman Bansal (Georgia Tech, USA), Bernhard Scholz (University of Sydney, Australia), and Nengkun Yu (University of Technology Sydney, Australia). The Program Committee also selected the recipient of the Radhia Cousot Young Researcher Best Paper Award, given to a paper with a significant contribution from a student. This award was instituted in memory of Radhia Cousot, for her fundamental contributions to static analysis and having been one of the main promoters and organizers of the SAS series of conferences.

The SAS program would not have been possible without the efforts of many people. We thank them all. The members of the Program Committee, the artifact evaluation committee, and the external reviewers worked tirelessly to select a strong program, offering constructive and helpful feedback to the authors in their reviews. The organizing committee of SPLASH 2022, chaired by Alex Potanin (Australian National University, Australia), and the hybridization committee, chaired by Jonathan Aldrich (CMU, USA) and Youyou Kong (Tokyo Institute of Technology, Japan), were tremendously helpful in navigating the conference through these difficult times. The SAS steering committee provided much-needed support and advice. Finally, we thank Springer for their support of this event as well as for publishing these proceedings.

October 2022

Caterina Urban
Gagandeep Singh

Organization

Program Committee Chairs

Gagandeep Singh   VMware Research and UIUC, USA
Caterina Urban   Inria and ENS|PSL, France

Steering Committee

Bor-Yuh Evan Chang   University of Colorado Boulder, USA
Patrick Cousot   New York University, USA
Cezara Dragoi   Inria and ENS|PSL and Informal Systems, France
Kedar Namjoshi   Nokia Bell Labs, USA
David Pichardie   Meta, France
Andreas Podelski   University of Freiburg, Germany
Francesco Ranzato   University of Padua, Italy
Mihaela Sighireanu   ENS Paris-Saclay, France

Program Committee

Sebastien Bardin   CEA-List, France
Liqian Chen   National University of Defense Technology, China
Patrick Cousot   New York University, USA
Arlen Cox   IDA and CCS, USA
Dana Drachsler Cohen   Technion, Israel
Jerome Feret   Inria and ENS|PSL, France
Pietro Ferrara   Ca' Foscari University of Venice, Italy
Roberto Giacobazzi   University of Verona, Italy
Kihong Heo   KAIST, South Korea
Paddy Krishnan   Oracle Labs, Australia
Isabella Mastroeni   University of Verona, Italy
Antoine Miné   Sorbonne Université, France
Raphaël Monat   Sorbonne Université, France
David Monniaux   CNRS and VERIMAG, France
Jorge A. Navas   SRI International, USA
Francesco Ranzato   University of Padua, Italy
Daniel Schoepe   Amazon, UK
Mihaela Sighireanu   ENS Paris-Saclay, France
Manu Sridharan   University of California, Riverside, USA
Benno Stein   Meta, USA
Laura Titolo   National Institute of Aerospace, USA

Artifact Evaluation Chair

Marc Chevalier   Snyk, Switzerland

Artifact Evaluation Committee

Vincenzo Arceri	University of Parma, Italy
Anna Becchi	Fondazione Bruno Kessler, Italy
Dorra Ben Khalifa	Université de Perpignan, France
Denis Bueno	Sandia National Laboratories, USA
Marco Campion	University of Verona, Italy
Madhurima Chakraborty	University of California, Riverside, USA
Christiane Goltz	Snyk, Switzerland
Kai Jia	MIT, USA
Sifis Lagouvardos	University of Athens, Greece
Jacob Laurel	UIUC, USA
Denis Mazzucato	Inria and ENS|PSL, France
Luca Negrini	Corvallis Srl and Ca' Foscari University of Venice, Italy
Vivek Notani	University of Verona, Italy
Luca Olivieri	University of Verona, Italy
Francesco Parolini	Sorbonne Université, France
Ilina Stoilkovska	Amazon, UK

Additional Reviewers

Christophe Alias   Victor Nicolet
Vincenzo Arceri   Rei Odaira
Roberto Blanco   Andreas Pavlogiannis
Loris D'Antoni   Quentin Stievenart
Stefania Dumbrava   Marco Zanella
Pierre Karpman   Linpeng Zhang
Yi Lu

Contents

Invited Talks

Specification-Guided Reinforcement Learning

Suguman Bansal[✉]

Georgia Institute of Technology, Atlanta, USA
suguman@seas.upenn.edu

Abstract. The problem of reinforcement learning (RL) is to generate an optimal policy w.r.t. a given task in an unknown environment. Traditionally, the task is encoded in the form of a reward function which becomes cumbersome for long-horizon goals. An appealing alternate is to use logical specifications, opening the direction of RL from logical specifications. This paper summarizes the trials and triumphs in developing highly performant algorithms and obtain theoretical guarantees in RL from logical specifications.

1 Introduction

The problem of *Reinforcement Learning* (RL) is to generate a policy for a given task in an unknown environment by continuously interacting with it [30]. When combined with neural-networks (NN), RL has made remarkable strides in control synthesis in real-world domains, including challenging continuous (infinite-state) environments with non-linear dynamics or unknown models. Few examples include tasks such as walking [6] and grasping [3], control of multi-agent systems [17,21,26], and control from visual inputs [23].

Yet, current RL approaches are poorly suited for control synthesis for long-horizon tasks. A critical challenge facing RL is that the desired task is encoded in the form of a reward. Specifying a long-horizon task in the form of a reward can be highly non-intuitive; Poor reward specification could hinder the performance and correctness of the learning algorithm. An appealing alternative is to express the task in the form of a high-level logical specification, such as a temporal logic [8,9,19,27], as opposed to a reward function. Logical specifications combine temporal operators with boolean connectives, enabling more natural encoding of a large class of desirable properties. Furthermore, logical specifications facilitate testing and verification, which could be used to rigorously evaluate the correctness of the learned policy.

This paper provides a brief overview of recent progress in RL from logical specifications. Formally, the problem is to learn a policy that optimizes the probability to satisfy the given specification in an environment modeled by a *Markov Decision Processs (MDP)*. The defining assumption in RL is that the transition probabilities of the MDP are unknown. Thus, the policy is learnt via

G. Singh and C. Urban (Eds.): SAS 2022, LNCS 13790, pp. 3–9, 2022.
https://doi.org/10.1007/978-3-031-22308-2_1

exploration via repeated sampling of the environment. We briefly summarize performance of existing algorithms and known theoretical guarantees[1].

2   Reinforcement Learning from Logical Specifications

Markov Decision Process. A Markov Decision Process (MDP) is a tuple $M = (S, A, \eta, P)$, where S is a set of states, $\eta : S \to [0,1]$ is the initial state distribution, A is a finite set of actions, and $P : S \times A \times S \to [0,1,]$ is the transition probability function with $\Sigma_{s' \in S} P(s, a, s') = 1$ for all $s \in S$.

An infinite run $\zeta \in (S \times A)^\omega$ is the sequence $\zeta = s_0, a_0, s_1, a_1 \ldots$, where $s_0 \sim \eta$ and $P(s_i, a_i, s_{i+1}) > 0$ for all $i \geq 0$. Similarly, a finite run $\zeta \in (S \times A)^* \times S$ is a sequence $\zeta = s_0, a_0, s_1, a_1 \ldots a_{t-1} s_t$. For any run of length at least j, we let $\zeta_{i:j} = s_i, a_i, \ldots a_{j-1}, s_j$ be a sub-sequence of ζ for $i, j \in \mathbb{N}$.

Let Runs_f denote the set of all finite runs in the MDP. Let $D(A) = \{\Delta : A \to [0,1] \text{ s.t. } \Sigma_{a \in A} \Delta(a) = 1\}$ be the set of all distributions on actions A. Then, a policy $\pi : \mathsf{Runs}_f \to D(A)$ maps a history of finite runs to a distribution on actions. Let Π denote the set of all policies.

Task Specifications. There are different ways in which one can specify the objective of the learning algorithm. We define a *reinforcement learning task* to be a pair (M, ϕ) where M is an MDP and ϕ is a specification for M. In general, a specification ϕ for $M = (S, A, s_0, P)$ defines a function $J_\phi^M : \Pi(S, A) \to \mathbb{R}$ and the reinforcement learning objective is to compute a policy π that maximizes $J_\phi^M(\pi)$. Below, we define RL tasks traditionally using rewards and using logical specifications.

Discounted-Sum Rewards. Traditionally, the specifications is a reward function that maps transitions in M to real values. The specification consists of a reward function $R : S \times A \times S \to \mathbb{R}$ and a discount factor $\gamma \in]0,1[$—i.e., $\phi = (R, \gamma)$. The value of a policy π is

$$J_\phi^M(\pi) = \mathbb{E}_{\zeta \sim D_\pi^M} \left[\sum_{i=0}^\infty \gamma^i R(s_i, a_i, s_{i+1}) \right],$$

where s_i and a_i denote the state and the action at the ith step of ζ, respectively. Limit-average instead of discounted-sum is also commonly used.

Logical Specifications. Rewards are defined w.r.t. a given set of states S and actions A, and can only be interpreted over MDPs with the same state and action spaces. Logical specifications are defined independently of S and A. To achieve this, a common assumption is that there is a fixed set of propositions Prop, and a labeling function $L : S \to 2^{\mathsf{Prop}}$ denoting which propositions hold in a given state.

---

[1] Parts of the paper is based on joint work with Rajeev Alur, Osbert Bastani, and Kishor Jothimurugan.

Given a run $\zeta = s_0 a_0 s_1 a_1 \ldots$, we let $L(\zeta)$ denote the corresponding sequence of labels $L(\zeta) = L(s_0)L(s_1)\ldots$. A *labeled MDP* is a tuple $M = (S, A, s_0, P, L)$. Wlog, we only consider labeled MDPs in the rest of the paper.

Formal languages are used to specify qualitative properties about runs of the system. A logical specification $\phi = \mathcal{L} \subseteq (2^{\mathsf{Prop}})^\omega$ is a set of "desirable" sequences of labels. The value of a policy π is the probability of generating a sequence in $\mathcal{L}$—i.e.,

$$J_\phi^M(\pi) = D_\pi^M(\{\zeta \in \mathsf{Runs}(S, A) \mid L(\zeta) \in \mathcal{L}\}).$$

Examples of logical specifications are reachability properties, safety properties, and temporal logics such as LTL [27], LTL over finite-traces [8], or SpectRL [19].

Reinforcement Learning. Given an RL task (M, ϕ), assuming the transition probabilities of M are unknown, the problem of RL is to generate a policy

$$\pi^* = \arg\max_{\pi \in \Pi} J_\phi^M(\pi).$$

3   Algorithms

Recently, a myriad of algorithms have been proposed for learning from logical specifications [1,4,5,7,10,12,14–16,18,24,31,32,34]. These methods can be categorized into two broad classes, as described below:

Specification to Rewards. Many early works on RL from logical specifications took a natural approach to solve the problem. Here, the goal is to automatically synthesize rewards from a given formal specification and then to use a traditional RL algorithm to learn an optimal policy from the synthesized rewards. The simplest reward function would be to assign a positive reward to executions that satisfy the specification and a zero reward to the rest. This naive reward function results in poor performance of the learning algorithm due to the sparsity of rewards. Thus, most algorithms are modified to provide informative intermediate rewards that also guide the search of an optimal policy. Few methods include policy-preserving reward shaping and rewards based on distance metrics.

Mostly, these algorithms demonstrate merit in learning *stateful policies*. For example, if the task was to learn to return to the initial state after visiting a goal, then the movement of the agent along the path connecting the initial state to the goal state depends on whether the goal has been visited or not. Since most specification-to-reward conversion schemes are *stateful*, such information automatically gets encoded in the learnt policy. By and large, these methods have shown to learn high-quality policies in finite-state environments, and for simple tasks in infinite-state environments.

Compositional Algorithm. These methods build on early progress of naïve approach of converting specifications to rewards with the objective to scale to complex long-horizon specifications in complex infinite-state environments. An example of a task that proves to be too complex for early works is illustrated in

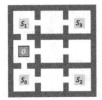

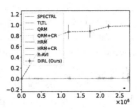

(achieve (reach S_1) or achieve (reach S_2);
achieve (reach S_3)) ensuring avoid O

Fig. 1. Left: The 9-rooms environment, with initial region S_0 in the bottom-left, an obstacle O in the middle-left, and three subgoal regions S_1, S_2, S_3 in the remaining corners. Middle: A user-provided specification ϕ. Right: Learning curves for compositional approach DiRL [20] and some baselines; x-axis is number of steps and y-axis is probability of achieving ϕ.

Fig. 1. Specification-to-reward based approaches fail on such examples due to the inherent greedy nature of RL algorithms. In this example, the algorithms learn to reach S_2 instead of S_1 as the former is easier to learn due to the absence of any obstacle. However, this is not fruitful towards satisfaction of the original specification as there is no direct path from S_2 to S_3.

Compositional approaches for learning from specifications leverage the structure of a given specification to first decompose the original task into several simpler and easier-to-learn tasks and then compose the policies learnt for these subtasks to obtain a policy that maximizes satisfaction of the original specification. This way these algorithms combine planning on the high-specification with learning on low-level tasks to scale to large and complex specifications. The structure of the specification could be exploited further for significant improvements in the performance of learning algorithms along the metrics of scalability in specification, sample complexity, and quality of solutions.

4   Theoretical Guarantees

We present the theoretical foundations of RL from logical specifications. The formal guarantees associated with the specification-to-reward approach of learning algorithms have been studied [11,13,28]. We will discuss PAC learning in the context of RL from logical specifications. We then discuss recent results [2,33] showing that PAC algorithms do not exist for Linear Temporal Logic (LTL) specifications and present a high-level overview of a proof.

For this section, we assume an MDP is has finitely many states S and actions A, and there is a unique initial state s_0, i.e., $\eta(s_0) = 1$ and $\eta(s) = 0$ for all $s \in S \setminus \{s_0\}$. A learning algorithm $\mathcal{A}$ can be thought of as an iterative process that in each iteration (i) either resets the MDP state to an initial state or takes a step in M, and (ii) outputs its current estimate of an optimal policy π. A learning algorithm $\mathcal{A}$ induces a random sequence of output policies $\{\pi_n\}_{n=1}^{\infty}$ where π_n is the policy output in the nth iteration.

Let $\mathcal{J}^*(M, \phi) = \sup_\pi J_\phi^M(\pi)$ denote the maximum value of J_ϕ^M. We let $\Pi_{opt}(M, \phi)$ denote the set of all optimal policies in M w.r.t. ϕ—i.e.,

$\Pi_{opt}(M, \phi) = \{\pi | J_\phi^M(\pi) = \mathcal{J}^*(M, \phi)\}$. In many cases, it is sufficient to compute an ε-optimal policy $\tilde{\pi}$ with $J_\phi^M(\tilde{\pi}) \geq \mathcal{J}^*(M, \phi) - \varepsilon$; we let $\Pi_{opt}^\varepsilon(M, \phi)$ denote the set of all ε-optimal policies in M w.r.t. ϕ.

Definition 1. *A learning algorithm $\mathcal{A}$ is said to be PAC-MDP for a class of specifications $\mathcal{C}$ if, there is a function h such that for any $p > 0$, $\varepsilon > 0$, and any RL task (M, ϕ) with $M = (S, A, s_0, P)$ and $\phi \in \mathcal{C}$, taking $N = h(|S|, |A|, |\phi|, \frac{1}{p}, \frac{1}{\varepsilon})$, with probability at least $1 - p$, we have*

$$\left| \left\{ n \mid \pi_n \notin \Pi_{opt}^\varepsilon(M, \phi) \right\} \right| \leq N.$$

We say a PAC-MDP algorithm is *efficient* if the *sample complexity* function h is polynomial in $|S|, |A|, \frac{1}{p}$ and $\frac{1}{\varepsilon}$. There are efficient PAC-MDP algorithms for discounted-sum rewards [22,29]. Unfortunately, we show that that it is not possible to obtain PAC-MDP algorithms for safety specifications.

Theorem 1 [2]. *There does not exist a PAC-MDP algorithm for the class of safety specifications.*

Intuitively, Theorem 1 follows from that fact that, when learning from simulation, it is highly likely that the learning algorithm will encounter identical transitions when the underlying MDP is modified slightly. This makes it impossible to infer an ε-optimal policy using a number of samples that is independent of the transition probabilities since safety specifications are not robust [25]. For a full proof, see [2].

References

1. Aksaray, D., Jones, A., Kong, Z., Schwager, M., Belta, C.: Q-learning for robust satisfaction of signal temporal logic specifications. In: Conference on Decision and Control (CDC), pp. 6565–6570. IEEE (2016)
2. Alur, R., Bansal, S., Bastani, O., Jothimurugan, K.: A framework for transforming specifications in reinforcement learning. https://arxiv.org/abs/2111.00272 (2021)
3. Andrychowicz, O.M., et al.: Learning dexterous in-hand manipulation. Int. J. Rob. Res. **39**(1), 3–20 (2020)
4. Bozkurt, A.K., Wang, Y., Zavlanos, M.M., Pajic, M.: Control synthesis from linear temporal logic specifications using model-free reinforcement learning. In: 2020 IEEE International Conference on Robotics and Automation (ICRA), pp. 10349–10355. IEEE (2020)
5. Brafman, R., De Giacomo, G., Patrizi, F.: Ltlf/ldlf non-markovian rewards. In: Proceedings of the AAAI Conference on Artificial Intelligence, vol. 32 (2018)
6. Collins, S., Ruina, A., Tedrake, R., Wisse, M.: Efficient bipedal robots based on passive-dynamic walkers. Science **307**(5712), 1082–1085 (2005)
7. De Giacomo, G., Iocchi, L., Favorito, M., Patrizi, F.: Foundations for restraining bolts: reinforcement learning with ltlf/ldlf restraining specifications. In: Proceedings of the International Conference on Automated Planning and Scheduling, vol. 29, pp. 128–136 (2019)

8. De Giacomo, G., Vardi, M.Y.: Linear temporal logic and linear dynamic logic on finite traces. In: IJCAI 2013 Proceedings of the Twenty-Third International Joint Conference on Artificial Intelligence, pp. 854–860. Association for Computing Machinery (2013)

9. Donzé, A.: On signal temporal logic. In: Legay, A., Bensalem, S. (eds.) RV 2013. LNCS, vol. 8174, pp. 382–383. Springer, Heidelberg (2013). https://doi.org/10.1007/978-3-642-40787-1_27

10. Fu, J., Topcu, U.: Probably approximately correct MDP learning and control with temporal logic constraints. In: Robotics: Science and Systems (2014)

11. Hahn, E.M., Perez, M., Schewe, S., Somenzi, F., Trivedi, A., Wojtczak, D.: Reward shaping for reinforcement learning with omega-regular objectives. arXiv preprint arXiv:2001.05977 (2020)

12. Hahn, E.M., Perez, M., Schewe, S., Somenzi, F., Trivedi, A., Wojtczak, D.: Omega-regular objectives in model-free reinforcement learning. In: Tools and Algorithms for the Construction and Analysis of Systems, pp. 395–412 (2019)

13. Hahn, E.M., Perez, M., Schewe, S., Somenzi, F., Trivedi, A., Wojtczak, D.: Omega-regular objectives in model-free reinforcement learning. In: Vojnar, T., Zhang, L. (eds.) TACAS 2019. LNCS, vol. 11427, pp. 395–412. Springer, Cham (2019). https://doi.org/10.1007/978-3-030-17462-0_27

14. Hasanbeig, M., Kantaros, Y., Abate, A., Kroening, D., Pappas, G.J., Lee, I.: Reinforcement learning for temporal logic control synthesis with probabilistic satisfaction guarantees. In: Conference on Decision and Control (CDC), pp. 5338–5343 (2019)

15. Hasanbeig, M., Abate, A., Kroening, D.: Logically-constrained reinforcement learning. arXiv preprint arXiv:1801.08099 (2018)

16. Icarte, R.T., Klassen, T., Valenzano, R., McIlraith, S.: Using reward machines for high-level task specification and decomposition in reinforcement learning. In: International Conference on Machine Learning, pp. 2107–2116. PMLR (2018)

17. Inala, J.P., et al.: Neurosymbolic transformers for multi-agent communication. arXiv preprint arXiv:2101.03238 (2021)

18. Jiang, Y., Bharadwaj, S., Wu, B., Shah, R., Topcu, U., Stone, P.: Temporal-logic-based reward shaping for continuing learning tasks (2020)

19. Jothimurugan, K., Alur, R., Bastani, O.: A composable specification language for reinforcement learning tasks. Adv. Neural Inf. Process. Syst. **32** (2019)

20. Jothimurugan, K., Bansal, S., Bastani, O., Alur, R.: Compositional reinforcement learning from logical specifications. Adv. Neural Inf. Process. Syst. **34**, 10026–10039 (2021)

21. Jothimurugan, K., Bansal, S., Bastani, O., Alur, R.: Specification-guided learning of nash equilibria with high social welfare (2022)

22. Kearns, M., Singh, S.: Near-optimal reinforcement learning in polynomial time. Mach. Learn. **49**(2), 209–232 (2002)

23. Levine, S., Finn, C., Darrell, T., Abbeel, P.: End-to-end training of deep visuomotor policies. J. Mach. Learn. Res. **17**(1), 1334–1373 (2016)

24. Li, X., Vasile, C.I., Belta, C.: Reinforcement learning with temporal logic rewards. In: IEEE/RSJ International Conference on Intelligent Robots and Systems (IROS), pp. 3834–3839. IEEE (2017)

25. Littman, M.L., Topcu, U., Fu, J., Isbell, C., Wen, M., MacGlashan, J.: Environment-independent task specifications via GLTL. arXiv preprint arXiv:1704.04341 (2017)

26. Lowe, R., Wu, Y., Tamar, A., Harb, J., Abbeel, P., Mordatch, I.: Multi-agent actor-critic for mixed cooperative-competitive environments. arXiv preprint arXiv:1706.02275 (2017)

27. Pnueli, A.: The temporal logic of programs. In: 18th Annual Symposium on Foundations of Computer Science, pp. 46–57. IEEE (1977)
28. Somenzi, F., Trivedi, A.: Reinforcement learning and formal requirements. In: Zamani, M., Zufferey, D. (eds.) NSV 2019. LNCS, vol. 11652, pp. 26–41. Springer, Cham (2019). https://doi.org/10.1007/978-3-030-28423-7_2
29. Strehl, A.L., Li, L., Wiewiora, E., Langford, J., Littman, M.L.: PAC model-free reinforcement learning. In: Proceedings of the 23rd International Conference on Machine Learning, pp. 881–888 (2006)
30. Sutton, R.S., Barto, A.G.: Reinforcement Learning: An Introduction. MIT press, Cambridge (2018)
31. Vaezipoor, P., Li, A.C., Icarte, R.A.T., Mcilraith, S.A.: Ltl2action: generalizing ltl instructions for multi-task rl. In: International Conference on Machine Learning, pp. 10497–10508. PMLR (2021)
32. Xu, Z., Topcu, U.: Transfer of temporal logic formulas in reinforcement learning. In: International Joint Conference on Artificial Intelligence, pp. 4010–4018 (7 2019)
33. Yang, C., Littman, M.L., Carbin, M.: Reinforcement learning for general LTL objectives is intractable. CoRR abs/2111.12679 (2021). https://arxiv.org/abs/2111.12679
34. Yuan, L.Z., Hasanbeig, M., Abate, A., Kroening, D.: Modular deep reinforcement learning with temporal logic specifications. arXiv preprint arXiv:1909.11591 (2019)

Towards Efficient Reasoning of Quantum Programs

Nengkun Yu[(✉)]

Stony Brook University, Stony Brook, NY 11794, USA
nengkun.yu@stonybrook.edu

Abstract. Qubit is the basic unit of information in quantum computing. It takes exponential time in the number of qubits to simulate the evolution of general quantum programs. This fact makes simulation infeasible beyond 50 qubits on current supercomputers. This observation motivates us to use static techniques to understand larger programs. We will briefly overview our recent efforts to develop static methods for quantum programming.

Keywords: Quantum programs · Abstract interpretation · Efficient reasoning

1 First Section

The idea of quantum computing emerged in the 1980s:s: Feynman [20,21] noted that a classical computer requires exponential time and space to simulate the behaviour of an n-particle system that evolves according to the laws of quantum mechanics. One can regard the particles themselves as a *quantum computer* that appears to be exponentially more efficient. Benioff described the quantum model of Turing machines in [8]. Deutsch resolved how quantum gates can function like classical logical gates in [16,17].

Driven by a desire for great computational power, there have been significant efforts to build quantum computers. We will likely have quantum computers with hundreds of qubits by 2024 [23]. Besides the efforts from the hardware aspect, the software research for quantum computing also attracted lots of attention, including the design of quantum programming languages [4,25,29,33–35] and develop quantum programming platforms such as Scaffold [1], Quipper [22], QWIRE [30], Silq [10], Microsoft's LIQUi| [38] and Q# [36], Google's Cirq [37], and IBM's Qiskit [3]. Using these languages, researchers have implemented programs for variational quantum algorithms [28,32] applied to quantum chemistry [13], quantum machine learning [9], and quantum approximate optimization algorithms [5,19].

To show the quantum advantage in computation, we usually working with quantum programs with many qubits.

How to check that a quantum program satisfies key correctness criteria?

G. Singh and C. Urban (Eds.): SAS 2022, LNCS 13790, pp. 10–15, 2022.
https://doi.org/10.1007/978-3-031-22308-2_2

There are many many approaches for checking correctness of classical pro-grams. How do they carry over to quantum computing?

We may first look at dynamic techniques such as *simulation*. On the one hand, it is not feasible to simulate a quantum program with a quantum computer since we are still in the noisy intermediate-scale quantum (NISQ) era. On the other hand, it is also infeasible to simulate a general quantum program with current supercomputers because the simulation of a general quantum program with n qubits requires working with 2^n complex numbers. The number can go beyong the number of atoms in the known universe as the number n goes to 300.

Many works take static verification techniques into quantum programming [2]. Recent works have used Coq and why3 for checking the correctness of the proof for a variety of quantum programs by Hietala et al. [24] and by Chareton et al. [14]. The static techniques also include logical methods. Indeed, attempts to develop Hoare-like logic for verification of quantum programs have been made in a series of papers [2,6,7,12]. In particular, D'Hondt and Panangaden [18] proposed to use quantum observables as predicates of quantum programs. Based on this, they presented the the the notion of quantum weakest precondition. Ying [39] established quantum Hoare logic (QHL for short) for both partial correctness and total correctness with (relative) completeness:

$$\models \{P\}S\{Q\}$$

of a quantum program S are defined by an inequality between the expectations $tr(P\rho)$ and $tr(Q[\![S]\!](\rho))$ of precondition and postcondition observables P and Q in the input state ρ and the output state $[\![S]\!](\rho)$, respectively.

QHL is attractive because of its (relatively) completeness. However, there is an obvious gap between its theoretical characterization and practical use:

1. It is not friendly for testing purposes as measurements could destroy the quantum state.
2. It involves complicated matrix calculations.
3. It does not provide an interpretation of approximation.

The many mathematical properties of projections make them versatile for thinking about the correctness of quantum programs and resolving the above questions [11,26]. In [43], we employed projections for static verification. Later, we used projections for run-time verification in [27]. In [40], we used projections to define temporal logic for quantum programs.

we only consider a special class of quantum Hoare triples $\{P\}S\{Q\}$, where both precondition P and postcondition Q are projections, and all measurement in program S are projective.

There is a one-onto-one correspondence between the closed subspaces of a Hilbert space and projectors in it, and moreover, the inclusion between closed subspaces is coincident with the Löwner order between their projectors. The restriction to projective Hoare triples can significantly simplify the definition of their correctness.

Projective Hoare triple $\{P\}S\{Q\}$ is true in the sense of partial correctness in aQHL, written

$$\models^{\mathrm{a}} \{P\}S\{Q\},$$

if for all ρ:

$$\rho \models P \Rightarrow [\![S]\!](\rho) \models Q,$$

where we say that ρ satisfies P, written $\rho \models P$, if $\mathrm{supp}(\rho) \subseteq P$; that is, $P\rho = \rho$.

However, all those methods require exponential space, which limits scalability.

In [41], we break through the exponential barrier for deriving useful information about quantum programs. Our approach rests on a central idea:

Rather than focusing on the whole quantum state, we focus on parts.

Our notion of a *part* is a well-known and extensively used concept in quantum science: the *reduced density matrix*. Intuitively, a density matrix represents the whole quantum state, while a reduced density matrix can represent a part of the state. For example, a program with 20 qubits means that the state can be represented by 2^{20} complex numbers, we might track just 19 small $2^2 \times 2^2$ reduced density matrices that focus on the qubit pairs $\{1,2\}, \{2,3\}, \cdots, \{19,20\}$. For comparison, 2^{20} is about a million, while $19 \times 2^2 \times 2^2 = 304$. When the number of qubits grows beyond fifty, tracking the whole state becomes infeasible, while tracking reduced density matrices stays tractable.

Here is an analogy with static analysis of integer variables in classical computing. The full-density matrix is like a polyhedron that approximates the program variables' values. On the other hand, a tuple of reduced density matrices is like a tuple of polyhedra, each over a subset of those program variables.

We can approximate each reduced density matrix by a projection. This approximation enables us to define an abstract state as a tuple of projections. The rest is to define a notion of state transition between such abstract states, checked so we bring in abstract interpretation [15], which has been done mainly for classical computing.

Perdrix [31] presented an abstract interpretation of quantum programs that is sound but lacks a Galois connection between the concrete and abstract domains.

In [41], we present a new abstract interpretation of quantum programs. For our notion of abstract states, we present abstraction and concretization functions that form a Galois connection and use them to define abstract operations. Each abstract step first concretizes to a more fine-grained abstract domain, then does an abstract operation on that domain, and finally abstracts back to the original abstract domain. We avoid concretizing to the concrete domain where we would need exponential space.

Another method of reaching local reasoning is separation logic. In [42], we propose a model of the substructural logic of Bunched Implications that is suitable for reasoning about quantum states. In our model, the separating conjunction of BI describes separable quantum states. We develop a program logic where pre- and post-conditions are BI formulas representing quantum states-the program logic can be seen as a counterpart of separation logic for imperative quantum programs. Intuitively, we take the tensor product of two quantum states with disjoint domains, a quantum analogue of probabilistic independence, as separation.

References

1. Abhari, A.J., et al.: Scaffold: quantum programming language. Technical Report TR-934-12, Dept. of Computer Science, Princeton University NJ (2012). ftp://ftp.cs.princeton.edu/reports/2012/934.pdf
2. Akatov, D.: The Logic of Quantum Program Verification. Master's thesis, Oxford University Computing Laboratory (2005). http://www.academia.edu/download/7563948/thesis-1.1.ps
3. Aleksandrowicz, G., et al.: Qiskit: an open-source framework for quantum computing (2019). https://doi.org/10.5281/zenodo.2562110
4. Altenkirch, T., Grattage, J.: A functional quantum programming language. In: Proceedings of the 20th Annual IEEE Symposium on Logic in Computer Science (LICS 2005), pp. 249–258. IEEE (2005)
5. Arute, F., et al.: Quantum approximate optimization of non-planar graph problems on a planar superconducting processor (2020). https://arxiv.org/abs/2004.04197
6. Baltag, A., Smets, S.: The logic of quantum programs. In: Selinger, P. (ed.) Proceedings of the 2nd International Workshop on Quantum Programming Languages (QPL 2004), pp. 39–56 (2004)
7. Baltag, A., Smets, S.: LQP: the dynamic logic of quantum information. Math. Struct. Comput. Sci. $16(3)$, 491–525 (2006)
8. Benioff, P.: Computer as a physical system: a microscopic quantum mechanical hamiltonian model of computers represented by turing machines. J. Stat. Phys.; (United States) $22(5)$, 525–532 (1980)
9. Biamonte, J., Wittek, P., Pancotti, N., Rebentrost, P., Wiebe, N., Lloyd, S.: Quantum machine learning. Nature $549(7671)$, 195–202 (2017). https://doi.org/10.1038/nature23474
10. Bichsel, B., Baader, M., Gehr, T., Vechev, M.: Silq: a high-level quantum language with safe uncomputation and intuitive semantics. In: Proceedings of the 40th ACM SIGPLAN Conference on Programming Language Design and Implementation. PLDI 2020. ACM, New York (2020)
11. Birkhoff, G., Von Neumann, J.: The logic of quantum mechanics. Ann. Math. $37(4)$, 823–843 (1936)
12. Brunet, O., Jorrand, P.: Dynamic quantum logic for quantum programs. Int. J. Quant. Inf. $2(01)$, 45–54 (2004)
13. Cao, Y., et al.: Quantum chemistry in the age of quantum computing. Chem. Rev. $119(19)$, 10856–10915 (2019). pMID: 31469277
14. Chareton, C., Bardin, S., Bobot, F., Perrelle, V., Valiron, B.: An automated deductive verification framework for circuit-building quantum programs. In: ESOP 2021. LNCS, vol. 12648, pp. 148–177. Springer, Cham (2021). https://doi.org/10.1007/978-3-030-72019-3_6
15. Cousot, P., Cousot, R.: Abstract interpretation: a unified lattice model for static analysis of programs by construction or approximation of fixpoints. In: Fourth ACM Symposium on Principles of Programming Languages, pp. 238–252 (1977)

16. Deutsch, D.: Quantum theory, the church-turing principle and the universal quantum computer. Proc. Roy. Soc. Lond. Ser. A **400**(1818), 97–117 (1985)
17. Deutsch, D.: Quantum computational networks. Proc. Roy. Soc. Lond. Ser. A, Math. Phys. Sci. **425**(1868), 73–90 (1989). http://www.jstor.org/stable/2398494
18. D'hondt, E., Panangaden, P.: Quantum weakest preconditions. Math. Struct. Comput. Sci. **16**(3), 429–451 (2006)
19. Farhi, E., Goldstone, J., Gutmann, S.: A quantum approximate optimization algorithm (2014). https://arxiv.org/abs/1411.4028
20. Feynman, R.P.: Simulating physics with computers. Int. J. Theor. Phys. **21**, 467–488 (1982)
21. Feynman, R.P.: Quantum mechanical computers. Found. Phys. **16**, 507–531 (1986)
22. Green, A.S., Lumsdaine, P.L., Ross, N.J., Selinger, P., Valiron, B.: Quipper: a scalable quantum programming language. In: Proceedings of the 34th ACM SIGPLAN Conference on Programming Language Design and Implementation, PLDI 2013, pp. 333–342. ACM, New York (2013)
23. Grumbling, E., Horowitz, M.: Quantum computing: Progress and prospects. Tech. Rep. National Academies of Sciences, Engineering, and Medicine, The National Academies Press, Washington, D.C. (2019). https://doi.org/10.17226/25196
24. Hietala, K., Rand, R., Hung, S.H., Li, L., Hicks, M.: Proving quantum programs correct (2020). arXiv:2010.01240
25. Hietala, K., Rand, R., Hung, S.H., Wu, X., Hicks, M.: A verified optimizer for quantum circuits. No. POPL 2021 (2021)
26. Kalmbach, G.: Orthomodular Lattices, vol. 18. Academic Press, Cambridge (1983)
27. Li, G., Zhou, L., Yu, N., Ding, Y., Ying, M., Xie, Y.: Projection-based runtime assertions for testing and debugging quantum programs. Proc. ACM Program. Lang. **4**(OOPSLA) (2020)
28. McClean, J.R., Romero, J., Babbush, R., Aspuru-Guzik, A.: The theory of variational hybrid quantum-classical algorithms. New J. Phys. **18**(2), 023023 (2016)
29. Ömer, B.: Structured quantum programming. Ph.D. thesis, Institute for Theoretical Physics, Vienna University of Technology (2003)
30. Paykin, J., Rand, R., Zdancewic, S.: Qwire: a core language for quantum circuits. In: Proceedings of the 44th ACM SIGPLAN Symposium on Principles of Programming Languages, POPL 2017, pp. 846–858. ACM, New York (2017)
31. Perdrix, S.: Quantum entanglement analysis based on abstract interpretation. In: Alpuente, M., Vidal, G. (eds.) SAS 2008. LNCS, vol. 5079, pp. 270–282. Springer, Heidelberg (2008). https://doi.org/10.1007/978-3-540-69166-2_18
32. Peruzzo, A., et al.: A variational eigenvalue solver on a photonic quantum processor. Nat. Commun. **5**(1), 4213 (2014)
33. Sabry, A.: Modeling quantum computing in haskell. In: Proceedings of the 2003 ACM SIGPLAN Workshop on Haskell (2003)
34. Sanders, J.W., Zuliani, P.: Quantum programming. In: Backhouse, R., Oliveira, J.N. (eds.) MPC 2000. LNCS, vol. 1837, pp. 80–99. Springer, Heidelberg (2000). https://doi.org/10.1007/10722010_6
35. Selinger, P.: Towards a quantum programming language. Math. Struct. Comput. Sci. **14**(4), 527–586 (2004)
36. Svore, K., et al.: Q#: Enabling scalable quantum computing and development with a high-level dsl. In: Proceedings of the Real World Domain Specific Languages Workshop 2018, RWDSL 2018, pp. 7:1–7:10. ACM, New York (2018)
37. The Cirq Developers: quantumlib/cirq: A python framework for creating, editing, and invoking noisy intermediate scale quantum (nisq) circuits (2018). https://github.com/quantumlib/Cirq

38. Wecker, D., Svore, K.M.: Liqui|⟩: A software design architecture and domain-specific language for quantum computing (2014)
39. Ying, M.: Floyd-hoare logic for quantum programs. ACM Trans. Program. Lang. Syst. (TOPLAS) **33**(6), 19:1–19:49 (2011)
40. Yu, N.: Quantum temporal logic (2019)
41. Yu, N., Palsberg, J.: Quantum abstract interpretation. In: Proceedings of the 42nd ACM SIGPLAN International Conference on Programming Language Design and Implementation, PLDI 2021, pp. 542–558. Association for Computing Machinery, New York (2021). https://doi.org/10.1145/3453483.3454061
42. Zhou, L., Barthe, G., Hsu, J., Ying, M., Yu, N.: A quantum interpretation of bunched logic & quantum separation logic. In: 2021 36th Annual ACM/IEEE Symposium on Logic in Computer Science (LICS), pp. 1–14 (2021). https://doi.org/10.1109/LICS52264.2021.9470673
43. Zhou, L., Yu, N., Ying, M.: An applied quantum hoare logic. In: Proceedings of the 40th ACM SIGPLAN Conference on Programming Language Design and Implementation, PLDI 2019, pp. 1149–1162. ACM, New York (2019)

Regular Papers

Solving Invariant Generation
for Unsolvable Loops

Daneshvar Amrollahi, Ezio Bartocci, George Kenison[(⊠)], Laura Kovács,
Marcel Moosbrugger, and Miroslav Stankovič

TU Wien, Vienna, Austria
amrollahi.daneshvar@gmail.com,
{ezio.bartocci,george.kenison,laura.kovacs,
marcel.moosbrugger}@tuwien.ac.at, miroslav.ms.stankovic@gmail.com

Abstract. Automatically generating invariants, key to computer-aided
analysis of probabilistic and deterministic programs and compiler optimisation, is a challenging open problem. Whilst the problem is in general
undecidable, the goal is settled for restricted classes of loops. For the
class of *solvable* loops, introduced by Kapur and Rodríguez-Carbonell in
2004, one can automatically compute invariants from closed-form solutions of recurrence equations that model the loop behaviour. In this
paper we establish a technique for invariant synthesis for loops that are
not solvable, termed *unsolvable* loops. Our approach automatically partitions the program variables and identifies the so-called *defective* variables
that characterise unsolvability. We further present a novel technique that
automatically synthesises polynomials, in the defective variables, that
admit closed-form solutions and thus lead to polynomial loop invariants.
Our implementation and experiments demonstrate both the feasibility
and applicability of our approach to both deterministic and probabilistic
programs.

Keywords: Invariant synthesis · Algebraic recurrences · Verification ·
Solvable operators

1   Introduction

With substantial progress in computer-aided program analysis and automated
reasoning, several techniques have emerged to automatically synthesise loop
invariants, thus advancing a central challenge in the computer-aided verification
of programs with loops. In this paper, we address the problem of automatically
generating loop invariants in the presence of polynomial arithmetic, which is still
unsolved. This problem remains unsolved even when we restrict consideration to

This research was supported by the WWTF ICT19-018 grant ProbInG, the ERC Con-
solidator Grant ARTIST 101002685, the Austrian FWF project W1255-N23, and the
SecInt Doctoral College funded by TU Wien.

G. Singh and C. Urban (Eds.): SAS 2022, LNCS 13790, pp. 19–43, 2022.
https://doi.org/10.1007/978-3-031-22308-2_3

loops that are non-nested, without conditionals, and/or without exit conditions. Our work improves the state of the art under such and similar considerations.

Loop invariants, in the sequel simply *invariants*, are properties that hold before and after every iteration of a loop. As such, invariants provide the key inductive arguments for automating the verification of programs; for example, proving correctness of deterministic loops [16,21,22,27,29] and correctness of hybrid and probabilistic loops [1,13,17], or data flow analysis and compiler optimisation [26]. One challenging aspect in invariant synthesis is the derivation of *polynomial invariants* for arithmetic loops. Such invariants are defined by polynomial relations $P(x_1, \ldots, x_k) = 0$ among the program variables $x_1, \ldots, x_k$. While deriving polynomial invariants is, in general, undecidable [12], efficient invariant synthesis techniques emerge when considering restricted classes of polynomial arithmetic in so-called *solvable loops* [29], such as loops with (blocks of) affine assignments [16,21,22,27].

A common approach for constructing polynomial invariants, first pioneered in [7,18], is to (i) map a loop to a system of recurrence equations modelling the behaviour of program variables; (ii) derive closed-forms for program variables by solving the recurrences; and (iii) compute polynomial invariants by eliminating the loop counter n from the closed-forms. The central components in this setting follow. In step (i) a *recurrence operator* is employed to map loops to recurrences, which leads to closed-forms for the program variables as *exponential polynomials* in step (ii); that is, each program variable is written as a finite sum of the form $\sum_j P_j(n)\lambda_j^n$ parameterised by the nth loop iteration for polynomials P_j and algebraic numbers λ_j. From the theory of algebraic recurrences, this is the case if and only if the behaviour of each variable obeys a linear recurrence equation with constant coefficients [8,19]. Exploiting this result, the class of recurrence operators that can be linearised are called *solvable* [29]. Intuitively, a loop with a recurrence operator is solvable only if the non-linear dependencies in the resulting system of polynomial recurrences are acyclic (see Sect. 3). However, even simple loops may fall outside the category of solvable operators, but still admit polynomial invariants and closed-forms for combinations of variables. This phenomenon is illustrated in Fig. 1 whose recurrence operators are not solvable (i.e. unsolvable). In general, the main obstacle in the setting of unsolvable recurrence operators is the absence of "well-behaved" closed-forms for the resulting recurrences.

Related Work. To the best of our knowledge, the study of invariant synthesis from the viewpoint of recurrence operators is mostly limited to the setting of solvable operators (or minor generalisations thereof). In [28,29] the authors introduce solvable loops and mappings to model loops with (blocks of) affine assignments and propose solutions for steps (i)–(iii) for this class of loops: all polynomial invariants are derived by first solving linear recurrence equations and then eliminating variables based on Gröbner basis computation. These results have further been generalised in [16,22] to handle more generic recurrences; in particular, deriving arbitrary exponential polynomials as closed-forms of loop variables and allowing restricted multiplication among recursively updated loop variables. The authors

$z \leftarrow 0$
while $\star$ **do**
  $z \leftarrow 1 - z$
  $x \leftarrow 2x + y^2 + z$
  $y \leftarrow 2y - y^2 + 2z$
end while

Closed-form of $x + y$:
$x(n) + y(n) = 2^n(x(0) + y(0) + 2) - (-1)^n/2 - 3/2$

(a) The program $\mathcal{P}_\square$.

$x, y \leftarrow 1, 1$
while $\star$ **do**
  $w \leftarrow x + y$
  $x \leftarrow w^2$
  $y \leftarrow w^3$
end while

Polynomial Invariant:
$y^2(n) - x^3(n) = 0$

(b) The program $\mathcal{P}_{\mathrm{SC}}$.

Fig. 1. Two running examples with unsolvable recurrence operators. Nevertheless, $\mathcal{P}_\square$ admits a closed-form for combinations of variables and $\mathcal{P}_{\mathrm{SC}}$ admits a polynomial invariant. Herein we use $\star$ (rather than a loop guard or true) as loop termination is not our focus. For the avoidance of doubt, in this paper we consider standard mathematical arithmetic (e.g. mathematical integers) rather than machine floating-point and finite precision arithmetic.

of [9,21] generalise the setting: they consider more complex programs and devise abstract (wedge) domains to map the invariant generation problem to the problem of solving *C-finite recurrences*. (We give further details of this class of recurrences in Sect. 2). All the aforementioned approaches are mainly restricted to C-finite recurrences for which closed-forms always exist, thus yielding loop invariants. In [1,2] the authors establish techniques to apply invariant synthesis techniques developed for deterministic loops to probabilistic programs. Instead of devising recurrences describing the precise value of variables in step (i), their approach produces C-finite recurrences describing (higher) moments of program variables, yielding moment-based invariants after step (iii).

Pushing the boundaries in analyzing unsolvable loops is addressed in [10,21]. The approach of [21] extracts C-finite recurrences over linear combinations of loops variables from unsolvable loops. For example, the method presented in [21] can also synthesise the closed-forms identified by our work for Fig. 1a. However, unlike [21], our work is not limited to linear combinations (we can extract C-finite recurrences over *polynomial* relations in the loop variables). As such, the technique of [21] cannot synthesise the polynomial loop invariant in Fig. 1b, whereas our work can. A further related approach to our work is given in [10], yet in the setting of loop termination. However, our work is not restricted to solvable loops that are triangular, but can handle mutual dependencies among (unsolvable) loop variables, as evidenced in Fig. 1.

Related work in the literature introduces techniques from the theory of martingales in order to synthesise invariants in the setting of probabilistic programs [4]. Therein, the programming model is represented by a class of loop programs where all updates are linear and the synthesized invariants are given by linear templates. By contrast, our method allows us to handle polynomial arithmetic; in particular, we automatically generate invariants given by monomials in the program variables. On the other hand, the approach of [4] can also synthesise supermartingales whereas our work is restricted to invariants defined by equalities.

Our Contributions. In this paper we tackle the problem of invariant synthesis in the setting of unsolvable recurrence operators. We introduce the notions of *effective* and *defective* program variables where, figuratively speaking, the defective variables are those "responsible" for unsolvability. Our main contributions are summarized below.

1. Crucial for our synthesis technique is our novel characterisation of unsolvable recurrence operators in terms of defective variables (Theorem 1). Our approach complements existing techniques in loop analysis, by extending these methods to the setting of 'unsolvable' loops.
2. On the one hand, defective variables do not generally admit closed-forms. On the other hand, some polynomial combinations of such variables are well-behaved (see e.g., Fig. 1). We show how to compute the set of defective variables in polynomial time (Algorithm 1).
3. We introduce a new technique to synthesise valid polynomial relations among defective variables such that these relations admit closed-forms, from which polynomial loop invariants follow (Sect. 5).
4. We generalise our work to the analysis of probabilistic program loops (Sect. 6) and showcase further applications of unsolvable operators in such programs (Sect. 7).
5. We provide a fully automated approach in the tool Polar[1]. Our experiments demonstrate the feasibility of invariant synthesis for 'unsolvable' loops and the applicability of our approach to deterministic loops, probabilistic models, and biological systems (Sect. 8).

Beyond Invariant Synthesis. We believe our work can provide new solutions towards compiler optimisation challenges. *Scalar evolution*[2] is a technique to detect general induction variables. Scalar evolution and general induction variables are used for a multitude of compiler optimisations, for example inside the LLVM toolchain [23]. On a high-level, general induction variables are loop variables that satisfy linear recurrences. As we show in our work, defective variables do not satisfy linear recurrences in general; hence, scalar evolution optimisations cannot be applied upon them. However, some polynomial combinations of defective variables *do* satisfy linear recurrences, which opens avenues where we can apply scalar evolution techniques over such defective variables. Our work automatically computes polynomial combinations of some defective loop variables, which potentially enlarges the class of loops that, for example, LLVM can optimise.

---

[1] https://github.com/probing-lab/polar.
[2] https://llvm.org/docs/Passes.html.

Structure and Summary of Results. The rest of this paper is organised as follows. We briefly recall preliminary material in Sect. 2. Section 3 abstracts from concrete recurrence-based approaches to invariant synthesis via recurrence operators. Section 4 introduces effective and defective variables, presents Algorithm 1 that computes the set of defective program variables in polynomial time, and characterises unsolvable loops in terms of defective variables (Theorem 1). In Sect. 5 we present our new technique that synthesises polynomials in defective variables that admit well-behaved closed-forms. In Sect. 6 we detail the necessary changes to the invariant synthesis algorithm in Sect. 5 for probabilistic programs. We illustrate our approach with several case-studies in Sect. 7, and describe a fully-automated tool support of our work in Sect. 8. We also report on accompanying experimental evaluation in Sects. 7–8, and conclude the paper in Sect. 9.

2   Preliminaries

Throughout this paper, we write $\mathbb{N}$, $\mathbb{Q}$, and $\mathbb{R}$ to respectively denote the sets of natural, rational, and real numbers. We write $\overline{\mathbb{Q}}$, the algebraic closure of $\mathbb{Q}$, to denote the field of algebraic numbers. We write $\mathbb{R}[x_1, \ldots, x_k]$ and $\overline{\mathbb{Q}}[x_1, \ldots, x_k]$ for the polynomial rings of all polynomials $P(x_1, \ldots, x_k)$ in k variables $x_1, \ldots, x_k$ with coefficients in $\mathbb{R}$ and $\overline{\mathbb{Q}}$, respectively (with $k \in \mathbb{N}$ and $k \neq 0$). A *monomial* is a monic polynomial with a single term.

For a program $\mathcal{P}$, $\mathrm{Vars}(\mathcal{P})$ denotes the set of program variables. We adopt the following syntax in our examples. Sequential assignments in while loops are listed on separate lines (as demonstrated in Fig. 1). In programs where simultaneous assignments are performed, we employ vector notation (as demonstrated by the assignments to the variables x and y in program $\mathcal{P}_{\mathrm{MC}}$ in Example 2).

We refer to a directed graph with G, whose edge and vertex (node) sets are respectively denoted via $A(G)$ and $V(G)$. We endow each element of $A(G)$ with a label according to a labelling function $\mathcal{L}$. A *path* in G is a finite sequence of contiguous edges of G, whereas a *cycle* in G is a path whose initial and terminal vertices coincide. A graph that contains no cycles is *acyclic*. In a graph G, if there exists a path from vertex u to vertex v, then we say that v is *reachable* from vertex u and say that u is a *predecessor* of v.

C-Finite Recurrences. We recall relevant results on (algebraic) recurrences and refer to [8,19] for further details. A *sequence* in $\overline{\mathbb{Q}}$ is a function $u \colon \mathbb{N} \to \overline{\mathbb{Q}}$, shortly written also as $\langle u(n) \rangle_{n=0}^{\infty}$ or simply just $\langle u(n) \rangle_n$. A *recurrence* for a sequence $\langle u(n) \rangle_n$ is an equation $u(n+\ell) = \mathrm{Rec}(u(n+\ell-1), \ldots, u(n+1), u(n), n)$, for some function $\mathrm{Rec} \colon \mathbb{R}^{\ell+1} \to \mathbb{R}$. The number $\ell \in \mathbb{N}$ is the *order* of the recurrence.

A special class of recurrences we consider are the *linear recurrences with constant coefficients*, in short *C-finite recurrences*. A C-finite recurrence for a sequence $\langle u(n) \rangle_n$ is an equation of the form

$$u(n+\ell) = a_{\ell-1} u(n+\ell-1) + a_{\ell-2} u(n+\ell-2) + \cdots + a_0 u(n) \qquad (1)$$

where $a_0, \ldots, a_{\ell-1} \in \overline{\mathbb{Q}}$ are constants and $a_0 \neq 0$. A sequence $\langle u(n) \rangle_n$ satisfying a C-finite recurrence (1) is a *C-finite sequence* and is uniquely determined by its initial values $u_0 = u(0), \ldots, u_{\ell-1} = u(\ell-1)$. The *characteristic polynomial* associated with the C-finite recurrence relation (1) is

$$x^{n+\ell} - a_{\ell-1}x^{n+\ell-1} - a_{\ell-2}x^{n+\ell-2} - \cdots - a_0 x^n.$$

The terms of a C-finite sequence can be written in a closed-form as exponential polynomials, depending only on n and the initial values of the sequence. That is, if $\langle u(n) \rangle_n$ is determined by a C-finite recurrence (1), then $u(n) = \sum_{k=1}^{r} P_k(n)\lambda_k^n$ where $P_k(n) \in \overline{\mathbb{Q}}[n]$ and $\lambda_1, \ldots, \lambda_r$ are the roots of the associated characteristic polynomial. Importantly, closed-forms of (systems of) C-finite sequences always exist and are computable [8, 19].

Invariants. A loop invariant is a loop property that holds before and after each loop iteration [11]. In this paper, we are interested in *polynomial invariants* the class of invariants given by Boolean combinations of polynomial equations among loop variables. There is a minor caveat to our characterisation of (polynomial) loop invariants. We assume that a (polynomial) invariant consists of a finite number of initial values together with a closed-form expression of a monomial in the loop variables. Thus the closed-form of a loop invariant must eventually hold after a (computable) finite number of loop iterations. Let us illustrate this caveat with the following loop:

$x \leftarrow 0$
while $\star$ **do**
    $x \leftarrow 1$
end while

Here the loop admits the polynomial invariant given by the initial value $x(0) = 1$ of x and the closed-form $x(n) = 1$. For each $n \geq 1$, we denote by $x(n)$ the value of loop variable x at loop iteration n. Herein, we synthesise invariants that satisfy inhomogeneous first-order recurrence relations and it is straightforward to show that each associated closed-form holds for $n \geq 1$.

Polynomial Invariants and Invariant Ideals. A polynomial *ideal* is a subset $I \subseteq \overline{\mathbb{Q}}[x_1, \ldots, x_k]$ with the following properties: I contains 0; I is closed under addition; and if $P \in \overline{\mathbb{Q}}[x_1, \ldots, x_k]$ and $Q \in I$, then $PQ \in I$. For a set of polynomials $S \subseteq \overline{\mathbb{Q}}[x_1, \ldots, x_k]$, one can define the *ideal generated by S* by

$$I(S) := \{s_1 q_1 + \cdots + s_\ell q_\ell \mid s_i \in S, q_i \in \overline{\mathbb{Q}}[x_1, \ldots, x_k], \ell \in \mathbb{N}\}.$$

Let $\mathcal{P}$ be a program as before. For $x_j \in \mathrm{Vars}(\mathcal{P})$, let $\langle x_j(n) \rangle_n$ denote the sequence whose nth term is given by the value of x_j in the nth loop iteration. The set of polynomial invariants of $\mathcal{P}$ form an ideal, the *invariant ideal* of $\mathcal{P}$ [28]. If for each program variable x_j the sequence $\langle x_j(n) \rangle_n$ is C-finite, then a basis for the invariant ideal can be computed as follows. Let $f_j(n)$ be the exponential polynomial closed-form of variable x_j. The exponential terms $\lambda_1^n, \ldots, \lambda_s^n$ in each of the $f_j(n)$ are replaced by fresh symbols, yielding the polynomials $g_j(n)$. Next, with techniques from [20], the set R of all polynomial relations among $\lambda_1^n, \ldots, \lambda_s^n$ (that hold for each $n \in \mathbb{N}$) is computed. Then we express the polynomial relations in terms of the fresh constants, so that we can interpret R as a set of polynomials. Thus

$$I(\{x_j - g_j(n) \mid 1 \leq i \leq k\} \cup R) \cap \overline{\mathbb{Q}}[x_1, \ldots, x_k]$$

is precisely the invariant ideal of $\mathcal{P}$. Finally, we can compute a finite basis for the invariant ideal with techniques from Gröbner bases and elimination theory [20].

3   From Loops to Recurrences

Modelling properties of loop variables by algebraic recurrences and solving the resulting recurrences is an established approach in program analysis. Multiple works [9,15,16,21,22] associate a loop variable x with a sequence $\langle x(n) \rangle_n$ whose nth term is given by the value of x in the nth loop iteration. These works are primarily concerned with the problem of representing such sequences via recurrence equations whose closed-forms can be computed automatically, as in the case of C-finite sequences. A closely connected question to this line of research focuses on identifying classes of loops that can be modelled by solvable recurrences, as advocated in [29]. To this end, over-approximation methods for general loops are proposed in [9,21] such that solvable recurrences can be obtained from (over-approximated) loops.

In order to formalise the above and similar efforts in associating loop variables with recurrences, herein we introduce the concept of a *recurrence operator*, and then *solvable* and *unsolvable* operators. Intuitively, a recurrence operator maps program variables to recurrence equations describing some properties of the variables; for instance, the exact values at the nth loop iteration [9,22,29] or statistical moments in probabilistic loops [1].

Definition 1 (Recurrence Operator). *A recurrence operator $\mathcal{R}$ maps the program variables $\mathrm{Vars}(\mathcal{P})$ to the polynomial ring $\mathbb{R}[\mathrm{Vars}_n(\mathcal{P})]$. The set of equations $\{x(n{+}1) = \mathcal{R}[x] \mid x \in \mathrm{Vars}(\mathcal{P})\}$ constitutes a polynomial first-order system of recurrences. We call $\mathcal{R}$ linear if $\mathcal{R}[x]$ is linear for all $x \in \mathrm{Vars}(\mathcal{P})$.*

One can extend the operator $\mathcal{R}$ to $\mathbb{R}[\mathrm{Vars}(\mathcal{P})]$. Then, with a slight abuse of notation, for $P(x_1, \ldots, x_j) \in \mathbb{R}[\mathrm{Vars}(\mathcal{P})]$ we define $\mathcal{R}(P)$ by $P(\mathcal{R}[x_1], \ldots, \mathcal{R}[x_j])$.

For a program $\mathcal{P}$ with recurrence operator $\mathcal{R}$ and a monomial over program variables $M := \prod_{x \in \mathrm{Vars}(\mathcal{P})} x^{\alpha_x}$, we denote by $M(n)$ the product of sequences $\prod_{x \in \mathrm{Vars}(\mathcal{P})} x^{\alpha_x}(n)$. Given a polynomial P over program variables, $P(n)$ is defined by replacing every monomial M in P by $M(n)$. For a set T of polynomials over program variables let $T_n := \{P(n) \mid P \in T\}$.

Example 1. Consider the program $\mathcal{P}_{\mathrm{SC}}$ in Fig. 1b. One can employ a recurrence operator $\mathcal{R}$ in order to capture the values of the program variables in the nth iteration. For $v \in \mathrm{Vars}(\mathcal{P}_{\mathrm{SC}})$, $\mathcal{R}[v]$ is obtained by bottom-up substitution in the polynomial updates starting with v. As a result, we obtain the following system of recurrences:

$$w(n+1) = \mathcal{R}[w] = x(n) + y(n)$$
$$x(n+1) = \mathcal{R}[x] = x(n)^2 + 2x(n)y(n) + y(n)^2$$
$$y(n+1) = \mathcal{R}[y] = x(n)^3 + 3x(n)^2y(n) + 3x(n)y(n)^2 + y(n)^3.$$

Similarly, for the program $\mathcal{P}_\square$ of Fig. 1a, we obtain the following system of recurrences:

$$z(n+1) = \mathcal{R}[z] = 1 - z(n)$$
$$x(n+1) = \mathcal{R}[x] = 2x(n) + y(n)^2 - z(n) + 1$$
$$y(n+1) = \mathcal{R}[y] = 2y(n) - y(n)^2 - 2z(n) + 2.$$

Solvable Operators. Systems of linear recurrences with constant coefficients admit computable closed-form solutions as exponential polynomials [8,19]. This property holds for a larger class of recurrences with polynomial updates, which leads to the notion of *solvability* introduced in [29]. We adjust the notion of solvability to our setting by using recurrence operators. In the following definition, we make a slight abuse of notation and order the program variables so that we can transform program variables by a matrix operator.

Definition 2 (Solvable Operators [27,29]). *The recurrence operator $\mathcal{R}$ is solvable if there exists a partition of* Vars_n*; that is,* $\mathrm{Vars}_n = W_1 \uplus \cdots \uplus W_k$ *such that for* $x(n) \in W_j$,

$$\mathcal{R}[x] = M_j \cdot W_j^\top + P_j(W_1, \ldots, W_{j-1})$$

for some matrices M_j and polynomials P_j. A recurrence operator that is not solvable is said to be unsolvable.

This definition captures the notion of solvability in [29] (see the discussion in [27]).

We conclude this section by emphasising the use of (solvable) recurrence operators beyond deterministic loops, in particular relating its use to probabilistic program loops. As evidenced in [1], recurrence operators model statistical moments of program variables by essentially focusing on solvable recurrence operators extended with an expectation operator $\mathbb{E}(\cdot)$ to derive closed-forms of (higher) moments of program variables, as illustrated below.

Example 2. Consider the probabilistic program $\mathcal{P}_{\mathrm{MC}}$ of [5,31] modelling a non-linear Markov chain, where Bernoulli(p) refers to a Bernoulli distribution with parameter p. Here the updates to the program variables x and y occur simultaneously.

while $\star$ do
    $s \leftarrow$ Bernoulli(1/2)

if $s = 0$ **then**
$$\begin{pmatrix} x \\ y \end{pmatrix} \leftarrow \begin{pmatrix} x + xy \\ \frac{1}{3}x + \frac{2}{3}y + xy \end{pmatrix}$$
else
$$\begin{pmatrix} x \\ y \end{pmatrix} \leftarrow \begin{pmatrix} x + y + \frac{2}{3}xy \\ 2y + \frac{2}{3}xy \end{pmatrix}$$
end if
end while

One can construct recurrence equations, in terms of the expectation operator $\mathbb{E}(\,\cdot\,)$, for this program as follows:

$$\mathbb{E}(s_{n+1}) = \tfrac{1}{2}$$
$$\mathbb{E}(x_{n+1}) = \mathbb{E}(x_n) + \tfrac{1}{2}\mathbb{E}(y_n) + \tfrac{5}{6}\mathbb{E}(x_n y_n)$$
$$\mathbb{E}(y_{n+1}) = \tfrac{1}{6}\mathbb{E}(x_n) + \tfrac{4}{3}\mathbb{E}(y_n) + \tfrac{5}{6}\mathbb{E}(x_n y_n).$$

4   Defective Variables

To the best of our knowledge, existing approaches in loop analysis and invariant synthesis are restricted to solvable recurrence operators. In this section, we establish a new characterisation of unsolvable recurrence operators. Our characterisation pinpoints the program variables responsible for unsolvability, the *defective variables* (see Definition 5). Moreover, we provide a polynomial time algorithm to compute the set of defective variables (Algorithm 1), in order to exploit our new characterisation for synthesising invariants in the presence of unsolvable operators in Sect. 5.

For simplicity, we limit the discussion in this section to deterministic programs. We note however that the results presented herein can also be applied to probabilistic programs. The details of the necessary changes in this respect are given in Sect. 6.

In what follows, we write $\mathcal{M}_n(\mathcal{P})$ to denote the set of non-trivial *monomials* in $\mathrm{Vars}(\mathcal{P})$ *evaluated at the nth loop iteration* so that

$$\mathcal{M}_n(\mathcal{P}) := \left\{ \prod_{x \in \mathrm{Vars}(\mathcal{P})} x^{\alpha_x}(n) \mid \exists x \in \mathrm{Vars}(\mathcal{P}) \text{ with } \alpha_x \neq 0 \right\}.$$

We next introduce the notions of variable dependency and dependency graph, needed to further characterise defective variables.

Definition 3 (Variable Dependency). *Let $\mathcal{P}$ be a loop with recurrence operator $\mathcal{R}$ and $x, y \in \mathrm{Vars}(\mathcal{P})$. We say x depends on y if y appears in a monomial in $\mathcal{R}[x]$ with non-zero coefficient. Moreover, x depends linearly on y if all monomials with non-zero coefficients in $\mathcal{R}[x]$ containing y are linear. Analogously, x depends non-linearly on y if there is a non-linear monomial with non-zero coefficient in $\mathcal{R}[x]$ containing y.*

Furthermore, we consider the transitive closure for variable dependency. If z depends on y and y depends on x, then z depends on x and, if in addition, one of these two dependencies is non-linear, then z depends non-linearly on x. We otherwise say the dependency is linear.

For each program with polynomial updates, we further define a *dependency graph* with respect to a recurrence operator.

Definition 4 (Dependency Graph). *Let $\mathcal{P}$ be a program with recurrence operator $\mathcal{R}$. The* dependency graph *of $\mathcal{P}$ with respect to $\mathcal{R}$ is the labelled directed graph $G = (\text{Vars}(\mathcal{P}), A, \mathcal{L})$ with vertex set $\text{Vars}(\mathcal{P})$, edge set $A := \{(x, y) \mid x, y \in \text{Vars}(\mathcal{P}) \wedge x \text{ depends on } y\}$, and a function $\mathcal{L}: A \rightarrow \{L, N\}$ that assigns a unique label to each edge such that*

$$\mathcal{L}(x, y) = \begin{cases} L & \text{if } x \text{ depends linearly on } y, \text{ and} \\ N & \text{if } x \text{ depends non-linearly on } y. \end{cases}$$

In our approach, we partition the variables $\text{Vars}(\mathcal{P})$ of the program $\mathcal{P}$ into two sets: *effective-* and *defective variables*, denoted by $E(\mathcal{P})$ and $D(\mathcal{P})$ respectively. Our partition builds on the definition of the dependency graph of $\mathcal{P}$, as follows.

Definition 5 (Effective-Defective). *A variable $x \in \text{Vars}(\mathcal{P})$ is* effective *if:*

1. *x appears in no directed cycle with at least one edge with an N label, and*
2. *x cannot reach a vertex of an aforementioned cycle (as in 1).*

A variable is defective *if it is not effective.*

Example 3. From the recurrence equations of Example 1 for the program $\mathcal{P}_{\text{SC}}$ (see Fig. 1b), one obtains the dependencies between the program variables of $\mathcal{P}_{\text{SC}}$: the program variable w depends linearly on both x and y, whilst x and y depend non-linearly on each other and on w. By definition, the partition into effective and defective variables is $E(\mathcal{P}_{\text{SC}}) = \emptyset$ and $D(\mathcal{P}_{\text{SC}}) = \{w, x, y\}$.

Similarly, we can construct the dependency graph for the program $\mathcal{P}_{\square}$ from Fig. 1a, as illustrated in Fig. 2. We derive that $E(\mathcal{P}_{\square}) = \{z\}$ and $D(\mathcal{P}_{\square}) = \{x, y\}$.

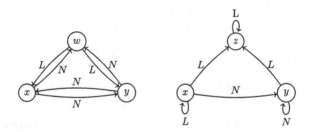

Fig. 2. The dependency graphs for $\mathcal{P}_{\text{SC}}$ and $\mathcal{P}_{\square}$ from Fig. 1.

The concept of effective, and, especially, defective variables allows us to establish a new characterisation of programs with unsolvable recurrence operators: *a recurrence operator is unsolvable if and only if there exists a defective variable* (as stated in Theorem 1 and automated in Algorithm 1). We formalise and prove this results via the following three lemmas.

Lemma 1. *Let $\mathcal{P}$ be a program with recurrence operator $\mathcal{R}$. If $D(\mathcal{P})$ is non-empty, so that there is at least one defective variable, then $\mathcal{R}$ is unsolvable.*

Proof. Let $x \in \text{Vars}(\mathcal{P})$ be a defective variable and $G = (\text{Vars}(\mathcal{P}), A, \mathcal{L})$ the dependency graph of $\mathcal{P}$ with respect to a recurrence operator $\mathcal{R}$. Following Definition 5, there exists a cycle C such that x is a vertex visited by or can reach said cycle and, in addition, there is an edge in C labelled by N.

Assume, for a contradiction, that $\mathcal{R}$ is solvable. Then there exists a partition $W_1, \ldots, W_k$ of $\text{Vars}_n(\mathcal{P})$ as described in Definition 2. Moreover, since C is a cycle, there exists $j \in \{1, \ldots, k\}$ such that each variable visited by C lies in W_j. Let $(w, y) \in C$ be an edge labelled with N. Since w depends on y non-linearly, and $\mathcal{R}[w] = M_j \cdot W_j^\top + P_j(W_1, \ldots, W_{j-1})$ (by Definition 2), it is clear that $y(n) \in W_\ell$ for some $\ell \neq j$. We also have that $y(n) \in W_j$ since C visits y. Thus we arrive at a contradiction as $W_1, \ldots, W_k$ is a partition of $\text{Vars}_n(\mathcal{P})$. Hence $\mathcal{R}$ is unsolvable. □

Given a program $\mathcal{P}$ whose variables are all effective, it is immediate that a pair of distinct mutually dependent variables are necessarily linearly dependent and, similarly, a self-dependent variable is necessarily linearly dependent on itself. Consider the following binary relation $\sim$ on program variables:

$$x \sim y \iff x = y \lor (x \text{ depends on } y \land y \text{ depends on } x).$$

Thus, any two mutually dependent variables are related by $\sim$. Under the assumption that all variables of a program $\mathcal{P}$ are effective, it is easily seen that $\sim$ defines an equivalence relation on $\text{Vars}(\mathcal{P})$. The partition of the equivalence classes Π of $\text{Vars}(\mathcal{P})$ under $\sim$ admits the following notion of dependence between equivalence classes: for $\pi, \hat{\pi} \in \Pi$ we say that π *depends on* $\hat{\pi}$ if there exist variables $x \in \pi$ and $y \in \hat{\pi}$ such that variable x depends on variable y.

Lemma 2. *Suppose that all variables of a program $\mathcal{P}$ are effective. Consider the graph $\mathcal{G}$ with vertex set given by the set of equivalence classes Π and edge set $A' := \{(\pi, \hat{\pi}) \mid (\pi \neq \hat{\pi}) \land (\pi \text{ depends on } \hat{\pi})\}$. Then $\mathcal{G}$ is acyclic.*

Proof. From the definition of $\mathcal{G}$, it is clear that the graph is directed and has no self-loops. Now assume, for a contradiction, that $\mathcal{G}$ contains a cycle. Since the relation $\sim$ is transitive, there exists a cycle C in $\mathcal{G}$ of length two. Moreover, the variables in a given equivalence class are mutually dependent. Thus the elements of the two classes in C are equivalent under the relation $\sim$, which contradicts the partition into distinct equivalence classes. Therefore the graph $\mathcal{G}$ is acyclic, as required. □

Lemma 3. *Let $\mathcal{P}$ be a program with recurrence operator $\mathcal{R}$. If each of the program variables of $\mathcal{P}$ is effective then $\mathcal{R}$ is solvable.*

Proof. By Lemma 2, the associated graph $\mathcal{G} = (\Pi, A')$ on the equivalence classes of $\text{Vars}(\mathcal{P})$ is directed and acyclic. Thus there exists a topological ordering of $\Pi = \{\pi_1, \ldots, \pi_{|\Pi|}\}$ such that for every $(\pi_i, \pi_j) \in A'$ we have $i > j$. Thus if $x \in \pi_i$

Algorithm 1. Construct $E(\mathcal{P})$ and $D(\mathcal{P})$ from program $\mathcal{P}$ with operator $\mathcal{R}$.

Let $G = (\text{Vars}(\mathcal{P}), A, \mathcal{L})$ be the dependency graph of $\mathcal{P}$ with respect to $\mathcal{R}$.
$D(\mathcal{P}) \leftarrow \emptyset$
for $(x, y) \in A$ where $\mathcal{L}(x, y) = N$ **do**
  if $x = y$ **then**
    $\text{predecessor} \leftarrow \emptyset$
    $\text{DFS}(x, \text{predecessor})$
    $D(\mathcal{P}) \leftarrow D(\mathcal{P}) \cup \text{predecessor}$
  end if
  if $x \neq y$ **then**
    $\text{predecessor} \leftarrow \emptyset$
    $\text{DFS}(y, \text{predecessor})$
    if $x \in \text{predecessor}$ **then**
      $D(\mathcal{P}) \leftarrow D(\mathcal{P}) \cup \text{predecessor}$
    end if
  end if
end for
$E(\mathcal{P}) \leftarrow \text{Vars}(\mathcal{P}) \setminus D(\mathcal{P})$

---

then x does not depend on any variables in class π_j for $j > i$. Moreover, for each $\pi_i \in \Pi$, if $x, y \in \pi_i$ then x cannot depend on y non-linearly because every variable is effective (and all the variables in π_i are mutually dependent). Thus Π evaluated at loop iteration n partitions $\text{Vars}_n(\mathcal{P})$ and satisfies the criteria in Definition 2. We thus conclude that $\mathcal{R}$ is solvable. $\square$

Together, Lemmas 1–3 yield a new characterisation of unsolvable operators.

Theorem 1 (Defective Characterisation). *Let $\mathcal{P}$ be a program with recurrence operator $\mathcal{R}$, then $\mathcal{R}$ is unsolvable if and only if $D(\mathcal{P})$ is non-empty.*

In Algorithm 1 we provide a polynomial time algorithm that constructs both $E(\mathcal{P})$ and $D(\mathcal{P})$ given a program and a recurrence operator. We use the initialism "DFS" for the *depth-first search* procedure. Algorithm 1 terminates in polynomial time as both the construction of the dependency graph and depth-first search exhibit polynomial time complexity. The procedure searches for cycles in the dependency graph with at least one non-linear edge (labelled by N). All variables that reach such cycles are, by definition, defective.

In what follows, we focus on programs with unsolvable recurrence operators, or equivalently by Theorem 1, the case where $D(\mathcal{P}) \neq \emptyset$. The characterisation of unsolvable operators in terms of defective variables and our polynomial algorithm to construct the set of defective variables is the foundation for our approach synthesising invariants in the presence of unsolvable recurrence operators in Sect. 5.

Remark 1. The recurrence operator $\mathcal{R}[x]$ for an effective variable x will admit a closed-form solution for every initial value x_0. For the avoidance of doubt, the same cannot be said for the recurrence operator of a defective variable. However, it is possible that a set of initial values will lead to a closed-form expression as a C-finite sequence: consider a loop with defective variable x and update $x \leftarrow x^2$ and initialisation $x_0 \leftarrow 0$ or $x_0 \leftarrow \pm 1$.

5   Synthesising Invariants

In this section we propose a new technique to *synthesise invariants for programs with unsolvable recurrence operators*. The approach is based on our new characterisation of unsolvable operators in terms of defective variables (Sect. 4). For the remainder of this section we fix a program $\mathcal{P}$ with an unsolvable recurrence operator $\mathcal{R}$, or equivalently with $D(\mathcal{P}) \neq \emptyset$. We start by extending the notions of *effective* and *defective* from program variables to monomials of program variables. Let $\mathcal{E}$ be the set of *effective monomials* given by

$$\mathcal{E}(\mathcal{P}) = \left\{ \prod_{x \in E(\mathcal{P})} x^{\alpha_x} \mid \alpha_x \in \mathbb{N} \right\}.$$

The complement, the *defective monomials*, is given by $\mathcal{D}(\mathcal{P}) := \mathcal{M}(\mathcal{P}) \setminus \mathcal{E}(\mathcal{P})$. The difficulty with defective variables is that in general they do not admit closed-forms. However, polynomials of defective variables may allow for closed-forms as illustrated in previous examples. The main idea of our technique for invariant synthesis in the presence of defective variables is to find such polynomials. We fix a *candidate polynomial* called $S(n)$ based on an arbitrary degree $d \in \mathbb{N}$:

$$S(n) = \sum_{W \in \mathcal{D}_n(\mathcal{P}) \restriction_d} c_W W, \tag{2}$$

where the coefficients $c_W \in \mathbb{R}$ are unknown real constants. We use $\mathcal{D}_n(\mathcal{P}) \restriction_d$ to indicate the set of *defective monomials of degree at most d*.

Example 4. For $\mathcal{P}_\square$ in Fig. 1a we have $\mathcal{D}_n(\mathcal{P}_\square) \restriction_1 = \{x, y\}$, and $\mathcal{D}_n(\mathcal{P}_\square) \restriction_2 = \{x, y, x^2, y^2, xy, xz, yz\}$.

On the one hand, all variables in $S(n)$ are defective; however, $S(n)$ may admit a closed-form. This occurs if $S(n)$ obeys a "well-behaved" recurrence equation; that is to say, an inhomogeneous recurrence equation where the inhomogeneous component is given by a linear combination of effective monomials. In such instances the recurrence takes the form

$$S(n+1) = \kappa S(n) + \sum_{M \in \mathcal{E}_n(\mathcal{P})} c_M M \tag{3}$$

where the coefficients c_M are unknown. Thus an intermediate step towards our goal of synthesising invariants is to determine whether there are constants $c_M, c_W, \kappa \in \mathbb{R}$ that satisfy the above equations. If such constants exist then we come to our final step: solving a first-order inhomogeneous recurrence relation.

There are standard methods available to solve first-order inhomogeneous recurrences of the form $S(n+1) = \kappa S(n) + h(n)$, where $h(n)$ is the closed-form of $\sum_{M \in \mathcal{E}_n(\mathcal{P})} c_M M$, see e.g., [19]. We note $h(n)$ is computable and an exponential polynomial since it is determined by a linear sum of effective monomials. Thus $\langle S(n) \rangle_n$ is a C-finite sequence.

Remark 2. Observe that the sum on the right-hand side of Eq. (3) is finite, since all but finitely many of the coefficients c_M are zero. Further, the coefficient c_M of monomial M is non-zero only if M appears in $\mathcal{R}[S]$.

Going further, in Eq. (3) we express $S(n+1)$ in terms of a polynomial in $\text{Vars}_n(\mathcal{P})$ with unknown coefficients c_M, c_W, and κ. An alternative expression for $S(n+1)$ in $\text{Vars}_n(\mathcal{P})$ is given by the recurrence operator $S(n+1) = \mathcal{R}[S]$. Taken in combination, we arrive at the following formula

$$\mathcal{R}[S] - \kappa S(n) - \sum_{M \in \mathcal{E}_n(\mathcal{P})} c_M M = 0,$$

yielding a polynomial in $\text{Vars}_n(\mathcal{P})$. Thus all the coefficients in the above formula are necessarily zero as the polynomial is identically zero. Therefore *all* solutions to the unknowns c_M, c_W, and κ are computed by solving a (quadratic) system of equations.

Example 5. We demonstrate our procedure for invariant synthesis by applying the method to an example. Recall program $\mathcal{P}_\square$ from Fig. 1a:

$$z \leftarrow 0$$
while $\star$ **do**
  $$z \leftarrow 1 - z$$
  $$x \leftarrow 2x + y^2 + z$$
  $$y \leftarrow 2y - y^2 + 2z$$
end while

From Algorithm 1 we obtain $E(\mathcal{P}_\square) = \{z\}$ and $D(\mathcal{P}_\square) = \{x, y\}$. Because $D(\mathcal{P}_\square) \neq \emptyset$, we deduce using Theorem 1 that the associated operator $\mathcal{R}$ is unsolvable. Consider the candidate $S(n) = ax(n) + by(n)$ with unknowns $a, b \in \mathbb{R}$. The recurrence for $S(n)$ given by $\mathcal{R}$ is

$$S(n+1) = \mathcal{R}[S] = a\mathcal{R}[x] + b\mathcal{R}[y]$$
$$= a + 2b + 2ax(n) + 2by(n) - (a + 2b)z(n) + (a - b)y^2(n).$$

We next express $S(n+1)$ in terms of an inhomogeneous recurrence equation (cf. Eq. (3)). When we substitute for $S(n)$, we obtain

$$S(n+1) = \kappa(ax(n) + by(n)) + (cz(n) + d)$$

where the coefficients in the inhomogeneous component are unknown. We then combine the preceding two equations (for brevity we suppress the loop counter n in the program variables x, y, z) and derive

$$(a + 2b - d) + (-a - c - 2b)z + (2a - \kappa a)x + (2b - \kappa b)y + (a - b)y^2 = 0.$$

Thus we have a polynomial in the program variables that is identically zero. Therefore, all the coefficients in the above equation are necessarily zero. We then solve the resulting system of quadratic equations, which leads to the non-trivial solution $a = b$, $\kappa = 2$, $d = 3a$, and $c = -3a$. We substitute this solution back into the recurrence for $\mathcal{R}[S]$ and find

$$S(n{+}1) = 2S(n) + 3a(1 - z(n)) = 2S(n) + 3a\frac{1 + (-1)^n}{2}.$$

Here, we have used the closed-form solution $z(n) = 1/2 - (-1)^n/2$ of the effective variable z. We can compute the solution of this inhomogeneous first-order recurrence equation. In the case that $a = 1$, we have $S(n) = 2^n(S(0) + 2) - (-1)^n/2 - 3/2$. Therefore, the following identity holds for each $n \in \mathbb{N}$:

$$x(n) + y(n) = 2^n(x(0) + y(0) + 2) - (-1)^n/2 - 3/2$$

and so we have synthesised the closed-form of $x + y$ for program $\mathcal{P}_\square$ of Fig. 1a.

5.1 Solution Space of Invariants for Unsolvable Operators

Given a program and a recurrence operator, our invariant synthesis technique is relative-complete with respect to the degree d of the candidate $S(n)$. This means, for a fixed degree $d \in \mathbb{N}$, our approach is in theory able to compute *all* polynomials of defective variables with maximum degree d that satisfy a "well-behaved" recurrence; that is, a first-order recurrence equation of the form (3). This holds because of our reduction of the problem to a system of quadratic equations for which all solutions are computable. Our technique can also rule out the existence of well-behaved polynomials of defective variables of degree at most d if the resulting system has no (non-trivial) solutions.

Let $\mathcal{P}$ be a program with program variables $\mathrm{Vars}(\mathcal{P}) = \{x_1, \ldots, x_k\}$. The set of polynomials P with $P(x_1(n), \ldots, x_k(n))=0$ for all $n \in \mathbb{N}$ form an ideal, the *invariant ideal* of $\mathcal{P}$. The requirement of closed-forms is the main obstacle for computing a basis for the invariant ideal in the presence of defective variables. Our work introduces a method that includes defective variables in the computation of invariant ideals, via the following steps of deriving the *polynomial invariant ideal of an unsolvable loop:*

- For every effective variable x_i, let $f_i(n)$ be its closed-form and assume $h(n)$ is the closed-form for some candidate S given by a polynomial in defective variables.
- Let $\lambda_1^n, \ldots, \lambda_s^n$ be the exponential terms in all $f_i(n)$ and $h(n)$. Replace the exponential terms in all $f_i(n)$ as well as $h(n)$ by fresh constants to construct the polynomials $g_i(n)$ and $l(n)$ respectively.
- Next, construct the set R of polynomial relations among all exponential terms, as explained in Sect. 2. Then, the ideal

$$I(\{x_i - g_i(n) \mid x_i \in E(\mathcal{P})\} \cup \{S - l(n)\} \cup R) \cap \overline{\mathbb{Q}}[x_1, \ldots, x_k]$$

contains precisely all polynomial relations among program variables implied by the equations $\{x_i = f_i(n)\} \cup \{S = g(n)\}$ in the theory of polynomial arithmetic.

- A finite basis for this ideal is computed using techniques from Gröbner bases and elimination theory. This step is similar to the case of the invariant ideal for solvable loops, see e.g., [22, 29].

In conclusion, we infer a *finite representation of the ideal of polynomial invariants for loops with unsolvable recurrence operators*.

6   Adjusting Defective Variables for Unsolvable Operators in Probabilistic Programs

The works [1, 25] defined recurrence operators for probabilistic loops. Specifically, a recurrence operator is defined for loops with polynomial assignments, probabilistic choice, and drawing from common probability distributions with constant parameters. Recurrences for deterministic loops model the precise values of program variables. For probabilistic loops, this approach is not viable, due to the stochastic nature of the program variables. Thus a recurrence operator for a probabilistic loop models *(higher) moments* of program variables. As illustrated in Example 2, the recurrences of a probabilistic loop are taken over expected values of program variable monomials.

   In [1, 25], the authors explicitly excluded the case of circular non-linear dependencies to guarantee computability. However, in contrast to our notions in Sects. 3, they defined variable dependence not on the level of recurrences but on the level of assignments in the loop body. To use the notions of effective and defective variables for probabilistic loops, we follow the same approach and base the dependency graph on assignments rather then recurrences. We illustrate the necessity of this adaptation in the following example.

Example 6. Consider the following probabilistic loop and associated set of first-order recurrence relations in terms of the expectation operator $\mathbb{E}(\,\cdot\,)$:

while ⋆ **do**
    $y \leftarrow 4y(1 - y)$
    $x \leftarrow x - y \ \{1/2\} \ x + y$
end while

$$\mathbb{E}(y_{n+1}) = 4\mathbb{E}(y_n) - 4\mathbb{E}(y_n^2)$$
$$\mathbb{E}(x_{n+1}) = \mathbb{E}(x_n)$$
$$\mathbb{E}(x_{n+1}^2) = \mathbb{E}(x_n^2) + \mathbb{E}(y_{n+1}^2)$$

It is straightforward to see that variable y is defective from the deterministic update $y \leftarrow 4y(1 - y)$ with its characteristic non-linear self-dependence. Moreover, y appears in the probabilistic assignment of x. However, due to the particular form of the assignment, the recurrence of $\mathbb{E}(x_n)$ does not contain y. Nevertheless, y appears in the recurrence of $\mathbb{E}(x_n^2)$. This phenomenon is specific to the probabilistic setting. For deterministic loops, it is always the case that if the values of a program variable w do not depend on defective variables, then neither do the values of any power of w.

In light of the phenomenon exhibited in Example 6, for probabilistic loops, we adapt our notion of *variable dependency*. Without loss of generality, we assume that every program variable has exactly one assignment in the loop body. Let $\mathcal{P}$ be a probabilistic loop and $x, y \in \text{Vars}(\mathcal{P})$. We say x *depends on* y, if y appears in the assignment of x. Additionally, the dependency is *linear* if all occurrences of y in the assignment of x are linear, else the dependency is *non-linear*. Further, we consider the transitive closure of variable dependency analogous to deterministic loops and Definition 3.

With variable dependency thus defined, the dependency graph and the notions of effective and defective variables follow immediately. Analogous to our characterisation of unsolvable recurrence operators in terms of defective variables for deterministic loops, *all (higher) moments* of effective variables of probabilistic loops can be described by a system of linear recurrences [1,25]. For defective variables this property will generally fail For instance, in Example 6, the variable x is now classified as defective and $\mathbb{E}(x_n^2)$ cannot be modelled by linear recurrences for some initial values.

The only necessary change to the invariant synthesis algorithm from Sect. 5 is that instead of program variable monomials, we consider expected values of program variable monomials. Now, our synthesis technique from Sect. 5 can also be applied to probabilistic loops to synthesise combinations of expected values of defective variable monomials that do satisfy a linear recurrence.

7   Applications of Unsolvable Operators Towards Invariant Synthesis

Our approach automatically generates invariants for programs with defective variables (Sect. 5), and pushes the boundaries of both theory and practice of invariant generation: we introduce and incorporate defective variable analysis into the state-of-the-art methodology of reasoning about solvable loops, complementing thus existing methods, see e.g., [16,21,22,29], in the area. As such, the class of unsolvable loops that can be handled by our work extends (aforementioned) existing approaches on polynomial invariant synthesis. The experimental results of our approach (see Sect. 8) demonstrate the efficiency and scalability of our work in deriving invariants for unsolvable loops. Since our approach to loops via recurrences is generic, we can deal with emerging applications of programming paradigms such as: transitions systems and statistical moments in probabilistic programs; and reasoning about biological systems. We showcase these applications in this section and also exemplify the limitations of our work. In the sequel, we write $\mathbb{E}(t)$ to refer to the expected value of an expression t, and denote by $\mathbb{E}(t_n)$ (or $\mathbb{E}(t(n))$) the expected value of t at loop iteration n.

Example 7. (Moments of Probabilistic Programs [31]). Recall the program $\mathcal{P}_{\text{MC}}$ of Example 2. One can easily verify that $\mathbb{E}(x_n - y_n) = \frac{5^n}{6^n}(x_0 - y_0)$ and so obtain an invariant for $\mathcal{P}_{\text{MC}}$. Closed-form solutions for higher order expressions are also available; for example,

$$\mathbb{E}((x_n - y_n)^d) = \frac{(2^d + 3^d)^n}{2^n \cdot 3^{dn}} (x_0 - y_0)^d$$

refers to the dth moment of $x(n) - y(n)$. While the work in [31] uses martingale theory to synthesise the above invariant (of degree 1), our approach automatically generates such invariants over higher-order moments (see Table 2). We note to this end that the defective variables in $\mathcal{P}_{MC}$ are precisely x and y as can be seen from their mutual non-linear interdependence. Namely, we have $D(\mathcal{P}_{MC}) = \{x, y\}$ and $E(\mathcal{P}_{MC}) = \{s\}$.

Example 8. (non-lin-markov-2). We give a second example of a non-linear Markov chain. We analyse the moments of this probabilistic program in the next section.

$x, y \leftarrow 0, 1$
while $\star$ **do**
    $s \leftarrow$ Bernoulli$(1/2)$
    if $s = 0$ **then**
$$\begin{pmatrix} x \\ y \end{pmatrix} \leftarrow \begin{pmatrix} \frac{4}{10}(x + xy) \\ \frac{4}{10}(13x + \frac{2}{3}y + xy) \end{pmatrix}$$
    else
$$\begin{pmatrix} x \\ y \end{pmatrix} \leftarrow \begin{pmatrix} \frac{4}{10}(x + y + \frac{2}{3}xy) \\ \frac{4}{10}(2y + \frac{2}{3}xy) \end{pmatrix}$$
    end if
end while

Example 9. (Biological Systems [3]). A model for the decision-making process of swarming bees choosing one nest-site from a selection of two is introduced in [3] and further studied in [6,30]. Previous works, motivated by reachability questions, have computed probability distributions for this model [30]. The (unsolvable) loop is a discrete-time model with five classes of bees (each represented by a program variable). The coefficient Δ is the length of the time-step in the model and the remaining coefficients parameterise the rates of change. All coefficients here are symbolic (representing any real number).

$$\begin{pmatrix} x \\ y_1 \\ y_2 \\ z_1 \\ z_2 \end{pmatrix} \leftarrow \begin{pmatrix} \text{Normal}(475, 5) \\ \text{Uniform}(350, 400) \\ \text{Uniform}(100, 150) \\ \text{Normal}(35, 1.5) \\ \text{Normal}(35, 1.5) \end{pmatrix}$$
while $\star$ **do**
$$\begin{pmatrix} x \\ y_1 \\ y_2 \\ z_1 \\ z_2 \end{pmatrix} \leftarrow \begin{pmatrix} x - \Delta(\beta_1 xy_1 + \beta_2 xy_2) \\ y_1 + \Delta(\beta_1 xy_1 - \gamma y_1 + \delta\beta_1 y_1 z_1 + \alpha\beta_1 y_1 z_2) \\ y_2 + \Delta(\beta_2 xy_2 - \gamma y_2 + \delta\beta_2 y_2 z_2 + \alpha\beta_2 y_2 z_1) \\ z_1 \leftarrow z_1 + \Delta(\gamma y_1 - \delta\beta_1 y_1 z_1 - \alpha\beta_2 y_2 z_1) \\ z_2 \leftarrow z_2 + \Delta(\gamma y_2 - \delta\beta_2 y_2 z_2 - \alpha\beta_1 y_1 z_2) \end{pmatrix}$$
end while

We note that the model in [30] uses truncated Normal distributions, as [30] is limited to finite supports for the program variables, which is not the case with our work.

In the loop above, each of the variables exhibits non-linear self-dependence, and so the variables are partitioned into $D(\mathcal{P}) = \{x, y_1, y_2, z_1, x_2\}$ and $E(\mathcal{P}) = \emptyset$. While the recurrence operator of the loop above is unsolvable, our approach infers polynomial loop invariants using defective variable reasoning (Sect. 5). Namely, we generate the following closed-form solutions over expected values of program variables:

$$\mathbb{E}(x(n) + y_1(n) + y_2(n) + z_1(n) + z_2(n)) = 1045,$$
$$\mathbb{E}((x(n) + y_1(n) + y_2(n) + z_1(n) + z_2(n))^2) = 3277349/3, \quad \text{and}$$
$$\mathbb{E}((x(n) + y_1(n) + y_2(n) + z_1(n) + z_2(n))^3) = 1142497455.$$

One can interpret such invariants in terms of the biological assumptions in the model. Take, for example, the fact that $\mathbb{E}(x(n) + y_1(n) + y_2(n) + z_1(n) + z_2(n))$ is constant. This invariant is in line with the assumption in the model that total population of the swarm is constant. In fact, our invariants reflect the behaviour of the system in the original *continuous-time* model proposed in [3], because our approach is able to process all coefficients (most importantly Δ) as symbolic constants.

Example 10. (Probabilistic Transition Systems [31]). Consider the following probabilistic loop modelling a *probabilistic transition system* from [31]:

while $\star$ **do**
$$\begin{pmatrix} a \\ b \end{pmatrix} \leftarrow \begin{pmatrix} \text{Normal}(0,1) \\ \text{Normal}(0,1) \end{pmatrix}$$
$$\begin{pmatrix} x \\ y \end{pmatrix} \leftarrow \begin{pmatrix} x + axy \\ y + bxy \end{pmatrix}$$
end while

While [31] uses martingale theory to synthesise a degree one invariant of the form $a\mathbb{E}(x_k) + b\mathbb{E}(y_k) = a\mathbb{E}(x_0) + b\mathbb{E}(y_0)$, our work automatically generates invariants over higher-order moments involving the defective variables x and y, as presented in Table 2.

The next example demonstrates an unsolvable loop whose recurrence operator cannot (yet) be handled by our work.

Example 11 (Trigonometric Updates). As our approach is limited to polynomial updates of the program variables, the loop below cannot be handled by our work:

while $\star$ **do**
$$\begin{pmatrix} x \\ y \end{pmatrix} \leftarrow \begin{pmatrix} \cos(x) \\ \sin(x) \end{pmatrix}$$
end while

Note the trigonometric functions are transcendental, from which it follows that one cannot generally obtain closed-form solutions for the program variables.

Nevertheless, this program does admit polynomial invariants in the program variables; for example, $x^2 + y^2 = 1$. Although our definition of a defective variables does not apply here, we could say the variable x here is *somehow defective*: while the exact value of $\sin(x)$ cannot be computed, it could be approximated using power series. Extending our work with more general notions of defective variables is an interesting line for future work.

We conclude this section with the following custom-made benchmarks. We have tailored these benchmarks to demonstrate the flexibility and applicability of our method to the current state of the art. Our experimental analysis is delayed to Sect. 8.

Example 12. (squares+).

$s, x, y, z \leftarrow 0, 2, 1, 0$
while $\star$ **do**
    $s \leftarrow$ Bernoulli(1/2)
    $z \leftarrow z - 1 \{1/2\}\ z + 2$
    $x \leftarrow 2x + y^2 + s + z$
    $y \leftarrow 2y - y^2 + 2s$
end while

Example 13. (prob-squares).

$g \leftarrow 1$
while $\star$ **do**
    $g \leftarrow$ Uniform$(g, 2g)$
$$\begin{pmatrix} a \\ b \\ c \end{pmatrix} \leftarrow \begin{pmatrix} a^2 + 2bc - df + b \\ df - a^2 + 2bd + 2c \\ g - bc - bd + \frac{1}{2}a \end{pmatrix}$$
end while

Example 14. (squares-squared).

while $\star$ **do**
$$\begin{pmatrix} x \\ y \\ z \\ m \end{pmatrix} \leftarrow \begin{pmatrix} xyz + x^2 \\ 2y + z - x^2 + 3ymz^2 \\ \frac{3}{2}x + \frac{3}{2}z + \frac{1}{2}y + \frac{1}{2}x^2 \\ \frac{2}{3}z + 3m - \frac{1}{3}x^2 - \frac{1}{3}xyz - ymz^2 \end{pmatrix}$$
end while

Example 15. (deg-d). The benchmarks deg-5, deg-6, deg-7, deg-8, deg-9, and deg-500 are parameterised by the degree d in the following program.

$x, y \leftarrow 1, 1$
while $\star$ **do**
    $z \leftarrow$ Normal$(0, 1)$
$$\begin{pmatrix} x \\ y \end{pmatrix} \leftarrow \begin{pmatrix} 2x^d + z + z^2 \\ 3x^d + z + z^2 + z^3 \end{pmatrix}$$
end while

8   Experiments

In this section we report on our implementation towards fully automating the analysis of unsolvable loops, and describe our experimental setting and results.

Implementation. Algorithm 1 together with our method for synthesising invariants involving defective variables is implemented in the `Polar` tool[3]. We use `python3` and the `sympy` package [24] for symbolic manipulations of algebraic expressions.

Benchmark Selection. While previous works [1,14,21,27–29] consider invariant synthesis, their techniques are only applicable in a restricted setting: the analysed loops are, for the most part, solvable; or, for unsolvable loops, the search for polynomial invariants is template-driven or employs heuristics. In contrast, the work herein complements and extends the techniques presented for solvable loops in [1,14,21,27–29]. Indeed, our automated approach turns the problem of polynomial invariant synthesis into a decidable problem for a larger class of unsolvable loops.

While solvable loops can clearly be analysed by our work, the main benefit of our work comes with handling unsolvable loops by translating them into solvable ones. For this reason, in our experimentation we are not interested in examples of solvable loops and so only focus on unsolvable loop benchmarks. There is therefore no sensible baseline that we can compare against, as state-of-the-art techniques cannot routinely synthesise invariants for unsolvable loops in the generality we present.

In our work we present a set of 15 examples of unsolvable loops, as listed in Table 1[4]. Common to all 15 benchmarks from Table 1 is the exhibition of circular non-linear dependencies within the variable assignments. We display features of our benchmarks in Table 1 (for example, column 3 of Table 1 counts the number of defective variables for each benchmark).

Three examples from Table 1 are challenging benchmarks taken from the invariant generation literature [5,6,30,31]; full automation in analysing these examples was not yet possible. These examples are listed as `non-lin-markov-1`, `pts`, and `bees` in Table 1, respectively corresponding to Example 2 (and hence Example 7), Example 10, and Example 9 from Sect. 7.

The remaining 12 examples of Table 1 are self-constructed benchmarks to highlight the key ingredients of our work in synthesising invariants associated with unsolvable recurrence operators.

Experimental Setup. We evaluate our approach in `Polar` on the examples from Table 1. All our experiments were performed on a machine with a 1.80 GHz Intel i7 processor and 16 GB of RAM.

---

[3] https://github.com/probing-lab/polar.

[4] each benchmark in Table 1 references, in parentheses, the respective example from our paper.

Table 1. Features of the benchmarks. VAR = Total number of loop variables; DEF = Number of defective variables; TERM = Total number of terms in assignments; DEG = Maximum degree in assignments; CAND-7 = Number of monomials in candidate with degree 7; EQN-7 = Size of the system of equations associated with a candidate of degree 7; - = Timeout (60 s).

BENCHMARK	VAR	DEF	TERM	DEG	CAND-7	EQN-7
squares (Fig. 1a)	3	2	8	2	35	113
squares+ (Ex. 12)	4	2	12	2	35	204
non-lin-markov-1 (Ex. 2)	2	2	11	2	35	64
non-lin-markov-2 (Ex. 8)	2	2	11	2	35	64
prob-squares (Ex. 13)	4	3	13	2	119	–
squares-and-cube (Fig. 1b)	3	3	4	3	119	337
pts (Ex. 10)	4	2	6	3	35	57
squares-squared (Ex. 14)	4	4	15	4	329	–
bees (Ex. 9)	5	5	21	5	791	–
deg-5 (Ex. 15)	3	2	8	5	35	42
deg-6 (Ex. 15)	3	2	8	6	35	42
deg-7 (Ex. 15)	3	2	8	7	35	42
deg-8 (Ex. 15)	3	2	8	8	35	43
deg-9 (Ex. 15)	3	2	8	9	35	43
deg-500 (Ex. 15)	3	2	8	500	35	43

Evaluation Setting. The landscape of benchmarks in the invariant synthesis literature for solvable loops can appear complex with: high numbers of variables, high degrees in polynomial updates, and multiple update options. However, we do not intend to compete on these metrics for solvable loops. The power of Algorithm 1 lies in its ability to handle 'unsolvable' loop programs: those with cyclic inter-dependencies and non-linear self-dependencies in the loop body. While the benchmarks of Table 1 may be considered simple, the fact that previous works cannot systematically handle such *simple models* crystallises that even simple loops can be unsolvable, limiting the applicability of state-of-the-art methods, as illustrated in the example below.

Example 16. Consider the question: *does the unsolvable loop program* deg-9 *in Table 1 (i.e. Example 15) possess an invariant of degree 3?* The program variables for deg-9 are x, y, and z. The variables x and y are defective. Using Polar, we derive that the cubic, non-trivial polynomial $p(x_n, y_n, z_n)$ given by

$$12(ay_n + by_n^2 + cy_n^3 + dx_n + ex_ny_n + fx_ny_n^2) - (3a + 24b + 117c + 2d + 17e + 26f)x_n^2$$
$$- (6a - 6b + 315c + 4d - 2e + 88f)x_n^2y_n + 3(3a - 3b + 144c + 2d - e + 35f)x_n^3$$

yields a polynomial loop invariant of degree 3, where a, b, c, d, e, and f are symbolic constants. Moreover, for $n \geq 1$, the expectation of this polynomial (deg-9 is a probabilistic loop) in the nth iteration is given by

$$\mathbb{E}(p(x_n, y_n, z_n)) = -108a + 312b - 1962c - 68d + 52e - 68f.$$

Table 2. The time elapsed to automatically synthesise candidates with closed-forms (results in seconds).

	Candidate degree						
BENCHMARK	1	2	3	4	5	6	7
squares (Fig. 1a)	*1.03	1.22	1.07	2.36	5.34	14.05	39.36
squares+ (Ex. 12)	*0.88	1.06	0.90	2.14	5.89	13.85	32.51
non-lin-markov-1 (Ex. 2)	*0.46	*0.94	*2.25	*3.84	*6.45	*12.29	*21.35
non-lin-markov-2 (Ex. 8)	*0.54	*1.06	*2.35	*4.43	*8.02	*14.07	*24.32
prob-squares (Ex. 13)	*0.80	0.93	4.29	22.50	–	–	–
squares-and-cube (Fig. 1b)	0.31	*0.72	*1.40	*3.11	*7.07	*25.74	–
pts (Ex. 10)	*0.33	*0.55	*0.93	*1.12	*1.78	*2.63	*3.75
squares-squared (Ex. 14)	*0.52	1.75	10.38	–	–	–	–
bees (Ex. 9)	*0.73	*4.80	*53.97	–	–	–	–
deg-5 (Ex. 15)	*0.43	*0.87	*1.83	*4.50	*9.88	*22.81	*45.58
deg-6 (Ex. 15)	*0.41	*0.85	*1.83	*4.39	*10.19	*23.00	*44.29
deg-7 (Ex. 15)	*0.42	*0.85	*1.79	*4.72	*10.04	*25.06	*47.27
deg-8 (Ex. 15)	*0.43	*0.93	*1.89	*4.38	*10.20	*23.91	*49.10
deg-9 (Ex. 15)	*0.43	*0.93	*1.91	*4.49	*10.83	*22.85	*51.97
deg-500 (Ex. 15)	*0.43	*0.85	*1.96	*4.55	*9.75	*23.46	*50.04

– = Timeout (60 s); * = Found invariant of the corresponding degree.

Experimental Results. Our experiments using Polar to synthesise invariants are summarised in Table 2, using the examples of Table 1. Patterns in Table 2 show that, if time considerations are the limiting factor, then the greatest impact cannot be attributed to the number of program variables nor the maximum degree in the program assignments (Table 1). Three of the examples in Table 1 exhibit timeouts (60 s) in the final column. The property common to each of these examples is the high number of monomial terms in any polynomial candidate of degree 7. In turn, this property feeds into a large system of simultaneous equations, which we solve to test for invariants. Indeed, time elapsed is not so strongly correlated with either of these program features. As supporting evidence we note the specific attributes of benchmark deg-500 whose assignments include polynomial updates of large degree and yet returns synthesised invariants with relatively low time elapsed in Table 2. We note the significantly longer running times associated with the benchmark bees (Example 9). This suggests that mutual dependencies between program variables in the loop assignment explain this phenomenon: such inter-relations lead to the construction of larger systems of equations, which itself feeds into the problem of resolving the recurrence equation associated with a candidate.

Experimental Summary. Our experiments illustrate the feasibility of synthesising invariants using our approach for programs with unsolvable recurrence operators from various domains such as biological systems, probabilistic loops and classical programs (see Sect. 5). This further motivates the theoretical characterisation of unsolvable operators in terms of defective variables (Sect. 4).

9   Conclusion

We establish a new technique that synthesises invariants for loops with unsolvable recurrence operators and show its applicability for deterministic and probabilistic programs. The technique is based on our new characterisation of unsolvable loops in terms of effective and defective variables: the presence of defective variables is equivalent to unsolvability. In order to synthesise invariants, we provide an algorithm to isolate the defective program variables and a new method to compute polynomial combinations of defective variables admitting exponential polynomial closed-forms. The implementation of our approach in the tool `Polar` and our experimental evaluation demonstrate the usefulness of our alternative characterisation of unsolvable loops and the applicability of our invariant synthesis technique to systems from various domains.

References

1. Bartocci, E., Kovács, L., Stankovic, M.: Automatic generation of moment-based invariants for Prob-solvable loops. In: Proceedings of ATVA, pp. 255–276 (2019)
2. Bartocci, E., Kovács, L., Stankovic, M.: Analysis of Bayesian networks via Prob-solvable loops. In: Proceedings of ICTAC, pp. 221–241 (2020)
3. Britton, N.F., Franks, N.R., Pratt, S.C., Seeley, T.D.: Deciding on a new home: how do honeybees agree? Proceedings of the Royal Society of London. Series B: Biological Sciences, vol. 269(1498), pp. 1383–1388 (2002)
4. Chakarov, A., Sankaranarayanan, S.: Probabilistic program analysis with martingales. In: Sharygina, N., Veith, H. (eds.) Computer Aided Verification, pp. 511–526. Springer, Berlin Heidelberg (2013). https://doi.org/10.1007/978-3-642-39799-8_34
5. Chakarov, A., Voronin, Y.L., Sankaranarayanan, S.: Deductive proofs of almost sure persistence and recurrence properties. In: Proceedings of TACAS, pp. 260–279 (2016)
6. Dreossi, T., Dang, T., Piazza, C.: Parallelotope bundles for polynomial reachability. In: Proceedings of HSCC, pp. 297–306 (2016)
7. Elspas, B., Green, M., Levitt, K., Waldinger, R.: Research in Interactive Program-Proving Techniques. Technical report, SRI (1972)
8. Everest, G., van der Poorten, A., Shparlinski, I., Ward, T.: Recurrence Sequences, Math. Surveys Monogr., vol. 104. Amer. Math. Soc., Providence, RI (2003)
9. Farzan, A., Kincaid, Z.: Compositional recurrence analysis. In: FMCAD, pp. 57–64 (2015)
10. Frohn, F., Hark, M., Giesl, J.: Termination of polynomial loops. In: Proceedings of SAS, pp. 89–112 (2020)
11. Hoare, C.A.R.: An axiomatic basis for computer programming. Commun. ACM **12**(10), 576–580 (1969)
12. Hrushovski, E., Ouaknine, J., Pouly, A., Worrell, J.: Polynomial invariants for affine programs. In: Proceedings of the 33rd Annual ACM/IEEE Symposium on Logic in Computer Science (LICS 2018). Association for Computing Machinery, New York, NY, USA, pp. 530–539 (2018). https://doi.org/10.1145/3209108.3209142
13. Huang, Z., Fan, C., Mereacre, A., Mitra, S., Kwiatkowska, M.Z.: Invariant verification of nonlinear hybrid automata networks of cardiac cells. In: Proceedings of CAV, pp. 373–390 (2014)

14. Humenberger, A., Jaroschek, M., Kovács, L.: Aligator.jl - A Julia package for loop invariant generation. In: Proceedings of CICM, pp. 111–117 (2018)

15. Humenberger, A., Jaroschek, M., Kovács, L.: Automated generation of non-linear loop invariants utilizing hypergeometric sequences. In: Proceedings of ISSAC, pp. 221–228 (2017)

16. Humenberger, A., Jaroschek, M., Kovács, L.: Invariant generation for multi-path loops with polynomial assignments. In: Proceedings of VMCAI, pp. 226–246 (2018)

17. Kaminski, B.L., Katoen, J., Matheja, C., Olmedo, F.: Weakest precondition reasoning for expected run-times of probabilistic programs. In: Proceedings of ESOP, pp. 364–389 (2016)

18. Katz, S., Manna, Z.: Logical analysis of programs. Commun. ACM **19**(4), 188–206 (1976)

19. Kauers, M., Paule, P.: The Concrete Tetrahedron. Texts and Monographs in Symbolic Computation. Springer Vienna (2011). https://doi.org/10.1007/978-3-211-99314-9

20. Kauers, M., Zimmermann, B.: Computing the algebraic relations of C-finite sequences and Multisequences. J. Symb. Comput. **43**, 787–803 (2008)

21. Kincaid, Z., Cyphert, J., Breck, J., Reps, T.W.: Non-linear reasoning for invariant synthesis. In: Proceedings of POPL, pp. 54:1–54:33 (2018)

22. Kovács, L.: Reasoning algebraically about P-solvable loops. In: Proceedings of TACAS, pp. 249–264 (2008)

23. Lattner, C., Adve, V.S.: LLVM: A compilation framework for lifelong program analysis & transformation. In: Proceedings of CGO, pp. 75–88 (2004)

24. Meurer, A., et al.: SymPy: symbolic computing in Python. Peer J. Comput. Sci. **3**, e103 (2017)

25. Moosbrugger, M., Stankovic, M., Bartocci, E., Kovács, L.: This is the moment for probabilistic loops. CoRR abs/2204.07185 (2022). To appear in the proceedings of OOPSLA 2022

26. Müller-Olm, M., Seidl, H.: Computing polynomial program invariants. Inf. Process. Lett. **91**(5), 233–244 (2004)

27. de Oliveira, S., Bensalem, S., Prevosto, V.: Polynomial invariants by linear algebra. In: Proceedings of ATVA, pp. 479–494 (2016)

28. Rodríguez-Carbonell, E., Kapur, D.: Generating all polynomial invariants in simple loops. J. Symb. Comput. 443–476 (2007)

29. Rodríguez-Carbonell, E., Kapur, D.: Automatic generation of polynomial loop invariants: algebraic foundations. In: Proceedings of ISSAC, p. 266–273 (2004)

30. Sankaranarayanan, S., Chou, Y., Goubault, E., Putot, S.: Reasoning about uncertainties in discrete-time dynamical systems using polynomial forms. In: Proceedings of NeurIPS, pp. 17502–17513 (2020)

31. Schreuder, A., Ong, C.L.: Polynomial Probabilistic Invariants and the Optional Stopping Theorem. CoRR abs/1910.12634 (2019)

Principles of Staged Static+Dynamic Partial Analysis

Aditya Anand[ID] and Manas Thakur[✉][ID]

Indian Institute of Technology Mandi, Kamand, India
ud21002@students.iitmandi.ac.in, manas@iitmandi.ac.in

Abstract. In spite of decades of static-analysis research behind developing precise whole-program analyses, languages that use just-in-time (JIT)
compilers suffer from the imprecision of resource-bound analyses local to
the scope of compilation. Recent promising approaches bridge this gap by
splitting program analysis into two phases: a static phase that identifies
interprocedural dependencies across program elements, and a dynamic
phase that resolves those dependencies to generate final analysis results.
Though this approach is capable of generating precise analysis results
without incurring analysis cost in JIT compilers, such "staged analyses" lack a theoretical backing. In particular, it is unclear if one could
transform a general whole-program analysis (that resolves dependencies
across all program elements) to a staged one that involves evaluation of
statically generated partial results later. Similarly, it would be interesting
if one could generate such "partial-result evaluators" in a way that can
also be used to argue about their correctness. In this paper, we propose
a novel model of static+dynamic partial analysis that addresses all these
points, based on the classic theory of partial evaluation.

We begin by shedding light on the enigmatic idea of partial evaluation
as well as the associated notion of Futamura projections to generate specialized program interpreters. We then describe *partial analysis* as the
process of evaluating dependencies across program elements with respect
to the statically available parts of a program, resulting into *partial results*.
Next, we devise a strategy (by deriving a novel notion of *AM projections*
from Futamura projections) to statically generate specialized evaluators
that can process partial results using dynamic dependencies, at run-
time. Later, we use our proposed model to straightforwardly establish
the correctness and precision properties of the idea of staging, independent of the program analysis under consideration. We demonstrate the
applicability of our model by showcasing examples from non-trivial Java
program analyses, implementing the pipeline for one of them, and also
discussing future possibilities to extend the same. We believe that our
contributions in formulating this theory of partial analysis will significantly extend the usage of existing partial analyzers, as well as promote
the design of new ones, for and even beyond Java.

Keywords: Staged analysis · Partial evaluation · Partial analysis

This research was partially supported by the project IITM/SERB/MTH/311 funded
by the Science and Engineering Research Board (SERB), Government of India.

G. Singh and C. Urban (Eds.): SAS 2022, LNCS 13790, pp. 44–73, 2022.
https://doi.org/10.1007/978-3-031-22308-2_4

1   Introduction

A lion's share of research in the programming language community is focused on devising novel compilation technologies for performance. In order to generate a performant binary, compilers for various programming languages perform a series of program analyses and optimizations on the program being compiled. The quality of the optimizations performed depends on the precision of the underlying program analyses. The holy grail in the space of precise program analyses is the ability to analyze the whole program. However, in case of languages such as Java and C#, where the complete program is available only during run-time (e.g., in Java Virtual Machines), performing whole-program analysis during just-in-time (JIT) compilation is prohibitively expensive. On the other hand, owing to the separate compilation assumption [2], it is possible to "partially analyze" various parts of the program statically.

Partial analysis is a program analysis technique used in compilation systems where the whole program is not available for analysis [8,9,18,28]. Traditionally, this implies generating analysis results without the ability to incorporate the effects of the unavailable parts of the program, which again loses precision. However, for languages like Java and C# where program translation is spread across static and JIT compilation, it is a promising idea to "stage" the program analysis itself across the static and the dynamic phases of compilation. Recent approaches such as the PYE framework [28] use this idea to statically generate "dependencies" from various elements of the known program to the unknown parts of the program, which are then resolved during JIT compilation. As an example, consider the Java code snippet shown in Fig. 1; say the object(s) allocated at line l are represented using the abstract object O_l. Here, what happens to the object O_3 depends on what happens to the respective first parameters in methods A.bar and B.bar. Assuming all the code of class A is available statically whereas that of class B is available only during run-time, we can resolve the dependencies related to A.bar statically, but for B.bar only during run-time. The idea behind staging is to generate such dependencies, resolve them as much as possible statically, and then complete the analysis results by resolving the residual dependencies during run-time. A point worth noting though is that this promising approach has stark similarities with the idea of *partial evaluation*.

Partial evaluation [14] is a well-known program optimization technique that specializes a given program with respect to its statically available inputs. The resultant partially evaluated program can later be executed with the dynamic inputs, to generate the final output. The advantage of performing partial evaluation is that the specialized program often executes faster compared to executing the original program provided both static and dynamic inputs together. Apart from specializing a program with its static inputs, partial evaluation has also been used to specialize interpreters and their generators, based on the notion of Futamura projections [12]. In this paper, drawing inspirations from the theory of partial evaluation, we devise a model to stage the process of obtaining the results of a whole-program analysis, by staging the same into static and dynamic components, independent of the analysis being performed.

```
1 class A {
2     void foo(A a1) {
3         A a2 = new A(); // Object O₃
4         a1.bar(a2);
5     }
6     void bar(A p) {...} }
```

```
7 class B extends A {
8     void bar(A q) {...}
9 }
```

Fig. 1. A Java code snippet to demonstrate generation of dependencies.

Observe that staging a whole-program analysis based on prior evaluation of static dependencies and residual evaluation of dynamic dependencies, as noted above and as illustrated in Fig. 2, would require a special component (say a "partial-result evaluator"), which is capable of consuming dynamic inputs and completing the analysis results. An important question that begs an answer here is whether and how could one generate such special evaluators that can "process partial results". Further, in order to hold the efficiency advantages of staging, it is important that the generation of such evaluators is itself efficient and if possible, offloaded to the static compiler. The next question thence is, can we design a "generator" that efficiently generates partial-result evaluators, given the standard evaluator for a particular whole-program analysis. Finally, assuming these components exist, can we assert that the staged analysis would generate the same result as the corresponding whole-program analysis. In this paper, we answer all these questions with a strong affirmation by modeling the staging scheme based on the classic theory of partial evaluation.

We begin by formulating whole-program analysis as the process of computing and resolving dependencies of various elements on different parts of the program. Followed by this, we define partial analysis as the process of partially evaluating those dependencies with respect to the statically available parts of a program, thus generating partial results for the analysis being performed. We then devise a strategy (called *first AM projection*) to "generate" an evaluator that can process these partial results by performing residual resolution using the evaluated values of dynamically available dependencies. Later, to improve the efficiency of generating such partial-result evaluators for different analyses, we propose a series of specializations (called *second and third AM projections*). Finally, illuminating the similarities between our model of partial analysis and the theory of partial evaluation, we prove that the results generated by an analysis staged using our scheme would be the same as the ones generated by its whole-program version.

In order to validate the concepts presented in our manuscript, we implemented prototypes of the different components of our staging scheme. Specifically, we first designed a simple evaluator that could resolve a set of dependencies and generate the analysis result for a given program element. This evaluator is written in a way that in case of staged analysis (where only static dependencies can be resolved initially), it generates a partial result. We next implemented a

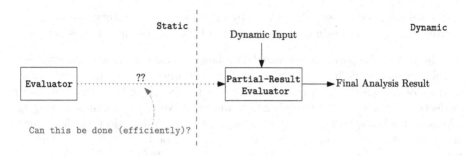

Fig. 2. Generation of partial-result evaluators.

specializer that takes the above evaluator and specializes it with the given partial result, to generate the partial-result evaluator. This partial-result evaluator can take evaluated values of dynamic dependencies as input and generate the final analysis result(s). Notably, such partial-result evaluators are independent of the way dependencies are generated for a particular analysis, agnostic of the tiered nature of modern managed runtimes, and can be invoked as soon as the values of dynamic dependencies are available. Our prototype demonstrates this by using dependencies generated for escape analysis [7,27] of Java programs, generating partial-result evaluators for abstract objects therein, and invoking them for dependencies on methods from the Java class library. Further, though the example analysis is based on method summaries, the idea of staging can be applied to other models of program analysis as well (as long as the dependencies can be categorized into static and dynamic components).

Having described partial-result evaluators and their generators in the said form (which describes standard staging), we observe that certain ways modern tiered runtimes (such as JVMs) operate raise few interesting questions. For example: "Can residual dependencies be always resolved?" "What if at certain execution points all the dynamic inputs are not available?" "In case resolution cannot proceed, can we generate a more precise value than falling back to the most conservative solution?" We discuss possible directions to address these questions, along with drawing connections with few other ways of performing program analysis, as interesting future extensions to the foundational model of staged static+dynamic partial analysis proposed in this paper.

Contributions:

- We explain partial evaluation and Futamura projections in context of speeding up the execution of programs and of the generation of program translators, in a lucid and easy-to-understand manner.
- We formalize the definition of partial analysis and devise a scheme to stage whole-program analyses into static and dynamic components, along with a novel notion of AM projections.
- We establish the correctness and precision properties of our staging scheme, based on results from the theory of partial evaluation.

– We validate the presented concepts by implementing a prototype that generates partial-result evaluators independent of the analysis under consideration.

The rest of the paper is organized as follows. In Sect. 2, we give an overview of relevant concepts from an existing staging framework required for further reading of the paper. In Sect. 3, we describe partial evaluation and Futamura projections in a readily comprehensible manner. We then present our staging scheme for whole-program analysis, along with the AM projections for generating partial-result evaluators, in Sect. 4. We describe the details of our prototype implementation to validate the presented concepts in Sect. 5. In Sect. 6, we highlight few of the challenges posed by contemporary programming-language runtimes, possible ways to deal with the same, as well as connections of our staging scheme with few other ways of performing program analysis. Finally, we discuss related work in Sect. 7, and conclude the paper in Sect. 8.

2   Background: The PYE Framework

To address the problem of imprecision of program analysis in JIT compilers, Thakur and Nandivada [28] propose a two-step solution called the PYE (Precise Yet Efficient) framework. PYE uses the concept of partial analysis [9] to generate partial results for all the statically analyzable parts of a program, and uses those results during run-time to generate the final result. In order to account for the unavailability of libraries while analyzing applications (and vice-versa) without losing precision, PYE generates dependencies across the elements of a program as *conditional values* statically, and evaluates them during run-time. We next describe the generation and evaluation of such conditional values, along with a representation that fits in with the notations that we use throughout this paper.

2.1   Conditional Values

Given a method m in a program P, a traditional whole-program analysis ψ generates a summary f_m mapping each program element $x \in m$ in the domain $\mathcal{D}$ of the analysis to one of the values in the set of dataflow values Val for that analysis. Thus, $f_m(x)$ denotes the *analysis result* for the element x present in method m. As an instance, for escape analysis [7], the set $\mathcal{D}$ could consist of all the abstract objects allocated in the method m and the set Val could be $\{D, E\}$, denoting *DoesNotEscape* and *Escapes*, respectively.

On the other hand, let $g_m(x)$ represent the set of conditional values for a program element x present in method m. A conditional value denotes dependence on another program element, and is defined in PYE as a 3-length tuple $\langle \Theta, v, v' \rangle$, where $\Theta = \langle u, y \rangle$ represents the dependee element y in method u, and v and v' are values from the lattice Val of the traditional analysis. A conditional value $\langle \langle n, y \rangle, v, v' \rangle$ can be evaluated to obtain v' if the analysis result $f_n(y)$ equals v.

For example, consider the code shown in Fig. 3. If the analysis ψ being performed is escape analysis, then the set $g_{\texttt{A.foo}}(O_4)$ of conditional values that determines the escape status of the abstract object O_4 allocated at line 4 is:

```
1  class A {
2      void foo(B b) {
3          A a1 = new A(); // Object O₃
4          A a2 = new A(); // Object O₄
5          a1.bar(a2);
6          L l1 = new L(); // Object O₆
7          l1.lib(a2); }
8      void  bar(A p1) {
9          // no assignment to p1
10     } }
```

```
1  class L {
2      // A library class
3      void lib(A r1) {
4          // A library method
5          ...
6      } }
```

Fig. 3. A Java code snippet to demonstrate static+JIT analysis. Class L is a library class not available during the analysis of the application class A.

$$g_{\text{A.foo}}(O_4) = \{\langle\langle\text{A.bar},\text{p1}\rangle, D, D\rangle, \langle\langle\text{L.lib},\text{r1}\rangle, D, D\rangle,$$
$$\langle\langle\text{A.bar},\text{p1}\rangle, E, E\rangle, \langle\langle\text{L.lib},\text{r1}\rangle, E, E\rangle\} \tag{1}$$

Here, the set of conditional values indicates that the escape status of O_4 depends on the escape statuses of the first parameters of the methods A.bar and L.lib. The conditional values denoting dependence on class A can be resolved statically, whereas those depending on the library class L are resolved at runtime. Note that we are directly using the names of parameters (that is, p1 and r1) in the conditional values for brevity; in practice they would be placeholders representing the first parameter of the corresponding method.

2.2 Evaluation of Conditional Values

Given a set $g_m(x)$ of conditional values generated for an analysis ψ, PYE evaluates them at run-time using an *evaluator*; we denote the same as CEval_ψ (see Fig. 4). CEval_ψ takes $g_m(x)$ along with the analysis results for all the dependencies contained therein ($\text{IN}_{g_m(x)}$ in Fig. 4), and generates $f_m(x)$ as follows:

$$f_m(x) = \sqcap_{\forall T \in g_m(x)} [\![T]\!] \tag{2}$$

where $T = \langle\langle\text{n},\text{y}\rangle, v, v'\rangle$ is resolved as:

$$[\![\langle\langle\text{n},\text{y}\rangle, v, v'\rangle]\!] = (f_n(y) == v) ? v' : \perp \tag{3}$$

$\perp$ being the most precise element in the lattice of the analysis ψ.

Using Eqs. 2 and 3, CEval_ψ can evaluate the conditional values for each program element and generate final results for the analysis ψ. Note that when a dependence in $g_m(x)$ cannot be evaluated statically, PYE takes *meet* simply as a union of the conditional values present therein.

For example, evaluating $T = \langle\langle\text{A.bar},\text{p1}\rangle, D, D\rangle$ in $g_{\text{A.foo}}(O_4)$ amounts to analyzing the method A.bar (to obtain $f_{\text{A.bar}}$), then looking up the escape status

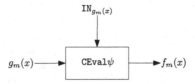

Fig. 4. Whole-program analysis.

of the abstract object pointed-to by p1 (i.e. the escape status $f_{\text{A.bar}}(O_{p1})$, if p points to O_{p_1}), and then checking if it equals D; if yes, then $\mathcal{T}$ gets evaluated to D, else to the most precise element of the analysis lattice (which also happens to be D for escape analysis). Finally, after evaluating each conditional value in $g_{\text{A.foo}}(O_4)$, we can use Eq. 2 to compute the meet of the individual evaluated values, in order to obtain the final analysis result $f_{\text{A.foo}}(O_4)$.

The approach of offloading complex analyses to static time and finishing the results during run-time can be used to perform various kinds of program analyses, and has been used in the past for escape analysis to elide synchronization and points-to analysis to elide null-checks [28], and even to perform dependence analysis for parallelizing loops [25]. In general, this approach can be used for any analysis with a finite lattice (to generate a finite number of conditional values), as discussed in detail in prior work [28].

In this paper, we develop a model of staged static+dynamic partial analyses, which allows us to straightforwardly prove the correctness and precision of the idea of staging as discussed above. We start with shedding light on the enigmatic [23] theory of partial evaluation and Futamura projections in a novel way (Sect. 3), and then use it to describe our model for partial analysis (Sect. 4).

3   Partial Evaluation and Futamura Projections

Partial evaluation [14] is a program evaluation technique that specializes a program with respect to its available inputs. The specialized program can take the remaining input[1] and generate the same output as the original program. The program that specializes other programs in this manner is called a *partial evaluator* (traditionally referred to as Mix). This way of specializing a program P with respect to a statically available input in_1 to generate the specialized program P_{in_1} that can take the remaining input in_2, often speeds up the overall execution as well. Thus, if the time taken by Mix to specialize P is $T_{\text{Mix}}(P, \text{in}_1)$, the time taken by P_{in_1} to generate the final output is $T_{P_{\text{in}_1}}(\text{in}_2)$, and the time taken by the original program P to generate the output in a single run is $T_P(\text{in}_1, \text{in}_2)$, then partial evaluation is often advantageous, as:

$$T_{\text{Mix}}(P, \text{in}_1) + T_{P_{\text{in}_1}}(\text{in}_2) < T_P(\text{in}_1, \text{in}_2)$$

---

[1] Note that at the machine level, there is an interpreter that actually executes the program along with its input; we are simply avoiding verbosity here.

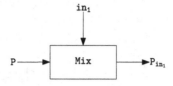

Fig. 5. Partial evaluation of program P using in_1.

In context of just-in-time (JIT) compilers, the time spent in performing program analysis gets added to the execution time of the program, thus making whole-program analysis during JIT compilation practically infeasible. Consequently, JIT compilers resort to very imprecise (e.g., intraprocedural) analyses. Thus, motivated by the possible efficiency advantages of partial evaluation, a promising way to obtain whole-program analysis results efficiently during JIT compilation is to perform partial analysis of the statically available program, and then complete the partial results during JIT compilation. In order to establish that this way of staging whole-program analysis across static and JIT compilation is correct, in this paper, we formalize a theory of partial analysis based on the prior theory of partial evaluation.

We now present an intuitive formulation of partial evaluation, along with the projections proposed by Futamura [12] to describe the generation of various partial evaluators; we extend this formulation to partial analysis in Sect. 4.

3.1 Partial Evaluation

Consider the partial evaluation scheme shown in Fig. 5. For a given program P and its available input in_1, the partial evaluator Mix generates the residual program P_{in_1}. This partially evaluated program, when given the remaining input in_2, yields the same result as running the original program on all of the inputs:

$$[\![P_{in_1}]\!](in_2) = [\![P]\!](in_1, in_2)$$

where $[\![P_{in_1}]\!](in_2)$ denotes the evaluation of P_{in_1} with in_2 as input, and $[\![P]\!](in_1, in_2)$ denotes the evaluation of P with in_1 and in_2 as inputs. The idea behind partial evaluation is that if the input in_2 changes more frequently than the input in_1, then evaluating the partially evaluated program P_{in_1} on in_2 will be faster than evaluating P on the complete input.

Partial evaluation can also be used to generate specialized versions of higher levels of abstraction in the program translation ecosystem. For example, an interpreter is a program that takes other programs along with their inputs and generates the output for those programs. "What if we use the idea of partial evaluation to specialize an interpreter with respect to a given input program? We get a faster interpreter for that program!" This specialization was described by Futamura as the first Futamura projection (FP), as discussed next.

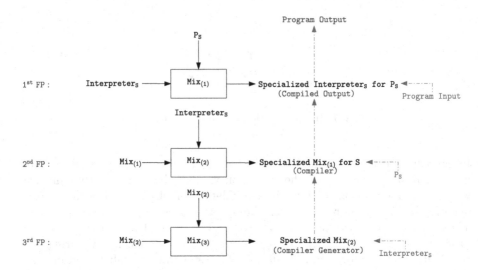

Fig. 6. Futamura projections in partial evaluation. Note that the three Mixes are the same specializers; we have added subscripted numbers for brevity in referencing them.

3.2   First Futamura Projection

The first Futamura projection describes how to specialize an interpreter for a given source program; see Fig. 6 (1st FP). Here, the partial evaluator ($\texttt{Mix}_{(1)}$) essentially applies the interpreter for a language S to a given source program $\texttt{P}_S$ and generates a specialized interpreter, as illustrated by the equation below:

$$[\![\texttt{Mix}_{(1)}]\!](\texttt{Interpreter}_S)(\texttt{P}_S) = \texttt{Specialized Interpreter}_S \texttt{ for } \texttt{P}_S$$

The generated specialized interpreter can directly take the inputs of the program for which it was specialized and produce the final output. Observe that the behavior of the specialized interpreter is similar to how the binary produced by a compiler (i.e. Compiled Output, see Fig. 6) takes the input of the source program and generates final output. "Can we use the idea of partial evaluation to generate a higher order program, which when given a source program as input, generates its compiled version faster?" This is achieved using the second Futamura projection, as discussed next.

3.3   Second Futamura Projection

The second Futamura projection describes how to specialize the specializer ($\texttt{Mix}_{(1)}$) used in first Futamura projection with the interpreter for a given programming language S; see Fig. 6 (2nd FP). Here, the specializer ($\texttt{Mix}_{(2)}$) takes the specializer itself as one of the inputs along with the interpreter, and generates a specialized $\texttt{Mix}_{(1)}$ for language S as the output, as shown below:

$$[\![\texttt{Mix}_{(2)}]\!](\texttt{Mix}_{(1)})(\texttt{Interpreter}_S) = \texttt{Specialized Mix}_{(1)} \texttt{ for } S$$

The generated specialized $\text{Mix}_{(1)}$ can directly take a program P_S in the language S as input and generate a specialized interpreter for P_S. Observe that the behavior of the specialized $\text{Mix}_{(1)}$ is similar to how a source program P_S written in a language S is compiled. Hence the output of the second Futamura projection can also be called a `Compiler` (see Fig. 6). "Can we again use the idea of partial evaluation to generate another higher order program, which when given an interpreter for programs written in S, efficiently generates a compiler for programs in S?" This is achieved using the third Futamura projection, as discussed next.

3.4   Third Futamura Projection

The third Futamura projection describes how to specialize the specializer ($\text{Mix}_{(2)}$) used in second Futamura projection with itself; see Fig. 6 (3rd `FP`). Here, the specializer ($\text{Mix}_{(3)}$) takes the specializer itself as both the inputs, and generates a specialized $\text{Mix}_{(2)}$ as the output, as illustrated by the equation below:

$$[\![\text{Mix}_{(3)}]\!](\text{Mix}_{(2)})(\text{Mix}_{(2)}) = \text{Specialized Mix}_{(2)}$$

The generated specialized $\text{Mix}_{(2)}$ can directly take an interpreter for a language S as input and generate a compiler for programs written in S as the output. Hence the specialized $\text{Mix}_{(2)}$ can also be called a `Compiler Generator` for programs written in the language S. Note that it is possible to extend this idea further and describe a fourth Futamura projection to generate a compiler-generator generator, and so on.

In a nutshell, the idea of partial evaluation can be used to automatically generate specialized tools in the program translation ecosystem. Though we could not find a standard implementation of the specializer `Mix`, Jones [14] describes it as a two-phase process: first a *division prepass* classifies program inputs into `static` and `dynamic`, followed by which the division and the static inputs are used to *compress* the program, to the extent possible, statically. Further, note that though higher levels of Futamura projections do make sense, the literature finds practical use primarily of the first projection [16], and sometimes the second projection [5]. We next highlight how even staged partial analysis is similar to partial evaluation, and then come up with novel projections that allow one to stage a whole-program analysis into static and dynamic components.

4   Staged Partial Analysis

As described in Sect. 2, a promising way to avoid incurring the cost of performing precise (whole-program) analysis during JIT compilation is to first analyze the available program statically, and then complete the results when the statically unavailable (or *dynamic*) dependencies are available (could be done either during program execution in a VM, or possibly for each version of the unavailable program, i.e., libraries, ahead of time). In one way, this implies that the evaluation of conditional values for a given analysis ψ, as performed by the conditional-value evaluator CEval_ψ, has to be split across static and dynamic components.

Notation	Description
$g_m(x)$	Set of conditional values for element x in method m
$\text{IN}_{g_m(x)}$	Set of all dependencies for evaluating $g_m(x)$
CEval_ψ	A conditional-value evaluator for analysis ψ
$f_m(x)$	Final analysis result for element x in method m
S_x	Set of statically available dependencies of x
D_x	Set of dynamically available dependencies of x
$[g_m(x)]_{S_x}$	Set of conditional values specialized with S_x
Mix	Specializer program used in partial evaluation

Fig. 7. A reference to the notations used in rest of the sections.

The consequence of this splitting (or *staging*) is that the static analysis can only compute *partial results*. Such a static analysis, which works on part of the whole program, is called *partial analysis*, and the corresponding module to perform partial analysis can be called a *partial analyzer*. Subsequently, the partial results generated by the partial analyzer need to be completed by resolving the dynamically available dependencies. This in turn requires a *special evaluator* that can take partial results along with the evaluated values of dynamic dependencies, to generate final analysis results.

As one of the key contributions of this paper, we now present a novel description of the process of performing partial analysis using statically resolved conditional values, followed by a series of specializations to efficiently generate the dynamic component of the conditional-value evaluator.

4.1   Partial Analysis

Recall (from Fig. 4) that computing the final analysis result (of analysis ψ) for a program element x in a method m requires supplying the evaluated values of all the dependencies of x to the conditional-value evaluator CEval_ψ. Whereas for languages like Java, several of these dependencies might not be available statically. We now define partial analysis in context of evaluating the set of dependencies available statically; see Fig. 7 for a list of the notations used throughout this section.

Definition 1 *(Partial analysis). For a program element x in method m with a set $g_m(x)$ of conditional values, let the set S_x denote the statically available dependencies of x. Here, while trying to evaluate $g_m(x)$, if we supply S_x to the partial evaluator* Mix *(see Sect. 3), we get the result of partially evaluating $g_m(x)$ with respect to the dependencies present in S_x. This process can also be seen as "specializing" the set of conditional values for the statically available inputs. We formally term this specialization as "partial analysis", illustrated in Fig. 8.*

When we perform partial analysis of the statically available program, using the schema shown in Fig. 8, we obtain a specialized set of conditional val-

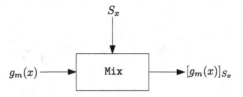

Fig. 8. Partial analysis: specializing $g_m(x)$ using the set S_x of static dependencies to obtain partial result.

ues ($[g_m(x)]_{S_x}$), which can be termed as the[2] *partial result* for the given element x. For example, in the code shown in Fig. 3, as class L is a library class not available for partial analysis, the dependencies in $g_{\text{A.foo}}(O_4)$ related to L.lib are not available statically (whereas those related to A.bar are available, forming the set S_{O_4}). Thus, the partial result $[g_{\text{A.foo}}(O_4)]_{S_{O_4}}$ generated after resolving the statically available dependencies S_{O_4} in Eq. 1, can be computed as:

$$= \ \sqcap \ \{D, D, \langle\langle\text{L.lib}, \text{r1}\rangle, D, D\rangle, D, D, \langle\langle\text{L.lib}, \text{r1}\rangle, E, E\rangle\}$$
$$(\because f_n(y) \neq v, so\ T = \bot\ i.e.\ D)$$
$$= \ \sqcap \ \{D, \langle\langle\text{L.lib}, \text{r1}\rangle, D, D\rangle, \langle\langle\text{L.lib}, \text{r1}\rangle, E, E\rangle\}$$
$$(\because D \sqcap D = D)$$
$$= \ \sqcap \ \{\langle\langle\text{L.lib}, \text{r1}\rangle, D, D\rangle, \langle\langle\text{L.lib}, \text{r1}\rangle, E, E\rangle\}$$
$$(\because D \sqcap X = X) \tag{4}$$

Given such a partial result, we need a special evaluator that can consume the runtime (dynamic) inputs to generate final analysis results for the element x. We now present a novel notion of *AM projections* that generate these special evaluators that can be used to accomplish the same.

4.2 First AM Projection

As discussed in Sect. 4.1, the output of performing partial analysis for a given program element x is a partial result (comprising of specialized conditional values $[g_m(x)]_{S_x}$). However, in order to be able to perform any optimization or transformation involving x, we need the final analysis result $f_m(x)$. Thus, we require a new evaluator that can take the partial result $[g_m(x)]_{S_x}$ as input, resolve the residual dependencies based on the evaluated values of dynamically available dependencies (say D_x), and generate $f_m(x)$. We now describe how can we generate such a "partial-result evaluator" for any program element x.

Recall the conditional-value evaluator (CEval_ψ) from Fig. 4, which, when given the set $g_m(x)$ of conditional values for an element x and the set $\text{IN}_{g_m(x)}$ of all dependencies of x, generates the final analysis result $f_m(x)$ for the analysis ψ. The first AM projection (see 1st AMP in Fig. 9) specializes CEval_ψ with

---

[2] We obtain a result later (Corollary 2) which implies that this is the only possible partial result for a given set S_x of statically available dependencies.

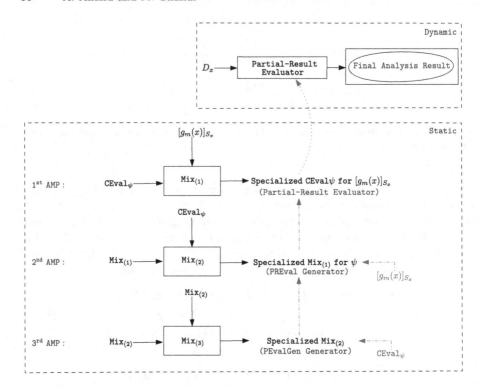

Fig. 9. AM projections in partial analysis. Note that $\texttt{Mix}_{(1)}$, $\texttt{Mix}_{(2)}$ and $\texttt{Mix}_{(3)}$ are the same specializers as used in partial evaluation; also, we have added subscripted numbers for brevity in referencing them.

respect to the partial result $[g_m(x)]_{S_x}$. The output is a specialized conditional-value evaluator that can take the set D_x of dynamically available dependencies of x to generate the final analysis result $f_m(x)$. This process of specializing the conditional-value evaluator can be summarized as follows:

$$\llbracket\texttt{Mix}_{(1)}\rrbracket(\texttt{CEval}_\psi)([g_m(x)]_{S_x}) = \texttt{Specialized CEval}_\psi \text{ for } [g_m(x)]_{S_x}$$

Note that the specialized conditional-value evaluator obtained above can be used (see the **Dynamic** module in Fig. 9) to complete the staging of the whole-program analysis ψ for the program element x. As this evaluator eventually evaluates a given partial result, we name the output of the first AM projection as **Partial-Result Evaluator**.

As an example, for the object O_4 of method $\texttt{A.foo}$ from Fig. 3, consider the partial result obtained in Eq. 4. Once the analysis result for the library class L is available, the **Partial-Result Evaluator** takes D_{O_4} (which is formed by the analysis result available for $\texttt{L.lib(r1)}$) and generates the final analysis result for O_4, as follows:

$$f_{\text{A.foo}}(O_4) = \sqcap (D, D) \quad (\text{assuming } f_{\text{L.lib}}(\text{r1}) = D, \text{ and } \because \perp = D)$$
$$= D$$

Thus, the consequence of the first AM projection is not only the fact that it is possible to derive a partial-result evaluator, but also that it can be generated statically. Further, the first AM projection also tells that for a given whole-program analysis, there also exists a component that can serve as the generator for such partial-result evaluators (which is the specializer Mix from the theory of partial evaluation). Note that the first AMP thus parallels the first Futamura projection; we next show that it is sensible to also extend the latter Futamura projections in the world of partial analysis.

4.3   Second AM Projection

Observe that the partial-result evaluator generated by the first AM projection is obtained by specializing the conditional-value evaluator for a single element in the domain of the analysis being staged. However, program analyses often generate results for multiple elements in a given program, implying that one may need to perform this specialization multiple times. To improve the efficiency of generating such specialized evaluators, we next propose a higher level of specialization, as the second AM projection.

The second AM projection (see 2nd AMP in Fig. 9) specializes the specializer $\text{Mix}_{(1)}$ itself with respect to the conditional-value evaluator CEval_ψ. The output is a specialized mix for analysis ψ that takes the specialized set of conditional values $[g_m(x)]_{S_x}$ for each element x and generates the specialized evaluator CEval_ψ for that x. This process of specializing $\text{Mix}_{(1)}$ with CEval_ψ can be summarized as follows:

$$[\![\text{Mix}_{(2)}]\!](\text{Mix}_{(1)})(\text{CEval}_\psi) = \text{Specialized Mix}_{(1)} \text{ for } \psi$$

As the output of the second AM projection can directly be used to generate the specialized CEval_ψ for each program element x, the second AM projection is a faster way of generating the partial-result evaluator compared to the first. Hence we name the output of the second AM projection as PREval Generator. We hypothesize that though this generator would give the same partial-result evaluator as the first AM projection, one could adopt the second AM projection in case of time constraints during static compilation.

4.4   Third AM Projection

Observe that the PREval Generator obtained by second AM projection can generate the partial-result evaluator for any partial result (of the form $[g_m(x)]_{S_x}$), for a particular analysis ψ. However, typical compilers perform many different program analyses. Consequently, in order to perform multiple analyses in a staged manner, one may need to perform the specialization of $\text{Mix}_{(1)}$ each time with different CEval_ψ, for varying ψ. To improve the efficiency of generating such specialized generators, we next propose a higher level of specialization, as the third AM projection.

The third AM projection (see 3rd AMP in Fig. 9) specializes the specializer Mix$_{(2)}$ with itself. The output is a specialized mix that can take as input the CEval$_\psi$ for any analysis ψ, and generate the specialized mix for that analysis ψ. This process of specializing Mix$_{(2)}$ with itself can be summarized as follows:

$$[\![\text{Mix}_{(3)}]\!](\text{Mix}_{(2)})(\text{Mix}_{(2)}) = \text{Specialized Mix}_{(2)}$$

A noteworthy point is that just by providing a conditional-value evaluator for any analysis ψ, the specialized mix can directly be used to generate the PREval Generator for that analysis ψ. Hence we name the output of the third AM projection as PREvalGen Generator.

In a nutshell, the three AM projections describe ways to efficiently generate the dynamic components required for staged static+dynamic whole-program analyses. We can summarize the specializations proposed in the three projections as follows:

1. **Partial-Result Evaluator**
   $= [\![\text{Mix}_{(1)}]\!](\text{CEval}_\psi, \text{Partial Result}) = [\![\text{PREval Generator}]\!](\text{Partial Result})$

2. **PREval Generator** $= [\![\text{Mix}_{(2)}]\!](\text{Mix}_{(1)}, \text{CEval}_\psi) = [\![\text{PREvalGen Generator}]\!](\text{CEval}_\psi)$

3. **PREvalGen Generator** $= [\![\text{Mix}_{(3)}]\!](\text{Mix}_{(2)}, \text{Mix}_{(2)})$

Thus, provided the conditional-value evaluator CEval$_\psi$ for a whole-program analysis ψ, a **PREvalGen Generator** can be used to generate a **PREval Generator**, which, when given a statically obtained partial result, can generate the corresponding **Partial Result Evaluator**, which can further be used to obtain the final analysis result given the evaluated values of dynamic dependencies. In Sect. 5, we discuss our implementation of these components using the first AM projection; the higher-order AM projections can be used to generate partial-result evaluators and their generators statically for multiple analyses.

4.5 Correctness, Precision, and Efficiency of Staging

In the previous subsections, we have seen how can we stage a whole-program analysis into static and dynamic components, based on ideas taken from the theory of partial evaluation. We now state and prove (by construction) few important properties of such a staging scheme, with respect to the correctness of staging and the precision of the results obtained, and comment on the overall efficiency of the process.

Lemma 1. *If the set of statically available dependencies is empty, then the specialization performed by the first AM projection for a conditional-value evaluator can be seen in same light as the specialization performed by the first Futamura projection for a program interpreter.*

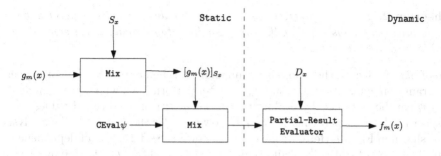

Fig. 10. A complete staging of whole-program analysis.

Proof Sketch. The first AM projection (see Fig. 9) specializes the conditional-value evaluator CEval$_\psi$ with a set $[g_m(x)]_{S_x}$ of conditional values that itself is specialized with the statically available dependencies (S_x). On the other hand, if S_x is empty (that is, the program element x does not have any static dependency), then the first AM projection would specialize CEval$_\psi$ just with $g_m(x)$, similar to the way the first Futamura projection specializes the interpreter (*evaluator* of programs) with a given source program P$_S$ (see Fig. 6).

Corollary 1. *The Partial-Result Evaluator specialized just with $g_m(x)$ is similar to the specialized interpreter obtained by the first Futamura projection, as both need to take the complete static+dynamic input (dependencies) for generating the final output (analysis result).*

Lemma 2. *Partial evaluation of a program with a statically available input implies that the program is specialized to the extent possible (that is, maximally specialized) with respect to that input.*

Proof Sketch. A partial evaluator specializes a program P with respect to some input in$_1$ by precomputing all expressions that depend on in$_1$, and then folding P to the extent possible [14], that is, in a loop until fixed point. Thus, the output of a partial evaluator is *maximal* in terms of evaluation of the program for the given set of inputs.

Corollary 2. *If the first Futamura projection uses the partially evaluated program P$_{in_1}$ (instead of the original program P) for specialization, then the obtained interpreter is maximally specialized with respect to P$_{in_1}$.*

Theorem 1. *For a given program element and its statically available dependencies, the partial-result evaluator obtained by the first AM projection is maximal in terms of the conditional-value evaluation that can be performed statically.*

Proof Sketch. Follows from Lemma 1 and Lemma 2, for a given set of statically available dependencies passed in for generating the partial-result evaluator.

Theorem 2. *For any program element, the analysis results generated by a whole-program analysis and by the corresponding staged analysis (as summarized in Fig. 10), are the same.*

Proof Sketch. Recall the whole-program analysis schema from Fig. 4. For a given program element x, its final result $f_m(x)$ after performing a whole-program analysis ψ can be obtained by evaluating the set $g_m(\mathbf{x})$ of conditional values with respect to all the dependencies $\text{IN}_{g_m(x)}$. Now consider the staging of the analysis ψ as shown in Fig. 10. Here, we have broken down the set $\text{IN}_{g_m(x)}$ of dependencies into the set S_x of statically available dependencies and the set D_x of dynamically available dependencies. The static component is a specializer (`Mix`) that generates the specialized conditional-value evaluator (`Partial-Result Evaluator`) by specializing the whole-program analysis evaluator CEval_ψ with respect to the partial result $[g_m(x)]_{S_x}$. The generated `Partial-Result Evaluator` forms the dynamic component of the staged analysis, and generates $f_m(\mathbf{x})$ using D_x. As established by the theory of partial evaluation, the result obtained by evaluating a program with respect to all of its inputs is same as the result obtained by evaluating the specialized program with respect to its dynamic input. It can be seen by construction that the way Fig. 10 stages a whole-program analysis is similar to the way partial evaluation stages the evaluation of a program. Hence, the analysis result generated by our staged analysis would be the same as the one generated by the whole-program analysis. This equality can be summarized as follows:

$$[\![g_m(x)]\!](\text{IN}_{g_m(x)}) = f_m(x) = [\![[g_m(x)]_{S_x}]\!](D_x)$$

Theorem 2 establishes the correctness and precision of the proposed staging scheme, and Theorem 1 establishes the efficiency (indicating maximal evaluation during static compilation) achieved by using the staging scheme. Observe that the proofs became straightforward due to two important illustrations: (i) that a whole-program analysis could be modeled as the evaluation of dependencies across program elements; and (ii) that for languages like Java with statically unavailable program parts, the evaluation of static and dynamic dependencies could be modeled based on the theory of partial evaluation.

We next describe our experience implementing a specializer for generating partial-result evaluators from given conditional-value evaluators for the whole program, similar to the `Mix` described by Jones in his classic book on partial evaluation. We approach this problem by describing a language of conditional values, such that programs in the world of partial analysis become sets of conditional values and program interpretation becomes conditional-value evaluation.

5   Specializers for Partial-Result Evaluation

In this section, similar to a language of programs, we first describe a language of conditional values that could be used to generate sets of conditional values (denoting dependence on various kinds of elements) for different program elements (Sect. 5.1). Next, similar to program interpreters, we design a simple

```
<Start>     ::= <ProgElem> : <CV>*
<ProgElem> ::= <Class> <Method> <Type> <Ref> <Fields>
<CV>        ::= <ProgElem> <DepVal> <ResVal>
<Type>      ::= LOCAL | PARM | ARG | RETVAL | FIELD
<DepVal>    ::= D | E
<ResVal>    ::= D | E
```
(a)

```
<Start>     ::= <ProgElem> : <TaggedCV>*
<TaggedCV> ::= <Tag> <CV>
<Tag>       ::= STATIC | DYNAMIC
```
(b)

Fig. 11. (a) The grammar for our division prepass; (b) extended grammar for conditional-value evaluation.

evaluator that could resolve those dependencies to generate the final analysis result for various program elements. We then mirror the process of specializing a program interpreter by designing a Mix that could specialize conditional-value evaluators to generate partial-result evaluators (Sect. 5.2). We also compiled and ran the generated partial-result evaluators, by supplying the statically evaluated values of Java libraries (computed using the same conditional-value evaluator discussed above); Sect. 5.3 describes our experience with the same.

Note that though our efforts are independent of the program analysis being staged, we need a set of conditional values generated for a given program analysis. In this section, we have chosen a publicly available conditional-value generator for escape analysis, Stava [27], written in Soot [29]. Stava generates a list of dependencies for each abstract object (program element), denoting its dependence on other program elements towards computing its escape status: one of *Escapes* (E) and *DoesNotEscape* (D).

5.1   A Grammar for Conditional Values

Based on the kinds of elements on which the analysis result for a given program element could depend on, Fig. 11 shows a grammar to generate sets of conditional values (denoting those dependencies) for various program elements. Each program element ProgElem belongs to a Class and a Method, and could be of one of the five Types: (i) local object in current method; (ii) parameter taken by current method; (iii) argument passed to another method; (iv) return value of current method; and (v) field of any other element. Ref is a number, denoting the line number of allocation for LOCAL, parameter and argument number respectively for PARM and ARG, and simply a filler for the rest. Fields contains a list of fields (e.g., f1, f2 to denote the element pointed to by X.f1.f2 for any abstract object X). A conditional value (CV) denotes dependence on a program element. Essentially, a conditional value <P1 X1 X2> evaluates to X2 if the element P1 resolves to X1; see Sect. 2.1). For example, for escape analysis, DepVal and ResVal could either be D or E. Thus, pairs comprising of program elements

```
1  Procedure CEval(gm(x), INgm(x))
2  │   Initialize a list L of statically known dependencies.
3  │   foreach d ∈ INgₐ(x) do
4  │   │   Add d to L.
5  │   └   Add the transitive dependencies of d to L.
6  │   Form strongly connected components (SCCs) in the list L.
7  │   repeat
8  │   │   foreach strongly connected component S formed above do
9  │   │   │   if ∄e ∈ S s.t. e depends on another SCC then
10 │   │   │   └   ∀e ∈ S, resolve e to ⊥.
11 │   │   │   Take a meet of the resolved values in each SCC as per the meet
   │   │   └   operation defined in Section 2.2.
12 └   until fixed point;
```

Fig. 12. Algorithm to perform conditional-value evaluation.

and the conditional values generated for those elements (e.g., by Stava) are the valid members of the language generated by this grammar. (Note that we had to make cosmetic changes in Stava to print its output in a form that can be parsed by our conditional-value grammar.)

5.2   Conditional-Value Evaluators and Specialization

Specialization using the theory of partial evaluation uses an auxiliary "division" routine to classify program inputs as static and dynamic. Having described a language of conditional values in the previous section, we next wrote a division prepass that classifies each conditional value as static or dynamic (based on whether it denotes a library dependency while analyzing applications, and vice-versa). We have implemented the division prepass as a JavaCC [26] visitor (about 300 lines of code) over the abstract syntax trees generated for the sets of conditional values prescribing to the grammar described above. We encode the result of division by prefixing each conditional value with a tag STATIC or DYNAMIC, resulting into a set of conditional values recognizable using the extended conditional-value grammar shown in Fig. 11(b). This extended grammar describes the language of conditional values that can be evaluated by our conditional-value evaluator CEval$_\Psi$.

Figure 12 gives an overview of the computation performed by CEval$_\Psi$. The evaluator takes as input the set of conditional values $g_m(x)$ for a program element x belonging to a method m and its dependencies $IN_{g_m(x)}$, and generates the partial result $[g_m(x)]_{S_x}$. First, the evaluator transitively adds all the dependencies of the given element into a list L (lines 2–5). Next, treating the various dependencies as a graph, the evaluator forms strongly-connected components (SCCs), denoting sets of equivalent resolved values. In case no element in an SCC depends on an element from another SCC, all the elements in that SCC are resolved to the bottom (most precise value) of the lattice of the analysis

```
1     class SpecializedCode1 {
2        public static void main(String[] args) {
3           // Read the values for dynamic dependencies
4           x1 = Resolved value of <L.lib, r1> // first dependence
5           x2 = Resolved value of <L.lib, r1> // second dependence
6           res = x1 ⊓ₑₐ x2
7           print(res);
8        }
9     }
```

Fig. 13. Schema of the partial-result evaluator emitted for $g_{A.foo}(O_4)$.

under consideration (lines 9–10). Finally, for the program element x, the evaluator takes a meet as described in Sect. 2.2, generating partial result in case of dynamic dependencies (line 11). The last two steps (lines 8 to 11) are performed till a fixed point. Our evaluator is also implemented as a JavaCC pass over the extended conditional-value grammar (from Fig. 11(b)), and spans about 1000 lines of code. Note that the only part of the evaluator that depends on the analysis for which the conditional-values are generated is the meet operation (to access its lattice); thus, the evaluator is essentially parametric over the analysis being performed. Hence, for escape analysis (ea), we denote the evaluator as $CEval_{ea}$.

Next we have implemented a Mix that takes as input our conditional-value evaluator and a partial result $[g_m(x)]_{S_x}$, and specializes the evaluator for the given partial result. Our Mix works similar to the partial-evaluation Mix proposed by Jones [14], but for Java programs of the kind of $CEval_{ea}$ (we could not find any existing implementation that we could reuse). Our Mix is implemented in JavaCC (for a grammar that covers the subset of Java required to parse $CEval_{ea}$), and spans about 1500 lines of code. The output of our Mix is a partial-result evaluator for the given partial result.

The fundamental idea behind specializing the evaluator is that its code should be executed as much as possible for the static dependencies, and the residual code should take the evaluated values of dynamic dependencies as input to generate the final analysis-result. Observe that Line 11 in Fig. 12 involves taking the meet (over the lattice Val) of the resolved dependencies. However, if any dependence is dynamic, its resolution cannot be performed statically. Hence, in order to specialize the evaluator for a given partial result, we first check the kind of dependence (populated by the division prepass), and for each dynamic dependence, we emit code to read and resolve the same. Next, we emit code to perform meet over the resolved values obtained therein. Finally, we enclose the emitted code as the main method of a uniquely named specialized-code class (say SpecializedCodeN for a unique N), to obtain the corresponding partial-result evaluator. For example, Fig. 13 shows the schema of the code emitted by our Mix for the element $g_{A.foo}(O_4)$ (see Eq. 4, Sect. 4.1).

Before we could use the partial-result evaluators generated for different program elements, we need to obtain the evaluated values of the dynamic dependen-

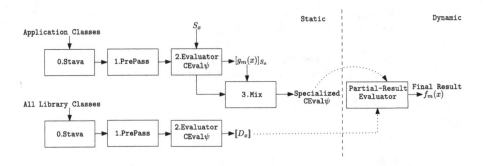

Fig. 14. Schema for prototype implementation of staged analysis

cies (libraries in case of Java). We do so by running an offline pass of $CEval_{ea}$ on the libraries, and obtaining the evaluated values therein. Finally, one can supply these evaluated values to the specialized codes comprising the partial-result evaluators for various program elements, to obtain the final analysis-result. Figure 14 shows the complete scheme of our prototype implementation for generating and executing partial-result evaluators.

Observe that partial-result evaluation over the evaluated values of dynamic dependencies, as per our proposed model, can be performed by executing the specialized code as soon as the dynamic dependencies can be resolved. Thus, we have the following options:

- Simply place the partial-result evaluators in a JIT compiler.
- As the partial-result evaluators are generated statically for all the program elements, place them in a VM agnostic to the methods/code-portions that are JIT compiled.
- For the evaluated dependencies corresponding to each version of the libraries, invoke the partial-result evaluators ahead-of-time (i.e., statically itself).

The first option can be mapped to the kind of scheme adopted by staging frameworks such as PYE [28]; however, it would mean we can perform optimizations for only those elements that belong to methods/regions that are JIT compiled (usually very few in tiered runtime systems such as the HotSpot JVM [21]). On the other hand, the second option could be used to obtain analysis results in the VM irrespective of the tiered nature and mode of compilation (by implementing corresponding optimization passes). Finally and most interestingly, the third option makes the process of generating analysis results even independent of the runtime system, and can also be used to demonstrate the full impact a staging scheme could make over performing a whole-program analysis.

5.3   Running the Partial-Result Evaluators

In this section, we try to validate the observation staging schemes reduce the amount of computation one may have to perform at run-time to obtain whole-program analysis results, significantly. In order to do so, we tried to perform a static whole-program escape analysis of a small benchmark `moldyn` from the JGF suite [10] (12 application and 3509 referenced library classes), by forcing `Stava` to analyze both application and libraries together. We found that for the whole-program analysis, though `Stava` generated conditional values for all the program elements in 4 h, their evaluation (using $CEval_{ea}$) did not terminate even in 20 h (on an Intel Xeon E5-2630 2.4 GHz system with 32 cores and 64 GB RAM, running Cent OS version 7), owing to the large number of residual dependencies (in the order of tens of thousands).

On the other hand, using the staged scheme (where we evaluate application and library dependencies separately), `Stava` took ∼30 s to generate the conditional-values for the application code, the division prepass (Step 1 in Fig. 14) took just a second, the evaluation of statically available dependencies (Step 2) took ∼3 min, the generation of partial-result evaluators (Step 3) took about a minute – all performed statically. Correspondingly, for the library classes referenced to by `moldyn`, Stava took ∼30 min, division and the evaluation took ∼90 min each – again performed statically. Finally, the execution of partial-result evaluators to generate final analysis-results, given the partial results for `moldyn` and the evaluated values of libraries – that is, the computation that needs to be performed dynamically – took only ∼35 s.

Thus, we can notice that a staged scheme may not only allow one to obtain the results of otherwise infeasible whole-program analysis during run-time, but also do so efficiently, that is, by reducing the actual amount of computation to be performed during run-time significantly. However, we looked into the list of dynamic dependencies generated for various program elements and found a scope to improve this time even further. In particular, we found that multiple program elements shared several dependencies; we attribute this to the fact that multiple parts of a Java application might use common library methods (for example, multiple objects being passed to the method `add` of `java.util.ArrayList`). To leverage this commonality, we modified our `Mix` to enclose the code generated for each partial-result evaluator in a separate function, and to concatenate all those functions in a single `PartialResultEvaluator` class. To obtain the final analysis results for all the program elements, we invoke the individual partial-result-evaluator functions present therein, using the Java reflection API; this reduced the time required to a mere ∼4 s.

Noting the improvement in the potential time required during run-time using the staged approach, we conclude that staging partial analyses into static and dynamic components, backed by a theoretical model presented in our paper, not only opens up avenues in languages with managed runtimes to perform existing optimizations more aggressively than present, but can also be used to perform novel analyses and optimizations that were otherwise practically infeasible.

6   Directions and Connections

Having drawn parallels between the classic theory of partial evaluation and a promising way to stage program analyses into static and dynamic components, we now turn our attention to various recent features and challenges pertaining to contemporary programming languages. In particular, we address topics of interest that could lead to further work built upon our model of partial analysis for languages with static and dynamic compilers. We also discuss connections with few other ways of performing program analysis in managed runtimes. In effect, we believe this discussion would be useful in driving multiple future directions, not only for the Java world but also for the wider community interested in.

6.1   Runtime Features: Challenges and Possibilities

In this section, we discuss few challenges posed by modern static+dynamic compilation systems, and discuss the kinds of techniques that could be used to improve the precision of the analysis results obtained therein.

As described in Sect. 2 (see Eqs. 2 and 3), standard resolution and conditional-value evaluation assume that all the dependencies can be resolved at run-time (that is, *closed world assumption*). However, there could be scenarios because of the way tiered JIT compilation works in modern JVMs where the results for few dependencies may not be available at the point of need. For example, if the program being analyzed uses reflective calls, state-of-the-art static-analysis frameworks (such as Soot [29]) miss edges in the call-graph for the program, as a result of which few methods may not get analyzed altogether. On another note, features such as dynamic classloading [15] in JVMs may bring up classes in a statically non-deterministic order. For example, in the partial result for element O_4 (see Eq. 4), if the class L is not loaded when the corresponding evaluation is invoked, the conditional values dependent on L1.lib cannot be resolved. The only possible sound option in this case would be to take the least precise value E as the resolved value.

On the other hand, for analyses such as control-flow analysis that have a richer lattice, it is possible to improve the precision for unresolvable dependencies. Consider the code snippet shown in Fig. 15. In method A.foo, the set of conditional values representing the possible types of objects that can be pointed-to by the reference variable z is $\{\langle\langle A.foo, b\rangle, B, Z1\rangle, \langle\langle A.foo, b\rangle, C, Z2\rangle\}$. Under the existing evaluation scheme, where all the required dependencies are available, the type of z will get assigned to either Z1 if b's type is B, or to Z2 if b's type is C. However, say in presence of dynamic classloading, if the class C has not been loaded when the conditional values for z need to be evaluated, then assuming the least precise value of the lattice (which, for control-flow analysis, is the set of all types in the program) is highly conservative and may affect many other optimizations such as method inlining and virtual-call resolution. We now discuss a solution to address this problem.

While performing partial-result evaluation, in case a certain dependency cannot be resolved, instead of always falling back to the least precise value in the lattice, we can statically generate some "fallback values" that can be used as the fallback option during resolution. Observe that the set of possible values that can be obtained as the analysis result for a given program element x, can be formed only from the third elements (say resolution values) of the tuples present

```
 1 class A {                          11 class B {
 2     void foo(B b) {                12     Z bar() {
 3         Z z = b.bar();             13         return new Z1() ;
 4     }                              14     }
 5 }                                  15 }
 6                                    16 class C extends B {
 7 interface Z {...}                  17     Z bar() {
 8 class Z1 implements Z { ... }      18         return new Z2();
 9 class Z2 implements Z { ... }      19     }
10 class Z3 implements Z { ... }      20 }
```

Fig. 15. A Java code snippet to demonstrate control-flow analysis.

in the set of conditional values for x. Thus, we can obtain a fallback value $fb(x)$ by taking the meet of all such resolution values:

$$fb(x) = \sqcap_{\forall \mathcal{T} \in g_m(x)} \mathcal{T}[3]$$

where $\mathcal{T}[3]$ gives the third element in each conditional value. As an example, for the reference variable z in Fig. 15, $fb(z)$ would be the set $\{Z1, Z2\}$.

In order to support fallback values, the staging scheme presented in Sect. 4 (see Fig. 10) can be modified as follows. In the static component, for each element x, apart from the partial result $[f_m(x)]_{S_x}$, we additionally need to store $fb(x)$. On the other hand, in the dynamic component, we can modify the partial-result evaluation as:

$$f_m(x) = \sqcap_{\forall \mathcal{T} \in g_m(x)} [\![\mathcal{T}]\!]$$

$$[\![\langle\langle \mathbf{n}, \mathbf{y}\rangle, v, v'\rangle]\!] = (\textit{is\_available}(f_\mathbf{n}(\mathbf{y}))) \; ? \; ((f_\mathbf{n}(\mathbf{y}) == v) \; ? \; v' \; : \; \bot) \; : \; fb(x)$$

Here, for a given element x, while trying to resolve a conditional value $\mathcal{T} = \langle\langle n, y\rangle, v, v'\rangle \in g_m(x)$, we first check if $f_n(y)$ is available; if yes, we proceed with normal resolution, else we use $fb(x)$ as the fallback value. Thus, for the example shown in Fig. 15, even if the runtime has no information about the caller of A.foo (that is, no knowledge about the type of the objects pointed-to by b), using statically computed $fb(z)$, we can resolve the conditional values for z generated above to obtain the set $\{Z1, Z2\}$ as the analysis result for z.

Apart from the challenges posed by runtime features discussed above, another important consideration for static+dynamic analyses is to guarantee/verify that the static-analysis results correspond to the bytecodes being executed. In case of a difference, one may need to invalidate the partial-result evaluator for the corresponding and dependent methods. This can at a simpler level be done by maintaining a list of affected methods with the statically resolved dependencies, and be improved by precisely identifying the effect on various program elements. We believe this to be an interesting future research direction.

6.2   Drawing Newer Connections

In this section, we first discuss few interesting aspects related to cross-pollination of ideas between Futamura and AM projections, along with few subtle points related to generation of conditional values in partial analysis. We then highlight how our staged analysis scheme can be used along with various other applications involving static and dynamic analyses.

1. Cross-pollination of Specialization Ideas. We have mentioned previously that AM projections are similar to yet different from Futamura projections. To elucidate this point, note that the partial-result evaluator generated by the first AM projection is a result of specializing the conditional-value evaluator for an already specialized set of conditional values (see Fig. 9). On the other hand, the output of the first Futamura projection is a result of specializing the interpreter for the original source program (see Fig. 6). It is possible to take cue from the first AM projection and modify the first Futamura projection to specialize the interpreter too with a partially evaluated program. Doing so would generate a faster interpreter, as the input program can anyway be specialized with the statically available input. Similarly, the compiler generated by the second Futamura projection can also take a specialized program as input to efficiently generate the specialized interpreter obtained in the first Futamura projection.

As another possibility to explore in the space of specialization, it can be seen in Sect. 4 (Figs. 4 and 10) that the input taken by our model of whole-program as well as partial analyses is the set of conditional values, denoting dependencies, for a given program element. It is possible to visualize the process of generating these conditional values: from a given program analysis specified as an abstract interpreter, we can identify the set of statements required to compute the final analysis result for a particular program element x, as the dependencies of x. This process of generating conditional values can be made faster: one could model program analyses as "conditional-value generators", and then specialize them with respect to a given program, similar to the specialization of conditional-value evaluators done by AM projections. Also note that though this "per element" modeling is a bit different from the way usual iterative dataflow analyses [20] are implemented (as aggregate transfer functions over all the variables in the domain), it fits well with various recently popular ways of writing program analyses, as discussed next.

2. Query- and Feedback-Driven Analyses. In general, whole-program analyses generate results for all the program elements in all the methods of a program. On the other hand, one of the growingly popular ways to scale precise analyses in resource-constrained environments is to compute information only for elements that are of interest, often specified as a set of queries generated by various client optimizations [13,24]. These analyses are called "query-driven analyses". Staged schemes of the kind proposed in this paper can be integrated directly with such analyses: First, the client can generate the list of program elements that are of interest for the query under consideration, based on which the partial analysis can generate the relevant sets of conditional values. Afterwards, our staging scheme can be used to specialize the corresponding set of conditional values and further generate the `Partial-Result Evaluator` only for the elements of interest.

For languages that support static+dynamic compilation, one of the ways to improve the outcomes produced by static analyses is to perform profiling in the dynamic compiler and give feedback to the static compiler [6,11,30]. As an instance, Bastani et al. [6] make optimistic assumptions for the unavailable portions of a program, detect during runtime if an assumption goes wrong, abort execution if it does, and then refine the static analysis accordingly; this process is repeated until no assumptions fail. The staged scheme of our kind suits such analyses particularly well: the feedback from runtime can be used to obtain the list of affected elements that need to be re-specialized by the static analysis for subsequent runs of the re-created partial evaluator, thus requiring the (partial) static analysis to be re-performed only for the affected elements.

7   Related Work

In this section, we discuss relevant related work in four categories: (i) partial evaluation; (ii) partial program analysis; (iii) other applications of partial evaluation; and (iv) staged analysis. To the best of our knowledge, ours is the first scheme that maps the staging of whole-program analysis across static and dynamic compilation to the theory of partial evaluation.

7.1   Partial Evaluation

Partial evaluation is a well-known technique to specialize programs with statically available inputs. Jones [14] formalized the theory of partial evaluation in context of constructing compilers and compiler generators by specializing subsequent levels of interpreters, using Futamura projections [12]. Perugini and Williams [23] underlined the difficulty in understanding partial evaluation and Futamura projections, and devised a diagrammatic approach to visualize the working of partial evaluation, by modeling program execution using a box-substitution notation. In this paper, we have also tried to explain the three Futamura projections, particularly by showing the connections among the outputs and inputs of the subsequent projections. Our goal behind this visualization is to later build a mapping from our proposed model of partial analysis, to generate partial-result evaluators.

7.2   Partial Program Analysis

The idea of analyzing partial programs was first formalized in a tool called PPA [9], wherein the goal was to infer types for incomplete Java programs. In presence of ambiguities, PPA uses heuristics based on the structure of a program to generate imprecise but sound results. Similarly, Melo et al. [18] generate missing type annotations for incomplete C programs, while handling challenges imposed by C's weak type system using "placeholder pre-types". In presence of ambiguities, Melo et al. fill the placeholder with an "orphan" type in the lattice of pre-types. Our staged scheme, though performs an analysis of the partial program to generate partial results statically, is able to generate sound as well as precise answers based on dynamic inputs, wherein the components needed to evaluate and complete partial results are generated statically, using novel AM projections based on the theory of partial evaluation.

There have been prior works [19,22,32] that generate results for incomplete programs by trying to obtain possible solutions based on examples and then ranking them for suitability. The limitation of these techniques is that they may generate unsound results. Our staged scheme, on the other hand, would always generate sound results, with varying precision based on the dynamic features supported by a given runtime.

Allen et al. [4] present a scheme to analyze Java libraries in absence of application code. They model concrete objects using allocation sites, while approximating unknown objects using static types, thus generating a combined lattice. Our approach, though different in the sense that it works for both application and library code, uses the idea of using static types as fallback values in absence of dynamic inputs. On the other end of the spectrum, Ali and Lhoták [3] generate call-graphs to analyze Java application code in absence of libraries, by approximating library methods as stubs. In comparison, our staging approach, instead of approximating the libraries, uses their analysis results (obtained offline) to complete application results during dynamic compilation.

7.3   Other Applications of Partial Evaluation

There have been works that use partial evaluation to speed up different parts of a program's execution lifecycle. One such implementation [16] speeds up the execution of code during JIT compilation by specializing the AST interpreter for a given language specified in the Truffle [31] framework. This avoids redundancy in code generation during JIT compilation. Marr and Ducasse [17] compare the performance of the previous approach with that of tracing JIT compilation (which optimizes a program by JIT-compiling traces obtained by profiling). On the other hand, in this paper, we have used the idea of partial evaluation to speed up the process of obtaining whole-program analysis results (possible during or just before JIT compilation). Our scheme can be augmented to the Truffle approach by performing partial analysis of the available program during AST specialization, and refining the results during JIT compilation.

7.4   Staged Analysis

Staging, though a general idea, has not often found place in static+dynamic analysis systems. Chug et al. [8] compute and check information-flow properties for Javascript programs statically, while leaving residual checks that depend on dynamic inputs for the runtime. Albarghouthi et al. [1] develop specifications for unknown methods in context of program synthesis. In context of Java, Thakur and Nandivada [28] recently proposed the PYE framework, which uses the idea of conditional values to denote dependencies on dynamic input and resolves them to generate final results during JIT compilation. In this paper, we have proposed a general staging framework based on the theory of partial evaluation that can be used not only to model both the above works, but also to establish and prove the correctness and precision of the same. Importantly, our base scheme (Sect. 4) is independent of the language and framework under consideration, and the extensions for Java runtimes (Sect. 6) can be used to devise corresponding strategies for other runtimes with novel dynamic features.

8   Conclusion

In this paper, we presented a formal model to stage whole-program analyses into static and dynamic components. Our staging scheme took inspiration from the theory of partial evaluation and specialized the evaluators for whole-program analysis with partial results to generate partial-result evaluators. Similarly, based on the notion of Futamura projections for partial evaluation, we proposed a novel notion of AM projections that describe the generation of partial-result evaluators and their generators. The generated partial-result evaluators can also be placed in managed runtimes to generate final analysis results using the dependencies that become available dynamically. This model allowed us to establish the correctness and precision of the idea of staging in a straightforward manner. Moreover, in order to address the challenges presented by the dynamic nature of modern tiered runtimes, we also discussed possible future directions to extend the staging scheme further. To the best of our knowledge, ours is the first scheme that backs the staging of whole-program analysis into static and dynamic components, using the established theory of partial evaluation. We envisage that our formulated theory of partial analysis would be used not only to promote the design of staged partial analyzers, but to also perform erstwhile infeasible optimizations, for and beyond Java.

References

1. Albarghouthi, A., Dillig, I., Gurfinkel, A.: Maximal specification synthesis. In: Proceedings of the 43rd Annual ACM SIGPLAN-SIGACT Symposium on Principles of Programming Languages. POPL 2016, pp. 789–801. Association for Computing Machinery, New York (2016). https://doi.org/10.1145/2837614.2837628
2. Ali, K.: The Separate Compilation Assumption. Ph.D. thesis, University of Waterloo, Waterloo, Ontario, Canada (2014)
3. Ali, K., Lhoták, O.: AVERROES: Whole-program analysis without the whole program. In: Castagna, G. (ed.) ECOOP 2013. LNCS, vol. 7920, pp. 378–400. Springer, Heidelberg (2013). https://doi.org/10.1007/978-3-642-39038-8_16
4. Allen, N., Krishnan, P., Scholz, B.: Combining type-analysis with points-to analysis for analyzing Java library source-Code. In: Proceedings of the 4th ACM SIGPLAN International Workshop on State Of the Art in Program Analysis. SOAP 2015, pp. 13–18. Association for Computing Machinery, New York (2015). https://doi.org/10.1145/2771284.2771287

5. Ancona, D., Ancona, M., Cuni, A., Matsakis, N.D.: RPython: a step towards reconciling dynamically and statically typed OO languages. In: Proceedings of the 2007 Symposium on Dynamic Languages. DLS 2007, pp. 53–64. Association for Computing Machinery, New York (2007). https://doi.org/10.1145/1297081.1297091
6. Bastani, O., Sharma, R., Clapp, L., Anand, S., Aiken, A.: Eventually sound points-to analysis with specifications. In: Donaldson, A.F. (ed.) 33rd European Conference on Object-Oriented Programming (ECOOP 2019). Leibniz International Proceedings in Informatics (LIPIcs), vol. 134, pp. 11:1–11:28. Schloss Dagstuhl-Leibniz-Zentrum fuer Informatik, Dagstuhl, Germany (2019). https://doi.org/10.4230/LIPIcs.ECOOP.2019.11
7. Blanchet, B.: Escape analysis for JavaTM: theory and practice. ACM Trans. Program. Lang. Syst. **25**(6), 713–775 (2003). https://doi.org/10.1145/945885.945886
8. Chugh, R., Meister, J.A., Jhala, R., Lerner, S.: Staged information flow for Javascript. In: Proceedings of the 30th ACM SIGPLAN Conference on Programming Language Design and Implementation. PLDI 2009, pp. 50–62. Association for Computing Machinery, New York (2009). https://doi.org/10.1145/1542476.1542483
9. Dagenais, B., Hendren, L.: Enabling static analysis for partial Java programs. SIGPLAN Not. **43**(10), 313–328 (2008). https://doi.org/10.1145/1449955.1449790
10. Daly, C., Horgan, J., Power, J., Waldron, J.: Platform independent dynamic Java virtual machine analysis: the Java grande forum benchmark suite. In: Proceedings of the 2001 Joint ACM-ISCOPE Conference on Java Grande. JGI 2001, pp. 106–115. ACM, New York (2001). https://doi.org/10.1145/376656.376826
11. Dean, J., Chambers, C., Grove, D.: Selective specialization for object-oriented languages. In: Proceedings of the ACM SIGPLAN 1995 Conference on Programming Language Design and Implementation. PLDI 1995, pp. 93–102. Association for Computing Machinery, New York (1995). https://doi.org/10.1145/207110.207119
12. Futamura, Y.: Partial evaluation of computation process - an approach to a compiler-compiler. Higher Order Symbol. Comput. **12**(4), 381–391 (1999). https://doi.org/10.1023/A:1010095604496
13. Heintze, N., Tardieu, O.: Demand-driven pointer analysis. In: Proceedings of the ACM SIGPLAN 2001 Conference on Programming Language Design and Implementation. PLDI 2001, pp. 24–34. Association for Computing Machinery, New York (2001). https://doi.org/10.1145/378795.378802
14. Jones, N.D.: An introduction to partial evaluation. ACM Comput. Surv. **28**(3), 480–503 (1996). https://doi.org/10.1145/243439.243447
15. Kotzmann, T., Mössenböck, H.: Escape analysis in the context of dynamic compilation and deoptimization. In: Proceedings of the ACM/USENIX International Conference on Virtual Execution Environments. VEE 2005, pp. 111–120. ACM, New York (2005). https://doi.org/10.1145/1064979.1064996
16. Latifi, F.: Practical second futamura projection: partial evaluation for high-performance language interpreters. In: Proceedings Companion of the 2019 ACM SIGPLAN International Conference on Systems, Programming, Languages, and Applications: Software for Humanity. SPLASH Companion 2019, pp. 29–31. Association for Computing Machinery, New York (2019). https://doi.org/10.1145/3359061.3361077
17. Marr, S., Ducasse, S.: Tracing vs. partial evaluation: comparing meta-compilation approaches for self-optimizing interpreters. In: Proceedings of the 2015 ACM SIGPLAN International Conference on Object-Oriented Programming, Systems, Languages, and Applications. OOPSLA 2015, pp. 821–839. Association for Computing Machinery, New York (2015). https://doi.org/10.1145/2814270.2814275

18. Melo, L.T.C., Ribeiro, R.G., de Araújo, M.R., Pereira, F.M.Q.A.: Inference of static semantics for incomplete C programs. Proc. ACM Program. Lang. **2**(POPL) (2017). https://doi.org/10.1145/3158117
19. Mishne, A., Shoham, S., Yahav, E.: Typestate-based semantic code search over partial programs. In: Proceedings of the ACM International Conference on Object Oriented Programming Systems Languages and Applications. OOPSLA 2012, pp. 997–1016. Association for Computing Machinery, New York (2012). https://doi.org/10.1145/2384616.2384689
20. Muchnick, S.S.: Advanced Compiler Design and Implementation. Morgan Kaufmann, Burlington (1997)
21. Paleczny, M., Vick, C., Click, C.: The Java hotspot server compiler. In: Proceedings of the 2001 Symposium on JavaTM Virtual Machine Research and Technology Symposium. JVM 2001, vol. 1, p. 1. USENIX Association, USA (2001)
22. Perelman, D., Gulwani, S., Ball, T., Grossman, D.: Type-directed completion of partial expressions. In: Proceedings of the 33rd ACM SIGPLAN Conference on Programming Language Design and Implementation. PLDI 2012, pp. 275–286. Association for Computing Machinery, New York (2012). https://doi.org/10.1145/2254064.2254098
23. Perugini, S., Williams, B.: Revisiting the Futamura projections: a diagrammatic approach. Theor. Appl. Inform. **28**, 15–32 (2017). https://doi.org/10.20904/284015
24. Rama, G.M., Komondoor, R., Sharma, H.: Refinement in object-sensitivity points-to analysis via slicing. Proc. ACM Program. Lang. **2**(OOPSLA), 142:1–142:27 (2018). https://doi.org/10.1145/3276512
25. Sharma, R., Kulshreshtha, S., Thakur, M.: Can we run in parallel? Automating loop parallelization for TornadoVM (2022). https://doi.org/10.48550/arXiv.2205.03590
26. Succi, G., Wong, R.: The application of JAVACC to develop a C/C++ preprocessor. ACM SIGAPP Appl. Comput. Rev. **7**, 11–18 (1999). https://doi.org/10.1145/333630.333633
27. Nikhil, T.R., Yadav, D., Thakur, M.: Stava (2021). https://github.com/CompL-IITMandi/stava
28. Thakur, M., Nandivada, V.K.: PYE: a framework for precise-yet-efficient just-in-time analyses for Java programs. ACM Trans. Program. Lang. Syst. **41**(3), 16:1–16:37 (2019). https://doi.org/10.1145/3337794
29. Vallée-Rai, R., Co, P., Gagnon, E., Hendren, L., Lam, P., Sundaresan, V.: Soot - a Java bytecode optimization framework. In: Proceedings of the 1999 Conference of the Centre for Advanced Studies on Collaborative Research. CASCON 1999, pp. 13–23. IBM Press (1999). http://dl.acm.org/citation.cfm?id=781995.782008
30. Vivien, F., Rinard, M.: Incrementalized pointer and escape analysis. In: Proceedings of the ACM SIGPLAN Conference on Programming Language Design and Implementation. PLDI 2001, pp. 35–46. ACM, New York (2001). https://doi.org/10.1145/378795.378804
31. Würthinger, T., et al.: Practical partial evaluation for high-performance dynamic language runtimes. In: Proceedings of the 38th ACM SIGPLAN Conference on Programming Language Design and Implementation. PLDI 2017, pp. 662–676. Association for Computing Machinery, New York (2017). https://doi.org/10.1145/3062341.3062381
32. Zhong, H., Wang, X.: Boosting complete-code tool for partial program. In: Proceedings of the 32nd IEEE/ACM International Conference on Automated Software Engineering. ASE 2017, pp. 671–681. IEEE Press (2017)

SecWasm: Information Flow Control for WebAssembly

Iulia Bastys[1](✉), Maximilian Algehed[1], Alexander Sjösten[2],
and Andrei Sabelfeld[1]

[1] Chalmers University of Technology, Gothenburg, Sweden
bastys@chalmers.se
[2] TU Wien, Vienna, Austria
alexander.sjoesten@tuwien.ac.at

Abstract. We introduce SecWasm, the first general purpose information-flow control system for WebAssembly (Wasm), thus extending the safety guarantees offered by Wasm with guarantees that applications manipulate sensitive data in a secure way. SecWasm is a hybrid system enforcing termination-insensitive noninterference which overcomes the challenges posed by the uncommon characteristics for machine languages of Wasm in an elegant and thorough way.

1 Introduction

WebAssembly (Wasm) [22] is gaining popularity as a new standard for near-native low-level code and is becoming a popular compilation target for languages like C, C++, and Rust. Designed to enable high-performance web applications, Wasm is currently supported by all major browsers [48]. Wasm also boasts support to standalone environments such as Node.js and it has been deployed for decentralized cloud computing [24], smart contracts [1], and IoT [40,51].

Consider a password meter website *PM* which needs to communicate with a third-party website *TP* to fetch a password dictionary. *PM* would fetch the dictionary in the beginning and signal the end of a successful run at the end. Current Wasm security guarantees are able to prevent direct exfiltration, but cannot ensure the password is not leaked (through URL parameter encoding or otherwise) given a malicious developer providing module *PM*.

More specifically, Wasm security relies on the browser's same-origin policy and a memory-safe sandboxed execution environment [2] with separate memory and code space [22]. Wasm has an unstructured linear memory which can be grown dynamically. To ensure memory safety, all memory accesses are dynamically checked against the memory bounds, trapping any out-of-bounds access. Furthermore, Wasm applications have structured control flow, therefore disallowing jumps to arbitrary locations. In this way, Wasm ensures *control-flow integrity* (CFI) [3], such that Wasm code can be compiled and validated in a single pass.

While Wasm offers CFI, it remains an open challenge to ensure a *secure flow of information* through its applications. A promising technique addressing this is *information-flow control* (IFC) [36], which tracks both explicit and implicit

G. Singh and C. Urban (Eds.): SAS 2022, LNCS 13790, pp. 74–103, 2022.
https://doi.org/10.1007/978-3-031-22308-2_5

information flows. While first valuable steps have been taken in this direction [19, 41,43,49], prior work is yet to address implicit flows [19,41], provide formal guarantees [19,43], handle flows via the memory [41], or apply beyond specialized scenarios of constant-time Wasm for cryptographic algorithms [49].

A *general* and *sound IFC* approach to Wasm suitable for *general-purpose applications* is pending. Moreover, it is a prerequisite for further progress in IFC techniques for WebAssembly. Although several IFC systems for other machine languages have been proposed [5,7,10,11,13,20,21,25,29,30,52], they cannot be immediately repurposed here. Wasm is not a regular low-level language. Its *structured* control flow mechanisms and *unstructured* linear memory are uncommon. And when it comes to IFC, they prove to be quite challenging on certain aspects.

The structured control flow allows us to design an IFC system which leverages Wasm's syntax to compute the control flow regions directly. This in contrast to IFC approaches for other machine languages which resorted to employing external tools [5,10,13,25,52] or adding artificial syntactic constructs [13,29,52] to achieve some structure at the low-level. However, Wasm's handling of the operand stack which, to the best of our knowledge, is unique among machine languages requires some innovation when it comes to defining the security properties enforced by the IFC system.

Dealing with an unstructured linear memory entails an analysis in itself, not only on what labeling tactic to apply, but also on what type of IFC enforcement to design—both quite intermingled. While choosing the type of enforcement may seem trivial, choosing the right memory labeling approach does not. When it comes to the former, the reasoning is straightforward. On the one hand, Wasm's well-developed type system makes it suitable for static IFC. On the other hand, managing dynamic flows such as memory accesses statically would lead to a restrictive and rigid system, tipping the balance in favor of dynamic IFC. Yet, a purely dynamic IFC approach usually bearing significant execution overhead is not necessary for Wasm, since the language does not exhibit dynamic features. Thus, the challenge remains in labeling the memory such that it minimizes the dynamic checks while still maintaining permissiveness and expressiveness.

In this paper, we propose SecWasm, a hybrid IFC system addressing the challenges above in an elegant and thorough way. As is common [5,10,13,25, 29,49,52], our focus is on *confidentiality*, with the security goal of preventing information from secret inputs to leak to public outputs. However, we envision our mechanisms to be suitable for tracking some facets of integrity, thanks to the duality of confidentiality and information-flow integrity [12].

Non-goals. To delimit the scope of the paper, we emphasize the non-goals of SecWasm, pertaining to handling the sources of non-determinism in WebAssembly: lack of bit pattern for NaN values, resource exhaustion, and imported host functions [22]. While we acknowledge that non-determinism can lead to illicit information-flows through side channels (e.g., via the micro-architectural state of the processor [44], or termination and progress channels [4]), we consider it a worthwhile subject for future work and not crucial for laying the foundations of general IFC in Wasm, which is the goal of this paper.

Contributions. In brief, we make the following contributions:

- We discuss the key aspects of IFC for Wasm, to back up and give an intuition for the design of SecWasm (Sect. 3).
- We present SecWasm, the first general IFC system for Wasm (Sect. 4).
- We formally prove SecWasm to enforce termination insensitive noninterference (Sect. 5).

2 Background on Wasm

This section gives a brief overview of the Wasm specifics required to understand SecWasm. In particular, we present the basic features and discuss important aspects such as *structured control flow, linear memory*, and *security characteristics*. For more details on Wasm, we refer the reader to the initial publication [22] or official live documentation [50]. In the following and the rest of the paper, we focus on Wasm v1.0 [47].

2.1 Basics

We begin by presenting the syntactic features of WebAssembly most relevant for SecWasm (Fig. 1).

Modules. Wasm programs are organized into modules. A module is composed of a list of function types, a list of functions, a table identifying function pointers with functions, a linear memory of raw bytes[1], and a list of typed global variables.

A module is instantiated through an embedder, which is a host environment usually attached to the JavaScript engine in a web browser. When instantiating a module, the embedder must provide definitions for everything that should be imported, such as host functions, and an initial linear memory m. The module can also export Wasm functions the embedder can invoke, and the embedder can read the linear memory of the module.

Each function *func* has a type specifying its signature by reference to a function type defined in the module. Functions may have local variables and consist of a sequence of instructions comprising the function body. Functions are not first-class, meaning they cannot be used as arguments to or returned from other functions, nor assigned to variables. However, functions can call other functions, including themselves recursively. Functions can be invoked directly using the **call** instruction which takes as argument the index of the function in the functions vector, or indirectly with the **call_indirect** instruction via the function pointer table *tbl* mapping integers to functions.

Global variables *gbl* may be either mutable or immutable and are in scope to the entire module. Local variables are always mutable and only in scope to the executing function.

Types. Wasm supports four primitive value types t: 32 and 64-bit integers (i32 and i64) and single and double precision floating-point numbers (f32 and f64). Complex data types such as arrays or pointers do not exist in Wasm, and any

---

[1] Wasm 1.0 only has support for a single memory per module.

(modules)	$module$	$::=$ {types ft^*, funcs $func^*$, tables tbl, mems m^1, globals glb}
(functions)	$func$	$::=$ {type idx, locals t^*, body $expr$}
(immediates)	i	$::= nat$
(value types)	t	$::=$ i32 | i64 | f32 | f64
(global types)	gt	$::=$ mut$^?$ t
(function types)	ft	$::= t^* \to t^*$
(block types)	bt	$::= t^* \to t^*$
(constants)	k	$::= \ldots$
(instructions)	$instr$	$::= data$ | mem | $ctrl$ | $admin$
	$data$	$::= t.\mathbf{const}\ n$ | $t.unop$ | $t.binop$ | **drop** | **select** | **local.get** i | **local.set** i
		| **local.tee** i | **global.get** i | **global.set** i
	mem	$::= t.\mathbf{load}\ a\ o$ | $t.\mathbf{store}\ a\ o$ | **memory.size** | **memory.grow**
	$ctrl$	$::=$ **nop** | **unreachable** | **block** (bt) $expr$ **end** | **loop** (bt) $expr$ **end**
		| **if** (bt) $expr$ **else** $expr$ **end** | **br** i | **br_if** i | **br_table** i^+ | **return** | **call** i
		| **call_indirect** ft
	$admin$	$::=$ **trap** | **label**$_n$\{$expr$\} $expr$ **end** | **frame**$_n$\{$frame$\} $expr$ **end** | **invoke** a
(expressions)	$expr$	$::= instr$ | $expr; expr$

Fig. 1. Selected Wasm abstract syntax. Non-empty sequences are denoted with exponent $^+$, possibly empty ones with exponent *, possibly empty singleton sequences with exponent ^{1}, and optional arguments with exponent $^?$.

representation of these types in the source language is compiled down to a primitive type. Function types ft (as well as block types bt) define a sequence of Wasm values taken as parameters and a sequence of values to return.

Instructions. Wasm bytecode is executed as a stack-machine, where instructions pop argument values off and push result values onto an operand stack.

Instructions are partitioned into $data$, mem, $ctrl$, and $admin$. Data instructions either manipulate the operand stack directly ($t.\mathbf{const}\ n$, **drop**, **select**), the local variables (**local.get** i, **local.set** i, **local.tee** i), or the global variables (**global.get** i, **global.set** i). Memory instructions are used for interaction with the linear memory. Instructions **store** and **load** write to and read from the linear memory, respectively. **memory.size** returns the current size of the memory, and **memory.grow** extends it dynamically. Control instructions comprise scoping constructs (**block**), loops (**loop**), conditionals (**if**), structured unconditional (**br**, **br_table**, **return**) and conditional jumps (**br_if**), and direct (**call**) and indirect function calls (**call_indirect**). Finally, **nop** does nothing, while **unreachable** causes an unconditional, uncatchable trap exception. When a trap occurs, the entire computation is aborted, and no other changes to the state are allowed. Wasm does not handle the traps, but propagates them to the embedder. Traps are expressed by the administrative instruction **trap**. Other $admin$ instructions express reduction of control instructions. As such, **block**, **loop**, and **if** reduce to **label**s, and **call**s to **invoke**, which further reduce to **frame**s. Labels **label**$_n$\{$expr_1$\} $expr_2$ **end** carry the return arity n of the block, the block's body $expr_2$, and the continuation $expr_1$ to execute when a jump occurs within the block. **invoke** represents the invocation of a function instance identified by its address a. Finally, frames **frame**$_n$\{$frame$\} $expr$ **end** carry the return arity n and body $expr$ of the function and the values of its arguments stored in $frame$.

2.2 Structured Control Flow

Unlike other machine languages, the control flow in Wasm is structured and this guarantees a program cannot jump to arbitrary locations. The structured control flow is obtained by a combination of nested block constructs and jumping instructions permitted only from within the blocks, and only as far out as the nesting depth allows.

Blocks. Blocks are formed by standard control flow constructs **if** and **loop**, and scoping construct **block**. Each such construct terminates with an **end** opcode indicating where the construct's lexical scope ends.

Branches. Wasm further implements its structured control flow with several branching instructions: **br**, **br_table**, and **return**—unconditional, and **br_if**—conditional. The crux of these branching instructions is that unlike unstructured control flow, such as `goto` in C, they can only be executed inside nested blocks. Branches have *label* immediates referencing outer blocks by their relative nesting depth. This makes the labels scoped and able to reference only constructs in which their corresponding branches are nested. Depending on the type of construct, the effect of taking a branch differs. For a **block** or **if** instruction, a *forward* jump occurs that resumes execution *after* the matching **end**. On the other hand, a **loop** has a *backward* jump that *restarts* the loop.

Operand Stack Unwinding. In Wasm, the operand stack contains three types of entries: values $t.$**const** n, labels **label**$_n\{expr\}$, and frames **frame**$_n\{frame\}$, with the latter two modeled by their respective administrative instructions. As such, when a block (or **call**) instruction executes, the top values corresponding to the block (or function) arguments are temporarily popped, a label (or frame) is pushed, and the value arguments are pushed back, order preserved.

Branching retains the values on top of the operand stack corresponding to the return values of the current block (but also to the argument values of the continuation) and pops *all* entries off the stack until and including the label entry corresponding to the continuation. Basically, this amounts to popping a number of labels off the stack equal to branching immediate +1 and all other value entries in between.

A **return** from a function keeps the top values on the stack denoting the function return values and pops everything off the stack until and including the first frame, which represents the frame of the current function.

Example. Consider the code in Fig. 2a and assume an initial operand stack containing only value i32.**const** 0. The evolution of the stack during the execution of the code is depicted in Fig. 2b. In the following, we will go through each instruction in the code of Fig. 2a and explain the behavior of the stack. Blocks are labeled $0 and $1 for easier referencing.

Note the type of block $0 is i32 $\rightarrow$ i32. This means the block takes one argument and has only one return value, both of type i32. More specifically, before entering and leaving the block, the operand stack requires on top a value of type i32. Block $1 of type i32 $\rightarrow$ ε only takes an argument of type i32 and has no return values.

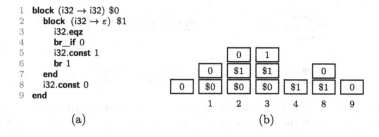

```
1  block (i32 → i32) $0
2     block (i32 → ε) $1
3        i32.eqz
4        br_if 0
5        i32.const 1
6        br 1
7     end
8     i32.const 0
9  end
```

(a)

(b)

Fig. 2. Branching example (a) and the evolution of the operand stack during its execution (b). The stack and index i below denote the operand stack after the execution of the instruction on line i. Values are depicted as n instead of t.**const** n. $0 = $ **label**$_1\{\varepsilon\}$; $1 = $ **label**$_0\{$i32.**const** $0\}$;

When block $0 is entered, value i32.**const** 0 is popped off the stack, label **label**$_1\{$i32.**const** $0\}$ is pushed, then i32.**const** 0 is pushed back in. The same behavior arises for instruction 2. i32.**eqz** pops the top value off the stack and checks if it equals 0. It does, so it pushes back i32.**const** 1, otherwise it would have pushed i32.**const** 0. **br_if** 0 is a conditional jump which executes if the top of the operand stack is i32.**const** 1. It is (step 3), so control is given to the instruction at the end of block $1. When this happens, the label of block $1 is popped off the stack. Note i32.**const** 1 was popped off during the execution of **br_if** 0. Instruction 8 simply pushes i32.**const** 0 on the operand stack. Since block $0 needs to return an i32 value, when leaving it on line 9, i32.**const** 0 is temporarily popped off, the block label is removed and i32.**const** 0 is pushed back in.

2.3 Linear Memory

The main storage for a Wasm program is an unmanaged linear memory representing a contiguous mutable array of raw bytes [50] which uses the little-endian byte order [22]. The memory is instantiated with an initial size and initialized with zeros. It can be grown dynamically with instruction **memory.grow** and queried for the current size with **memory.size**. The memory can be accessed through **load** and **store** instructions, with the addresses being unsigned integers of type i32. Whenever a memory access occurs, a dynamic check ensures the address is within the memory bounds. If it is not, a trap occurs.

Writing to and Reading from Memory. Figure 3 depicts instances of memory access. Initially, linear memory m_0 of size **memory.size** $= n$ contains only zeros. We store 32-bit integer 10752 on array positions 0 to 3, as the value takes four bytes, and get a new memory m_1. Reading a 32-bit integer from m_1 (starting) at location 1 means converting bytes 2A000000 to 42. Observe bytes from values stored at adjacent positions in the memory can be interpreted as a new value, as the raw data in the memory can be used to represent other numbers [50].

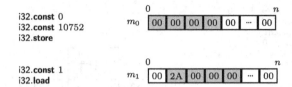

Fig. 3. Illustrative memory accesses for reads and writes. Highlighted memory locations denote the positions in the memory array where the value is written to/read from.

Security Specifications. The linear memory is disjoint from the code space, the execution stack, and the runtime engine's data structures. As the memory is unmanaged, Wasm does not provide garbage collection. Moreover, being the only unmanaged part of Wasm, the linear memory becomes the only component of the execution environment prone to corruption by buggy or malicious Wasm code. Thus, untrusted Wasm code can safely execute in the same address space as other code.

Unfortunately, this does not do away with buggy programs susceptible to attacks *via* the memory. Specifically, certain memory vulnerabilities in C code can persist when compiled to Wasm [27]. While these vulnerabilities do not allow the attacker to corrupt the execution environment, meaning they are *memory-safe*, they can still lead to insecure information flows that, e.g., may breach confidentiality; in other words, they are *information-flow unsafe*.

3   Challenges and Design Choices

Next, we highlight the challenges arising from building an IFC system for Wasm and give an intuition for the design choices taken when modeling it.

3.1   Attacker Model

As usual when designing an IFC system, we consider a join semi-lattice $(\mathcal{L}, \sqsubseteq)$ of security levels ℓ, where data at level $\ell_d \in \mathcal{L}$ can flow to an observer at level $\ell_o \in \mathcal{L}$ if and only if $\ell_d \sqsubseteq \ell_o$.

The attacker is thus able to observe information below their security level $\mathcal{A}$. In addition, they have the ability to execute a Wasm program, and have access to the final state of the global variables whose labels ℓ may flow to $\mathcal{A}$ ($\ell \sqsubseteq \mathcal{A}$). The attacker does not have access to the linear memory, nor to the operand stack after the execution of the Wasm program. However, as customary, in our noninterference proofs we also show $\mathcal{A}$-equivalence on the operand stacks and linear memories of two runs to get the appropriate induction invariants.

While these requirements may seem restrictive, they are in line with previous work [10] and we argue our model allows for a realistic attacker, external to the system in which the Wasm code is running. Recall the attacker providing the malicious *PM* module in the password meter example in the introduction.

The attacker is able to supply malicious Wasm code, but cannot control the surrounding JavaScript context, is able to see external events (such as web requests) emanating from the Wasm code, but cannot usurp the entire surrounding execution context and thus cannot see the whole linear memory at the end of the execution. As Wasm does not have a notion of web requests or channel communication with the surrounding execution context, we model external events by the final value of global variables.

Finally, as already mentioned, we ignore information leaks stemming from other side channels or from the interaction with the environment.

3.2   Unstructured Linear Memory

When it comes to the linear memory, we point out three properties we want our IFC enforcement to fulfill, all necessary to achieve a more expressive and permissive system. The system should: 1) handle dynamic data structures compiled down from the high-level language, such as objects and arrays; 2) allow for a dynamic memory reuse; and 3) provide an IFC-sound memory.

In addition, for the IFC enforcement *per se*, two aspects need to be considered: type of enforcement and memory labeling strategy (including granularity and sensitivity). While tightly bound, we address them separately in the following paragraphs.

Type of IFC Enforcement. In theory, we could model our system as a static, dynamic, or hybrid enforcement. In practice, enforcing IFC in Wasm dynamically could be an overkill since the language does not have dynamic features, e.g., in the style of JavaScript[2]. Leveraging Wasm's type system and building a fully static IFC enfocement is not an option either because of the unstructured nature of the memory. Statically, we do not have access to the memory address we are reading from/writing to, so we cannot propagate memory taints via the type system. A static enforcement can be indeed forced by either labeling the entire memory upfront, or by using one memory for every security level in the lattice, as previously suggested [49]. However, the former approach leads to a rigid system breaking points 1) and 2), while the latter suffers from several drawbacks. Firstly, it does not scale well to larger lattices and secondly, objects in the high-level language with differently labeled fields would have to be split across different memories. Finally, handling implicit flows in a meaningful way is not obvious.

Thus, the solution we adopt in this paper is hybrid IFC enforcement. More specifically, we design a mainly static enforcement augmented with dynamic security checks on memory access instructions. This is consistent with previous work on IFC for other low-level languages without dynamic features [5,13,25,29, 30,52], which are fully static as they do not handle a linear memory, but rely entirely on a heap. Hybrid IFC systems have also been discussed for TAL-like languages [21] and even JavaScript [23,38], the former to increase expressiveness of previous static enforcements, the latter to reduce the overhead of the dynamic monitor.

---

[2] Wasm does exhibit some dynamism through `importObject`, but since we do not handle imported host functions in this paper, we do not consider it further here.

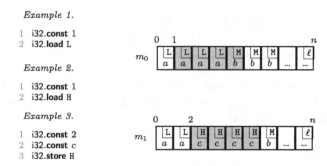

Fig. 4. Illustrative examples for memory access rules. Locations ⌊L/a⌋ denote bytes of value a labeled L. Highlighted locations are read from/written to.

Labeling the Linear Memory. Recall Wasm's linear memory is a contiguous array of raw bytes. To achieve more flexibility, we opt for a fine-grained approach of labeling the memory and assign a label to every memory location. As such, each memory location l maps in SecWasm to a pair (b, ℓ) of byte b and security level ℓ.

The fine-grained labeling allows for a straightforward handling of arrays and objects when compiled down to Wasm, as they can occupy a contiguous sequence of memory locations, instead of non-adjacent ranges of locations (a first step in satisfying point 1). For the same reason, but also for satisfying point 2), we pursue a flow-sensitive approach. Flow-insensitivity would again require the memory to be statically labeled upfront, without possibility of changing its taints. As mentioned earlier, this is a rigid approach we do not consider further.

Security Considerations. One consequence of these choices is that memory access instructions become adorned with a security label ℓ. Then t.**load** ℓ (t.**store** ℓ) reads from (writes to) the memory a value of type t and security level ℓ.

Further, to reduce the dynamic overhead, we employ dynamic checks only when reading from the memory. Checks when writing to the memory are not needed. First, because the labels in the memory are updated upon a write, and second, because the security type system ensures the security labels of the value to be written, of the execution context, and of the address to write at all have lower sensitivity than the instruction's label. As such, while writing to memory will always succeed, given the instruction does not trap due to insufficient resources, reading from memory needs to additionally ensure the security labels of all memory locations required to form the value read are below level ℓ of the instruction. Thus, given memory m_0 in Fig. 4, the program in Example 1 will trap (M $\not\sqsubseteq$ L), while the one in Example 2 will not (L $\sqcup$ M $\sqsubseteq$ H). Finally, executing the program in Example 3 with memory m_0 produces memory m_1.

Another consequence of our memory labeling strategy is that *new* memory locations require a security label as well. (Recall Wasm's memory can be extended dynamically with construct **memory.grow**.) Thus, for security reasons the newly created memory locations are labeled with the bottom label L of the lattice.

Moreover, calls to **memory.grow** can only take place in public contexts and by a public value. Allowing other levels would leak private information, as depicted in the code snippets in Example 4 and Example 5. In both examples, by comparing the global values stored at positions 0 and 1 in the final state, the attacker can learn the secret read on line 3 in Example 4, respectively line 4 in Example 5.

Example 4.

```
1  memory.size
2  global.set 0
3  i32.load H
4  memory.grow
5  memory.size
6  global.set 1
```

Example 5.

```
1  memory.size
2  global.set 0
3  i32.const 1
4  i32.load H
5  if (memory.grow)
6  else (i32.const 0)
7  memory.size
8  global.set 1
```

3.3   Structured Control Flow

One of the challenges of extending Wasm with IFC is computing the control flow regions for handling implicit flows.

Wasm has scoped control flow instructions, similarly to high-level languages, and branching instructions which extend their lexical scope, similarly to other low-level languages. Computing the scope extension is what sets SecWasm apart, as employing external tools or performing additional computations [5,10] does not seem to be necessary for it. Instead, we benefit from branching instructions arising only within *nested* blocks and use their immediates to compute the scope extension.

Consider the code snippet in Example 7. It contains three nested **blocks** (labeled $B0-$B2 and whose types we omit for clarity) and two conditional branching instructions inside block $B2, with **br_if** 1 (line 8) extending $B2's scope until the end of block $B1. The first branch (line 8) is conditioned by the medium-labeled value read on line 7. Then, instructions on lines 8–13 will be in medium context. However, since the second branch (line 10) is conditioned by the high-labeled value read on line 9, the execution of instructions on lines 10–11 will be in high context. We assume $expr_n$, with $0 \leq n \leq 4$, are not branching instruction. Note $expr_4$ is not highlighted in red, nor $expr_5$ in blue. The reason for this is that $expr_4$ is executed irrespective of whether $expr_3$ gets executed or not. Similarly, $expr_5$ is not in a medium context as it is always executed.

Example 6.

```
1  block $B0
2     expr_0
3     block $B1
4        expr_1
5        block $B2
6           expr_2
7           t.load M
8           br_if 1
9           t.load H
10          br_if 0
11          expr_3
12        end
13        expr_4
14     end
15     expr_5
16  end
17  expr_6
```

In brief, immediate i of a branching instruction extends the scope of the current block until the end of the ith-1 block, where counting starts at 0 from the current block. We further use this information to compute the control flow regions without resorting to other additional tools.

The *pc* upgrading and downgrading around the control flow regions is not surprising, and this is usually dealt with by adopting a stack of security levels [53], with the top *pc* being the effective one. We follow a similar tactic and push a *pc* entry onto the stack whenever we enter a block. What SecWasm does differently

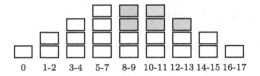

0   1-2   3-4   5-7   8-9   10-11 12-13 14-15 16-17

Fig. 5. pc stack progression for Example 7. Indices denote code line numbers, white denotes a low program counter, blue medium, and red high. (Color figure online)

next, is to use a *flow-sensitive* stack, i.e., a stack whose entry sensitivity can change during typing (Fig. 5), in contrast to most previous approaches employing a flow-insensitive one. More specific details on this are discussed in Sect. 4.3.

3.4 $\mathcal{A}$-Equivalences

The final challenge we face is not to ensure the design of SecWasm is sound, information flow in Wasm is comparatively straight forward, but *proving* it is sound. A first step in this direction is coming up with the *right* definitions to get the appropriate induction invariants for proving noninterference.

While we are interested in global variables equivalence with respect to the attacker (Sect. 3.1), we need to show some kind of $\mathcal{A}$-equivalence holds throughout the program's execution for other parameters as well, such as memory and operand stack, even though the attacker *does not have access to them*.

Memory $\mathcal{A}$-Equivalence. Traditionally, ℓ-equivalence on memories m_0 and m_1 (denoted $m_0 \sim_\ell m_1$) is defined such that for every memory location l, if $m_0(l) = (k_0, \ell_0)$ and $m_1(l) = (k_1, \ell_1)$ and both $\ell_0, \ell_1 \sqsubseteq \ell$, then $k_0 = k_1$ and $\ell_0 = \ell_1$.

However, this relation is not an equivalence relation, as it is not transitive. Given memories $m_1 = \{0 \mapsto (1, \text{L}), 1 \mapsto (1, \text{L}), 2 \mapsto (3, \text{H})\}$, $m_2 = \{0 \mapsto (1, \text{L}), 1 \mapsto (1, \text{H}), 2 \mapsto (2, \text{H})\}$, and $m_3 = \{0 \mapsto (1, \text{L}), 1 \mapsto (2, \text{L}), 2 \mapsto (1, \text{H})\}$, $m_1 \sim_\text{L} m_2$ and $m_2 \sim_\text{L} m_3$, but $m_1 \not\sim_\text{L} m_3$. Due to this, the classical formulation for confinement will not be strong enough to hold true, as after typing a program in a high context, executing it will not necessarily result in ℓ-equivalent memories. Because of the flow-sensitivity, the program execution in a high context is confined to strictly making more memory locations secret.

This means we need a stronger relation for memories, an ordered-equivalence $\blacktriangleleft_\mathcal{A}$ which says two memories m_0 and m_1 are $\blacktriangleleft_\mathcal{A}$-equivalent if m_1 has strictly more high-labeled indices and all low-labeled indices are the same between m_0 and m_1 (see Definition 6 in Sect. 5).

Operand Stack $\mathcal{A}$-Equivalence. Defining $\mathcal{A}$-equivalence for two unwinding operand stacks is more involved.

Consider the Wasm code in Example 7 prepending the code in Fig. 2a with instructions 1–2 for reading value of secret x_H. This also corresponds to C code if (x_H) {return 0;} else {return 1;}. Figure 6 depicts the evolution of the operand stack during the execution of this program for both cases when $x_\text{H} = 0$ and $x_\text{H} \neq 0$.

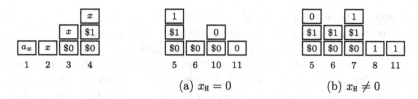

(a) $x_{\mathrm{H}} = 0$ (b) $x_{\mathrm{H}} \neq 0$

Fig. 6. Evolution of the operand stack for Example 7. The stack and index i below denote the operand stack after the execution of the instruction on line i. Values are depicted as n instead of t.**const** n. $\$0 = \mathbf{label}_1\{\epsilon\}$; $\$1 = \mathbf{label}_0\{\text{i32.const } 0\}$; x is the value read from memory starting at location a_x.

Since we consider x to be high, running the program with values for x_{H} from the two cases gives us two different operand stacks which at the end of the execution must be indistinguishable to an attacker. We say the end of the execution since instructions 6-11 will be in high context. (**br_if** 0 sets a high context for instructions 6-9 and **br** 1 on line 8 extends it until line 11.)

Example 7.

```
 1  i32.const aₓ
 2  i32.load H
 3  block  (i32 → i32) $0
 4    block  (i32 → ε) $1
 5      i32.eqz
 6      br_if 0
 7      i32.const 1
 8      br 1
 9    end
10    i32.const 0
11  end
```

Generally, we show this indistinguishability by first relating through an equivalence relation $\sim_{\mathcal{A}}$ two operand stacks with the same shape OS_1 and OS_2 and second, by relating through an ordered equivalence $\blacktriangleleft_{\mathcal{A}}$ and a *confinement* lemma two operand stacks OS_1 and OS_1' (OS_2 and OS_2', respectively) when entering and leaving a high-context area. Finally, a *triangle* lemma proves the two final operand stacks OS_1' and OS_2' $\mathcal{A}$-equivalent.

Recall the elements on the operand stack are values, frames, and labels, and none of which contains security levels. Before relating the operand stacks in attacker-equivalence relations, we need to relate them to another structure containing security levels, and this is a type stack

$$OS_1 \blacktriangleleft_{\mathcal{A}} OS_1'$$
$$\sim_{\mathcal{A}} \qquad \sim_{\mathcal{A}}$$
$$OS_2 \blacktriangleleft_{\mathcal{A}} OS_2'$$

TS of labeled types $t\langle\ell\rangle$. Then, $TS \Vdash OS$ (Definition 3 in Sect. 5) says that OS is in agreement with TS, meaning that if disconsidering frames and labels, then for every labeled type $t\langle\ell\rangle$ in TS there is a corresponding value t.**const** k on the same position in OS.

Defining relation $\sim_{\mathcal{A}}$ simply means ensuring the operand stacks satisfy certain requirements given their corresponding labeled type stacks. Figure 7a illustrates this relation. Cells denote values on the operand stack, and gray cells denote values whose corresponding labeled type on the type stack has a high label. Basically, $\sim_{\mathcal{A}}$ says that any two operand stacks of the same shape (without frames and labels) and with equal low values (the label of the corresponding type is low) on the

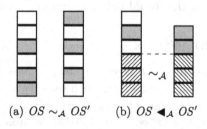

(a) $OS \sim_{\mathcal{A}} OS'$ (b) $OS \blacktriangleleft_{\mathcal{A}} OS'$

Fig. 7. Operand stack equivalence relations in SecWasm. White is low, gray is high, striped is either.

same positions are attacker-equivalent (Definition 4 in Sect. 5).

Defining relation $\blacktriangleleft_\mathcal{A}$ is particularly challenging, as we need to specify what happens to the operand stack during the high-context execution. If it unwinds, how much does it unwind? If it grows, what gets added to it? When a program executes in a high context, one of three things can happen (and all three things can happen during different parts of the execution). Firstly, the program can branch and pop the appropriate number of entries off the stack. Secondly, the program can pop some number of entries off the stack without branching. Thirdly, the program can push elements onto the stack. In the first two cases, the bottom of the stack will remain unchanged between the beginning and the end of the execution. In the third case, there is still some part at the bottom of the stack that remains unchanged (this may however be empty) and the top of the stack will contain only values labeled at or above the high pc-label. Relation $\blacktriangleleft_\mathcal{A}$ in Fig. 7b captures all three cases (Definition 5 in Sect. 5).

3.5 Big-Step Semantics

To conclude this section, we make a final note on a decision related to the semantic model we take to obtain proof clarity and simplicity.

In this paper, we opt for a big-step operational semantics for (Sec)Wasm, in contrast to previous work using a small-step operational semantics [22], due to two principal reasons. Firstly, our goal is to provide an IFC system that is mostly static and, therefore, we do not find the choice of semantics to be crucial, as long as it remains faithful to the Wasm specification. Secondly, our IFC system aims to provide end-to-end noninterference for full program executions. In this setting, big-step semantics naturally accommodates clean proofs of noninterference for Wasm's structured control flow primitives.

4 SecWasm

This section presents the technical details of SecWasm, our information flow-aware variant of Wasm. Recall we focus on WebAssembly 1.0 [47]. Consequently, we disregard language extensions in the current version [50]. However, to the best of our knowledge, the extensions do not fundamentally alter Wasm in a way that could not be accommodated in SecWasm.

4.1 Syntax

As already discussed in the previous section, SecWasm extends several of Wasm syntactic constructs with security levels, all highlighted in Fig. 8. We append a security label ℓ to each value type, and augment all types t in Wasm to labeled types τ in SecWasm. Further, we annotate function types ft with a security label ℓ specifying an upper bound on the information that may flow into the execution of a function. As mentioned in Sect. 3, instructions for reading from/writing to memory also carry a security label ℓ. We omit alignment immediates for these instructions as they do not affect the semantics [50]. As seen in Sect. 2,

(security labels)	ℓ	::=	$\mathsf{L} \mid \mathsf{H} \mid \ldots$
(labeled types)	τ	::=	$t\langle \ell \rangle$
(global types)	gt	::=	$\mathsf{mut}^? \ \tau$
(function types)	ft	::=	$\tau^* \xrightarrow{\ell} \tau^*$
(block types)	bt	::=	$\tau^* \to \tau^*$
(memory instructions)	mem	::=	$t.\mathsf{load} \ \ell \mid t.\mathsf{store} \ \ell$
(admin instructions)	$admin$	::=	trap

Fig. 8. SecWasm's extensions over Wasm syntax.

administrative instructions are an artifact of small-step semantics. Due to the big-step semantics paradigm we employ, all administrative operators except for **trap** become irrelevant in SecWasm.

As our extensions are only related to information-flow, we do not explicitly distinguish between SecWasm and Wasm when we discuss about the syntax and semantics the two systems share. We use SecWasm only when we refer to the information-flow extensions to Wasm.

4.2 Semantics

Since our IFC enforcement is mostly static, this subsection provides mainly a glimpse into (Sec)Wasm's semantic behavior.

Notation. If a is a sequence or stack of items, then we use notation $a[i]$ to denote the i:th element of the stack (counting from top and starting from 0), $a[i :]$ to denote all elements from $a[i]$ through the end of a, and $a[i : j]$ to denote all elements from $a[i]$ to $a[j]$ inclusive (the empty sequence is $j < i$ and $a[i : \infty]$ is equivalent to $a[i :]$). Furthermore, we write $a[i : j \to k^*]$ to denote the sequence in a with all data at indices between (inclusive) i and j replaced by the sequence of values k^*. We use :: as a stack entry separator. Note in SecWasm, we represent the top of the stack on the left, i.e., $a[0] :: a[1 :]$, unlike in pure Wasm, where it is denoted on the right.

By e^n we denote a sequence of length n with all free variables in e replaced by x_i for each $i \in [0, n-1]$.

Following Wasm, we make heavy use of record-like syntactic constructs in SecWasm. A grammatical category consisting of records is declared, e.g., as $R :: = \{\mathsf{key}_1 \ n, \mathsf{key}_2 \ expr\}$ and if $r \in R$ then $r = \{\mathsf{key}_1 \ n, \mathsf{key}_2 \ expr\}$ for some number n and expression $expr$, and $r.\mathsf{key}_1 = n$. Furthermore, we use syntax $r\{\mathsf{key}_1 \ 0\}$ to denote a record that is like r except "field" key_1 now has value 0.

Evaluation Judgment. As discussed in Sect. 3, we employ a big-step semantics paradigm due to its cleaner representation and ease of reasoning. As such, we have a big-step evaluation judgment $\ll\sigma, S, expr\gg \Downarrow \ll\sigma', S', \theta\gg$ relating an initial configuration to a final configuration. In the initial configuration, a sequence of instructions $expr$ is executed in current state S by interacting with the operand stack σ, leading to the final configuration containing the updated state S' and

(values)	v	$::= t.\textbf{const } k$
(addresses)	a	$::= 0 \mid 1 \mid 2 \mid \ldots$
(store)	S	$::= \{\text{funcs } func^*_{inst}, \text{tables } table^*_{inst}, \text{globals } global^*_{inst}, \text{mems } mem^*_{inst}\}$
(function instances)	$func_{inst}$	$::= \{\text{type } i, \text{module } module_{inst}, \text{code } func\}$
(memory instances)	mem_{inst}	$::= \{\text{data } (byte, \ell)^*, \text{max } k^?\}$
(operand stack)	σ	$::= \varepsilon \mid v :: \sigma \mid L_k :: \sigma \mid \textbf{frame}_k\{frame\} :: \sigma$
(frames)	$frame$	$::= \{\text{locals } v^*, \text{module } module_{inst}\}$

Expression evaluation: $\boxed{\ll \sigma, S, expr \gg \Downarrow \ll \sigma', S', \theta \gg}$

E-LOAD
$$j = i + S.\text{mem.offset}$$
$$\frac{j + |t|/8 \le S.\text{mem.data} \qquad S.\text{mem}[j : j + |t|/8] = (b, \ell)^* \qquad bytes_t(n) = b^* \qquad \boxed{\bigsqcup \ell \sqsubseteq \ell_m}}{\ll \text{i32.const } i :: \sigma, S, t.\textbf{load } \boxed{\ell_m} \gg \Downarrow \ll t.\textbf{const } n :: \sigma, S, no\text{-}br \gg}$$

E-STORE
$$j = i + S.\text{mem.offset}$$
$$\frac{j + |t|/8 \le S.\text{mem.data} \qquad bytes_t(n) = b^* \qquad S' = S.\text{mem}[j : j + |t|/8 \mapsto (b, \boxed{\ell_m})^*]}{\ll t.\textbf{const } n :: \text{i32.const } i :: \sigma, S, t.\textbf{store } \boxed{\ell_m} \gg \Downarrow \ll \sigma, S', no\text{-}br \gg}$$

E-MEMORY-GROW
$$\frac{\sigma|_F[0].\text{module.memaddrs}[0] = a \quad S.\text{mems}[a] = m \quad sz = |m.\text{data}|/64 \text{ Ki} \quad len = k + sz}{\ll \text{i32.const } k :: \sigma, S, \textbf{memory.grow} \gg \Downarrow \ll \text{i32.const } sz :: \sigma, S', no\text{-}br \gg}$$
with middle premise: $len \le 2^{16} \quad (m.\text{max} = null \ \lor \ len \le m.\text{max}) \quad S' = S.\text{mems}[a][sz : len \to (0, \boxed{\text{L}})]$

E-BLOCK
$$\ll v_1^n :: L_m :: \sigma_{init}, S, expr \gg \Downarrow \ll \sigma, S', \theta \gg$$
$$\frac{\theta \ne no\text{-}br \Rightarrow \sigma_{fin} = \sigma \qquad \theta = no\text{-}br \Rightarrow (\sigma = \sigma' :: L_m^0 :: \sigma'' \land \sigma_{fin} = \sigma' :: \sigma'')}{\ll v_1^n :: \sigma_{init}, S, \textbf{block } (\tau_1^n \to \tau_2^m) \ expr \ \textbf{end} \gg \Downarrow \ll \sigma_{fin}, S', \text{pred}(\theta) \gg}$$

E-LOOP-EVAL
$$\frac{\ll v_1^n :: L_n :: \sigma, S, expr \gg \Downarrow \ll \sigma', S', 0 \gg \qquad \ll \sigma', S', \textbf{loop } (\tau_1^n \to \tau_2^m) \ expr \ \textbf{end} \gg \Downarrow \ll \sigma'', S'', \theta \gg}{\ll v_1^n :: \sigma, S, \textbf{loop } (\tau_1^n \to \tau_2^m) \ expr \ \textbf{end} \gg \Downarrow \ll \sigma'', S'', \theta \gg}$$

E-BR-IF-JUMP
$$\frac{}{\ll \text{i32.const } k + 1 :: v^n :: \sigma_0 :: L_n^{i-1} :: \sigma, S, \textbf{br\_if } i \gg \Downarrow \ll v^n :: \sigma, S, i \gg}$$

E-BR-IF-NO-JUMP
$$\frac{}{\ll \text{i32.const } 0 :: \sigma, S, \textbf{br\_if } i \gg \Downarrow \ll \sigma, S, no\text{-}br \gg}$$

E-RETURN
$$\frac{}{\ll v^n :: \sigma :: F_n, S, \textbf{return} \gg \Downarrow \ll v^n :: F_n, S, return \gg}$$

E-CALL
$$f = S.\text{funcs}[i] \qquad f.\text{type} = \tau_1^n \xrightarrow{\ell} \tau_2^m \qquad f.\text{code.locals} = \tau^p \qquad f.\text{code.body} = expr$$
$$\frac{F_m = \{\text{locals } v_1^n : (t.\textbf{const } 0)^p, \text{module } f.\text{module}\} \qquad \ll F_m, S, expr \gg \Downarrow \ll v_2^m :: F_m, S', \theta \gg}{\ll v_1^n :: \sigma, S, \textbf{call } i \gg \Downarrow \ll v_2^m :: \sigma, S', no\text{-}br \gg}$$

E-SEQ-JUMP
$$\frac{\ll \sigma_0, S_0, expr_0 \gg \Downarrow \ll \sigma_1, S_1, \theta \gg \qquad \theta \ne no\text{-}br}{\ll \sigma_0, S_0, expr_0; expr_1 \gg \Downarrow \ll \sigma_1, S_1, \theta \gg}$$

E-SEQ
$$\frac{\ll \sigma_0, S_0, expr_0 \gg \Downarrow \ll \sigma_1, S_1, no\text{-}br \gg \qquad \ll \sigma_1, S_1, expr_1 \gg \Downarrow \ll \sigma_2, S_2, \theta \gg}{\ll \sigma_0, S_0, expr_0; expr_1 \gg \Downarrow \ll \sigma_2, S_2, \theta \gg}$$

Fig. 9. SecWasm selected evaluation rules. Security extensions are highlighted.

operand stack σ'. The essence of this paradigm is the third component θ of a final configuration. θ evaluates to either a natural number j denoting a branch out of j contexts (blocks, loops, or conditionals), *no-br* if there was no jump, or *return* if a **return** instruction executed. θ allows to do away with the administrative instructions in Wasm. More on this in the next paragraph when we discuss selected evaluation rules.

Metavariable S represents the store or the global state and comprises of instances for all functions, globals, tables, and memories that have been allocated. Just like in pure Wasm, operand stack σ contains three types of entries: values, labels, and frames. In SecWasm, we diverge slightly from Wasm by denoting branch target labels as L_n instead of **label**$_n\{expr\}$, as in SecWasm we do not need to keep track of the continuation expression *expr*. As a simplifying choice, we also use the syntax $\sigma :: L_n^{i-1} :: \sigma'$ to represent the case where L_n is the i:th label (counting from top and starting from 0) on the compound stack $\sigma :: L_n :: \sigma'$. Frames remain as defined in Wasm, **frame**$_n\{frame\}$, with *frame* keeping track of the values for the function's local variables.

Another point of divergence from Wasm is that in SecWasm there is only one frame on the operand stack at any given time. The reason for this change is that it simplifies our formalization. Thus, instead of having an operand stack containing several frames, in SecWasm every function call creates another (sub-)stack, where its corresponding frame is on the bottom. This is in line with function behavior in WebAssembly, as jumps from inside a function are either branching from within nested blocks, giving control at the end of the corresponding block, or **return**s, giving control back to the caller function. This will become more obvious when discussing rules E-CALL-*.

Similar to Wasm, abnormal termination of a program results in a trap, denoted $\ll\sigma, S, expr\gg \Downarrow$ **trap**. When a trap occurs, the computation is aborted and no further modifications to the state can be made. In SecWasm, the execution of an instruction traps under the same conditions as in Wasm, but failure to satisfy the additional security checks also leads to a trap. Thus, SecWasm introduces additional rules for handling the error cases which result in a trap due to the IFC-checks. These rules are presented in the technical report [6].

Selected Evaluation Rules. Figure 9 depicts the most important evaluation rules, while the full set of rules is presented in the technical report [6]. Since we opt for a mostly static enforcement, note only few semantic rules carry security checks.

The intuition for the memory access rules was given in Sect. 3, so we do not discuss the rules in detail here. However, recall Examples 1 and 2 and note premise $\bigsqcup \ell \sqsubseteq \ell_m$ in rule E-LOAD ensuring all security levels ℓ of memory locations read from are below the immediate label ℓ_m for the **load** instruction. Due to this check, in SecWasm the execution of Example 1 will trap, while the execution of Example 2 will succeed. Further, recall Example 3 and note that rule E-STORE updates the security levels of the memory locations written into with no additional checks.

Before we discuss the rules for achieving structured control flow, few things are worth mentioning. First, recall that branching can only happen from within the block constructs **block**, **loop**, and **if**. Second, the end of every such block is a valid branch target for code executing inside the block, with the exception of loops where the target can also be at the start of the loop. Finally, recall θ specifies how far out of a series of nested blocks to jump. We further introduce the notion of predecessor of θ ($\mathsf{pred}(\theta)$) specifying how to update θ when we exit a block: $\mathsf{pred}(no\text{-}br) = \mathsf{pred}(0) = no\text{-}br$, $\mathsf{pred}(j+1) = j$, $\mathsf{pred}(return) = return$.

When entering a **block** of type $\tau_1^n \rightarrow \tau_2^m$ and body $expr$, label L_m is added in between the top n values v_1^n of the operand stack corresponding to the block's input arguments and the rest of the stack. Exiting a block can happen either by trapping (rule E-BLOCK-TRAP), by jumping (when a branch/return instruction is executed inside the block), or by reaching its end without a jump. Rule E-BLOCK distinguishes between the latter two cases by inspecting marker θ. If no jump occurred ($\theta = no\text{-}br$), we remove the label L_m from the operand stack and return the result $\sigma' :: \sigma''$. Otherwise, we return the operand stack as is, since the stack unwinding has been dealt with already by the jumping instruction (See below rule E-BR-IF-JUMP.) Finally, function pred adjusts θ to account for the fact that a block has been exited.

Consider again Example 7 when $x \neq 0$ and the instruction on line 8 is about to be executed. **br** 1 unconditionally jumps out of the two blocks and gives control at the end of instruction on line 11. θ is set to 1 after executing line 8 and exiting block \$1 updates it to $\mathsf{pred}(1) = 0$ (rule E-BLOCK). Since $\theta \neq no\text{-}br$, all remaining instructions in block \$0 will be ignored (rule E-SEQ-JUMP). Reaching the end of block \$0 updates θ again to $\mathsf{pred}(0) = no\text{-}br$. If present, executing all subsequent instructions would continue according to rule E-SEQ until the next branching or function return.

loop and **if** statements constitute **block**s with slightly specialized rules to reflect their different function. This can also be seen in the semantic behavior of pure Wasm, where **if**s and **loop**s reduce in one step to a **block** [22]. For this reason we only present rules E-LOOP-SKIP (for leaving a loop) and E-IF in the technical report [6], as they differ only slightly from rule E-BLOCK. What differs is that **if** statements choose the expression to execute based on the value on top of the operand stack, while E-LOOP-SKIP requires θ to be different than 0, as $\theta = 0$ restarts the loop (rule E-LOOP-EVAL). Note from rule E-LOOP-EVAL another perk of Wasm, namely **loop** blocks are evaluated at least once.

A conditional branch **br_if** i executes when the value on top of the operand stack is different than 0 (rule E-BR-IF-JUMP). In this case, Wasm requires the top of the stack to contain at least n other values, as illustrated by the index of the i:th label L_n^{i-1} on the input stack. Recall the index specifies the number of values expected by the branch target. Next, the rule drops everything between the top $n+1$ entries on the stack down to and including label L_n^{i-1} and finishes with $\theta = i$. If the top value of the operand stack is 0, then the conditional branch does not execute (rule E-BR-IF-NO-JUMP), and the computation proceeds sequentially, finishing with $\theta = no\text{-}br$. Unconditional branching **br** i (rule E-BR) works in a similar way as executing conditional branching.

When a function is **call**ed (rules E-CALL-*), we create an empty operand stack and push on it a frame instantiated with values v_1^n for the function arguments and initial values 0 for the function's local variables. When returning from a function, we only retain the return values, discarding everything else, including the frame. Note in Wasm, the frame is popped off when executing a **return**, but in SecWasm it is not (rule E-RETURN).

Finally, rules E-SEQ-* distinguish between the cases when a jump occurred, i.e., $\theta \neq no\text{-}br$ in rule E-SEQ-JUMP, and when the execution proceeds sequentially in rule E-SEQ. In the former case, rule E-SEQ-JUMP simply ignores the subsequent instructions until θ becomes $no\text{-}br$. And the block rules ensure θ indeed decreases to $no\text{-}br$, by computing its predecessor every time a block is exited. Thus, either the same number of blocks have been exited as the initial value of $\theta + 1$, or all instructions after a **return** statement have been ignored.

4.3   Security Type System

As our enforcement is mostly static, SecWasm's type system is heavily populated with security checks. Before discussing the type system, we first give an intuition for the constructs SecWasm uses to track the information flows, and then briefly discuss the typing judgment.

Tracking Flows—an Intuition. As the bedrock for static IFC in Wasm, SecWasm's type system tracks both explicit and implicit information flows. For tracking explicit flows, we assign a security label to each value in the operand stack via a *type stack st* denoting a stack of labeled types. As discussed in Sect. 3.3, for tracking implicit flows we use a stack of *pc* labels, with a label entry for every block context. We then combine the *pc* stack with the type stack in a *stack-of-stacks* γ with entries $\langle st, pc \rangle$. Upon entering a block, γ is augmented with a new pair $\langle st, pc \rangle$, with *st* denoting the input stack for the block, and *pc* the initial program counter label for the block's execution. The security labels in γ may get upgraded, and after leaving a block, the top two entries are merged.

Typing Judgments. The type system assumes a typing security context C containing e.g., the type of functions and local variables. C is defined as in Wasm, but where value types t have been adorned with labels to labeled types τ.

Previous presentations of Wasm [22] depict the type system using a judgment of the form $C \vdash expr : t^n \rightarrow t^m$ that only says how *expr* affects the top elements on the stack and leaves the rest to a subtyping-like rule. Instead, we use a more explicit judgment form passing the entire γ around while updating its program counters: $\gamma, C \vdash expr \dashv \gamma'$. The judgment reads as follows: Assuming input type stack γ.fst and security context C, *expr* produces (possibly) updated output type stack γ'.fst. For $\gamma = \langle st_0, pc_0 \rangle :: \dots :: \langle st_n, pc_n \rangle$, γ.fst denotes the stack formed by the first elements of each entry in γ, i.e., $\gamma.\text{fst} \triangleq st_0 :: \dots :: st_n$.

We extend the type system with a simple subtyping judgment for types to capture when a type is less sensitive than another and write $\tau \sqsubseteq \tau'$ whenever the label of τ can flow to the label of τ'. We further extend this notion to sequences of labeled types as $st \sqsubseteq st'$ if st and st' are of the same length and $\tau_i \sqsubseteq \tau_i'$ for $\tau_i = st[i]$ and $\tau_i' = st'[i]$, respectively.

(Security contexts) $C ::= \{\text{globals } (\text{mut}^? \ \tau \ )^*, \text{locals } \tau \ ^*, \text{return } (\ \tau \ ^*)^?, \text{labels } (\ \tau \ ^*)^*, \dots\}$

(Security-labeled type stack) $st ::= \varepsilon \mid \tau :: st$

(Stack-of-stacks) $\gamma ::= \varepsilon \mid (st, pc) :: \gamma$

Expression typing: $\boxed{\gamma, C \vdash expr \dashv \gamma'}$

T-UNREACHABLE
$$\gamma, C \vdash \textbf{unreachable} \dashv \gamma$$

T-LOAD
$$\frac{C.\text{mem} = n \qquad \ell_v = \ell_a \sqcup \ell \sqcup pc}{\langle \text{i32}\langle \ell_a \rangle :: st, \ pc \rangle :: \gamma, C \vdash t.\textbf{load} \ \ell \dashv \langle t\langle \ell_v \rangle :: st, \ pc \rangle :: \gamma}$$

T-STORE
$$\frac{C.\text{mem} = n \qquad pc \sqcup \ell_a \sqcup \ell_v \sqsubseteq \ell}{\langle t\langle \ell_v \rangle :: \text{i32}\langle \ell_a \rangle :: st, \ pc \rangle :: \gamma, C \vdash t.\textbf{store} \ \ell \dashv \langle st, \ pc \rangle :: \gamma}$$

T-MEMORY-GROW
$$\frac{C.\text{mem} = n}{\langle \text{i32}\langle L \rangle :: st, \ L \rangle :: \gamma, C \vdash \textbf{memory.grow} \dashv \langle \text{i32}\langle L \rangle :: st, \ L \rangle :: \gamma}$$

T-BLOCK
$$\frac{\langle \tau_1^n, \ pc \rangle :: \langle st, pc \rangle :: \gamma, \text{label}(\tau_2^m) : C \vdash expr \dashv \langle \tau_2^m, \ pc' \rangle :: \langle st', \ pc'' \rangle :: \gamma'}{\langle \tau_1^n :: st, \ pc \rangle :: \gamma, C \vdash \textbf{block} \ (\tau_1^n \to \tau_2^m) \ expr \ \textbf{end} \dashv \langle \tau_2^m :: st', \ pc \sqcup pc'' \rangle :: \gamma'}$$

T-LOOP
$$\frac{pc \sqsubseteq pc' \qquad \gamma \sqsubseteq \gamma' \qquad pc \sqsubseteq pc'' \qquad st \sqsubseteq st' \qquad \langle \tau_1^n, \ pc' \rangle :: \langle st', \ pc'' \rangle :: \gamma', \text{label}(\tau_1^n) : C \vdash expr \dashv \langle \tau_2^m, \ pc' \rangle :: \langle st', \ pc'' \rangle :: \gamma'}{\langle \tau_1^n :: st, \ pc \rangle :: \gamma, C \vdash \textbf{loop} \ (\tau_1^n \to \tau_2^m) \ expr \ \textbf{end} \dashv \langle \tau_2^m :: st', \ pc \sqcup pc'' \rangle :: \gamma'}$$

T-BR-IF
$$\frac{C.\text{labels}[i] = st \qquad \gamma \sqsubseteq \gamma' \qquad pc \sqcup \ell \sqsubseteq st \qquad \gamma^* = \text{lift}_{\ell \sqcup pc}(\langle st :: st', pc \rangle :: \gamma'[0 : i-1])}{\langle \text{i32}\langle \ell \rangle :: st :: st', \ pc \rangle :: \gamma, C \vdash \textbf{br\_if} \ i \dashv \gamma^* :: \gamma'[i :]}$$

T-RETURN
$$\frac{C.\text{return} = st \qquad \gamma \sqsubseteq \gamma' \qquad pc \sqsubseteq st \qquad \gamma'' = \text{lift}_{pc}(\langle st'', \ell \rangle :: \gamma')}{\langle st :: st', \ pc \rangle :: \gamma, C \vdash \textbf{return} \dashv \gamma''}$$

T-CALL
$$\frac{C.\text{funcs}[i] = f : \tau_1^n \xrightarrow{\ell} \tau_2^m \qquad pc \sqsubseteq \ell}{\langle \tau_1^n :: st, \ pc \rangle :: \gamma, C \vdash \textbf{call} \ i \dashv \langle \tau_2^m :: st, \ pc \rangle :: \gamma}$$

T-CALL-INDIRECT
$$\frac{pc \sqcup \ell \sqsubseteq \ell_f}{\langle \text{i32}\langle \ell \rangle :: \tau_1^n :: st, \ pc \rangle :: \gamma, C \vdash \textbf{call\_indirect} \ \tau_1^n \xrightarrow{\ell_f} \tau_2^m \dashv \langle \tau_2^m :: st, \ pc \rangle :: \gamma}$$

Fig. 10. SecWasm type system (Selected rules). Security extensions and static checks are highlighted.

Selected Typing Rules. In the following, we discuss the most interesting rules of the type system, depicted in Fig. 10. The full set of rules is presented in the technical report [6].

First, note that abuses of non-termination channel such as in snippet $t.\textbf{load}$ H; **br_if** 0; **unreachable** are outside the scope of this work, as we further focus on enforcing termination-insensitive noninterference. Thus, we add no restrictions on the program context in rule T-UNREACHABLE.

An intuition for the memory access instructions was given in Sect. 3. Here, we reiterate that static security checks are employed only when writing to the memory ($pc \sqcup \ell_a \sqcup \ell_v \sqsubseteq \ell$ in T-STORE), as the semantics are responsible for the dynamic security checks when reading. Finally, **memory.grow** executes in a public context and only if the amount to extend the memory with is also public.

Typing the **block** instruction (rule T-BLOCK) requires the current type stack to contain at least n labeled types, corresponding to the block type. Since we enter a new block, we split the arguments off and push pair $\langle \tau_1^n, pc \rangle$ containing the n labeled types and the same program counter pc on the stack-of-stacks $\langle st, pc \rangle :: \gamma$. We also push τ_2^m on the label-stack C.labels in context C to denote the branch target at the end of the block ($\textsf{label}(\tau_2^m) : C$). The sequence of instructions $expr$ is required to produce m correctly typed output values and a new stack of stacks $\langle st', pc'' \rangle :: \gamma'$ possibly with higher labels. Finally, on the output stack-of-stacks, τ_2^m is merged with st'.

Recall **if** and **loop** are just special types of **block**s. As a consequence, rules T-IF and T-LOOP only bear minor differences to rule T-BLOCK. For the former, inner expressions $expr_1$ and $expr_2$ are type-checked under a program counter *tainted* by the information flow from the condition operand, and for the latter, the labels of type stacks and program counter need to be in a fixed-point over the loop.

In rule T-BR-IF, all types on the stack-of-stacks $\langle st, pc \rangle :: \gamma$ until and including the i:th+1 entry are tainted by label ℓ of the top element on the input stack deciding whether a branch will happen, as illustrated in Example 7. (This is represented by operator $\texttt{lift}$ upgrading all security levels present in its argument.) Furthermore, we require $pc \sqcup \ell \sqsubseteq C.\textsf{labels}[i]$ to avoid implicit flows. This rule is important because it rejects leaky programs like the one in Example 8 that copies the truth-value of local variable y_H to local variable x_L by skipping all the way to the end with **br_if** 1.

Example 8.

```
1  block
2    block
3      i32.const 0
4      local.get y_H
5      br_if 1
6    end
7    drop
8    i32.const 1
9  end
10 local.set x_L
```

All other jumping rules entail a similar taint propagation. In rule T-RETURN, for example, the entire stack-of-stacks is tainted by the function program counter. Note that premise $pc \sqsubseteq st$ in the jumping rules is synthetic and we resort to using it as it considerably simplifies the proofs.

Rule T-CALL is standard for function calls in IFC type systems. The input type stack is required to be a subtype of the input type stack for the caller function, the function program counter label ℓ needs to be at least as high as current callee pc, and the output type stack of the function needs to be a subtype of the expected output type stack.

T-CALL-INDIRECT works in almost the same way as rule T-CALL, with the difference that indirect calls require a 32-bit integer labeled ℓ on top of the input stack acting as the function pointer and thus the function also needs to check ℓ flows to the function program counter ℓ_f.

5 Security Properties

This section presents the security properties enforced by SecWasm. All proofs are manual and presented in the technical report [6], a mechanization thereof being left for future work.

We begin by stating two well-formedness properties for operand stacks $C \vdash \sigma$ and stores $C \vdash S$, specifying that local and global variables are well-typed in σ and S, respectively, with respect to the types declared in context C.

Definition 1 (Context-Stack Well-Formedness). *Operand stack σ is well-formed with respect to context C, denoted $C \vdash \sigma$, if:*

1. *For all i in the domain of C.labels there exists some σ_0, σ_1, and m such that $\sigma = \sigma_0 :: L_m^i :: \sigma_1$ and C.labels$[i] = \tau^m$ for some τ^m.*
2. *C.return $= \tau^m$ for some m and $\sigma|_F[0] = F_m$, for the bottom frame F_m and F_m.locals is well typed with respect to C.locals.*

Definition 2 (Context-Store Well-Formedness). *Store S is well-formed with respect to context C, denoted $C \vdash S$, if:*

1. *For every function f in S.funcs we have $C \vdash f$.*
2. *For every variable in C.globals there is a corresponding well-typed entry in S.globals.*

Next, we state what it means for an operand stack and labeled type stacks to be in agreement. (Recall Fig. 7a.)

Definition 3 (Operand Stack and Type Stack Agreement). *Given operand stack σ and type stack st, we define σ agreement with st (denoted $st \Vdash \sigma$) inductively as:*

$$\frac{}{[] \Vdash e} \qquad \frac{st \Vdash \sigma}{t\langle \ell \rangle :: st \Vdash t.\textbf{const } k :: \sigma} \qquad \frac{st \Vdash \sigma}{st \Vdash L :: \sigma} \qquad \frac{st \Vdash \sigma}{st \Vdash F :: \sigma}.$$

Now, we can define what it means for two operand stacks to be equivalent with respect to the attacker, i.e., relations $\sim_{\mathcal{A}}$ and $\blacktriangleleft_{\mathcal{A}}$, as discussed in Sect. 3. Recall security label $\mathcal{A}$ simply captures the level at or below which the attacker can read information.

Definition 4 (Operand Stack and Type Stack Agreement Equivalence).
For two operand stacks σ_0 and σ_1 and type stacks st_0 and st_1 such that $st_i \Vdash \sigma_i$, we define operand stack equivalence $st_0 \Vdash \sigma_0 \sim_{\mathcal{A}}^{C} st_1 \Vdash \sigma_1$ inductively as:

$$\frac{}{[] \Vdash e \sim_{\mathcal{A}}^{C} [] \Vdash e} \qquad \frac{st_0 \Vdash \sigma_0 \sim_{\mathcal{A}}^{C} st_1 \Vdash \sigma_1 \qquad \ell_0 \sqsubseteq \mathcal{A} \wedge \ell_1 \sqsubseteq \mathcal{A} \Rightarrow v_0 = v_1}{t\langle \ell_0 \rangle :: st_0 \Vdash v_0 :: \sigma_0 \sim_{\mathcal{A}}^{C} t\langle \ell_1 \rangle :: st_1 \Vdash v_1 :: \sigma_1}$$

$$\frac{st_0 \Vdash \sigma_0 \sim_{\mathcal{A}}^{C} st_1 \Vdash \sigma_1 \qquad F \sim_{\mathcal{A}}^{C} F'}{st_0 \Vdash F :: \sigma_0 \sim_{\mathcal{A}}^{C} st_1 \Vdash F' :: \sigma_1} \qquad \frac{st_0 \Vdash \sigma_0 \sim_{\mathcal{A}}^{C} st_1 \Vdash \sigma_1}{st_0 \Vdash L :: \sigma_0 \sim_{\mathcal{A}}^{C} st_1 \Vdash L :: \sigma_1}.$$

The two type stacks st_0 and st_1 must have the same *shape*, but may differ in their security labels. This allows us to relate prefixes of stacks before and after program execution (when security labels may have been upgraded due to a branch). In other words, this part of the definition does not come into effect when considering a "traditional" noninterference theorem statement.

Ideally, when proving noninterference one would show that if two configurations, including stacks and memories, are $\mathcal{A}$-equivalent then the output configurations that result after executing the same program on both these configurations are also $\mathcal{A}$-equivalent. However, this property cannot easily be extended to be inductive and instead a *confinement* lemma is required. This lemma relates the configurations before and after a single execution in a high context. Specifically, it usually says that when you execute a well-typed program in a high context it only alters high data. However, this statement is not sufficient in SecWasm, as we also have to specify what happens to the operand stack during this execution.

And this is how we define ordered equivalence $\blacktriangleleft_{\mathcal{A}}$, by introducing judgment $\gamma \Vdash \sigma \blacktriangleleft_{\mathcal{A}}^{C} \gamma' \Vdash \sigma'$ stating that stack σ' is the result of executing a high (w.r.t. the attacker-label $\mathcal{A}$) program that starts off with σ. To prove σ and σ' are related in this way one needs to prove there is some common $\mathcal{A}$-equivalent bottom of the two stacks (that may be empty) and that all elements on top of this bottom part of σ' are labeled high in γ'.

Definition 5 (Operand Stack and Stack-of-Stacks Agreement Ordered Equivalence).

$$\frac{\gamma \Vdash \sigma_t :: \sigma_b \quad \gamma' \Vdash \sigma_t' :: \sigma_b' \quad \gamma.\mathsf{fst} = st_t :: st_b}{\gamma' .\mathsf{fst} = st_t' :: st_b' \quad st_b \sqsubseteq st_b' \quad \mathsf{high}(st_t') \quad st_b \Vdash \sigma_b \sim_{\mathcal{A}}^{C} st_b' \Vdash \sigma_b'}{\gamma \Vdash \sigma_t :: \sigma_b \blacktriangleleft_{\mathcal{A}}^{C} \gamma' \Vdash \sigma_t' :: \sigma_b'}$$

Note the *pcs* are not used in the ordered equivalence, although they are part of γ. The reason for this is that in our proofs we only require the structure of $\gamma.\mathsf{fst}$ given by γ.

Recall from the discussion in Sect. 3 that the classical memory equivalence is not strong enough for our setting, so we use an ordered-equivalence relation $\blacktriangleleft_{\mathcal{A}}$ which says that two linear memories m and m' are $\blacktriangleleft_{\mathcal{A}}$-ordered equivalent if m has strictly more high-labeled indices and all the low-labeled indices are the same between m and m'.

Definition 6 ($\mathcal{A}$-Ordered Memory Equivalence). *Two memories m_0 and m_1 are $\mathcal{A}$-ordered equivalent (denoted $m_0 \blacktriangleleft_{\mathcal{A}} m_1$) iff $\forall l. \ m_1(l) = (k, \ell) \wedge \ell \sqsubseteq \mathcal{A} \Rightarrow m_0(l) = (k, \ell)$ and $\forall l. \ m_1(l) = (k_1, \ell_1) \wedge \ell_1 \not\sqsubseteq \mathcal{A} \Rightarrow m_0(l) = (k_0, \ell_0) \wedge \ell_1 \not\sqsubseteq \ell_0$.*

Further, we also need to consider what happens to the linear memory, global and local variables, i.e., the state of the program. Fortunately, the flow-insensitive nature of the global and local variables means that these will just be $\mathcal{A}$-equivalent before and after execution.

Definition 7 ($\mathcal{A}$-Ordered Store Equivalence). *Two stores S_0 and S_1 are $\mathcal{A}$-ordered equivalent given security context C:*

$$S_0 \blacktriangleleft_{\mathcal{A}}^{C} S_1 \ iff \ \begin{cases} S_0.\text{funcs} = S_1.\text{funcs} \\ S_0.\text{tables} = S_1.\text{tables} \\ S_0.\text{globals} \sim_{\mathcal{A}}^{C} S_1.\text{globals} \\ S_0.\text{mems} \blacktriangleleft_{\mathcal{A}}^{C} S_1.\text{mems}. \end{cases}$$

Confinement. Usually, these definitions are sufficient for stating confinement. Yet, in SecWasm we need to deal with an unwinding stack too. Ideally, confinement would be that given $\gamma, C \vdash expr \dashv \gamma'$ where $\gamma[0].\text{snd} \not\sqsubseteq \mathcal{A}$ and $\ll\sigma, S, expr\gg \Downarrow \ll\sigma', S', \theta\gg$, then $\gamma \Vdash \sigma \blacktriangleleft_{\mathcal{A}}^{C} \gamma' \Vdash \sigma'$ and $S \blacktriangleleft_{\mathcal{A}}^{C} S'$. However, this definition implicitly assumes $\theta = no\text{-}br$! For example, if $\theta = j + 1$ then a branch executed in $expr$ and the stack σ' is not well-typed with respect to γ' anymore. We take this dependency of the type of σ' on θ with the following definition.

Definition 8 (θ-Variant Typing Contexts).

$$\Delta(C, \gamma, \theta) \triangleq \begin{cases} \gamma & if \ \theta = no\text{-}br \\ merge(C, \gamma, j) & if \ \theta = j \\ \langle C.\text{return}, \gamma[0].\text{snd} \rangle & if \ \theta = return, \end{cases}$$

where $merge(C, \gamma, j) \triangleq \langle C.\text{labels}[j] :: \gamma[j+1].\text{fst}, \gamma[0].\text{snd} \sqcup \gamma[j+1].\text{snd} \rangle :: \gamma[j+2:]$.

Finally, we introduce an order on θs to capture the fact that if we branch in a high context we know something about the pc-labels in the output γ. Specifically, we have $no\text{-}br < 0 < 1 < \ldots < return$. We also need to define a translation of θs to integers with infinity where $\text{nat}(no\text{-}br) = -1$, $\text{nat}(j) = j$, and $\text{nat}(return) = \infty$.

We are now ready to state our confinement lemma.

Lemma 1 (Confinement.) *For any typing context C, store S_0, operand stack σ_0, stack-of-stacks γ_0, and expression $expr$, such that $C \vdash S_0$, $C \vdash \sigma_0$, and $\gamma_0 \Vdash \sigma_0$, if $\ll\sigma_0, S_0, expr\gg \Downarrow \ll\sigma_1, S_1, \theta\gg$, $\gamma_0, C \vdash expr \dashv \gamma_1$, and $\gamma_0[0].\text{snd} \not\sqsubseteq \mathcal{A}$, then the following statements hold:*

1. $\gamma_0 \Vdash \sigma_0 \blacktriangleleft_{\mathcal{A}}^{C} \Delta(C, \gamma_1, \theta) \Vdash \sigma_1$,

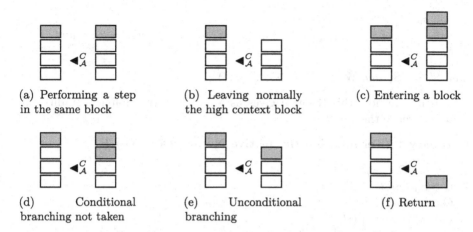

(a) Performing a step in the same block

(b) Leaving normally the high context block

(c) Entering a block

(d) Conditional branching not taken

(e) Unconditional branching

(f) Return

Fig. 11. Pictorial representation of the confinement lemma. Each box represents an element $\langle st, pc \rangle$ of γ before (left) or after (right) the execution in the high context. White means $pc \sqsubseteq \mathcal{A}$, gray $pc \not\sqsubseteq \mathcal{A}$.

2. $S_0 \blacktriangleleft_{\mathcal{A}}^{C} S_1$, and
3. $\gamma_1[0 : \mathsf{nat}(\mathsf{pred}(\theta))].\mathsf{snd} \not\sqsubseteq \mathcal{A}$.

The confinement lemma as stated above and proven in the technical report [6], captures the intuition laid out previously. Furthermore, the different cases one needs to consider in the proof are illustrated in Fig. 11.

Noninterference. Next we turn our attention to stating and proving noninterference. We would like to state a classical theorem along the lines "if you start off with two $\mathcal{A}$-equivalent configurations and execute the same program in both, you end up with two $\mathcal{A}$-equivalent configurations." However, this is not a strong enough statement to induct over the evaluation of expressions in SecWasm because the two different executions may end up branching differently in a high context. For this reason we need a weaker notion of stack similarity than the strong equivalence given above.

Definition 9 (Weak Stack Similarity). *Stacks σ_0 and σ_1 with respective thetas θ_0 and θ_1 are weakly similar given γ and C (written $WS_{\gamma,C}(\langle \sigma_0, \theta_0 \rangle, \langle \sigma_1, \theta_1 \rangle))$ iff $\Delta(\gamma, C, \theta_0) \Vdash \sigma_0 \blacktriangleleft_{\mathcal{A}}^{C} \Delta(\gamma, C, \theta_1) \Vdash \sigma_1$ or $\Delta(\gamma, C, \theta_1) \Vdash \sigma_1 \blacktriangleleft_{\mathcal{A}}^{C} \Delta(\gamma, C, \theta_0)\gamma \Vdash \sigma_0$, and if $\theta_0 \neq \theta_1$ then $\gamma[0 : |\mathsf{pred}(max(\theta_0, \theta_1))|].\mathsf{snd} \not\sqsubseteq \mathcal{A}$.*

This is enough to let us state and prove a sufficiently strong noninterference statement:

Theorem 1 (Noninterference) *If*

1. $\gamma, C \vdash expr \dashv \gamma'$,
2. $C \vdash S_0$ and $C \vdash S_1$,
3. $C \vdash \sigma_0$ and $C \vdash \sigma_1$,

4. $\gamma \Vdash \sigma_0 \sim_{\mathcal{A}}^{C} \gamma \Vdash \sigma_1$,
5. $\ll\sigma_0, S_0, expr\gg \Downarrow \ll\sigma_0', S_0', \theta_0\gg$ and $\ll\sigma_1, S_1, expr\gg \Downarrow \ll\sigma_1', S_1', \theta_1\gg$, and
6. $S_0 \sim_{\mathcal{A}}^{C} S_1$,

then $S_0' \sim_{\mathcal{A}}^{C} S_1'$ and $WS_{\gamma',C}(\langle\sigma_0',\theta_0\rangle, \langle\sigma_1',\theta_1\rangle)$.

Finally, we note this theorem gives us a corollary resembling a traditional noninterference theorem.

Corollary 1 (Termination Insensitive Noninterference) *If*

1. $\langle st, pc\rangle, C \vdash expr \dashv \langle C.\text{return}, pc'\rangle$,
2. $C \vdash S_0$ and $C \vdash S_1$,
3. $C \vdash \sigma_0$ and $C \vdash \sigma_1$,
4. $\langle st, pc\rangle \Vdash \sigma_0 \sim_{\mathcal{A}}^{C} \langle st, pc\rangle \Vdash \sigma_1$,
5. $\ll\sigma_0, S_0, expr\gg \Downarrow \ll\sigma_0', S_0', \theta_0\gg$ and $\ll\sigma_1, S_1, expr\gg \Downarrow \ll\sigma_1', S_1', \theta_1\gg$, and
6. $S_0 \sim_{\mathcal{A}}^{C} S_1$,

then $S_0' \sim_{\mathcal{A}}^{C} S_1'$ and $\langle C.\text{return}, pc'\rangle \Vdash \sigma_0' \sim_{\mathcal{A}}^{C} \langle C.\text{return}, pc'\rangle \Vdash \sigma_1'$.

This corollary holds because if the program *expr* terminates without trapping, then it terminates with either $\theta = no\text{-}br$ or $\theta = return$ and both of these guarantee that the two output stacks are typed *with the same stack type*. When they do, $\blacktriangleleft_{\mathcal{A}}^{C}$ boils down to $\sim_{\mathcal{A}}^{C}$.

6 Discussion

Several points we have not addressed in the paper are worth discussing. These are implementation, overhead, usability, and declassification. Before addressing them below, we stress that they are extensions to our work and important avenues for future exploration and not mandatory for foundational IFC in Wasm.

Implementation and Overhead. It is difficult to judge the overhead our framework would entail without having an actual implementation. We have argued for and justified the hybrid design of SecWasm as a trade-off between achieving permissiveness and expressiveness, and incurring some runtime overhead. While the semantics carry only few dynamic checks, the type system is heavily populated with additional IFC constraints which might slow-down the type-checking mechanism. However, as in prior work, the concern is not on the static overhead, but on the dynamic one. As we keep dynamic checks to a minimum, we are confident future benchmarks will not reveal considerate overheads.

Usability. We expect the use of SecWasm to be straightforward. The developer would have to manually annotate the function types and the **load** and **store** operations with security labels, and then to verify if any detected illicit information flows are due to buggy implementations or imported malicious modules (such as the password meter module *PM*).

Declassification. Certain situations require sensitive data to be released, an operation known as declassification [31]. When designing a declassification mechanism, one should aim to have it *robust*, meaning not allowing public data to influence what data to be declassified [32].

Sabelfeld and Sands presented four dimensions of declassification: *what* information is released, *who* is releasing information, *where* in the system information is released, and *when* information can be released [37]. To allow declassification in a static IFC system for Wasm, Watt *et al.* allowed functions marked as trusted to declassify data through a declassification primitive [49]. In order to extend SecWasm with a declassification construct, the formalization of the security properties enforced by the current system must be altered, as some information about the secret data could be learned by a public observer. In this sense, a password checker is different from a password meter because the latter leaks some information about the password. Although we leave it for future work, we believe our approach can be straightforwardly extended to handle the *what* dimension from Sabelfeld and Sands by guaranteeing that the system cannot leak more secrets than allowed by externally-specified escape hatches.

7 Related Work

IFC for Low-Level Languages. There has been much work on securing (subsets of) Java bytecode [5,7,11,20,25], or on enforcing security in TAL (Typed Assembly Language) [13,21,29,30,52] which models the RISC architecture, and even on JavaScript bytecode [10]. These approaches dealt with languages with unstructured control flow and heap memory, with TAL also employing registers. Due to lack of structured control flow at the low-level, prior work resorted to mimicking the block structure of the original high-level languages and computing dependence regions: linear continuations and continuation stacks [13], static code labels [29], control regions [5,10,25], type annotations [29,52]. Due to the structured control flow inherited from Wasm, in SecWasm the language's constructs proved sufficient for computing the dependence regions.

Most previous approaches dealt with Java bytecode or TAL, both languages without dynamic features. Thus, the preferred IFC enforcement was static, through security type systems [5,13,25,29,52]. More recently, a hybrid system was suggested for TAL-like languages [21], in an attempt to increase permissiveness over previous fully static approaches. Due to being a language heavily-charged with dynamic features, JavaScript bytecode was instrumented through a dynamic monitor, although prior static analysis is required for computing the control flow graphs and immediate post-dominators [10]. Although Wasm does not exhibit the same dynamism as JavaScript does, the nature of memory accesses requires a dynamic handling if a more expressive and permissive system is desired. Thus, SecWasm is designed to be mainly static and introduces dynamic checks in key places to increase permissiveness.

Cassel *et al.* present FlowNotation to find information flow violations in C programs [15], and De Francesco and Martini use abstract interpretation for instruction-level information-flow analysis [16]. Both have similar handling of the memory as SecWasm. With FlowNotation, each pointer (i.e., heap location) and its corresponding value are labeled with security policies which are joined upon dereferencing the pointer, and De Francesco and Martini label each memory location with a label to represent the maximum security level of the data to be stored. However, since FlowNotation does not handle pointer arithmetic and the memory in the system by De Francesco and Martini is a map of variables to abstract values, neither of those solutions have an unstructured memory as in SecWasm with partial re-writes of data (such as Example 3, where part of the 32-bit integer value starting at position 0 is overwritten).

Hybrid IFC. While hybrid analyses were not so popular amongst low-level languages, they have been employed for high-level languages [8,23,26,35,46]. Our hybrid mechanism draws on the basic principles laid out in prior work, such as establishing what paths are reachable by dynamic analysis and inferring what dependencies arise from non-taken branches by static analysis [26,35]. A key contribution of SecWasm is extending these principles to deal with the challenges of an unstructured linear memory.

Wasm Security. Lehmann et al. [27] prove vulnerabilities with well-known mitigations in the original high-level code propagate down to Wasm code. As a vulnerable program in C/C++ compiled to Wasm can translate the memory vulnerabilities, Disselkoen et al. introduce MS-Wasm, an extension to Wasm allowing developers to capture low-level C/C++ memory semantics in Wasm at compile time [18]. Swivel is a compiler framework to harden Wasm against Spectre attacks [33]. These works, however, do not focus on information-flow control.

Different language-based security techniques for Wasm perform taint-tracking. Szanto et al. propose a Wasm virtual machine in JavaScript [43], TaintAssembly presents a taint-tracking engine for interpreted Wasm implemented in V8 [19], while Wasabi is an expressive framework for dynamically analyzing and taint-tracking in Wasm [28]. Lastly, Stiévenart and De Roover [41] use taint-tracking to create function summaries, i.e., descriptions of where information from the function parameters and global variables can flow to when a function is invoked. Compared to these techniques, SecWasm not only tracks explicit and implicit flows, but also memory accesses.

Vivienne is an open-source tool that performs symbolic analysis and constraint solving for analyzing constant-time properties in Wasm programs [45]. Watt et al. introduce CT-Wasm [49], a type-driven extension to Wasm for constant-time cryptographic applications. To achieve constant-time, CT-Wasm disallows secret-dependent control instructions, being thus more restrictive than SecWasm. Furthermore, CT-Wasm introduces a separate memory for storing secret data, while in SecWasm we annotate individual memory cells with security labels, an approach that scales to general lattices.

Gradual Typing. Gradual typing allows programmers to control the combination of dynamic and static approaches *at the programming level* [39]. Swamy et al. [42] presented TS* that adds a static static type system over JavaScript and Rastogi *et al.* [34] presented Safe TypeScript to catch any dynamic type errors while not altering the semantics of type-safe TypeScript code.

Gradual typing has also been used for IFC. Disney and Flanagan described an IFC type system for λ-calculus that defers cast checks that cannot be determined statically to the runtime [17]. In HLIO, Buiras *et al.* used gradual typing to allow programmers to defer some IFC checks to runtime in Haskell [14]. Bichhawat *et al.* investigated the tension between noninterference and gradual guarantees and defined a simple imperative languages that provides both noninterference and gradual guarantees [9].

Although there are high-level connections with gradual typing, there are also important differences. Indeed, gradual typing gives the developer the control of when to use static and when to use dynamic types. In our approach, the split is taken care of by the enforcement mechanism.

8 Conclusions

This paper presented SecWasm, the first general-purpose information-flow enforcement mechanism for Wasm. The synergy of static and dynamic IFC enforcement in SecWasm is the result of a thorough design analysis that leverages the already existing Wasm type system, while also ensuring permissiveness for Wasm's dynamic features. SecWasm overcomes the challenges imposed by the combination of uncommon characteristics for machine languages of structured control flow and linear memory in an elegant way. Finally, SecWasm provably enforces termination-insensitive noninterference.

In line with other foundational work on hybrid IFC (e.g., [8,23,26,35]), we leave implementation and experiments with performance overhead as an important track for future work.

Acknowledgements. This work was partially supported by the Wallenberg AI, Autonomous Systems and Software Program (WASP) funded by the Knut and Alice Wallenberg Foundation, the Swedish Foundation for Strategic Research (SSF), the Swedish Research Council (VR), Meta, the European Research Council (ERC) under the Horizon 2020 research (grant 771527-BROWSEC), and by the Vienna Business Agency through the project Vienna Cybersecurity and Privacy Research Center (VISP).

References

1. Ethereum WebAssembly (ewasm). http://ewasm.readthedocs.io/en/mkdocs
2. WebAssembly Security. http://webassembly.org/docs/security
3. Abadi, M., Budiu, M., Erlingsson, U., Ligatti, J.: Control-flow integrity principles, implementations, and applications. Trans. Inf. Syst. Sec. **13**, 1–40 (2009)
4. Askarov, A., Hunt, S., Sabelfeld, A., Sands, D.: Termination-insensitive noninterference leaks more than just a bit. In: ESORICS (2008)
5. Barthe, G., Pichardie, D., Rezk, T.: A certified lightweight non-interference java bytecode verifier. Math. Struct. Comput. Sci. **23**(05), 125–140 (2013)

6. Bastys, I., Algehed, M., Sjösten, A., Sabelfeld., A.: SecWasm: Information Flow Control in WebAssembly–Full version (2022). http://www.cse.chalmers.se/research/group/security/secwasm/
7. Bernardeschi, C., De Francesco, N.: Combining abstract interpretation and model checking for analysing security properties of Java Bytecode. In: VMCAI (2002)
8. Besson, F., Bielova, N., Jensen, T.P.: Hybrid information flow monitoring against web tracking. In: CSF (2013)
9. Bichhawat, A., McCall, M., Jia, L.: Gradual security types and gradual guarantees. In: CSF (2021)
10. Bichhawat, A., Rajani, V., Garg, D., Hammer, C.: Information flow control in Webkit's javascript bytecode. In: POST (2014)
11. Bieber, P., Cazin, J., Girard, P., Lanet, J., Wiels, V., Zanon, G.: Checking secure interactions of smart card applets: extended version. J. Comput. Secur. **10**, 369–398 (2002)
12. Birgisson, A., Russo, A., Sabelfeld, A.: Unifying facets of information integrity. In: ICISS (2010)
13. Bonelli, E., Compagnoni, A., Medel, R.: SIFTAL: a typed assembly language for secure information flow analysis. Technical report (2004)
14. Buiras, P., Vytiniotis, D., Russo, A.: HLIO: mixing static and dynamic typing for information-flow control in Haskell. In: ICFP (2015)
15. Cassel, D., Huang, Y., Jia, L.: FlowNotation: uncovering information flow policy violations in C Programs. CoRR, abs/1907.01727 (2019)
16. De Francesco, N., Martini, N.: Instruction-level security analysis for information flow in stack-based assembly languages. Inf. Comput. **205**, 1334–1370 (2007)
17. Disney, T., Flanagan, C.: Gradual information flow typing. In: STOP (2011)
18. Disselkoen, C., Renner, J., Watt, C., Garfinkel, T., Levy, A., Stefan, D.: Position paper: progressive memory safety for WebAssembly. In: HASP@ISCA (2019)
19. Fu, W., Lin, R., Inge, D.: TaintAssembly: taint-based information flow control tracking for WebAssembly. CoRR, abs/1802.01050 (2018)
20. Genaim, S., Spoto, F.: Information flow analysis for java bytecode. In: VMCAI (2005)
21. Geraldo, E., Santos, J.F., Seco, J.C.: Hybrid information flow control for low-level code. In: SEFM (2021)
22. Haas, A., et al.: Bringing the web up to speed with webassembly. In: PLDI (2017)
23. Hedin, D., Bello, L., Sabelfeld, A.: Value-sensitive hybrid information flow control for a javascript-like language. In: CSF (2015)
24. Hoffman, K.: WebAssembly in the cloud. http://medium.com/@KevinHoffman/webassembly-in-the-cloud-2f637f72d9a9
25. Kobayashi, N., Shirane, K.: Type-based information analysis for low-level languages. In: APLAS (2002)
26. Le Guernic, G.: Automaton-based confidentiality monitoring of concurrent programs. In: CSF (2007)
27. Lehmann, D., Kinder, J., Pradel, M.: Everything old is new again: binary security of WebAssembly. In: USENIX Security (2020)
28. Lehmann, D., Pradel, M.: Wasabi: a framework for dynamically analyzing WebAssembly. In: ASPLOS (2019)
29. Medel, R., Compagnoni, A.B., Bonelli, E.: A typed assembly language for noninterference. In: ICTCS (2005)
30. Morrisett, J.G., Walker, D., Crary, K., Glew, N.: From system F to typed assembly language. ACM Trans. Progr. Lang. Sys. **21**, 527–568 (1999)

31. Myers, A.C., Liskov, B.: A decentralized model for information flow control. In: SOSP (1997)
32. Myers, A.C., Sabelfeld, A., Zdancewic, S.: Enforcing robust declassification and qualified robustness. J. Comput. Secur. **14**, 157–196 (2006)
33. Narayan, S., et al.: Swivel: hardening WebAssembly against Spectre. In: USENIX Security (2021)
34. Rastogi, A., Swamy, N., Fournet, C., Bierman, G.M., Vekris, P.: Safe & efficient gradual typing for TypeScript. In: POPL (2015)
35. Russo, A., Sabelfeld, A.: Dynamic vs. static flow-sensitive security analysis, In: CSF (2010)
36. Sabelfeld, A., Myers, A.C.: Language-based information-flow security. J. Select. Areas Commun. **21** (2003)
37. Sabelfeld, A., Sands, D.: Declassification: dimensions and principles. In: 18th IEEE Workshop on Computer Security Foundations, 2009. CSFW-18 (2009)
38. Fragoso Santos, J., Jensen, T., Rezk, T., Schmitt, A.: Hybrid typing of secure information flow in a JavaScript-like language. In: Ganty, P., Loreti, M. (eds.) TGC 2015. LNCS, vol. 9533, pp. 63–78. Springer, Cham (2016). https://doi.org/10.1007/978-3-319-28766-9_5
39. Siek, J., Taha, W.: Gradual typing for functional languages. In: Scheme and Functional Programming Workshop (SFP) (2006)
40. Singh, R.G., Scholliers, C.: WARDuino: a dynamic WebAssembly virtual machine for programming microcontrollers. In: MPLR (2019)
41. Stiévenart, Q., De Roover, C.: Compositional information flow analysis for WebAssembly programs. In: SCAM (2020)
42. Swamy, N., et al.: Gradual Typing embedded securely in JavaScript. In: POPL (2014)
43. Szanto, A., Tamm, T., Pagnoni, A.: Taint tracking for WebAssembly. CoRR, abs/1807.08349 (2018)
44. Szefer, J.: Survey of microarchitectural side and covert channels, attacks, and defenses. J. Hardw. Syst. Secur. **3**, 219–234 (2019)
45. Tsoupidi, R., Balliu, M., Baudry, B.: Vivienne: relational verification of cryptographic implementations in WebAssembly. In IEEE Secure Development Conference, SecDev 2021, Atlanta, GA, USA, 18–20 October 2021, pp. 94–102. IEEE (2021)
46. Vogt, P., et al.: Cross site scripting prevention with dynamic data tainting and static analysis. In: NDSS (2007)
47. W3C. WebAssembly Core Specification. https://www.w3.org/TR/wasm-core-1/
48. Wagner, L.: WebAssembly consensus and end of browser preview. https://lists.w3.org/Archives/Public/public-webassembly/2017Feb/0002.html
49. Watt, C., Renner, J., Popescu, N., Cauligi, S., Stefan, D.: CT-WASM: type-driven secure cryptography for the web ecosystem. In: POPL (2019)
50. WebAssembly Community Group. WebAssembly Specification, current version. https://webassembly.github.io/spec/core/'
51. Wen, E., Weber, C.: Wasmachine: Bring IoT up to speed with a WebAssembly OS. In: PerCom Workshops (2020)
52. Yu, D., Islam, N.: A typed assembly language for confidentiality. In: ESOP (2006)
53. Zdancewic, S.A.: Programming languages for information security. Ph.D. Thesis, Cornell University (2002)

Lifting Numeric Relational Domains to Algebraic Data Types

Santiago Bautista$^{1,2(\boxtimes)}$ (iD), Thomas Jensen^{1,2}(iD), and Benoît Montagu^{1,2}

^{1} Univ Rennes, 263 Avenue Général Leclerc, 35000 Rennes, France
`Santiago.Bautista@ens-rennes.fr`
^{2} Inria, Rennes, France
`{Thomas.Jensen,Benoit.Montagu}@inria.fr`

Abstract. We present RAND, an input-output relational abstract domain that expresses relations between values of non-recursive algebraic data types (ADTs), and numeric relations between their scalar parts. RAND is parametrised on a user-provided numeric relational domain, that we lift to pairs of variables and projection paths. It is constructed as a disjunctive completion of a reduced product of domains for numeric relations, for equalities, and for cases of variant constructors. Using RAND, we define a modular, inter-procedural, input-output relational analysis for a `while` language with ADTs and function calls. The analysis computes function summaries, that describe relations between the inputs of programs and their outputs.

Keywords: Static analysis · Abstract interpretation · Relational abstract domains · Algebraic data types · Input-output relations · Function summaries

1 Introduction

Research in static analysis has successfully developed automatic techniques to ensure the safety and security of programs, by detecting bugs *before* a program actually runs. In particular, there exists a substantial number of analyses that target programs with numeric or pointer-based computations and which can detect frequent bugs that arise from arithmetic overflows or memory safety issues. Another important class of programs are those manipulating algebraic data types (ADTs). ADTs form the core of modern programming languages—such as OCaml, Haskell, Scala, Rust or Swift—that have been adopted by the software industry. The static analysis of this class of programs has seen important progress too, with the development of type systems [38,39] or by leveraging

G. Singh and C. Urban (Eds.): SAS 2022, LNCS 13790, pp. 104–134, 2022.
https://doi.org/10.1007/978-3-031-22308-2_6

tree automata techniques [7] for approximating the tree structures described by ADTs [18,30,37].

In this paper, we focus on the automatic analysis of programs that perform numeric operations *and* manipulate ADTs. So far, few works [16,25,26] have put emphasis on the analysis of such programs. They provide additional safety guarantees specifically related to this combination—such as the unreachability of branches of a pattern matching. Such static analyses can also alleviate the interactive verification of large, critical programs that compute over ADTs, by automatically discharging a substantial number of proof obligations [1].

To this end, we first develop a novel relational abstract domain that can express relations between numeric-algebraic values of a program state (Sect. 3). We build this abstract domain in a generic way, by taking as a parameter *any* relational abstract domain that fulfils an Apron-like interface [24] to handle the numeric properties. One difficulty in designing this domain is to handle soundly and precisely the mutually exclusive cases that an algebraic value may take. We tackle this issue using *projection paths* that point inside algebraic values, and by devising a notion of *compatibility* between paths: two paths are compatible when they make consistent assumptions over the constructors of variant values. The resulting abstract domain can describe sets of states of algebraic data structures with scalar data.

Then, we show how to turn our abstract domain into RAND—the Relational Algebraic-Numeric Domain—an abstract domain that can express *relations* between *different* states (Sect. 4). For an example process management program from an idealised operating system (Fig. 1), RAND can express that the input and output processes p and p' satisfy the constraint p'.status@Running.count = p.status@Asleep.count + 1, meaning that the status fields of p and p' differ by 1, whenever the process p has a *running* status, and p' a *sleeping* status. This is indicated by the projections on constructor cases @Running and @Sleeping. We discuss this example further in the paper (Sect. 2.3).

Using RAND, we define a *relational* analysis for a while language that features non-recursive ADTs (Sect. 5). Our analysis infers relations between the inputs and the outputs of programs. In particular, we explain how a standard static analysis for reachable states can be turned into an analysis for input-output relations. This relational analysis is well suited for designing an inter-procedural analysis based on function summaries.

Our work offers the following contributions:

- We present a novel abstract domain that expresses relations between values of non-recursive ADTs (Sect. 3 and 4). Our abstract domain can be instantiated with any numeric relational domain. This offers the possibility to choose domains with different precision *vs* cost balances, and allows to capture numeric inequalities. This improves upon the correlation domain [1], that is restricted to information about equality and reachability.
- Our abstract domain uses a form of *disjunctive completion* (Sect. 3.6), where we limit the number of disjuncts by *merging* some of them. Our merging strategy is guided by observing the different *cases* of algebraic values.

- We give a formal justification to the folklore assertion that *"a static analysis can be made relational by duplicating variables"*, by showing that a non input-output relational and an input-output relational analysis actually share the same *structure* (Lemma 1) and by showing how any relational domain can express relations between different stores (Sect. 4.2).
- We formally define a relational analysis (Sect. 5) that infers relations between inputs and outputs of programs, and propose a modular inter-procedural extension that is based on function summaries. We illustrate the analyser's results on a running example taken from an idealised operating system.
- We provide an OCaml implementation [3] of our analyser, for a while language with algebraic types; together with 43 test cases, some of which are inspired from an operating system code (Sect. 6). We briefly discuss the complexity of our implementation.

2   Syntax and Semantics

Our programming language is an extension of a classic while language with algebraic data types (products and sums). Sect. 2.1 presents algebraic types, Sect. 2.2 presents the language and its semantics, and Sect. 2.3 introduces our running example.

2.1   Algebraic Types and Values

ADTs are pervasively used in functional languages like OCaml, Haskell, Coq, or F*, and have become a central feature of more recent programming languages, such as Swift or Rust, just to name a few. We briefly recall the definitions of algebraic types, and of the *structured values* that inhabit them.

Definition 1 (Algebraic types and structured values). Algebraic types *and* structured values *are inductively defined as follows:*

$$\tau \in \text{Types} \quad ::= \quad \text{N} \quad | \quad \{\overline{f_i \to \tau_i}^{i \in I}\} \quad | \quad [\overline{A_i \to \tau_i}^{i \in I}]$$
$$v \in \text{Values} \quad ::= \quad \underline{n} \quad | \quad \{\overline{f_i = v_i}^{i \in I}\} \quad | \quad A(v)$$

Here, N is the type of numbers, the $(f_i)_{i \in I}$ are field names, the $(A_i)_{i \in I}$ are constructor names, and I ranges over finite sets. The compound type $\{\overline{f_i \to \tau_i}^{i \in I}\}$ is a *record type*, in which a type τ_i is associated to each field f_i. The type $[\overline{A_i \to \tau_i}^{i \in I}]$ is a *sum type* containing values formed with a head constructor that must be one of the A_i, and whose argument must be of type τ_i. $\{\overline{f_i = v_i}^{i \in I}\}$ denotes a *record value* where each field f_i has value v_i for every $i \in I$. $A(v)$ denotes a *variant value*, built by applying the constructor A to the value v. Constructors expect exactly one argument. Constructors with arities other than 1, as typically found in functional languages, are encoded by providing a (possibly empty) record value as argument to constructors. The numeric type N and the record type with no fields {} are the two base cases for types.

We use *projection paths* to refer to a part of a structured value (*i.e.*, to a value embedded *inside* another structured value). A path is either the empty path ε, or the path $p.f$, that first accesses the value at path p and then accesses the record field f, or the path $p@A$, that first accesses the value at path p and then accesses the argument of variant constructor A.

Definition 2 (Paths). *Paths are inductively defined as follows:*

$$p \in \text{Paths} \quad ::= \quad \varepsilon \quad | \quad p.f \quad | \quad p@A$$

Because paths are simply sequences of atomic paths (.f or @A) we allow their creation or destruction from either side, and write for example .fp to denote a path that starts with .f.

The *projection of the value v on the path p*, written $v \Downarrow^{\text{val}} p$, is the value pointed to by p inside v. It is defined as follows:

Definition 3 (Projection of a value on a path).

$$
v \Downarrow^{\text{val}} p = \begin{cases}
v & \text{if } p = \varepsilon \\
v' \Downarrow^{\text{val}} p' & \text{if } p = @Ap' \text{ and } v = A(v') \\
v_i \Downarrow^{\text{val}} p' & \text{if } p = .f_i p' \text{ and } v = \{\overline{f_j = v_j}^{j \in I}\} \text{ and } i \in I \\
\text{Undef} & \text{otherwise}
\end{cases}
$$

Our definition returns Undef when a path does not make sense for some value.

2.2 A Language with Algebraic Data Types

The syntax of the language consists of expressions t, boolean conditions b, and commands c. Vars denotes the set of variables that may appear in commands. Expressions include the projection of a variable $x \in$ Vars over a path $p \in$ Paths, written $x.p$. The expression $t_1 \boxplus t_2$ denotes some arithmetic operations on the expressions t_1 and t_2, and $t_1 \bowtie t_2$ ranges over arithmetic comparisons.

$$
\begin{array}{llll}
t \in \text{Exp} & ::= & \underline{n} \quad | \quad A(t) \quad | \quad \{\overline{f_i = t_i}^{i \in I}\} \quad | \quad x.p \quad | \quad t_1 \boxplus t_2 \\
b \in \text{BExp} & ::= & t_1 \bowtie t_2 \quad | \quad b_1 \wedge b_2 \quad | \quad b_1 \vee b_2 \quad | \quad \neg b \\
c \in \text{Cmd} & ::= & \text{skip} \quad | \quad c_1 ; c_2 \quad | \quad \text{branch } c_1 \text{ or } \dots \text{ or } c_n \text{ end} \quad | \\
& & \text{while } b \text{ do } c \text{ end} \quad | \quad \text{assert } b \quad | \quad x := t
\end{array}
$$

We restrict our attention to well-typed commands (that we call *programs*), following a standard structural type system [39]. For instance, well-typedness ensures that arithmetic tests and operations receive arguments of integer type, and that every projection $x.p$ is consistent with the type of the variable x.

Programs operate on *stores*, denoted by s, that are finite maps from Vars to Values. We define the semantics of programs using a standard small-step semantics that specifies the effects of commands on stores. The relation $(c, s) \rightarrow (c', s')$ tells that the command c transforms the store s into a store s', and that command c' is to be executed next. We briefly explain the semantics of each command, and refer the reader to the extended version [4] for technical details.

The command skip performs no operation, whereas the sequence $c_1 ; c_2$ executes c_1 followed by c_2. The branching command branch c_1 or ... or c_n end nondeterministically chooses one of the commands c_i and executes it, discarding the other branches. The command while b do c end executes the command c as long as the condition b holds, and successfully terminates otherwise.

The command assert(b) tests whether the condition b holds, in which case the command succeeds, and the execution of the program continues. When b is not satisfied, assert(b) fails, *i.e.*, the program remains stuck. We can express the conditional construct if b then c_1 else c_2 as branch assert(b) ; c_1 or assert($\neg b$) ; c_2 end.

Finally, the assignment command $x := t$ evaluates t to some value v and updates the variable x with v. We write $s(x \mapsto v)$ to denote the store s in which the variable x is associated to the value v. If there was an entry for x in s already, then it is replaced with the value v. Otherwise, a new entry is created.

The evaluation $[\![t]\!]_s^{\mathrm{exp}}$ of an expression t in a store s proceeds by induction on the structure of t to evaluate sub-expressions, and reads in the store s the values of variables. $[\![t]\!]_s^{\mathrm{exp}}$ is either a singleton, which denotes normal execution, or the empty set, which denotes a failure, such as an invalid projection $x.p$. For example, if $s(x) = A(v)$ then $[\![x@B]\!]_s^{\mathrm{exp}} = \emptyset$, because the constructors A and B are different. The evaluation of booleans $[\![b]\!]_s^{\mathrm{bool}}$ is standard.

Importantly, records and variants are *immutable* in our language: it is not possible to update some field f of a record *in-place*, for example. Instead, the programmer must follow the functional idiom, and create a new record value, that contains a different value for the field f.

We recover the *pattern matching* construct match t with $A_1(x_1) \rightarrow c_1 \mid \cdots \mid$ $A_n(x_n) \rightarrow c_n$ end as a syntactic sugar for command $z := t$; branch $x_1 :=$ $z@A_1 ; c_1$ or ... or $x_n := z@A_n ; c_n$ end for a freshly chosen variable z.

2.3   Running Example

Figure 1 shows an example program for which we would like to infer precise input-output properties. This program features algebraic data types that represent the meta-data of a process, as usually found in operating system implementations. Here, a process is a record composed of an identifier, some incoming message that was sent by another process and finally a piece of data that describes the status of the process. The message is a record that contains some payload and whether it needs a reply (and to whom). The process status is either running, in which case it records how many times the process has been activated, or it is asleep, in which case it also records how many seconds the process should remain asleep before waking up again. The function do_ticks(p, n) simulates the action of n clock ticks on a process p: a clock tick leaves the process p unchanged if p is already running, or, if it is asleep, decrements the sleeping budget of p. If that budget is already zero, the clock tick promotes p into a running process.

The important properties of do_ticks(p, n) that we intend to infer *automatically* are the following:

```
type status = [
(* Scheduling status *)
  | Running of { count: int }
    (* Running: activation times *)
  | Asleep of { secs: int; count: int }
    (* Sleeping: remaining seconds, activation times *)
]
type msg = {              (* Messages *)
  data : int ;            (* Payload *)
  reply : [               (* Whether to reply or not *)
    | Reply of int        (* Who to reply to *)
    | DontReply of {}     (* No reply expected *)
  ]
}
type process = { id: int; msg: msg; status: status }
(* Process structure *)

def do_ticks(process p, int n) : process = {
(* Performs n clock ticks on the process p *)
  int count; int secs; int i
  assert (n > 0)
  i = 0
  while (i < n) do (* loop n times, i.e.: perform n clock ticks *)
    branch (* case where p is running *)
      count = p.status@Running.count
    or (* case where p is asleep and can sleep longer *)
      assert (p.status@Asleep.secs > 0)
      count = p.status@Asleep.count
      secs = p.status@Asleep.secs
      p = { id = p.id; msg = p.msg;
            status = Asleep { secs = secs - 1; count = count } }
    or (* case where p is asleep and has no more sleeping budget *)
      assert (p.status@Asleep.secs = 0)
      count = p.status@Asleep.count
      p = { id = p.id; msg = p.msg;
            status = Running { count = count + 1 } }
    end
    i = i + 1
  end
  return p
}
```

Fig. 1. Example: performing clock ticks on a process' meta-data.

1. If p is initially running, then it remains unchanged;
2. If p is initially sleeping, then it *might* wake up: in this case, its original sleeping budget was less than n, and count—its number of activations—has been incremented by one;
3. If p is initially sleeping, then it *might* remain sleeping: in this case, its sleeping budget decreased by n, and its number of activations remains the same;
4. The field id, of integer type, of the process p has not changed;
5. The field msg, of record type, of the process p has not changed either.

Sections Sects. 3 to 5 explain in detail how we express and capture these properties by presenting the structure of the RAND abstract domain. The correlation abstract domain [1] was also designed to handle programs that manipulate algebraic data types, but cannot express, on numbers, properties other than binary equalities. Using the correlation domain, we could infer all the properties listed above, *except* the ones that involve arithmetics: properties 2 and 3.

3   Extending Numeric Domains to Algebraic Types

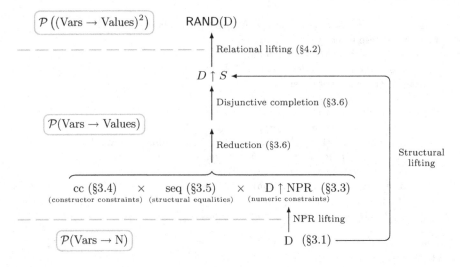

Fig. 2. The construction of the RAND abstract domain. The frame-enclosed sets are the sets the abstract domains concretize to.

In this section, we introduce an abstract domain that is able to express equality and numeric constraints between parts of structured values. Our construction is summarised in Fig. 2. It is parametric with respect to a numeric abstract domain D, so that we can instantiate it on domains with different precision versus cost trade-offs. We expect the numeric domain D to provide the operations described in Sect. 3.1, which are a subset of the API offered by Apron [24]. An essential ingredient of our construction is the use of *extended variables* (Sect. 3.2), *i.e.*, regular program variables equipped with a projection path. Our example `do_ticks` on Fig. 1 features extended variables, such as `p.status@Asleep.secs`. Using extended variables, we define in Sect. 3.3 a first way to lift numeric domains to languages with algebraic types: the *Numeric Path Relations* lifting, or *NPR lifting* for short. This first lifting builds on the ideas of [2], but achieves a better precision. It can express, for example, that a call to `do_ticks` can only decrease the value in the field `secs` of processes (that denotes the number of seconds for which a process should remain asleep), thanks to the constraint on extended variables `p.status@Asleep.secs` $\geq$ `p'.status@Asleep.secs`. We improve the precision of the *NPR lifting* by combining it with two other domains (Sect. 3.4 and 3.5) in a product domain (Sect. 3.6). A first domain of *constructor constraints* tracks which constructors are used for values of sum types (Sect. 3.4). Constructor constraints allow us to distinguish between different cases, by stating which extended variables are valid in each case. For the `do_ticks` program, a possible case is when the input process `p` is sleeping—*i.e.*, `p.status@Asleep` is valid—and the output process `p'` is running—*i.e.*, `p'.status@Running` is valid. Another domain, called *structural equalities* (Sect. 3.5), uses equality constraints between extended variables to express equalities that *must* hold between arbitrary parts—of any type—of structured values. With this domain, we can tell for the `do_ticks` program that the `msg` field of processes cannot change, by saying that the extended variables `p.msg` and `p'.msg` are equal. Finally, in order to obtain additional precision when analysing pattern-matching, we use a *disjunctive completion* of the product of these domains (Sect. 3.6): we obtain the *structural lifting* of the numeric abstract domain. Each value of the structural lifting can contain multiple cases, and each case has three components: one that expresses constructor constraints, one that expresses structural equalities, and one that expresses numeric constraints. Sect. 3.3 to 3.5 also define abstractions for assignments and conditionals, that are needed in Sect. 5 to define the analysis of our language.

3.1 Background: Numeric Abstract Domains

We first review the structure of traditional numeric domains [35] such as intervals, octagons and polyhedra. The domains are parametrised by a set of variables, and describe sets of *numeric stores* over those variables, *i.e.*, sets of maps from variables to numbers.

Given a set of variables V, we expect a numeric abstract domain $D(V)$ to provide the operations listed below (which are included in the user interface of the Apron library [24]) in such a way that the standard soundness properties of abstract interpretation [9,10] are met: A set of abstract values $D(V)$ with a concretisation function $\gamma^{D(V)} \in D(V) \to \mathcal{P}(V \to \mathbb{N})$, a pre-order on abstract values $\sqsubseteq^{D(V)}$, abstract union $\sqcup^{D(V)}$ and intersection $\sqcap^{D(V)}$, and a widening operator $\nabla^{D(V)}$. The domain must also offer abstractions for boolean conditions $\text{Cond}^{D(V)} \in \text{BExp} \to D(V) \to D(V)$ and for assignment $\text{Assign}^{D(V)} \in V \times \text{Arith}(V) \to D(V) \to D(V)$ (where $\text{Arith}(V)$ is the set of arithmetic expressions over the variables V), satisfying the soundness properties:

$$\gamma^{D(V)}(\text{Assign}^{D(V)}(x := t)(d)) \supseteq \{s(x \mapsto v) \mid s \in \gamma^{D(V)}(d) \wedge v \in [\![t]\!]_s^{\exp}\}$$
$$\gamma^{D(V)}(\text{Cond}^{D(V)}(b)(d)) \qquad \supseteq \{s \in \gamma^{D(V)}(d) \mid \mathbf{t} \in [\![b]\!]_s^{\text{bool}}\}$$

We also assume the existence of "variable management" operators for removing, adding and renaming variables. Operator $\text{Rem}_{V'}^{D(V)}$ projects an element of $D(V)$ onto $D(V \setminus V')$. Operator $\text{Add}_{V'}^{D(V)}$ embeds an element of $D(V)$ into the domain $D(V \cup V')$. Given a bijection $r : V_1 \to V_2$, the operator $\text{Rename}_r^{D(V_1)}$ translates an element of $D(V_1)$ into $D(V_2)$. These operators satisfy the soundness properties:

$$\gamma^{D(V \setminus V')}(\text{Rem}_{V'}^{D(V)}(d)) \supseteq \{s|_{(V \setminus V')} \mid s \in \gamma^{D(V)}(d)\}$$
$$\gamma^{D(V \cup V')}(\text{Add}_{V'}^{D(V)}(a)) \supseteq \{s : (V \cup V') \to \mathbb{N} \mid s|_V \in \gamma^{D(V)}(a)\}$$
$$\gamma^{D(V_2)}(\text{Rename}_r^{D(V_1)}(d)) \supseteq \{s \mid s \circ r \in \gamma^{D(V_1)}(d)\}$$

3.2 Extended Variables

We call *extended variable* the pair of a variable and a path. Extended variables designate some values that are located *inside* a structured value. We only consider paths that make sense for the given variables, *i.e.*, paths whose projections on a variable's type are valid in the following sense:

Definition 4 (Projection of a type on a path). *The judgement $\tau \Downarrow^{\text{typ}} p$ defines when a path p is consistent with a type τ, and is inductively defined by:*

$$\frac{}{\tau \Downarrow^{\text{typ}} \varepsilon} \qquad \frac{\tau_i \Downarrow^{\text{typ}} p \qquad i \in I}{\{f_j \to \tau_j^{j \in I}\} \Downarrow^{\text{typ}} .f_i p} \qquad \frac{\tau_i \Downarrow^{\text{typ}} p \qquad i \in I}{[A_j \to \tau_j^{j \in I}] \Downarrow^{\text{typ}} @A_i p}$$

Typing contexts, written Γ, are mappings from variables to types. We write $\mathcal{E}(\Gamma) = \{x.p \mid x \in \text{dom}\,\Gamma \wedge \Gamma(x) \Downarrow^{\text{typ}} p\}$ for the set of extended variables $x.p$ such that p is consistent with the type of x in Γ.

We say that two extended variables $x.p_1$ and $x.p_2$ are *incompatible*—written $x.p_1 <> x.p_2$—if they would force a value (or part of a value) to be in two different variants of a sum type. Definition 5 formalises this notion of incompatibility, using the prefix order $\preccurlyeq$ on extended variables ($x.p \preccurlyeq y.q$ iff $x = y$ and p is a prefix of q).

Definition 5 (Incompatibility and inconsistency). *Two extended variables $x_1.p_1$ and $x_2.p_2$ are incompatible, written $x_1.p_1 <> x_2.p_2$, if and only if $x_1 = x_2$ and there is a path p and two distinct constructors A_1 and A_2, such that $x_1.p@A_1 \preccurlyeq x_1.p_1$ and $x_2.p@A_2 \preccurlyeq x_2.p_2$. A set of extended variables E is inconsistent if it contains two or more incompatible extended variables. Two sets of extended variables are incompatible, written $E_1 <> E_2$, if their union is inconsistent.*

In Sect. 3.4, we use the fact that inconsistent sets of extended variables denote empty sets of stores. Such inconsistent sets correspond to unreachable program points, and can be safely removed from the disjunctive completion of Sect. 3.6.

Assignment Decomposition. To easily define the abstract transfer functions for assignment in the next subsections, it is useful to decompose an assignment command $x := t$—where t can be a compound expression—into an equivalent set of *parallel* assignments of the form $x.p := t'$, where t' is either an expression of numeric type or an extended variable. The idea is to model the effect of the assignment as a set of parallel assignments on the paths of variable x.

Definition 6. *The decomposition of the assignment $x := t$ is defined by:*

$$\text{Decomp}\,(x.p := t) = \begin{cases} \bigcup_{i \in I} \text{Decomp}\,(x.p.f_i := t_i) & \text{if } t = \{\overline{f_i = t_i}^{\,i \in I}\} \\ \text{Decomp}\,(x.p@A := t') & \text{if } t = A(t') \\ \{x.p := t\} & \text{if } \Gamma \vdash t : \mathsf{N} \vee t \in \mathcal{E} \end{cases}$$

We write $\text{Decomp}\,(x := t)$ as a shorthand for $\text{Decomp}\,(x.\varepsilon := t)$.

For the different objects defined in this paper, we write $\text{Env}\,(\bullet)$ for the set of extended variables that appear in them.

3.3 Numeric Domains over Extended Variables

In this section, extending ideas from [2], we define the *Numeric Path Relations lifting* $\mathrm{D} \uparrow \mathrm{NPR}$ as a generic way to lift a domain D that is numeric—*i.e.*, that denotes sets of stores that map variables to numbers—to a domain that denotes sets of stores that map variables to *structured values* (Definition 1). The main idea is to use *extended variables* as the variables of the underlying numeric domain.

For a typing context Γ, the abstract values of $\mathrm{D} \uparrow \mathrm{NPR}(\Gamma)$ are pairs of a set E of extended variables that are valid in Γ, and a numeric abstract value from $\mathrm{D}(E)$—*i.e.*, whose variables are the extended variables in E.

Definition 7. $\mathrm{D} \uparrow \mathrm{NPR}(\Gamma) = \{(d, E) \mid E \in \mathcal{P}(\mathcal{E}(\Gamma)) \wedge d \in \mathrm{D}(E)\}$

In this definition, an abstract numeric value d can refer to any extended variable $x.p$ declared in E, and does not need to reason on whether $x.p$ is a valid projection. In practice, though, the complete domain of Sect. 3.6 will only consider sets E that are consistent. When writing examples in the rest of the paper, we may omit the set E when it can be deduced from context, for example when E is exactly the set of extended variables used in d.

Intuitively, an abstract value (d, E) denotes a set of stores that map regular variables to structured values, such that the paths listed in E point to integer values, and such that those integers are related by the numeric abstract value d. Using the projection function for values (Definition 3), it is easy to transform a store whose indices are variables into a store whose indices are *extended variables*:

Definition 8 (Projection of a store). *The projection of a store $s \in \text{Vars} \to$ Values on a set of extended variables $E \in \mathcal{P}(\mathcal{E})$ is a store in $E \to$ (Values $\cup$ {Undef}), written $s \Downarrow^{\text{sto}} E$, and is defined by:* $(s \Downarrow^{\text{sto}} E)(x.p) = s(x) \Downarrow^{\text{val}} p$.

The concretisation of an element $(d, E) \in D \uparrow \mathrm{NPR}(\Gamma)$ easily follows: it is the set of well-typed stores whose projections on E satisfy the numeric constraints d. The typing judgement $\Gamma \vdash s$ means that $s(x)$ has type $\Gamma(x)$ for every x.

Definition 9. $\gamma^{D \uparrow \mathrm{NPR}(\Gamma)}(d, E) = \{s \mid \Gamma \vdash s \wedge s \Downarrow^{\mathrm{sto}} E \in \gamma^{D(E)}(d)\}$

We briefly explain how to define the abstract intersection in $D \uparrow \mathrm{NPR}(\Gamma)$. The intersection of (d_1, E_1) and (d_2, E_2) denotes the conjunction of the constraints d_1 and d_2. Therefore, the extended variables that appear in the conjunction are in $E_1 \cup E_2$. Thus, one must inject d_1 and d_2 in $E_1 \cup E_2$ using the $\mathrm{Add}_{E_j}^{D(E_i)}$ operators, before actually taking their intersection in the numeric domain:

$$(d_1, E_1) \sqcap^{D \uparrow \mathrm{NPR}(\Gamma)} (d_2, E_2) = \left(\mathrm{Add}_{E_2}^{D(E_1)}(d_1) \sqcap^{D(E_1 \cup E_2)} \mathrm{Add}_{E_1}^{D(E_2)}(d_2), E_1 \cup E_2 \right)$$

The pre-order, union and widening are defined in a similar way :

$$(d_1, E_1) \sqsubseteq^{D \uparrow \mathrm{NPR}(\Gamma)} (d_2, E_2) \text{ iff } E_2 \subseteq E_1 \wedge \mathrm{Rem}_{E_1 \backslash E_2}^{D(E_1)}(d_1) \sqsubseteq^{D(E_2)} d_2$$

$$(d, E) \sqcap^{D \uparrow \mathrm{NPR}(\Gamma)} (d', E') = \left(\mathrm{Add}_{E'}^{D(E)}(d) \sqcap^{D(E \cup E')} \mathrm{Add}_{E}^{D(E')}(d'), E \cup E' \right)$$

$$(d, E) \sqcup^{D \uparrow \mathrm{NPR}(\Gamma)} (d', E') = \left(\mathrm{Rem}_{E \backslash E'}^{D(E)}(d) \sqcup^{D(E \cap E')} \mathrm{Rem}_{E' \backslash E}^{D(E')}(d'), E \cap E' \right)$$

$$(d, E) \bigtriangledown^{D \uparrow \mathrm{NPR}(\Gamma)} (d', E') = \left(\mathrm{Rem}_{E \backslash E'}^{D(E)}(d) \bigtriangledown^{D(E \cap E')} \mathrm{Rem}_{E' \backslash E}^{D(E')}(d'), E \cap E' \right)$$

Transfer Functions. The transfer function for assignment $x := t$ works by temporarily introducing a new variable x' (that represents the value of x *after* assignment). First, it applies the transfer function for assignment on every numeric assignment in the decomposition of $x' := t$ (Definition 6). Then, it removes the references to the paths of x, and finally renames x' into x. The auxiliary variable x' is introduced to avoid clashes between the paths that are valid for x *before* the assignment and those that are valid *after* the assignment.

$$\mathrm{Assign}^{D \uparrow \mathrm{NPR}(\Gamma)}(x := t)(d, E) = \mathrm{Rename}_{[x' \mapsto x]}^{D \uparrow \mathrm{NPR}(\Gamma)}(\mathrm{Rem}_{E_x}^{D \uparrow \mathrm{NPR}(\Gamma)}(d_1, E_1))$$

$$\text{where} \begin{cases} E_x = \{y.p \in E \mid y = x\} \\ d_1 = \bigcap_{x'.p := u \in \mathrm{Decomp}(x' := t), \Gamma \vdash u : \mathrm{N}}^{D(E_1)} \mathrm{Assign}^{D(E_1)}(x'.p := u)(\mathrm{Add}_{E_0}^{D(E)}(d)) \\ E_1 = E \cup E_0 \\ E_0 = \{y.p \in \mathrm{Env}\,(\mathrm{Decomp}\,(x' := t)) \mid \Gamma \vdash y.p : \mathrm{N}\} \end{cases}$$

The transfer function for conditionals is simpler: negation is eliminated using De Morgan laws, whereas conjunctions and disjunctions are handled by abstract intersection and union, respectively. The remaining case is the one of a numeric test $t_1 \bowtie t_2$: it suffices to call the transfer function of domain D for conditionals, and to extend the extended variables with those that occur in the test.

$$\mathrm{Cond}^{D \uparrow \mathrm{NPR}(\Gamma)}(b)(d, E) = $$
$$\left(\mathrm{Cond}^{D(E \cup \mathrm{Env}(b))}(b)(\mathrm{Add}_{\mathrm{Env}(b)}^{D(E)}(d)), E \cup \mathrm{Env}\,(b) \right) \text{ if } b = t_1 \bowtie t_2$$

3.4 Constructor Constraints

We introduce the abstract domain of *constructor constraints*, that intuitively describes in which *cases* the values of a store might be, *i.e.*, which are the allowed variant constructors of the values of a store. We write $\mathrm{cc}(\Gamma)$ for the set of constructor constraints for a typing environment Γ. An element $E \in \mathrm{cc}(\Gamma)$ is a set of extended variables, that restricts the possible sets of stores to those that are compatible with *every* path in E. In other words, if a path in E mentions some constructor, then the corresponding value in any store of the concretisation must be built using that constructor. Constructor constraints are a key ingredient of the disjunctive completion of Sect. 3.6, as they serve as hints for which disjuncts need to be kept separate, and which should be merged.

An element $E \in \mathrm{cc}(\Gamma)$ is either the bottom value $\perp^{\mathrm{cc}(\Gamma)}$, or must be a set of extended variables that is both *consistent* and *closed under the prefix order* $\preccurlyeq$.

Definition 10 (Constructor constraints). *The domain of constructor constraints is defined by* $\mathrm{cc}(\Gamma) = \{E \subseteq \mathcal{E}(\Gamma) \mid E \preccurlyeq \text{-closed and consistent}\} \cup \{\perp^{\mathrm{cc}(\Gamma)}\}$ *and is equipped with the ordering* $\sqsubseteq^{\mathrm{cc}(\Gamma)}$ *defined as* $E_1 \sqsubseteq^{\mathrm{cc}(\Gamma)} E_2$ *iff* $E_1 = \perp^{\mathrm{cc}(\Gamma)}$ *or* $E_1 \supseteq E_2$.

We write $\mathrm{clos}^{\mathrm{cc}(\Gamma)}(E)$ to denote the prefix-closure of E, *i.e.*, the smallest $\preccurlyeq$-closed set that contains E. For a given Γ, the domain $\mathrm{cc}(\Gamma)$ is *finite*: because our types are not recursive, the valid paths necessarily have finite lengths.

The concretisation $\gamma^{\mathrm{cc}(\Gamma)}$ defines the stores denoted by constructor constraints.

Definition 11 (Concretisation for constructor constraints).

$$\gamma^{\mathrm{cc}(\Gamma)}(\perp^{\mathrm{cc}(\Gamma)}) = \emptyset \qquad \gamma^{\mathrm{cc}(\Gamma)}(E) = \{s \mid \Gamma \vdash s \wedge \forall x.p \in E, s(x) \Downarrow^{\mathrm{val}} p \neq \mathrm{Undef}\}$$

The concretisation of a set E produces a set of well-typed stores such that the values in the stores can be projected along the paths in E.

The abstract union and intersection for the $\mathrm{cc}(\Gamma)$ domain are easily obtained:

$$\perp^{\mathrm{cc}(\Gamma)} \sqcup^{\mathrm{cc}(\Gamma)} E = E \sqcup^{\mathrm{cc}(\Gamma)} \perp^{\mathrm{cc}(\Gamma)} = E \qquad E_1 \sqcup^{\mathrm{cc}(\Gamma)} E_2 = E_1 \cap E_2 \text{ otherwise}$$

$$E_1 \sqcap^{\mathrm{cc}(\Gamma)} E_2 = \begin{cases} \perp^{\mathrm{cc}(\Gamma)} & \text{if } E_1 = \perp^{\mathrm{cc}(\Gamma)} \text{ or } E_2 = \perp^{\mathrm{cc}(\Gamma)} \text{ or } E_1 <> E_2 \\ E_1 \cup E_2 & \text{otherwise} \end{cases}$$

Because the domain is finite, there is no issue with infinite ascending chains, and we can simply define the widening as the abstract union.

Transfer Functions. We express the abstract transfer function for assignment in the $\mathrm{cc}(\Gamma)$ domain in a standard *"kill-gen"* form as follows:

$\mathrm{Assign}^{\mathrm{cc}(\Gamma)}(x := t)(E) = (E \setminus \mathrm{Kill}^{\mathrm{cc}(\Gamma)}(x)(E)) \sqcap^{\mathrm{cc}(\Gamma)} \mathrm{Gen}^{\mathrm{cc}(\Gamma)}(x := t)(E)$
where $\mathrm{Kill}^{\mathrm{cc}(\Gamma)}(x)(E) = \{y.p \in E \mid y = x\}$
and $\mathrm{Gen}^{\mathrm{cc}(\Gamma)}(x := t)(E) =$
   $\mathrm{clos}^{\mathrm{cc}(\Gamma)}(\{y.q \in \mathrm{Env}\,(t) \mid y \neq x\} \cup \{x.p \mid \exists t', x.p := t' \in \mathrm{Decomp}\,(x := t)\})$

The extended variables that must be removed are those that have x as root, since the new value for x might be modified by the assignment. The newly added extended variables are those of t that are still live after x is updated, and the ones that are effectively assigned, as given by the decomposition of the assignment. We ensure that the added variables remain prefix-closed thanks to a call to $\text{clos}^{\text{cc}(\Gamma)}$.

The transfer function for conditionals is straightforward: it only adds the extended variables of the boolean expression:

$$\text{Cond}^{\text{cc}(\Gamma)}(b)(E) = E \sqcap^{\text{cc}(\Gamma)} \text{clos}^{\text{cc}(\Gamma)}(\text{Env}\,(b))$$

3.5   Structural Equalities

The NPR lifting of Sect. 3.3 can only express relations between the *numeric* parts of values. It can't record whether some non-numeric part of a value has not changed. In our example of Fig. 1, this is the case of the msg field of processes, that is not modified, and is of record type. We introduce in this section the domain $\text{seq}(\Gamma)$, that tracks *structural equalities*. The domain $\text{seq}(\Gamma)$ tells which parts of the values of a store *must* be identical.

One could argue that any equality between structured values could be replaced with a conjunction of equalities between the integer fields of those values, and, consequently, that the $\text{seq}(\Gamma)$ domain is hardly useful. Such a decomposition could lead, however, to more verbose abstract values, and could also introduce extra disjunctions when dealing with values of sum types. Thus, our choice of handling equality constraints between structured values is beneficial, as it helps keep our abstract values small in size. The extended version [4] provides an example of this decomposition of equalities into a conjunction of equalities.

We give here a simplified definition of the domain, where the abstract values of $\text{seq}(\Gamma)$ are either the bottom element—denoting the empty set of stores—or a finite set of pairs of extended variables $(x.p, y.q)$—denoting a set of stores s in which the value at path p in $s(x)$ is equal to the one at path q in $s(y)$. In practice, our implementation uses a map from extended variables to equivalence class indices, to ensure we remain closed by reflexivity, symmetry and transitivity.

Definition 12 (Domain of structural equalities). *The domain of structural equalities* $\text{seq}(\Gamma) = \mathcal{P}(\mathcal{E}(\Gamma) \times \mathcal{E}(\Gamma)) \cup \{\bot^{\text{seq}(\Gamma)}\}$ *is equipped with the concretisation function* $\gamma^{\text{seq}(\Gamma)} \in \text{seq}(\Gamma) \to \mathcal{P}(\text{Vars} \to \text{Values})$ *that is defined as follows:*

$$\gamma^{\text{seq}(\Gamma)}(\bot^{\text{seq}(\Gamma)}) = \emptyset$$

$$\gamma^{\text{seq}(\Gamma)}(C) = \{s \mid \Gamma \vdash s \wedge \forall (x.p, y.q) \in C,\, s(x) \Downarrow^{\text{val}} p = s(y) \Downarrow^{\text{val}} q \neq \text{Undef}\}$$

Abstract values in this domain might carry some implicit information. For example, if x and y have type $\{f \to \mathbb{N}; g \to \mathbb{N}\}$, the abstract value $\{(x, y)\}$ also *implicitly* implies that $x.f = y.f$ and $x.g = y.g$. To avoid losing precision, it is sometimes necessary to *saturate* an abstract value by congruence, so that it contains all the valid equalities that mention *a given set of extended variables*. For this purpose, we define the following closure operator.

Definition 13 (Closure of structural equalities). *The closure of a set of structural equalities C with respect to a set of extended variables E, written $\mathrm{clos}_E^{\mathrm{seq}(\Gamma)}(C)$, is the smallest set that is larger than C, that mentions the variables in E, is closed under symmetry, reflexivity and transitivity, and satisfies the following congruence property:*

$$\left.\begin{array}{l} (x.p, y.q) \in \mathrm{clos}_E^{\mathrm{seq}(\Gamma)}(C) \\ (x.pr) \in \mathrm{Env}\left(\mathrm{clos}_E^{\mathrm{seq}(\Gamma)}(C)\right) \end{array}\right\} \Rightarrow (x.pr, y.qr) \in \mathrm{clos}_E^{\mathrm{seq}(\Gamma)}(C)$$

The need for a closure operator is not surprising, as it occurs in other relational domains, like octagons [34]. We use this closure operator to gain precision in the transfer function for assignment, and in the reduction operator of the product domain of Sect. 3.6.

Transfer Functions. The transfer function for assignment $x := t$ for the $\mathrm{seq}(\Gamma)$ domain exploits the decomposition of assignments from Definition 6. It considers only the assignments of the form $x.p := y.q$, where the right-hand side is an extended variable. We express the transfer function in a *"kill-gen"* form, where we kill every equality that involves x, and add the new equalities $x.p = y.q$ where we are careful to avoid any use of x that refers to the state *before* the assignment.

$$\mathrm{Assign}^{\mathrm{seq}(\Gamma)}(x := t)(C) = \left(C \setminus \mathrm{Kill}^{\mathrm{seq}(\Gamma)}(x)(C)\right) \cup \mathrm{Gen}^{\mathrm{seq}(\Gamma)}(x := t)(C)$$
where $\mathrm{Kill}^{\mathrm{seq}(\Gamma)}(x)(C) = \{(y.p, z.q) \in C \mid y = x \lor z = x\}$
and $\mathrm{Gen}^{\mathrm{seq}(\Gamma)}(x := t)(C) =$
$$\bigcup\nolimits_{x.p := y.q \in \mathrm{Decomp}(x := t)} \{(x.p, z.r) \mid z \neq x \land (y.q, z.r) \in \mathrm{clos}_{\{y.q\}}^{\mathrm{seq}(\Gamma)}(C)\}$$

The transfer functions for conditionals can only exploit equality tests between extended variables: $\mathrm{Cond}^{\mathrm{seq}(\Gamma)}(b)(C) = C \sqcap^{\mathrm{seq}(\Gamma)} \{(x.p, y.q)\}$ if b is $x.p = y.q$.

3.6 Bringing Everything Together: Product Domain and Disjunctive Completion

In this section, we describe the remaining steps of our construction, that lead to the *structural lifting* $D \uparrow S$ of the numeric domain D that we have considered. We combine the domains we have defined in the previous sections—the constructor constraints (Sect. 3.4), the structural equalities (Sect. 3.5), and the NPR lifting (Sect. 3.3)—into a *reduced product*, and then add a disjunctive completion layer on top of that product. We will ultimately obtain the domain of relations RAND once we apply the relational lifting defined in Sect. 4.2.

Reduced Product. Our reduced product is based on a reduction operator ρ, that enables information transfer between the different domains of the product.

Definition 14 (Reduction operator). *The reduction operator ρ for the product of constructor constraints, structural equalities and the NPR lifting is defined as follows:*

$$\rho(E, C, N) = \begin{pmatrix} E \sqcap^{cc(\Gamma)} \mathrm{clos}^{cc(\Gamma)}(\mathrm{Env}\,(C')), \\ C', \\ \mathrm{Cond}^{D\uparrow \mathrm{NPR}(\Gamma)}(\bigwedge_{(x.p, y.q) \in C' \wedge \Gamma \vdash x.p:N} x.p = y.q)(N) \end{pmatrix}$$

where $C' = \mathrm{clos}^{\mathrm{seq}(\Gamma)}_{\mathrm{clos}^{cc(\Gamma)}(\mathrm{Env}((E,C,N)))}(C)$

The reduction operator ρ transfers the following pieces of information between the three components of the product:

- Structural equalities are completed with additional constraints, so that all the extended variables that are used in the constructor constraints and the numeric constraints are mentioned (this is the role of C').
- If some equalities between integers are deduced from the structural equalities, then they are added to the numeric constraints.
- The extended variables from the structural equalities and the numeric constraints are added to the constructor constraints, which may reveal some inconsistent cases.

Union, intersection and widening for the reduced product domain add variables to the structural equalities component, use component-wise operations and use the reduction operator. For widening, reduction is only applied to the right-hand side argument to avoid interfering with convergence. We invite the reader to look at the extended version [4] for further details. The transfer functions for assignment and conditionals use the transfer functions of each component.

Using Disjunctions to Handle Incompatible Cases. Pattern matching performs a case analysis on the different constructors a value may start with: these cases are pairwise incompatible. To analyse pattern matching with precision, we add disjunctions to our abstract domain by means of a disjunctive completion, so that each pattern matching case has a distinct disjunct. Hence, for any numeric domain D, we take the disjunctive completion [9] of the reduced product of constructor constraints, structural equalities and the NPR lifting of D. We call this the *structural lifting* of D, written $D \uparrow S(\Gamma)$, and defined as $D \uparrow S(\Gamma) = \mathcal{P}(cc(\Gamma) \times seq(\Gamma) \times D \uparrow \mathrm{NPR}(\Gamma))$. To control the number of disjuncts, however, we *merge* some cases together: merging is performed when the constructor constraints of two abstract values concretise to the same sets of stores—*i.e.*, when they impose the same constraints on the constructors used for variant values. The technical details are provided in the extended version [4].

4   A Collecting Semantics of Relations

The term *"relational analysis"* is widely used in the literature, and may refer to two different notions. In a majority of related works, a "relational analysis" designates a static analysis that infers relations that hold between variables of a *single* program point, *i.e.*, relations *in space*. In other works, a "relational analysis" denotes a static analysis that infers relations between (variables of) *different* states, *i.e.*, relations *in time*. In the rest of this paper, the term "relational" mostly refers to to *input-output* relational analysis, that computes relations between the input states and the output states of a program.

In this section, we define an input-output *relational* semantics of programs, that forms the semantic basis of an input-output relational analysis. Our relational semantics determines relations that relate the input stores of a program with its output stores, *i.e.*, the stores that are obtained when there are no more commands to evaluate.

Definition 15 (Relational semantics). *The relational semantics of a command c is defined as follows:* $\mathbb{S}[\![c]\!] = \{(s_1, s_2) \mid (c, s_1) \rightarrow^* (\textsf{skip}, s_2)\}$.

$\mathbb{S}[\![c]\!]$ is a binary relation that may be employed to derive fully compositional static analyses, such as CRA [14,28]. Indeed, it enjoys equations (*e.g.*, $\mathbb{S}[\![c_1 \, ; c_2]\!] = \mathbb{S}[\![c_1]\!];\mathbb{S}[\![c_2]\!]$) that help defining the analysis of a compound command from the *independent* analyses of its constituents. A drawback of this approach, however, is its inability to exploit any information about the states that have been reached so far, which may degrade the precision of an analysis. The following piece of code illustrates this issue: `assert (x > 1 && y > 1); x := y * x`. If we analyse the assignment `x := y * x` with no knowledge that the preceding assertion succeeded, then, using a linear relational domain—*e.g.*, octagons or polyhedra—we will not obtain any precise information about how the value of x has changed, as the domain cannot express non-linear relations. The relational collecting semantics of the next section waives this limitation, as it allows to exploit the information that has so far been obtained for the current program point.

4.1   Relational Collecting Semantics

In this section, we build a collecting relational semantics on top of $\mathbb{S}[\![c]\!]$, that can exploit the information about the states that have been reached. Let us consider again the example from the previous paragraph: with the knowledge that the assertion succeeded, then a linear relational domain will be able to express that x has strictly increased, for example. Our collecting semantics $\mathbb{P}[\![c]\!]$ is a function from relations to relations: given some initial relation a that holds between initial stores s_i and the stores s_b at the current program point (*before* the execution of c), $\mathbb{P}[\![c]\!](a)$ computes a relation between the initial stores s_i and the final stores s_f that are produced by evaluating the command c from the stores s_b. Thus, $\mathbb{P}[\![c]\!]$ *extends* the relations *in time* by composing on the right-hand side with the behaviour of command c. Our collecting semantics is defined as follows:

Definition 16 (Collecting semantics). $\mathbb{P}[\![c]\!](a) = a; \mathbb{S}[\![c]\!]$

$\mathbb{P}[\![c]\!]$ is an abstraction of a semantics of computation traces [8], that collects the intermediate stores that a program may reach. The collecting semantics $\mathbb{P}[\![c]\!]$

enjoys the equations listed in the next lemma, that shows how it decomposes by following the syntax of commands.

Lemma 1. *The following equations hold:*

$$\mathbb{P}[\![skip]\!](a) = a$$
$$\mathbb{P}[\![c_1 ; c_2]\!](a) = \mathbb{P}[\![c_2]\!](\mathbb{P}[\![c_1]\!](a))$$
$$\mathbb{P}[\![branch\ c_1\ or\ \ldots\ or\ c_n\ end]\!](a) = \bigcup_{1 \le i \le n} \mathbb{P}[\![c_i]\!](a)$$
$$\mathbb{P}[\![while\ b\ do\ c\ end]\!](a) = \mathbb{P}[\![assert(\neg b)]\!](\mathrm{lfp}\, f_a)$$
$$where\ f_a(r) = a \cup \mathbb{P}[\![c]\!](\mathbb{P}[\![assert(b)]\!](r))$$
$$\mathbb{P}[\![assert(b)]\!](a) = \{(s_1, s_2) \mid (s_1, s_2) \in a \wedge [\![b]\!]_{s_2}^{\mathrm{bool}} = \{\mathrm{tt}\}\}$$
$$\mathbb{P}[\![x := t]\!](a) = \{(s_1, s_2(x \mapsto v)) \mid (s_1, s_2) \in a \wedge v \in [\![t]\!]_{s_2}^{\mathrm{exp}}\}$$

Lemma 1 will serve as the semantic basis for the analysis that we describe in Sect. 5.2. The proof of Lemma 1 is available in the extended version [4].

Lemma 1 shows that the syntax-directed decomposition of the relation transformer $\mathbb{P}[\![c]\!]$ follows the same *structure* as the standard set-based collecting semantics, that collects the set of reachable states. Most transfer functions of our collecting semantics are the same, but they operate on different objects (binary relations on stores instead of sets of stores). The two transfer functions that are specific to this relational semantics are the ones for assertion and for assignment. We show in Sect. 4.2 how to define those two transfer functions—that transform relations that relate stores in *different* program points—using *any* relational abstract domain that represents sets of stores for one program point. Using these two results, we can turn a folklore technique into a formal claim: transforming a non input-output relational analysis into an input-output relational one is "as simple as" duplicating variables [5, 19].

4.2 Leveraging Relations in Space to Express Relations in Time

In this section we show that any relational domain—*i.e.*, that denotes sets of stores and can express binary relations between different variables of a single store—can be lifted to a domain for pairs of stores, that is able to express relations between input stores and output stores. The main idea is simple: a pair of stores $(s_1, s_2) \in (\mathrm{Vars} \to \mathrm{Values})^2$ can be represented as a single store, provided we can distinguish the variables in s_1 from those in s_2.

Formally, this is achieved by assuming two bijections *prime* : Vars $\to$ Vars′ and *second* : Vars $\to$ Vars″ where Vars′ and Vars″ are disjoint "copies" of Vars, that intuitively contain the "primed" and "seconded" versions of the variables of Vars. We write x' as a shorthand for $prime(x)$, and x'' for $second(x)$, and use the same convention as in [14], *i.e.*, we use regular variables for the left-hand sides of relations—the input stores—and primed variables for the right-hand sides—the output stores. For any map f, we write f' as a shorthand for $f \circ prime^{-1}$, and we write $f \cup g$ for the union of maps with disjoint domains. This allows us to represent any pair (s_1, s_2) of stores as a single store $s_1 \cup s_2'$. We use this encoding to transform any relational domain that represents a set of stores into a domain that represents a binary relation over stores.

Definition 17 (Relational lifting). *Let* A *be an abstract domain, such that for any typing context* Γ, $A(\Gamma)$ *is equipped with concretisation function* $\gamma^{A(\Gamma)} \in A(\Gamma) \to \mathcal{P}(\text{Vars} \to \text{Values})$. *For any two typing contexts* Γ_1 *and* Γ_2, *the relational lifting* $A \uparrow R(\Gamma_1, \Gamma_2)$ *of* A *and its concretisation function are defined as follows:*

$$A \uparrow R(\Gamma_1, \Gamma_2) = A(\Gamma_1 \cup \Gamma_2')$$
$$\gamma^{A \uparrow R(\Gamma_1, \Gamma_2)}(a) = \{(s_1, s_2) \mid s_1 \cup s_2' \in \gamma^{A(\Gamma_1 \cup \Gamma_2')}(a)\}$$

The relational lifting expects two typing contexts—one for the input stores, and one for the output stores. This flexibility will prove useful in Sect. 5.3 to define the abstract relational composition in order to analyse function calls.

The lifted domain $A \uparrow R(\Gamma_1, \Gamma_2)$ is naturally equipped with a pre-order relation, abstract union, intersection and widening, by reusing those of $A(\Gamma_1 \cup \Gamma_2')$.

As we remarked in Sect. 4.1, only two pieces are missing to get a relational input-output analysis: now that we can express relations on stores, the question remains of how to express the transfer functions for conditionals and assignments. We show in Fig. 3 how to do so in a generic way, by exploiting the transfer functions of the underlying domain.

$$\text{Cond}^{A \uparrow R(\Gamma_1, \Gamma_2)}(b)(a) = \text{Cond}^{A(\Gamma_1 \cup \Gamma_2')}(b')(a)$$
$$\text{Assign}^{A \uparrow R(\Gamma_1, \Gamma_2)}(x := t)(a) = \text{Rem}_{\Gamma_2''}^{A(\Gamma)} \left(\begin{array}{l} \text{Assign}^{A(\Gamma)}(x' := t'') \left(\text{Add}_{\Gamma_2'}^{A(\Gamma_1 \cup \Gamma_2'')} c \right) \\ \sqcap^{A(\Gamma)} \sqcap_{y \in \text{dom } \Gamma \setminus \{x\}}^{A(\Gamma)} \text{Cond}^{A(\Gamma)}(y'' = y') \end{array} \right)$$
$$\text{where } \Gamma = \Gamma_1 \cup \Gamma_2' \cup \Gamma_2'' \text{ and } c = \text{Rename}_{second \circ prime^{-1}}(a)$$

Fig. 3. Relational transfer functions for conditionals and assignment.

The transfer function for conditionals $\text{Cond}^{A \uparrow R(\Gamma_1, \Gamma_2)}(b)(a)$ constrains the right-hand side of the relation a to satisfy the boolean expression b. This is achieved by calling the transfer function for conditions of the underlying domain on b', to enforce that the variables of b refer to the outputs of a.

The transfer function for assignment $\text{Assign}^{A \uparrow R(\Gamma_1, \Gamma_2)}(x := t)(a)$ first renames the output variables y' of a into y''. The variables y'' belong to the state that lies just *before* the assignment. Then, we call the transfer function for assignment from the underlying domain for the command $x' := t''$. This has the effect of extending a with relations that express the link between t and the new variable x. Then, we add the equalities $y'' = y'$ for all the variables other than x, because none of them was modified by the assignment. Finally, we eliminate the auxiliary variables y''. This effectively builds a relation between the input state and the state that is obtained *after* the assignment.

This concludes our justification of the folklore claim that, "*to turn a static analysis for the sets of final states into an analysis for input-output relations, it suffices to duplicate variables*". We have built our justification on the following remarks: 1. Duplicating variables turns a non input-output relational domain— *i.e.*, a relation between variables of the stores of a *single* program point—into a

```
Function summary for function do_ticks(p, n) returning p' :
 (Constructor constraints : p.status@Running; p'.status@Running ...
  with structural equalities : p = p' ; ...
  and numeric constraints : n >= 1 ; ... )
 Or (Constructor constraints : p.status@Asleep; p'.status@Running ...
  with structural equalities : p.msg = p'.msg
  and numeric constraints :
     p.id = p'.id; p'.status@Running.count = p.status@Asleep.count + 1;
     p.status@Asleep.secs >= 0; n >= p.status@Asleep.secs + 1 )
 Or (Constructor constraints : p.status@Asleep; p'.status@Asleep ...
  with structural equalities : p.msg = p'.msg
  and numeric constraints :
     p.id = p'.id; p.status@Asleep.secs >= n; n >= 1;
     p.status@Asleep.count = p'.status@Asleep.count;
     p'.status@Asleep.secs = p.status@Asleep.secs - n )
```

Fig. 4. Result of our analysis on the example of Fig. 1. Ellipses mark information that is also present in other components of the same case and is elided.

domain of binary relations between stores of *two* different program points. 2. An input-output relational analysis has the same structure as an analysis for final states. 3. The transfer functions that are specific to the input-output relational analysis can be defined in a generic way, using those of the analysis for final states.

In the rest of this article, we use the relational lifting of the abstract domain from Sect. 3, that we call RAND—short for *Relational Algebraic and Numeric Domain*.

5   Analysis

This section explains how to use the abstract domain built in Sects. 3 and 4, to analyse the language described in Sect. 2.2. After providing an example that illustrates what the analysis computes (Sect. 5.1), we first describe an intra-procedural analysis (Sect. 5.2) and then extend it to support function calls, yielding a modular, summary-based, inter-procedural analysis (Sect. 5.3).

The inter-procedural version of our analysis does not currently handle recursive or mutually recursive functions, as we chose to focus solely on the topic of handling algebraic values and arithmetic relations. Nevertheless, we expect that the analysis of recursive functions can be achieved by performing a widened fixpoint iteration sequence at the level of function summaries.

5.1   Analysis Result for the do_ticks Function

Before giving the formal description of the analysis, we give an example of the properties that it can infer. Figure 4 shows the result of running our analyser on the example from Sect. 2.3 using polyhedra as a numeric domain. We see that our disjunctive completion considers three different cases, and contains all five properties that we wanted to infer automatically. In the first case, both the input and the output are running processes and the structural equality $p = p'$ tells us that the process remained unchanged (property 1). In the two other cases, the structural equality $p.msg = p'.msg$ conveys that the msg field has not changed (property 5) while numeric constraints indicate that the id field has not changed (property 4). In the second case, the input process is asleep while the output process is running. The numeric properties tell us that the wake up count has increased by one and the sleeping budget of the input process is lower than argument n (property 2). In the third case, both the input and output process are asleep. The numeric relations tell us that the initial sleeping budget was greater than n and has decreased by n; also, the wake up count remains unchanged (property 3).

5.2 Intra-procedural Analysis

We define a function Analyze that takes a program c and an abstract value a—representing the relation gathered so far between the input states and the current state—and returns the abstract value $\text{Analyze}(c)(a)$ that over-approximates the effect of running c *after* a. This section deals with basic constructs, while Sect. 5.3 explains how we analyse functions.

Definition 18 (Intra-procedural version of the analysis function).

$$\text{Analyze}(\mathsf{assert}(b))(a) = \text{Cond}^{D\uparrow S\uparrow R(\Gamma,\Gamma)}(b)(a)$$
$$\text{Analyze}(x := t)(a) = \text{Assign}^{D\uparrow S\uparrow R(\Gamma,\Gamma)}(x := t)(a)$$
$$\text{Analyze}(c_1\,;c_2)(a) = \text{Analyze}(c_2)\,(\text{Analyze}(c_1)(a))$$
$$\text{Analyze}(\mathsf{branch}\ c_1\ \mathsf{or}\ \dots\ \mathsf{or}\ c_n\ \mathsf{end})(a) = \bigsqcup_{i\in 1,\dots,n}^{D\uparrow S\uparrow R(\Gamma,\Gamma)} \text{Analyze}(c_i)(a)$$
$$\text{Analyze}(\mathsf{while}\ b\ \mathsf{do}\ c\ \mathsf{end})(a) = \text{Cond}^{D\uparrow S\uparrow R(\Gamma,\Gamma)}(\neg b)\,(\lim_{n\to\infty} a_n)$$
$$\textit{where }a_0 = a\textit{ and }a_{n+1} = a_n\ \nabla^{D\uparrow S\uparrow R(\Gamma,\Gamma)}\ \text{Analyze}(\mathsf{assert}(b);c)(a_n)$$

Assertion and assignment use the transfer functions we built in previous sections. Sequence and branching follow the structure outlined in Lemma 1.

We analyse loops in a standard way, using a widening-based Kleene iteration, which ensures that we reach a post-fixpoint in a finite number of iterations. In practice, our implementation performs a *loop unrolling* [40, p.131] of the first iteration, so as to obtain better precision.

The Analyze function is *sound*, in the sense that it over-approximates the relational collecting semantics.

Theorem 1 (Soundness w.r.t. the collecting semantics). *For any command c and abstract value $a \in D \uparrow S \uparrow R(\Gamma,\Gamma)$,*

$$\mathbb{P}[\![c]\!]\left(\gamma^{D\uparrow S\uparrow R(\Gamma,\Gamma)}(a)\right) \subseteq \gamma^{D\uparrow S\uparrow R(\Gamma,\Gamma)}\,(\text{Analyze}(c)(a))$$

By instantiating Theorem 1 with the abstraction of the identity relation, we get a soundness result with respect to the relational semantics of commands:

Corollary 1 (Soundness w.r.t. the relational semantics). *For any command c,* $\mathbb{S}[\![c]\!] \subseteq \gamma^{D\uparrow S\uparrow R(\Gamma,\Gamma)} \left(\text{Analyze}(c) \left(\text{Id}^{D\uparrow S\uparrow R(\Gamma,\Gamma)} \right) \right).$

5.3 Analysis of Function Calls

In this section, we add function definitions and function calls to our language, and extend the intra-procedural analysis of Sect. 5.2 into a modular inter-procedural analysis, based on function summaries.

Extended Syntax and Semantics for Functions. We extend our language to support function calls in commands and function declarations:

$$
\begin{aligned}
c \in \text{Cmd} &::= \quad \ldots \quad | \quad x := f(x_1, \ldots, x_n) \\
d \in \text{Decl} &::= \text{def } f(\tau_1 \; x_1, \ldots, \tau_n \; x_n) : \tau = \{c\,; \text{return } x\} \\
P \in \text{Prog} &::= d_1; \ldots; d_n
\end{aligned}
$$

For simplicity, the command for function calls $y := f(x_1, \ldots, x_n)$ immediately saves in a variable y the result of calling a function f. This restriction forbids to call functions within expressions, so that the semantics of expressions and the transfer function for assignment remain unchanged.

A program is a sequence of function declarations $\text{def } f(\tau_1 \; x_1, \ldots, \tau_n \; x_n) : \tau = \{c\,; \text{return } r\}$, that specify for the function f what are its input and output variables and their types, and defines its body c. A program effectively defines a map Δ, that associates to every declared function f a quadruplet $\Delta(f) = ((x_1, \ldots, x_n), c, r, \Gamma)$ that holds the formal parameters x_i of f, its body c, its formal return variable r, and the typing context Γ that specifies the types of its formal and local variables.

The operational semantics is extended in a standard manner to support function calls and returns, by augmenting states with a call stack. The new rules are given in the extended version [4].

Analysing Functions. We have chosen to develop a modular analysis, by analysing each function *only once* and computing a *function summary*, that summarises a function's behaviour. This summary is then reused and instantiated each time that function is called. Such a modular analysis allows to better scale to large code bases [11].

Definition 19 (Function summaries). *For a function f defined by $\Delta(f) = ((x_1, \ldots, x_n), c_f, y_f, \Gamma_f)$, we call* summary *of f the quadruplet given by:*

$$
\left((x_1, \ldots, x_n), \text{Analyze}(c_f) \left(\text{Id}^{D\uparrow S\uparrow R(\Gamma_f)} \right), y_f, \Gamma_f \right)
$$

The second component of the summary of a function f is an abstract value summarising f's behaviour by over-approximating the input-output relation between its formal arguments and its formal return variable. Thus, this abstract value deals with the variables that are *local* to the execution of f: no information about the caller's environment is recorded in the summary. This abstract value is obtained by analysing the body of f, starting with the identity relation. This means that we make no assumption on the actual arguments that will be given to f, hence we can reuse the *same* summary in *every* calling context.

To use a function summary at some call site, we *instantiate* the summary on the actual arguments and output variable used at the call site. Our method to instantiate summaries is based on an abstraction of relational composition, that sequentially chains together two abstract values that represent binary relations.

Definition 20 (Abstract composition). *Let Γ_1, Γ_2 and Γ_3 be typing contexts. Let $a_1 \in A \uparrow R(\Gamma_1, \Gamma_2)$ and $a_2 \in A \uparrow R(\Gamma_2, \Gamma_3)$ be two abstract values. The abstract composition $a_1 \;;^A a_2$ of the abstract values a_1 and a_2 is defined by:*

$$a_1 \;;^A a_2 = \underset{\Gamma_2''}{\text{Remove}} \left(\underset{\Gamma_3'}{\text{Add}\, c_1} \; \sqcap^{A(\Gamma_1 \cup \Gamma_2'' \cup \Gamma_3')} \underset{\Gamma_1}{\text{Add}\, c_2} \right)$$

where $c_1 = \text{Rename}_{second \circ prime^{-1}}\, a_1$ and $c_2 = \text{Rename}_{second}\, a_2$.

Abstract composition chains the effects of a_1 and a_2 by introducing auxiliary names—*i.e.*, variables of the form y''—for the states that are in the output of a_1 and the input of a_2, before taking the intersection, and then removing the temporarily introduced variables. The calls to Add are necessary name management steps, that ensure that the abstract values deal with the same sets of variables. Abstract composition is a sound approximation of relational composition, as stated by the following lemma:

Lemma 2 (Soundness of composition). *Let $a_1 \in A \uparrow R(\Gamma_1, \Gamma_2)$ and $a_2 \in A \uparrow R(\Gamma_2, \Gamma_3)$ be two abstract values. We have:*

$$\gamma^{A \uparrow R(\Gamma_1, \Gamma_2)}(a_1); \gamma^{A \uparrow R(\Gamma_2, \Gamma_3)}(a_2) \subseteq \gamma^{A \uparrow R(\Gamma_1, \Gamma_3)}(a_1 \;;^A a_2)$$

Based on abstract composition, we express summary instantiation as follows:

Definition 21 (Summary instantiation). *The* instantiation *of the function summary $S_f = ((x_1, \ldots, x_n), a_f, y_f, \Gamma_f)$ on the actual parameters $(z_1, \ldots, z_n)$, the actual return variable y and the caller typing context Γ is defined as follows:*

$$\text{Inst}(S_f, (z_1, \ldots, z_n), y, \Gamma) = ins \;;^{D \uparrow S} a_f \;;^{D \uparrow S} outs$$
$$\text{where } ins = \text{Cond}^{D \uparrow S \uparrow R(\Gamma, \Gamma_f)} \left(\bigwedge\nolimits_{i \in \{1, \ldots, n\}} z_i = x_i' \right)$$
$$\text{and } outs = \text{Cond}^{D \uparrow S \uparrow R(\Gamma_f, \Gamma)}(y_f = y')$$

Summary instantiation simply works by composing three abstract values, using abstract composition. Instantiation first ties each actual parameter to its formal parameter by *pre*-composing the abstract value a_f for f's body with the *ins* abstract value, and then ties the formal output to the actual output by *post*-composing with the *outs* value. The values *ins* and *outs* are simply expressed as mere conjunctions of equalities. The first composition deals with the *call* of the function, whereas the second composition handles the *return*.

During a function call $y := f(z_1, \ldots, z_n)$, the instantiation of f's summary deals with which variables might have changed and how, but does not deal with the fact that *only* the variable y may have changed: every other variable that is available before the call remains the same after the call. Thus, the transfer function for function call augments the instantiation of the function summary S_f with equalities for the unaltered variables, before extending the so far gathered relation a with the effect of the call to f:

$$\text{Analyze}(y := f(z_1, \ldots, z_n))(a) =$$
$$a \; ;^{\text{D}\uparrow\text{S}} \left(\begin{array}{c} \text{Inst}(S_f, (z_1, \ldots, z_n), y, \Gamma) \sqcap^{D\uparrow S\uparrow R(\Gamma,\Gamma)} \\ \sqcap^{D\uparrow S\uparrow R(\Gamma,\Gamma)}_{x \neq y} \text{Cond}^{D\uparrow S\uparrow R(\Gamma,\Gamma)}(x = x') \end{array} \right)$$

The transfer function for function calls is sound:

Lemma 3 (Soundness of function call analysis). *For every function definition* $\Delta(f) = ((x_1, \ldots, x_n), c_f, y_f, \Gamma_f)$ *in a program, and any function summary* $S_f = ((x_1, \ldots, x_n), a_f, y_f, \Gamma_f)$ *such that* $\mathbb{S}[\![c_f]\!] \subseteq \gamma^{D\uparrow S\uparrow R(\Gamma_f, \Gamma_f)}(a_f)$, *we have:*

$$\mathbb{P}[\![y := f(z_1, \ldots, z_n)]\!](\gamma^{D\uparrow S\uparrow R(\Gamma,\Gamma)}(a)) \subseteq \gamma^{D\uparrow S\uparrow R(\Gamma,\Gamma)}(\text{Analyze}(y := f(z_1, \ldots, z_n))(a))$$

Lemma 3 ensures that the soundness result for the intra-procedural analysis (Theorem 1) extends to the language with function calls that we have described in this section. We give in the extended version [4] a proof of Lemma 3.

6   Implementation, Experimental Results and Complexity

We have implemented our analyser in approximately 5000 lines of OCaml. Our implementation together with instructions on how to add new test cases and run the tests cases is packaged and published as a virtual machine artefact [3]. Similarly to our formal development, our analyser is parametrised by an abstract domain for integers. A command-line option allows to choose among numeric domains provided by Apron [24], such as intervals, octagons or polyhedra.

We have tested our analyser on a total of 43 programs (summarised on Table 1), that comprise some complex examples: some sorting algorithms, the `do_ticks` function from Sect. 2.3, and 6 functions inspired from the abstract specification of the seL4 micro-kernel [29]. We now review the results that our analyser computed for these examples, using polyhedra as numeric domain.

Sorting Integer Arrays. To circumvent the absence of support for arrays in our language and in our abstract domain, we modelled arrays of fixed length using tuples, and we defined `get` and `set` functions. With this encoding, we wrote several sorting algorithms for arrays of integers, for arrays of size 5. The analyser could not infer that the output array was sorted. Still, it was able to infer that the sum of the values of the array was preserved by the sorting function.

The do_ticks function. The do_ticks function (Sect. 2.3) is inspired from a process scheduler from operating system code. As reported in Sect. 5.1, the analysis result for do_ticks captures all the properties we expected.

seL4-Inspired Functions. We have extracted from the abstract specification of the seL4 formally verified micro-kernel [29] several functions, that work both on ADTs and on scalar values, and translated them in our while language. Specifically, those functions are related to either thread management, capability management or scheduling (decode_set_priority, check_prio, mask_cap, validate_vm_rights, cap_rights_update, timer_tick). Our analyser infers exact abstractions for all of them, except for timer_tick. This program is slightly different from do_ticks: when a thread's time budget is over, this budget is reset to its original value, and the thread is then re-scheduled, which might select a new current thread. The case constraints of our abstract domain cannot distinguish whether the current thread remains the same or not, so a join of those two cases is performed. This results in some expected information loss on the thread's time.

For the mask_cap program, we experimented with two encodings of bitmasks, using either integers or ADTs to represent booleans. The integer-based encoding produced a function summary that is compact—only 4 cases—but hard to understand for a human being, whereas the summary produced with the ADT-based encoding was easy to interpret, but large—it involved 324 disjunctions.

We consider that the precision we obtained on the seL4 examples is satisfying. Still, the last example illustrates a limitation of our approach. Indeed the function summaries can significantly grow when the analysed program pattern matches on many distinct variables. Abstract domains that leverage BDDs have been successfully used to reduce analysis costs by sharing common results [12,13,21, 41], and could also help in our situation.

Complexity of Our Analysis. Each domain that constitutes RAND, with the exception of the disjunctive completion layer, features operators and transfer functions whose complexity is polynomial in program parameters, *e.g.*, the number of variables, or the maximum depth of the defined types. For the disjunctive completion, however, the complexity is polynomial in the number of possible cases, which can itself be exponential in program parameters. The number of cases is asymptotically bounded by c^{xf^p}, where x is the number of variables in the program, c is the maximum number of different constructors per sum type, f is the maximum number of fields in any product type and p is the maximum depth of the types being defined. While it is possible to write a program that reaches this bound, we have not found any program, even in seL4, that makes the number of cases explode.

There are two different scenarios that render our analysis costly: either when the number of different cases is high—in which case our disjunctive comple-

Table 1. Test cases used for experimental evaluation. We use the * symbol for families of similar tests, whose names start identically. The columns indicate whether the tests involve **sum** types, **numeric** operations, while **loops** or function **calls**, as well as the analysis **time**, and the maximum number of **cases** per function summary. Analysis times are given in milliseconds, with the exception of longer durations, that are given in seconds and printed with a bold face. Measures were performed on an Intel® Core™ i7 @2.30GHz × 16. The accompanying artefact [3] includes instructions to reproduce the results.

Name	Sums	Numeric	Loops	Calls	Time	Cases
Hand-crafted tests:						
do_ticks	Yes	Yes	Yes	No	166 ms	3
nondeterministic_ bubble_sort	Yes	Yes	Yes	Yes	**2.1 s**	5
selection_sort	Yes	Yes	Yes	Yes	**10.9 s**	25
Inspired from SeL4:						
decode_set_priority	Yes	Yes	No	Yes	10 ms	2
mask_cap_boolean	Yes	No	No	Yes	**7.4 s**	324
mask_cap_int	Yes	Yes	No	Yes	**1.5 s**	4
timer_tick_scheduling	Yes	Yes	Yes	Yes	**41.2 s**	81
Simple tests:						
assert*	Yes	Yes	No	No	1 ms	1
call_inside_loop_*	No	Yes	Yes	Yes	15 ms	1
drift	Yes	Yes	Yes	Yes	24 ms	2
exchange	No	No	No	No	2 ms	1
facto*	No	Yes	Yes	No	8 ms	1
false_type_collision	No	No	No	Yes	3 ms	1
fibonacci	No	Yes	Yes	Yes	51 ms	1
gauss*	No	Yes	Yes	No	15 ms	1
ghost_equality	No	No	No	No	<1 ms	1
hidden_incompat	Yes	No	No	No	2 ms	0
id	No	No	No	No	<1 ms	1
if	No	Yes	No	No	2 ms	1
incompat	Yes	No	No	No	<1 ms	0
indirect_swap	Yes	No	No	Yes	3 ms	2
long_id	Yes	No	No	Yes	5 ms	2
modulo	No	Yes	Yes	Yes	33 ms	2
multiplication_larger	No	Yes	No	No	2 ms	1
or_constructor	Yes	No	No	No	< 1 ms	0
plus_*	Yes	Yes	No	No	< ms	1
record_assignment*	No	Yes	No	No	2 ms	1
reduction	No	Yes	No	No	3 ms	1
struct_exchange	Yes	No	No	No	<1 ms	1
swap	Yes	No	No	No	<1 ms	2
test_loop	No	Yes	Yes	No	3 ms	1
two_by_two	No	Yes	Yes	No	3 ms	1
while_true	No	No	Yes	No	<1 ms	0
widening_convergence	No	Yes	Yes	No	49 ms	1
xor	Yes	No	No	Yes	8 ms	3

tion can be the bottleneck—or when many *numeric* extended variables are considered—in which case the underlying numeric domain can be the bottleneck. A solution for the first scenario could be to adopt a different merging strategy, so that more cases are merged, at the risk of losing precision. In the second scenario, the generic aspect of our domain allows to choose between numeric domains with different precision versus cost trade-offs. In addition, techniques based on partitioning the set of variables could also be leveraged.

7   Related Work

The idea of exploiting an input-output *relational* semantics to verify `while` programs was developed by Kozen [31]. He introduced Kleene Algebra with Tests, an extension of relation algebra [44] with co-reflexive relations named *tests*, that serves as a foundation for the semantics of imperative programs, their verification, and as an effective formal tool for proving the correctness of program transformations.

A number of static analyses for approximating the input-output relation of a program have been proposed. Cousot and Cousot [11] used abstract interpretation for designing modular and relational analyses, and argue that compositionality can improve the scalability of analysers. Compositional Recurrence Analysis (CRA) [14] is a *compositional* static analysis that infers numeric relations between the inputs and the outputs of programs. CRA first builds a regular expression to describe the set of program paths, that is then interpreted as an input-output *relation* in a compositional way, in a second stage. Their approach is context insensitive, and is similar to the relational semantics of Definition 15. Whereas we follow the standard iteration-based analysis of loops, they use a special operator to compute the reflexive transitive closure of a relation, that is specialised on linear recurrence equations. Interestingly, they discuss in their benchmarks a variation of their analysis, named CRA+OCT, that *"uses an intra-procedural octagon analysis to gain some contextual information, but which is otherwise compositional"*, and that leads to more precise results than pure CRA. Although no precise definition is given for CRA+OCT, we believe that it follows our *relational collecting semantics* of Definition 16, again with the exception of the treatment of loops. As we have also observed, exploiting the information available at loop entries is crucial to obtain sufficiently precise results. ICRA [28] is an inter-procedural extension of CRA, where function summaries are computed once and for all, independently of their calling contexts—an approach we have followed too in Sect. 5.3. In contrast to CRA and ICRA, our analysis can deal with programs that are not purely numeric, and that can handle algebraic data types. We have not found any detailed description of *how* the function summaries of CRA and ICRA are instantiated. We are therefore not able to compare the way we instantiate function summaries (Sect. 5.3) with CRA or ICRA. In contrast to CRA and ICRA, our analysis does not yet support recursively defined functions.

The same approach of computing context-insensitive function summaries was followed in the context of correlation analysis [1]. This analysis infers binary equalities between the parts of structured inputs and outputs of programs, using the *correlation abstract domain*. We improve on that work because we can also express numeric relations between parts of structured values, and n-ary equalities. Our domain differs significantly from the correlation domain, in the sense that correlations are recursively defined so that parts of abstract values relate parts of structured values, whereas our domain is not a recursive structure, and instead exploits *extended variables* to relate the parts of structured values that are accessible through projection paths. We published a preliminary version of our approach in [2]. In this previous work, the analysis was not input-output relational, since it inferred approximations of the final states, as opposed to the relations between input and output states that the current paper is dealing with. Moreover, our previous work did not include the domain for structural equalities, and was thus unable to express concisely n-ary equality relations between parts of structured values. Finally, no implementation and experimental evaluation was provided. Our implementation effort helped identify several precision issues in our previous approach, that motivated the addition of the structural equality domain (Sect. 3.5) and of the relational lifting (Sect. 4.2).

Several relational analyses were developed for the inter-procedural analysis of numeric programs [5,23,36,42], and in the context of inter-procedural shape analysis [20,22,43]. They all feature a form of function summary, that helps reduce the analysis cost of large programs, by enabling modular analyses. A domain that supports both shape abstraction and numeric constraints was developed by [6]. It is defined in a modular fashion, based on the cofibered abstract domain [45]. As in our construction, theirs also features a disjunctive completion, but leaves open the question of how to keep the number of disjuncts under control.

In the context of the static analysis of languages with algebraic data types, techniques based on tree automata [7] have been developed. Tree automata are well suited to represent regular sets of trees, and several works propose to extend their expressive power further. Lattice tree automata [16,17] augment tree automata with elements of an arbitrary abstract domain at their leaves, and allow to express *non-relational* integer constraints on the leaves of trees. More recently, [25,26] use a combination of tree automata and of a relational domain whose keys are regular expressions to express relational constraints between the numeric leaves of trees. They use regular expressions to denote sets of access paths within those trees, and thus to support structures of unbounded heights.

As a particular case of algebraic values, the analysis of programs with *optional* numerical values was handled in [33] by associating to optional variables two *avatars*, that respectively model lower- and upper-constraints on that variable. When the avatars of some variable x induce a contradictory constraint, this denotes that x is in the None case. It is unclear how this approach generalises to deeply nested algebraic values.

Controlling the number of disjuncts in a disjunctive completion is admittedly difficult, as a cost *vs* precision balance must be found. Since we deal with finite types only, our number of disjuncts is bounded by the products of the sizes of types used in a program. Other works have used *silhouettes* [32]—abstractions of the shapes of the abstract values—to control disjunctions. Following [27], our disjunctions, that are guided by paths in values, can be understood as a form of *control sensitivity*. It is worth noticing that our disjuncts do not form a *partition* since some disjuncts may overlap—a degree of freedom that is advocated by [27]. Based on our present work, we will investigate whether we can re-cast our disjuncts as *conjunctions of implications*, which could both improve precision and lead to a more parsimonious representations of abstract values.

8   Conclusion and Future Work

In the context of programs that combine arithmetic operations and algebraic data types, we have shown how to construct an abstract domain that extends *any* abstract domain for numeric relations into an abstract domain for relations between algebraic values. The main idea is to consider extended variables—*i.e.*, a variable, and an access path—as the variables used in the numeric abstract domain. To reduce the size of abstract values, we add a domain that keeps track of equalities between non-numeric values. The domains are combined using a reduced product that propagates equalities. Additional expressiveness and precision is obtained using an adaptation of disjunctive completion for handling the different, incompatible cases that an algebraic value can exhibit. This abstract domain is called RAND—the Relational Algebraic Numeric Domain—and can be exploited in a static analyser.

We have given a formal justification to the folklore result of static analysis that *"an analysis can be made relational by duplicating variables"*, by effectively turning a non input-output relational analysis into an input-output relational one. One key observation is that the input-output relational analyser and the non input-output relational one share the same *structure*: only a few transfer functions need to be redefined. The second observation is that any relational domain can easily be used to express relations between different stores: the necessary transfer functions can be redefined once and for all, in a generic manner.

Finally, we have exploited our abstract domain to design and implement [3] a static analyser for a `while` language with algebraic data types and function calls that exploits the relational feature of RAND to infer function summaries. Summaries express the input-output behaviours of functions, and enable a *modular* inter-procedural analysis of programs: every function is analysed *exactly once*.

Further work will address the challenging problem of handling *recursive* algebraic data types and functional arrays. To that end, we will need to adapt our language of *paths*, *e.g.*, by using regular languages, or by extending techniques based on tree automata [26]. Another direction of research is to analyse recursive programs, which will require the computation of a fixpoint at the level of function summaries for groups of mutually defined functions.

Finally, we intend to apply our analyser to help the verification of programs, by mixing automatic techniques based on abstract interpretation with standard deductive verification tools, such as Why3 [15]. Previous work [1] have indeed demonstrated that a large number of proof obligations could be discharged automatically in such a way, and could alleviate the verification of large programs.

References

1. Andreescu, O.F., Jensen, T., Lescuyer, S., Montagu, B.: Inferring frame conditions with static correlation analysis. POPL (2019). https://doi.org/10.1145/3290360
2. Bautista, S., Jensen, T., Montagu, B.: Numeric domains meet algebraic data types. NSAD (2020). https://doi.org/10.1145/3427762.3430178
3. Bautista, S., Jensen, T., Montagu, B.: Artifact for the "Lifting Numeric Relational Domains to Algebraic Data Types" article of the SAS 2022 symposium (2022). https://doi.org/10.5281/zenodo.6977156
4. Bautista, S., Jensen, T., Montagu, B.: Lifting Numeric Relational Domains to Algebraic Data Types (extended version) (2022). https://hal.inria.fr/hal-03765357
5. Boutonnet, R., Halbwachs, N.: Disjunctive relational abstract interpretation for interprocedural program analysis. VMCAI (2019). https://doi.org/10.1007/978-3-030-11245-5_7
6. Chang, B.Y.E., Rival, X.: Modular construction of shape-numeric analyzers. Festschrift for Dave Schmidt (2013). https://hal.inria.fr/hal-00926948
7. Comon, H., et al.: Tree Automata Techniques and Applications (2008). https://hal.inria.fr/hal-03367725
8. Cousot, P.: Constructive design of a hierarchy of semantics of a transition system by abstract interpretation (extended abstract). MFPS (1997). https://doi.org/10.1016/s1571-0661(05)80168-9
9. Cousot, P.: Principles of Abstract Interpretation. The MIT Press, Cambridge (2021)
10. Cousot, P., Cousot, R.: Abstract interpretation: a unified lattice model for static analysis of programs by construction or approximation of fixpoints. In: POPL (1977). https://doi.org/10.1145/512950.512973
11. Cousot, P., Cousot, R.: Modular static program analysis. In: Horspool, R.N. (ed.) CC 2002. LNCS, vol. 2304, pp. 159–179. Springer, Heidelberg (2002). https://doi.org/10.1007/3-540-45937-5_13
12. Dimovski, A.S.: Lifted static analysis using a binary decision diagram abstract domain. In: GPCE (2019). https://doi.org/10.1145/3357765.3359518
13. Dimovski, A.S., Apel, S., Legay, A.: Several lifted abstract domains for static analysis of numerical program families. Sci. Comput. Program. **213** (2022). https://doi.org/10.1016/j.scico.2021.102725
14. Farzan, A., Kincaid, Z.: Compositional recurrence analysis. In: FMCAD (2015). https://doi.org/10.1109/FMCAD.2015.7542253
15. Filliâtre, J.-C., Paskevich, A.: Why3 — where programs meet provers. In: Felleisen, M., Gardner, P. (eds.) ESOP 2013. LNCS, vol. 7792, pp. 125–128. Springer, Heidelberg (2013). https://doi.org/10.1007/978-3-642-37036-6_8
16. Genet, T., Le Gall, T., Legay, A., Murat, V.: A completion algorithm for lattice tree automata. In: Konstantinidis, S. (ed.) CIAA 2013. LNCS, vol. 7982, pp. 134–145. Springer, Heidelberg (2013). https://doi.org/10.1007/978-3-642-39274-0_13
17. Genet, T., Le Gall, T., Legay, A., Murat, V.: Tree regular model checking for lattice-based automata. In: CIAA (2013). https://hal.inria.fr/hal-00924849
18. Haudebourg, T., Genet, T., Jensen, T.P.: Regular language type inference with term rewriting. In: ICFP (2020). https://doi.org/10.1145/3408994

19. Illous, H., Lemerre, M., Rival, X.: A relational shape abstract domain. In: NASA Formal Methods (2017). https://doi.org/10.1007/978-3-319-57288-8_15
20. Illous, H., Lemerre, M., Rival, X.: Interprocedural shape analysis using separation logic-based transformer summaries. In: Pichardie, D., Sighireanu, M. (eds.) SAS 2020. LNCS, vol. 12389, pp. 248–273. Springer, Cham (2020). https://doi.org/10.1007/978-3-030-65474-0_12
21. Jeannet, B.: The BDDAPRON logico-numerical abstract domains library (2009). https://pop-art.inrialpes.fr/~bjeannet/bjeannet-forge/bddapron/
22. Jeannet, B.: Relational interprocedural verification of concurrent programs. Softw. Syst. Model. **12** (2013). https://doi.org/10.1007/s10270-012-0230-7
23. Jeannet, B., Loginov, A., Reps, T., Sagiv, M.: A relational approach to interprocedural shape analysis. In: Giacobazzi, R. (ed.) SAS 2004. LNCS, vol. 3148, pp. 246–264. Springer, Heidelberg (2004). https://doi.org/10.1007/978-3-540-27864-1_19
24. Jeannet, B., Miné, A.: Apron: a library of numerical abstract domains for static analysis. CAV (2009). https://doi.org/10.1007/978-3-642-02658-4_52
25. Journault, M.: Precise and modular static analysis by abstract interpretation for the automatic proof of program soundness and contracts inference. (Analyse statique modulaire précise par interprétation abstraite pour la preuve automatique de correction de programmes et pour l'inférence de contrats.). Ph.D. thesis, Sorbonne University, France (2019). https://tel.archives-ouvertes.fr/tel-02947214
26. Journault, M., Miné, A., Ouadjaout, A.: An abstract domain for trees with numeric relations. In: Caires, L. (ed.) ESOP 2019. LNCS, vol. 11423, pp. 724–751. Springer, Cham (2019). https://doi.org/10.1007/978-3-030-17184-1_26
27. Kim, S., Rival, X., Ryu, S.: A theoretical foundation of sensitivity in an abstract interpretation framework. In: TOPLAS (2018). https://doi.org/10.1145/3230624
28. Kincaid, Z., Breck, J., Boroujeni, A.F., Reps, T.: Compositional recurrence analysis revisited. In: PLDI (2017). https://doi.org/10.1145/3062341.3062373
29. Klein, G., et al.: seL4: Formal verification of an OS kernel. In: SOSP (2009). https://doi.org/10.1145/1629575.1629596
30. Kobayashi, N., Tabuchi, N., Unno, H.: Higher-order multi-parameter tree transducers and recursion schemes for program verification. In: POPL (2010). https://doi.org/10.1145/1706299.1706355
31. Kozen, D.: Kleene algebra with tests. In: TOPLAS (1997). https://doi.org/10.1145/256167.256195
32. Li, H., Berenger, F., Evan Chang, B., Rival, X.: Semantic-directed clumping of disjunctive abstract states. In: POPL (2017). https://doi.org/10.1145/3009837.3009881
33. Liu, J., Rival, X.: Abstraction of optional numerical values. In: Feng, X., Park, S. (eds.) APLAS 2015. LNCS, vol. 9458, pp. 146–166. Springer, Cham (2015). https://doi.org/10.1007/978-3-319-26529-2_9
34. Miné, A.: The octagon abstract domain. High. Order Symb. Comput. **19** (2006). https://doi.org/10.1007/s10990-006-8609-1
35. Miné, A.: Tutorial on static inference of numeric invariants by abstract interpretation. Found. Trends Program. Lang. **4** (2017). https://doi.org/10.1561/2500000034
36. Müller-Olm, M., Seidl, H.: Analysis of modular arithmetic. In: TOPLAS (2007). https://doi.org/10.1145/1275497.1275504
37. Ong, C.L., Ramsay, S.J.: Verifying higher-order functional programs with pattern-matching algebraic data types. In: POPL (2011). https://doi.org/10.1145/1926385.1926453

38. Pierce, B.: Advanced Topics in Types and Programming Languages. MIT Press, Cambridge (2005)
39. Pierce, B.C.: Types and Programming Languages. MIT Press, Cambridge (2002)
40. Rival, X., Yi, K.: Introduction to Static Analysis: An Abstract Interpretation Perspective. The MIT Press, Cambridge (2020)
41. Schrammel, P., Jeannet, B.: Logico-numerical abstract acceleration and application to the verification of data-flow programs. In: Yahav, E. (ed.) SAS 2011. LNCS, vol. 6887, pp. 233–248. Springer, Heidelberg (2011). https://doi.org/10.1007/978-3-642-23702-7_19
42. Sharma, T., Reps, T.: A new abstraction framework for affine transformers. Formal Methods Syst. Des. **54**(1), 110–143 (2018). https://doi.org/10.1007/s10703-018-0325-z
43. Sotin, P., Jeannet, B.: Precise Interprocedural Analysis in the Presence of Pointers to the Stack. In: Barthe, G. (ed.) ESOP 2011. LNCS, vol. 6602, pp. 459–479. Springer, Heidelberg (2011). https://doi.org/10.1007/978-3-642-19718-5_24
44. Tarski, A.: On the calculus of relations. J. Symbol. Logic **6** (1941). https://doi.org/10.2307/2268577
45. Venet, A.: Abstract cofibered domains: application to the alias analysis of untyped programs. In: Cousot, R., Schmidt, D.A. (eds.) SAS 1996. LNCS, vol. 1145, pp. 366–382. Springer, Heidelberg (1996). https://doi.org/10.1007/3-540-61739-6_53

Automated Synthesis
of Asynchronizations

Sidi Mohamed Beillahi[1]([✉]), Ahmed Bouajjani[2], Constantin Enea[3],
and Shuvendu Lahiri[4]

[1] University of Toronto, Toronto, Canada
`sm.beillahi@utoronto.ca`
[2] Université Paris Cité, IRIF, CNRS, Paris, France
`abou@irif.fr`
[3] LIX, Ecole Polytechnique, CNRS and Institut Polytechnique de Paris, Paris, France
`cenea@lix.polytechnique.fr`
[4] Microsoft Research Lab - Redmond, Redmond, USA
`shuvendu@microsoft.com`

Abstract. Asynchronous programming is widely adopted for building responsive and efficient software, and modern languages such as C# provide async/await primitives to simplify the use of asynchrony. In this paper, we propose an approach for refactoring a sequential program into an asynchronous program that uses async/await, called asynchronization. The refactoring process is parametrized by a set of methods to replace with asynchronous versions, and it is constrained to avoid introducing data races. We investigate the delay complexity of enumerating all data race free asynchronizations, which quantifies the delay between outputting two consecutive solutions. We show that this is polynomial time modulo an oracle for solving reachability in sequential programs. We also describe a pragmatic approach based on an interprocedural dataflow analysis with polynomial-time delay complexity. The latter approach has been implemented and evaluated on a number of non-trivial C# programs extracted from open-source repositories.

1 Introduction

Asynchronous programming is widely adopted for building responsive and efficient software. As an alternative to explicitly registering callbacks with asynchronous calls, C# 5.0 [4] introduced the `async/await` primitives. These primitives allow the programmer to write code in a familiar sequential style without explicit callbacks. An asynchronous procedure, marked with `async`, returns a task object that the caller uses to "await" it. Awaiting may suspend the execution of the caller, but does not block the thread it is running on. The code after `await` is the continuation called back when the callee result is ready. This paradigm has become popular across many languages, C++, JavaScript, Python.

The `async/await` primitives introduce concurrency which is notoriously complex. The code in between a call and a matching `await` (referring to the same

© The Author(s), under exclusive license to Springer Nature Switzerland AG 2022
G. Singh and C. Urban (Eds.): SAS 2022, LNCS 13790, pp. 135–159, 2022.
https://doi.org/10.1007/978-3-031-22308-2_7

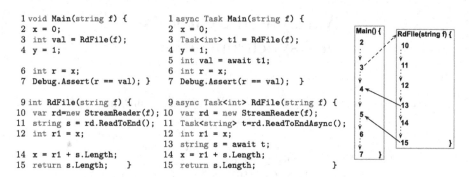

```
1 void Main(string f) {        1 async Task Main(string f) {
2   x = 0;                      2   x = 0;
3   int val = RdFile(f);        3   Task<int> t1 = RdFile(f);
4   y = 1;                      4   y = 1;
                                5   int val = await t1;
6   int r = x;                  6   int r = x;
7   Debug.Assert(r == val); }   7   Debug.Assert(r == val);  }

9 int RdFile(string f) {         9 async Task<int> RdFile(string f) {
10  var rd=new StreamReader(f); 10  var rd = new StreamReader(f);
11  string s = rd.ReadToEnd();  11  Task<string> t=rd.ReadToEndAsync();
12  int r1 = x;                 12  int r1 = x;
                                13  string s = await t;
14  x = r1 + s.Length;          14  x = r1 + s.Length;
15  return s.Length;    }       15  return s.Length;              }
```

Fig. 1. Synchronous and asynchronous C# programs (x, y are static variables).

task) may execute before some part of the awaited task or after the awaited task finished. For instance, on the middle of Fig. 1, the assignment y=1 at line 4 can execute before or after RdFile finishes. The await for ReadToEndAsync in RdFile (line 13) may suspend RdFile's execution because ReadToEndAsync did not finish, and pass the control to Main which executes y=1. If ReadToEndAsync finishes before this await executes, then the latter has no effect and y=1 gets executed after RdFile finishes. The resemblance with sequential code can be especially deceitful since this non-determinism is opaque. It is common that awaits are placed immediately after the corresponding call which limits the benefits that can be obtained from executing steps in the caller and callee concurrently [25].

In this paper, we address the problem of writing efficient asynchronous code that uses async/await. We propose a procedure for automated synthesis of asynchronous programs *equivalent* to a given synchronous (sequential) program *P*. This can be seen as a way of refactoring synchronous code to asynchronous code. Solving this problem in its full generality would require checking equivalence between arbitrary programs, which is known to be hard. Therefore, we consider a restricted space of asynchronous program candidates defined by substituting synchronous methods in *P* with asynchronous versions (assumed to be behaviorally equivalent). The substituted methods are assumed to be leaves of the call-tree (they do not call any method in *P*). Such programs are called *asynchronizations* of *P*. A practical instantiation is replacing IO synchronous calls for reading/writing files or managing http connections with asynchronous versions.

For instance, the sequential C# program on the left of Fig. 1 contains a Main that invokes a method RdFile that returns the length of the text in a file. The file name input to RdFile is an input to Main. The program uses a variable x to aggregate the lengths of all files accessed by RdFile; this would be more useful when Main calls RdFile multiple times which we omit for simplicity. Note that this program passes the assertion at line 7. The time consuming method ReadToEnd for reading a file is an obvious choice for being replaced with an equivalent *asynchronous* version whose name is suffixed with Async. Performing such tasks asynchronously can lead to significant performance boosts. The program on the middle of Fig. 1 is an example of an asynchronization defined by this substitution. The syntax of async/await imposes that every method that transitively calls one of the substituted methods, i.e., Main and RdFile, must also be

declared as asynchronous. Then, every asynchronous call must be followed by an
`await` that specifies the control location where that task should have completed.
For instance, the `await` for `ReadToEndAsync` is placed at line 13 since the next
instruction (at line 14) uses the computed value. Therefore, synthesizing such
refactoring reduces to finding a correct placement of `await`s (that implies equivalence) for every call of a method that transitively calls a substituted method
(we do not consider "deeper" refactoring like rewriting conditionals or loops).

We consider an equivalence relation between a synchronous program and an
asynchronization that corresponds to absence of data races in the asynchronization. Data race free asynchronizations are called *sound*. Relying on absence of
data races avoids reasoning about equality of sets of reachable states which is
harder in general, and an established compromise in reasoning about concurrency. For instance, the asynchronization in Fig. 1 is sound because the call to
`RdFile` accessing x finishes before the read of x in `Main` (line 6). Therefore,
accesses to x are performed in the same order as in the synchronous program.

The asynchronization on the right of Fig. 1 is not the only sound (data-race
free) asynchronization of the program on the left. The `await` at line 13 can
be moved one statement up (before the read of x) and the resulting program
remains equivalent to the sequential one. In this paper, we investigate the problem of enumerating *all* sound asynchronizations of a sequential program P w.r.t.
substituting a set of methods with asynchronous versions. This makes it possible to deal separately with the problem of choosing the best asynchronization in
terms of performance based on some metric (e.g., performance tests).

Identifying the most efficient asynchronization is difficult and can not be done
syntactically. It is tempting to consider that increasing the distance between calls
and matching `await`s so that more of the caller code is executed while waiting for
an asynchronous task to finish increases performance. However, this is not true
in general. We use the programs in Fig. 2 to show that the best `await` placement
w.r.t. performance depends on execution times of code blocks in between calls
and `await`s in a non-trivial manner. Note that estimating these execution times,
especially for IO operations like http connections, can not be done statically.

The programs in Fig. 2 use `Thread.Sleep(n)` to abstract sequential code
executing in n milliseconds and `Task.Delay(n)` to abstract an asynchronous call
executing in n milliseconds on a different thread. The functions named `Foo` differ
only in the position of `await t`. We show that modifying this position worsens
execution time in each case. For the left program, best performance corresponds
to maximal distance between `await t` in `Foo` and the corresponding call. This
allows the IO call to execute in parallel with the caller, as depicted on the bottom-
left of Fig. 2. The executions corresponding to the other two positions of `await`
t are given just above. For the middle program, placing `await t` in between the
two code blocks in `Foo` optimizes performance (note the extra IO call in `Main`):
the IO call in `Foo` executes in parallel with the first code block in `Foo` and the
IO call in `Main` executes in parallel with the second one. This is depicted on the
bottom-middle of Fig. 2. The execution above shows that placing `await t` as on
the left (after the two code blocks) leads to worse execution time (placing `await`
t immediately after the call is also worse). Finally, for the right program, placing

```
 1 async Task Main() {        1 async Task Main() {        1 async Task Main() {
 2   var t1 = Foo();           2   var t1 = Foo();           2   var t1 = Foo();
                               3   var t2 = IO();            3   var t2 = IO();
 4   await t1;                 4   await t1;                 4   await t1;
 5               }             5   await t2;       }         5   await t2;       }

 7 async Task Foo() {          7 async Task Foo() {          7 async Task Foo() {
 8   var t = IO();             8   var t = IO();             8   var t = IO();
                                                             9   await t;
10   Thread.Sleep(200);       10   Thread.Sleep(200);       10   Thread.Sleep(200);
                              11   await t;
12   Thread.Sleep(200);       12   Thread.Sleep(200);       12   Thread.Sleep(200);
13   await t;       }         13               }            13               }

15 async Task IO() {          15 async Task IO() {          15 async Task IO() {
16   var t0 = Task.Delay(300);16   var t0 = Task.Delay(300);16   var t0 = Task.Delay(300);
                                                            17   Thread.Sleep(150);
18   await t0;      }         18   await t0;      }         18   await t0;      }
```

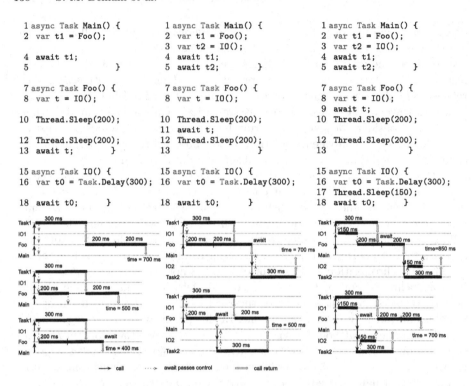

Fig. 2. Asynchronous C# programs and executions. On the bottom, time durations of executing code blocks from the same method are aligned horizontally, and time goes from left to right. Vertical single-line arrows represent method call steps, dashed arrows represent `awaits` passing control to the caller, and double-line arrows represent a call return. Total execution time is marked `time=....`

`await t` immediately after the call is best (note that `IO` executes another code block before `await`). The `IO` call in `Main` executes in parallel with `Foo` as shown on the bottom-right of Fig. 2. The execution above shows the case where `await` `t` is placed in the middle (the await has no effect because `IO` already finished, and `Foo` continues to execute). This leads to worse execution time (placing `await` `t` after the two code blocks is also worse). These differences in execution times have been confirmed by running the programs on a real machine.

As demonstrated by the examples in Fig. 2, the performance of an asynchronization depends on the execution environment, e.g., the overhead of IO operations like http connections and disk access (in Fig. 2, we use `Thread.Sleep(n)` or `Task.Delay(n)` to model such overheads). Since modeling the behavior of an execution environment w.r.t. performance is difficult in general, selecting the most performant asynchronization using static reasoning is also difficult. As a way of sidestepping this difficulty, we focus on enumerating *all* sound asynchronizations that allows to evaluate performance separately in a dynamic manner using performance tests for instance (for each sound asynchronization).

In the worst-case, the number of (sound) asynchronizations is exponential in the number of method calls in the program. Therefore, we focus on the *delay complexity* of the problem of enumerating sound asynchronizations, i.e., the complexity of the delay between outputting two consecutive (distinct) solutions, and show that this is polynomial time modulo an oracle for solving reachability (assertion checking) in *sequential* programs. Note that a trivial enumeration of all asynchronizations and checking equivalence for each one of them has an exponential delay complexity modulo an oracle for checking equivalence.

As an intermediate step, we consider the problem of computing *maximal* sound asynchronizations that maximize the distance between every call and its matching `await`. We show that rather surprisingly, there exists a *unique* maximal sound asynchronization. This is not trivial since asynchronizations can be incomparable w.r.t. distances between calls and `await`s (i.e., better for one `await` and worse for another, and vice-versa). This holds even if maximality is relative to a given asynchronization P_a imposing an upper bound on the distance between awaits and calls. In principle, avoiding data races could reduce to a choice between moving one await or another closer to the matching call. We show that this is not necessary because the maximal asynchronization is required to be equivalent to a *sequential* program, which executes statements in a fixed order.

As a more pragmatic approach, we define a procedure for computing sound asynchronizations which relies on a bottom-up interprocedural data-flow analysis. The placement of awaits is computed by traversing the call graph bottom up and using a data-flow analysis that computes read or write accesses made in the callees. We show that this procedure computes maximal sound asynchronizations of abstracted programs where every Boolean condition is replaced with a non-deterministic choice. These asynchronizations are sound for the concrete programs as well. This procedure enables a polynomial-time delay enumeration of sound asynchronizations of abstracted programs.

We implemented the asynchronization enumeration based on data-flow analysis in a prototype tool for C# programs. We evaluated this implementation on a number of non-trivial programs extracted from open source repositories to show that our techniques have the potential to become the basis of refactoring tools that allow programmers to improve their usage of async/await primitives.

In summary, this paper makes the following contributions:

- Define the problem of data race-free (sound) asynchronization synthesis for refactoring sequential code to equivalent asynchronous code (Sect. 3).
- Show that the problem of computing a sound asynchronization that maximizes the distance between calls and awaits has a unique solution (Sect. 4).
- The delay complexity of sound asynchronization synthesis (Sects. 5–6).
- A pragmatic algorithm for computing sound asynchronizations based on a data-flow analysis (Sect. 7).
- A prototype implementation of this algorithm and an evaluation of this prototype on a benchmark of non-trivial C# programs (Sect. 8).

Additional formalization and proofs are included in [3].

$\langle prog \rangle$ ::= **program** $\langle md \rangle$

$\langle md \rangle$ ::= **method** $\langle m \rangle$ { $\langle inst \rangle$ } | **async method** $\langle m \rangle$ { $\langle inst \rangle$ } | $\langle md \rangle$ $\langle md \rangle$

$\langle inst \rangle$ ::= $\langle x \rangle$:= $\langle le \rangle$ | $\langle r \rangle$:= $\langle x \rangle$ | $\langle r \rangle$:= **call** $\langle m \rangle$ | **return** | **await** $\langle r \rangle$
     | **await** * | **if** $\langle le \rangle$ {$\langle inst \rangle$} **else** {$\langle inst \rangle$} | **while** $\langle le \rangle$ {$\langle inst \rangle$} |
     $\langle inst \rangle$; $\langle inst \rangle$

Fig. 3. Syntax. $\langle m \rangle$, $\langle x \rangle$, and $\langle r \rangle$ represent method names, program and local variables, resp. $\langle le \rangle$ is an expression over local variables, or * which is non-deterministic choice.

2 Asynchronous Programs

We consider a simple programming language to formalize our approach, shown in Fig. 3. A *program* is a set of methods, including a distinguished **main**, which are classified as *synchronous* or *asynchronous*. Synchronous methods run continuously until completion when they are invoked. Asynchronous methods, marked using the keyword **async**, can run only partially and be interrupted when executing an **await**. Only asynchronous methods can use **await**, and all methods using **await** must be defined as asynchronous. We assume that methods are not (mutually) recursive. A program is called *synchronous* if it is a set of synchronous methods.

A method is defined by a name from a set $\mathbb{M}$ and a list of statements over a set $\mathbb{PV}$ of *program variables*, which can be accessed from different methods (ranged over using $x, y, z, \ldots$), and a set $\mathbb{LV}$ of method *local variables* (ranged over using $r, r_1, r_2, \ldots$). Input/return parameters are modeled using program variables. Each method call returns a *unique task identifier* from a set $\mathbb{T}$, used to record control dependencies imposed by **await**s (for uniformity, synchronous methods return a task identifier as well). Our language includes assignments, **await**s, **return**s, loops, and conditionals. Assignments to a local variable $r := x$, where x is a program variable, are called *reads* of x, and assignments to a program variable $x := le$ (le is an expression over local variables) are called *writes* to x. A *base* method is a method whose body does *not* contain method calls.

Asynchronous Methods. Asynchronous methods can use **await**s to wait for the completion of a task (invocation) while *the control is passed to their caller*. The parameter r of the **await** specifies the id of the awaited task. As a sound abstraction of awaiting the completion of an IO operation (reading or writing a file, an http request, etc.), which we do not model explicitly, we use a variation **await** *. This has

```
async method ReadToEndAsync() {
  await *;
  ind = Stream.index;
  len = Stream.content.Length;
  if (ind >= len)
    retVal = ""; return
  Stream.index = len;
  retVal = Stream.content(ind,len);
  return                          }
```

Fig. 4. An IO method.

a non-deterministic effect of either continuing to the next statement in the same method (as if the IO operation already completed), or passing the control to the caller (as if the IO operation is still pending).

Figure 4 lists our modeling of the IO method ReadToEndAsync used in Fig. 1. We use program variables to represent system resources such as the file system. The await for the completion of accesses to such resources is modeled by **await**

∗. This enables capturing racing accesses to system resources in asynchronous executions. Parameters or return values are modeled using program variables. ReadToEndAsync is modeled using reads/writes of the index/content of the input stream, and await ∗ models the await for their completion.

We assume that the body of every asynchronous method m satisfies several well-formedness syntactic constraints, defined on its control-flow graph (CFG). We recall that each node of the CFG represents a basic block of code (a maximal-length sequence of branch-free code), and nodes are connected by directed edges which represent a possible transfer of control between blocks. Thus,

1. every call $r :=$ call m' uses a distinct variable r (to store task identifiers),
2. every CFG block containing an await r is dominated by the CFG block containing the call $r :=$ call ... (i.e., every CFG path from the entry to the await has to pass through the call),
3. every CFG path starting from a block containing a call $r :=$ call ... to the exit has to pass through an await r statement.

The first condition simplifies the technical exposition, while the last two ensure that r stores a valid task identifier when executing an await r, and that every asynchronous invocation is awaited before the caller finishes. Languages like C# or Javascript do not enforce the latter constraint, but it is considered bad practice due to possible exceptions that may arise in the invoked task and are not caught. We forbid passing task identifiers as method parameters (which is possible in C#). A statement await r is said to *match* a statement $r :=$ call m'.

In Fig. 5, we give three examples of programs to explain in more details the well-formedness syntactic constraints. The program on the left of Fig. 5 does not satisfy the second condition since

```
async method m {
    while ∗
        r = call m1;

    await r;
}
```

```
async method m {
    r = call m1;

    if ∗
        await r;
}
```

```
async method m {
    r = call m1;
    while ∗
        r' = call m1;
        await r';
    await r;
}
```

Fig. 5. Examples of programs

await r can be reached without entering the loop. The program in the center of Fig. 5 does not satisfy the third condition since we can reach the end of the method without entering the if branch and thus, without executing await r. The program on the right of Fig. 5 satisfies both conditions.

Semantics. A program configuration is a tuple (g, stack, pend, cmpl, c-by, w-for) where g is composed of the valuation of the program variables excluding the program counter, stack is the call stack, pend is the set of asynchronous tasks, e.g., continuations predicated on the completion of some method call, cmpl is the set of completed tasks, c-by represents the relation between a method call and its caller, and w-for represents the control dependencies imposed by await statements. The activation frames in the call stack and the asynchronous tasks are represented using triples (i, m, ℓ) where $i \in \mathbb{T}$ is a task identifier, $m \in \mathbb{M}$ is a method name, and ℓ is a valuation of local variables, including as usual a dedicated program counter. The set of completed tasks is represented as a function cmpl : $\mathbb{T} \to \{\top, \bot\}$ such that cmpl$(i) = \top$ when i is completed and cmpl$(i) = \bot$, otherwise. We define c-by and w-for as partial functions $\mathbb{T} \rightharpoonup \mathbb{T}$

with the meaning that c-by$(i) = j$, resp., w-for$(i) = j$, iff i is called by j, resp., i is waiting for j. We set w-for$(i) = *$ if the task i was interrupted because of an `await *` statement.

The semantics of a program P is defined as a labeled transition system (LTS) $[P] = (\mathbb{C}, \text{Act}, \text{ps}_0, \rightarrow)$ where $\mathbb{C}$ is the set of program configurations, Act is a set of transition labels called *actions*, ps_0 is the initial configuration, and $\rightarrow \subseteq \mathbb{C} \times \text{Act} \times \mathbb{C}$ is the transition relation. Each program statement is interpreted as a transition in $[P]$. The set of actions is defined by (Aid is a set of action identifiers):

$$\text{Act} = \{(aid, i, ev) : aid \in \text{Aid}, i \in \mathbb{T}, ev \in \{\text{rd}(x), \text{wr}(x), \text{call}(j), \text{await}(k), \text{return},$$
$$\text{cont} : j \in \mathbb{T}, k \in \mathbb{T} \cup \{*\}, x \in \mathbb{PV}\}\}$$

The transition relation $\rightarrow$ is defined in Fig. 6. Transition labels are written on top of $\rightarrow$.

Transitions labeled by $(aid, i, \text{rd}(x))$ and $(aid, i, \text{wr}(x))$ represent a read and a write accesses to the program variable x, respectively, executed by the task (method call) with identifier i. A transition labeled by $(aid, i, \text{call}(j))$ corresponds to the fact that task i executes a method call that results in creating a task j. Task j is added on the top of the stack of currently executing tasks, declared pending (setting cmpl(j) to $\bot$), and c-by is updated to track its caller (c-by$(j) = i$). A transition (aid, i, return) represents the return from task i. Task i is removed from the stack of currently executing tasks, and cmpl(i) is set to $\top$ to record the fact that task i is finished.

A transition $(aid, i, \text{await}(j))$ relates to task i waiting asynchronously for task j. Its effect depends on whether task j is already completed. If this is the case (i.e., cmpl$[j] = \top$), task i continues and executes the next statement. Otherwise, task i executing the await is removed from the stack and added to the set of pending tasks, and w-for is updated to track the waiting-for relationship (w-for$(i) = j$). Similarly, a transition $(aid, i, \text{await}(*))$ corresponds to task i waiting asynchronously for the completion of an unspecified task. Non-deterministically, task i continues to the next statement, or task i is interrupted and transferred to the set of pending tasks (w-for(i) is set to $*$).

A transition (aid, i, cont) represents the scheduling of the continuation of task i. There are two cases depending on whether i waited for the completion of another task j modeled explicitly in the language (i.e., w-for$(i) = j$), or an unspecified task (i.e., w-for$(i) = *$). In the first case, the transition is enabled only when the call stack is empty and j is completed. In the second case, the transition is always enabled. The latter models the fact that methods implementing IO operations (waiting for unspecified tasks in our language) are executed in background threads and can interleave with the main thread (that executes the `Main` method). Although this may seem restricted because we do not allow arbitrary interleavings between IO methods and Main, this is actually sound when focusing on the existence of data races as in our approach. As shown later in Table 1, any two instructions that follow an `await *` are not happens-before related and form a race.

$$\frac{\texttt{r := x} \in \mathsf{inst}(\ell(\mathsf{pc})) \quad aid \in \mathsf{Aid\ fresh} \quad \ell' = \ell[r \mapsto \mathsf{g}(x), \mathsf{pc} \mapsto \mathsf{next}(\ell(\mathsf{pc}))]}{(\mathsf{g}, (i, m, \ell) \circ \mathsf{stack}, \_, \_, \_, \_) \xrightarrow{(aid,\, i,\, \mathsf{rd}(x))} (\mathsf{g}, (i, m, \ell') \circ \mathsf{stack}, \_, \_, \_, \_)}$$

$$\frac{\texttt{x := le} \in \mathsf{inst}(\ell(\mathsf{pc})) \quad aid \in \mathsf{Aid\ fresh} \quad \ell' = \ell[\mathsf{pc} \mapsto \mathsf{next}(\ell(\mathsf{pc}))] \quad \mathsf{g}' = \mathsf{g}[x \mapsto \ell(\texttt{le})]}{(\mathsf{g}, (i, m, \ell) \circ \mathsf{stack}, \_, \_, \_, \_) \xrightarrow{(aid,\, i,\, \mathsf{wr}(x))} (\mathsf{g}', (i, m, \ell') \circ \mathsf{stack}, \_, \_, \_, \_)}$$

$$\frac{\begin{array}{c}\texttt{r := call } m \in \mathsf{inst}(\ell(\mathsf{pc})) \quad aid \in \mathsf{Aid\ fresh} \quad \ell_0 = \mathsf{init}(\mathsf{g}, m) \quad j \in \mathbb{T}\ \mathsf{fresh}\\ \ell' = \ell[r \mapsto j, \mathsf{pc} \mapsto \mathsf{next}(\ell(\mathsf{pc}))] \quad \mathsf{cmpl}' = \mathsf{cmpl}[j \mapsto \bot] \quad \mathsf{c\text{-}by}' = \mathsf{c\text{-}by}[j \mapsto i]\end{array}}{(\mathsf{g}, (i, m', \ell) \circ \mathsf{stack}, \_, \mathsf{cmpl}, \mathsf{c\text{-}by}, \_) \xrightarrow{(aid,\, i,\, \mathsf{call}(j))} (\mathsf{g}, (j, m, \ell_0) \circ (i, m', \ell') \circ \mathsf{stack}, \_, \mathsf{cmpl}', \mathsf{c\text{-}by}', \_)}$$

$$\frac{\texttt{return} \in \mathsf{inst}(\ell(\mathsf{pc})) \quad aid \in \mathsf{Aid\ fresh} \quad \mathsf{cmpl}' = \mathsf{cmpl}[i \mapsto \top]}{(\mathsf{g}, (i, m, \ell) \circ \mathsf{stack}, \_, \mathsf{cmpl}, \_, \_) \xrightarrow{(aid,\, i,\, \mathsf{return})} (\mathsf{g}, \mathsf{stack}, \_, \mathsf{cmpl}', \_, \_)}$$

$$\frac{\texttt{await r} \in \mathsf{inst}(\ell(\mathsf{pc})) \quad aid \in \mathsf{Aid\ fresh} \quad \mathsf{cmpl}(\ell(r)) = \top \quad \ell' = \ell[\mathsf{pc} \mapsto \mathsf{next}(\ell(\mathsf{pc}))]}{(\mathsf{g}, (i, m, \ell) \circ \mathsf{stack}, \_, \mathsf{cmpl}, \_, \_) \xrightarrow{(aid,\, i,\, \mathsf{await}(\ell(r)))} (\mathsf{g}, (i, m, \ell') \circ \mathsf{stack}, \_, \mathsf{cmpl}, \_, \_)}$$

$$\frac{\begin{array}{c}\texttt{await r} \in \mathsf{inst}(\ell(\mathsf{pc})) \quad aid \in \mathsf{Aid\ fresh} \quad \mathsf{cmpl}(\ell(r)) = \bot \quad \mathsf{w\text{-}for}' = \mathsf{w\text{-}for}[i \mapsto \ell(r)]\\ \ell' = \ell[\mathsf{pc} \mapsto \mathsf{next}(\ell(\mathsf{pc}))]\end{array}}{(\mathsf{g}, (i, m, \ell) \circ \mathsf{stack}, \mathsf{pend}, \mathsf{cmpl}, \_, \mathsf{w\text{-}for}) \xrightarrow{(aid,\, i,\, \mathsf{await}(\ell(r)))} (\mathsf{g}, \mathsf{stack}, \{(i, m, \ell')\} \uplus \mathsf{pend}, \mathsf{cmpl}, \_, \mathsf{w\text{-}for}')}$$

$$\frac{\texttt{await *} \in \mathsf{inst}(\ell(\mathsf{pc})) \quad aid \in \mathsf{Aid\ fresh} \quad \ell' = \ell[\mathsf{pc} \mapsto \mathsf{next}(\ell(\mathsf{pc}))]}{(\mathsf{g}, (i, m, \ell) \circ \mathsf{stack}, \_, \_, \_, \_) \xrightarrow{(aid,\, i,\, \mathsf{await}(*))} (\mathsf{g}, (i, m, \ell') \circ \mathsf{stack}, \_, \_, \_, \_)}$$

$$\frac{\texttt{await *} \in \mathsf{inst}(\ell(\mathsf{pc})) \quad aid \in \mathsf{Aid\ fresh} \quad \mathsf{w\text{-}for}' = \mathsf{w\text{-}for}[i \mapsto *] \quad \ell' = \ell[\mathsf{pc} \mapsto \mathsf{next}(\ell(\mathsf{pc}))]}{(\mathsf{g}, (i, m, \ell) \circ \mathsf{stack}, \mathsf{pend}, \_, \_, \mathsf{w\text{-}for}) \xrightarrow{(aid,\, i,\, \mathsf{await}(*))} (\mathsf{g}, \mathsf{stack}, \{(i, m, \ell')\} \uplus \mathsf{pend}, \_, \_, \mathsf{w\text{-}for}')}$$

$$\frac{aid \in \mathsf{Aid\ fresh} \quad \mathsf{w\text{-}for}(i) = j \quad \mathsf{cmpl}(j) = \top}{(\mathsf{g}, \epsilon, \{(i, m, \ell)\} \uplus \mathsf{pend}, \mathsf{cmpl}, \_, \mathsf{w\text{-}for}) \xrightarrow{(aid,\, i,\, \mathsf{cont})} (\mathsf{g}, (i, m, \ell), \mathsf{pend}, \mathsf{cmpl}, \_, \mathsf{w\text{-}for})}$$

$$\frac{aid \in \mathsf{Aid\ fresh} \quad \mathsf{w\text{-}for}(i) = *}{(\mathsf{g}, \mathsf{stack}, \{(i, m, \ell)\} \uplus \mathsf{pend}, \_, \_, \mathsf{w\text{-}for}) \xrightarrow{(aid,\, i,\, \mathsf{cont})} (\mathsf{g}, (i, m, \ell) \circ \mathsf{stack}, \mathsf{pend}, \_, \_, \mathsf{w\text{-}for})}$$

Fig. 6. Program semantics. For a function f, we use $f[a \mapsto b]$ to denote a function g such that $g(c) = f(c)$ for all $c \neq a$ and $g(a) = b$. The function inst returns the instruction at some given control location while next gives the next instruction to execute. We use $\circ$ to denote sequence concatenation and init to denote the initial state of a method call.

By the definition of $\rightarrow$, every action $a \in \mathsf{Act} \setminus \{(\_, \_, \mathsf{cont})\}$ corresponds to executing some statement in the program, which is denoted by $\mathsf{S}(a)$.

An execution of P is a sequence $\rho = \mathsf{ps}_0 \xrightarrow{a_1} \mathsf{ps}_1 \xrightarrow{a_2} \ldots$ of transitions starting in the initial configuration ps_0 and leading to a configuration ps where the call stack and the set of pending tasks are empty. $\mathbb{C}[P]$ denotes the set of all program variable valuations included in configurations that are reached in executions of P. Since we are only interested in reasoning about the sequence of actions $a_1 \cdot a_2 \cdots$ labeling the transitions of an execution, we will call the latter an execution as well. The set of executions of a program P is denoted by $\mathbb{E}\mathrm{x}(P)$.

Traces. The *trace* of execution $\rho \in \mathbb{E}\mathrm{x}(P)$ is a tuple $\mathsf{tr}(\rho) = (\rho, \mathsf{MO}, \mathsf{CO}, \mathsf{SO}, \mathsf{HB})$ of strict partial orders between the actions in ρ defined in Table 1. The *method invocation order* MO records the order between actions in the same invocation, and the *call order* CO is an extension of MO that additionally orders actions before an invocation with respect to those inside that invocation. The *syn-*

chronous happens-before order SO orders the actions in an execution as if all the invocations were synchronous (even if the execution may contain asynchronous ones). It is an extension of CO where additionally, every action inside a callee is ordered before the actions following its invocation in the caller. The (asynchronous) *happens-before order* HB contains typical control-flow constraints: it is an extension of CO where every action a inside an asynchronous invocation is ordered before the corresponding await in the caller, and before the actions following its invocation in the caller if a precedes the first[1] await in MO (an invocation can be interrupted only when executing an await) or if the callee does not contain an await (it is synchronous). $\mathbb{Tr}(P)$ is the set of traces of P.

Table 1. Strict partial orders included in a trace. CO, SO, and HB are the smallest satisfying relations.

$a_1 <_\rho a_2$	a_1 occurs before a_2 in ρ and $a_1 \neq a_2$
$a_1 \sim a_2$	$a_1 = (\_, i, \_)$ and $a_2 = (\_, i, \_)$
$(a_1, a_2) \in$ MO	$a_1 \sim a_2 \wedge a_1 <_\rho a_2$
$(a_1, a_2) \in$ CO	$(a_1, a_2) \in$ MO $\vee$ $(a_1 = (\_, i, \mathsf{call}(j)) \wedge a_2 = (\_, j, \_))$
	$\vee (\exists a_3. (a_1, a_3) \in$ CO $\wedge (a_3, a_2) \in$ CO$)$
$(a_1, a_2) \in$ SO	$(a_1, a_2) \in$ CO $\vee (\exists a_3. (a_1, a_3) \in$ SO $\wedge (a_3, a_2) \in$ SO$)$
	$\vee (a_1 = (\_, j, \_) \wedge a_2 = (\_, i, \_) \wedge \exists a_3 = (\_, i, \mathsf{call}(j)). a_3 <_\rho a_2)$
$(a_1, a_2) \in$ HB	$(a_1, a_2) \in$ CO $\vee (\exists a_3. (a_1, a_3) \in$ HB $\wedge (a_3, a_2) \in$ HB$)$
	$\vee (a_1 = (\_, j, \_) \wedge a_2 = (\_, i, \_) \wedge \exists a_3 = (\_, i, \mathsf{await}(j)). a_3 <_\rho a_2)$
	$\vee (a_1 = (_, j, \mathsf{await}(i')) $ is the first await in $j \wedge$
	$a_2 = (\_, i, \_) \wedge \exists a_3 = (\_, i, \mathsf{call}(j)). a_3 <_\rho a_2)$
	$\vee (a_1 = (\_, j, \_) \wedge \nexists (\_, j, \mathsf{await}(\_)) \in \rho \wedge$
	$a_2 = (\_, i, \_) \wedge \exists a_3 = (\_, i, \mathsf{call}(j)). a_3 <_\rho a_2)$

On the right of Fig. 1, we show a trace where two statements (represented by the corresponding lines numbers) are linked by a dotted arrow if the corresponding actions are related by MO, a dashed arrow if the corresponding actions are related by CO but not by MO, and a solid arrow if the corresponding actions are related by the HB but not by CO.

3   Synthesizing Asynchronous Programs

Given a synchronous program P and a subset of *base* methods $L \subseteq P$, our goal is to synthesize *all* asynchronous programs P_a that are equivalent to P and that are obtained by substituting every method in L with an equivalent *asynchronous* version. The base methods are considered to be models of standard library calls (e.g., IO operations) and asynchronous versions are defined by inserting await * statements in their body. We use $P[L]$ to emphasize a subset of base methods L in a program P. Also, we call L a *library*. A library is called (a)synchronous when all methods are (a)synchronous.

---

[1] Code in between two awaits can execute before or after the control is returned to the caller, depending on whether the first awaited task finished or not.

Asynchronizations of a Synchronous Program. Let $P[L]$ be a synchronous program, and L_a a set of asynchronous methods obtained from those in L by inserting at least one `await *` statement in their body (and adding the keyword `sync`). Each method in L_a corresponds to a method in L with the same name, and vice-versa. $P_a[L_a]$ is called an *asynchronization* of $P[L]$ with respect to L_a if it is a syntactically correct program obtained by replacing the methods in L with those in L_a and adding `await` statements as necessary.

More precisely, let $L^* \subseteq P$ be the set of all methods of P that transitively call methods of L. Formally, L^* is the smallest set of methods that includes L and satisfies the following: if a method m calls $m' \in L^*$, then $m \in L^*$. Then, $P_a[L_a]$ is an *asynchronization* of $P[L]$ w.r.t. L_a if it is obtained from P as follows:

```
method m {            async method m {       async method m {
    r1 = call m1;         r1 = call m1;          r1 = call m1;
                          await r1;
    r2 = x;               r2 = x;                r2 = x;
                      }                      }      await r1;        }
method m1 {           async method m1 {      async method m1 {
                          await *                await *
    retVal = x;           retVal = x;            retVal = x;
    x = input;            x = input;             x = input;
    return;    }          return;        }       return;        }
```

Fig. 7. A program and its asynchronizations.

- Each method in L is replaced with the corresponding method from L_a.
- All methods in $L^* \setminus L$ are declared as asynchronous (because every call to an asynchronous method is followed by an `await` and any method using `await` must be asynchronous).
- For each invocation $r := $ `call` m of $m \in L^*$, add `await` statements `await` r satisfying the well-formedness syntactic constraints described in Sect. 2.

Figure 7 lists a synchronous program and its two asynchronizations, where $L = \{m1\}$ and $L^* = \{m, m1\}$. Asynchronizations differ only in the await placement.

$\mathsf{Asy}[P, L, L_a]$ is the set of all asynchronizations of $P[L]$ w.r.t. L_a. The *strong* asynchronization $\mathsf{strongAsy}[P, L, L_a]$ is an asynchronization where every `await` *immediately* follows the matching call. It reaches exactly the same set of program variable valuations as P.

Problem Definition. We investigate the problem of enumerating *all* asynchronizations of a given program w.r.t. a given asynchronous library, which are *sound*, in the sense that they do not admit data races. Two actions a_1 and a_2 in a trace $\tau = (\rho, \mathsf{MO}, \mathsf{CO}, \mathsf{SO}, \mathsf{HB})$ are *concurrent* if $(a_1, a_2) \notin \mathsf{HB}$ and $(a_2, a_1) \notin \mathsf{HB}$.

An ansynchronous program P_a admits a *data race* (a_1, a_2), where $(a_1, a_2) \in \mathsf{SO}$, if a_1 and a_2 are two concurrent actions of a trace $\tau \in \mathsf{Tr}(P_a)$, and a_1 and a_2 are read or write accesses to the same program variable x, and at least one of them is a write. We write data races as ordered pairs w.r.t. SO to simplify the definition of the algorithms in the next sections. Also, note that traces of *synchronous* programs can *not* contain concurrent actions, and therefore they do not admit data races. $\mathsf{strongAsy}[P, L, L_a]$ does not admit data races as well.

$P_a[L_a]$ is called *sound* when it does not admit data races. The absence of data races implies equivalence to the original program, in the sense of reaching the same set of configurations (program variable valuations).

Definition 1. *For a synchronous program $P[L]$ and asynchronous library L_a, the* asychronization synthesis problem *asks to enumerate all sound asynchronizations in* $\mathsf{Asy}[P, L, L_a]$.

4   Enumerating Sound Asynchronizations

We present an algorithm for solving asynchronization synthesis, which relies on a partial order between asynchronizations that guides the enumeration of possible solutions. The partial order takes into account the distance between calls and corresponding awaits. Figure 8 pictures the partial order for asynchronizations of the program on the left of Fig. 1. Each asynchronization is written as a vector of distances, the first (second) element is the number of statements between await t1 (await t) and the matching call (we count only statements that appear in the sequential program). The edges connect comparable elements, smaller elements being below bigger elements. The asynchronization on the middle of Fig. 1 corresponds to the vector $(1,1)$. The highlighted elements constitute the set of all sound asynchronizations. The strong asynchronization corresponds to the vector $(0,0)$.

$(2,1)$

$(2,0)$ $(1,1)$

$(1,0)$ $(0,1)$

$(0,0)$

Fig. 8. The partially-ordered set of asynchronizations of the program on the left of Fig. 1.

Formally, an await statement s_w in a method m of an asynchronization $P_a[L_a] \in \mathsf{Asy}[P, L, L_a]$ *covers* a read/write statement s in P if there exists a path in the CFG of m from the call statement matching s_w to s_w that contains s. The set of statements covered by an await s_w is denoted by $\mathsf{Cover}(s_w)$. We compare asynchronizations in terms of sets of statements covered by awaits that match the same call from the synchronous program $P[L]$. Since asynchronizations are obtained by adding awaits, every call in asynchronization $P_a[L_a] \in \mathsf{Asy}[P, L, L_a]$ corresponds to a *fixed* call in $P[L]$. Therefore, for two asynchronizations $P_a, P'_a \in \mathsf{Asy}[P, L, L_a]$, P_a is *smaller* than P'_a, denoted by $P_a \leq P'_a$, iff for every await s_w in P_a, there exists an await s'_w in P'_a that matches the same call as s_w, such that $\mathsf{Cover}(s_w) \subseteq \mathsf{Cover}(s'_w)$. For example, the two asynchronous programs in Fig. 7 are ordered by $\leq$ since $\mathsf{Cover}(\text{await } r1) = \{\}$ in the first and $\mathsf{Cover}(\text{await } r1) = \{r2 = x\}$ in the second. Note that the strong asynchronization is smaller than every other asynchronization. Also, note that $\leq$ has a unique maximal element that is called the weakest asynchronization and denoted by $\mathsf{wkAsy}[P, L, L_a]$. In Fig. 8, the weakest asynchronization corresponds to the vector $(2,1)$.

In the following, we say *moving an await down (resp., up)* when moving the await further away from (resp. closer to) the matching call while preserving well-formedness conditions in Sect. 2. Further away or closer to means increasing or decreasing the set of statements that are covered by the await. For instance, if an await s_w in a program P_a is preceded by a while loop, then *moving it up* means moving it before the whole loop and not inside the loop body. Otherwise, the third well-formedness condition would be violated.

Relative Maximality. A crucial property of this partial order is that for every asynchronization P_a, there exists a *unique* maximal asynchronization that is smaller than P_a and that is sound. Formally, an asynchronization P'_a is called a *maximal asynchronization of P relative to P_a* if (1) $P'_a \leq P_a$, P'_a is sound, and (2) $\forall\, P''_a \in \mathsf{Asy}[P, L, L_a]$. P''_a is sound and $P''_a \leq P_a \Rightarrow P''_a \leq P'_a$.

Algorithm 1. An algorithm for enumerating all sound asynchronizations (these asynchronizations are obtained as a result of the **output** instruction). MAXREL returns the maximal asynchronization of P relative to P_a

```
1: procedure ASYSYN(P_a, s_w)
2:     P'_a ← MAXREL(P_a);
3:     output P'_a;
4:     P ← ImPred(P'_a, s_w);
5:     for each (P''_a, s''_w) ∈ P
6:         ASYSYN(P''_a, s''_w);
```

Lemma 1. *Given an asynchronization $P_a \in \mathsf{Asy}[P, L, L_a]$, there exists a unique program P'_a that is a maximal asynchronization of P relative to P_a.*

The asynchronization P'_a exists because the bottom element of $\leq$ is sound. To prove uniqueness, assume by contradiction that there exist two incomparable maximal asynchronizations P^1_a and P^2_a and select the first await s^1_w w.r.t. the control-flow of the sequential program that is placed in different positions in the two programs. Assume that s^1_w is closer to its matching call in P^1_a. Then, we move s^1_w in P^1_a further away from its matching call to the same position as in P^2_a. This modification does not introduce data races since P^2_a is data race free. Thus, the resulting program is data race free, bigger than P^1_a, and smaller than P_a w.r.t. $\leq$ contradicting the fact that P^1_a is a maximal asynchronization.

4.1 Enumeration Algorithm

Our algorithm for enumerating all sound asynchronizations is given in Algorithm 1 as a recursive procedure ASYSYN that we describe in two phases.

First, ignore the second argument of ASYSYN (in blue), which represents an **await** statement. For an asynchronization P_a, ASYSYN outputs *all* sound asynchronizations that are smaller than P_a. It uses MAXREL to compute the maximal asynchronization P'_a of P relative to P_a, and then, calls itself recursively for all immediate predecessors of P'_a. ASYSYN outputs all sound asynchronizations of P when given as input the weakest asynchronization of P.

Recursive calls on immediate predecessors are necessary because the set of sound asynchronizations is not downward-closed w.r.t. $\leq$. For instance, the asynchronization on the right of Fig. 9 is an immediate predecessor of the sound asynchronization on the left but it has a data race on x.

The delay complexity of this algorithm remains exponential in general, since a sound asynchronization may be outputted multiple times. Asynchroniza-

```
async method m {        async method m {
    r1 = call m1;            r1 = call m1;
    r2 = x;                  r2 = x;
    await r1;      }         await r1;      }
async method m1 {       async method m1 {
    r3 = call m2;            r3 = call m2;
    x = x + 1;              await r3;
    await r3;      }         x = x + 1;     }
async method m2 {       async method m2 {
    await *                  await *
    retVal = input;         retVal = input;
    return;        }         return;        }
```

Fig. 9. Asynchronizations.

tions are only partially ordered by $\leq$ and different chains of recursive calls starting in different immediate predecessors may end up outputting the same solution. For instance, for the asynchronizations in Fig. 8, the asynchronization $(0,0)$ will be outputted twice because it is an immediate predecessor of both $(1,0)$ and $(0,1)$.

To avoid this redundancy, we use a refinement of the above that *restricts* the set of immediate predecessors available for a (recursive) call of AsySyn. This is based on a *strict total order* $\prec_w$ between awaits in a program P_a that follows a topological ordering of its inter-procedural CFG, i.e., if s_w occurs before s'_w in the body of a method m, then $s_w \prec_w s'_w$, and if s_w occurs in a method m and s'_w occurs in a method m' s.t. m (indirectly) calls m', then $s_w \prec_w s'_w$. Therefore, AsySyn takes an await statement s_w as a second parameter, which is initially the maximal element w.r.t. $\prec_w$, and it calls itself only on immediate predecessors of a solution obtained by *moving up* an await s''_w *smaller than or equal to* s_w w.r.t. $\prec_w$. The recursive call on that predecessor will receive as input s''_w. Formally, this relies on a function ImPred that returns pairs of immediate predecessors and await statements defined as follows:

$$\mathsf{ImPred}(P'_a, s_w) = \{(P''_a, s''_w) : P''_a < P'_a \text{ and } \forall P'''_a \in \mathsf{Asy}[P, L, L_a].P'''_a < P'_a \Rightarrow P'''_a \le P''_a$$
$$\text{and } s''_w \preceq_w s_w \text{ and } P''_a \in P'_a \uparrow s''_w \}$$

($P'_a \uparrow s''_w$ is the set of asynchronizations obtained from P'_a by changing *only* the position of s''_w, moving it up w.r.t. the position in P'_a). For instance, looking at immediate predecessors of $(1,1)$ in Fig. 8, $(0,1)$ is obtained by moving the *first* await in $\prec_w$. Therefore, the recursive call on $(0,1)$ computes the maximal asynchronization relative to $(0,1)$, which is $(0,1)$, and stops (ImPred returns $\emptyset$ because the input s_w is the minimal element of $\prec_w$, and already immediately after the call). Its immediate predecessor is explored when recursing on $(1,0)$.

Algorithm 1 outputs all sound asynchronizations because after having computed a maximal asynchronization P'_a in a recursive call with parameter s_w, any smaller sound asynchronization is smaller than a predecessor in $\mathsf{ImPred}(P'_a, s_w)$. Also, it can not output the same asynchonization twice. Let P^1_a and P^2_a be two predecessors in $\mathsf{ImPred}(P'_a, s_w)$ obtained by moving up the awaits s^1_w and s^2_w, respectively, and assume that $s^1_w \prec_w s^2_w$. Then, all solutions computed in the recursive call on P^1_a will have s^2_w placed as in P'_a while all the solutions computed in the recursive call on P^2_a will have s^2_w closer to the matching call. Therefore, the sets of solutions computed in these two recursion branches are distinct.

Theorem 1. AsySyn*(wkAsy$[P, L, L_a]$, s_w) where s_w is the maximal await in* wkAsy$[P, L, L_a]$ *w.r.t.* $\prec_w$ *outputs all sound asynchronizations of $P[L]$ w.r.t.* L_a.

The delay complexity of Algorithm 1 is polynomial time modulo an oracle that returns a maximal asynchronization relative to a given one. In the next section, we show that the latter problem can be reduced in polynomial time to the reachability problem in sequential programs.

5   Computing Maximal Asynchronizations

In this section, we present an implementation of the procedure MaxRel that relies on a reachability oracle. In particular, we first describe an approach for computing the maximal asynchronization relative to a given asynchronization P_a, which can be seen as a way of repairing P_a so that it becomes data-race free. Intuitively, we repeatedly eliminate data races in P_a by moving certain await statements closer to the matching calls. The data races in P_a (if any) are enumerated in a certain order that prioritizes data races between actions that occur first in executions of the original synchronous program. This order allows to avoid superfluous repair steps.

5.1   Data Race Ordering

An action a representing a read/write access in a trace τ of an asynchronization P_a of P is *synchronously reachable* if there is an action a' in a trace τ' of P that represents the same statement, i.e., $\mathsf{S}(a) = \mathsf{S}(a')$. It can be proved that any trace of an asynchronization contains a data race if it contains a data race between two synchronously reachable actions (see Appendix C in [3]). In the following, we focus on data races between actions that are synchronously reachable.

We define an order between such data races based on the order between actions in executions of the original synchronous program P. This order relates data races in possibly different executions or asynchronizations of P, which is possible because each action in a data race corresponds to a statement in P.

For two read/write statements s and s', $s \prec s'$ denotes the fact that there is an execution of P in which the *first* time s is executed occurs before the *first* time s' is executed. For two actions a and a' in an execution/trace of an asynchronization, generated by two read/write statements $s = \mathsf{S}(a)$ and $s' = \mathsf{S}(a')$, $a \prec_{\mathsf{SO}} a'$ holds if $s \prec s'$ and either $s' \not\prec s$ or s' is reachable from s in the interprocedural[2] control-flow graph of P without taking any back edge[3]. For a *deterministic* synchronous program (admitting a single execution), $a \prec_{\mathsf{SO}} a'$ iff $\mathsf{S}(a) \prec \mathsf{S}(a')$. For non-deterministic programs, when $\mathsf{S}(a)$ and $\mathsf{S}(a')$ are contained in a loop body, it is possible that $\mathsf{S}(a) \prec \mathsf{S}(a')$ and $\mathsf{S}(a') \prec \mathsf{S}(a)$. In this case, we use the control-flow order to break the tie between a and a'.

The order between data races corresponds to the colexicographic order induced by $\prec_{\mathsf{SO}}$. This is a partial order since actions may originate from different control-flow paths and are incomparable w.r.t. $\prec_{\mathsf{SO}}$.

Definition 2 (Data Race Order). *Given two races (a_1, a_2) and (a_3, a_4) admitted by (possibly different) asynchronizations of a synchronous program P, we have that $(a_1, a_2) \prec_{\mathsf{SO}} (a_3, a_4)$ iff $a_2 \prec_{\mathsf{SO}} a_4$, or $a_2 = a_4$ and $a_1 \prec_{\mathsf{SO}} a_3$.*

Repairing a minimal data race (a_1, a_2) w.r.t. $\prec_{\mathsf{SO}}$ removes any other data race (a_1, a_4) with $(a_2, a_4) \in \mathsf{HB}$ (note that we cannot have $(a_4, a_2) \notin \mathsf{HB}$ since $a_2 \prec_{\mathsf{SO}} a_4$). The repair will enforce that $(a_1, a_2) \in \mathsf{HB}$ which implies that $(a_1, a_4) \in \mathsf{HB}$.

---

[2] The interprocedural graph is the union of the control-flow graphs of each method along with edges from call sites to entry nodes, and from exit nodes to return sites.
[3] A back edge points to a block that has already been met during a depth-first traversal of the control-flow graph, and corresponds to loops.

5.2 Repairing Data Races

Repairing a data race (a_1, a_2) reduces to modifying the position of a certain await. We consider only repairs where awaits are moved up (closer to the matching call). The "completeness" of this set of repairs follows from the particular order in which we enumerate data races.

Let s_1 and s_2 be the statements generating a_1 and a_2. In general, there exists a method m that (transitively) calls another asynchronous method $m1$ that contains s_1 and before awaiting for $m1$ it (transitively) calls a method $m2$ that executes s_2. This is pictured in Fig. 10. It is also possible that m itself contains s_2 (see the program on the right of Fig. 7). The repair consists in moving the await for $m1$ before

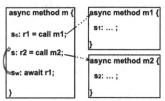

Fig. 10. A data race repair.

the call to $m2$ since this implies that s_1 will always execute before s_2 (and the corresponding actions are related by happens-before).

Formally, any two racing actions have a common ancestor in the call order CO which is a call action. The least common ancestor of a_1 and a_2 in CO among call actions is denoted by $\mathsf{LCA_{CO}}(a_1, a_2)$. In Fig. 10, it corresponds to the call statement s_c. More precisely, $\mathsf{LCA_{CO}}(a_1, a_2)$ is a call action $a_c = (\_, i, \mathsf{call}(j))$ s.t. $(a_c, a_1) \in \mathsf{CO}$, $(a_c, a_2) \in \mathsf{CO}$, and for each other call action a_c', if $(a_c, a_c') \in \mathsf{CO}$ then $(a_c', a_1) \notin \mathsf{CO}$. This call action represents an asynchronous call for which the matching await s_w must move to repair the data race. The await should be moved before the last statement in the same method generating an action which precedes a_2 in the reflexive closure of call order (statement s in Fig. 10). This way every statement that follows s_c in call order will be executed before s and before any statement which succeeds s in call order, including s_2. Note that moving the await s_w anywhere after s will not affect the concurrency between a_1 and a_2.

The pair (s_c, s) is called the *root cause* of the data race (a_1, a_2). We denote by $\mathsf{RDR}(P_a, s_c, s)$ the maximal asynchronization P_a' smaller than P_a w.r.t. $\leq$, s.t. no await statement matching s_c occurs after s on a CFG path.

5.3 A Procedure for Computing Maximal Asynchronizations

Given an asynchronization P_a, the procedure MAXREL in Algorithm 2 computes the maximal asynchronization relative to P_a by repairing data races iteratively until the program becomes data race free. The sub-procedure $\mathsf{RCMINDR}(P_a')$ computes the root cause of a minimal data race (a_1, a_2) of P_a' w.r.t. $\prec_{\mathsf{so}}$ such that the two actions are synchronously reachable. If P_a' is data race free, then $\mathsf{RCMINDR}(P_a')$ returns $\perp$. The following theorem states the correctness of MAXREL.

Theorem 2. *Given an asynchronization $P_a \in \mathsf{Asy}[P, L, L_a]$, MAXREL($P_a$) returns the maximal asynchronization of P relative to P_a.*

Algorithm 2. The procedure MaxRel to find the maximal asynchronization of P relative to P_a.

```
1: procedure MaxRel(P_a)
2:     P'_a ← P_a
3:     root ← RCMinDR(P'_a)
4:     while root ≠ ⊥
5:         P'_a ← RDR(P'_a, root)
6:         root ← RCMinDR(P'_a)
7:     return P'_a
```

MaxRel(P_a) repairs a number of data races which is linear in the size of the input. Indeed, each repair results in moving an await closer to the matching call and before at least one more statement from the original program P.

The problem of computing root causes of minimal data races is reducible to reachability (assertion checking) in sequential programs. This reduction builds on a program instrumentation for checking if there exists a data race that involves two given statements (s_1, s_2) that are reachable in an executions of P. This instrumentation is used in an iterative process where pairs of statements are enumerated according to the colexicographic order induced by $\prec$. For lack of space, we present only the main ideas of the instrumentation (see Appendix D in [3]). The instrumentation simulates executions of an asynchronization P_a using non-deterministic synchronous code where methods may be only partially executed (modeling await interruptions). Immediately after executing s_1, the current invocation t_1 is interrupted (by executing a return added by the instrumentation). The active invocations that transitively called t_1 are also interrupted when reaching an await for an invocation in this call chain (the other invocations are executed until completion as in the synchronous semantics). When reaching s_2, if s_1 has already been executed and at least one invocation has been interrupted, which means that s_1 is concurrent with s_2, then the instrumentation stops with an assertion violation. The instrumentation also computes the root cause of the data race using additional variables for tracking call dependencies.

6   Asymptotic Complexity of Asynchronization Synthesis

We state the complexity of the asynchronization synthesis problem. Algorithm 1 shows that the delay complexity of this problem is polynomial-time in the number of statements in input program modulo the complexity of computing a maximal asynchronization, which Algorithm 2 shows to be polynomial-time reducible to reachability in sequential programs. Since the reachability problem is PSPACE-complete for finite-state sequential programs [16], we get the following:

Theorem 3. *The output complexity[4] and delay complexity of the asynchroniza- tion synthesis problem is polynomial time modulo an oracle for reachability in sequential programs, and PSPACE for finite-state programs.*

This result is optimal, i.e., checking whether there exists a sound asynchro- nization which is different from the trivial strong synchronization is PSPACE- hard (follows from a reduction from the reachability problem). See Appendices D and E in [3] for the detailed formal proofs.

7   Asynchronization Synthesis Using Data-Flow Analysis

In this section, we present a refinement of Algorithm 2 that relies on a bottom- up inter-procedural data flow analysis. The analysis is used to compute maximal asynchronizations for abstractions of programs where every Boolean condition (in if-then-else or while statements) is replaced with the non-deterministic choice $*$, and used as an implementation of MAXREL in Algorithm 1.

For a program P, we define an abstraction $P^{\#}$ where every conditional if $\langle le \rangle$ $\{S_1\}$ else $\{S_2\}$ is rewritten to if $*$ $\{S_1\}$ else $\{S_2\}$, and every while $\langle le \rangle$ $\{S\}$ is rewritten to if $*$ $\{S\}$. Besides adding the non-deterministic choice $*$, loops are unrolled exactly once. Every asynchronization P_a of P corresponds to an abstraction $P_a^{\#}$ obtained by applying exactly the same rewriting. $P^{\#}$ is a sound abstraction of P in terms of sound asynchronizations it admits. Unrolling loops once is sound because every asynchronous call in a loop iteration should be awaited for in the same iteration (see the syntactic constraints in Sect. 2).

Theorem 4. *If $P_a^{\#}$ is a sound asynchronization of $P^{\#}$ w.r.t. L_a, then P_a is a sound asynchronization of P w.r.t. L_a.*

The procedure for computing maximal asynchronizations of $P^{\#}$ relative to a given asynchronization $P_a^{\#}$ traverses methods of $P_a^{\#}$ in a bottom-up fash- ion, detects data races using summaries of read/write accesses computed using a straightforward data-flow analysis, and repairs data races using the schema presented in Sect. 5.2. Applying this procedure to a real programming language requires an alias analysis to detect statements that may access the same memory location (this is trivial in our language which is used to simplify the exposition).

We consider an enumeration of methods called *bottom-up order*, which is the reverse of a topological ordering of the call graph[5]. For each method m, let $\mathcal{R}(m)$ be the set of program variables that m can read, which is defined as the union of $\mathcal{R}(m')$ for every method m' called by m and the set of program variables read in statements in the body of m. The set of variables $\mathcal{W}(m)$ that m can write is defined in a similar manner. We define RW-var$(m) = (\mathcal{R}(m), \mathcal{W}(m))$. We extend the notation RW-var to statements as follows: RW-var$(\langle r \rangle := \langle x \rangle) = (\{x\}, \emptyset)$, RW-var$(\langle x \rangle := \langle le \rangle) = (\emptyset, \{x\})$, RW-var$(r := \text{call } m) = \text{RW-var}(m)$,

---

[4] Note that all asynchronizations can be enumerated with polynomial space.
[5] The nodes of the call graph are methods and there is an edge from a method m_1 to a method m_2 if m_1 contains a call statement that calls m_2.

and RW-var$(s) = (\emptyset, \emptyset)$, for any other type of statement s. Also, let CRW-var(m) be the set of read or write accesses that m can do and that can be concurrent with accesses that a caller of m can do after calling m. These correspond to read/write statements that follow an `await` in m, or to accesses in CRW-var(m') for a method m' called by m. These sets of accesses can be computed using the following data-flow analysis: for all methods $m \in P_a^{\#}$ in bottom-up order, and for each statement s in the body of m from begin to end,

- if s is a call to m' and s is *not* reachable from an `await` in the CFG of m
  - CRW-var$(m) \leftarrow$ CRW-var$(m) \cup$ CRW-var(m')
- if s is reachable from an `await` statement in the CFG of m
  - CRW-var$(m) \leftarrow$ CRW-var$(m) \cup$ RW-var(s)

We use $(\mathcal{R}_1, \mathcal{W}_1) \bowtie (\mathcal{R}_2, \mathcal{W}_2)$ to denote the fact that $\mathcal{W}_1 \cap (\mathcal{R}_2 \cup \mathcal{W}_2) \neq \emptyset$ or $\mathcal{W}_2 \cap (\mathcal{R}_1 \cup \mathcal{W}_1) \neq \emptyset$ (i.e., a conflict between read/write accesses). We define the procedure MAXREL$^{\#}$ that given an asynchronization $P_a^{\#}$ works as follows:

- for all methods $m \in P_a^{\#}$ in bottom-up order, and for each statement s in the body of m from begin to end,
  - if s occurs between $r := $ `call` m' and `await` r (for some m'), and RW-var$(s) \bowtie$ CRW-var(m'), then $P_a^{\#} \leftarrow$ RDR$(P_a^{\#}, r := $ `call` $m', s)$
- return $P_a^{\#}$

Theorem 5. *The procedure* MAXREL$^{\#}(P_a^{\#})$ *returns a maximal asynchronization relative to* $P_a^{\#}$.

Since MAXREL$^{\#}$ is based on a single bottom-up traversal of the call graph of the input asynchronization $P_a^{\#}$ we get the following result.

Theorem 6. *The delay complexity of the asynchronization synthesis problem restricted to abstracted programs* $P^{\#}$ *is polynomial time.*

8   Experimental Evaluation

We present an empirical evaluation of our asynchronization synthesis approach, where maximal asynchronizations are computed using the data-flow analysis in Sect. 7. Our benchmark consists mostly of asynchronous C# programs from open-source GitHub projects. We evaluate the effectiveness in reproducing the original program as an asynchronization of a program where asynchronous calls are reverted to synchronous calls, along with other sound asynchronizations.

Implementation. We developed a prototype tool that uses the Roslyn .NET compiler platform [27] to construct CFGs for methods in a C# program. This prototype supports C# programs written in static single assignment (SSA) form that include basic conditional/looping constructs and async/await as concurrency primitives. Note that object fields are interpreted as program variables in the terminology of Sect. 2 (data races concern accesses to object fields). It assumes that alias information is provided apriori; these constraints can be removed in the future with more engineering effort. In general, our synthesis procedure is compatible with any sound alias analysis. The precision of this analysis impacts only the set (number) of asynchronizations outputted by the procedure (a more precise analysis may lead to more sound asynchronizations).

The tool takes as input a possibly asynchronous program, and a mapping between synchronous and asynchronous variations of base methods in this program. It reverts every asynchronous call to a synchronous call, and it enumerates sound asynchronizations of the obtained program (using Algorithm 1).

Benchmark. Our evaluation uses a benchmark listed in Table 2, which contains 5 synthetic examples (variations of the program in Fig. 1), 9 programs extracted from open-source C# GitHub projects (their name is a prefix of the repository name), and 2 programs inspired by questions on stackoverflow.com about async/await in C# (their name ends in Stackoverflow). Overall, there are 13 base methods involved in computing asynchronizations of these programs (having both synchronous and asynchronous versions), coming from 5 C#

Table 2. Empirical results. Syntactic characteristics of input programs: lines of code (loc), number of methods (m), number of method calls (c), number of asynchronous calls (ac), number of awaits that *could* be placed at least one statement away from the matching call ($\text{await}_{\#}$). Data concerning the enumeration of asynchronizations: number of awaits that *were* placed at least one statement away from the matching call (await), number of races discovered and repaired (races), number of statements that the awaits in the maximal asynchronization are covering *more than* in the input program (cover), number of computed asynchronizations (async), and running time (t).

Program	loc	m	c	ac	$\text{await}_{\#}$	await	races	cover	async	t(s)
SyntheticBenchmark-1	77	3	6	5	4	4	5	0	9	1.4
SyntheticBenchmark-2	115	4	12	10	6	3	3	0	8	1.4
SyntheticBenchmark-3	168	6	16	13	9	7	4	0	128	1.5
SyntheticBenchmark-4	171	6	17	14	10	8	5	0	256	1.9
SyntheticBenchmark-5	170	6	17	14	10	8	9	0	272	2
Azure-Remote	520	10	14	5	0	0	0	0	1	2.2
Azure-Webjobs	190	6	14	6	1	1	0	1	3	1.6
FritzDectCore	141	7	11	8	1	1	0	1	2	1.6
MultiPlatform	53	2	6	4	2	2	0	2	4	1.1
NetRpc	887	13	18	11	4	1	3	0	3	2
Scoreboards	43	3	3	3	0	0	0	0	1	1.5
VBForums-Viewer	275	7	10	7	3	2	1	1	6	1.8
Voat	178	3	5	5	2	1	1	1	3	1.2
WordpressRESTClient	133	3	10	8	4	2	1	0	4	1.7
ReadFile-Stackoverflow	47	2	3	3	1	0	1	0	1	1.5
UI-Stackoverflow	50	3	4	4	3	3	3	0	12	1.5

libraries (*System.IO*, *System.Net*, *Windows.Storage*, *Microsoft.WindowsAzure.-
Storage*, and *Microsoft.Azure.Devices*). They are modeled as described in Sect. 2.

Evaluation. The last five columns of Table 2 list data concerning the application
of our tool. The column async lists the number of outputted sound asynchronizations. In general, the number of asynchronizations depends on the number
of invocations (column ac) and the size of the code blocks between an invocation
and the instruction using its return value (column await$_\#$ gives the number of
non-empty blocks). The number of *sound* asynchronizations depends roughly, on
how many of these code blocks are racing with the method body. These asynchronizations contain awaits that are at a non-zero distance from the matching
call (non-zero values in column await) and for many Github programs, this distance is bigger than in the original program (non-zero values in column cover).
This shows that we are able to increase the distances between awaits and their
matching calls for those programs. The distance between awaits and matching
calls in maximal asynchronizations of non synthetic benchmarks is 1.27 statements on average. A statement representing a method call is counted as one
independently of the method's body size. With a single level of inlining, the
number of statements becomes 2.82 on average. However, these statements are
again, mostly IO calls (access to network or disk) or library calls (string/bytes
formatting methods) whose execution time is not negligible. The running times
for the last three synthetic benchmarks show that our procedure is scalable when
programs have a large number of sound asynchronizations.

   With few exceptions, each program admits multiple sound asynchronizations
(values in column async bigger than one), which makes the focus on the delay
complexity relevant. This leaves the possibility of making a choice based on
other criteria, e.g., performance metrics. As shown by the examples in Fig. 2,
their performance can be derived only dynamically (by executing them). These
results show that our techniques have the potential of becoming the basis of a
refactoring tool allowing programmers to improve their usage of the async/await
primitives. The artifact is available at [2].

9   Related Work

There are many works on synthesizing or repairing concurrent programs in the
standard multi-threading model, e.g., automatic parallelization in compilers [1,
7,19], or synchronization synthesis [6,10–12,18,24,30,31]. We focus on the use
of async/await which poses specific challenges not covered in these works.

   Our semantics without await * instructions is equivalent to the semantics
defined in [4,28]. But, to simplify the exposition, we consider a more restricted
programming language. For the modeling of asynchronous IO operations, we
follow [4] with the restriction that the code following an await * is executed
atomically. This is sound when focusing on data-race freedom because even if
executed atomically, any two instructions from different asynchronous IO operations (following await *) are not happens-before related.

Program Refactoring. Program refactoring tools have been proposed for converting C# programs using explicit callbacks into async/await programs [25] or Android programs using AsyncTask into programs that use IntentService [22]. The C# tool [25], which is the closest to our work, makes it possible to repair misusage of async/await that might result in deadlocks. This tool cannot modify procedure calls to be asynchronous as in our work. A static analysis based technique for refactoring JavaScript programs is proposed in [17]. As opposed to our work, this refactoring technique is unsound in general. It requires that programmers review the refactoring for correctness, which is error-prone. Also, in comparison to [17], we carry a formal study of the more general problem of finding all sound asynchronizations and investigate its complexity.

Data Race Detection. Many works study dynamic data race detection using happens-before and lock-set analysis, or timing-based detection [14,20,21,26,29]. They could be used to approximate our reduction from data race checking to reachability in sequential programs. Some works [5,13,23] propose static analyses for finding data races. [5] designs a compositional data race detector for multi-threaded Java programs, based on an inter-procedural analysis assuming that any two public methods can execute in parallel. Similar to [28], they precompute method summaries to extract potential racy accesses. These approaches are similar to the analysis in Sect. 7, but they concern a different programming model.

Analyzing Asynchronous Programs. Several works propose program analyses for various classes of asynchronous programs. [8,15] give complexity results for the reachability problem, and [28] proposes a static analysis for deadlock detection in C# programs that use both asynchronous and synchronous wait primitives. [9] investigates the problem of checking whether Java UI asynchronous programs have the same set of behaviors as sequential programs where roughly, asynchronous tasks are executed synchronously.

10   Conclusion

We proposed a framework for refactoring sequential programs to equivalent asynchronous programs based on async/await. We determined precise complexity bounds for the problem of computing all sound asynchronizations. This problem makes it possible to compute a sound asynchronization that maximizes performance by separating concerns – enumerate sound asynchronizations and evaluate performance separately. On the practical side, we have introduced an approximated synthesis procedure based on data-flow analysis that we implemented and evaluated on a benchmark of non-trivial C# programs.

The asynchronous programs rely exclusively on async/await and are deadlock-free by definition. Deadlocks can occur in a mix of async/await with "explicit" multi-threading that includes blocking `wait` primitives. Extending our approach for such programs is an interesting direction for future work.

References

1. Bacon, D.F., Graham, S.L., Sharp, O.J.: Compiler transformations for high-performance computing. ACM Comput. Surv. **26**(4), 345–420 (1994). https://doi.org/10.1145/197405.197406
2. Beillahi, S.M., Bouajjani, A., Enea, C., Lahiri, S.: Artifact for the SAS 2022 paper: Automated Synthesis of Asynchronizations (May 2022). DOI: https://doi.org/10.5281/zenodo.7055422,https://doi.org/10.5281/zenodo.7055422
3. Beillahi, S.M., Bouajjani, A., Enea, C., Lahiri, S.: Automated synthesis of asynchronizations. CoRR abs/2209.06648 (2022), https://arxiv.org/abs/2209.06648
4. Bierman, G., Russo, C., Mainland, G., Meijer, E., Torgersen, M.: Pause n play: formalizing asynchronous $C^\sharp$. In: Noble, J. (ed.) ECOOP 2012. LNCS, vol. 7313, pp. 233–257. Springer, Heidelberg (2012). https://doi.org/10.1007/978-3-642-31057-7_12
5. Blackshear, S., Gorogiannis, N., O'Hearn, P.W., Sergey, I.: Racerd: compositional static race detection. Proc. ACM Program. Lang. **2**(OOPSLA), 144:1–144:28 (2018). https://doi.org/10.1145/3276514
6. Bloem, R., Hofferek, G., Könighofer, B., Könighofer, R., Ausserlechner, S., Spork, R.: Synthesis of synchronization using uninterpreted functions. In: Formal Methods in Computer-Aided Design, FMCAD 2014, Lausanne, Switzerland, 21–24 October 2014. pp. 35–42. IEEE (2014). https://doi.org/10.1109/FMCAD.2014.6987593
7. Blume, W., et al.: Parallel programming with Polaris. Computer **29**(12), 81–87 (1996). https://doi.org/10.1109/2.546612
8. Bouajjani, A., Emmi, M.: Analysis of recursively parallel programs. In: Field, J., Hicks, M. (eds.) Proceedings of the 39th ACM SIGPLAN-SIGACT Symposium on Principles of Programming Languages, POPL 2012, Philadelphia, Pennsylvania, USA, 22–28 January 2012, pp. 203–214. ACM (2012). https://doi.org/10.1145/2103656.2103681
9. Bouajjani, A., Emmi, M., Enea, C., Ozkan, B.K., Tasiran, S.: Verifying robustness of event-driven asynchronous programs against concurrency. In: Yang, H. (ed.) ESOP 2017. LNCS, vol. 10201, pp. 170–200. Springer, Heidelberg (2017). https://doi.org/10.1007/978-3-662-54434-1_7
10. Černý, P., Clarke, E.M., Henzinger, T.A., Radhakrishna, A., Ryzhyk, L., Samanta, R., Tarrach, T.: From Non-preemptive to preemptive scheduling using synchronization synthesis. In: Kroening, D., Păsăreanu, C.S. (eds.) CAV 2015. LNCS, vol. 9207, pp. 180–197. Springer, Cham (2015). https://doi.org/10.1007/978-3-319-21668-3_11
11. Černý, P., Henzinger, T.A., Radhakrishna, A., Ryzhyk, L., Tarrach, T.: Regression-free synthesis for concurrency. In: Biere, A., Bloem, R. (eds.) CAV 2014. LNCS, vol. 8559, pp. 568–584. Springer, Cham (2014). https://doi.org/10.1007/978-3-319-08867-9_38
12. Clarke, E.M., Emerson, E.A.: Design and synthesis of synchronization skeletons using branching time temporal logic. In: Kozen, D. (ed.) Logic of Programs 1981. LNCS, vol. 131, pp. 52–71. Springer, Heidelberg (1982). https://doi.org/10.1007/BFb0025774
13. Engler, D.R., Ashcraft, K.: Racerx: effective, static detection of race conditions and deadlocks. In: Scott, M.L., Peterson, L.L. (eds.) Proceedings of the 19th ACM Symposium on Operating Systems Principles 2003, SOSP 2003, Bolton Landing, NY, USA, 19–22 October 2003, pp. 237–252. ACM (2003). https://doi.org/10.1145/945445.945468

14. Flanagan, C., Freund, S.N.: Fasttrack: efficient and precise dynamic race detection. In: Hind, M., Diwan, A. (eds.) Proceedings of the 2009 ACM SIGPLAN Conference on Programming Language Design and Implementation, PLDI 2009, Dublin, Ireland, 15–21 June 2009, pp. 121–133. ACM (2009). https://doi.org/10.1145/1542476.1542490

15. Ganty, P., Majumdar, R.: Algorithmic verification of asynchronous programs. ACM Trans. Program. Lang. Syst. **34**(1), 6:1–6:48 (2012). https://doi.org/10.1145/2160910.2160915

16. Godefroid, P., Yannakakis, M.: Analysis of Boolean programs. In: Piterman, N., Smolka, S.A. (eds.) TACAS 2013. LNCS, vol. 7795, pp. 214–229. Springer, Heidelberg (2013). https://doi.org/10.1007/978-3-642-36742-7_16

17. Gokhale, S., Turcotte, A., Tip, F.: Automatic migration from synchronous to asynchronous javascript apis. Proc. ACM Program. Lang. **5**(OOPSLA), 1–27 (2021). https://doi.org/10.1145/3485537

18. Gupta, A., Henzinger, T.A., Radhakrishna, A., Samanta, R., Tarrach, T.: Succinct representation of concurrent trace sets. In: Rajamani, S.K., Walker, D. (eds.) Proceedings of the 42nd Annual ACM SIGPLAN-SIGACT Symposium on Principles of Programming Languages, POPL 2015, Mumbai, India, 15–17 January 2015, pp. 433–444. ACM (2015). https://doi.org/10.1145/2676726.2677008

19. Han, H., Tseng, C.: A comparison of parallelization techniques for irregular reductions. In: Proceedings of the 15th International Parallel & Distributed Processing Symposium (IPDPS-01), San Francisco, CA, USA, 23–27 April 2001, p. 27. IEEE Computer Society (2001). https://doi.org/10.1109/IPDPS.2001.924963

20. Kini, D., Mathur, U., Viswanathan, M.: Dynamic race prediction in linear time. In: Cohen, A., Vechev, M.T. (eds.) Proceedings of the 38th ACM SIGPLAN Conference on Programming Language Design and Implementation, PLDI 2017, Barcelona, Spain, 18–23 June 2017, pp. 157–170. ACM (2017). https://doi.org/10.1145/3062341.3062374

21. Li, G., Lu, S., Musuvathi, M., Nath, S., Padhye, R.: Efficient scalable thread-safety-violation detection: finding thousands of concurrency bugs during testing. In: Brecht, T., Williamson, C. (eds.) Proceedings of the 27th ACM Symposium on Operating Systems Principles, SOSP 2019, Huntsville, ON, Canada, 27–30 October 2019. pp. 162–180. ACM (2019). https://doi.org/10.1145/3341301.3359638

22. Lin, Y., Okur, S., Dig, D.: Study and refactoring of android asynchronous programming (T). In: Cohen, M.B., Grunske, L., Whalen, M. (eds.) 30th IEEE/ACM International Conference on Automated Software Engineering, ASE 2015, Lincoln, NE, USA, 9–13 November 2015, pp. 224–235. IEEE Computer Society (2015). https://doi.org/10.1109/ASE.2015.50

23. Liu, B., Huang, J.: D4: fast concurrency debugging with parallel differential analysis. In: Foster, J.S., Grossman, D. (eds.) Proceedings of the 39th ACM SIGPLAN Conference on Programming Language Design and Implementation, PLDI 2018, Philadelphia, PA, USA, 18–22 June 2018, pp. 359–373. ACM (2018). https://doi.org/10.1145/3192366.3192390

24. Manna, Z., Wolper, P.: Synthesis of communicating processes from temporal logic specifications. ACM Trans. Program. Lang. Syst. **6**(1), 68–93 (1984). https://doi.org/10.1145/357233.357237

25. Okur, S., Hartveld, D.L., Dig, D., van Deursen, A.: A study and toolkit for asynchronous programming in c#. In: Jalote, P., Briand, L.C., van der Hoek, A. (eds.) 36th International Conference on Software Engineering, ICSE 2014, Hyderabad, India - May 31–June 07, 2014, pp. 1117–1127. ACM (2014). https://doi.org/10.1145/2568225.2568309

26. Raman, R., Zhao, J., Sarkar, V., Vechev, M., Yahav, E.: Efficient data race detection for Async-finish parallelism. In: Barringer, H., et al. (eds.) RV 2010. LNCS, vol. 6418, pp. 368–383. Springer, Heidelberg (2010). https://doi.org/10.1007/978-3-642-16612-9_28

27. Roslyn: (2022). https://github.com/dotnet/roslyn

28. Santhiar, A., Kanade, A.: Static deadlock detection for asynchronous c# programs. In: Cohen, A., Vechev, M.T. (eds.) Proceedings of the 38th ACM SIGPLAN Conference on Programming Language Design and Implementation, PLDI 2017, Barcelona, Spain, 18–23 June 2017, pp. 292–305. ACM (2017). https://doi.org/10.1145/3062341.3062361

29. Smaragdakis, Y., Evans, J., Sadowski, C., Yi, J., Flanagan, C.: Sound predictive race detection in polynomial time. In: Field, J., Hicks, M. (eds.) Proceedings of the 39th ACM SIGPLAN-SIGACT Symposium on Principles of Programming Languages, POPL 2012, Philadelphia, Pennsylvania, USA, 22–28 January 2012, pp. 387–400. ACM (2012). https://doi.org/10.1145/2103656.2103702

30. Vechev, M., Yahav, E., Yorsh, G.: Inferring synchronization under limited observability. In: Kowalewski, S., Philippou, A. (eds.) TACAS 2009. LNCS, vol. 5505, pp. 139–154. Springer, Heidelberg (2009). https://doi.org/10.1007/978-3-642-00768-2_13

31. Vechev, M.T., Yahav, E., Yorsh, G.: Abstraction-guided synthesis of synchronization. In: Hermenegildo, M.V., Palsberg, J. (eds.) Proceedings of the 37th ACM SIGPLAN-SIGACT Symposium on Principles of Programming Languages, POPL 2010, Madrid, Spain, 17–23 January 2010, pp. 327–338. ACM (2010). https://doi.org/10.1145/1706299.1706338

Case Study on Verification-Witness Validators: Where We Are and Where We Go

Dirk Beyer[1] and Jan Strejček[2]

[1] LMU Munich, Munich, Germany
[2] Masaryk University, Brno, Czechia

Abstract. Software-verification tools sometimes produce incorrect answers, which can be a false alarm or a wrong claim of correctness. To increase the reliability of verification results, many verifiers now accompany their answers by witnesses in an interoperable standard format. There exist witness validators that can examine the witnesses and potentially confirm the verification results. This case study analyzes the quality of existing witness validators for C programs using the witnesses produced by a wide variety of 40 verification tools that participated in SV-COMP 2022. In particular, we show that many witness validators sometimes confirm witnesses that are invalid. To remedy this situation, we suggest some advances in witness validation, including a regular comparative evaluation of validators. Our suggestions were recently adopted by the SV-COMP community for the next edition of the competition.

Keywords: Software verification · Program analysis · Software validation · Software bugs · Verification witnesses · Evaluation · Benchmarking

1 Introduction

There are now many tools for verification of computer programs, but as far as we know, none of them claims to always produce correct results. The results of the *Competition on Software Verification (SV-COMP)* show that out of the 57 verifiers participating in the main category called *Overall* in the last five years (there were 10, 13, 11, 10, and 13 participants in this category in years 2018–2022, respectively), only four provide no incorrect results, namely ULTIMATE KOJAK in 2018, CPA-SEQ and SYMBIOTIC in 2019, and GOBLINT in 2022. Moreover, communication with industrial developers reveals that even a relatively small portion of incorrect results can devaluate credibility of a verification tool. As a solution, many verifiers now accompany their verification results by some evidence in the form of *verification witnesses*. These verification witnesses can be independently analyzed and potentially confirmed by *witness validators*. Industrial developers can use witness validation to triage the verification results: the results with unconfirmed witnesses are ignored and attention is focused on the confirmed ones.

Independent validation of verification witnesses is possible thanks to a machine-readable exchange format for witnesses. The first such format [11] was introduced in 2015. It supported only *violation witnesses* (also called *counterexamples*)

© The Author(s) 2022
G. Singh and C. Urban (Eds.): SAS 2022, LNCS 13790, pp. 160–174, 2022.
https://doi.org/10.1007/978-3-031-22308-2_8

produced when a verifier reports that a given program violates a considered safety specification. The authors of this format also extended the verification tools CPACHECKER and ULTIMATE AUTOMIZER to support validation of these witnesses. In 2016, the format was extended to accommodate also witnesses for the cases when a verifier decides that a given program satisfies a given specification [9]. Such witnesses are called *correctness witnesses*, and they should contain some hints for the proof of program correctness. In the same year, the two mentioned tools were extended to support validation of correctness witnesses as well. In 2018, a new (execution-based) approach for checking of violation witnesses was introduced and implemented in tools CPA-WITNESS2TEST and FSHELL-WITNESS2TEST [12]. Another two witness validators called METAVAL [14] and NITWIT [21] were introduced in 2020, followed by validators DARTGNAN [19] and SYMBIOTIC-WITCH [1] introduced in 2022. The evolution of the witness format and validators is driven by the SV-COMP community. Since SV-COMP 2021, the competition rewards with points only the verification results with witnesses confirmed by at least one witness validator (with the exception of several categories for which witness confirmation is not required for correctness witnesses due to unavailability of suitable witness validators).

The witness format [10,11] is based on GraphML. Each witness contains information about the corresponding verification task (in particular, the program and the specification) and the verification result it witnesses. The main part of the witness resembles an automaton decorated with additional information. Hence, we talk about *witness automata*. A violation witness automaton represents a set of program paths and it is *valid* if at least one of these paths is feasible and violates the considered specification. Figure 1 provides an example of a C program that violates the specification that function reach_error is never called, and three different violation witnesses. In general, a violation witness automaton describes a set of program paths by specifying passed program locations (depicted by line numbers on edges), called functions, taken branches, constraints on variable values, etc. Each violation witness automaton has to contain at least one error state representing a specification violation (depicted in red). Further, it can also contain sink states (depicted in blue) saying that the represented paths violating the specification are elsewhere. A witness can represent a single program path by specifying all program inputs (as in Fig. 1b), it can say nothing about input values and prescribe taken branches (as in Fig. 1c), or it can combine some branching information with restrictions on input values (as in Fig. 1d).

A correctness witness automaton represents program invariants and it is *valid* if all these invariants hold and the corresponding program satisfies the considered specification. Ideally, a correctness witness contains a minimal set of invariants implying that the program satisfies the specification. Figure 2 shows a fixed version of the C program (see the rectangle), which can be proven correct, and the correctness witness shows invariants (depicted in green) that help to re-establish the proof of correctness.

The examples of witnesses are adopted from literature [10] which provides their detailed description: in Sect. 4.2, Examples 7 and 8 explain the violation

```
1 void reach_error (){}
2 extern unsigned char
  ↪ __VERIFIER_nondet_uchar (void);
3 int main () {
4   unsigned char n =
    ↪ __VERIFIER_nondet_uchar ();
5   if (n == 0) {
6     return 0;
7   }
8   unsigned char v = 0;
9   unsigned char s = 0;
10  unsigned int i = 0;
11  while (i < n) {
12    v = __VERIFIER_nondet_uchar ();
13    s += v;
14    ++i;
15  }
16  if (s < v) {
17    reach_error ();
18    return 1;
19  }
20  if (s > 65025) {
21    reach_error ();
22    return 1;
23  }
24  return 0;
25 }
```

(a) Unsafe program linear-inequality-inv-b.c

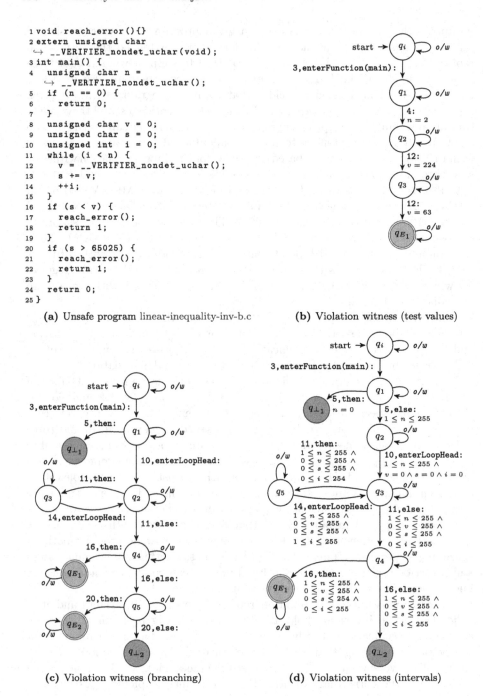

(b) Violation witness (test values)

(c) Violation witness (branching)

(d) Violation witness (intervals)

Fig. 1. Example C program with a bug (a) and violation witnesses for it: with test values (b), with branching information (c) and with intervals (d); taken from [10]

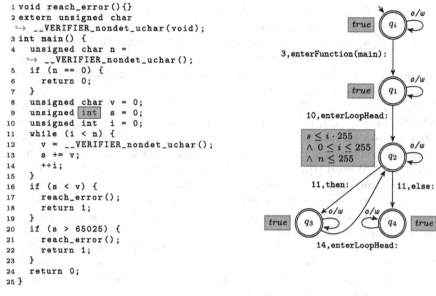

```
1 void reach_error(){}
2 extern unsigned char
  ↪ __VERIFIER_nondet_uchar(void);
3 int main() {
4   unsigned char n =
    ↪ __VERIFIER_nondet_uchar();
5   if (n == 0) {
6     return 0;
7   }
8   unsigned char v = 0;
9   unsigned int s = 0;
10  unsigned int i = 0;
11  while (i < n) {
12    v = __VERIFIER_nondet_uchar();
13    s += v;
14    ++i;
15  }
16  if (s < v) {
17    reach_error();
18    return 1;
19  }
20  if (s > 65025) {
21    reach_error();
22    return 1;
23  }
24  return 0;
25 }
```

(a) Safe program linear-inequality-inv-a.c   (b) Correctness witness

Fig. 2. Corrected C program (a) and a correctness witness for it (b); the only difference to Fig. 1a is the corrected type in line 9 (highlighted); taken from [10]

witnesses (pages 21–27), and in Sect. 4.3., Example 9 explains the correctness witness (pages 31–33). The witness format admits also *trivial witnesses* that provide no useful information. A trivial violation witness represents all program paths and a trivial correctness witness provides no invariant. Validation of a trivial witness is as hard as the original verification task.

Overview and Outline. A witness validator is given a witness and the corresponding verification task, and it aims at confirming the verification result by proving that the witness is valid.[1] On one side, the addition of the witness-validation step to the verification process increases the reliability of the confirmed verification results. On the other side, the reliability of witness validators is not challenged or even properly studied. As validators are often implemented using the same techniques as their corresponding verifiers (and by the same development teams), it is reasonable to expect that they also sometimes produce incorrect results.

In Sect. 2, we focus on the first goal of this paper, namely to evaluate the performance and reliability of current witness validators for C programs.[2] There are currently 8 such validators which can be divided into several categories according to their approach.

---

[1] Note that the current SV-COMP rules use the term *invalid* for witnesses that are not syntactically correct. In our case study, we ignore such witnesses as they can be filtered out by WITNESSLINT (https://github.com/sosy-lab/sv-witnesses/tree/svcomp22/lint).

[2] There are only very few validators that support other languages. We know only about GWIT [18] and WIT4JAVA [20] for Java programs.

- CPACHECKER [11], METAVAL [14], and ULTIMATE AUTOMIZER [11] create a product of a witness automaton and the original program and analyze it. A violation witness is confirmed if the product exhibits the specification violation described by the witness. A correctness witness is confirmed if the product satisfies the specification and the invariants in the witness are valid (cf. [16], Sect. 4.3).
- CPA-WITNESS2TEST[12], CPROVER-WITNESS2TEST (originally called FSHELL-WITNESS2TEST) [12], and NITWIT [21] can handle only violation witnesses. They derive a single test from a given witness automaton and execute it. The witness is confirmed if the execution violates the considered specification.
- SYMBIOTIC-WITCH [1] can process also only violation witnesses. It performs symbolic execution of the given program and tracks the corresponding set of states in the witness automaton. A witness is confirmed if the symbolic execution violates the considered specification and the tracked set contains an error state of the witness automaton.
- DARTGNAN [19] is a bounded model checker for parallel programs, which has been extended with the ability to analyze violation witnesses. It transforms the violation witness and the program into an SMT query, and it confirms the witness if the query is satisfiable.

We evaluate the validators on witnesses produced in SV-COMP 2022. As various validators support different specifications and program features, they are applicable only to witnesses created for verification tasks of selected SV-COMP categories. Verification tasks with C programs are currently divided into 6 main categories, which can be roughly characterized as follows.

- *ReachSafety* contains sequential programs that should be checked for unreachability of a given error function.
- *MemSafety* consists of sequential programs that should be checked to contain no invalid dereference, no invalid deallocation, and no memory leaks.
- *ConcurrencySafety* contains parallel programs that should be checked for unreachability of a given error function.
- *NoOverflows* collects sequential programs that should contain no overflow of a signed integer.
- *Termination* consists of sequential programs that should be checked to have no infinite execution.
- *SoftwareSystems* collects more complex programs that are usually a part of real software projects and they should be checked for specifications described in *ReachSafety*, *MemSafety*, or *NoOverflows*.

The applicability of the considered validators to violation and correctness witnesses of individual SV-COMP categories is summarized in Table 1. Please note that even if the table indicates that a certain validator is applicable to violation or correctness witnesses of a certain category, it does not mean that the validator can handle all such witnesses of this category (for example, a validator may not support a specific feature of some programs).

Verification tasks in SV-COMP are labelled with expected verification results. We consider the labelling with expected results as highly reliable due

Table 1. Applicability of validators to violation and correctness witnesses from individual SV-COMP categories; some validator names are abbreviated

Category	violation-witness validators								correctness-witness validators		
	CPACHECKER [11]	CPA-w2T [12]	CPROVER-w2T [12]	DARTGNAN [19]	METAVAL [14]	NITWIT [21]	UAUTOMIZER [11]	SYMBIOTIC-WITCH [1]	CPACHECKER [9]	METAVAL [14]	UAUTOMIZER [9]
ReachSafety	✓	✓	✓		✓	✓	✓	✓	✓	✓	✓
MemSafety	✓	✓	✓		✓		✓	✓	✓		✓
ConcurrencySafety	✓			✓							
NoOverflows	✓	✓	✓		✓		✓	✓	✓	✓	✓
Termination	✓				✓		✓				
SoftwareSystems	✓	✓	✓		✓	✓	✓	✓	✓	✓	✓

to the following penalty mechanism of SV-COMP and competitiveness of its community. In SV-COMP, if a verifier produces an incorrect result (i.e., the opposite to the expected one), it immediately gets many penalty points. If the authors of the verifier are confident that the result is correct, they can (and often do) challenge the expected result. The verification task is then discussed and potentially relabelled.[3] Unfortunately, there is no set of witnesses labelled as valid or invalid, and we cannot safely assume that all witnesses accompanying correct verification results are valid. In fact, there are known cases of correct verification results accompanied by invalid witnesses. For example, this is the case of some violation witnesses produced by SYMBIOTIC 9 for some *MemSafety* benchmarks [17]. However, when a verifier produces an incorrect verification result, the corresponding witness has to be invalid. In our experiments, we apply the existing witness validators on all relevant witnesses of both correct and incorrect verification results computed in SV-COMP 2022.

Section 3 is devoted to the second goal of this paper: to initiate qualitative improvement of witness validators. In particular, we suggest extending the semantics of possible validator outcomes and we propose a formula for evaluating validators. Our suggestions have been recently accepted by the SV-COMP community and a new competition track for witness validators has been announced starting from SV-COMP 2023.

Related Work. Existing papers on witness validators typically present only the confirmation rates of considered validators on the set of witnesses accompanying correct verification results, which are implicitly assumed to be valid

---

[3] For example, see Merge Request 1336 of the SV-Benchmarks repository.

witnesses [10,14,19,21]. Evaluation of validators on invalid witnesses accompanying incorrect verification results has been previously done only twice: in 2015 for a limited set of invalid violation witnesses and the initial versions of witness validators CPACHECKER and ULTIMATE AUTOMIZER [11] and in 2018 for a larger set of invalid violation witnesses and initial versions of witness validators CPA-WITNESS2TEST and CPROVER-WITNESS2TEST and then-current versions of CPACHECKER and ULTIMATE AUTOMIZER [12]. In contrast, we consider invalid verification witnesses for both violation and correctness results and all 8 currently available witness validators in their versions used in SV-COMP 2022.

More information about witnesses and their validation in the context of SV-COMP can be found in regular competition reports [5,6]. There is also a study [4] on violation and correctness witnesses produced in SV-COMP 2019.

2   Evaluation

We would like to investigate the state of the art of witness validation. Therefore, we take a large set of 158 848 known syntactically correct witnesses from SV-COMP 2022 and validate all those witnesses using all available witness validators for C programs and report the results.

Execution Environment. We executed all experiments on a cluster with 167 machines, each with a CPU of type Intel Xeon E3-1230 v5, 3.4 GHz, with 8 processing units (virtual cores), 33 GB RAM, operating system Ubuntu 20.04 (Linux 5.4.0-94-generic). Each validation run (execution of one validator on one verification task and witness) was limited to 2 processing units, 7 GB memory, and 900 s of CPU time for correctness validators and 90 s of CPU time for violation validators. We chose this configuration because it was used in SV-COMP 2022. In order to ensure reliable measurement and control of the computing resources and isolation of processes, we used the benchmarking framework BENCHEXEC [13].

Evaluated Validators. In this evaluation, we consider all eight witness validators for C programs that participated in SV-COMP 2022. Table 1 lists the validators and the categories for which they can validate witnesses.

Data Set and Benchmark. The witnesses and the verification tasks (program and specification) are taken from the data set of SV-COMP 2022 at Zenodo [8]. SV-COMP organizes the verification tasks with C programs into six categories. We take all witnesses produced for these tasks by all participating verification tools. Then we remove the witnesses for which WITNESSLINT produced an exception. Exceptions are typically caused by syntax problems or too large witness files.

We classify each violation witness for a correct program as invalid (because the competition classified the result of the verifier as false alarm), and we classify each correctness witness for a buggy program as invalid (because the competition classified the result of the verifier as wrong claim of correctness). All other witnesses are classified as valid*, because they do not contradict the expected result. We use the term valid* with asterisk because there are witnesses that do not contradict the expected result but are still invalid (e.g., there can be a violation witness

Table 2. Validation of violation witnesses by eight violation validators; the numbers are hyperlinked to the tables generated by BENCHEXEC

Category	Witnesses	CPACHECKER	CPA-w2T	CPROVER-w2T	DARTGNAN	METAVAL	NITWIT	SYMBIOTIC-WITCH	UAUTOMIZER
ReachSafety									
valid*	26 797	14 908	8628	14 168	–	0	15 507	11 176	8592
invalid	5177	28	12	2	–	0	10	0	0
MemSafety									
valid*	16 984	12 594	231	954	–	116	–	8394	4197
invalid	2804	0	0	26	–	2	–	0	0
ConcurrencySafety									
valid*	4746	2700	–	–	1464	–	–	–	–
invalid	1293	40	–	–	0	–	–	–	–
NoOverflows									
valid*	2808	2334	887	1436	–	1982	–	2609	2468
invalid	167	0	0	0	–	0	–	0	0
Termination									
valid*	3652	2580	–	–	–	598	–	–	960
invalid	56	21	–	–	–	0	–	–	0
SoftwareSystems									
valid*	2102	621	6	33	–	0	0	179	26
invalid	5903	5	0	27	–	0	0	51	4

representing no feasible path violating the considered specification, even if such a path exists). However, there is currently no reliable way to automatically identify invalid witnesses that do not contradict the expected result. Tables 2 and 3 report in column 'Witnesses' the number of valid* and invalid witnesses for each category.

Results. We report the results of our validation experiments in two tables. The results on violation witnesses are presented in Table 2 and the results on correctness witnesses in Table 3. For each category and validator, row 'valid*' reports the number of valid* witnesses confirmed by the validator, and row 'invalid' reports the number of invalid witnesses erroneously confirmed by the validator. Due to the source of invalid witnesses described above, each erroneous confirmation of an invalid witness here means that the validator either confirmed a violation witness, but the program does not violate the specification, or it confirmed a correctness witness, but the program does violate the specification. In the following we highlight a few observations revealed by the results.

Table 3. Validation of correctness witnesses by three correctness validators; the numbers are hyperlinked to the tables generated by BENCHEXEC

Category	Witnesses	CPACHECKER	METAVAL	UAUTOMIZER
ReachSafety				
valid*	31 013	17 312	19 655	19 632
invalid	894	0	**315**	**3**
MemSafety				
valid*	16 948	–	227	14 384
invalid	326	–	0	0
ConcurrencySafety				
valid*	3177	–	–	–
invalid	389	–	–	–
NoOverflows				
valid*	2089	1718	1608	1713
invalid	300	0	**36**	0
Termination				
valid*	4502	–	–	–
invalid	14	–	–	–
SoftwareSystems				
valid*	25 819	6771	20 624	19 343
invalid	888	0	**403**	0

Soundness of validators. There is only one validator, namely DARTGNAN, that does not confirm any invalid violation witness. The validator participated only in category *ConcurrencySafety* as it is specialized in parallel programs (Table 2). CPACHECKER does not confirm any invalid correctness witness (Table 3).

There seems to be a particularly difficult category. The category SoftwareSystems has a large number of invalid violation witnesses (Table 2, 'Witnesses' column). This means that in this category, many verification runs report a false alarm for a correct program, accompanied by an invalid violation witness. The violation witnesses in this category seem to be difficult for validation, as only CPACHECKER confirmed more than 10 % of valid* violation witnesses. Moreover, all validators that confirmed at least ten valid* violation witnesses confirmed also some invalid violation witnesses.

Our evaluation revealed technical problems. The validator METAVAL does not confirm any violation witness (Table 2) in categories ReachSafety and SoftwareSystems and confirms a large number of invalid correctness witnesses (Table 3) in these categories. The reason for those incorrect validation results is that the validator was not adapted to a new rule of SV-COMP that was introduced for SV-COMP 2021: All verification tasks in those categories were changed to using a new logic to encode invalid function calls. Other specifications are not affected by this change.

Summary. Most of the invalid witnesses that were incorrectly confirmed were due to bugs in validators. The conclusion is that the quality of validators should be increased by establishing means to stimulate the inspection and quality control of validation tools. A competition track for validators suggested in the following section could help drawing the attention of developers to inspecting results of validators. Currently, SV-COMP uses validators for confirmation of verification results, but does not evaluate the quality of their results.

Threats to Validity. Regarding internal validity, the main threat to our results is that we rely on the expected results for verification tasks. If those were incorrectly specified, our classification of validator results would also be incorrect. But the verification tasks in the benchmark collection that we use are actively maintained by the community and the participating teams inspected the results of their verifiers. The 33 actively participating teams in SV-COMP 2022 have approved the results of their verifiers before the results were published.

For executing the experiments, we used the publicly-available benchmarking framework BENCHEXEC [13], which gives us access to the modern features of the Linux kernel for controling the resources and for isolating executions. This framework is used by several competitions and is actively maintained. For job distribution on the cluster we use VERIFIERCLOUD, which is also used by several competitions and research groups for their lab work. It is unlikely that a bug in the benchmarking infrastructure causes wrong results.

Regarding external validity, our results are specific to witness validators for the programming language C, because this is the only language for which a large set of verification and validation tools exist. The first two validators [18, 20] for Java were introduced for SV-COMP 2022. Further, our results are specific to validators that participated in SV-COMP and to the verification tasks from the SV-Benchmarks collection. We are not aware of any validators besides those participating in the competition, and we are not aware of a benchmark that is better suited for the evaluation than what is used by the competition. Therefore, we assume that our results are still significant because SV-COMP is comprehensive.

3 Suggestions for Advances in Witness Validation

Extended Semantics of Validator Outcomes. Possible validator answers recognized by SV-COMP are the same as possible answers of verifiers, which are

- `false`, meaning that the given program violates the given specification and a violation witness was generated,
- `true`, meaning that the given program satisfies the given specification and a correctness witness was generated, and
- `unknown`, meaning that the verifier was unable to decide.

The interpretation of a witness-validator answer depends on the kind of the analyzed witness. A violation witness is confirmed if a validator outputs `false`. All other answers (including `true` and `unknown`) mean that the witness is not confirmed by this validator. Similarly, a correctness witness is confirmed if a validator outputs `true` and all other answers mean that the validator did not confirm the witness. In other words, even if a validator has the confidence to say that some witness is invalid, the competition rules give it the same semantics as `unknown`. As a consequence, there is no difference between witnesses that are not confirmed due to insufficient power of validators and those that were refuted by some validators.

We suggest to explicitly state the semantics of a validator output as follows. On violation witnesses, a validator should produce

- `false` to confirm that there exists a program execution represented by the witness such that it violates the considered specification,
- `true` to refute the witness as there is no program execution represented by the witness that violates the considered specification, or
- `unknown` to indicate that it is unable to decide.

On correctness witnesses, a validator produces

- `false` to refute the witness as there exists some execution violating the considered specification or some invariant given in the witness,
- `true` to confirm the witness as the validator can prove that the program satisfies the considered specification with help of the invariants given in the witness and that all invariants given in the witness are valid, or
- `unknown` to indicate that it is unable to decide.

Evaluation of Validators. One can find many areas of computer science (e.g., SMT solving), where some kind of competition or regular evaluation led to a rapid improvement of the state of the art. With this motivation, we suggest to extend SV-COMP with a comparative evaluation of witness validators, and we propose the following scoring schema for this evaluation.

Assume that we are given a witness validator, a set of valid* witnesses, and a set of invalid witnesses. Our scoring schema is inspired by the established scoring schema for evaluating verifiers in SV-COMP. The community agreed that showing that a system satisfies a given specification deserves more credit than showing that the specification is violated. Hence, SV-COMP rewards correct (and confirmed) answers `true` with 2 points and correct (and confirmed) answers `false` with 1 point. The penalty factor for incorrect answers is -16, which means that incorrect `true` yields -32 points and incorrect `false` -16 points.

The proposed scoring schema for validators is depicted in Fig. 3. We first describe the scores for invalid violation witnesses (the right side of the figure). Refutation of an invalid witness is rewarded with 2 points as it means to decide that all program paths represented by the witness satisfy the specification, which is an analogy to showing that a program satisfies its specification. Refutation of an invalid correctness witness is rewarded with 1 point as it corresponds to finding a violation of the specification or some invariant given in the witness. Confirmation of an invalid witness yields the penalty p for a violation witness and $2p$ for a correctness witness, where p is the *penalty factor* (with $p < 0$). Points and penalties for invalid witnesses are accumulated in p_{invalid}. The proposed scores for valid* witnesses (the left side of the figure) reflect the fact that these witnesses

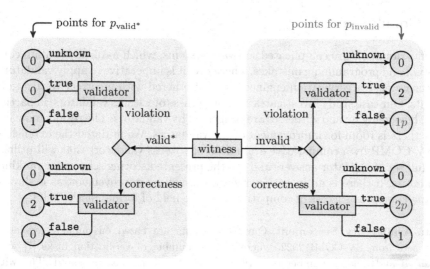

Fig. 3. Proposed scoring schema for evaluation of validators (with $p < 0$)

are only assumed to be valid and some of them can be actually invalid. Hence, we suggest to reward only confirmation of valid* witnesses: 2 points for each confirmed correctness witness and 1 point for each confirmed violation witness. Points for valid* witnesses are accumulated in p_{valid^*}.

One can observe in Tables 2 and 3 that the number of incorrect witnesses is typically one or two orders of magnitude lower than the number of valid* witnesses and this disbalance is assumed to increase if verifiers produce less incorrect verification results. Further, the p_{invalid} deserves a higher impact than p_{valid^*} as we do not really know whether valid* witnesses are indeed valid. Hence, we propose to compute the score as the sum

$$score = \frac{p_{\text{valid}^*}}{|\text{valid}^*|} + q \cdot \frac{p_{\text{invalid}}}{|\text{invalid}|}$$

where the points in p_{valid^*} and p_{invalid} are normalized by the cardinality of the corresponding witness sets and p_{invalid} is given a higher weight using the factor q.

We suggest to compute the validator scores separately for witnesses of each category. The overall score of a validator can be computed by the normalization used in SV-COMP to compute the overall scores of verifiers (see [3], page 597).

Our proposal of a comparative evaluation of witness validators based on the scoring schema above was presented and discussed at the SV-COMP community meeting on April 7, 2022. The community decided to establish a witness-validation track from SV-COMP 2023 onwards. The community further decided to use the suggested scoring schema and set the parameters to $p = -16$ and $q = 2$.

4 Conclusion

Verification tools are complicated software systems, which naturally contain conceptual and programming mistakes. Therefore, it is imperative to apply validators to ensure that a verification engineer is not bothered with incorrect verification results. Our case study investigates the correctness of witness validators, in particular, how many invalid witnesses are confirmed by validators. The results indicate that there is room for improvement of the validators. We initiated the extension of SV-COMP by a comparative evaluation of witness validators that will utilize the full set of validator answers and use the presented scoring schema for ranking validators. If there is an incentive, then there will be improvement, as is shown by the enormous success of competitions in the field of formal methods [2].

Data-Availability Statement. Our experiments are based on publicly available data sets from SV-COMP 2022, where a large number of verification tasks [7] was executed and a large number of verification witnesses [8] was produced. The witness format is maintained in a GitHub repository: https://github.com/sosy-lab/sv-witnesses/tree/svcomp22/. Our experimental results are available on a supplementary web page (https://sv-comp.sosy-lab.org/2022/results/validators/) as tables produced by BENCHEXEC [13] (also linked to from Tables 2 and 3). The log output is available by clicking on the status of a result in the tables. All experimental results (raw data, tables) and scripts are available in our reproduction package [15].

References

1. Ayaziová, P., Chalupa, M., Strejček, J.: SYMBIOTIC-WITCH: A Klee-based violation witness checker (competition contribution). In: Proc. TACAS (2). pp. 468–473. LNCS 13244, Springer (2022). https://doi.org/10.1007/978-3-030-99527-0_33
2. Bartocci, E., Beyer, D., Black, P.E., Fedyukovich, G., Garavel, H., Hartmanns, A., Huisman, M., Kordon, F., Nagele, J., Sighireanu, M., Steffen, B., Suda, M., Sutcliffe, G., Weber, T., Yamada, A.: TOOLympics 2019: An overview of competitions in formal methods. In: Proc. TACAS (3). pp. 3–24. LNCS 11429, Springer (2019). https://doi.org/10.1007/978-3-030-17502-3_1
3. Beyer, D.: Second competition on software verification (Summary of SV-COMP 2013). In: Proc. TACAS. pp. 594–609. LNCS 7795, Springer (2013). https://doi.org/10.1007/978-3-642-36742-7_43
4. Beyer, D.: A data set of program invariants and error paths. In: Proc. MSR. pp. 111–115. IEEE (2019). https://doi.org/10.1109/MSR.2019.00026
5. Beyer, D.: Software verification: 10th comparative evaluation (SV-COMP 2021). In: Proc. TACAS (2). pp. 401–422. LNCS 12652, Springer (2021). https://doi.org/10.1007/978-3-030-72013-1_24
6. Beyer, D.: Progress on software verification: SV-COMP 2022. In: Proc. TACAS (2). pp. 375–402. LNCS 13244, Springer (2022). https://doi.org/10.1007/978-3-030-99527-0_20
7. Beyer, D.: SV-Benchmarks: Benchmark set for software verification and testing (SV-COMP 2022 and Test-Comp 2022). Zenodo (2022). https://doi.org/10.5281/zenodo.5831003

8. Beyer, D.: Verification witnesses from verification tools (SV-COMP 2022). Zenodo (2022). https://doi.org/10.5281/zenodo.5838498
9. Beyer, D., Dangl, M., Dietsch, D., Heizmann, M.: Correctness witnesses: Exchanging verification results between verifiers. In: Proc. FSE. pp. 326–337. ACM (2016). https://doi.org/10.1145/2950290.2950351
10. Beyer, D., Dangl, M., Dietsch, D., Heizmann, M., Lemberger, T., Tautschnig, M.: Verification witnesses. ACM Trans. Softw. Eng. Methodol. **31**(4), 57:1–57:69 (2022). https://doi.org/10.1145/3477579
11. Beyer, D., Dangl, M., Dietsch, D., Heizmann, M., Stahlbauer, A.: Witness validation and stepwise testification across software verifiers. In: Proc. FSE. pp. 721–733. ACM (2015). https://doi.org/10.1145/2786805.2786867
12. Beyer, D., Dangl, M., Lemberger, T., Tautschnig, M.: Tests from witnesses: Execution-based validation of verification results. In: Proc. TAP. pp. 3–23. LNCS 10889, Springer (2018). https://doi.org/10.1007/978-3-319-92994-1_1
13. Beyer, D., Löwe, S., Wendler, P.: Reliable benchmarking: Requirements and solutions. Int. J. Softw. Tools Technol. Transfer **21**(1), 1–29 (2017). https://doi.org/10.1007/s10009-017-0469-y
14. Beyer, D., Spiessl, M.: METAVAL: Witness validation via verification. In: Proc. CAV. pp. 165–177. LNCS 12225, Springer (2020). https://doi.org/10.1007/978-3-030-53291-8_10
15. Beyer, D., Strejček, J.: Reproduction package for article 'case study on verification-witness validators: Where we are and where we go'. Zenodo (2022). https://doi.org/10.5281/zenodo.7096382
16. Beyer, D., Wehrheim, H.: Verification artifacts in cooperative verification: Survey and unifying component framework. In: Proc. ISoLA (1). pp. 143–167. LNCS 12476, Springer (2020). https://doi.org/10.1007/978-3-030-61362-4_8
17. Chalupa, M., Řechtáčková, A., Mihalkovič, V., Zaoral, L., Strejček, J.: SYMBIOTIC 9: String analysis and backward symbolic execution with loop folding (competition contribution). In: Proc. TACAS (2). pp. 462–467. LNCS 13244, Springer (2022). https://doi.org/10.1007/978-3-030-99527-0_32
18. Howar, F., Mues, M.: GWIT (competition contribution). In: Proc. TACAS (2). pp. 446–450. LNCS 13244, Springer (2022). https://doi.org/10.1007/978-3-030-99527-0_29
19. Ponce-De-Leon, H., Haas, T., Meyer, R.: DARTAGNAN: Smt-based violation witness validation (competition contribution). In: Proc. TACAS (2). pp. 418–423. LNCS 13244, Springer (2022). https://doi.org/10.1007/978-3-030-99527-0_29
20. Wu, T., Schrammel, P., Cordeiro, L.: WIT4JAVA: A violation-witness validator for Java verifiers (competition contribution). In: Proc. TACAS (2). pp. 484–489. LNCS 13244, Springer (2022). https://doi.org/10.1007/978-3-030-99527-0_36
21. J. Švejda, Berger, P., Katoen, J.P.: Interpretation-based violation witness validation for C: NITWIT. In: Proc. TACAS. pp. 40–57. LNCS 12078, Springer (2020). https://doi.org/10.1007/978-3-030-45190-5_3

Deciding Program Properties
via Complete Abstractions on Bounded
Domains

Roberto Bruni[1], Roberta Gori[1], and Nicolas Manini[1,2,3(✉)]

[1] Dipartimento di Informatica, Università di Pisa, Largo B. Pontecorvo 3, Pisa, Italy
{roberto.bruni,roberta.gori}@unipi.it
[2] IMDEA Software Institute, Madrid, Spain
nicolas.manini@imdea.org
[3] Universidad Politécnica de Madrid, Madrid, Spain

Abstract. Abstract interpretation provides an over-approximation of
program behaviours that is used to prove the absence of bugs. When the
computed approximation in the chosen abstract domain is as precise as
possible, we say the analysis is complete and false alarms cannot arise.
Unfortunately for any non trivial abstract domain there is some program
whose analysis is incomplete. In this paper we want to characterize the
classes of complete programs on some non-trivial abstract domains for
studying their expressiveness. To this aim we introduce the notion of
bounded domains for posets with ascending chains of bounded length
only. We show that any complete program on bounded domains can
be rewritten in an equivalent canonical form without nontrivial loops.
This result proves that program termination on the class of complete
programs on bounded domain is decidable. Moreover, semantic equivalence between programs in the above class can be reduced to determining
the equivalence of a set of guarded statements. We show how our approach can be applied to a quite large class of programs. Indeed, abstract
domains defined on Boolean abstractions that are complete for the same
functions can be composed by preserving boundedness and completeness also w.r.t. any expressible guard. This suggests that new complete
bounded abstract domains can be tailored on the guards and functions
appearing in the program. Their existence is sufficient to prove decidability of termination and program equivalence for such programs.

Keywords: Abstract interpretation · Complete abstraction · Bounded
domains · Program transformation · Termination · Program
equivalence

Research supported by MIUR PRIN Project 201784YSZ5 ASPRA–Analysis of Program
Analyses. Partially funded by RYC-2016-20281, by ESF Investing in your future and
by Madrid regional government as part of the program S2018/TCS-4339 co-funded by
EIE Funds of the European Union.

G. Singh and C. Urban (Eds.): SAS 2022, LNCS 13790, pp. 175–200, 2022.
https://doi.org/10.1007/978-3-031-22308-2_9

1   Introduction

The current spread of software-driven computing devices and the fact that our daily activities and lives are dependent on them makes program verification extremely important to prevent crashes that may involve millions of users (see, for example, [2,10,12,18,23]). Formal methods and static analysis techniques [19,21] are a useful tool to verify program properties before deployment and to gain confidence on programs behaviour without running the actual code. Unfortunately the founding fathers of Computer Science had well established the limits of such approaches, by showing that all interesting problems about Turing equivalent programming languages are undecidable, like program termination and extensional equivalence [20,22], so that the pretension of devising universal analysis procedures that works fine for any program is deemed to fail. Intensional analysis is more subtle, because it takes into account *how a program is written* and not just *what a program computes*.

Abstract Interpretation [5,7,16,21] is an intensional, sound-by-construction static analysis method whose precision depends very much on the way in which the program is coded. The basic idea of Abstract Interpretation is to execute the program over an abstract domain that over-approximate the concrete program semantics. In this sense, each set of concrete stores is approximated by its least superset available in the abstract domain. For example, if one is interested in sign analysis, the abstract domain can be the finite set $\{\varnothing, \mathbb{Z}_{<0}, \mathbb{Z}_{\geq 0}, \mathbb{Z}\}$ such that the empty set is approximated by $\varnothing$, any set of negative values, like $\{-4, -2\}$, is approximated by $\mathbb{Z}_{<0}$, any set of non-negative values by $\mathbb{Z}_{\geq 0}$ and any other (non-empty) set by $\mathbb{Z}$. The symbolic execution of the program on the abstract domain is performed by a so-called abstract interpreter that may loose precision because it operates on abstract elements only. The abstract interpreter is sound-by-construction in the sense that it is guaranteed to return an over-approximation of the concrete result. Completeness of the abstract interpreter would ensure that the abstract result is the least representative available in the abstract domain of the concrete result, that is the abstract result is as much precise as possible. Recent work has shown that only trivial abstract domains can be complete for all programs of a Turing equivalent language [3,14]. However, if the abstract analysis is complete for all primitives appearing in a program then we can conclude that, for that particular program, the analysis is also complete-by-construction. Consequently, if we consider the sublanguage consisting of all programs composed by complete primitives, then Abstract Interpretation gives us an analysis framework that is sound-and-complete by construction.

Contribution. In this paper, we investigate the connections between completeness in Abstract Interpretation and decidability of program termination and (extensional) equivalence. The idea is to fix some constraints over the abstract domain that guarantees the decidability of relevant properties for any program for which the analysis is complete-by-construction. The notion we put forward is that of *bounded abstract domain* (see Definition 13), where the termination of the abstract interpreter is always guaranteed. Note that, in the general case, termination of the abstract interpreter does not imply termination of the concrete program.

As a first result we show that for programs that are complete-by-construction on a bounded abstract domain termination is decidable. This is obtained by showing that each such program can be rewritten in an equivalent form by unrolling each loop a finite number of times, possibly ending up in a trivial loop. Since the equivalent form can only contain trivial loops, which are immediate to detect, it follows that program termination is decidable.

As a second main result, we show a convenient way of attacking program equivalence for programs that are complete-by-construction on a bounded abstract domain. This can be done by unrolling each program as specified above and by then rewriting the code in a so-called *reduced select normal form* (see Definition 32) that is essentially a series of nested if-then-else structures whose basic commands are assignments and trivial loops. Finally, we give a procedure to decide whether two programs in reduced select normal form are equivalent or not by reducing the problem to the validity of a set of guarded statements defined using the primitives appearing in the programs only.

To support the applicability of our approach we prove how abstract domains defined on Boolean abstractions complete for the same functions can be composed to obtain new bounded domains complete for the same functions and for any guard expressible in one of the original domain. By composing different domains each one complete for a different guard of the program we may end up in designing a new abstract domain complete for *any* guard appearing in the program.

Structure of the Paper: In Sect. 2 we introduce the notation and recall the basic concepts of Abstract Interpretation. The notion of bounded abstract domain is introduced in Sect. 3, together with some results on their composition. In Sect. 4 we prove that any program whose analysis is complete on a bounded domain can be transformed in an equivalent one for which termination is decidable. We conclude Sect. 4 by discussing the applicability of the approach when Boolean abstractions are used. Section 5 shows that equivalence between complete programs on abstract bounded domain is decidable. Finally, Sect. 6 draws some conclusions and discusses future work. All technical proofs are collected in the Appendix for reviewers' convenience.

2   Background

2.1   Notation

We let $\mathbb{N}$ be the set of natural numbers, $\mathbb{Z}$ the set of integers and $\mathbb{B}$ the set of Booleans and write $X \cup Y$ for the union of X and Y, $X \cap Y$ for their intersection, $X \backslash Y$ for their difference, $X \times Y$ for their cartesian product, and X^n for the cartesian product of X with itself n times. The powerset of X is denoted by $\mathcal{P}(X)$. Set inclusion is denoted as $X \subseteq Y$ and strict inclusion as $X \subset Y$.

The identity function over a set X is written $id_X : X \to X$ and we omit the subscript when it is clear from the context. The composition of two functions $f : X \to Y$ and $g : Y \to Z$ is denoted by $g \circ f : X \to Z$ or more concisely by gf.

We also define the iterated application of a function $f : X \to X$ as $f^0 \stackrel{\text{def}}{=} id_X$ and $f^n \stackrel{\text{def}}{=} f \circ f^{n-1}$. Abusing the notation, we extend function application to denote its lifting to sets of elements $f(X) \stackrel{\text{def}}{=} \{f(x) \mid x \in X\}$. Tuples will be denoted by $\tilde{x} = \langle x_1, \ldots, x_n \rangle \in X^n$, however, by overloading the notation $\tilde{x}$ will also denote the set $\{x_1, \ldots, x_n\}$ when no ambiguity arises, moreover, let $\tilde{x}' \in X^m$ we denote as $\tilde{x} + \!\!\!+\, \tilde{x}'$ the concatenation $\langle x_1, \ldots, x_n, x'_1, \ldots, x'_m \rangle$. $\tilde{X} \cap Y$ indicates the tuple $\langle X_1 \cap Y, \ldots, X_n \cap Y \rangle$ when each X_i is a set itself.

We formally define a partitioning of a set U where each partition does not need to be nonempty.

Definition 1 (Partitioning). *Given $n \in \mathbb{N}$, we say that $P = \{P_1, \ldots, P_n\}$ is a partitioning of a set U iff $U = \bigcup_{i=1}^{n} P_i$ and $P_i \cap P_j = \varnothing$ for $i \neq j$.*

We will refer to complete lattices as $\mathcal{C} = \langle C, \leq_C, \vee_C, \wedge_C, \top_C, \bot_C \rangle$ where $\vee_C, \wedge_C$ are the lub and glb respectively and $\top_C, \bot_C$ are the top and bottom elements. When clear from the context the subscripts will be omitted. We define an order on functions $f, g : C \to D$ between lattices, denoted by $f \leq g$, iff for all $c \in C$ it holds that $f(c) \leq_D g(c)$.

We say that a function f between posets is monotone if it is order preserving. The function f is called additive if it is lub preserving and co-additive if it preserves glbs. Moreover, we say that a mapping $f : X \to X$ on a poset is extensive (or reductive) iff for all x it holds that $x \leq f(x)$ (resp. $f(x) \leq x$). We also denote with lfp (f) the least fixpoint of f (w.r.t. $\leq$) when it exists.

2.2 Abstract Interpretation

Abstract interpretation [7] is based on the notion of Galois connections/insertions. We recall the basic concepts here, but see [5–7,9] for further details.

Given two complete lattices $\mathcal{C}$ and $\mathcal{A}$, a pair of functions $\alpha : \mathcal{C} \to \mathcal{A}$ and $\gamma : \mathcal{A} \to \mathcal{C}$ forms a Galois connection (GC) iff for all $a \in A, c \in C$:

$$\alpha(c) \leq_A a \iff c \leq_C \gamma(a)$$

holds. The two domains $\mathcal{C}$ and $\mathcal{A}$ are called the concrete and the abstract domain, respectively. α is the abstraction map while γ is the concretization map.

The elements of the abstract domain are usually denoted by using the symbol $\sharp$, as $S^\sharp$. As some relevant properties: $\gamma\alpha$ is extensive and $\alpha\gamma$ is reductive, both α and γ are monotone, and α is additive, while γ is co-additive.

Definition 2 (Galois Insertion). *A Galois connection where $\alpha\gamma = id_A$ is called a Galois Insertion (GI), in this case α is onto and γ is one-to-one.*

An abstract domain $\mathcal{A}$ is said to be strict when $\gamma(\bot_A) = \bot$. In a GI the property $\gamma(S^\sharp) = \bot \iff S^\sharp = \bot_A$ also holds. From now on we consider GIs on strict abstract domains (unless otherwise specified).

Some elements of the concrete domain can be approximated without any loss of informations: we call them expressible values.

Definition 3 (Expressible Value). *We say that a concrete element $c \in C$ is expressible in $\mathcal{A}$ when $\gamma\alpha(c) = c$. When instead $c \prec \gamma\alpha(c)$ we say that c is strictly approximated in $\mathcal{A}$.*

Also functions need to be approximated on abstract domains.

Definition 4 (Correct Approximation). *Given a concrete function $f : C \to C$, we say that $f^\sharp : A \to A$ is a correct approximation of f iff $\alpha f \leq f^\sharp \alpha$.*

It is known that if $f^\sharp$ is a correct approximation of f then we also have fixpoint correctness when least fixpoints exist, i.e., $\alpha(\text{lfp}\,(f)) \leq \text{lfp}\,(f^\sharp)$ holds.

Between all abstract functions that approximate a concrete one we can define the most precise one.

Definition 5 (Best Correct Approximation). *We define the best correct approximation (BCA) of a concrete function f as $f^A \overset{\text{def}}{=} \alpha f \gamma$.*

Such function is called best correct approximation because it holds $f^A \leq f^\sharp$ for any other correct approximation $f^\sharp$ of f.

Definition 6 (Complete approximation). *A correct approximation $f^\sharp$ is complete iff $\alpha f = f^\sharp \alpha$ holds.*

Analogously to soundness, completeness transfers to fixpoints, meaning that if $f^\sharp$ is complete for f then fixpoint completeness $\alpha(\text{lfp}\,(f)) = \text{lfp}\,(f^\sharp)$ holds.

An abstract domain is said to be complete for f if there exists a complete approximation for f in that domain. A known result is that a complete abstraction exists iff $\alpha f = \alpha f \gamma \alpha$, or equivalently $\gamma \alpha f = \gamma f^A \alpha$.

We use $\mathbb{C}^A(f)$ to indicate that f admits a complete approximation in A (the abstraction domain will be omitted when clear from the context), this notation naturally extends to sets of functions F in the sense that we write $\mathbb{C}^A(F)$ when all the functions in F admit a complete approximation in A.

Abstract domains can be finite or infinite with some desirable properties that ensure the termination of the abstract semantics computation.

Definition 7 (ACC Poset). *A poset is ACC (satisfies the Ascending Chain condition) if it has no infinite strictly increasing chain.*

Any analysis through abstract interpretation over an ACC domain is guaranteed to terminate, since by definition it follows that any fixpoint computation will converge in a finite number of steps.

2.3   Programs

Syntax. We consider the usual definitions for Boolean and integer expressions, where, for simplicity we omit expressions that can generate runtime errors, like division by zero. At the level of the concrete collecting semantics, runtime errors could be handled either with the introduction of distinguished elements in the domain or by using the bottom element (the empty set of results). In the former case, runtime errors are distinguished from divergence and must be propagated ad hoc in the semantic definitions, while in the latter case they are just handled as absence of result. We let:

$$AExp \ni a ::= v \in \mathbb{Z} \mid x \in Var \mid a+a \mid a-a \mid a*a \mid a \div k$$
$$BExp \ni b ::= \mathbf{tt} \mid \mathbf{ff} \mid a=a \mid a>a \mid b \wedge b \mid \neg b.$$

where Var is a denumerable set of program variables and $k \in \mathbb{Z}$ is different from 0. We will introduce some syntax sugar whenever required to keep the notation short by writing e.g. $x \leqslant y$ instead of $\neg(x > y)$ or $(x \vee y)$ instead of $\neg(\neg x \wedge \neg y)$.

Moreover, we define the syntactic substitution of all the occurrences of a variable x with an expression a' inside the expression a, denoted by $a[a'/x]$, as:

$$v[a'/x] \stackrel{\text{def}}{=} v, \qquad\qquad y[a'/x] \stackrel{\text{def}}{=} \begin{cases} a' & \text{if } y = x \\ y & \text{otherwise} \end{cases}$$

$$(a_1 \; op \; a_2)[a'/x] \stackrel{\text{def}}{=} a_1[a'/x] \; op \; a_2[a'/x], \qquad \text{for } op \in \{+, -, *\}$$

$$(a \div k)[a'/x] \stackrel{\text{def}}{=} a[a'/x] \div k.$$

Such definition extends naturally to Boolean expressions in $BExp$.

Given any subset of arithmetic expressions $A \subseteq AExp$ and of Boolean expressions $B \subseteq BExp$, we define two sets of programs: $Imp(A, B)$ the set of imperative programs on A and B, and $Imp^-(A, B)$ a set of programs using only trivial loops of the form **while tt do skip**, for which we use the shorthand $\mathbf{w}_\perp$.

The set of programs $Imp(A, B)$ and $Imp^-(A, B)$ are generated by the following grammars, where $a \in A$ and $b \in B$:

$$Imp \ni c ::= \mathbf{skip} \mid x := a \mid c;c \mid \mathbf{if} \; b \; \mathbf{then} \; c \; \mathbf{else} \; c \mid \mathbf{while} \; b \; \mathbf{do} \; c$$
$$Imp^- \ni c ::= \mathbf{skip} \mid x := a \mid c;c \mid \mathbf{if} \; b \; \mathbf{then} \; c \; \mathbf{else} \; c \mid \mathbf{w}_\perp$$

The two sets A and B will be omitted when clear by the context.

Concrete Semantics. In order to define the semantics of an imperative program, we consider a store $\sigma \in \Sigma$ as a function from $V \subseteq Var$ to integers, that is, $\Sigma \stackrel{\text{def}}{=} V \to \mathbb{Z}$. We define the semantics for integer expressions $(\!|\cdot|\!) : AExp \times \Sigma \to \mathbb{Z}$ as:

$$(\!|v|\!)\sigma \stackrel{\text{def}}{=} v \qquad\qquad (\!|x|\!)\sigma \stackrel{\text{def}}{=} \sigma(x)$$

$$(\!|a_1 + a_2|\!)\sigma \stackrel{\text{def}}{=} (\!|a_1|\!)\sigma \oplus (\!|a_2|\!)\sigma \qquad (\!|a_1 - a_2|\!)\sigma \stackrel{\text{def}}{=} (\!|a_1|\!)\sigma \ominus (\!|a_2|\!)\sigma$$

$$(\!|a_1 * a_2|\!)\sigma \stackrel{\text{def}}{=} (\!|a_1|\!)\sigma \circledast (\!|a_2|\!)\sigma \qquad (\!|a \div k|\!)\sigma \stackrel{\text{def}}{=} (\!|a|\!)\sigma \oslash k$$

where $\oplus, \ominus, \circledast$ and $\oslash$ are the usual mathematical operations. Analogously we define the semantic of Boolean expressions $(\!|\cdot|\!) : BExp \times \Sigma \to \mathbb{B}$ corresponding to the usual comparison and logical operators $=, >, \wedge, \neg$.

We define the concrete collecting semantics by extending the previous seman-tics to sets of stores. Let $\mathbb{S} \stackrel{\text{def}}{=} \mathcal{P}(\Sigma)$, $[\![\cdot]\!] : AExp \times \mathbb{S} \to \mathcal{P}(\mathbb{Z})$ and $[\![\cdot]\!] : BExp \times \mathbb{S} \to \mathbb{S}$ where $[\![a]\!]S \stackrel{\text{def}}{=} \{(\![a]\!)\sigma \mid \sigma \in S\}$ and $[\![b]\!]S \stackrel{\text{def}}{=} \{\sigma \in S \mid (\![b]\!)\sigma = \mathbf{tt}\}$. The concrete collecting semantics for programs in Imp (and Imp^-) is defined as follows:

$$[\![x := a]\!]S \stackrel{\text{def}}{=} \{\sigma[x \mapsto (\![a]\!)\sigma] \mid \sigma \in S\}$$

$$[\![\mathbf{skip}]\!]S \stackrel{\text{def}}{=} S$$

$$[\![c_1; c_2]\!]S \stackrel{\text{def}}{=} [\![c_2]\!][\![c_1]\!]S$$

$$[\![\mathbf{if}\ b\ \mathbf{then}\ c_1\ \mathbf{else}\ c_2]\!]S \stackrel{\text{def}}{=} [\![c_1]\!][\![b]\!]S \cup [\![c_2]\!][\![\neg b]\!]S$$

$$[\![\mathbf{while}\ b\ \mathbf{do}\ c]\!]S \stackrel{\text{def}}{=} [\![\neg b]\!]\mathrm{lfp}\left(\Gamma_S^{b,c}\right)$$

where $\Gamma_S^{b,c} \stackrel{\text{def}}{=} \lambda X.S \cup [\![c]\!][\![b]\!]X$. We also denote with b the set $[\![b]\!]\Sigma$ of all stores satisfying b. By this convention, abusing the notation, $[\![b]\!]S = b \cap S$.

Abstract Semantics. By considering A as an abstract domain for $\mathbb{S}$, we can define the abstract collecting semantics as follows. For integer and Boolean expressions, consider the best correct approximations $[\![a]\!]_A^{\sharp} \stackrel{\text{def}}{=} [\![a]\!]^A$ and $[\![b]\!]_A^{\sharp} \stackrel{\text{def}}{=} [\![b]\!]^A$. The semantics for Imp and Imp^- is defined as follows:

$$[\![x := a]\!]_A^{\sharp} S^{\sharp} \stackrel{\text{def}}{=} \alpha[\![x := a]\!]\gamma S^{\sharp}$$

$$[\![\mathbf{skip}]\!]_A^{\sharp} S^{\sharp} \stackrel{\text{def}}{=} S^{\sharp}$$

$$[\![c_1; c_2]\!]_A^{\sharp} S^{\sharp} \stackrel{\text{def}}{=} [\![c_2]\!]_A^{\sharp}[\![c_1]\!]_A^{\sharp} S^{\sharp}$$

$$[\![\mathbf{if}\ b\ \mathbf{then}\ c_1\ \mathbf{else}\ c_2]\!]_A^{\sharp} S^{\sharp} \stackrel{\text{def}}{=} [\![c_1]\!]_A^{\sharp}[\![b]\!]_A^{\sharp} S^{\sharp} \vee_A [\![c_2]\!]_A^{\sharp}[\![\neg b]\!]_A^{\sharp} S^{\sharp}$$

$$[\![\mathbf{while}\ b\ \mathbf{do}\ c]\!]_A^{\sharp} S^{\sharp} \stackrel{\text{def}}{=} [\![\neg b]\!]_A^{\sharp}\mathrm{lfp}\left(\mathbb{A}_{S^{\sharp}}^{b,c}\right)$$

where $\mathbb{A}_{S^{\sharp}}^{b,c} \stackrel{\text{def}}{=} \lambda X^{\sharp}.S^{\sharp} \vee_A [\![c]\!]_A^{\sharp}[\![b]\!]_A^{\sharp} X^{\sharp}$. For our following applications we need to observe the following straightforward property, which is a consequence of [14].

Lemma 8. *If all assignments in A and all guards in B are complete on $\mathcal{A}$, then any program in $Imp(A, B)$ (and in $Imp^-(A, B)$) is complete on $\mathcal{A}$.*

Note that for any $X \in \mathbb{S}$, $X^{\sharp} \in A$, we have $[\![\mathbf{w}_\perp]\!]X = \varnothing$ and $[\![\mathbf{w}_\perp]\!]_A^{\sharp} X^{\sharp} = \bot$.

The concrete semantics is additive and, moreover, when A and B are sets of respectively complete assignments and guards, then for any $c \in Imp^-(A, B)$, $[\![c]\!]_A^{\sharp}$ is also additive.

In the paper we will exploit Boolean abstraction domains [1]. They are defined by mapping concrete elements into sets of bitvectors as follows (we use $\sigma \models p$ for a given predicate p and a concrete state σ to denote that p holds in σ):

Definition 9 (Boolean abstraction). *Given a set of Boolean predicates $\mathcal{P} = \{p_1, \ldots, p_n\}$ defined over concrete states, we define the associated Boolean*

abstraction on the abstract domain $\text{Bool}(\mathcal{P}) \overset{\text{def}}{=} \langle \mathcal{P}(\{0,1\}^n), \subseteq, \cup, \cap, \{0,1\}^n, \varnothing \rangle$
via the following abstraction/concretization maps, where $1 \cdot p_i \overset{\text{def}}{=} p_i$ *and* $0 \cdot p_i \overset{\text{def}}{=} \neg p_i$:

$$\alpha_{\mathcal{P}}(S) \overset{\text{def}}{=} \{\langle v_1, \ldots, v_n \rangle \mid S \cap \{\sigma \mid \sigma \vDash v_1 \cdot p_1 \wedge \cdots \wedge v_n \cdot p_n\} \neq \varnothing\}$$

$$\gamma_{\mathcal{P}}(S^\sharp) \overset{\text{def}}{=} \{\sigma \mid \exists \langle v_1, \ldots, v_n \rangle \in S^\sharp . \sigma \vDash v_1 \cdot p_1 \wedge \cdots \wedge v_n \cdot p_n\}$$

2.4 Conditions for Completeness of Guards

The only abstract domains that are complete for all programs in any Turing complete programming language are the trivial ones[1] (see [3,14]). In [14] the authors further observed that the completeness of (the semantic functions associated with) assignments and Boolean guards occurring in a program is a sufficient condition to guarantee the completeness of the whole program (see Lemma 8 above). While the completeness of assignments has been extensively studied (e.g., the completeness conditions for assignments in major numerical domains such as intervals, congruences, octagons and affine relations have been fully settled [14,16], while the case of Boolean guards is more troublesome and has been studied in [4], from which we report below the main results we exploit here. Formally, completeness of guards is defined as follows:

Definition 10 (Complete Guard). *We say that a guard b is complete (in short $\mathbb{C}(b)$) to indicate that the filtering functions for both b and $\neg b$ are complete, that is, letting $F_b \overset{\text{def}}{=} \{\lambda X \in \mathcal{S} . b \cap X, \lambda X \in \mathcal{S} . \neg b \cap X\}$, then $\mathbb{C}(b) \iff \mathbb{C}(F_b)$.*

Both b and $\neg b$ being expressible is a necessary condition for $\mathbb{C}(b)$ to hold. Moreover:

Theorem 11 (cf. [4]). *If b and $\neg b$ are expressible in A, then:*

$$\mathbb{C}(b) \iff \forall S \in \mathbb{S} . \left(\alpha(S \cap b) = \alpha(S) \wedge_A \alpha(b) \quad \wedge \quad \alpha(S \cap \neg b) = \alpha(S) \wedge_A \alpha(\neg b) \right)$$

$$\iff \forall S_1^\sharp, S_2^\sharp \in A . \left(S_1^\sharp \leq \alpha(b) \wedge S_2^\sharp \leq \alpha(\neg b) \implies \gamma(S_1^\sharp \vee_A S_2^\sharp) = \gamma(S_1^\sharp) \cup \gamma(S_2^\sharp) \right)$$

Theorem 11 offers a convenient way to check guard completeness: it is necessary and sufficient to check that the join of every two points under b and $\neg b$ respectively is expressible in the domain. Theorem 11 also gives a way to compute the completeness closure w.r.t. to a guards b, by enforcing the presence in the abstract domain of the elements b and $\neg b$ together with the (concrete) join of every two (abstract) points under b and $\neg b$.

3 Bounded Domains

We first introduce the notion of bounded (abstract) domain in order to characterize the class of programs that we will manipulate in order to remove any nontrivial loop.

---

[1] Namely, the identical abstraction, making abstract and concrete semantics the same, and the top abstraction, making all programs equivalent by abstract semantics.

Definition 12 (k-ACC Poset). *A poset is k-ACC iff all ascending chain lengths are bound by a value $k \in \mathbb{N}$.*

Definition 13 (Bounded domain). *A poset is said to be bounded if there exists some value k for which it is k-ACC.*

Whenever a complete abstract interpretation can be conducted on a bounded domain, then we can exploit the parameter k which gives us an upper bound to the number of iterations required to compute any abstract fixpoint.

Focusing on the chain of iterates produced when computing $\mathrm{lfp}\left(\mathbb{A}_{S^{\sharp}}^{b,c}\right)$ we observe that if our abstract domain is bounded, then it is (k+1)-ACC for some k, thus it holds that the produced chain contains no more than $k + 1$ distinct values, meaning that the fixpoint computation converges in no more than $k + 1$ steps, that is $\mathrm{lfp}\,(\mathbb{A}) = \mathbb{A}^{(k)}(\bot_A)$.

An interesting result about complete abstractions is the following:

Lemma 14. *Let $\mathcal{A}$ be a strict domain for which $[\![c_1]\!]$ and $[\![c_2]\!]$ are complete. If $[\![c_1]\!]_A^{\sharp} = [\![c_2]\!]_A^{\sharp}$ it holds that:*

$$[\![c_1]\!]S = \bot \iff [\![c_2]\!]S = \bot$$

We present two well-known abstract domains *Sign* and *Mod3* in Fig. 1 which are both bounded and will be used in the upcoming examples.

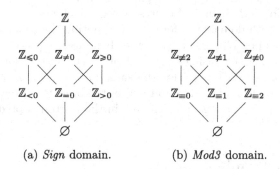

(a) *Sign* domain.   (b) *Mod3* domain.

Fig. 1. Abstract domains

Note that we use the symbol $\equiv_3$, or $\equiv$ when no ambiguity arises, to identify modulo 3 congruences.

The abstraction function for the *Sign* domain is defined by mapping each set X of concrete values based on the sign of its elements, let us define an auxiliary function $sgn(x) : \mathbb{Z} \to \{\mathbb{Z}_{<0}, \mathbb{Z}_{=0}, \mathbb{Z}_{>0}\}$ which maps concrete values based on their sign (and zero in $\mathbb{Z}_{=0}$), the abstraction map is then defined as:

$$\alpha_{Sign}(S) \stackrel{\text{def}}{=} \bigvee_{x \in S} sgn(x)$$

The concretization map is then defined intuitively over $\mathbb{Z}_{<0}$ as

$$\gamma_{Sign}(\mathbb{Z}_{<0}) \stackrel{\text{def}}{=} \{x \in \mathbb{Z} \mid x < 0\}$$

and following a similar approach for all the other abstract values.

Both the abstract and the concretization maps for the *Mod3* domain are defined in a similar fashion, by mapping every concrete value based on its modulo 3 reminder as classically defined.

Multiplication is a complete operation in both domains, while addition and difference are complete in *Mod3* only.

We now show that Boolean abstractions give rise to bounded domains which can be composed via predicate union while preserving functional completeness.

Lemma 15. *Let* $\mathcal{P} \stackrel{\text{def}}{=} \{p_1, \ldots, p_n\}$, $\mathcal{Q} \stackrel{\text{def}}{=} \{q_1, \ldots, q_m\}$ *be sets of predicates, and let* $P \stackrel{\text{def}}{=} \text{Bool}(\mathcal{P})$ *and* $Q \stackrel{\text{def}}{=} \text{Bool}(\mathcal{Q})$ *be the Boolean abstraction domains built over the two predicate sets, respectively, and let* $f : \Sigma \to \Sigma$ *be a complete function over both* P *and* Q. *Then, the Boolean abstraction domain* $D \stackrel{\text{def}}{=} \text{Bool}(\mathcal{P} \cup \mathcal{Q})$ *built over the set of predicates* $\mathcal{P} \cup \mathcal{Q}$ *is such that:*

1. *D is bounded*
2. *The predicate filter for every predicate in* $\mathcal{P} \cup \mathcal{Q}$ *is complete*
3. *f is complete over D*

We also note that the class of bounded domains is closed under reduced product [8, Section 10.1] (which also preserves completeness for functions which are complete on both domains). Moreover, computing the completeness closure w.r.t. to guards as per Theorem 11 preserves boundedness, too.

It is worth noting that using Cartesian predicate abstraction [1] instead of Boolean abstraction would not offer the same guarantees about completeness for predicate filters. Indeed Lemma 15 requires the presence of the disjunction of predicate filters, which is in general missing in the Cartesian predicate abstraction.

4   Program Termination

In this section we explore the connections between complete abstractions in bounded domains and program termination on a given input. Formally, given a command $c \in Imp(A, B)$ and an input set S, the termination problem corresponds to deciding whether $[\![c]\!]S = \bot$ or not, i.e., we want to establish if there is some input in S where c terminates or not.[2] We show that the bound on the length of any ascending chain in the abstract domain can be used to infer the largest number of times each loop must be unrolled. This allows us to define a program transformation that replaces each loop with its bounded unrolling

---

[2] Note that this is different from establishing termination for all input in S, which should be addressed separately.

while preserving the concrete collecting semantics. While the original program belongs to $Imp(A, B)$, the transformed program will belong to $Imp^-(A, B)$, that is the only loops have the form $\mathbf{w}_\perp$, which is the only source of divergence. As a main result, termination is thus decidable for any complete program (and any input).

The first observation is that in any $(k + 1)$-ACC domain and for any $Imp(A, B)$ program **while** b **do** c we have that, for all $S^\sharp$,

$$\llbracket \textbf{while } b \textbf{ do } c \rrbracket_A^\sharp S^\sharp = \llbracket \textbf{if}_{b,c}^{(k-1)} \rrbracket_A^\sharp S^\sharp \tag{1}$$

where $\textbf{if}_{b,c}^{(k-1)}$ is the $Imp^-(A, B)$ command inductively defined as:

$$\textbf{if}_{b,c}^{(0)} \stackrel{\text{def}}{=} \textbf{if } b \textbf{ then } \mathbf{w}_\perp \textbf{ else skip}$$

$$\textbf{if}_{b,c}^{(n+1)} \stackrel{\text{def}}{=} \textbf{if } b \textbf{ then } \left(c; \textbf{if}_{b,c}^{(n)}\right) \textbf{ else skip}$$

To see this, we exploit the equality

$$\mathbb{A}^{(k+1)}(\perp_A) = \left(\bigvee_{i=0}^{k} (\llbracket c \rrbracket_A^\sharp \llbracket b \rrbracket_A^\sharp)^{(i)} S^\sharp\right) \vee_A \perp_A \tag{2}$$

which can be immediately proved by induction on k. Then, the equality (1) can be proved as follows:

$$\llbracket \textbf{while } b \textbf{ do } c \rrbracket_A^\sharp S^\sharp = \llbracket \neg b \rrbracket_A^\sharp \text{lfp}(\mathbb{A}) = \qquad \{\text{Hypothesis}\}$$

$$\llbracket \neg b \rrbracket_A^\sharp \mathbb{A}^{(k)}(\perp_A) = \qquad \{\text{Equation 2}\}$$

$$\llbracket \neg b \rrbracket_A^\sharp \left(\left(\bigvee_{i=0}^{k-1} (\llbracket c \rrbracket_A^\sharp \llbracket b \rrbracket_A^\sharp)^{(i)} S^\sharp\right) \vee_A \perp_A\right) = \qquad \{\text{Additivity of } \llbracket \neg b \rrbracket_A^\sharp\}$$

$$\left(\bigvee_{i=0}^{k-1} \llbracket \neg b \rrbracket_A^\sharp (\llbracket c \rrbracket_A^\sharp \llbracket b \rrbracket_A^\sharp)^{(i)} S^\sharp\right) \vee_A \llbracket \neg b \rrbracket_A^\sharp \perp_A = \qquad \{\text{Definition of } \llbracket \textbf{skip} \rrbracket_A^\sharp, \llbracket \neg b \rrbracket_A^\sharp\}$$

$$\left(\bigvee_{i=0}^{k-1} \llbracket \textbf{skip} \rrbracket_A^\sharp \llbracket \neg b \rrbracket_A^\sharp (\llbracket c \rrbracket_A^\sharp \llbracket b \rrbracket_A^\sharp)^{(i)} S^\sharp\right) \vee_A \perp_A = \qquad \{\text{By induction on } k\}$$

$$\llbracket \textbf{if}_{b,c}^{(k-1)} \rrbracket_A^\sharp S^\sharp$$

This process of "unrolling" **while** loops introduces a sequence of nested **if-else** commands of depth k; unrolling a **while** loop having $d - 1$ nested loops inside produces a program having a total of k^d **if-else** commands. Equation 1 proves that the transformed program will exhibit an equivalent behaviour as the original one on the abstract domain $\mathcal{A}$ (for any abstract input).

Next we exploit the notion of complete abstraction. Assuming that the set A contains only complete assignments and B only complete guards on the abstract domain $\mathcal{A}$, we have that every program in $Imp(A, B)$ is complete as well as its transformed version in $Imp^-(A, B)$, because the transformation does not introduce any new guard or assignment (see Lemma 8). By Lemma 14 and Eq. (1), we conclude that, from a divergence perspective, the **while** command is equivalent to its transformed version in **if-else** form, that is, the concrete semantics of the first one diverges if and only the concrete semantics of the second does.

Theorem 16 (Termination). *Let A contain only complete assignments and B only complete guards on the abstract domain $\mathcal{A}$. For any guard $b \in B$ and any command $c \in Imp(A, B)$ we have*

$$[\![\textbf{while } b \textbf{ do } c]\!]S = \bot \iff [\![\textbf{if}_{b,c}^{(k-1)}]\!]S = \bot \tag{3}$$

In fact, a much stronger result can be obtained, namely that the concrete collecting semantics of the program and its transformation coincide.

Theorem 17 (Unrolling). *Let A contains only complete assignments and B only complete guards on the abstract domain $\mathcal{A}$. For any guard $b \in B$ and any command $c \in Imp(A, B)$ we have*

$$[\![\textbf{while } b \textbf{ do } c]\!] = [\![\textbf{if}_{b,c}^{(k-1)}]\!] \tag{4}$$

Proof. By applying $k - 1$ expansions

$$[\![\textbf{while } b \textbf{ do } c]\!] = [\![\textbf{if } b \textbf{ then } (c; \textbf{while } b \textbf{ do } c) \textbf{ else skip}]\!]$$

we get an equivalent command which is identical to $\textbf{if}_{b,c}^{(n)}$ except for the $\textbf{if}_{b,c}^{(0)}$ element which is replaced by **while** b **do** c. Moreover, by Eq. (3), we obtain the thesis. $\qquad\qquad\qquad\qquad\qquad\qquad\qquad\qquad\qquad\qquad\qquad\qquad\qquad\qquad\Box$

This result lets us conclude that:

Corollary 18. *For any complete program $c \in Imp(A, B)$ on a bounded strict abstract domain there exists an $Imp^-(A, B)$ program which is equivalent under the concrete semantics.*

The above procedure also gives us a constructive way to obtain such an equivalent program that will also be complete.

4.1   Deciding Program Termination

We now use our results to solve the program termination problem, which consists of, given a program c and an input σ, determining if $[\![c]\!]\{\sigma\} = \varnothing$.

Let us consider the command $c' \in Imp^-$ obtained by the previous transformation of c. The result builds on the fact that for any Imp^- program, termination is decidable since it can only involve trivial loops $\mathbf{w}_\bot$, i.e., we can safely state that any nonterminating computation will reach some $\mathbf{w}_\bot$ in a finite number of steps.

In fact, for any input, we can safely execute the semantics of the equivalent Imp^- program c' and as soon as we enter any loop we can safely conclude that the program diverges on such input.

On the other hand, executing c' on any terminating input will never enter any loop, since that would lead to divergence. Observing that the number of executed steps in absence of any loop is bounded by the program length (since no program line can be executed more than once) concludes that termination will be decided in a finite number of steps.

Putting it all together:

Theorem 19 (Deciding termination). *Let $c \in Imp(A, B)$ be any program which admits a complete approximation in a bounded strict abstract domain, then program termination of c is decidable for any input σ.*

This gives some interesting insight in characterizing the expressiveness of the class of programs for which such an analysis is effective, since classical results such as Rice's Theorem and the undecidability of the halting problem state that program termination is, in general, undecidable. This result can also be applied in a different way: given a program c for which we want to investigate termination, we aim at finding a bounded abstract domain in which all of the guards and assignments appearing in c are complete. By exhibiting such a domain we are able to conclude that termination is decidable for c.

We now show an example to give an idea of the manipulations occurring during the proposed program transformation.

Example 20. Consider the program w_1 defined as follows:

$$w_1 \overset{\text{def}}{=} \textbf{while } (x \neq_3 0) \textbf{ do } (x := 2 * x)$$

where $x \neq_3 0$ is a shorthand for $\neg(x - 3 * (x \div 3) = 0)$. The program w_1 does not contain any other **while** loops inside its body and admits a complete approximation in the domain *Mod3*, which is 4-ACC thus we conclude that termination is decidable on w_1, and its equivalent form is:

$$\llbracket w_1 \rrbracket = \llbracket \textbf{if}^{(2)}_{(x \neq_3 0),(x:=2*x)} \rrbracket$$

that is, $\textbf{if}^{(2)}_{(x \neq_3 0),(x:=2*x)} =$

```
if  x ≠₃ 0  then
      x := 2 * x;
    if  x ≠₃ 0  then
          x := 2 * x;
        if  x ≠₃ 0  then
                while true do skip
            else skip
        else skip
else skip
```

For example, it is now immediate to check that if initially $x = 1$, then we multiply x by 2 twice and we reach the innermost **if** with $x = 4$, thus entering the trivial non-terminating loop. Similarly, for $x = 5$ we reach the innermost **if** with $x = 20$ and detect divergence.

4.2   Exploiting Boolean Abstractions

The decidability result presented in Theorem 19 (but the same considerations will also hold for Theorem 35) can be applied whenever we can prove the existence of a bounded domain satisfying the required hypotheses. Lemma 15 suggests a strong approach to proving the existence of such a domain. The idea is to tailor some boolean abstraction domain to each fragment of the program, possibly using different guards, but complete w.r.t. the same kinds of assignments, and then derive the existence of a complete bounded abstract domain for the whole program from Lemma 15.

As a notable example, we observe that domains built over congruences modulo some given number, like *Mod3*, are complete w.r.t. sum, difference and product. They are also complete w.r.t. all the guards testing the remainder of the division modulo the given number. As they are all boolean abstractions, it follows that both termination and program equivalence are decidable for programs in which all guards test for congruences, and assignments apply arithmetic operations.

5   Program Equivalence

In this section we address the problem of checking program equivalence, which can formally be stated as follows: given two programs $c_1, c_2 \in Imp(A, B)$ we want to decide whether $[\![c_1]\!] = [\![c_2]\!]$ or not. Thanks to the results in Sect. 4, we define here a program transformation that produces a so-called reduced select normal form, such that program equivalence reduces to decide the validity of a set of guarded statements. The technique presented here applies to deterministic programs as the ones in *Imp*. Its extension to more general analysis frameworks where nondeterministic languages are also considered may not be trivial and needs further investigation.

First, we introduce an intermediate syntax defining a **select** command which constitutes a generalization of **if-else** as a n-way conditional.

Definition 21 (select). *Given two vectors $\tilde{b} \in BExp^n, \tilde{c} \in (Imp^-)^n$ such that $\tilde{b}$ forms a partitioning of Σ, we call n the branching factor of the **select** construct with a semantics defined as:*

$$[\![\mathbf{select}(\tilde{b} : \tilde{c})]\!]S \overset{\text{def}}{=} \bigcup_{i=1}^{n} [\![c_i]\!][\![b_i]\!]S$$

This can be seen as a generalized multi-way **if** command, like Dijkstra's guarded statements, and can be expressed as a sequence of nested **if-else** by following a nested structure of the form **if** b_1 **then** c_1 **else** (**if** b_2 **then** c_2 **else** ...). Since $\tilde{b}$

forms a partitioning of Σ, the order in which the various disjoint cases are nested is not important: semantic equivalence holds under any arbitrary permutation applied to the entries of both $\tilde{b}$ and $\tilde{c}$. We note that as a special case:

$$[\![\text{if } b \text{ then } c_1 \text{ else } c_2]\!] = [\![\text{select}(\langle b, \neg b \rangle : \langle c_1, c_2 \rangle)]\!].$$

By this observation we can define a new auxiliary grammar:

$$Select \ni c ::= \textbf{skip} \mid x := a \mid c; c \mid \textbf{select}(\tilde{b} : \tilde{c}) \mid \textbf{w}_\perp$$

In the following we refer to $\textbf{skip}$, $\textbf{w}_\perp$ and assignments as *basic commands*. We will also use the notation $Select(A, B)$ to explicitly indicate the sets of expressions and guards used to construct the $Select$ commands, as we did for Imp and Imp^-. We will show that every Imp^- program can be translated in an equivalent $Select$ one (and every $Select$ program can be translated into an Imp^- one by applying the above definition of $\textbf{select}$ as nested $\textbf{if}$ statements).

The program transformation is defined in two phases: first we transform the Imp^- program in a so-called select normal form (see Definition 29) that consists of at most one $\textbf{select}$ statement and then we compress series of assignments into a single one (called reduced select normal form, see Definition 32). The transformation to select normal form requires the ability to invert the order in which assignments and guards are applied, so to move all guards upfront. The next section on backward computation introduces the main concepts and notation exploited in the reduction to normal form. Finally, in Sect. 5.4 it is explained how to compare two programs in reduced select normal forms.

5.1   Backward Computation

In order to manipulate the program structure obtained in the previous section we are going to introduce a concept of inverse semantics for Imp^- commands, which is a function mapping a command c and a set of states S to all possible states for which the execution of the semantics of c may lead to some state in S, also called the *weakest liberal precondition* [11].

Definition 22 (Inverse Concrete Semantics). *We define* $X = [\![c]\!]^{-1}S$ *as the largest set* X *such that* $[\![c]\!]X \subseteq S$, *this can be computed as:*

$$[\![x := a]\!]^{-1}S \stackrel{\text{def}}{=} \{\sigma' \mid \sigma \in S, \sigma' \in (\![a]\!)^{-1}\sigma(x)\}$$

$$[\![\textbf{skip}]\!]^{-1}S \stackrel{\text{def}}{=} S$$

$$[\![c_1; c_2]\!]^{-1}S \stackrel{\text{def}}{=} [\![c_1]\!]^{-1}[\![c_2]\!]^{-1}S$$

$$[\![\text{if } b \text{ then } c_1 \text{ else } c_2]\!]^{-1}S \stackrel{\text{def}}{=} [b][\![c_1]\!]^{-1}S \cup [\neg b][\![c_2]\!]^{-1}S$$

$$[\![\textbf{w}_\perp]\!]^{-1}S \stackrel{\text{def}}{=} \Sigma$$

where $(\![a]\!)^{-1}(x) = \{\sigma \mid (\![a]\!)\sigma = x\}$.

In general $[\![\cdot]\!]^{-1}$ is not the inverse function (in the mathematical sense) of the concrete semantics, this can be observed for example as:

$$[\![\textbf{if } x = 0 \textbf{ then } (x := x + 1) \textbf{ else } (x := x + 2)]\!]\{0\} = \{1\}$$
$$\text{but } [\![\textbf{if } x = 0 \textbf{ then } (x := x + 1) \textbf{ else } (x := x + 2)]\!]^{-1}\{1\} = \{0, -1\} \neq \{0\}$$

This is due to the fact that we can loose some information related to the previous state at each conditional branching. We also note that the function $(\!|a|\!)^{-1}$ in the definition maps each post-value to a set of possible pre-states, this is needed in cases such as that of constant assignment, since we loose any information about the previous value of x after we assign a constant value to it:

$$[\![x := 0]\!]^{-1}\{0\} = \top$$

Moreover, let us notice that the inverse semantics could give us a set of values smaller (in cardinality) than the input, as for:

$$[\![x := 0]\!]^{-1}\{1\} = \bot$$

In general, it holds for all Imp^- commands c that $[\![c]\!]^{-1}$ is additive, implying that it is also monotone, that $[\![c]\!]^{-1}[\![c]\!]$ is extensive and dually $[\![c]\!][\![c]\!]^{-1}$ is reductive.

We now observe that, in general, $[\![c]\!][\![c]\!]^{-1}S \neq S$ whenever there exists some $x \in S$ such that x is not reachable through $[\![c]\!]$ from any input, then $x \notin [\![c]\!][\![c]\!]^{-1}S$, for example:

$$[\![x := 0]\!][\![x := 0]\!]^{-1}\{0, 1\} = [\![x := 0]\!]\top = \{0\}.$$

The following result follows from the literature.

Lemma 23 (Adjointness). *For any $c \in Imp^-$ and $X, S \subseteq \Sigma$ it holds*

$$X \subseteq [\![c]\!]^{-1}S \iff [\![c]\!]X \subseteq S$$

We now show an important result that arises whenever we apply $[\![c]\!]^{-1}$ to sets which constitute a partitioning. In our case we will apply this result to the partitioning $\{b, \neg b\}$ whenever b is a valid guard.

Lemma 24. *For any $c \in Imp^-$ and any partitioning $P = \{P_1, \ldots, P_n\}$ of Σ it holds that:*

$$\Sigma = \bigcup_{i=1}^{n}[\![c]\!]^{-1}P_i$$

Lemma 25. *For any Imp^- command c and any partitioning $P = \{P_1, \ldots, P_n\}$ of Σ it holds that:*

$$[\![c]\!]\{\sigma\} = \bot \iff \sigma \in \left([\![c]\!]^{-1}P_i \cap [\![c]\!]^{-1}P_j\right) \qquad \text{for any } i \neq j$$

We now introduce $b^{-c} \overset{\text{def}}{=} [\![c]\!]^{-1}b$ as a shorthand which we will use in the upcoming sections.

Another key result which can be obtained by using the inverse semantics enables us to swap the order of a command execution and a filtering as follows:

Lemma 26. *For any guard b and command c:*

$$[\![b]\!][\![c]\!]S = [\![c]\!]\left([\![c]\!]^{-1}b \cap S\right)$$

that is, in a more succinct notation: $[\![b]\!][\![c]\!]S = [\![c]\!][\![b^{-c}]\!]S$.

We now address the problem of guaranteeing that the process of applying the inverse semantics of c to any guard b produces some b^{-c} which is contained in our language $Imp^-(A,B)$. In the upcoming sections we will show that the only commands for which we will need to apply Lemma 26 are those where c is a basic command. Of these three cases, **skip** is trivial and does not need any manipulation, since $[\![b]\!][\![\textbf{skip}]\!] = [\![\textbf{skip}]\!][\![b]\!] = [\![b]\!]$, and the same holds for $[\![b]\!][\![\mathbf{w}_\perp]\!] = [\![\mathbf{w}_\perp]\!][\![b]\!] = [\![\mathbf{w}_\perp]\!]$.

The case for assignment can be resolved by applying the following property.

Theorem 27. *For any $a \in AExp$ and $b \in BExp$ it holds:*

$$[\![b]\!][\![x := a]\!] = [\![x := a]\!][\![b[a/x]]\!]$$

The previous theorem together with the previous observations allow us to conclude the main result of this section.

Corollary 28. *If the set of guards B is closed under syntactical substitution, in the sense that for any $a \in A$ and $b \in B$ we have $b[a/x] \in B$, then for any $c \in Imp^-$ and $b \in B$, there exists some $b' \in B$ such that $[\![b]\!][\![c]\!] = [\![c]\!][\![b']\!]$.*

5.2   Select Normal Form

Next, we define select normal form and prove that any *Select* command can be put in such format by a semantic-preserving transformation.

Definition 29 (Select normal form, SNF). *We say that a program $c \in Select$ is in normal form (in short, SNF) if either:*

- *c is $\mathbf{w}_\perp$;*
- *c is a sequential composition of **skip**s and assignments;*
- *c is in the form $\textbf{select}(\tilde{b} : \tilde{c})$ and every c_i is $\mathbf{w}_\perp$ or a sequential composition of **skip**s and assignments.*

We also use $\tilde{c}; c$ as a shorthand for the vector $\langle (c_1; c), \dots, (c_n; c) \rangle$ obtained by post-composing c to every command c_i in a sequential way, and the same goes for $c; \tilde{c}$ using pre-composition. We now introduce some rewriting rules involving **select** which are helpful in manipulating *Select* programs:

Post-composition with Arbitrary c: The case $[\![\textbf{select}(\tilde{b} : \tilde{c}); c]\!]$ can be rewritten as $[\![\textbf{select}(\tilde{b} : \tilde{c}; c)]\!]$, post-composing c to every c_i sequentially; the equality holds in a straightforward way by expanding the definition and applying additivity.

*Pre-composition with $\mathbf{w}_\perp$ and **skip**:* These two cases are trivial, since:

$$[\![\textbf{skip}; \textbf{select}(\tilde{b} : \tilde{c})]\!] = [\![\textbf{select}(\tilde{b} : \tilde{c})]\!]$$
$$[\![\mathbf{w}_\perp; \textbf{select}(\tilde{b} : \tilde{c})]\!] = [\![\mathbf{w}_\perp]\!]$$

Pre-composition with an Assignment: In the case $[\![x := a; \mathbf{select}(\tilde{b} : \tilde{c})]\!]$ we can safely observe that $x := a$ is always terminating, thus by expanding the definitions:

$$[\![x := a; \mathbf{select}(\tilde{b} : \tilde{c})]\!]S = \bigcup_{i=1}^{n}[\![c_i]\!][\![b_i]\!][\![x := a]\!]S = \bigcup_{i=1}^{n}[\![c_i]\!][\![x := a]\!][\![b_i^{-x:=a}]\!]S$$

where the fact that the set of states on which $x := a$ diverges is empty ensures that $\tilde{b}^{-x:=a} \overset{\text{def}}{=} [\![x := a]\!]^{-1}\tilde{b} = \langle b_1^{-x:=a}, \ldots, b_n^{-x:=a}\rangle$ forms a partitioning by means of Lemmas 24 and 25, thus $[\![x := a; \mathbf{select}(\tilde{b} : \tilde{c})]\!] = [\![\mathbf{select}(\tilde{b}^{-x:=a} : c; \tilde{c})]\!]$.

Nested **select** *Commands:* Let us consider the case $\mathbf{select}(\tilde{b} : \tilde{c})$ where some $c_i = \mathbf{select}(\tilde{b}' : \tilde{c}')$, with $|\tilde{b}| = n$ and $|\tilde{b}'| = m$, we take $i = 1$ (without loss of generality, since the semantics is preserved under permutation of the indexes) and by expanding the definition we get:

$$[\![\mathbf{select}(\tilde{b} : \tilde{c})]\!]S = [\![\mathbf{select}(\tilde{b}' : \tilde{c}')]\!][\![b_1]\!]S \cup \bigcup_{i=2}^{n}[\![c_i]\!][\![b_i]\!]S$$

and expanding the isolated term: $[\![\mathbf{select}(\tilde{b}' : \tilde{c}')]\!][\![b_1]\!]S = \bigcup_{j=1}^{m}[\![c_j']\!][\![b_j']\!][\![b_1]\!]S$.

Since $\tilde{b}'$ is a partitioning of Σ, then $\tilde{b}' \cap b_1$ is a partitioning of b_1, thus $\tilde{b}'' = \langle b_1' \cap b_1, \ldots, b_m' \cap b_1, b_2, \ldots, b_n\rangle$ is a partitioning of Σ and defining $\tilde{c}'' = \langle c_1', \ldots, c_m', c_2, \ldots, c_n\rangle$ gives the equality $[\![\mathbf{select}(\tilde{b} : \tilde{c})]\!] = [\![\mathbf{select}(\tilde{b}'' : \tilde{c}'')]\!]$ which has one less **select** command and $|\tilde{b}''| = n + m - 1$.

Sequence of **select** *Commands:* We now consider the case where for some $\tilde{b}, \tilde{b}', \tilde{c}, \tilde{c}'$ s.t. $|\tilde{b}| = n$ and $|\tilde{b}'| = m$ we have a sequential composition of $\mathbf{select}(\tilde{b} : \tilde{c})$ and $\mathbf{select}(\tilde{b}' : \tilde{c}')$. We first give an intuitive reasoning for this case: we can expand this term by applying the post-composition rule and we get a new command of the form $\mathbf{select}(\tilde{b} : (\tilde{c}; \mathbf{select}(\tilde{b}' : \tilde{c}')))$ and by (recursively) applying these rules we can obtain a new command such that $[\![\mathbf{select}(\tilde{b}_i'' : \tilde{c}_i'')]\!] = [\![c_i; \mathbf{select}(\tilde{b}' : \tilde{c}')]\!]$ for each $i = 1 \ldots n$, thus allowing us to apply the rule for nested **select**s to each of the n branches, successfully producing a single **select** command.

We now consider the case where $\mathbf{select}(\tilde{b} : \tilde{c})$ is in normal form, in order to get an explicit formula to rewrite these terms we observe that:

$$[\![\mathbf{select}(\tilde{b} : \tilde{c}); \mathbf{select}(\tilde{b}' : \tilde{c}')]\!]S = \bigcup_{j=1}^{m}[\![c_j']\!][\![b_j']\!]\bigcup_{i=1}^{n}[\![c_i]\!][\![b_i]\!]S$$

which by additivity of $[\![\cdot]\!]$ can be rewritten as $\bigcup_{j=1}^{m}\bigcup_{i=1}^{n}[\![c_j']\!][\![b_j']\!][\![c_i]\!][\![b_i]\!]S$.

Since we are in normal form, then the vector $\tilde{c}$ does not contain any **select** command and each of its entries is either $\mathbf{w}_\perp$ or a composition of assignments and **skip**s.

We now consider the case where $c_i = \mathbf{w}_\perp$ and we notice that the corresponding terms are $\bigcup_{j=1}^{m}[\![c_j']\!][\![b_j']\!][\![\mathbf{w}_\perp]\!][\![b_i]\!]S = \bigcup_{j=1}^{m}[\![\mathbf{w}_\perp]\!][\![b_i]\!]S = [\![\mathbf{w}_\perp]\!][\![b_i]\!]S$ by definition of $\mathbf{w}_\perp$.

When considering any other $c_i \neq c_j$, then c_i converges for any input since it consist of a composition of assignments and **skips**, thus the corresponding term can be rewritten as

$$\bigcup_{j=1}^{m} [\![c_j']\!] [\![b_j']\!] [\![c_i]\!] [\![b_i]\!] S = \bigcup_{j=1}^{m} [\![c_j']\!] [\![c_i]\!] [\![b_j'^{-c_i}]\!] [\![b_i]\!] S$$

Since c_i is always terminating, by Lemmas 24–25 the sets $b_j'^{-c_i}$ form a partitioning of Σ. Thus we conclude that the sets $b_j'^{-c_i} \cap b_i$ form a partitioning of b_i.

The assumption we made on **select**$(\tilde{b} : \tilde{c})$ being in normal form can always be achieved, since by these rules we can always rewrite in normal form the innermost **select** constructs first and proceed our way merging them with the outer ones (a more detailed proof of how we can reduce every *Select* program to normal form is given in Lemma 30). We thus conclude that every composition of two **select** commands can be substituted with a single **select** command having a branching factor less or equal than nm (equality holds when no $\mathbf{w}_\perp$ appear).

Successive applications of the above rewriting rules give us an effective way to reduce every *Select* program to a normal form, in fact:

Lemma 30. *Every Select command c can be reduced in normal form using the above rules.*

We note that the reduction procedure is guaranteed to terminate, therefore giving an effective procedure to obtain a SNF. We also introduce some auxiliary rules which are not necessary in order to reach a normal form but which could help in simplifying some program structures:

Select Branch Pruning: If we have a command of the form **select**$(\tilde{b} : \tilde{c})$ such that there exists b_i for which $[\![b_i]\!] = [\![\mathbf{ff}]\!]$, then we can drop the corresponding branch by removing both b_i and c_i from $\tilde{b}$ and $\tilde{c}$.

Select Branch Merging: If we have a command of the form **select**$(\tilde{b} : \tilde{c})$ such that there exist two indexes $i \neq j$ and $[\![c_i]\!] = [\![c_j]\!]$ we can safely merge the two branches by removing b_j and c_j from $\tilde{b}$ and $\tilde{c}$ respectively and updating $b_i = b_i \vee b_j$.

Select Removal: This rule is dual to the select introduction one: every command of the form **select**$(\langle b \rangle : \langle c \rangle)$ (thus having branching factor 1) can be rewritten by removing the **select** construct as $[\![c]\!]$; this follows directly observing that since $\{b\}$ forms a partitioning then $[\![b]\!] = [\![\mathbf{tt}]\!]$ and by expanding the definition.

Newly Introduced Guards: We now examine the new guards which are introduced by the aforementioned manipulations, let $a \in A$ be an arithmetic expression and $b, b_1, b_2 \in B$ be guards in the program we are rewriting, then the newly introduced guards will be of the forms:

$b[a/x]$: If we are applying either the rule for pre-composition with an assignment or that for a sequence of **select** commands;

194   R. Bruni et al.

$b_1 \wedge b_2$: If we are applying the rule for nested **select** commands.

$b_1 \vee b_2$: If we are applying the **select** branch merging rule, this guard can be rewritten as $\neg(\neg b_1 \wedge \neg b_2)$ by means of De Morgan.

tt: If we are applying the **select** introduction rule.

We now observe that main rules (that is, the non-auxiliary ones) only introduce new guards in the form of $b[a/x]$ or $b_1 \wedge b_2$ and we observe that:

Lemma 31. *If* $\mathbb{C}(b_1), \mathbb{C}(b_2)$, *then the filtering function for* $b_1 \wedge b_2$ *is also complete:*

This lets us conclude that, under the hypothesis:

$$\mathbb{C}(a) \wedge \mathbb{C}(b) \implies \mathbb{C}(b[a/x]) \tag{5}$$

the rewriting process we defined to reduce every *Select* program into normal form produces new guards by preserving completeness of their filtering functions. Moreover, if B is closed under syntactical substitution for every $a \in A$ to x and forms a Boolean algebra (i.e. is closed under $\wedge$, $\vee$ and $\neg$), then for every $c \in Select(A, B)$ its rewritten normal form c' is such that $c' \in Select(A, B)$.

5.3   Normal Form Scaling in Combined Domains

In order to discuss how the normal form may scale when different abstract domains are combined, we consider the following program p, whose conditions of termination are not easy to detect.

```
while x ≠₂ 0:
    x := 5 * x
    while x ≠₃ 0:
        x := 2 * x + 1
```

We can observe that each assignment is complete w.r.t. modulo k congruences and this allows us to build a complete bounded domain following the approach of Lemma 15. Given the guards in the program p, the idea is to consider the sets of predicates $M_2 \stackrel{\text{def}}{=} \{\text{“}x \equiv_2 1\text{”}\}$ and $M_3 \stackrel{\text{def}}{=} \{\text{“}x \equiv_3 1\text{”}, \text{“}x \equiv_3 2\text{”}\}$ so that the predicates in M_2 ensure completeness of the outer while-guard and those in M_3 ensure completeness for the inner while-guard. Note that the Boolean domain $\text{Bool}(M_3)$ has 16 elements (it is a powerset of four 2-bitvectors) but only 8 elements are relevant, because the 2-bitvector associated with “$x \equiv_3 1$” and “$x \equiv_3 2$” corresponds to false. In fact $\text{Bool}(M_3)$ is equivalent to $Mod3$ and its ascending chains have at most 4 elements. For similar reasons, the resulting bounded abstract domain $\text{Bool}(M_2 \cup M_3)$ is $7 - ACC$, since it is defined as the powerset over the set of 3-bitvectors corresponding to value assignments for each of the predicates in M_2 and M_3.

The result of this paper assures us that we can detect the inputs for which p terminates by investigating its SNF form obtained considering $k = 7$. However, computing the SNF form of p leads to select form with a quite high branching factor. Even if we are interested in characterizing the diverging executions only, the computed SNF will contain several thousands of diverging branches (assuming that the select branch pruning rule is never applied). Also the size of the guards corresponding to such branches will grow rapidly due to the subsequent syntactical substitutions. For example, for program p there will be one diverging branch whose guard is semantically equivalent to "$x \equiv_2 1 \wedge x \equiv_3 0$", but its syntactical expression is more complex. This poses a challenge to gaining useful insight on the program behavior by analyzing the SNF.

We can observe, however, that even if the different branches of the SNF contain syntactically different guards, the number of such guards that are semantically distinct ones is limited by the number of elements in the abstract domain (which in the case of the example is at most 32). This allows us to conclude that many guards appearing in the SNF will be semantically equivalent. Moreover, since the guards in any select command are mutually exclusive, we can be sure that all such redundant guards are indeed semantically equivalent to false. Of course, the problem to detect such false guards must be entrusted to a SMT solver that should support an effective SNF reduction tool implementation. This would allows us to maintain a concise select structure during the rewriting process.

5.4   Deciding Program Equivalence

The problem of deciding semantic equivalence is defined as, given two programs c_1 and c_2, determining whether $[\![c_1]\!] = [\![c_2]\!]$, that is, the two diverge on the same set of inputs and for every converging input, they give the same result.

We now present the main idea to solving program equivalence for programs containing a single variable x. This approach can be straightforwardly generalized to multiple variables by extending our language with a notion of multi-assignments (i.e. every assignment is defined by a tuple of variable-expression pairs and its semantics executes every variable assignment at the same time), but we prefer to keep the notation simpler for the sake of exposition.

The notion of a reduced normal form is as follows.

Definition 32 (Reduced select normal form (RSNF)). *We say that a program $c \in Select$ is in reduced select normal form (in short RSNF) if either:*

- *c is a basic command (that is either $\mathbf{w}_\perp$, **skip** or an assignment);*
- *c has the form **select**$(\tilde{b} : \tilde{c})$ where every c_i is a basic command.*

We first observe that *Select* programs in this form do not allow for arbitrary sequences of assignments and **skip** to occur either inside (or outside) any select branch, but every sequence $c = c_1; c_2; \ldots; c_3$ of said commands can always be reduced into either one single **skip** or one single assignment as follows:

- If for every i it holds $c_i = $ **skip**, then $[\![c]\!] = [\![\mathbf{skip}]\!]$

– Otherwise, we remove every c_i for which $c_i = $ **skip** and merge the remaining assignments observing that:

$$[\![x := a_1; x := a_2]\!] = [\![x := a_2[a_1/x]]\!] \qquad (6)$$

which follows directly from the definition.

We also note that the process of merging two complete assignments preserves completeness.

Lemma 33. $\mathbb{C}([\![x := a_1]\!]) \wedge \mathbb{C}([\![x := a_2]\!]) \implies \mathbb{C}([\![x := a_2[a_1/x]]\!])$.

These observations let us conclude that any SNF program can be easily transformed into RSNF by collapsing every sequence of assignments (and **skip**s) into one single command, and the procedure is guaranteed to terminate.

More in detail, given any program $c \in Select(A, B)$ we can compute its SNF $c' \in Select(A, B^*)$ where B^* is the closure of B under $\wedge$ and substitution $b[a/x]$ for $a \in A$, then we can rewrite c' as some RSNF $c'' \in Select(A^*, B^*)$ where A^* is the closure of A under substitution $a[a'/x]$.

When considering two RSNF programs, proving their semantic equivalence can be done by observing that (RSNF programs not containing any **select** construct can be checked as if they contained a single branch):

Lemma 34. *Given two RSNF programs* $c = $ **select**$(\tilde{b} : \tilde{c})$ *and* $c' = $ **select**$(\tilde{b}' : \tilde{c}')$ *such that* $|\tilde{b}| = n$ *and* $|\tilde{b}'| = m$, *then semantic equivalence between* c *and* c' *holds iff every formula in the set* $E = \bigcup_{i=1}^{n} \bigcup_{j=1}^{m} \mathcal{E}(i, j)$ *is valid, where* $\mathcal{E}(i, j)$ *is defined according to:*

– *If* $c_i = c'_j = \mathbf{w}_\perp$, *then* $\mathcal{E}(i, j) = \varnothing$
– *If* $c_i \neq c'_j$ *and* $\mathbf{w}_\perp \in \{c_i, c_j\}$ *then* $\mathcal{E}(i, j) = \{\neg(b_i \wedge b'_j)\}$
– *If* $c_i = c'_j = $ **skip**, *then* $\mathcal{E}(i, j) = \varnothing$
– *If* $\{c_i, c_j\} = \{$**skip**$, x := a\}$ *then* $\mathcal{E}(i, j) = \{b_i \wedge b'_j \implies a = x\}$
– *If* $\{c_i, c_j\} = \{x := a, x := a'\}$ *then* $\mathcal{E}(i, j) = \{b_i \wedge b'_j \implies a = a'\}$

We can now make use of our previous results to conclude that:

Theorem 35. *Let* $c_1 \in Imp(A_1, B_1)$, $c_2 \in Imp(A_2, B_2)$ *be any two single-variable programs admitting complete approximation in some (possibly different) bounded strict abstract domains, then the problem of deciding semantic equivalence between* c_1 *and* c_2 *can be reduced to that of determining the validity of a set of formulas built by using only Boolean and arithmetic expressions contained in the closures (by substitution)* A_1^*, A_2^*, B_1^* *and* B_2^*.

Proof. By applying the program transformation defined in Sect. 4, both c_1 and c_2 can be reduced to some $c'_1 \in Imp^-(A_1, B_1)$, $c'_2 \in Imp^-(A_2, B_2)$. Those two programs can then be expressed as $Select$ commands and reduced to SNF by means of Lemma 30 and further reduced to RSNF as discussed in 5.4. Applying Lemma 34 completes the proof.   □

In a similar way to what we proposed for Theorem 19 we can apply the result given in Theorem 35 whenever we want to investigate the decidability of semantic equivalence between programs: if we are able to exhibit a domain for each program in which all the guards and assignments are complete, then we have successfully proven that their equivalence is reducible to checking a set of guarded statements, which can be done, e.g., by exploiting SMT solvers like Z3 [17].

Example. We consider the following *Imp* program:

$$w \stackrel{\text{def}}{=} x := -1 * x; \textbf{while } x < 0 \textbf{ do } x := 2 * x$$

In order to reduce w to RSNF we first transform w is SNF. In fact, since it is complete in *Sign* we can find an equivalent *Imp⁻* which can be translated into a select program as:

```
x := -1 * x;
select (
x < 0:   x := 2 * x;
         select (
         x < 0:   x := 2 * x;
                  select (
                  x < 0:   w⊥ ,
                  x ⩾ 0:   skip )
         x ⩾ 0:   skip )
x ⩾ 0:   skip )
```

we can now reduce this program to RSNF and obtain:

```
select (
x > 0:   w⊥ ,
x ⩽ 0:   x := -1*x  )
```

Now, by taking another equivalent program such as:

```
if  x ≠ 0 then
    x := x + 1;
    if x < 1 then
        x := -1 * x + 1;
    else
        while x ⩽ 0 do
            x := x - 2;
else skip
```

which gets reduced to the following RSNF:

```
select (
¬(x ⩽ 0): w⊥ ,
x = 0:   skip ,
x < 0:   x := -1*(x+1)+1  )
```

we can reduce the problem of determining their semantic equivalence to that of proving the validity of the following set of guarded statements:

$$E = \left\{ \begin{array}{l} \neg((x > 0) \wedge (x = 0)) \\ \neg((x > 0) \wedge (x < 0)) \\ \neg((x \leqslant 0) \wedge \neg(x \leqslant 0)) \\ (x \leqslant 0) \wedge (x = 0) \implies (-1 * x) = x \\ (x \leqslant 0) \wedge (x < 0) \implies (-1 * x) = (-1 * (x + 1) + 1) \end{array} \right\}$$

Since they are all tautologies, the two programs are equivalent.

The same considerations of Sect. 4.2 about the applicability of the method based on Boolean abstractions for deciding termination are straightforwardly extended to the case of program equivalence.

6   Conclusions

We have investigated the relationship between completeness in Abstract Interpretation and expressiveness of programs, showing that several important properties become decidable for the class of complete programs in certain domains. In particular, we have given a notion of bounded domain and we have studied classes of programs that are parametric on sets of guards and assignments whose abstract semantics is complete on such domains.

In order to study the expressiveness of this class, we have considered two well-known problems: program termination and semantic equivalence, which are of course not decidable in the general case. Our findings seem interesting: as a first result we have shown that under the above hypotheses the termination problem becomes decidable for complete programs. This, of course, severely limits the expressiveness of our class of programs. Then, we defined an intermediate *Select* syntax and a notion of inverse semantics in order to derive a set of rewriting rules for *Select* programs. Applying such rules gives an effective way to express every program from our target class in a canonical form that highlights the program semantics. By further program transformations to the so-called reduced select normal form we are also able to rephrase the problem of deciding semantic equivalence to that of proving the validity of a set of formulas constructed using the original guards and assignments (along with their composition as needed by normalization), giving an effective procedure to solve the semantic equivalence problem. We have developed a proof-of-concept Haskell implementation that has been used to check the program transformations reported in the examples. The tool takes an input program and the bound k of the abstract domain and transforms it in (reduced) select normal form. Note that completeness has to be checked beforehand, as the tool just assumes the existence of the bounded abstract domain.

We have also investigated the applicability of our approach by proposing a method to compose Boolean abstractions, each one designed for being complete for all functions and for some guards appearing in the program. The proposed approach is structural, in the sense that it builds on the functions and guards used in programs, for which suitable complete bounded domains must be detected. Here the main limitation is therefore the completeness requirement: although abstract domains can always be refined to achieve completeness for a given set of functions [13], it is often the case that this process leads to the whole (unbounded) concrete domain. On the other hand, once a library of bounded domains is available, Boolean abstractions could be used to compose them and make the technique applicable to larger sets of programs.

The process described in this work focused on an imperative language with standard single-variable assignments, and reduction to normal form has been defined for single-variable programs only. Considering a more general notion of multi-assignments $\tilde{x} := \tilde{a}$ (i.e. where multiple variables are assigned simultaneously to corresponding expressions) gives a direct generalization of our approach to programs with more than one variable (observing that every assignment is a trivial case of multi-assignment). The select normal form we used can be seen as a star-free fragment of Kleene Algebra with Test (KAT) [15]. In this sense, it is worth pushing the analogy even further and consider the full KAT instead of *Imp* as a reference language, finding suitable conditions under which star expressions can be equivalently iterated only a bounded number of times.

We think that further studies could be conducted on several aspects, such as investigating whether weakening the constraint over boundedness of the domain (that is, when considering ACC domains with finite but not bounded chains) makes program termination undecidable.

References

1. Ball, T., Podelski, A., Rajamani, S.K.: Boolean and Cartesian abstraction for model checking C programs. In: Margaria, T., Yi, W. (eds.) TACAS 2001. LNCS, vol. 2031, pp. 268–283. Springer, Heidelberg (2001). https://doi.org/10.1007/3-540-45319-9_19
2. Barringer, H.: A Survey of Verification Techniques for Parallel Programs. Springer, Heidelberg (1985). https://doi.org/10.1007/3-540-15239-3
3. Bruni, R., Giacobazzi, R., Gori, R., Garcia-Contreras, I., Pavlovic, D.: Abstract extensionality: on the properties of incomplete abstract interpretations. Proc. ACM on Program. Lang. 4(POPL), 1–28 (2019)
4. Bruni, R., Giacobazzi, R., Gori, R., Ranzato, F.: A logic for locally complete abstract interpretations. In: Proceedings of LICS 2021, 36th Annual ACM/IEEE Symposium on Logic in Computer Science, pp. 1–13. IEEE (2021). https://doi.org/10.1109/LICS52264.2021.9470608, distinguished paper
5. Cousot, P.: Principles of Abstract Interpretation. MIT Press, Cambridge (2021)
6. Cousot, P.: Abstract interpretation based formal methods and future challenges. In: Wilhelm, R. (ed.) Informatics. LNCS, vol. 2000, pp. 138–156. Springer, Heidelberg (2001). https://doi.org/10.1007/3-540-44577-3_10
7. Cousot, P., Cousot, R.: Abstract interpretation: a unified lattice model for static analysis of programs by construction or approximation of fixpoints. In: Proceedings of the 4th ACM SIGACT-SIGPLAN Symposium on Principles of programming Languages, pp. 238–252 (1977)

8. Cousot, P., Cousot, R.: Systematic design of program analysis frameworks. In: Proceedings of the 6th ACM SIGACT-SIGPLAN Symposium on Principles of Programming Languages, pp. 269–282 (1979)
9. Cousot, P., Cousot, R.: Basic concepts of abstract interpretation. In: Jacquart, R. (ed.) Building the Information Society. IIFIP, vol. 156, pp. 359–366. Springer, Boston, MA (2004). https://doi.org/10.1007/978-1-4020-8157-6_27
10. Das, M., Lerner, S., Seigle, M.: ESP: path-sensitive program verification in polynomial time. In: Proceedings of the ACM SIGPLAN 2002 Conference on Programming Language Design and Implementation, pp. 57–68 (2002)
11. Dijkstra, E.W.: A Discipline Of programming. Series in Automatic Computation, Prentice-Hall, Hoboken (1976)
12. D'silva, V., Kroening, D., Weissenbacher, G.: A survey of automated techniques for formal software verification. IEEE Trans. Comput. Aided Des. Integr. Circuits Syst. 27(7), 1165–1178 (2008)
13. Giacobazzi, R., Ranzato, F., Scozzari., F.: Making abstract interpretation complete. J. ACM 47(2), 361–416 (2000). https://doi.org/10.1145/333979.333989
14. Giacobazzi, R., Logozzo, F., Ranzato, F.: Analyzing program analyses. ACM SIGPLAN Not. 50(1), 261–273 (2015)
15. Kozen, D.: Kleene algebra with tests. ACM Trans. Program. Lang. Syst. 19(3), 427–443 (1997). https://doi.org/10.1145/256167.256195
16. Miné, A.: Tutorial on static inference of numeric invariants by abstract interpretation. Found. Trends Program. Lang. 4(3–4), 120–372 (2017)
17. de Moura, L., Bjørner, N.: Z3: an efficient SMT solver. In: Ramakrishnan, C.R., Rehof, J. (eds.) TACAS 2008. LNCS, vol. 4963, pp. 337–340. Springer, Heidelberg (2008). https://doi.org/10.1007/978-3-540-78800-3_24
18. Nelson, C.G.: Techniques for Program Verification. Stanford University, Stanford (1980)
19. Nielson, F., Nielson, H., Hankin, C.: Principles of Program Analysis. Springer, Cham (2010). https://doi.org/10.1007/978-3-662-03811-6
20. Rice, H.G.: Classes of recursively enumerable sets and their decision problems. Trans. Am. Math. Soc. 74(2), 358–366 (1953)
21. Rival, X., Yi, K.: Introduction to Static Analysis - An Abstract Interpretation Perspective. MIT Press, Cambridge (2020)
22. Turing, A.M.: On computable numbers, with an application to the entscheidungsproblem. A correction. Proc. Lond. Math. Soc. 2(1), 544–546 (1938)
23. Vardi, M.Y., Wolper, P.: An automata-theoretic approach to automatic program verification. In: Proceedings of the First Symposium on Logic in Computer Science, pp. 322–331. IEEE Computer Society (1986)

Invariant Inference with Provable Complexity from the Monotone Theory

Yotam M. Y. Feldman$^{(\boxtimes)}$ and Sharon Shoham

Tel Aviv University, Tel Aviv, Israel
yotam.feldman@gmail.com, sharon.shoham@gmail.com

Abstract. Invariant inference algorithms such as interpolation-based inference and IC3/PDR show that it is feasible, in practice, to find inductive invariants for many interesting systems, but non-trivial upper bounds on the computational complexity of such algorithms are scarce, and limited to simple syntactic forms of invariants. In this paper we achieve invariant inference algorithms, in the domain of propositional transition systems, with *provable upper bounds* on the number of SAT calls. We do this by building on the *monotone theory*, developed by Bshouty for exact learning Boolean formulas. We prove results for two invariant inference frameworks: (i) *model-based interpolation*, where we show an algorithm that, under certain conditions about reachability, efficiently infers invariants when they have both short CNF and DNF representations (transcending previous results about monotone invariants); and (ii) *abstract interpretation* in a domain based on the monotone theory that was previously studied in relation to *property-directed reachability*, where we propose an efficient implementation of the best abstract transformer, leading to overall complexity bounds on the number of SAT calls. These results build on a novel procedure for computing least monotone overapproximations.

1 Introduction

In a fruitful, recent trend, many that aspire to innovate in verification seek advice from research in machine learning [e.g. 11–13,18,21,22,24,36–38]. The topic of this paper is the application of the *monotone theory*, developed by Bshouty in exact concept learning, to improve theoretical complexity results for *inductive invariant inference*.

One of the *modi operandi* for automatically proving that a system is safe— that it cannot reach a state it should not—is an *inductive invariant*, which is an assertion that (i) holds for the initial states, (ii) does not hold in any bad state, and (iii) is closed under transitions of the system. These properties are reminiscent of a data classifier, separating good from bad points, prompting the adaptation of algorithms from classical classification to invariant inference [e.g. 11,13,18,19,35–38]. In this paper we focus on inductive invariants for propositional transition systems, which are customary in hardware verification and also applicable to software systems through predicate abstraction [17,20].

The *monotone theory* by Bshouty [5] is a celebrated achievement in learning theory (most notably in exact learning with queries [1]) that is the foundation

© The Author(s), under exclusive license to Springer Nature Switzerland AG 2022
G. Singh and C. Urban (Eds.): SAS 2022, LNCS 13790, pp. 201–226, 2022.
https://doi.org/10.1007/978-3-031-22308-2_10

for learning Boolean formulas with complex syntactic structures. At its core, the monotone theory studies the *monotonization* $\mathcal{M}_b(\varphi)$ of a formula φ w.r.t. a valuation b, which is the smallest b-monotone formula that overapproximates φ. (This concept is explained in Sect. 3.) In Bshouty's work, several monotonizations are used to efficiently reconstruct φ.

Recently, the monotone theory has been applied to theoretical studies of invariant inference in the context of two prominent SAT-based inference approaches. In this paper, we solve open problems in each, using a new efficient algorithm to compute monotonizations.

Efficient Interpolation-Based Inference. The study [13] of interpolation-based invariant inference—a hugely influential approach pioneered by McMillan [26]—identified the fence condition as a property of systems and invariants under which the success of a model-based inference algorithm [3,6] is guaranteed. (We explain the fence condition in Sect. 5.1.) Under this condition, the number of SAT calls (specifically, bounded model checking queries) of the original model-based interpolation algorithm was shown to be polynomial in the DNF size (the number of terms in the smallest DNF representation) of the invariant, but only when the invariant is *monotone* (containing no negated variables) [13]. Based on the monotone theory, the authors of [13] further introduced an algorithm that, under the same fence condition, could efficiently infer invariants that were *almost* monotone (containing $O(1)$ terms with negated variables). However, their techniques could not extend to mimic the pinnacle result of Bshouty's paper: the CDNF algorithm [5], which can learn formulas in a number of queries that is polynomial in their DNF size, their CNF size (the number of clauses in their smallest CNF representation), and the number of variables. It was unclear whether an analogous result is possible in invariant inference without strengthening the fence condition, e.g. to assume that the fence condition holds both forwards and backwards (see Sect. 7).

We solve this question, and introduce an algorithm that can infer an invariant in a number of SAT queries (specifically, bounded model checking queries) that is polynomial in the invariant's DNF size, CNF size, and the number of variables, under the assumption that the invariant satisfies the fence condition, without further restrictions (Therorm 5). In particular, this implies that invariants that are representable by a small decision tree can be inferred efficiently. The basic idea is to learn an invariant I as a conjunction of monotonizations $\mathcal{M}_\sigma(I)$ where σ are chosen as counterexamples to induction. The challenge is that I is unknown, and the relatively weak assumption on the transition system of the fence condition does not allow the use of several operations (e.g. membership queries) that learning algorithms rely on to efficiently generate such a representation.

Efficient Abstract Interpretation. The study of IC3/PDR [4,9] revealed that part of the overapproximation this sophisticated algorithm performs is captured by an abstract interpretation procedure, in an abstract domain founded on the monotone theory [14]. In this procedure, dubbed Λ-PDR, each iteration involves several monotonizations of the set of states reachable in one step from the value of the previous iteration. Upper bounds on the number of iterations in Λ-PDR were investigated to shed light on the number of frames of PDR [14]. However, it was unclear whether the abstract domain itself can be implemented in an efficient manner, and whether efficient complexity bounds on the number of SAT queries (and not just the number of iterations) in Λ-PDR can be obtained.

We solve this question, and show that Λ-PDR can be implemented to yield an overall upper bound on the number of SAT calls which is polynomial in the same quantity that was previously used to bound the number of iterations in Λ-PDR (Theorem 7). This is surprising because, until now, there was no way to compute monotonizations of the post-image of the previous iteration that did not suffer from the fact that the exact post-image of a set of states may be much more complex to represent than its abstraction.

Super-efficient Monotonization. Bshouty [5] provided an algorithm to compute the monotonization $\mathcal{M}_b(\varphi)$, but the complexity of this algorithm depends on the DNF size of the original formula φ. Our aforementioned results build on a new algorithm for the same task, whose complexity depends on the DNF size of the monotonization $\mathcal{M}_b(\varphi)$ (Theorem 2), which may be much smaller (and never larger). This enables our efficient interpolation-based inference algorithm and our efficient implementation of abstract interpretation, although each result requires additional technical sophistication: For our efficient model-based interpolation result, the key idea is that the monotonization of an invariant satisfying the fence condition can be computed through the monotonization of the set of states reachable in at most s steps, and our new monotonization algorithm allows to do this efficiently even when the latter set is complex to represent exactly. For our efficient abstract interpretation result, the key idea is that the DNF size of an abstract iterate is bounded by a quantity related to monotonizations of the transition relation, and our new monotonization algorithm allows to compute it efficiently w.r.t the same quantity even though the DNF size of the exact post-image of the previous iterate may be larger.

Overall, we make the following contributions:

- We introduce a new efficient algorithm to compute monotonizations, whose complexity in terms of the number of SAT queries is proportional to the DNF size of its output (Sect. 4).
- We prove that an invariant that satisfies the fence condition can be inferred in a number of SAT (bounded model checking) queries that is polynomial in its CNF size, its DNF size, and the number of variables; in particular, invariants represented by small decision trees can be efficiently inferred (Sect. 5).
- We prove an efficient complexity upper bound for the number of SAT queries performed by abstract interpretation in a domain based on the monotone theory (Sect. 6).

Section 2 sets preliminary notation and Sect. 3 provides background on the monotone theory. Section 7 discusses related work and Sect. 8 concludes.

2   Preliminaries

We work with propositional transition systems defined over a vocabulary $\Sigma = \{p_1, \ldots, p_n\}$ of n Boolean variables. We identify a formula with the set of its valuations, and at times also identify a set of valuations with an arbitrary formula that represents it which is chosen arbitrarily (one always exists in propositional logic). $\varphi \implies \psi$ denotes the validity of the formula $\varphi \to \psi$. **States, Transition**

Systems, Inductive Invariants. A *state* is a *valuation* to Σ. If x is a state, $x[p]$ is the value (*true/false* or 1/0) that x assigns to the variable $p \in \Sigma$. A *transition system* is a triple $(Init, \delta, Bad)$ where $Init, Bad$ are formulas over Σ denoting the set of initial and bad states respectively, and the *transition relation* δ is a formula over $\Sigma \uplus \Sigma'$, where $\Sigma' = \{x' \mid x \in \Sigma\}$ is a copy of the vocabulary used to describe the post-state of a transition. If $\tilde{\Sigma}, \tilde{\Sigma}'$ are distinct copies of Σ, $\delta[\tilde{\Sigma}, \tilde{\Sigma}']$ denotes the substitution in δ of each $p \in \Sigma$ by its corresponding in $\tilde{\Sigma}$ and likewise for $\Sigma', \tilde{\Sigma}'$. Given a set of states S, the *post-image* of S is $\delta(S) = \{\sigma' \mid \exists \sigma \in S. \ (\sigma, \sigma') \models \delta\}$. A transition system is *safe* if all the states that are reachable from $Init$ via any number of steps of δ satisfy $\neg Bad$. An *inductive invariant* is a formula I over Σ such that (i) $Init \implies I$, (ii) $I \wedge \delta \implies I'$, and (iii) $I \implies \neg Bad$, where I' denotes the result of substituting each $x \in \Sigma$ for $x' \in \Sigma'$ in I.

In the context of propositional logic, a transition system is safe iff it has an inductive invariant.

Use of SAT in Invariant Inference. Given a candidate, the requirements for being an inductive invariant can be verified using SAT; we refer to the SAT query that checks requirement ii by the name *inductiveness check*. When an inductiveness checks fails, a SAT solver returns a *counterexample to induction*, which is a transition (σ, σ') with $\sigma \models I$ but $\sigma' \not\models I$. Another important check in invariant inference algorithms that can be implemented using SAT is *bounded model checking (BMC)* [2], which asks whether a set of states described by a formula ψ is forwards unreachable in a bounded number $s \in \mathbb{N}$ of steps; we write this as the check $\underline{\delta}^s(Init) \cap \psi \overset{?}{=} \emptyset$. Using SAT it is also possible to obtain a counterexample $\sigma \in \underline{\delta}^s(Init) \cap \psi$ if it exists.

We measure the *complexity* of a SAT-based inference algorithm by the number of SAT calls it performs (including inductiveness checks, BMC, and other SAT calls), and the number of other steps, when each SAT call is considered one step (an oracle call).

Literals, Cubes, Clauses, CNF, DNF. A *literal* ℓ is a variable p or its negation $\neg p$. A *clause* c is a disjunction of literals. The empty clause is *false*. A formula is in *conjunctive normal norm (CNF)* if it is a conjunction of clauses. A *cube* or *term* d is a conjunction of a consistent set of literals; at times, we also refer directly to the set and write $\ell \in d$. The empty cube is *true*. A formula is in *disjunctive normal form (DNF)* if it is a disjunction of terms. The *domain*, $dom(d)$, of a cube d is the set of variables that appear in it (positively or negatively). Given a state σ, we use the state and the (full) cube that consists of all the literals that are satisfied in σ interchangeably. $|\varphi|_{dnf}$ is the minimal number of terms in any DNF representation of φ. $|\varphi|_{cnf}$ is the minimal number of clauses in any CNF representation of φ.

3   Background: The Monotone Theory

This section provides necessary definitions and results from the monotone theory by Bshouty [5] as used in this paper. Our presentation is based on [13,14] (lemmas that are stated here slightly differently are proved in the extended version [15]).

Boolean functions which are *monotone* are special in many ways; one is that they are easier to learn [e.g. 1,41]. Syntactically, a monotone function can be written in DNF so that all variables appear positively. This is easily generalized to b-monotone formulas, where each variable appears only at one polarity specified by b (Definition 2). The *monotone theory* aims to handle functions that are not monotone through the conjunction of b-monotone formulas. Section 3.1 considers the (over)approximation of a formula by a b-monotone formula, the "monotonization" of a formula; Sect. 3.2 studies the conjunction of several such monotonizations through the *monotone hull* operator.

3.1   Least b-Monotone Overapproximations

Definition 1 (b-Monotone Order). *Let b be a cube. We define a partial order over states where $v \leq_b x$ when x, v agree on all variables not present in b, and x disagrees with b on all variables on which also v disagrees with b:* $\forall p \in \Sigma. \ x[p] \neq v[p]$ *implies* $p \in dom(b) \wedge v[p] = b[p]$.

Intuitively, $v \leq_b x$ when x can be obtained from v by flipping bits to the opposite of their value in b.

Definition 2 (b-Monotonicity). *A formula ψ is b-monotone for a cube b if* $\forall v \leq_b x. \ v \models \psi$ *implies* $x \models \psi$.

That is, if v satisfies ψ, so do all the states that are farther away from b than v. For example, if ψ is 000-monotone and $100 \models \psi$, then because $100 \leq_{000} 111$ (starting in 100 and moving away from 000 can reach 111), also $111 \models \psi$. In contrast, $100 \not\leq_{000} 011$ (the same process cannot flip the 1 bit that already disagrees with 000), so 011 does not necessarily belong to ψ. (000-monotonicity corresponds to the usual notion of monotone formulas.)

Definition 3 (Least b-Monotone Overapproximation). *For a formula φ and a cube b, the* least b-monotone overapproximation *of φ is a formula $\mathcal{M}_b(\varphi)$ defined by*

$$x \models \mathcal{M}_b(\varphi) \ \textit{iff} \ \exists v. \ v \leq_b x \wedge v \models \varphi.$$

For example, if $100 \models \varphi$, then $100 \models \mathcal{M}_{000}(\varphi)$ because $\mathcal{M}_{000}(\varphi)$ is an overapproximation, and hence $111 \models \mathcal{M}_{000}(\varphi)$ because it is 000-monotone, as above. Here, thanks to minimality, 011 does not belong to $\mathcal{M}_{000}(\varphi)$, unless 000, 001, 010, or 011 belong to φ.

The minimality property of $\mathcal{M}_b(\varphi)$ is formalized as follows:

Lemma 1. $\mathcal{M}_b(\varphi)$ (Definition 3) is the least b-monotone formula ψ (Definition 2) s.t. $\varphi \implies \psi$ (i.e., for every other b-monotone formula ψ, if $\varphi \implies \psi$ then $\mathcal{M}_b(\varphi) \implies \psi$).

An immediate but useful fact is that $\mathcal{M}_b(\cdot)$ is a monotone operator:

Lemma 2. If $\varphi_1 \implies \varphi_2$ then $\mathcal{M}_b(\varphi_1) \implies \mathcal{M}_b(\varphi_2)$.

Syntactic Intuition. Ordinary monotone formulas are $\bar{0}$-monotone; for general b, a formula ψ in DNF is b-monotone if interchanging $p, \neg p$ whenever $b[p] = true$ results in a formula that is monotone DNF per the standard definition.[1] When φ is not b-monotone, the monotonization $\mathcal{M}_b(\varphi)$ is the "closest thing", in the sense that it is the smallest b-monotone ψ s.t. $\varphi \implies \psi$. As we shall see, $\mathcal{M}_b(\varphi)$ can be efficiently obtained from φ by deleting literals. The syntactic viewpoint is key for our results in Sect. 4 and Sect. 5.

Geometric Intuition. Geometrically, ψ is b-monotone if $v \models \psi \implies x \models \psi$ for every states v, x s.t. $v \leq_b x$; the partial order $\leq_b$ indicates that x is "farther away" from b in the Hamming cube than v from b, namely, that there is a shortest path w.r.t. Hamming distance from b to x (or from $\pi_b(x)$—the projection of x onto b—to x, when b is not a full cube) that goes through v. A formula ψ is b-monotone when it is closed under this operation, of getting farther from b. In this way, $\mathcal{M}_b(\varphi)$ corresponds to the set of states x to which there is a shortest path from b that intersects φ.[2] The geometric viewpoint is key for our results in Sect. 4 and for the abstract domain in Sect. 6.

Disjunctive Form. The monotone overapproximation can be obtained from a DNF representation of the original formula, a fact that is useful for algorithms that compute the monotone overapproximation. Starting with a DNF representation of φ, we can derive a DNF representation of $\mathcal{M}_b(\varphi)$ by dropping in each term the literals that agree with b. Intuitively, if ℓ agrees with b, the "constraint" that $\sigma \models \ell$ is dropped from $\mathcal{M}_b(t)$ because if $\sigma \models \mathcal{M}_b(t)$ then flipping the value of ℓ in σ results in a state $\tilde{\sigma}$ such that $\sigma \leq_b \tilde{\sigma}$ and hence also $\tilde{\sigma} \models \mathcal{M}_b(t)$.

Lemma 3. Let $\varphi = t_1 \vee \ldots \vee t_m$ in DNF. Then the monotonization $\mathcal{M}_b(\varphi) \equiv \mathcal{M}_b(t_1) \vee \ldots \vee \mathcal{M}_b(t_m)$ where $\mathcal{M}_b(t_i) \equiv t_i \setminus b = \bigwedge \{\ell \in t_i \wedge \ell \notin b\}$.

This fact has several useful corollaries. First, for the important special case of a state (full cube) v, the monotonization $\mathcal{M}_b(v)$ is the conjunction of all literals that hold in v except those that are present in b, written

$$cube_b(v) \stackrel{\text{def}}{=} \mathcal{M}_b(v) = \bigwedge \{p \mid v[p] = true, p \notin b\} \wedge \bigwedge \{\neg p_i \mid v[p] = false, \neg p \notin b\}.$$

---

[1]   When b is a full cube, another way to say this is that ψ is b-monotone if it is monotone in the ordinary sense under the translation [42] specified by b.

[2]   This is reminiscent of visibility in Euclidean geometry [e.g. 29]: picturing b as a guard, the source of visibility, then $\mathcal{M}_b(\varphi)$ is the set of states that are visible in $\neg\varphi$, that is, the set of states σ s.t. the "line segment" $[b, \sigma]$ is contained in $\neg\varphi$. Here $[b, \sigma]$ is the Hamming interval [e.g. 42] between b, σ, the union of all the multiple shortest paths between the states (each path corresponds to a different permutation of the variables on which the states disagree).

In particular, if $v \models \varphi$ then $cube_b(v) \implies \mathcal{M}_b(\varphi)$ (follows from Lemma 3 thinking about the representation $v \vee \varphi$). A similar property holds under the weaker premise that v is known to belong to the monotonization:

Lemma 4. *If* $v \models \mathcal{M}_b(\varphi)$ *then* $cube_b(v) \implies \mathcal{M}_b(\varphi)$.

Another corollary is that the DNF size cannot increase from φ to $\mathcal{M}_b(\varphi)$:

Lemma 5. $|\mathcal{M}_b(\varphi)|_{\mathrm{dnf}} \leq |\varphi|_{\mathrm{dnf}}$.

3.2   Monotone Hull

We now define the monotone hull, which is a conjunction of b-monotone overapproximations over all the b's from a fixed set of states B.

Definition 4 (Monotone Hull). *The* monotone hull *of a formula* φ *w.r.t. a set of states* B *is* $\mathrm{MHull}_B(\varphi) = \bigwedge_{b \in B} \mathcal{M}_b(\varphi)$.

The monotone hull can be simplified to use a succinct DNF representation of the basis B instead of a conjunction over all states.

Lemma 6. *If* $B \equiv b_1 \vee \ldots \vee b_m$ *where* $b_1, \ldots, b_m$ *are cubes, then* $\mathrm{MHull}_B(\varphi) \equiv \mathcal{M}_{b_1}(\varphi) \wedge \ldots \wedge \mathcal{M}_{b_m}(\varphi)$.

Note that when $B = b$ is a single cube, $\mathrm{MHull}_b(\varphi) = \mathcal{M}_b(\varphi)$.
   Similarly to $\mathcal{M}_b(\varphi)$, the monotone hull is an overapproxmation:

Lemma 7. $\varphi \implies \mathrm{MHull}_B(\varphi)$.

In general, $\mathrm{MHull}_B(\varphi)$ is not equivalent to φ. However, we can always choose B so that $\mathrm{MHull}_B(\varphi) \equiv \varphi$. A set B that suffices for this is called a basis:

Definition 5 (Monotone Basis). *A* monotone basis *is a set of states* B. *It is a basis for a formula* φ *if* $\varphi \equiv \mathrm{MHull}_B(\varphi)$.

Conversely, given a set B, we are interested in the set of formulas for which B forms a basis:

Definition 6 (Monotone Span). $\mathrm{MSpan}(B) = \{\mathrm{MHull}_B(\varphi) \mid \varphi$ *over* $\Sigma\}$, *the set of formulas for which* B *is a monotone basis.*

The following theorem provides a syntactic characterization of $\mathrm{MSpan}(B)$, as the set of all formulas that can be written in CNF using clauses that exclude states from the basis. The connection between CNF and the monotone basis is useful in Sect. 5 where a monotone basis is constructed automatically, and in Sect. 6 where it is used to define an abstract domain.

Theorem 1 ([5]). $\varphi \in \mathrm{MSpan}(B)$ *iff there exist clauses* $c_1, \ldots, c_s$ *such that* $\varphi \equiv c_1 \wedge \ldots \wedge c_s$ *and for every* $1 \leq i \leq s$ *there exists* $b_j \in B$ *such that* $b_j \not\models c_i$.

In particular, a basis B for φ can be constructed by writing a CNF representation of φ and choosing for B a state $b_j \not\models c_j$ for each clause c_j.

Exact Learning Using the Monotone Theory. The monotone theory was first developed by Bshouty for the purpose of exact learning formulas that are not monotone. Essentially, the idea is to reconstruct the formula φ by finding a monotone basis $B = \{b_1, \ldots, b_t\}$ for it, and constructing $\mathrm{MHull}_B(\varphi)$ while using equivalence and membership queries. The CDNF Algorithm [5] achieves efficient learning in terms of the DNF & CNF size of the target formula, and its code is shown in the extended version [15]. Our CDNF invariant inference algorithm (Sect. 5) is inspired by it, although it departs from it in significant ways (see Remark 3).

4   Super-Efficient Monotonization

In this section we develop an efficient procedure to compute $\mathcal{M}_b(\varphi)$, which is a technical enabler of the results in following sections. The algorithm, presented in Algorithm 1, satisfies the following:

Theorem 2. *Let φ be a formula and b a cube. The algorithm* MONOTONIZE (φ, b) *computes* $\mathcal{M}_b(\varphi)$ *in* $O(n^2 |\mathcal{M}_b(\varphi)|_{\mathrm{dnf}})$ *SAT queries and time.*

(Throughout this paper, n denotes the number of propositional variables $|\Sigma|$.)

What distinguishes Theorem 2 is that the complexity bound depends on the DNF size of the *output*, the monotonization $\mathcal{M}_b(\varphi)$, and *not* on the size of the *input* φ, in contrast to the algorithm by Bshouty [5] (see Remark 1).

Algorithm 1. Super-Efficient Monotonization

1: **procedure** MONOTONIZE(φ, b)	12: **procedure** GENERALIZE(φ, b, σ_r)
2: $H \leftarrow$ *false*	13: $v \leftarrow \sigma_r$; walked $\leftarrow$ *true*
3: **while** SAT($\varphi \wedge \neg H$) **do**	14: **while** walked **do**
4: **let** $\sigma_r \models \varphi \wedge \neg H$	15: walked $\leftarrow$ *false*
5: $v \leftarrow$ GENERALIZE(φ, b, σ_r)	16: **for** $j = 1, \ldots, n$ **do**
6: $H \leftarrow H \vee cube_b(v)$	17: **if** $b[p_j] = v[p_j]$ **then**
7: **return** H	18: **continue**
8:	19: $x \leftarrow v[p_j \mapsto b[p_j]]$
9:	20: **if** SAT($\varphi \wedge \boxed{x, \pi_b(x)}$) **then**
10:	21: $v \leftarrow x$; walked $\leftarrow$ *true*
11:	22: **return** v

Starting from the candidate $H = $ *false*, the algorithm iteratively samples—through satisfying models of a SAT query—states that belong in φ but not yet included in H. Every such state σ_r generates a new term in H. Since H is supposed to be b-monotone, the minimal term to include is $cube_b(\sigma_r)$. To be efficient, the algorithm generalizes each example, trying to flip bits to find an example v that also should be included in $\mathcal{M}_b(\varphi)$ and is closer in Hamming distance to b, which would result in a smaller term $cube_b(v)$, thereby including more states in each iteration and converging faster. The criterion for v is that a bit cannot be flipped if this would result in a state x where the Hamming interval $\boxed{x, \pi_b(x)}$ does not intersect φ. Here, $\pi_b(x)$, the projection [e.g. 42] of x onto the (possibly partial) cube b is the state s.t.

$$\pi_b(x) = \begin{cases} b[p] & p \in dom(b) \\ x[p] & \text{otherwise} \end{cases},$$

and the Hamming interval $\boxed{\sigma_1, \sigma_2}$ between two states σ_1, σ_2 is the smallest cube that contains both—the conjunction of the literals where these agree. In sum, $\boxed{x, \pi_b(x)}$ is the conjunction of the literals where x, b agree and the literals of x over variables that are not present in b. As we will show, $\boxed{x, \pi_b(x)}$ intersecting with φ is an indicator for x belonging to the monotonization of φ.

The use of SAT queries in the algorithm does not necessarily assume that φ is given explicitly, and indeed in Sect. 5 we apply this algorithm with an implicit representation of φ (using additional copies of the vocabulary).

The rest of this section proves Theorem 2. First, the result v of generalization is so that when we disjoin the term $cube_b(v)$, we do not "overshoot" to include states that do not belong to the true monotonization:

Lemma 8. *If $\sigma_r \models \varphi$, then* GENERALIZE(φ, b, σ_r) *returns* v *s.t.* $cube_b(v) \Longrightarrow \mathcal{M}_b(\varphi)$.

Proof. v is chosen s.t. $\boxed{v, \pi_b(v)} \cap \varphi \neq \emptyset$—note that this holds trivially in the initial choice of v which is $\sigma_r \models \varphi$. Let $\tilde{\sigma} \models \varphi$ s.t. $\tilde{\sigma} \models \boxed{v, \pi_b(v)}$. The latter means that $\tilde{\sigma} \leq_b v$, because $\boxed{v, \pi_b(v)}$ consists of all the literals in v except for those that disagree with b, so σ agrees with v whenever v, b agree. In more detail, $\tilde{\sigma}$ agrees with v on all $p \notin dom(b)$ (because $\pi_b(v)[p] = v[p]$ on such variables), and for $p \in dom(p)$, if $\tilde{\sigma}[p] \neq v[p]$, if v, b agree on p then likewise $\tilde{\sigma}$ agrees with them (because then $v[p] = \pi_b(v)[p]$ and p is retained in the conjunction that forms the Hamming interval), which satisfies Definition 2. As also $\tilde{\sigma} \models \varphi$, this implies that $v \models \mathcal{M}_b(\varphi)$ per Definition 3. Hence $cube_b(v) \Longrightarrow \mathcal{M}_b(\varphi)$, by Lemma 4. $\square$

This shows that it is reasonable to disjoin the term $cube_b(v)$ to H in the hope of eventually obtaining $H = \mathcal{M}_b(\varphi)$. The following lemma argues that the algorithm continues to sample states until it converges to the true monotonization.

Lemma 9. MONOTONIZE(φ, b) *terminates and returns* $\mathcal{M}_b(\varphi)$.

Proof. First we show that when it terminates, the result is correct. Always $H \subseteq \mathcal{M}_b(\varphi)$, because in each iteration we disjoin to H a formula that satisfies the same property, by Lemma 8. The algorithm terminates when $\varphi \subseteq H$, and H is always a b-monotone formula (by Lemma 3 the monotonization of H is H itself, which is b-monotone as in Lemma 1). From the minimality of $\mathcal{M}_b(\varphi)$ (Lemma 1), necessarily also $\mathcal{M}_b(\varphi) \subseteq H$.

To show termination it suffices to show that H strictly increases in each iteration (because the number of non-equivalent propositional formulas is finite). To see this, note that GENERALIZE(φ, b, σ_r) returns v s.t. $v \leq_b \sigma_r$, since the procedure starts with σ_r and only flips literals to agree with b. This implies that $\sigma_r \models cube_b(v)$, so after the iteration $\sigma_r \models H$ whereas previously $\sigma_r \not\models H$.   □

The novelty of the algorithm is its efficiency, which we now turn to establish. The crucial point is the generalization is able to produce, term by term, a minimal representation of $\mathcal{M}_b(\varphi)$. To this end, we first show that $cube_b(v)$ that the algorithm computes in lines 5 to 6 is a *prime implicant* of $\mathcal{M}_b(\varphi)$. Recall that a term t is an *implicant* of a formula ψ if $t \implies \psi$, and it is *prime* if this no longer holds after dropping a literal, that is, for every $\ell \in t$ (as a set of literals), $(\wedge (t \setminus \{\ell\})) \not\implies \psi$. It is *non-trivial* if $t \not\equiv false$ (not an empty set of literals).

Lemma 10. *If $\sigma_r \models \varphi$, then GENERALIZE(φ, b, σ_r) returns v s.t. $cube_b(v)$ is a non-trivial prime implicant of $\mathcal{M}_b(\varphi)$.*

Proof. Lemma 8 shows that it is an implicant. It is non-trivial because σ_r is a model of it, as shown as part of the proof of Lemma 9. Suppose that $cube_b(v)$ is not prime. Then there a literal over some variable p that can be dropped. It is present in $cube_b(v)$, which means that $p \in dom(b)$ and $v[p] \neq b[p]$. Then the cube obtained from dropping the literal can be written as $cube_b(x)$ where $x = v[p \mapsto \neg v[p]]$. If this cube is an implicant of $\mathcal{M}_b(\varphi)$, then, because $x \models cube_b(x)$, in particular $x \models \mathcal{M}_b(\varphi)$. By Definition 3, there is $\tilde{\sigma} \models \varphi$ such that $\tilde{\sigma} \leq_b x$. But the latter implies that $\tilde{\sigma} \in \boxed{x, \pi_b(x)}$, because, by Definition 2, for every $p \notin dom(b)$, $\tilde{\sigma}[p] = x[p] = \pi_b(x)[p]$ and for every $p \in dom(b)$ where $x, \pi_b(x)$ agree also $\tilde{\sigma}, b$ agree (because $\pi_b(x)[p] = b[p]$). Thus $\boxed{x, \pi_b(x)} \cap \varphi \neq \emptyset$, in contradiction to the choice of v, according to the check in line 20.   □

Thanks to the fact that $\mathcal{M}_b(\varphi)$ is b-monotone, through one of the basic properties of monotone functions that dates back to Quine [30], a prime implicant reproduces a term from the (unique) minimal representation of $\mathcal{M}_b(\varphi)$. We use this to show that the monotonization is computed in few iterations:

Lemma 11. *The number of iterations of the loop in line 3 of* MONOTONIZE(φ, b) *is at most* $|\mathcal{M}_b(\varphi)|_{\mathrm{dnf}}$.

Proof. Lemma 10 shows that in each iteration we disjoin a prime implicant. It is a property of monotone functions that they have a unique DNF representations with irredundant, which consists of the disjunction of all non-trivial prime implicants [30], and this extends to b-monotone functions (through a simple renaming of variables to make the function monotone). Thus the non-trivial prime implicant we disjoin is a term of the minimal DNF representation of $\mathcal{M}_b(\varphi)$. Each additional σ_r produces a new term, as shown in Lemma 9.   □

We are now ready to prove that the algorithm overall is efficient.

Proof of Theorem 2. By Lemma 11 the number of iterations of the loop in line 3 is bounded by $|\mathcal{M}_b(\varphi)|_{\mathrm{dnf}}$. Each iteration calls GENERALIZE, which performs at most n iterations of the loop in line 14 because the same variable is never flipped twice. Each iteration of this loop performs n SAT queries in line 20. Note that the cube $\boxed{x, \pi_b(x)}$ is straightforward to compute in linear time.   □

Remark 1. Bshouty [5] used an algorithm for computing $\mathcal{M}_b(\varphi)$ whose complexity is bounded by the DNF input size $|\varphi|_{\mathrm{dnf}}$, whereas Algorithm 1's complexity is bounded by the DNF *output* size, $|\mathcal{M}_b(\varphi)|_{\mathrm{dnf}}$, which is never worse (Lemma 5), and sometimes significantly smaller. When considered as learning algorithms, the improved complexity of Algorithm 1 comes at the expense of the need for richer queries: Bshouty's algorithm is similar to Algorithm 1 (using an equivalence query in line 3 that produces a positive example—see the extended version [15]), except that the condition in line 20 is replaced by checking whether $x \models \varphi$. This is a membership query to φ, whereas our check amounts to a disjointness query [1].

5   Efficient Inference of CDNF Invariants

Algorithm 2 . Dual of model-based interpolation-based inference [3,6]	**Algorithm 3** . Interpolation-based inference of CDNF invariants
1: **procedure** Dual-MB-ITP($Init,\delta,Bad,s$)	1: **procedure** CDNF-ITP($Init,\delta,Bad,s$)
2: **if** $\underline{\delta}^s(Init) \cap Bad \neq \emptyset$ **then**	2: **if** $\underline{\delta}^s(Init) \cap Bad \neq \emptyset$ **then**
3: unsafe	3: unsafe
4: $\varphi \leftarrow \neg Bad$	4: $\varphi \leftarrow \neg Bad$
5: **while** φ not inductive **do**	5: **while** φ not inductive **do**
6: let $\sigma,\sigma' \models \varphi \wedge \delta \wedge \neg\varphi'$	6: let $\sigma,\sigma' \models \varphi \wedge \delta \wedge \neg\varphi'$
7: **if** $\underline{\delta}^s(Init) \cap \{\sigma\} \neq \emptyset$ **then**	7: **if** $\underline{\delta}^s(Init) \cap \{\sigma\} \neq \emptyset$ **then**
8: restart with larger s	8: restart with larger s
9: take minimal clause $c \subseteq \neg\sigma$ s.t. $\underline{\delta}^s(Init) \Longrightarrow c$	9: $H \leftarrow$ MONOTONIZE($\underline{\delta}^s(Init), \sigma$)
10: $\varphi \leftarrow \varphi \wedge c$	10: $\varphi \leftarrow \varphi \wedge H$
11: **return** φ	11: **return** I

In this section we build on the algorithm of Sect. 4 to devise a new model-based interpolation-based algorithm that can efficiently infer invariants that have poly-size CNF and DNF representations (dubbed "CDNF invariants"). We start with background on the theoretical condition that guarantees the success of the original model-based algorithm for simpler forms of invariants.

5.1   Background: Interpolation with the Fence Condition

The essence of interpolation-based invariant inference (ITP) is to generalize a proof of *bounded* unreachability—i.e., bounded model checking [2]—into a proof of *un*bounded reachability, that is, a part of the inductive invariant. The reader is more likely to be familiar with the structure of the original algorithm by McMillan [26], which uses bounded unreachability *to* the *bad* states, where in each iteration the algorithm adds states to the candidate by *disjoining* a formula from which it is impossible to reach a bad state in s steps. However, for our purposes here, it is more convenient to consider the *dual* version, which uses bounded unreachability *from* the *initial* states, where in each iteration the algorithm excludes states from the candidate by *conjoining* a formula which does not exclude any state that the system can reach in s steps from an initial state (i.e., the candidate φ is updated by $\varphi \leftarrow \varphi \wedge H$ where H is a formula s.t. $\underline{\delta}^s(Init) \subseteq H$).

The original interpolation-based algorithm by McMillan uses a procedure that relies on the internals of the SAT solver [26]. Complexity bounds on interpolation-based algorithms analyze later approaches that exercise control on how interpolants are generated, and do this in a model-based fashion [3,6] inspired by IC3/PDR [4,9]. The dual version is presented in Algorithm 2. After starting the candidate φ as $\neg Bad$, each iteration checks for a counterexample to induction (line 6), whose pre-state σ is excluded from φ at the end of the iteration (line 10). Many states are excluded in each iteration beyond the counterexample, by conjoining to the candidate a minimal *clause* that excludes σ but retains all the states that are reachable in the system in s steps (line 9—this involves up to n queries of s-BMC, each time dropping a literal and checking whether the clause is still valid). If the counterexample cannot be blocked, because it is in fact reachable in s steps, this is an indication that s needs to be larger (line 7) to find a proof or a safety violation. The algorithm detects that the transition system is unsafe in line 3 when s is enough to find an execution from $Init$ to Bad with at most s transitions. (Our analysis of the algorithms in the paper focuses on the safe case, the complexity of finding an invariant.)

A condition that guarantees that s is large enough for Algorithm 2 to successfully find an inductive invariant, called the *fence condition*, was recently put forward [13], involving the Hamming-geometric boundary of the invariant.

Definition 7 (Boundary). *Let I be a set of states. Then the (inner) boundary of I, denoted $\partial^+(I)$, is the set of states $\sigma^+ \models I$ s.t. there is a state σ^- that differs from σ in exactly one variable, and $\sigma^+ \models I, \sigma^- \not\models I$.*

Definition 8 (Fence Condition). *Let I be an inductive invariant for a transition system $(Init, \delta, Bad)$ and $s \in \mathbb{N}$. Then I is s-forwards fenced if $\partial^+(I) \subseteq \underline{\delta}^s(Init)$.*

Example 1. Let I be the set of all states where at least two bits are 0 *and* at least two bits are 1. Then $\partial^+(I)$ is the set where exactly two bits are 0 (and at least two bits are 1) or exactly two bits are 1 (and at least two bits are 0). Note that $I \setminus \partial^+(I)$ contains many (most) states—those where three or more bits are 0 and three or more bits are 1. The fence condition requires only from the states in $\partial^+(I)$ to be reachable in s steps.

The fence condition guarantees that throughout the algorithm's execution, φ contains the fenced invariant, giving rise to the following correctness property:

Theorem 3 *([13]).* *If there exists an s-forwards fenced invariant for* $(Init, \delta, Bad)$, *then* Dual-MB-ITP$(Init, \delta, Bad, s)$ *successfully finds an invariant.*

The idea is that the property that $I \implies \varphi$ is maintained because the fence condition ensures that it suffices to verify that the clause that GENERALIZE computes, starting from a state $\sigma \models \varphi$ that is outside of I, does not exclude a state from $\underline{\delta}^s(Init)$ to guarantee that it also does not exclude a state from I. (Note that the fence condition does not provide a way to know whether an *arbitrary* state belongs to I.).

The fence condition ensures the algorithm's success, but not that it is efficient—the number of iterations until convergence may be large, even when there is a fenced inductive invariant that has a short representation in CNF. (Note that in Algorithm 2, φ is always in CNF.) This was ameliorated in [13] by the assumption that the invariant is *monotone*:

Theorem 4 *([13]).* *If I is an s-forwards fenced inductive invariant for* $(Init, \delta, Bad)$ *and I is* monotone *(can be written in CNF/DNF with all variables un-negated), then* Dual-MB-ITP$(Init, \delta, Bad, s)$ *successfully finds an inductive invariant in* $O(|I|_{\mathrm{cnf}})$ *inductiveness checks, and* $O(n \cdot |I|_{\mathrm{cnf}})$ *checks of s-BMC and time.*[3]

However, when I is *not* monotone, it is possible for the algorithm to require an exponential number of iterations even though $|I|_{\mathrm{cnf}}$ is small (and in fact, even though *every* representation of I without redundant clauses is small).

The challenge that we address in this section is to create an invariant inference algorithm that efficiently infers inductive invariants that are not monotone, while relying only on the fence condition.

5.2 CDNF Inference with the Fence Condition

We now present our new invariant inference algorithm (Algorithm 3), that is guaranteed to run in time polynomial in $n, |I|_{\mathrm{cnf}}, |I|_{\mathrm{dnf}}$ of a fenced invariant I:

Theorem 5. *Let I be a forwards s-fenced inductive invariant for* $(Init, \delta, Bad)$. *Then* CDNF-ITP$(Init, \delta, Bad, s)$ *finds an inductive invariant in at most* $|I|_{\mathrm{cnf}} \cdot |I|_{\mathrm{dnf}} \cdot n^2$ *of s-BMC checks,* $|I|_{\mathrm{cnf}}$ *inductiveness checks, and* $O(|I|_{\mathrm{cnf}} \cdot |I|_{\mathrm{dnf}} \cdot n^2)$ *time.*

Example 2. I from Example 1 has poly-size representations in both CNF and DNF. We write:

---

[3] A similar result applies when the invariant is *unate*, that is, can be written in CNF/DNF so that every variable is either always negated or always un-negated.

DNF: there is a choice of four bits with two 0's and two 1's,

$$I \equiv \bigvee_{1 \leq i_1 \neq i_2 \neq i_3 \neq i_4 \leq n} (x_{i_1} = 0 \wedge x_{i_2} = 0 \wedge x_{i_3} = 1 \wedge x_{i_4} = 1).$$

CNF: it is impossible that $n-1$ bits or more are 1, likewise for 0,

$$I \equiv \left(\bigwedge_{i=1}^{n} \bigvee_{j \neq i} x_j = 0 \right) \wedge \left(\bigwedge_{i=1}^{n} \bigvee_{j \neq i} x_j = 1 \right).$$

The CNF formula has $2n$ clauses, and the DNF has $\binom{n}{4} = \Theta(n^4)$ terms. Theorem 5 shows that such I satisfying the fence condition can be inferred in a number of queries and time that is polynomial in n. Note that these formulas fall outside the classes that previous results can handle efficiently (see Sect. 7) as they are not monotone nor almost-monotone (the number of terms/clauses with negated variables is not constant).

As noted by Bshouty [5], the class of formulas with short DNF and CNF includes the formulas that can be expressed by a small *decision tree*: a binary tree in which every internal node is labeled by a variable and a leaf by *true/false*, and σ satisfies the formula if the path defined by starting from the root, turning left when the σ assigns *false* to the variable labeling the node and right otherwise, reaches a leaf *true*. The size of a decision tree is the number of leaves in the tree. We conclude that (see the proof in the extended version [15]):

Corollary 1. *Let I be a forwards s-fenced inductive invariant for $(Init, \delta, Bad)$, that can be expressed as a decision tree of size m. Then* CDNF-ITP *$(Init, \delta, Bad, s)$ finds an inductive invariant in at most $m^2 \cdot n^2$ of s-BMC checks, m inductiveness checks, and $O(m^2 \cdot n^2)$ time.*

The algorithm CDNF-ITP which attains Theorem 5 is presented in Algorithm 3. Its overall structure is similar to Algorithm 2, except the formula used to block a counterexample is the monotonization of the s-reachable states. Specifically, starting from the candidate $\varphi = true$ (line 4, the algorithm iteratively samples counterexamples to induction (line 6) and blocks the pre-state σ from φ by conjoining $\mathcal{M}_\sigma(\underline{\delta}^s(Init))$, computed by invoking Algorithm 1. The SAT queries of the form $\text{SAT}(\varphi \wedge \theta)$ that Algorithm 1 performs (see Sect. 4) have $\varphi = \underline{\delta}^s(Init)$, and they amount to the BMC checks of whether $\underline{\delta}^s(Init) \cap \theta \overset{?}{=} \emptyset$.

It is important for the efficiency result that Algorithm 3 uses Algorithm 1 as a subprocedure. Using Bshouty's procedure (see Remark 1) would yield a bound of $n \cdot |\underline{\delta}^s(Init)|_{\text{dnf}}$ checks of s-BMC, and it is likely that $\underline{\delta}^s(Init)$ is complex to capture in a formula when s is significant (as common for sets defined by exact reachability, such as the set of the reachable states).

We now proceed to prove the correctness and efficiency of the algorithm (Theorem 5). Throughout, assume that I is an inductive invariant for $(Init, \delta, Bad)$. I will be s-forwards fenced; we state this explicitly in the premise of lemmas where this assumption is used. The idea behind the correctness and efficiency of Algorithm 3 is that $\mathcal{M}_\sigma(I)$ is a stronger formula than the clauses that are produced in Algorithm 2, causing the candidate to converge down to the invariant in fewer iterations, while never excluding states that belong to I (because $I \subseteq \mathcal{M}_\sigma(I)$, as used in Lemma 14). As we will show (in Lemma 15), this strategy results in a number of iterations that is bounded by the CNF size of I (without further assumptions on the syntactic structure of I). The trick, however, is to show (in Lemma 13) that what the algorithm computes in line 9 is indeed $\mathcal{M}_\sigma(I)$, even though I is unknown. The crucial observation is that under the fence condition, the monotonization of the s-reachable states matches the monotonization of the invariant (even though these are different sets!). Note that this holds for any invariant that satisfies the fence condition. To prove this we need to recall a fact about the monotonization of the boundary of a set:

Lemma 12 ([14]). *Let I, S be sets of states s.t. $\partial^+(I) \subseteq S$ and σ a state s.t. $\sigma \not\models I$. Then $I \subseteq \mathcal{M}_\sigma(S)$.*

The idea is that for every $x \in I$, there is a state on the boundary $v \in \partial^+(I)$ s.t. $v \leq_\sigma x$ (where a shortest path between x, b crosses I), and because also $v \in S$ we would have that $x \in \mathcal{M}_\sigma(S)$.

We proceed to relate the monotonizations of $\underline{\delta}^s(Init), I$:

Lemma 13. *If I is forwards s-fenced for $(Init, \delta, Bad)$, and $\sigma \not\models I$, then we have that $\mathcal{M}_\sigma(\underline{\delta}^s(Init)) = \mathcal{M}_\sigma(I)$.*

Proof. Since I is an inductive invariant, $\underline{\delta}^s(Init) \subseteq I$, so $\mathcal{M}_\sigma(\underline{\delta}^s(Init)) \subseteq \mathcal{M}_s(I)$ from Lemma 2. For the other direction we use Lemma 12: by the fence condition, $\partial^+(I) \subseteq \underline{\delta}^s(Init)$ and hence, as $\sigma \not\models I$, we obtain $I \subseteq \mathcal{M}_\sigma(\underline{\delta}^s(Init))$. By Lemma 1, this implies that $\mathcal{M}_\sigma(I) \subseteq \mathcal{M}_\sigma(\underline{\delta}^s(Init))$. ☐

We use this to characterize the candidate invariant the algorithm constructs:

Lemma 14. *If I is forwards s-fenced for $(Init, \delta, Bad)$, then in each step of CDNF-ITP$(Init, \delta, Bad, k)$, $\varphi = \text{MHull}_{\mathcal{C}_i}(I) \wedge \neg Bad$, where $\mathcal{C}_i$ is the set of counterexamples σ the algorithm has observed so far. In particular, $I \subseteq \varphi$.*

Proof. First, $I \subseteq \varphi$ holds from the rest of the lemma because $I \subseteq \neg Bad$ (it is an inductive invariant), and $I \subseteq \text{MHull}_{\mathcal{C}_i}(I)$ by Lemma 7. The proof of $\varphi = \text{MHull}_{\mathcal{C}_i}(I) \wedge \neg Bad$ is by induction on iterations of the loop in line 5. Initially, $\mathcal{C} = \emptyset$ and indeed $\varphi = \neg Bad$. In each iteration, $I \subseteq \varphi$ using the argument above and the induction hypothesis. Hence, the counterexample to induction of line 6 has $\sigma \not\models I$ (otherwise $\sigma' \models I$ because I is an inductive invariant, and this would imply also $\sigma \models \varphi$, in contradiction). Then Lemma 9 ensures that $H = \mathcal{M}_\sigma(\underline{\delta}^s(Init))$. Lemma 13 shows that this is $\mathcal{M}_\sigma(I)$, as required. ☐

Essentially, the algorithm gradually learns a monotone basis (Definition 5) for I from the counterexamples to induction, and constructs I via the monotone hull w.r.t. this basis. The next lemma shows that the size of the basis that the algorithm finds is bounded by $|I|_{\text{cnf}}$.

Lemma 15. *If I is forwards s-fenced for $(Init, \delta, Bad)$, then CDNF-ITP$(Init, \delta, Bad, k)$ successfully finds an inductive invariant. Further, the number of iterations of the loop in line 5 is at most $|I|_{\mathrm{cnf}}$.*

Proof. Since $\sigma \not\models I$, also it is not a model of the monotonization w.r.t. to itself, $\sigma \not\models \mathcal{M}_\sigma(I)$ (because the only state $x \leq_\sigma \sigma$ is $x = \sigma$—see Definitions 1 and 3). This shows, using Lemma 14, that at least one state is excluded from the candidate φ in each iteration. By the same lemma always $I \implies \varphi$, and the algorithm terminates when φ is inductive, so this shows that the algorithm successfully converges to an inductive invariant.

To see that this occurs in at most $|I|_{\mathrm{cnf}}$ iterations, consider a minimal CNF representation of I, $I = c_1 \wedge \ldots \wedge c_{|I|_{\mathrm{cnf}}}$. We argue that in each iteration produces at least one new clause from that representation, in the sense that for some i, $\varphi \wedge \mathcal{M}_{\sigma_b}(I) \implies c_i$ whereas previously $\varphi \not\implies c_i$. Let c_i be the clause that $\sigma \not\models c_i$ (recall e.g. that $\sigma \not\models \varphi$ and $I \subseteq \varphi$). Then $\mathcal{M}_\sigma(I) \subseteq c_i$, since c_i is σ-monotone ($\mathcal{M}_\sigma(c_i) = c_i$, using Lemma 3, because all the literals disagree with σ) and $I \subseteq c_i$, and $\mathcal{M}_\sigma(I)$ is the smallest such (Lemma 1). Thus when we conjoin $H = \mathcal{M}_\sigma(I)$ to φ we conjoin at least one new c_i that was not present in a CNF representation of φ; this can happen at most $|I|_{\mathrm{cnf}}$ times.   □

Overall:

Proof of Theorem 5. The algorithm's success in finding an invariant is established in Lemma 15. As for efficiency, by Lemma 15, there are at most $|I|_{\mathrm{cnf}}$ iterations of the loop in CDNF-ITP, each performs a single inductiveness query, and calls MONOTONIZE. By Theorem 2 each such call performs at most $O(n^2|\mathcal{M}_\sigma(I)|_{\mathrm{dnf}})$ s-BMC queries. The claim follows because $|\mathcal{M}_\sigma(I)|_{\mathrm{dnf}} \leq |I|_{\mathrm{dnf}}$ (Lemma 5).   □

Remark 2 (Backwards fence condition). Our main theorem in this section, Theorem 5, also has a dual version that applies to a fence condition concerning *backwards* reachability. I is s-backwards fenced if every state in the *outer boundary* $\partial^-(I) \overset{\text{def}}{=} \partial^+(\neg I)$ can reach a state in Bad in at most s steps [13]. The dual of Theorem 5 is that there is an algorithm that achieves the same complexity bound under the assumption that I is s-*backwards* fenced (instead of s-forwards fenced). The dual-CDNF algorithm is obtained by running our CDNF algorithm on the dual transition system $(Bad, \delta^{-1}, Init)$ (see e.g. [[12], Appendix A]) and negate the invariant; notice that the CDNF class is closed under negation. This algorithm also achieves the same bound for decision trees as in Corollary 1, under the backwards fence assumption.

Remark 3 (Comparison to Bshouty's CDNF algorithm). Our CDNF algorithm, Algorithm 3, is inspired by Bshouty's CDNF algorithm [5], but diverges from it in several ways. The reason is the different queries available in each setting. (The code for Bshouty's CDNF algorithm is provided in the extended version [15].) Structurally, while the candidate in both algorithms is gradually constructed to be $\mathrm{MHull}_{\mathcal{C}_i}(I) = \bigwedge_{\sigma \in \mathcal{C}_i} \mathcal{M}_\sigma(I)$ (I being the unknown invariant/formula, and $\mathcal{C}_i$

the set of negative examples so far), Algorithm 3 constructs each monotonization separately, one by one, whereas Bshouty's algorithm increases all monotonizations simultaneously. Bshouty's design follows from having the source of
examples—both positive and negative—equivalence queries, checking whether
the candidate matches I. A membership query is necessary to decide whether
the differentiating example is positive or negative for I in order to decide whether
to add disjuncts to the existing monotonizations or to add a new monotonization, respectively. This procedure is problematic in invariant inference, because
we cannot in general decide, for a counterexample (σ, σ') showing that our candidate is not inductive, whether $\sigma \not\models I$ (negative) or $\sigma' \models I$ (positive) [12,18]. The
solution in previous work [13] was to assume that the invariant satisfies both the
forwards *and* backwards fence condition (see Remark 2). Under this assumption
it is possible to decide whether $\sigma \models I$ for an arbitrary state σ. However, this condition is much stronger than a one-sided version of the fence condition. Instead,
in our inference algorithm, the candidate is ensured to be an overapproximation
of the true I, so each counterexample to induction in line 6 yields a negative
example. Positive examples are obtained in line 4 from $\underline{\delta}^s(Init) \subseteq I$; there is no
obvious counterpart to that in exact learning, because in that setting we have no
a-priori knowledge of some set S that underapproximates I, let alone one where
we know—as the fence condition guarantees through Lemma 12—that covering
S in the monotonization is enough to cover I.

6   Efficient Implementation of Abstract Interpretation

In this section we build on the algorithm of Sect. 4 to prove a complexity upper
bound on abstract interpretation in the domain based on the monotone theory
(Theorem 7). We begin with background on this domain.

6.1   Background: Abstract Interpretation in the Monotone Theory

Recall that given a set of states B, the monotone span (Definition 6) of B,
$\mathrm{MSpan}(B)$, is the set of formulas φ s.t. $\mathrm{MHull}_B(\varphi) \equiv \varphi$, or, equivalently, the set
of formulas that can be written as conjunctions of clauses that exclude states
from B (Theorem 1). The *abstract domain* $\mathbb{M}[B] = \langle \mathrm{MSpan}(B), \Longrightarrow, \sqcup_B, false \rangle$,
introduced in [14], is a join-semilattice over the monotone span of B, ordered by
logical implication, with bottom element *false*. The lub $\sqcup_B$ exists because the
domain is finite and closed under conjunction (follows from Theorem 1). A Galois
connection $(2^{\mathrm{States}[\Sigma]}, \subseteq) \xleftarrow[\alpha_B]{\gamma} (\mathrm{MSpan}(B), \Longrightarrow)$ with the concrete domain is
obtained through the *concretization* $\gamma(\varphi) = \{\sigma \mid \sigma \models \varphi\}$ and the *abstraction*
$\alpha_B(\psi) = \mathrm{MHull}_B(\psi)$ [14].[4]

---

[4] $\mathbb{M}[B]$ is parametrized by a choice of a monotone basis B. When B is large, the
abstraction is more precise; it is precise enough to prove safety when there exists
an inductive invariant that can be expressed in CNF such that each clause excludes
at least one state from B (through Theorem 1). The fewer states B includes, the
more extrapolation is performed in each abstraction step. However, since B also

---

Algorithm 4. Kleene Iterations in $\mathbb{M}[B]$

1: **procedure** AI-$\mathbb{M}[B]$(*Init*, δ, *Bad*)
2:     $i \leftarrow 0$
3:     $\xi_{-1} \leftarrow \textit{false}$
4:     $\xi_0 \leftarrow \text{MHull}_B(\textit{Init})$
5:     **while** $\xi_i \not\Rightarrow \xi_{i-1}$ **do**
6:         $\xi_{i+1} = \text{MHull}_B(\delta(\xi_i) \cup \textit{Init})$
7:         $i \leftarrow i + 1$
8:     **return** ξ_i

Given a transition system $(\textit{Init}, \delta)$, iterations of abstract interpretation with the abstract transformer are given by $\xi_0 = \alpha_B(\textit{Init}), \xi_{i+1} = \alpha_B(\delta(\gamma(\xi_i)) \cup \textit{Init})$. Substituting γ, α_B yields the iterations as shown in Algorithm 4.

Each iterate in Algorithm 4 involves a monotone hull (lines 4 and 6), which is a conjunction of monotonizations. Using Algorithm 1 this can be computed efficiently. We follow on this idea to prove efficient complexity upper bounds on Algorithm 4.

6.2 Complexity Upper Bound

To obtain a complexity upper bound on Algorithm 4 we need to bound the time needed to compute each ξ_i as well as the number of ξ_i's. A bound for the latter is provided by [14]:

Theorem 6 (*[14]*). *Let* $(\textit{Init}, \delta, \textit{Bad})$ *be a transition system. Then the algorithm* AI-$\mathbb{M}[B](\textit{Init}, \delta, \textit{Bad})$ *converges in iteration number at most*

$$\zeta \overset{\text{def}}{=} \prod_{i=1}^{m} \left(\left| \mathcal{M}_{\textit{Ref}(\boxed{B}) \wedge b_i'}(\delta) \right|_{\text{dnf}} + \left| \mathcal{M}_{b_i}(\textit{Init}) \right|_{\text{dnf}} \right),$$

where B can be written in DNF as $b_1 \vee \ldots \vee b_m$, the cube $\boxed{B}$ consists of the literals that appear in all $b_1, \ldots, b_m$ (i.e., $\boxed{B} = \bigcap_{i=1}^{m} b_i$ as sets of literals), and the reflection of a cube $d = \ell_1 \wedge \ldots \wedge \ell_r$ is $\textit{Ref}(d) = \neg\ell_1 \wedge \ldots \wedge \neg\ell_r$.

We fix a DNF representation of $B = b_1 \vee \ldots \vee b_m$. For brevity, we use ζ to refer to the bound in Theorem 6. When ζ is small, it reflects the benefit of using abstract interpretation in MSpan(B) over exact reachability (even though ζ is not always a tight bound) [14]. An example of ζ for a simple system appears in Example 3.

---

changes the available inductive invariants, the overall convergence might actually be faster with a larger (less extrapolating) B. Understanding how to choose B is an important direction for future work. (In [14], B was obtained from the states that reach a bad state in a fixed number of steps, mimicking PDR's scheme for generating proof obligations.).

In this section we prove that it is possible to implement Algorithm 4 so that its overall complexity is polynomial in the same quantity ζ, the number of variables n, and the number m of terms in the representation of B:

Theorem 7. *Algorithm 4 can be implemented to terminate in $O(n^2\zeta + (n + m)\zeta^2)$ SAT queries and time.*

Example 3. Let n be an odd number. Consider a transition system over $\bar{x} = x_1, \ldots, x_n$, where *Init* is $\bar{x} = 00\ldots00$ and the transition relation chooses an even number of variables that are 0 from the initial state and turns them into 1. If we take B to be the singleton set containing the state $\bar{x} = 11\ldots11$ (hence, B is a cube and $m = 1$), then Lemma 3 yields that $\mathcal{M}_{\bar{x}=00\ldots00\wedge\bar{x}'=11\ldots11}(\delta) = \bigvee_{i=1}^{n}(x'_i = 0)$ (see the extended version [15] for details) so $\zeta = |\mathcal{M}_{\bar{x}=00\ldots00\wedge\bar{x}'=11\ldots11}(\delta)|_{\mathrm{dnf}} = O(n)$. Theorem 7 shows that an implementation of abstract interpretation in $\mathbb{M}[B]$ for this system terminates in $O(n^3)$ SAT queries and time. This is significant because a naive implementation of Algorithm 4 would start, for the first iteration of line 6, by computing the exact post-image $\delta(\textit{Init})$; in our example this is the set of states where the parity of $\bar{x}$ is 0, which cannot be represented in polynomial-size DNF nor CNF [e.g. 8]. Our implementation is able to compute the abstraction of the post-image without constructing the post-image and avoids the blowup in complexity. [14] contains other examples with small ζ.

At this point, the direct approach to implement Algorithm 4 is to perform $\mathrm{MHull}_B(\varphi)$ in lines 4 and 6 through $\bigwedge_{j=1}^{m}$ MONOTONIZE(φ, b_j), invoking Algorithm 1 on φ. Indeed, this achieves a bound that is only slightly worse than Theorem 7 (see Remark 4). In what follows we provide an implementation that both explicates the connection to ζ, and achieves exactly the bound of Theorem 7.

Algorithm 5. Efficient Kleene Iterations in $\mathbb{M}[B]$

1: **procedure** AI-$\mathbb{M}[B]$(*Init*, δ, *Bad*)
2:     $i \leftarrow 0$
3:     $\xi_{-1} \leftarrow \textit{false}$
4:     $\xi_0 \leftarrow \bigwedge_{j=1}^{m}$ MONOTONIZE(*Init*, b_j)
5:     **for** $j = 1..m$ **do**
6:         $\delta_j^{\mathsf{x}} \leftarrow$ MONOTONIZE($\delta \vee \textit{Init}'$, $\textit{Ref}(\mathbb{B}) \wedge b'_j$)
7:     **while** $\xi_i \not\Rightarrow \xi_{i-1}$ **do**
8:         $\xi_{i+1} = \bigvee \{(t_1|_{\Sigma'}) \wedge \ldots \wedge (t_m|_{\Sigma'}) \mid t_j$ a term of $\delta_j^{\mathsf{x}}, \exists \sigma_j \in \xi_i. \sigma_j \models (t_j|_{\Sigma})\}$
9:         $i \leftarrow i + 1$
10:    **return** ξ_i

Our implementation is displayed in Algorithm 5. The first iterate is computed as described above by invoking Algorithm 1 on *Init* (line 4). The SAT queries performed by Algorithm 1 are in this case straightforward, with $\varphi = \textit{Init}$.

To compute the next iterates, we first compute monotnizations of the concrete transformer, $\delta \vee Init'$ (line 6). This is a two-vocabulary formula, and accordingly the monotonizations are w.r.t. two-vocabulary cubes. The monotonizations are computed in DNF form and stored in $\delta_j^{\times}$. The next iterate ξ_{i+1} is formed from the $\delta_j^{\times}$'s by taking all the combinations of terms from $\delta_1^{\times}, \ldots, \delta_m^{\times}$ whose pre-state part is satisfied by at least one state in ξ_i, and forming the conjunction of the post-state parts: for a term $t = \ell_1 \vee \ldots \vee \ell_{i_1} \vee \ell'_{i_1+1} \vee \ldots \vee \ell'_{i_2}$ over $\Sigma \uplus \Sigma'$, the restriction $t\big|_{\Sigma} = \ell_1 \vee \ldots \vee \ell_{i_1}$ and $t\big|_{\Sigma'} = \ell'_{i_1+1} \vee \ldots \vee \ell'_{i_2}$.

The intuition is that in the original algorithm, given a set of states ξ_i, we find the set of states in ξ_{i+1} by taking the result of the transformer $\delta \vee Init'$ on the specific ξ_i, then, for the monotonization of the result, adding also the states that are required by the b_j-monotone order, and this we do for every disjunct b_j in B, letting ξ_{i+1} be the conjunction of the said monotonizations. Here, instead, we monotonize $\delta \vee Init'$ itself w.r.t. every b_j, such that for every pre-state we have ready the monotonization of the corresponding post-state. We then form ξ_{i+1} by picking and conjoining the right monotonizations—the ones whose pre-state is in the previous frame. (The monotonization of the pre-state w.r.t. $Ref(\mathbb{B})$ is useful for decreasing ζ, and hence the obtained bound, without altering ξ_{i+1}; the latter stems from the fact that the input ξ_i is also the result of such a procedure, so the presence of a pre-state in ξ_i indicates the presence all the states in its monotone hull w.r.t. $Ref(\mathbb{B})$ in ξ_i.)

The invocation of Algorithm 1 in line 6 is on a double-vocabulary formula; still, the SAT queries to be performed in the invocation of Algorithm 1 are simple SAT queries about two-vocabulary formulas (and a counterexample is a pair of states).

It is important for the efficiency result that Algorithm 3 uses Algorithm 1 as a subprocedure. Using Bshouty's procedure (see Remark 1) would yield a bound in terms of the DNF size of the original transition relation, which could be significantly larger, especially in cases where the abstract interpretation procedure terminates faster than exact forward reachability [14].

The rest of this section proves that Algorithm 5 realizes Theorem 7. To show that it correctly implements Algorithm 4, we need the following fact about Algorithm 4:

Lemma 16 ([14]). *In Algorithm 4, $\sigma' \models \xi_{i+1}$ iff there exist $\sigma_1, \ldots, \sigma_m \models \xi_i$ s.t.*

$$(\sigma_1, \sigma') \models \mathcal{M}_{Ref(\mathbb{B}) \wedge b'_1}(\delta \vee Init') \wedge \ldots \wedge (\sigma_m, \sigma') \models \mathcal{M}_{Ref(\mathbb{B}) \wedge b'_m}(\delta \vee Init'). \quad (1)$$

We use this to show the correctness of Algorithm 5:

Lemma 17. *ξ_i in Algorithm 5 is logically equivalent to ξ_i in Algorithm 4.*

Proof. By induction over i. The correctness of ξ_0 follows from the correctness of Algorithm 1 (Theorem 2). For the same reasons, $\delta_j^{\times}$ of Algorithm 5 is equivalent to $\mathcal{M}_{Ref(\boxdot)\wedge b'_j}(\delta \vee Init')$. Now for some DNF manipulation: for every σ',

$$\exists \sigma_1,\ldots,\sigma_m.(\sigma_1,\sigma') \models \delta_1^{\times} \wedge \ldots \wedge (\sigma_m,\sigma') \models \delta_m^{\times}$$

$$\Longleftrightarrow \quad \exists \sigma_1,\ldots,\sigma_m. \exists t_1 \text{ term of } \delta_1^{\times},\ldots,\exists t_m \text{ term of } \delta_m^{\times}.$$
$$(\sigma_1,\sigma') \models t_1 \wedge \ldots \wedge (\sigma_m,\sigma') \models t_m$$

$$\Longleftrightarrow \quad \exists \sigma_1,\ldots,\sigma_m. \exists t_1 \text{ term of } \delta_1^{\times},\ldots,\exists t_m \text{ term of } \delta_m^{\times}.$$
$$\sigma_1 \models \left(t_1\big|_{\Sigma}\right) \wedge \sigma' \models \left(t_1\big|_{\Sigma'}\right) \wedge \ldots \wedge \sigma_1 \models \left(t_m\big|_{\Sigma}\right) \wedge \sigma' \models \left(t_m\big|_{\Sigma'}\right)$$

$$\Longleftrightarrow \quad \exists \sigma_1, \exists t_1 \text{ term of } \delta_1^{\times}. \sigma_1 \models \left(t_m\big|_{\Sigma}\right) \wedge \sigma' \models \left(t_m\big|_{\Sigma'}\right)$$

$$\wedge \ldots \wedge$$

$$\exists \sigma_m, \exists t_m \text{ term of } \delta_m^{\times}. \sigma_m \models \left(t_m\big|_{\Sigma}\right) \wedge \sigma' \models \left(t_m\big|_{\Sigma'}\right).$$

Hence, $\exists \sigma_1,\ldots,\sigma_m \in \xi_i$ of Algorithm 5 that with σ' satisfy Eq. 1 iff $\sigma' \in \xi_{i+1}$ of Algorithm 5. Lemma 16 and the induction hypothesis complete the proof. $\square$

We can now proceed to prove the complexity bound for Algorithm 5.

Lemma 18. *Algorithm 5 terminates in $O(n^2\zeta + (n+m)\zeta^2)$ SAT queries and time.*

Proof. By Theorem 2, each invocation of Algorithm 1 in line 4 takes $O\left(n^2 \cdot |\mathcal{M}_{b_i}(Init)|_{\mathrm{dnf}}\right) = O(n^2\zeta)$ queries and time. Similarly, each invocation in line 6 takes

$$O\left((2n)^2 \cdot |\mathcal{M}_{Ref(\boxdot)\wedge b'_i}(\delta \vee Init')|_{\mathrm{dnf}}\right)$$

queries and time. This quantity is $O(n^2\zeta)$, because by Lemma 3

$$|\mathcal{M}_{Ref(\boxdot)\wedge b'_i}(\delta \vee Init')|_{\mathrm{dnf}} \leq |\mathcal{M}_{Ref(\boxdot)\wedge b'_i}(\delta)|_{\mathrm{dnf}} + |\mathcal{M}_{Ref(\boxdot)\wedge b'_i}(Init')|_{\mathrm{dnf}}$$
$$= |\mathcal{M}_{Ref(\boxdot)\wedge b'_i}(\delta)|_{\mathrm{dnf}} + |\mathcal{M}_{b_i}(Init)|_{\mathrm{dnf}}.$$

In each iteration, the number of combinations of terms in line 8 is at most $\prod_{i=1}^m |\mathcal{M}_{Ref(\boxdot)\wedge b'_i}(\delta \vee Init')|_{\mathrm{dnf}}$. For each of the m terms in the combination, we split the term to Σ, Σ' parts in time linear term size which is at most n, and perform a SAT check for whether the term intersects ξ_i. Overall this step involves $O(m \cdot \zeta)$ queries and $O((n+m) \cdot \zeta)$ time. This is the cost of each iteration; the number of iterations is bounded by ζ by Theorem 6. The claim follows. $\square$

The proof of Theorem 7 follows from Lemmas 17 and 18.

Remark 4. Lemmas 17 and 18 have the consequence that in Algorithm 4, $|\xi_i|_{\mathrm{dnf}} \leq \zeta$ (interestingly, this is true in particular for the resulting inductive invariant). This is a proof that the direct implementation of the monotone hull by m calls to Algorithm 1 amounts to $O(n^2m\zeta)$ SAT queries in each iteration, and $O(n^2m\zeta^2)$ time thanks to Theorem 6. Though asymptotically inferior, this implementation approach may be more efficient than Algorithm 5 when $|\xi_i|_{\mathrm{dnf}} \ll \zeta$.

7   Related Work

Complexity Bounds for Ivariant Inference. Conjunctive/disjunctive invariants can be inferred in a linear number of SAT calls [16,25]. On the other hand, inferring CNF/DNF invariants for general transition systems is **NP**-hard with access to a SAT solver [25], even when the invariants are restricted to monotone formulas [12]. Complexity results for model-based interpolation-based invariant inference (stemming from the analysis of the algorithm by [3,6]) were presented in [13], based on the (backwards) fence condition, which tames reachability enough to efficiently infer monotone and almost-monotone DNF invariants, or monotone and almost-monotone CNF invariants under the (forwards) fence condition with the dual algorithms. Our algorithm (Algorithm 5) can achieve the same bounds if, similar to [13], the monotone basis (set of counterexamples) is fixed in advance. (This alteration is needed because some short monotone DNF formulas have large CNF size [27].) Our algorithm is more versatile because it applies to CDNF formulas which are not monotone or almost-monotone, and alleviates the need to know a monotone basis in advance. A CDNF complexity bound similar to ours was obtained in [13] under the much stronger assumption that both the backwards and the forwards fence condition hold simultaneously (see Remark 2). Property-directed reachability algorithms [4,9] were shown efficient on several parametrized examples [14,34] and the very special case of maximal transition systems for monotone invariants [12]. We show (Sect. 6) that abstract interpretation in the monotone theory, studied under the name Λ-PDR [14] in relation to standard PDR, is efficient in broader circumstances, when the DNF size of certain monotonizations of the transition relation are small, using the same quantity ζ that in previous work [14] was established as an upper bound on the number of iterations (without an overall complexity result).

Monotone Theory in Invariant Inference. The monotone theory has been employed in previous works on invariant inference. The aforementioned previous results on inference under the fence condition [13] also employ the monotone theory, and are based on one-to-one translations of Bshouty's algorithms to invariant inference, replacing equivalence queries by inductiveness checks and membership queries by bounded model checking. For Bshouty's CDNF algorithm this only works under the stronger two-sided fence condition, which is why our algorithm differs significantly (see Remark 3). The one-sided fence condition suffices for the translation of Bshouty's Λ-algorithm, which is suitable when a monotone basis is known in advance, e.g. for almost-monotone invariants, whereas the CDNF algorithm learns a monotone basis on-the-fly. Another translation of Bshouty's algorithm to invariant inference is by Jung et al. [23], who combine the CDNF algorithm of Bshouty [5] with predicate abstraction and templates to infer quantified invariants. They overcome the problem of membership queries in the original algorithm (see Remark 3) heuristically, using under- and over-approximations and sometimes random guesses, which could lead to the need to restart. The monotone theory is also used in a non-algorithmic way in [14] to analyze overapproximation in IC3/PDR through abstract interpretation in the monotone theory, to which we prove a complexity upper bound.

Inferring Decision Tree Invariants. In machine learning, decision trees are a popular representation of hypotheses and target concepts. Garg et al. [19] adapt an algorithm by Quinlan [31] to infer invariants (later, general Horn clauses [11]) in the form of decision trees over numerical and Boolean attributes, which is guaranteed to converge, but not necessarily efficiently overall (even though the algorithm efficiently generates the candidates, the number of candidates could be large). Similarly to our algorithm, the translation of the CDNF algorithm to invariant inference in [13] is applicable also to Boolean decision trees, but, as previously mentioned, requires the stronger two-sided fence condition, whereas our result is the first to do so under the (one-sided) fence condition.

Complexity of Abstract Interpretation. The efficiency of the abstract transformers is crucial to the overall success of abstract interpretation, which is often at odds with the domain accuracy; a famous example is the octagon abstract domain [28], whose motivation is the prohibitive cost of the expressive polyhedra domain [7]. We provide a way to compute abstract transformers in the monotone span domain that is efficient in terms of the DNF size of the result (see also Remark 4). The computation of the abstract transformer in Algorithm 5 is inspired by works in symbolic abstraction [32,40] about finding *representations* of the best abstract transformer, rather than computing it anew per input [10,33,39].

8 Conclusion

This work has accomplished invariant inference algorithms with efficient complexity guarantees in two settings—model-based interpolation and property-directed reachability—resolving open problems where the missing component (as it turns out) was a new way to compute monotone overapproximations. A common theme is the use of rich syntactic forms of the formulas that the algorithms maintain: in our model-based interpolation algorithm, the candidate invariant is a conjunction of DNFs, even though the target invariant has both short CNF and DNF representations. In our efficient implementation of abstract interpretation, each iterate is again a conjunction of DNFs, although the natural definition (Theorem 1, and as inspired by PDR) is with CNF formulas. We hope that these ideas could inspire new interpolation-based and property-directed reachability algorithms that would benefit in practice from richer hypotheses and techniques from the monotone theory.

Acknowledgements. We thank the anonymous reviewers and Hila Peleg for insightful comments. The research leading to these results has received funding from the European Research Council under the European Union's Horizon 2020 research and innovation programme (grant agreement No. [759102-SVIS]). This research was partially supported by the Israeli Science Foundation (ISF) grant No. 1810/18.

References

1. Angluin, D.: Queries and concept learning. Mach. Learn. **2**(4), 319–342 (1987)
2. Biere, A., Cimatti, A., Clarke, E.M., Zhu, Y.: Symbolic model checking without BDDs. In: Tools and Algorithms for Construction and Analysis of Systems, 5th International Conference, TACAS 1999, Held as Part of the European Joint Conferences on the Theory and Practice of Software, ETAPS'99, Amsterdam, The Netherlands, 22–28 March 1999, pp. 193–207 (1999). https://doi.org/10.1007/3-540-49059-0_14,https://doi.org/10.1007/3-540-49059-0_14
3. Bjørner, N., Gurfinkel, A., Korovin, K., Lahav, O.: Instantiations, zippers and EPR interpolation. In: LPAR 2013, 19th International Conference on Logic for Programming, Artificial Intelligence and Reasoning, 12–17 December 2013, Stellenbosch, South Africa, Short Papers Proceedings, pp. 35–41 (2013). https://easychair.org/publications/paper/XtN
4. Bradley, A.R.: Sat-based model checking without unrolling. In: Verification, Model Checking, and Abstract Interpretation - 12th International Conference, VMCAI 2011, Austin, TX, USA, 23–25 January 2011. Proceedings, pp. 70–87 (2011). https://doi.org/10.1007/978-3-642-18275-4_7, https://dx.doi.org/10.1007/978-3-642-18275-4_7
5. Bshouty, N.H.: Exact learning Boolean function via the monotone theory. Inf. Comput. **123**(1), 146–153 (1995)
6. Chockler, H., Ivrii, A., Matsliah, A.: Computing interpolants without proofs. In: Hardware and Software: Verification and Testing - 8th International Haifa Verification Conference, HVC 2012, Haifa, Israel, 6–8 November 2012. Revised Selected Papers. pp. 72–85 (2012). https://doi.org/10.1007/978-3-642-39611-3_12,https://doi.org/10.1007/978-3-642-39611-3_12
7. Cousot, P., Halbwachs, N.: Automatic discovery of linear restraints among variables of a program. In: Aho, A.V., Zilles, S.N., Szymanski, T.G. (eds.) Conference Record of the Fifth Annual ACM Symposium on Principles of Programming Languages, Tucson, Arizona, USA, January 1978. pp. 84–96. ACM Press (1978). https://doi.org/10.1145/512760.512770,https://doi.org/10.1145/512760.512770
8. Crama, Y., Hammer, P.L.: Boolean Functions - Theory, Algorithms, and Applications, Encyclopedia of mathematics and its applications, vol. 142. Cambridge University Press, Cambridge(2011). https://www.cambridge.org/gb/knowledge/isbn/item6222210/?site_locale=en_GB
9. Eén, N., Mishchenko, A., Brayton, R.K.: Efficient implementation of property directed reachability. In: International Conference on Formal Methods in Computer-Aided Design, FMCAD 2011, Austin, TX, USA, October 30–November 02, 2011, pp. 125–134 (2011). https://dl.acm.org/citation.cfm?id=2157675
10. Elder, M., Lim, J., Sharma, T., Andersen, T., Reps, T.: Abstract domains of affine relations. In: Yahav, E. (ed.) SAS 2011. LNCS, vol. 6887, pp. 198–215. Springer, Heidelberg (2011). https://doi.org/10.1007/978-3-642-23702-7_17
11. Ezudheen, P., Neider, D., D'Souza, D., Garg, P., Madhusudan, P.: Horn-ice learning for synthesizing invariants and contracts. Proc. ACM Program. Lang. **2**(OOPSLA), 131:1–131:25 (2018)
12. Feldman, Y.M.Y., Immerman, N., Sagiv, M., Shoham, S.: Complexity and information in invariant inference. Proc. ACM Program. Lang. **4**(POPL), 5:1–5:29 (2020). https://doi.org/10.1145/3371073,https://doi.org/10.1145/3371073
13. Feldman, Y.M.Y., Sagiv, M., Shoham, S., Wilcox, J.R.: Learning the boundary of inductive invariants. Proc. ACM Program. Lang. **5**(POPL), 1–30 (2021). https://doi.org/10.1145/3434296,https://doi.org/10.1145/3434296

14. Feldman, Y.M.Y., Sagiv, M., Shoham, S., Wilcox, J.R.: Property-directed reachability as abstract interpretation in the monotone theory. Proc. ACM Program. Lang. **6**(POPL), 1–31 (2022). https://doi.org/10.1145/3498676,https://doi.org/10.1145/3498676

15. Feldman, Y.M.Y., Shoham, S.: Invariant inference with provable complexity from the monotone theory. CoRR (2022), https://arxiv.org/pdf/2208.07451.pdf

16. Flanagan, C., Leino, K.R.M.: Houdini, an annotation assistant for esc/java. In: FME 2001: International Symposium of Formal Methods Europe for Increasing Software Productivity, Berlin, Germany, March 12–16, 2001, Proceedings. pp. 500–517 (2001)

17. Flanagan, C., Qadeer, S.: Predicate abstraction for software verification. In: Conference Record of POPL 2002: The 29th SIGPLAN-SIGACT Symposium on Principles of Programming Languages, Portland, OR, USA, 16–18 January 2002. pp. 191–202 (2002). https://doi.org/10.1145/503272.503291,https://doi.acm.org/10.1145/503272.503291

18. Garg, P., Löding, C., Madhusudan, P., Neider, D.: ICE: A robust framework for learning invariants. In: Biere, A., Bloem, R. (eds.) CAV 2014. LNCS, vol. 8559, pp. 69–87. Springer, Cham (2014). https://doi.org/10.1007/978-3-319-08867-9_5

19. Garg, P., Neider, D., Madhusudan, P., Roth, D.: Learning invariants using decision trees and implication counterexamples. In: Proceedings of the 43rd Annual ACM SIGPLAN-SIGACT Symposium on Principles of Programming Languages, POPL 2016, St. Petersburg, FL, USA, 20–22 January 2016. pp. 499–512 (2016). https://doi.org/10.1145/2837614.2837664,https://doi.org/10.1145/2837614.2837664

20. Graf, S., Saïdi, H.: Construction of abstract state graphs with PVS. In: 9th International Conference on Computer Aided Verification, CAV 1997, Haifa, Israel, J22–25 June 1997, Proceedings. pp. 72–83 (1997). https://doi.org/10.1007/3-540-63166-6_10,https://doi.org/10.1007/3-540-63166-6_10

21. Jha, S., Gulwani, S., Seshia, S.A., Tiwari, A.: Oracle-guided component-based program synthesis. In: Proceedings of the 32nd ACM/IEEE International Conference on Software Engineering - Volume 1, ICSE 2010, Cape Town, South Africa, 1–8 May 2010, pp. 215–224 (2010). https://doi.org/10.1145/1806799.1806833,https://doi.org/10.1145/1806799.1806833

22. Jha, S., Seshia, S.A.: A theory of formal synthesis via inductive learning. Acta Inf. **54**(7), 693–726 (2017)

23. Jung, Y., Kong, S., David, C., Wang, B., Yi, K.: Automatically inferring loop invariants via algorithmic learning. Math. Struct. Comput. Sci. **25**(4), 892–915 (2015)

24. Koenig, J.R., Padon, O., Immerman, N., Aiken, A.: First-order quantified separators. In: Donaldson, A.F., Torlak, E. (eds.) Proceedings of the 41st ACM SIGPLAN International Conference on Programming Language Design and Implementation, PLDI 2020, London, UK, 15–20 June 2020. pp. 703–717. ACM (2020), https://doi.org/10.1145/3385412.3386018

25. Lahiri, S.K., Qadeer, S.: Complexity and algorithms for monomial and clausal predicate abstraction. In: Automated Deduction - CADE-22, 22nd International Conference on Automated Deduction, Montreal, Canada, 2–7 August 2009. Proceedings. pp. 214–229 (2009)

26. McMillan, K.L.: Interpolation and sat-based model checking. In: Computer Aided Verification, 15th International Conference, CAV 2003, Boulder, CO, USA, 8–12 July 2003, Proceedings, pp. 1–13 (2003)

27. Miltersen, P.B., Radhakrishnan, J., Wegener, I.: On converting CNF to DNF. Theor. Comput. Sci. **347**(1), 325–335 (2005)
28. Miné, A.: The octagon abstract domain. High. Order Symb. Comput. **19**(1), 31–100 (2006)
29. O'Rourke, J.: Visibility. In: Goodman, J.E., O'Rourke, J. (eds.) Handbook of Discrete and Computational Geometry, 2nd edn., pp. 643–663. Chapman and Hall/CRC (2004). https://doi.org/10.1201/9781420035315.ch28,https://doi.org/10.1201/9781420035315.ch28
30. Quine, W.: Two theorems about truth-functions. Boletín de la Sociedad Matemática Mexicana **10**(1–2), 64–70 (1954)
31. Quinlan, J.R.: Induction of decision trees. Mach. Learn. **1**(1), 81–106 (1986)
32. Reps, T.W., Sagiv, S., Yorsh, G.: Symbolic implementation of the best transformer. In: 5th International Conference on Verification, Model Checking, and Abstract Interpretation, VMCAI 2004, Venice, Italy, J11–13 January 2004, Proceedings, pp. 252–266 (2004). https://doi.org/10.1007/978-3-540-24622-0_21,https://doi.org/10.1007/978-3-540-24622-0_21
33. Reps, T., Thakur, A.: Automating Abstract interpretation. In: Jobstmann, B., Leino, K.R.M. (eds.) VMCAI 2016. LNCS, vol. 9583, pp. 3–40. Springer, Heidelberg (2016). https://doi.org/10.1007/978-3-662-49122-5_1
34. Seufert, T., Scholl, C.: Sequential verification using reverse PDR. In: Große, D., Drechsler, R. (eds.) Methoden und Beschreibungssprachen zur Modellierung und Verifikation von Schaltungen und Systemen, MBMV 2017, Bremen, Germany, February 8–9, 2017. pp. 79–90. Shaker Verlag (2017)
35. Sharma, R., Aiken, A.: From invariant checking to invariant inference using randomized search. Formal Methods Syst. Des. **48**(3), 235–256 (2016)
36. Sharma, R., Gupta, S., Hariharan, B., Aiken, A., Liang, P., Nori, A.V.: A data driven approach for algebraic loop invariants. In: Programming Languages and Systems - 22nd European Symposium on Programming, ESOP 2013, Held as Part of the European Joint Conferences on Theory and Practice of Software, ETAPS 2013, Rome, Italy, 16–24 March 2013. Proceedings. pp. 574–592 (2013). https://doi.org/10.1007/978-3-642-37036-6_31,https://doi.org/10.1007/978-3-642-37036-6_31
37. Sharma, R., Gupta, S., Hariharan, B., Aiken, A., Nori, A.V.: Verification as learning geometric concepts. In: Static Analysis - 20th International Symposium, SAS 2013, Seattle, WA, USA, June 20–22, 2013. Proceedings, pp. 388–411 (2013)
38. Sharma, R., Nori, A.V., Aiken, A.: Interpolants as classifiers. In: Computer Aided Verification - 24th International Conference, CAV 2012, Berkeley, CA, USA, 7–13 July 2012 Proceedings. pp. 71–87 (2012). https://doi.org/10.1007/978-3-642-31424-7_11,https://doi.org/10.1007/978-3-642-31424-7_11
39. Thakur, A.V., Elder, M., Reps, T.W.: Bilateral algorithms for symbolic abstraction. In: Miné, A., Schmidt, D. (eds.) Static Analysis - 19th International Symposium, SAS 2012, Deauville, France, 11–13 September 2012. Proceedings. Lecture Notes in Computer Science, vol. 7460, pp. 111–128. Springer (2012). https://doi.org/10.1007/978-3-642-33125-1_10,https://doi.org/10.1007/978-3-642-33125-1_10
40. Thakur, A.V., Lal, A., Lim, J., Reps, T.W.: Posthat and all that: automating abstract interpretation. Electr. Notes Theor. Comput. Sci. **311**, 15–32 (2015)
41. Valiant, L.G.: A theory of the learnable. Commun. ACM **27**(11), 1134–1142 (1984)
42. Wiedemann, D.H.: Hamming geometry. Ph.D. thesis, University of Waterloo (1987)

Efficient Modular SMT-Based Model Checking of Pointer Programs

Isabel Garcia-Contreras[1]([✉]) [iD], Arie Gurfinkel[1] [iD], and Jorge A. Navas[2] [iD]

[1] University of Waterloo, Waterloo, ON, Canada
{igarciac,agurfink}@uwaterloo.ca
[2] Certora, Seattle, WA, USA
jorge@certora.com

Abstract. Modularity is indispensable for scaling automatic verification to large programs. However, modularity also introduces challenges because it requires inferring and abstracting the behavior of functions as *summaries* – formulas that relate the function's inputs and outputs. For programs manipulating memory, summaries must include the function's *frame*, i.e., how the content memory is affected by the execution of the function. In SMT-based model-checking, memory is often modeled with (unbounded) logical arrays and expressing frames generally requires universally quantified formulas. Such formulas significantly complicate inference and subsequent reasoning and are thus to be avoided. In this paper, we present a technique to encode the memory that is bounded explicitly, eliminating the need for quantified summaries. We build on the insight that the size of frames can be statically known. This enables replacing unbounded arrays with *finite maps* – a finite collection of key-value pairs. Specifically, we develop a new static analysis to infer the finite parts of a function's frame. We then extend the theory of arrays to the theory of finite maps and show that satisfiability of Constrained Horn Clauses (CHCs) over finite maps is reducible to satisfiability of CHCs over the base theory. Finally, we propose a new encoding from imperative programs to CHCs that uses finite maps to model explicitly the finite memory passed in function calls. The result is a new verification strategy that preserves the advantages of modularity while reducing the need for quantified frames. We have implemented this approach in SEA-HORN, a state-of-the-art CHC-based software model checker for LLVM. An evaluation on Linux Drivers from SV-COMP shows the effectiveness of our technique.

Keywords: Modular verification · Software model checking · Constrained Horn clauses · Pointer analysis

Part of this work was done when third author worked for SRI International and first author was visiting him. The work was partially funded by FPU grant 16/04811, MICINN project PID2019-108528RB-C21 *ProCode*, and the Comunidad de Madrid P2018/TCS-4339 *BLOQUES-CM* program.

G. Singh and C. Urban (Eds.): SAS 2022, LNCS 13790, pp. 227–246, 2022.
https://doi.org/10.1007/978-3-031-22308-2_11

1   Introduction

Modularity is indispensable for scaling automatic verification, such as software model checking. Reasoning modularly about a program involves abstracting the behavior of its functions in the form of a summary. For programs manipulating memory inferring summaries can be especially challenging. The reason is that summaries need to express the *frame* of the function, i.e., how the function modifies memory in any execution.

We focus on automated modular program verification using Constrained Horn Clauses (CHCs). In this setting, program verification is reduced to satisfiability of a set of logical rules (or clauses) [6], where unknown predicates represent summaries and inductive invariants. Satisfiability of CHCs is in general undecidable but, in practice, it is solved using so-called CHC solvers (e.g., HoICE [8], and SPACER [16]). CHC solvers automatically synthesize inductive invariants and, in the case of modular verification, function summaries.

In CHCs, memory side-effects are encoded by first *purifying* program statements to make such side-effects explicit, and then, encoding memory content by (unbounded) logical arrays. Each summary predicate relates arrays representing input and output memory contents. While this encoding is simple to implement, it is challenging to solve because it requires the CHC solver to discover function frames, that are typically expressed using quantified formulas. Although reasoning with quantified formulas is supported by some CHC solvers (e.g., [12]), it remains very challenging and is best to be avoided whenever possible.

Quantifiers are needed to restrict arrays at an unbounded number of indices. This is required to express how the execution of a function affects the state of memory. A key observation is that modeling the finite parts of a function's memory does not require the full power of arrays. The memory that is finitely accessed can be modeled using only scalar variables, avoiding the need for quantifiers. In this paper, we present a fully automatic CHC encoding of C programs that alleviates the problem of quantified frames based on this observation.

First, we introduce a new static analysis to compute: (a) which memory regions used in a function are accessed only finitely by it, (b) how many bytes are accessed per region, and (c) what are all the access paths for the finitely accessed memory. Our analysis is based on an existing alias analysis that ensures the soundness of our approach. Second, we model bounded memory, i.e., finite associative arrays, within SMT. For this, we propose a *new* SMT theory of *finite maps*. Finite maps modify the theory of arrays to account for a fixed number of key-value pairs. We show that the theory of finite maps is reducible to underlying SMT theories, and extend the reduction to CHCs (i.e., reduce CHCs with finite maps, to CHCs without). Finally, we extend the CHC encoding of SEAHORN to use finite maps for finite memory regions passed to functions. The key difficulty is in the handling of call sites since they must explicitly express the frame conditions.

We implemented our encoding using SEAHORN and evaluated it on Linux Drivers from SV-COMP. We show that the new encoding improves the original, array-based, one of SEAHORN. However, we also noticed that arrays sometimes provide a beneficial abstraction. Therefore, we relax our encoding to allow mixing arrays and finite maps for best performance.

2 Related Work

The frame problem is a well-known problem in artificial intelligence [20] and program analysis. In this section, we discuss the related work in the areas of deductive verification and model checking.

Deductive Verification. Including the footprint of a function in its specification to deal with the frame problem is a common solution in deductive verification. This is done explicitly or implicitly. An example of explicit footprints is dynamic frames [15] and the **reads** and **modifies** annotations in Dafny [19]. Examples of implicit footprints are implicit dynamic frames [26], permissions [22], and Separation Logic [25]. Explicit approaches describe the heap using additional assertions in the base logic, while implicit approaches embed heap information in the assertions by extending the logic. These have been proven difficult to integrate into SMT-based software model checkers, due to the difficulty of using SMT solvers to reason about both heap shape and content (Piskac et al. [23]). Our approach can be seen as computing the footprint explicitly but partitioning it into bounded and unbounded. The footprint is computed automatically, similar in spirit to how procedure specifications are inferred in tools such as Infer [7]. Most significantly, our approach is tightly integrated with automatic invariant inference over the content of the heap.

Inlining-Based Model Checking. Tools based on bounded model checking (e.g., CBMC [9], LLBMC [21], and SMACK [24]) inline all procedures, which avoids the frame problem. Inlining is also implemented by unbounded tools such as UFO [2], SeaHorn [10], CPAChecker [5], and UAutomizer [13].

Summary-Based Model Checking. Unbounded model checkers such as CPAChecker, Whale [1], and UAutomizer use inter-procedural model checking techniques to compute procedure summaries. The technique proposed by Beyer and Friedberger [3] lifts the idea of *Block-Abstraction Memoization (BAM)* from basic blocks to procedure boundaries. Procedures can be analyzed by using any of the intra-procedural model checking algorithms available in CPAChecker. The technique then generates summaries and stores them in a cache for future reuse. Whale computes summaries by exploiting sequence interpolants generated from underapproximations (i.e., finite traces) of functions. Finally, UAutomizer relies on *Nested Interpolants* [14] to produce summaries but they depend on the calling context so they might be harder to reuse. Most importantly, none of these techniques tackle the problem of frame inference. Note also that this paper does not propose a new inter-procedural model-checking algorithm. Instead, our goal is to improve the encoding of verification conditions to reduce the need for quantifiers in CHC solvers.

Modeling Memory in SMT-Based Model Checking. Most existing software model checkers use some form of purification. In all cases, memory is modeled as either arrays [10] or lambdas [21]. Sometimes a finite abstraction of memory is used (see e.g., Blast [4]) modeling precisely only a few levels of pointer deference (e.g., *p and **p). In contrast, our modeling is precise – we use finite footprint wherever possible and arrays only if necessary. While the need for a finite map theory for program reasoning has been identified before [17], we propose a theory of finite maps that is more suitable for encoding finite memory in CHCs.

3   Motivating Example

We illustrate our approach with an example. We begin with *purification*. Figure 1a shows the definition of a data structure S with a field x in a C-like language and two functions over S: init_x, which stores the value 0 in the field x, and read_x, which returns the value of the field. In its purified version (Fig. 1b), memory operations are made explicit with a structure of type Memory (a special array) that represents an unbounded sequence of bytes. The signature of every function is extended to include a Memory parameter, and memory reads and writes are operations over it. Given a variable MEM of type Memory, and assuming that field x is at offset 0, s->x = v is encoded as MEM[s] = v, and s->x as MEM[s].

Consider the program defined by Figs. 1a and 1c. In Fig. 1c, the main procedure allocates two structures p and q of type S on lines 3 and 4. Line 6 models that the pointers p and q must be disjoint. Let us assume that after the execution of some arbitrary code the pointer analysis infers that p and q might alias (line 7). On line 10, some values are stored at p->x and q->x. Figure 1d shows the purified version of Fig. 1c. Note that memory allocations do not change the state of MEM. In this example, the property to be verified is assert(read_x(q, &MEM) == 20) (line 13). The semantics of the program together with this property is encoded by the following CHCs[1]:

$$r = m[s] \rightarrow read\_x(s, r, m) \quad \text{(CHC 1)}$$
$$m_2 = m_1[s \leftarrow 0] \rightarrow init\_x(s, m_1, m_2) \quad \text{(CHC 2)}$$
$$p + 4 < q \ \wedge m_1 = m[p \leftarrow 10] \wedge m_2 = m_1[q \leftarrow 20] \ \wedge \quad \text{(B3a)}$$
$$init\_x(p, m_2, m_3) \wedge read\_x(q, r, m_3) \rightarrow r = 20 \quad \text{(CHC 3)}$$

The summaries computed for read_x and init_x need to be precise enough to prove the satisfiability of CHC 3. For read_x, referring to the content of *one* memory location is enough: $\lambda s, r, m. \ r = m[s]$. Since m_3 is an argument of init_x, its summary needs to express how m_3 is related to m_2, i.e., how memory is updated:

$$\lambda p, m_2, m_3. \ m_3[p] = 0 \wedge \forall i \neq p. \ m_3[i] = m_2[i]$$

---

[1] We use the syntax $a[i]$ and $a' = a[i \leftarrow v]$ to denote, respectively, an array select at index i and an array store at index i with value v.

```
1  typedef struct S { int x; } S;
2  void init_x(S *s) {
3    s->x = 0;
4  }
5  int read_x(S *s) {
6    return s->x;
7  }
```

(a)

```
1  typedef struct S { int x; } S;
2  void init_x(S *s, Memory *MEM) {
3    (*MEM)[s] = 0;
4  }
5  int read_x(S *s, Memory *MEM) {
6    return (*MEM)[s];
7  }
```

(b) Purified functions from Fig. 1a

```
1   void main() {
2
3     S* p = malloc(sizeof(S));
4     S* q = malloc(sizeof(S));
5     // Model part of malloc semantics
6     assume(p + sizeof(S) < q);
7     // Code makes the analyzer think
8     // that p and q alias
9
10    p->x = 10;    q->x = 20;
11
12    init_x(p);
13    assert(read_x(q) == 20);
14  }
```

(c)

```
1   void main() {
2     Memory MEM;
3     S* p = malloc(sizeof(S));
4     S* q = malloc(sizeof(S));
5     // Model part of malloc semantics
6     assume(p + sizeof(S) < q);
7     // Code makes the analyzer think
8     // that p and q alias
9
10    MEM[p] = 10;    MEM[q] = 20;
11
12    init_x(p, &MEM);
13    assert(read_x(q, &MEM) == 20);
14  }
```

(d) Purified program from Fig. 1c

```
1   void main() {
2
3     S* p = malloc(sizeof(S));
4     S* q = malloc(sizeof(S));
5     // Model part of malloc semantics
6     assume(p + sizeof(S) < q);
7     // Code makes the analyzer think
8     // that p and q alias
9
10    p->x = 10;    q->x = 20;
11
12    S tmp;
13    tmp.x = p->x;
14    init_x(&tmp);
15    p->x = tmp.x;
16    assert(read_x(q) == 20);
17  }
```

(e)

```
1   void main() {
2     Memory MEM;
3     S* p = malloc(sizeof(S));
4     S* q = malloc(sizeof(S));
5     // Model part of malloc semantics
6     assume(p + sizeof(S) < q);
7     // Code makes the analyzer think
8     // that p and q alias
9
10    MEM[p] = 10;    MEM[q] = 20;
11
12    S tmp;    Memory AUX;
13    AUX[&tmp] = MEM[p];
14    init_x(&tmp, &AUX);
15    MEM[p] = AUX[&tmp];
16    assert(read_x(q, &MEM) == 20);
17  }
```

(f) Purified program from Fig. 1e

Fig. 1. Some functions (left) and their purified versions (right)

The first conjunct expresses the memory location that is modified by init_x, and the second expresses the frame, using a quantified formula.

We now show how a manual transformation in the C program eases the verification task by eliminating the need of inferring quantified summaries. Consider the program defined by Figs. 1a and 1e. The main function differs from Fig. 1c in that a new structure tmp is passed to init_x. The content of p->x is stored in tmp.x before calling init_x, and tmp.x is copied back to p->x right after the call returns. After purification (Fig. 1f), before the call, the memory contents accessed by the callee (MEM[p]) are copied into a new memory AUX, because the content tmp and p is known to be stored in different memory regions. After the call, the contents are copied back from AUX into MEM. It is not hard to see that the programs in Figs. 1d and 1f are equivalent. However, the latter is much easier to verify. The program in Figs. 1b and 1f is encoded by CHCs $\{1, 2\}$ and:

$$B3a \wedge aux_1 = aux[tmp \leftarrow m_2[p]] \wedge \tag{L4a}$$

$$init\_x(tmp, aux_1, aux_2) \wedge m_3 = m_2[p \leftarrow aux_2[tmp]] \wedge \tag{L4b}$$

$$read\_x(q, r, m_3) \rightarrow r = 20 \tag{CHC 4}$$

The difference between CHC 3 and CHC 4 is in the literals before and after the predicate call to `init_x`. In CHC 4, the array contents accessed by $init\_x$ are copied to a different array aux in L4a. The predicate $init\_x$ takes aux and tmp arguments instead of m_i, and finally, the values of aux are copied back to m. Note that CHCs $\{1, 2, 3\}$ and $\{1, 2, 4\}$ are *equisatisfiable*. However, the key advantage of CHCs $\{1, 2, 4\}$ is that the relation between m_2 and m_3 is explicit in CHC 4. Since aux arrays are not relevant to the property, the behavior of $init\_x$ can be abstracted with the trivial summary "true", which is not quantified.

This example showed how a manual transformation in the C program eases the verification task by eliminating the need of inferring quantified summaries. In the rest of the paper, we show how to encode automatically in the CHCs the idea behind this example, without any user intervention. This requires: (1) finding the finite memory footprint of a function (i.e., the candidates to be copied to an auxiliary variable) and (2) identifying the memory locations that are accessed, to copy their content to/from auxiliary memory objects.

Remarks. In this example, using auxiliary arrays to represent the finite memory accessed in `init_x` was enough to avoid a quantified summary. An alternative approach is to use partial array equalities from the *extensional* theory of arrays [28]. This, however, still uses arrays, and, therefore, does not eliminate the need for quantifiers. A more concise logic to represent finite memory is the theory of *finite maps*. In Sect. 5, we describe the theory of finite maps and how to extend CHCs with finite maps.

4   Static Analysis of Memory Footprints

The C memory model interprets a pointer as a pair (id, o) where id is an identifier that uniquely defines a memory object and o defines the byte in the object being pointed to. The number of objects is unbounded. Points-to analysis typically abstracts the unbounded set of concrete memory objects as a finite set of abstract objects (also called memory regions). A points-to analysis is sound if whenever a pointer p does not point to an abstract object, then there is no actual execution in which p points to any concrete object represented by the abstract object.

We rely on the Data Structure Analysis (DSA) of [11,18] which provides a unification-based, context- and field-sensitive points-to analysis, that supports pointer arithmetic. In DSA, a pointer can only point to one abstract object due to its unification-based nature [27]. The analysis results are presented in the

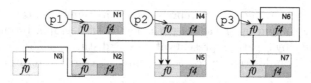

Fig. 2. Points-to graph of a function `foo(S *p1, S *p2, S *p3)`.

form of DSA graphs. A *DSA graph* is a triple (C, E, σ), where C is a finite set of abstract cells. Each *cell* is a pair of a memory region identifier and a byte offset; $E \subseteq C \times C$ is a set of edges between cells, denoting points-to relations; and environment $\sigma : Var \mapsto C$ maps pointer variables to cells.

As part of the DSA analysis, a summary graph is built for each function. A *summary* graph contains all the memory objects accessed by the function and its callees, and their points-to relationships, i.e., its *memory footprint*. These graphs, called henceforth DSA graphs, are computed ignoring how and where the function is called, assuming that there is no aliasing between input parameters.

Example 1 (DSA graph). Figure 2 shows a DSA graph generated from a function `foo` with parameters `p1`, `p2`, and `p3`. Each of the cells encodes an offset in the memory region that may be accessed during a concrete execution. For example, the memory object **N1** has 2 cells $f0$ and $f4$ (naming the offsets). This means that at some point of the execution of `foo` (or its callees), `p1->f0` and `p1->f4` may be accessed (read or written). The cells of **N2** are representing that `p1->f0->f0` and `p1->f0->f4` may be accessed. Since DSA graphs are over-approximations of the concrete memory used during any execution, the absence of a cell in the graph implies that a memory location is never accessed. For example, `p1->f0->f0->f4` is never accessed because there is not a field $f4$ in **N3**.

The goal is to determine which memory objects are bounded to make them explicit in the encoding. First, we define the paths in a DSA graph.

Definition 1 (A Path in the DSA Graph). *Let $g = (C, E, \sigma)$ be a graph. A sequence of cells $[c_1, c_2, \ldots, c_k]$ is a path in g iff for every $c_i, c_{i+1}, 1 \le i < k$:*

$$\exists x, y, n \cdot (c_i, (n, x)) \in E \wedge (c_{i+1} = (n, y)) \in C.$$

This is the standard definition of a path in a graph, modified to capture that when a memory object with id n is reachable by some path, all its fields (i.e., all the cells that have the same id n) are reachable as well. In Fig. 2, `p1` points to cell $(\mathbf{N1}, f0)$ but both fields, $f0$ and $f4$, are reachable. An *access path* is a base variable followed by a finite sequence of field accesses. That is, an access path is a pair (var, acc), where var is a variable of the function, and acc is either a sequence with a single cell or a path between two cells. E.g., the access path of the expression `p1->f0->f0` is $(p1, [(N2, f0), (N1, f0)])$.[2]

---

[2] For conciseness and presentation purposes, we use $[x_1, \ldots, x_n]$ to refer to $\texttt{cons}(x_1, (\ldots \texttt{cons}(x_n, \texttt{nil})))$ and write the paths reversed.

One way to determine if a cell represents a finite number of concrete memory locations is by computing the set of paths in the DSA graph. Intuitively, a cell that is reachable by n paths represents at most n distinct memory locations. The following definition describes a cell *being finitely accessed* in terms of its paths.

Definition 2 (Finitely Accessed Cell). *Let g be a graph with cells C and $C' \subseteq C$. A cell $c \in C$ is* finitely accessed *from C' if the number of paths from $c' \in C'$ to c is finite.*

This definition is based on paths starting from arbitrary cells in the graph. However, in practice, we are interested only in the cells pointed by the parameters of the function, because only those are reachable by callers. Finding the cells in a summary graph that meet the property of Definition 2 allows identifying the finitely accessed memory regions of a function assuming no aliasing relationships before the function call. However, cells that are distinct in the callee maybe the same in the caller. For example, in a call of the form `foo(s1,s1,s3)`, objects **N1** and **N4**, shown to be distinct in the summary graph of Fig. 2, are actually the same since the same pointer `s1` is passed as the first and second parameter of `foo`. Therefore, these aliasing relationships must be considered to produce a sound encoding. In the following, given the graph g of a function f the predicate $\mathtt{alias}_{call}(c, c')$ is true if c and c' (cells in g), may be the same in a *call* to f. The predicate $\mathtt{alias}_{call}$ induces an equivalence relation over the cells in the graph, where two cells are related if they are the same at the function call.

Definition 3 (Finitely Accessed Equivalence Class). *Let g be a graph with cells C, $C' \subseteq C$, and $\mathtt{alias}_{call}$ the aliasing relation of the cells. The* equivalence class of $c \in C$ is finitely accessed *from C' iff all the elements in the equivalence class are finitely accessed. That is, $\forall d \in C$ such that $\mathtt{alias}_{call}(c, d)$, d is finitely accessed from C'.*

Definition 3 lifts Definition 2 to the equivalence classes defined by $\mathtt{alias}_{call}$. The following example illustrates the concepts in Definitions 1, 2, and 3.

Example 2 (Bounded memory objects). Consider again the graph in Fig. 2 and a predicate $\mathtt{alias}_{call}$ that is true iff the cells in the graph have the same color. For example, $\mathtt{alias}_{call}((N1, f0), (N4, f0))$ and $\mathtt{alias}_{call}((N1, f4), (N4, f4))$ are facts. First, we determine which cells are finitely accessed (Def. 2). Memory objects that have self-loops are not finitely accessed, as they have an unbounded number of access paths. For example, the cell (**N6**, $f0$) has access paths `p3->f0`, `p3->f4->f0`, `p3->f4->f4->f0`,... For the same reason, cells that are reachable from memory objects with self-loops are also unbounded. For example, cell (**N7**, $f0$) can be accessed by `p3->f0->f0`, `p3->f4->f0->f0`, `p3->f4->f4->f0->f0`,... Thus, **N6** and **N7** encode unbounded memory accesses. For the remaining objects, **N1** to **N5**, all the cells in the same equivalence class need to be finitely accessed. Consider all the cells in green: **N1**, **N4**, and **N5**. All three objects are finitely accessed, so the equivalence classes of (**N1**, $f0$) and (**N1**, $f4$) are finitely accessed. **N2** is finitely accessed but its cells are in the same equivalence class as the cells in **N7** (red). Since **N7** is not finitely accessed, the classes of the cells of

compFiniteAPs$(g = (C, E, \sigma),$ alias, $\textit{fparams})$
1: $C' := \{\sigma(p) \mid p \in \textit{fparams}\}$
2: $U :=$ exploreGraph(g, C')
3: $APs := \emptyset$
4: **for all** $p \in \textit{fparams}$ **do**
5:    $ap_0 =$ nil
6:    recCompAPs$(\sigma(p), g, U,$ alias$, p, ap_0, APs)$
7: **return** APs

recCompAPs$(c, g, U,$ alias$, p, ap, APs)$
8: **if** $c \in U$ **then return**
9: **if not** aliasesUbnd$(c, U,$ alias$)$ **then**
10:    **for all** $fc \in$ Fields(c, g) **do**
11:       $APs := APs \cup \{(p, \text{cons}(fc, ap))\}$
12: **for all** $lc \in$ Links(c, g) **do**
13:    $ap' = \text{cons}(c, ap)$
14:    recCompAPs$(lc, g, U,$ alias$, p, ap', APs)$

aliasesUbnd$(c, U,$ alias$)$
15: **return** $\exists c' \in U.\text{alias}(c, c')$

exploreGraph$(g = (C, E, \sigma), C')$
16: **for all** $c \in C$ **do**
17:    $color[c] :=$ white
18: $U := \emptyset$
19: **for all** $c \in C'$ **do**
20:    exploreCell$(c, g, color, U)$
21: **return** U;

exploreCell$(c, g, color, U)$
22: $color[c] :=$ grey;
23: **for all** $d \in$ Links(c, g) **do**
24:    **if** $color[d] =$ grey **then**
25:       propagateUbnd$(d, g, color, U)$
26:    **else if** $color[d] =$ white **then**
27:       exploreCell$(d, g, color, U)$
28: $color[c] :=$ black;

propagateUbnd$(c, g, color, U)$
29: $U := U \cup \{c\}$
30: $color[c] :=$ black
31: **for all** $d \in$ Links(c, g) **do**
32:    **if not** $(color[d] =$ black
33:                  **and** $d \in U)$ **then**
34:       propagateUbnd$(d, g, color, U)$

Fig. 3. Algorithm to find finite memory objects and all their access paths.

N2 are not finitely accessed. Last, even if the classes of the cells of **N2** are not finitely accessed, **N3** is finitely accessed because its parents are finitely accessed.

We have shown intuitively how to determine if cells are reachable only by a *finite number of paths*. Figure 3 shows the proposed algorithm to find the finite memory objects used by a function and their access paths. Access paths are used later to encode the memory passed to a function at a call. The entry point is compFiniteAPs$(g,$ alias, *fparams*) which takes a DSA graph g, a relation of its cells alias, and the function parameters *fparams*. First, the set of cells, C', pointed by *fparams* is computed, which is the starting point for traversing the graph. The algorithm is split into two steps. The function exploreGraph computes the set of cells that have an unbounded number of paths in g. Second, recCompAPs computes all access paths to cells that belong to equivalence classes that are finitely accessed through paths starting from C'.

Function exploreGraph(g, C') is similar to standard cycle-detection algorithms. However, when a cycle is detected in a memory object, all the cells that are reached from that object are also stored as unbounded. In this function, *color* is a map from cells to exploration status, denoted with a color: white, grey, or black, respectively, not explored, exploring, and explored. U is the set of cells with an unbounded number of paths. Given a cell $c = (n, o)$ and a graph g, Links(c, g) denotes the set of cells that are reachable from any cell in the same region n, i.e., all the c_i such that there is an edge of the form $(n, \_) \to c_i$ in g. First, all the cells in g are marked as unexplored. Then, starting from every cell in C', the cell is marked as grey (*exploring*), and all the reachable cells in one step (given by Links) are explored. If the cell is currently being explored (grey), a cycle has been encountered and propagateUbnd is used to mark them. If the cell has not been explored yet, it is explored. Once all the links of the cell have been explored, the cell is marked as explored (black). The function propagateUbnd marks as explored and stores in U the cell c and all cells reachable from c.

After exploration, recCompAPs(c, g, U, alias, p, ap, APs) computes the set of access paths to cells in equivalence classes that represent bounded memory. The argument c is the cell to be processed, g is the graph, U is the set of cells in g that represent unbounded memory, alias determines the equivalence classes, i.e., which cells need to be considered together, p is the base variable of the access path, and ap is the path followed in the graph to access c. In the recursion, loops in the graph are avoided by checking U before exploring a cell. Equivalence classes are considered in aliasesUbnd, which determines if a cell belongs to the same class as an unbounded cell. Fields(c, g) denotes the set of cells in the same region as c. That is, Fields($(n, o), g$) = $\{c' \mid c' = (n, \_)$ in the cells of $g\}$. If c does not alias with unbounded cells, all the fields are stored in APs, together with how they were reached in ap (line 11 in Fig. 3). Last, the Links of the cell are explored, adding c to the path in the recursive call (line 14).

Example 3 (Access paths to cells encoding finite memory). Given the graph of Fig. 2 the following access paths to cells with finite access paths are found:

Class of (**N1**, $f0$): $\{(p1, [(N1, f0)]), (p2, [(N4, f0)]), (p2, [(N5, f0), (N4, f4)])\}$

Class of (**N1**, $f4$): $\{(p1, [(N1, f4)]), (p2, [(N4, f4)]), (p2, [(N5, f4), (N4, f4)])\}$

Class of (**N3**, $f0$): $\{(p1, [(N3, f0), (N2, f0), (N1, f0)]\}$

Remark. The correctness of our approach relies on the fact that DSA graphs over-approximate both the length and the number of access paths in the concrete memory graph. This follows from the fact that DSA graphs simulate all possible concrete memory graphs [11].

5   Theory of Finite Maps

We model the contents of finitely accessed memory through finite maps. This resembles an SMT-LIB unbounded array in that the map can have arbitrary keys, and a finite sequence, in that the number of entries is fixed. While the need for such a structure for program reasoning has been identified before [17], no theory is provided in the SMT-LIB standard. In this section, we propose a theory of finite maps that is suitable for encoding finite memory footprints. Our key contribution is a reduction procedure from CHCs defined over finite maps and integers to CHCs only over integers.

A *finite map* is composed of a set of key-value pairs. Its *sort* is defined by the sort of the keys, the sort of the values, and the *size* of the finite map, i.e., the maximum number of key-value pairs that it can store. For simplicity of presentation, we restrict ourselves to a finite map of size 2 but our implementation

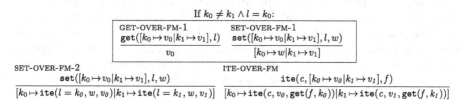

Fig. 4. Reduction rules.

If $k_0 \neq k_1 \wedge l = k_0$:

GET-OVER-FM-1	SET-OVER-FM-1
$\dfrac{\text{get}([k_0 \mapsto v_0 \mid k_1 \mapsto v_1], l)}{v_0}$	$\dfrac{\text{set}([k_0 \mapsto v_0 \mid k_1 \mapsto v_1], l, w)}{[k_0 \mapsto w \mid k_1 \mapsto v_1]}$

SET-OVER-FM-2
$$\frac{\text{set}([k_0 \mapsto v_0 \mid k_1 \mapsto v_1], l, w)}{[k_0 \mapsto \text{ite}(l = k_0, w, v_0) \mid k_1 \mapsto \text{ite}(l = k_1, w, v_1)]}$$

ITE-OVER-FM
$$\frac{\text{ite}(c, [k_0 \mapsto v_0 \mid k_1 \mapsto v_1], f)}{[k_0 \mapsto \text{ite}(c, v_0, \text{get}(f, k_0)) \mid k_1 \mapsto \text{ite}(c, v_1, \text{get}(f, k_1))]}$$

Fig. 5. Additional rules for optimization.

supports finite maps of arbitrary size. Similarly, we assume that finite maps are of the form $[k_0 \mapsto v_0 \mid k_1 \mapsto v_1]^3$. We define two operations over finite maps: *get*, denoted by $\text{get}(fm, k)$, which stands for the value of map fm for key k, and *set*, denoted by $\text{set}(fm, k, v)$, which stands for the map obtained after writing v at key k in fm. These operations are well-formed whenever the key used in the operation is in the range of the map. That is, it matches a key of an already stored key-value pair or the map contains a key-value pair that has not been initialized yet, and thus, has no key assigned. We always ensure that expressions are well-formed by construction, thus, we do not provide a well-formedness check. For well-formed formulas, these operations satisfy the usual array axioms:

- congruence: $k = l \implies \text{get}(fm, k) = \text{get}(fm, l)$
- get-over-set (1): $k = l \implies \text{get}(\text{set}(fm, k, v), l) = v$
- get-over-set (2): $k \neq l \implies \text{get}(\text{set}(fm, k, v), l) = \text{get}(fm, l)$

Reduction Procedure. Applying the rules in Fig. 4 exhaustively to a formula with finite maps results in an equisatisfiable formula without finite maps. No assumptions are made about how the keys within the map are related. The function toLmd transforms a finite map into a lambda term: $\text{toLmd}([k_0 \mapsto v_0 \mid k_1 \mapsto v_1]) = \lambda x.(\text{ite}(x = k_0, v_0, v_1))$. We do not support extensionality because it is not needed in our encoding.

Optimizations. Figure 5 defines rules for optimization for the cases in which information about the keys is available. The application of these rules can be used to update finite maps "in-place" during a sequence of *set* operations, which can avoid an exponential blow-up caused by introducing *ite* terms.

CHCs over Finite Maps. In general, a Constrained Horn Clause (CHC) is a first-order formula of the form $\forall V \cdot (\phi \wedge \bigwedge p_i(X_1^i, \ldots, X_{n_i}^i) \implies h(X_1^h, \ldots, X_n^h))$, where V are all the free variables, ϕ is a constraint in some background theory, p_i are n_i-ary predicates, and $p_i(X_1^i, \ldots, X_{n_i}^i)$ applications of predicates to

---

[3] A finite map variable can always be expressed in this form using the size in its sort.

first-order terms. The antecedent of the implication is called the *body* and the consequent is called the *head*.

CHCs over finite maps extend general CHCs by allowing finite maps to appear in both the constraint ϕ and in arguments to the predicates, and extending the background theory with finite maps. To reduce CHCs with finite maps to CHCs without them, we apply the rules from Fig. 4 and Fig. 5 exhaustively to remove fnite maps from ϕ. To eliminate finite maps from arguments, we expand each finite map argument to the scalars defining its keys and values. For example, if $F = [k_0 \mapsto E_0 | k_1 \mapsto E_1]$ with two key-value pairs, then all predicate applications $p(\ldots, F, \ldots)$, in bodies and heads, are expanded into $p(\ldots, k_0, E_0, k_1, E_1, \ldots)$.

6   A CHC Encoding with Finite Maps

In this section, we show how to extend the CHC encoding within SEAHORN to model memory using finite maps. Roughly, SEAHORN takes as input a C program with assertions (expressing the properties of interest) and produces a set of CHCs. Each CHC captures the semantics of one or multiple basic blocks (sequence of instructions) [6]. Loops are modeled by recursive CHCs and function calls are encoded as predicate calls in the body of a CHC, representing the effects of the call. In general, a CHC is of the form:

$$loc_n(s, a_0) \wedge fun(s, a_0, a_1) \wedge \phi(s, a_1, a_2) \implies loc_m(s, a_2) \qquad \text{(CHC}_A\text{)}$$

where every variable represents a vector of variables and is implicitly universally quantified. The symbols loc_n, loc_m, and fun are predicate names. This clause models how location loc_m in the program may be reached from location loc_n. The literal $fun(s, a_0, a_1)$ captures that there is a function call between the two locations, and ϕ encodes the semantics of all program statements other than function calls. s is a vector of scalar variables, and each a_i are array vectors that model the state of memory at the different locations. a_0 models the state at location n. It is passed to predicate fun, since it may modify memory, producing the next state a_1. The semantics of the remaining statements of the program, from loc_n to loc_m, is modeled by the constraint $\phi(s, a_1, a_2)$, with a_2 the state of the memory at loc_m, in the consequent of the clause. The number of variables in a_i is the number of disjoint memory regions discovered by the pointer analysis.

When encoding bounded memory regions as finite maps the cells that were identified to be bounded are represented using finite map terms, instead of arrays. In general, a clause with finite maps in our proposed encoding is of the form:

$$loc_n(s, b_0, f_0) \wedge fun(s, b_0', f_{in}, b_1', f_{out}) \wedge \phi_A(b_0, f_{out}, b_1) \wedge$$
$$\wedge \phi_{FM}(f_0, f_{out}, f_1) \wedge \phi(s, b_1, b_2, f_1, f_2) \implies loc_m(s, b_2, f_2)$$
$$\text{(CHC}_{FM}\text{)}$$

where s is the same as in CHC$_A$; each b_i is a subset of their respective a_i in CHC$_A$ (the cells encoded using arrays); b_0' and b_1' are, respectively, subsets of b_0 and b_1,

```
EncFunCall(g, alias, params)
 1:  APs := compFiniteAPs(g, alias, params)        encodeAP(ap, var, sorts)
 2:  φ := true
 3:  sorts := infer-sorts(APs, alias)              20:  match ap with
 4:  for all (var, ap) ∈ APs do                    21:    nil → return varToE(var)
 5:    match ap with cons(c, ap') →                22:    cons((n, o), ap') →
 6:      k := encodeAP(ap', var, sorts)            23:      MS := cellToE((n, o), sorts[(n, o)])
 7:      v := encodeAP(ap, var, sorts)             24:      idx' := encodeAP(ap', var, sorts)
 8:      c_r = alias-rep(alias, c)                 25:      idx := mk-add(idx', o)
 9:      Ps_in[c_r] := Ps_in[c_r] ∪ {(in(k), in(v))}  26:      return mk-read(MS, k)
10:      Ps_out[c_r] := Ps_out[c_r] ∪ {(out(k), mk-var())}  mk-read(mem, k)
11:  for all (c_r, Ps) ∈ Ps_in do
12:    Args_in[c_r] := mk-fm(Ps)                   27:  match sort(mem) with
13:  for all (c_r, Ps) ∈ Ps_out do                 28:    Array → return mem[k]
14:    Args_out[c_r] := mk-fm(Ps)                  29:    FiniteMap → return get(mem, k)
15:    φ' := in(cellToE(c_r, sorts[c_r]))
16:    for all (k, v) ∈ Ps_out do                  mk-write(mem, k, v)
17:      φ' := mk-write(φ', k, v)
18:    φ := φ ∧ mk-eq(out(cellToE(c_r, sorts[c_r])), φ')  30:  match sort(mem) with
19:  return (Args_in, Args_out, φ)                  31:    Array → return mem[k ← v]
                                                    32:    FiniteMap → return set(mem, k, v)
```

Fig. 6. Algorithm to encode the finite memory at a function call.

for the cells encoded using arrays in the function call fun; f_i are vectors of finite maps representing a subset of a_i; and f_{in}, f_{out} finite maps used as parameters in the function call. The constraint $\phi_A(b_0, f_{out}, b_1)$ describes how the values in the output finite maps f_{out} are related to the arrays b_1 in the caller. Such constraints are generated if a memory cell is inferred to be unbounded in the caller and bounded in the callee. The constraint $\phi_{FM}(f_0, f_{out}, f_1)$ describes how the values in the output finite maps are related to the finite maps f_1 in the caller. Such constraints are generated if a memory cell is inferred to be bounded both in the caller and in the callee but the caller may access more memory locations than the callee, and thus they have a different size.

Extending the Encoding. We present the parts of the CHC encoding related to memory. Memory accesses are modeled either with arrays or finite maps. The function $cellToE(c, sort)$ takes a memory cell c and its $sort$ and returns a logical variable of that sort. The sort is determined by the algorithm described in Fig. 3 (Sect. 4). If c is finitely accessed, its sort is a finite map of size the number of access paths to it, otherwise, it is an array.

Without function calls, for every memory operation, its associated memory cell c is obtained from the pointer analysis. Then, $cellToE$ is used to encode c as an array or finite map. The remaining operands are encoded by the function $varToE$, which takes a program variable and returns a logical variable (pointers are encoded as integers). The functions mk-read and mk-write, defined in Fig. 6, produce the array or finite map term for the corresponding memory operation.

Function calls require additional constraints. Namely, the formulas ϕ_A and ϕ_{FM} in CHC_{FM}, and the finite maps that represent the memory used by the function. Figure 6 shows how to encode a function call. EncFunCall takes as input the graph g of the called function, and the aliasing (alias) and the parameters (*params*) at the call site. It returns a triple $(Args_{in}, Args_{out}, \phi)$, with $Args_{in}, Args_{out}$ mappings from equivalence classes of cells to the corresponding finite map used to encode all the cells in the class (i.e., respectively, f_{in} and f_{out} in CHC_{FM}), and ϕ that expresses $\phi_A \wedge \phi_{FM}$ in CHC_{FM}. For simplicity, $Args_{in}$ and $Args_{out}$ are defined only for cells belonging to finitely accessed equivalence classes. The remaining cells are encoded as arrays.

Functions of the form mk-E build a logical expression of sort E. The functions mk-eq and mk-add are self-explanatory. mk-var returns a fresh integer variable. mk-fm builds a finite map out of a set of pairs of key-values. The function alias-rep(alias, c) returns the representative of the class of c induced by alias.

The algorithm proceeds as follows. First, all the access paths are computed on line 1 (described in Fig. 3). Based on these, on line 3, the sorts of the finite maps are inferred. The loop on lines 4–10 processes all access paths. On lines 6-7, the sequence of dereferences corresponding to the access path is encoded as key-value pair of logical expression. The value is the whole sequence and the key is the sequence except the last dereference. The algorithm produces *input* and *output* finite maps representing memory before and after the call (lines 12-14). The functions *in* and *out* rename logical terms on the set of input and output variables. Finally, lines 15-18 build ϕ_A and ϕ_{FM} described in CHC_{FM}.

In function encodeAP, if the access path (AP) is empty, the logical expression of the pointer *var* is returned using *varToE*. If not, first, the formula of the rest of the AP is computed, which is the index of the current level of the AP. MS is the logical expression for the cell of the current level of the AP. For example, if *cellToE* maps cells $(N3, f0)$, $(N2, f0)$, and $(N1, f0)$ respectively to a_3, a_2, and a_1, an expression of the form p1->f0->f0->f0 with the access path $(p1, [(N3, f0), (N2, f0), (N1, f0)])$ of Ex. 3 is encoded as: $a_3[a_2[a_1[p1]]]$.

The program defined by Figs. 1a and 1c encoded with finite maps is:

$$v = \text{get}([s \mapsto v_{in}], s) \rightarrow read\_x(s, v, [s \mapsto v_{in}]) \quad \text{(CHC 5)}$$

$$true \rightarrow init\_x(s, [s \mapsto v_{in}], \text{set}([s \mapsto v_{in}], s, 0)) \quad \text{(CHC 6)}$$

$$B3a \wedge init\_x(p, [p \mapsto m_2[p]], [p \mapsto v_{out}]) \wedge \quad \text{(L7a)}$$

$$m_3 = m_2[p \leftarrow \text{get}([p \mapsto v_{out}], p)] \wedge read\_x(q, r, [q \mapsto m_3[q]]) \rightarrow r = 20 \quad \text{(CHC 7)}$$

Up to literal L7a, the same constraints as in CHC 3 are produced. The arguments in L7a are generated on lines 12 and 14 of the algorithm. The last line of CHC 7 captures how the output finite map and the memory at the call m_3 are related (lines 15–18). After applying the rules in Sect. 5 to remove finite map expressions we obtain:

$$v = v_{in} \rightarrow read\_x(s, v, s, v_{in}) \quad \text{(CHC 5 without finite maps)}$$

$$true \rightarrow init\_x(s, s, v_{in}, s, 0) \quad \text{(CHC 6 without finite maps)}$$

$$B3a \wedge init\_x(p, p, m_2[p], p, v_{out}) \wedge \quad \text{(L7a without finite maps)}$$

$$m_3 = m_2[p \leftarrow v_{out}] \wedge read\_x(q, r, q, m_3[q]) \rightarrow r = 20 \quad \text{(CHC 7 without finite maps)}$$

Table 1. SEAHORN (mod, fmap-mod), and UAUTO on micro-benchmarks.

| | SEAHORN | | UAUTO | |
| | mod | fmap-mod | | |
	Time (s)	Time (s)	Time (s)	Quantified
bench1	1	1	8	Yes
bench2	–	1	20	Yes
bench3	–	1	18	Yes
bench4	–	1	120	Yes
bench5	–	1	–	–
bench6	–	8	–	–

7 Experimental Evaluation

We have implemented our new technique to encode bounded memory regions as finite maps using the CHC-based model-checker SEAHORN. The implementation is available in https://github.com/seahorn/seahorn/releases/tag/fmaps-sas22. We have evaluated it on two different sets of benchmarks.

Evaluation on Microbenchmarks. To evaluate our technique we handcrafted a set of benchmark problems.[4] This is a set of small but challenging benchmarks for modular, SMT-based model-checking. These examples can be easily verified by inlining the functions, however, as we can see later, inlining does not scale for larger programs. This means that if any of the patterns in these examples are present in some program, it will not be possible to verify it when inlining is not feasible. Table 1 shows the result of our evaluation. We compare SEAHORN with two different modular encodings: modeling memory only with arrays (mod) and our proposed technique, modeling memory with arrays and finite maps (fmap-mod). SEAHORN, regardless the encoding, can only produce quantifier-free summaries. As a result, it diverges in the cases where only quantified summaries exist. We also compare with UAutomizer [13] (UAUTO), which can also produce (quantified) function summaries[5]. Table 1 shows whether the summaries discovered by UAUTO are quantified. The symbol '–' denotes that tool did not produce an answer in 5 min.

Evaluation on SV-COMP Programs. We have also evaluated our approach on a selection of 745 Linux device drivers from SVCOMP 2019[6], after discarding

---

[4] Available at https://zenodo.org/record/4505518.

[5] In this evaluation, we used the online version of UAUTO because it is the one that computes function summaries.

[6] Available at https://zenodo.org/record/4498784.

Table 2. Instances solved out of 745 within 900 s and 8 GB of memory.

	UAuto	CPA	SeaHorn (mono)
false	2	17	41
true	94	226	218

all the benchmarks that were trivially proven by the SeaHorn front-end or produced some crash. These programs are large and use a variety of language features including pointers and aliasing. All experiments were run on Intel(R) Xeon(R) CPU E5-2680 v3 @ 2.50 GHz with 48 cores and 251 GB of RAM on Ubuntu 18.04.

Although SeaHorn is actively maintained, it does not participate in SVCOMP. Hence, we first compare SeaHorn with participants of SVCOMP 2021 which also focus on discovering safe inductive invariants. Table 2 shows a comparison with UAutomizer [13] (UAuto) and CPAChecker [5] (CPA). We compare with their most recent versions[7], customized to analyze Linux device drivers. For SeaHorn, we use monolithic encoding using arrays to model memory. The rows true and false show how many instances were proven and disproven (i.e., the property holds or is violated), respectively, without exhausting resources. In the rest, solved instances are those for which the verifier produced an answer. From this comparison, we can safely conclude that SeaHorn is competitive with UAuto and CPA on our benchmarks.

Tables 3, 4 and 5 show the main results of this paper by comparing our new encoding (fmap-mod) with two baseline encodings already available in SeaHorn: one monolithic encoding with multiple arrays (mono) where all functions have been inlined[8] and one modular encoding with multiple arrays (mod) without special treatment of statically-known finite memory. Since we are more interested in the comparison with mod, the column mod shows the best result after 5 runs on each program.

During our evaluation, we found out that representing all finite memory with finite maps can be expensive. We hypothesize that the correctness of some Linux device drivers does not depend much on memory (especially after the optimizations performed by the SeaHorn frontend). In those cases, the solver can avoid reasoning about most of the array expressions. However, our encoding with finite maps eagerly adds constraints about memory, regardless of whether they are relevant to prove the program correct or not.

For this reason, we limit the size of the finite maps (the number of key-value pairs), denoted by sX in Tables 3, 4 and 5, where each finite map of size X is encoded using $2X$ scalar variables, two per key-value pair. Moreover, when no

---

[7] Available at https://github.com/ultimate-pa/ultimate/releases/tag/v0.2.1 and https://cpachecker.sosy-lab.org/CPAchecker-2.0-unix.zip, respectively.

[8] Recursive functions are not relevant to prove the properties so that they are abstracted by functions without side-effects that return non-deterministic values.

Table 3. Instances solved by SEAHORN encoding as mono, mod, and fmap-mod.

| | mono | mod | fmap-mod | | | | | | | | | |
			s1-a1	s2-a1	s2-a2	s3-a1	s3-a2	s3-a3	s5-a1	s5-a2	s5-a3	s5-a5	best
false	41	107	94	91	93	89	91	90	90	90	90	87	110
true	218	278	265	268	262	270	263	263	265	256	261	262	297
Total	**259**	**385**	359	359	355	359	354	353	355	346	351	349	**405**

Table 4. Instances solved by SEAHORN with fmap-mod not solved by mono.

	s1-a1	s2-a1	s2-a2	s3-a1	s3-a2	s3-a3	s5-a1	s5-a2	s5-a3	s5-a5	best
false	61	59	59	56	59	58	58	59	59	57	73
true	85	91	82	89	82	84	88	79	82	83	110
Total	146	150	141	145	141	142	146	138	141	140	183

Table 5. Instances solved by SEAHORN with fmap-mod not solved by mod.

	s1-a1	s2-a1	s2-a2	s3-a1	s3-a2	s3-a3	s5-a1	s5-a2	s5-a3	s5-a5	best
false	2	1	2	2	4	1	1	1	2	1	5
true	6	11	11	8	11	13	8	15	13	14	24
Total	8	12	13	10	15	14	9	16	15	15	29

relations about the keys are known, all cases need to be considered. In the worst case, for a finite map of size Y, an *ite* term of depth $Y - 1$ is created for *get* operations, and Y *ite* terms of depth $Y - 1$ (one per key-value pair) are needed in predicate calls (see the reduction rules in Sect. 5). Therefore, we also limit this, denoted by aY in Tables 3, 4 and 5, informally meaning "encoding with finite maps only the memory objects pointed by at most Y pointer variables in the program". In these tables, the column best is equivalent to running in parallel all finite map configurations in a portfolio and stopping when the first one is solved. This is more resource intensive than other configurations. However, since the optimal finite map configuration for each program cannot be known a priori, it is a best effort to verify as many programs as possible.

Table 3 contains the number of solved instances per encoding (columns). The row **total** is the number of benchmarks solved by each configuration with the available resources. Tables 4 and 5 show how many instances the CHCs with finite maps (fmap-mod) were solved that, respectively, for mono and mod it was not possible to solve, split by false and true. For example, in Table 5, s3-a2 (finite maps of size 3 and at most 2 keys may alias) solves 4 false and 11 true instances that cannot be solved by mod. The best configuration of finite maps proves 183 benchmarks that mono could not, and 29 that mod could not. However, fmap-mod could not solve all the instances that mod solved. Table 6 shows the number

Table 6. Instances solved by SEAHORN with mod (best out of 5 runs) not solved by each configuration of fmap-mod.

	s1-a1	s2-a1	s2-a2	s3-a1	s3-a2	s3-a3	s5-a1	s5-a2	s5-a3	s5-a5	best
false	15	17	16	18	20	18	18	18	19	21	2
true	19	21	27	16	26	28	21	37	30	30	5
Total	34	38	43	36	46	46	39	55	49	51	7

of instances that were solved only by (the best out of five runs of) mod and not by each fmap-mod configuration (one run), represented in each of the columns. There were 7 instances proven by mod that no fmap-mod configuration proved (shown in the best column of Table 6). Lastly, were 35 mono instances that no mod or fmap-mod configuration proved.

We found that out of all the true instances solved by mod, 23% required arrays in the summaries. When encoding memory with fmap-mod configurations, only 9% of the summaries required arrays on average.

Finally, we do not report the time of the encoding phase because it is negligible compared with the time spent solving. SEAHORN already performs a whole-program pointer analysis so the overhead of our new encoding (Sect. 6) and the finite maps reduction (Sect. 5) is very low.

8   Conclusions

We presented a new CHC encoding that enables automatic modular proofs for programs with pointers without using quantified summaries. The main idea is to encode explicitly the finite parts of the frame of a function when they can be statically determined. We presented an algorithm to infer statically the size of the memory used by a function. To represent bounded memory succinctly, we proposed a new theory of finite maps, adapted to CHCs, and a reduction procedure to simpler theories supported by any SMT solver. We then extended a CHC encoding to represent finite memory using finite maps. We implemented our new technique in SEAHORN and evaluated it on Linux device drivers. Our results are encouraging and show that our new encoding can prove new programs that a previous encoding cannot. However, our evaluation also shows that a priori knowledge about the program and its properties can help to choose the most effective encoding of CHCs. We consider this problem an interesting future work.

References

1. Albarghouthi, A., Gurfinkel, A., Chechik, M.: Whale: an interpolation-based algorithm for inter-procedural verification. In: VMCAI, pp. 39–55 (2012). https://doi.org/10.1007/978-3-642-27940-9_4

2. Albarghouthi, A., Li, Y., Gurfinkel, A., Chechik, M.: UFO: a framework for abstraction- and interpolation-based software verification. In: CAV, pp. 672–678 (2012). https://doi.org/10.1007/978-3-642-31424-7_48
3. Beyer, D., Friedberger, K.: Domain-independent interprocedural program analysis using block-abstraction memoization. In: Devanbu, P., Cohen, M.B., Zimmermann, T. (eds.) ESEC/FSE, pp. 50–62. ACM (2020). https://doi.org/10.1145/3368089.3409718
4. Beyer, D., Henzinger, T.A., Jhala, R., Majumdar, R.: The software model checker blast. STTT **9**(5–6), 505–525 (2007). https://doi.org/10.1007/s10009-007-0044-z
5. Beyer, D., Keremoglu, M.E.: CPAchecker: a tool for configurable software verification. In: CAV, pp. 184–190 (2011). https://doi.org/10.1007/978-3-642-22110-1_16
6. Bjørner, N., Gurfinkel, A., McMillan, K.L., Rybalchenko, A.: Horn clause solvers for program verification. In: Fields of Logic and Computation II - Essays Dedicated to Yuri Gurevich on the Occasion of His 75th Birthday, pp. 24–51 (2015). https://doi.org/10.1007/978-3-319-23534-9_2
7. Calcagno, C., Distefano, D., O'Hearn, P.W., Yang, H.: Compositional shape analysis by means of bi-abduction. In: Shao, Z., Pierce, B.C. (eds.) POPL, pp. 289–300 (2009). https://doi.org/10.1145/1480881.1480917
8. Champion, A., Chiba, T., Kobayashi, N., Sato, R.: ICE-based refinement type discovery for higher-order functional programs. J. Autom. Reason. **64**(7), 1393–1418 (2020). https://doi.org/10.1007/s10817-020-09571-y
9. Clarke, E., Kroening, D., Lerda, F.: A Tool for Checking ANSI-C Programs. In: TACAS, pp. 168–176 (2004). https://doi.org/10.1007/978-3-540-24730-2_15
10. Gurfinkel, A., Kahsai, T., Komuravelli, A., Navas, J.A.: The SeaHorn verification framework. In: CAV, pp. 343–361 (2015). https://doi.org/10.1007/978-3-319-21690-4_20
11. Gurfinkel, A., Navas, J.A.: A context-sensitive memory model for verification of C/C++ programs. In: SAS, pp. 148–168 (2017). https://doi.org/10.1007/978-3-319-66706-5_8
12. Gurfinkel, A., Shoham, S., Vizel, Y.: Quantifiers on demand. In: ATVA, pp. 248–266 (2018). https://doi.org/10.1007/978-3-030-01090-4_15
13. Heizmann, M., et al.: Ultimate Automizer with SMTInterpol - (Competition Contribution). In: TACAS, pp. 641–643 (2013). https://doi.org/10.1007/978-3-642-36742-7_53
14. Heizmann, M., Hoenicke, J., Podelski, A.: Nested interpolants. In: Hermenegildo, M.V., Palsberg, J. (eds.) POPL, pp. 471–482. ACM (2010). https://doi.org/10.1145/1706299.1706353
15. Kassios, I.T.: Dynamic Frames: Support for Framing, Dependencies and Sharing Without Restrictions. In: Misra, J., Nipkow, T., Sekerinski, E. (eds.) FM 2006. LNCS, vol. 4085, pp. 268–283. Springer, Heidelberg (2006). https://doi.org/10.1007/11813040_19
16. Komuravelli, A., Gurfinkel, A., Chaki, S.: SMT-based model checking for recursive programs. In: CAV, pp. 17–34 (2014). https://doi.org/10.1007/978-3-319-08867-9_2
17. Kröning, D., Weissenbacher, G.: A proposal for a theory of finite sets, lists, and maps for the smt-lib standard (2009 (accessed October 13th, 2020)). http://www.philipp.ruemmer.org/publications/smt-lsm.pdf
18. Kuderski, J., Navas, J.A., Gurfinkel, A.: Unification-based pointer analysis without oversharing. In: Barrett, C.W., Yang, J. (eds.) FMCAD, pp. 37–45. IEEE (2019). https://doi.org/10.23919/FMCAD.2019.8894275

19. Leino, K.R.M.: Dafny: an automatic program verifier for functional correctness. In: Clarke, E.M., Voronkov, A. (eds.) LPAR 2010. LNCS (LNAI), vol. 6355, pp. 348–370. Springer, Heidelberg (2010). https://doi.org/10.1007/978-3-642-17511-4_20

20. McCarthy, J., Hayes, P.J.: Some philosophical problems from the standpoint of artificial intelligence. In: Meltzer, B., Michie, D. (eds.) Machine Intelligence 4, pp. 463–502. Edinburgh University Press (1969), reprinted in McC90

21. Merz, F., Falke, S., Sinz, C.: LLBMC: bounded model checking of C and C++ programs using a compiler IR. In: VSTTE, pp. 146–161 (2012). https://doi.org/10.1007/978-3-319-08867-9_7

22. Müller, P., Schwerhoff, M., Summers, A.J.: Viper: A Verification Infrastructure for Permission-Based Reasoning. In: Pretschner, A., Peled, D., Hutzelmann, T. (eds.) Dependable Software Systems Engineering, NATO Science for Peace and Security Series - D: Information and Communication Security, vol. 50, pp. 104–125. IOS Press (2017). https://doi.org/10.3233/978-1-61499-810-5-104

23. Piskac, R., Wies, T., Zufferey, D.: GRASShopper. In: Ábrahám, E., Havelund, K. (eds.) TACAS 2014. LNCS, vol. 8413, pp. 124–139. Springer, Heidelberg (2014). https://doi.org/10.1007/978-3-642-54862-8_9

24. Rakamaric, Z., Emmi, M.: SMACK: decoupling source language details from verifier implementations. In: CAV, pp. 106–113 (2014). https://doi.org/10.1007/978-3-319-08867-9_7

25. Reynolds, J.C.: Separation logic: a logic for shared mutable data structures. In: LICS, pp. 55–74 (2002). https://doi.org/10.1109/LICS.2002.1029817

26. Smans, J., Jacobs, B., Piessens, F.: Implicit dynamic frames: combining dynamic frames and separation logic. In: Drossopoulou, S. (ed.) ECOOP 2009. LNCS, vol. 5653, pp. 148–172. Springer, Heidelberg (2009). https://doi.org/10.1007/978-3-642-03013-0_8

27. Steensgaard, B.: Points-to analysis in almost linear time. In: POPL, pp. 32–41 (1996). https://doi.org/10.1145/237721.237727

28. Stump, A., Barrett, C.W., Dill, D.L., Levitt, J.R.: A decision procedure for an extensional theory of arrays. In: LICS, pp. 29–37. IEEE Computer Society (2001). https://doi.org/10.1109/LICS.2001.932480

Property-Driven Code Obfuscations Reinterpreting Jones-Optimality in Abstract Interpretation

Roberto Giacobazzi and Isabella Mastroeni[✉]

Computer Science Department, University of Verona, Verona, Italy
{roberto.giacobazzi,isabella.mastroeni}@univr.it

Abstract. Jones-optimality determines whether a specializer improves program performances. Reinterpreting this concept in terms of the precision of an abstract interpreter means to determine whether specializing a source program is able to improve the precision of a given static analysis. In the opposite direction, a specializer failing optimality (disoptimal) would decrease the precision of the analysis when applied to the specialized code. In this paper, we exploit this reinterpretation of Jones-optimality relatively to the precision of an abstract interpreter with the aim of systematically deriving obfuscated code. In line with the idea behind Futamura's projections, we factorize the construction of the obfuscated code by separating specialization and interpretation. An interpreter specializer is then systematically made disoptimal by means of language transduction. The result is a language agnostic code obfuscator which is able to foil any given static analyzer.

Keywords: Abstract interpretation · Code obfuscation · Program interpretation · Jones-optimality

1 Introduction

Code obfuscation relies upon the idea of making security inseparable from code: *a program, or parts of it, are transformed in order to make them hard to understand or analyze* [10]. This technology is increasingly relevant in software security, providing an effective way for facing the problem of code protection against reverse engineering. This contributes to comprehensive digital asset protection, with applications in DRM systems, IPP systems, tamper resistant applications, watermarking and fingerprinting, and white-box cryptography [8,9].

Obfuscation [2] exploits, by a suitably designed program transformation, the intensional nature of program analysis [4,24], namely the fact that the precision of a program analysis algorithm depends upon the way the program is written and on how data structures are used. The attack scenario here considers the protection of a program—the asset, from an attacker which is implemented by a program analysis algorithm—the so called hostile observer.

In this paper, we consider program analysis as implemented by an abstract interpreter [13]. This is general enough to include most effective sound program

© The Author(s), under exclusive license to Springer Nature Switzerland AG 2022
G. Singh and C. Urban (Eds.): SAS 2022, LNCS 13790, pp. 247–271, 2022.
https://doi.org/10.1007/978-3-031-22308-2_12

analysis algorithms. The abstraction here plays the role of constraining the interpreter (i.e., a Universal Turing Machine) within the boundaries of expressivity as given by the chosen abstract domain. On the one hand, this realizes a case principle in computer security, where the security of a system (e.g., an encryption protocol) is always proved relatively to a *constrained attacker*, (e.g., by computational complexity). On the other, because any effective attack on code cannot avoid some form of automation of program analysis, this model can fruitfully represent a relevant part of the action of code attack by reverse engineering.

It is known that, by transforming a code we can improve or reduce the precision of any analyzer. It is in general impossible to design a compiler that automatically removes from any program all the false alarms produced by a non straightforward abstract interpreter [4]. However it is instead always possible to inject arbitrary many false alarms by compilation. One of such obfuscating compilers can be simply designed by specializing a suitably designed (called distorted) interpreter [20]. The key observation relies upon the semantic equivalence between the source code and an interpreter specialized on this code. In this case, [26]: (1) The transformed program (resulting from the specialization process) inherits the *programming style* of the interpreter; (2) The transformed program inherits the *semantics* of the original program. The reason for (1) is that the transformed program is the result of the specialization of the code of the interpreter. The reason for (2) is that even though the transformed program may be a disguised form of the source code P, a correct interpreter must faithfully execute the operations that P specifies. It is therefore always possible to act on the intensional properties of programs, and hence on the precision of program analysis, by specializing a suitably designed interpreter [20].

Paper Contribution. In this paper we go deeper into building obfuscating compilers by considering the role of the specializer and its interplay with the given interpreter in the action of producing obfuscated code. The notion of Jones optimality [25,27] helps to give us the compass for understanding the role of program specialization in code obfuscation. Jones optimality was originally introduced to prove whether by compilation it is possible to improve program performance by removing the so called *interpretational overhead* [27]. We reinterpret Jones optimality in the light of the accuracy of an abstract interpreter. In particular, we show that obfuscating programs by specializing interpreters can be seen as a peculiar, and non-standard, case of Jones-(dis)optimality [25,27], where, instead of considering performances, we consider precision. We introduce a new notion of optimality (Sect. 5) stating that a specializer is optimal w.r.t. an abstract interpreter if the abstract interpreter is complete (viz. precise [22]) for the resulting program obtained by specializing the concrete interpreter with the source code. Of course, optimal specializers removing all false alarms cannot exist for all programs and non straightforward abstract interpreters, otherwise by the second Futamura projection such compiler would exist [4]. However the degree of optimality of the specializer shows how the specializer is able to remove the imprecision injected by a distorted interpreter. In the case of code flattening, the code obtained by specializing a vanilla interpreter with the source code produces a truly flattened code whenever the program counter is forced to be a dynamic structure [20]. This inhibits a simple specializer to reconstruct the source structure, hence forcing its disoptimal behavior.

On this basis, we derive a constructive technique for building obfuscating compilers which are driven by the property to hide. The distortion phase is built by means of suitable transducers (Sect. 3) that syntactically act on code in order to make a fixed abstract interpreter incomplete for the property to hide. The core structure of our property-driven obfuscating compilers (Sect. 6) is language and property independent. The main conceptual innovation is in the correspondence between a modified version of Jones optimality, where concrete execution time is replaced by the precision of the abstract interpreter, and the process of protecting a program from the analysis obtained by that abstract interpreter. In order to formally characterize this correspondence we need to rethink program interpretation by separating the syntactic parsing from the semantic interpretation (Sect. 4). This allows us to perform the distortion process on the syntactic phase only, without changing the semantic interpretation of code, hence further separating distortion from interpretation.

Related Works. The most related work is [20], based on the seminal paper [19], where obfuscation was formalized by means of completeness and interpreter specialization. Giacobazzi et al. [20] provide precisely the theoretical bases for obfuscating programs by interpreter specialization, in order to force intensional properties affecting the precision of a given static analysis. With respect to [20], we focus the attention on what we want to protect rather than on what the attacker can observe/analyze. Moreover, Giacobazzi et al. [20] did not provide any systematic approach for deriving the distorted interpreters. Our aim is to fill the gap between the identification of the property to make obscure and the process for building the distorted interpreter to specialize for obscuring the property.

Dalla Preda and Mastroeni [16] exploit the relation between obfuscation and completeness to design property-driven obfuscation strategies as program transformations *revealing* (preserving) some fixed semantic property while *concealing* a property to protect. In this work, it is also shown that the obfuscation approach based on distorted interpreters [20] is precisely a technique for revealing the I/O program semantics while concealing a given property to protect. The problem with this work is that it still does not provide a constructive method for obfuscating programs, but only a theoretical framework for designing obfuscation strategies. Finally, Giacobazzi et al. [21] exploit the relation between completeness and obfuscation for "measuring" obfuscation potency, namely the obfuscator capability of hiding properties.

2 Background

2.1 The Language £ and Control Flow Graphs

Following [5,30] (see also [37]) we consider the language £ of regular commands in Fig. 1 (where + denotes non-deterministic choice and ∗ is the Kleene closure),

$\text{Exp} \ni e ::= a \mid b$

$\text{AExp} \ni a ::= x \mid n \mid a + a \mid a - a \mid a * a$

$\text{BExp} \ni b ::= x \mid true \mid false \mid e = e \mid e > e \mid e < e \mid b \wedge b \mid \neg b$

$\text{Stm} \ni c ::= \mathbf{skip}; \mid x := e; \mid b;$

$\text{Stms} \ni C ::= c \mid C\,C \mid {}_+\langle C + C \rangle_+; \mid {}_*\langle C \rangle_*;$

$\mathfrak{L} \ni P ::= \{ C \}$ (programs) $Var \ni x$ (variables), $n \in \mathbb{Z}$ (values)

Fig. 1. Syntax of $\mathfrak{L}$

which is general enough to cover deterministic imperative languages. We complete the Bruni et al. grammar [5] with an expressions grammar, and we make some syntactic change in order to simplify the parsing and interpretation processes. In particular, we use ; not for composing statements (composition is made by concatenation of statements) but for delimiting the end of a statement. We use delimiters ${}_+\langle$ and $\rangle_+$ for determining the action range of +, we use ${}_*\langle$ and $\rangle_*$ for the range of *, and we use { and } for delimiting programs. Let $\mathfrak{L}$ denote also the set of programs in the language and $Var(P)$ the set of all the variables in $P \in \mathfrak{L}$.

Programs will be graphically represented by means of their control flow graphs (CFG for short). The definition is quite standard [33], but we recall it here in order to fix the notation we use. The CFG of $P \in \mathfrak{L}$ is the labeled directed graph whose nodes are program points Lab_P and whose edge labels are in the language $L_{sp} \ni 1 ::= x := e \mid \mathbf{skip} \mid b$. In order to build the CFG, in the following, we will use labeled programs in $\mathfrak{L}$, namely code in $\mathfrak{L}$ where program points are labeled with values in a set of labels Lab. The labels are not in the syntax since they can be considered as program annotations added by a labeling function. Formally, let $P = \{ C \} \in \mathfrak{L}$ its CFG is $\mathtt{Cfg}(C) \stackrel{\text{def}}{=} Edges({}^{q_0}C^{q_1}) \subseteq Lab_C \times L_{sp} \times Lab_C$, where $Edges({}^{q_0}C^{q_1})$ is inductively defined on the structure of C (we ignore the initial and final brackets).

$$Edges({}^{q_0}\mathbf{skip};{}^{q_1}) = \{\langle q_0, \mathbf{skip}, q_1 \rangle\}$$
$$Edges({}^{q_0}x := e;{}^{q_1}) = \{\langle q_0, x := e, q_1 \rangle\}$$
$$Edges({}^{q_0}{}_+\langle {}^{q_1}C_1{}^{q_2} + {}^{q_3}C_2{}^{q_4}\rangle_+;{}^{q_5}) = Edges({}^{q_1}C_1{}^{q_2}) \cup Edges({}^{q_3}C_2{}^{q_4}) \cup$$
$$\{\langle q_0, true, q_1 \rangle, \langle q_0, true, q_3 \rangle, \langle q_2, true, q_5 \rangle, \langle q_4, true, q_5 \rangle\}$$
$$Edges({}^{q_0}{}_*\langle {}^{q_1}C^{q_2}\rangle_*;{}^{q_3}) = Edges({}^{q_1}C^{q_2}) \cup$$
$$\{\langle q_0, true, q_1 \rangle, \langle q_2, true, q_0 \rangle, \langle q_0, true, q_3 \rangle\}$$
$$Edges({}^{q_0}C_1{}^{q_1}C_2{}^{q_2}) = Edges({}^{q_0}C_1{}^{q_1}) \cup Edges({}^{q_1}C_2{}^{q_2})$$

The nodes can be restricted to those involved in edges, i.e., $Nodes(\mathtt{Cfg}(C)) = \{q \mid \exists \langle q, 1, q' \rangle \in \mathtt{Cfg}(C)$ or $\langle q', 1, q \rangle \in \mathtt{Cfg}(C), 1 \in L_{sp}\}$. In Fig. 2 we have, on the right, an example of CFG extracted from a simple program and on the left we have a simplified version, where all the true transitions are omitted and states are relabeled.

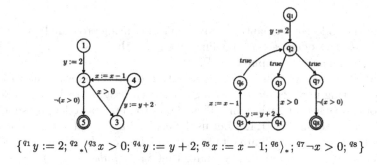

$$\{\, ^{q_1} y := 2; \, ^{q_2} \,_* \langle \, ^{q_3} x > 0; \, ^{q_4} y := y + 2; \, ^{q_5} x := x - 1; \, ^{q_6} \rangle_* ; \, ^{q_7} \neg x > 0; \, ^{q_8} \}$$

Fig. 2. Example of CFG construction.

2.2 The Language Semantics

Denotations are *memories*, i.e., partial functions $m : Var \longrightarrow \mathbb{V} \cup \{\$\} \in \mathbb{M}$ where $\mathbb{V}$ is a domain of values, e.g., $\mathbb{V} \stackrel{\text{def}}{=} \mathbb{Z} \cup \{true, false\}$ and $\$$ denotes an uninstantiated value. A memory assigns values in $\mathbb{V}$ only to a finite set of variables, i.e., it is a *variable finite memory* [4]. We abuse notation by denoting as $\mathbb{M}$ precisely the set of such memories. We define $var(m) \stackrel{\text{def}}{=} \{x \in Var \mid m(x) \neq \$\}$ and for $\mathbb{M} \subseteq \mathbb{M}$, we define $var(\mathbb{M}) = \bigcup_{m \in \mathbb{M}} var(m)$. As usual we will often represent a memory $m \in \mathbb{M}$ as a tuple $[x_1/v_1, \dots, x_n/v_n]$ of its defined variable/value pairs, i.e., such that $m(y) = \$$ if $y \notin \{x_1, \dots, x_n\}$ and $m(y) = v_i$ if $y = x_i$ for all $i \in [1, n]$. Memory update is written $m[x \mapsto v]$ and it associates with x the value v, while all the other associations remain the same. The concrete semantics of the program can be computed by a fine-grain small-step execution deriving the set of all the possible executions of programs. In the following, $\llbracket P \rrbracket \in \wp(\mathbb{M}^*)$ denotes the set of the (terminating) program computations modeled as finite traces of memories [12], while $(\!\![e]\!\!)\, m$ denotes the concrete evaluation of $e \in Exp$ in the memory m.

The Collecting Semantics. The *collecting big-step semantics* of programs in $\mathcal{L}$ (denoted by the subscript $\mathcal{C}$) is defined as the *additive lift* of the standard I/O semantics and it is inductively defined on program's syntax. We first define the collecting semantics for $a \in AExp$, $\llbracket a \rrbracket_c : \wp(\mathbb{M}) \longrightarrow \wp(\mathbb{V})$, as additive lift to sets of memories: $\llbracket a \rrbracket_c \mathbb{M} \stackrel{\text{def}}{=} \{(\!\![a]\!\!)\, m \mid m \in \mathbb{M}\}$. Similarly, for boolean expressions $b \in BExp$, $\llbracket b \rrbracket_c : \wp(\mathbb{M}) \longrightarrow \wp(\mathbb{M})$ is defined as $\llbracket b \rrbracket_c \mathbb{M} \stackrel{\text{def}}{=} \{m \in \mathbb{M} \mid (\!\![b]\!\!)\, m = true\}$. The semantics of $P = \{C\}$ is $\llbracket P \rrbracket_c = \llbracket C \rrbracket_c : \wp(\mathbb{M}) \longrightarrow \wp(\mathbb{M})$ defined inductively as follows [4][1] where $\llbracket C \rrbracket_c^1 \mathbb{M} \stackrel{\text{def}}{=} \llbracket C \rrbracket_c \mathbb{M}$ and $\forall n > 1.\ \llbracket C \rrbracket_c^{n+1} \mathbb{M} \stackrel{\text{def}}{=} \llbracket C \rrbracket_c \mathbb{M} \circ \llbracket C \rrbracket_c^n \mathbb{M}$:

$$\llbracket \mathbf{skip}; \, \rrbracket_c \mathbb{M}; \stackrel{\text{def}}{=} \mathbb{M}$$
$$\llbracket x := e; \, \rrbracket_c \mathbb{M} \stackrel{\text{def}}{=} \mathbb{M}[x \mapsto \llbracket e \rrbracket_c \mathbb{M}] \stackrel{\text{def}}{=} \{\, m[x \mapsto (\!\![e]\!\!)\, m] \mid m \in \mathbb{M} \,\}$$
$$\llbracket_+ \langle C_1 + C_2 \rangle_+; \, \rrbracket_c \mathbb{M} \stackrel{\text{def}}{=} \llbracket C_1 \rrbracket_c \mathbb{M} \cup \llbracket C_2 \rrbracket_c \mathbb{M}$$
$$\llbracket_* \langle C \rangle_*; \, \rrbracket_c \mathbb{M} \stackrel{\text{def}}{=} \bigcup \{\, \llbracket C \rrbracket_c^n \mathbb{M} \mid n \in \mathbb{N} \,\}$$
$$\llbracket C_1 C_2 \rrbracket_c \mathbb{M} \stackrel{\text{def}}{=} \llbracket C_2 \rrbracket_c (\llbracket C_1 \rrbracket_c \mathbb{M})$$

---

[1] We avoid labels and initial and final brackets being not used in the semantics.

Note that the collecting semantics of any non terminating program P is $[\![P]\!]_c = \varnothing$. In this case, if $\varnothing$ denotes the undefined memory, then $\lambda M \subseteq M$. $[\![P]\!]_c M$ is the collection of memories computed by P.

In the following we will use also the notion of store, allowing us to locally denote collecting updates by associating, with each program point the collection of memories reached at each point. This allows to define a collecting small-step semantics abstracting $[\![P]\!]$ [1,12]. Let us define, $S \overset{\text{def}}{=} Lab \rightarrow \wp(M) \cup \{\$\}$ such that for any $s \in S$ there exists a finite set of program labels $q \in Lab$ such that $s(q) \neq \$$, in particular, given a program P we have that $S_P = Lab_P \rightarrow \wp(M) \cup \{\$\}$ (when not necessary or when clear from the context, we will avoid the subscript P). In the following, we will denote by s^q the set of memories associated with $q \in Lab$, i.e., $s(q) \in \wp(M)$. For the sake of readability, we will also use the following update notation: $s[q \mapsto M](q') \overset{\text{def}}{=} M$ if $q = q'$, $s(q')$ otherwise. Moreover, we will denote by $s_\varnothing$ the store mapping each program point to the emptyset, i.e., $\forall q. s_\varnothing(q) = \varnothing$.

The Abstract Semantics. The abstract semantics of programs is an abstraction of the concrete small-step semantics [12–14], also called trace semantics. An abstract domain is a set of properties, here modeled as upper closure operators (uco for short), i.e., a monotone, extensive and idempotent operator on $\wp(M)$ [14]. If $\mathcal{A} \in uco(\wp(M^*))$ is an abstraction of program traces, then we can denote by $[\![P]\!]^{\mathcal{A}} \supseteq \mathcal{A}([\![P]\!])$ the fix-point computation (inductively defined on the language $\mathfrak{L}$) as the $\mathcal{A}$ observation of $[\![P]\!]$. In static analysis, it is quite common to define the semantic abstraction in terms of an abstraction of variable values $\mathbb{V}$. In general, if a program has n variables, then concrete values for the program are n-tuples of values. Hence, abstract domains must be parametric on the number n of variables of the program to analyze, i.e., we have to consider, as abstract domains, families of abstractions $\{\rho_n \in uco(\wp(\mathbb{V}^n))\}_{n \in \mathbb{N}}$ [4,15]. For the sake of readability, in the following we simply denote this family of abstraction as ρ, ignoring the technical aspect that it changes with the number of variables of the program to analyze, and we denote the corresponding abstract semantics as $[\![P]\!]^\rho$. Given a value abstraction ρ, we can define a memory abstraction, abstracting sets of memories in M in abstract memories in M^ρ. Define the memory abstraction as the tuple $\mathcal{A}_\rho = \langle \rho, M^\rho, \alpha_\rho, \gamma_\rho \rangle$, where we define $\alpha_\rho : \wp(M) \rightarrow M^\rho$ $(\alpha_\rho(M) \overset{\text{def}}{=} \lambda\langle x_1, \ldots, x_n \rangle . \rho(\{\langle v_1, \ldots, v_n \rangle \mid [x_1/v_1, \ldots, x_n/v_n] \in M\}))$, while the concretization is the function $\gamma_\rho : M^\rho \rightarrow \wp(M)$ (defined on abstract collecting memories as $\gamma_\rho(\overline{M}) \overset{\text{def}}{=} \{[x_1/v_1, \ldots, x_n/v_n] \mid \langle v_1, \ldots, v_n \rangle \in \overline{M}(x_1, \ldots, x_n)\})$.

In order to define the abstract semantics, we define the semantics of expressions $[\![e]\!]^\rho$ computing abstract operations in ρ, and then we define the abstract semantics of basic instructions: Let $\{x_i\}_{i \in I}$ be the set of defined variables ranging over i in the set of indexes $I = [1, n]$.

$$[\![x_i := e]\!]^\rho \overline{M} \overset{\text{def}}{=} \lambda\langle x_1, \ldots, x_n \rangle . \left\{ \langle v_1, \ldots, v_i, \ldots, v_n \rangle \middle| \begin{array}{l} \exists v \in \mathbb{V}. \langle v_1, \ldots, v, \ldots, v_n \rangle \in \\ \overline{M}(x_1, \ldots, x_n), v_i \in [\![e]\!]^\rho \overline{M} \end{array} \right\}$$

$$\overset{\text{def}}{=} \overline{M}[x_i \mapsto [\![e]\!]^\rho \overline{M}]$$

$$[\![\textbf{skip}]\!]^\rho \overline{M} \overset{\text{def}}{=} \overline{M}$$

In the assignment, we consider all the tuples where the potential relation among all the variables different from x_i remains unaltered, while x_i may have any value in $[\![e]\!]^\rho \overline{M}$. The abstract semantics, of a program $P = \{C\} \in \mathfrak{L}$, is simply denoted as $[\![P]\!]^\rho = [\![C]\!]^\rho : M^\rho \longrightarrow M^\rho$ and it is inductively defined on the syntax of commands (loops, conditionals and compositions) as the composition of the abstract semantics of their components [4]. It is well known that abstract interpretation is not compositional, namely the composition of two best correct approximation (bca for short) semantics is not the bca semantics of the composition. This is indeed the main source of imprecision in program analysis. Note that, also for abstract semantics we can use (abstract) stores S^ρ for defining abstract collecting rules where we associate with program points abstract memories in M^ρ.

Program Specialization. *Program specialization* is a source-to-source program transformation also known as *partial evaluation* [26]. A specializer is a program spec such that for $P \in \mathfrak{L}$ with "static" input $s \in D$ and "dynamic" input $d \in D$ $\mathcal{S}[P](s,d) = \mathcal{S}[\mathcal{S}[spec](P,s)]d$ where $\mathcal{S}[\cdot]$ denotes generic semantics associating I/O meaning to programs independently from the language, hence distinguishing the I/O semantics from the collecting semantics $[\![\cdot]\!]_c$. A specializer executes P in two stages: (1) P is specialized to its static input s yielding a "residual program" $spec(P,s) \stackrel{\text{def}}{=} \mathcal{S}[spec](P,s)$, (2) $spec(P,s)$ can be run on P's dynamic input d [26].

A trivial specializer spec is easy to build by "freezing" the static input s (Kleene's *s-m-n* Theorem of the 1930s s did specialization in this way.) A number of practical program specializers exist. Published partial evaluation systems include TEMPO, ECCE, LOGEN, UNMIX, SIMILIX and PGG [11,28,29,32,34].

3 Symbolic Finite State Machines

In this section, we define a generic notion of symbolic machine and symbolic transducer by generalizing the symbolic automata and transducers defined in the literature [17,35]. The idea consists in generalizing the *symbolic* approach (admitting potentially infinite alphabets) also to finite state machines/transducers equivalent to Turing Machines, namely with more than one stack and/or with writable input tape, while simplifying the notation, for instance by avoiding to introduce a further notion of interpretation for symbols. The following machines are non deterministic with ε transitions, where as usual ε is a special symbol used for executing transitions without reading symbols.

3.1 Finite State Machines

By finite state machines we mean any state machine with a finite number of states that reads an input sequence of symbols. Each symbol allows the execution of a transition, and final states decide which input sequences are accepted by the machine, accepted when the input reading leads to a final state. The notion is recalled only because we provide a unique parametric definition for automata and Turing machines.

Definition 1 (Finite state machines (FSM)). *A FSM is the tuple* $M = \langle \mathbb{Q}, q_\iota, q_\mathbf{f}, \Sigma, \Gamma, \mathsf{S}, \delta \rangle$ *where*

- $\mathbb{Q}$ *is a finite set of states* $(q_\iota \in \mathbb{Q}$ *initial state,* $q_\mathbf{f} \in \mathbb{Q}$ *final/accepting state)*[2];
- Σ *and* Γ *are* finite *input and stack alphabets, respectively;*
- $\mathsf{S} \subseteq \{Stack^n\} \cup \{Input\}$ *is a set of tapes which may contain* $n \geq 0$ *Stacks (if* $n = 0$ *there are no stacks), i.e., LIFO tapes, and one Input tape, a writable and readable input tape where we can stop or move left/right*[3];
- $\delta : \mathbb{Q} \times \Sigma \times \Gamma^n \rightarrow \wp(\mathbb{Q}) \times \{R, L, H\}^{\{0,1\}} \times (\Gamma^*)^n$ *is the transition function. The transition* $q \rightarrow q'$ *labeled with* $((s, M), \{t_i \rightarrow \gamma_i\}_{i \in [1,n]})$ *(read* $s \in \Sigma$ *in the state* q *with the top (popped) elements of the stacks* $\{t_i\}_{i \in [1,n]}$, *reach* q', *push* $\{\gamma_i\}_{i \in [1,n]}$ *on the* n *stacks, and move* $M \in \{R, L, H\}$)[4] *iff* $\langle q', M, \{\gamma_i\}_{i \in [1,n]} \rangle \in \delta(q, s, \{t_i\}_{i \in [1,n]})$.

In order to make such a machine symbolic, we simply consider infinite alphabets (both for input and stack) and a recursive enumerable set of decidable predicates on the alphabet symbols. In this way, transitions are labeled with predicates allowing all the symbols satisfying the property to be read in the transition (on the input tape or on the stack).

Definition 2 (Symbolic finite state machines (SFSM)). *A SFSM is the tuple* $\langle \mathbb{Q}, q_\iota, q_\mathbf{f}, \Psi_\Sigma, \Psi_\Gamma, \mathsf{S}, \delta \rangle$ *where*

- $\mathbb{Q}$ *is a finite set of states* $(q_\iota \in \mathbb{Q}$ *initial state,* $q_\mathbf{f} \in \mathbb{Q}$ *final/accepting state);*
- Σ *and* Γ *are* infinite *input and stack alphabets, respectively;*
- $\Psi_\Sigma \subseteq \wp(\Sigma)$ *and* $\Psi_\Gamma \subseteq \wp(\Gamma)$ *are recursive enumerable sets of predicates on* Σ *and* Γ *(closed under logic connectives)*[5];
- $\mathsf{S} \subseteq \{Stack^n\} \cup \{Input\}$ *(* $n \geq 0$ *number of stacks);*
- $\delta : \mathbb{Q} \times \Psi_\Sigma \times (\Psi_\Gamma)^n \rightarrow \wp(\mathbb{Q}) \times \{R, L, H\}^{\{0,1\}} \times (\Gamma^*)^n$, *where we have the transition* $q \rightarrow q'$ *labeled with* $((s, M), \{t_i \rightarrow \gamma_i\}_{i \in [1,n]})$ *iff* $\exists \Phi_\Sigma \in \Psi_\Sigma$, $\{\Phi_\Gamma^i\}_{i \in [1,n]} \subseteq \Psi_\Gamma$, $\gamma \in \Gamma^n$ *and* $M \in \{R, L, H\}$ *such that* $\langle q', M, \{\gamma_i\}_{i \in [1,n]} \rangle \in \delta(q, \Phi_\Sigma, \{\Phi_\Gamma^i\}_{i \in [1,n]})$, *with* $s \in \Phi_\Sigma$ *and* $\forall i \in [1, n]. t_i \in \Phi_\Gamma^i$.

3.2 Finite State Transducers

Finite state transducers are finite state machine providing an output sequence of symbols for each transition. The standard generalized notion is the following.

---

[2] Being the machine non deterministic with ϵ-transition, w.l.g., we can suppose to have only one final state.

[3] Every FSM has a (only) readable input tape, where it is possible only to move right after each step, a finite state pushdown automaton is an automaton with also one stack, in any other cases we have a Turing Machine.

[4] Where R stands for move-right, L for move-left, and H for halt, and $\{R, L, H\}^0$ means there is no writable input tape.

[5] We avoid the interpretation function [17] simply by denoting directly the predicates extensionally, as the sets of the elements satisfying the predicate.

Definition 3 (Finite state transducers (FST)). *A finite state transducer is a FSM with an output language, i.e., a tuple* $\langle Q, q_\iota, q_f, \Sigma, \Gamma, S, \tilde{\delta}, \Omega \rangle$, *where* $\langle Q, q_\iota, q_f, \Sigma, \Gamma, S, \delta \rangle$ *is a FSM,* Ω *is a finite output alphabet, and the transition function* $\tilde{\delta}$: $Q \times \Sigma \times \Gamma^n \rightarrow \wp(Q) \times \{R, L, H\}^{\{0,1\}} \times (\Gamma^*)^n \times \Omega^*$ *is* δ *extended by returning also an output string* $\omega \in \Omega^*$ *for each input symbol read, i.e.,* $\forall (q, s, \{t_i\}_{i \in [1,n]}) \in Q \times \Sigma \times \Gamma^n. \exists \omega \in \Omega^*. \tilde{\delta}(q, s, \{t_i\}_{i \in [1,n]}) \stackrel{\text{def}}{=} \langle \delta(q, s, \{t_i\}_{i \in [1,n]}), \omega \rangle$.

In this case, we have the transition $q \rightarrow q'$ labeled with $((s/\omega, M), \{t_i \rightarrow \gamma_i\}_{i \in [1,n]})$ (read $s \in \Sigma$ in the state q with the top (popped) elements of the i-th stack $t_i \in \Gamma$ ($i \in [1,n]$) and reach state q', push $\gamma_i \in \Gamma^*$ on the i-th stack ($i \in [1,n]$), move M and provide in output the sequence $\omega \in \Omega$) iff $\exists \langle q', M, \{\gamma_i\}_{i \in [1,n]} \rangle \in \delta(q, s, \{t_i\}_{i \in [1,n]})$, and therefore $\langle q', M, \{\gamma_i\}_{i \in [1,n]}, \omega \rangle \in \tilde{\delta}(q, s, \{t_i\}_{i \in [1,n]})$.

In the symbolic extension, following the Veanes et al. [35], we simply consider a function that for each input symbol read, provides a sequence of output symbols.

Definition 4 (Symbolic finite state transducers (SFST)). *A symbolic finite state transducers is a SFSM with an output language, i.e., it is defined as a tuple* $\langle Q, q_\iota, q_f, \Psi_\Sigma, \Psi_\Gamma, S, \tilde{\delta}, \Omega, f \rangle$, *where* $\langle Q, q_\iota, q_f, \Psi_\Sigma, \Psi_\Gamma, S, \delta \rangle$ *is a SFSM,* Ω *is an infinite output alphabet,* $f : \Sigma \rightarrow \Omega^*$, *and the transition function* $\tilde{\delta}$ *is defined as* $\langle \delta, f \rangle$.

In this case, we have the transition $q \rightarrow q'$ labeled with $((s/f(s), M), \{t_i \rightarrow \gamma_i\}_{i \in [1,n]})$ (read $s \in \Sigma$ in the state q with the top (popped) elements of the i-th stack $t_i \in \Gamma$ ($i \in [1,n]$) and reach state q', push $\gamma_i \in \Gamma^*$ ($i \in [1,n]$), move M and provide in output the symbols $f(s) \in \Omega^*$) iff $\exists \langle q', M, \{\gamma_i\}_{i \in [1,n]} \rangle \in \delta(q, \Phi_\Sigma, \{\Phi_\Gamma^i\}_{i \in [1,n]})$ and $s \in \Phi_\Sigma, \forall i \in [1,n]. t_i \in \Phi_\Gamma^i$.

When dealing with symbolic transducers we can characterize the corresponding transduction function.

Definition 5 (Transduction). [35] *The transduction of a symbolic transducer* T *is the function* $\mathfrak{T}_T : \Sigma^* \rightarrow \wp(\Omega^*)$ *where* $\mathfrak{T}_T(\sigma) \stackrel{\text{def}}{=} \{ \gamma \in \Omega^* \mid q_\iota \xrightarrow{\sigma/\gamma} q_f \}$[6].

Note that a symbolic machine $M = \langle Q, q_\iota, q_f, \Psi_\Sigma, \Psi_\Gamma, S, \delta \rangle$ can be always transformed in the transducer $T_M \stackrel{\text{def}}{=} \langle Q, q_\iota, q_f, \Psi_\Sigma, \Psi_\Gamma, S, \tilde{\delta}, \Sigma, \text{id} \rangle$, where the output language is precisely the input one.

We can compose transducers T_1 and T_2 by composing their transductions [35] $\mathfrak{T}_{T_1}$ and $\mathfrak{T}_{T_2}$ as:

$$\mathfrak{T}_{T_1} \diamond \mathfrak{T}_{T_2} \stackrel{\text{def}}{=} \lambda \sigma. \bigcup_{\gamma \in \mathfrak{T}_{T_1}(\sigma)} \mathfrak{T}_{T_2}(\gamma)$$

3.3 Example: Parser as *Symbolic* Pushdown Automaton

Being the language generated by a context free grammar, the parser can be modeled as a symbolic pushdown (non deterministic) automaton. In particular, it is the automaton $\text{pars} \stackrel{\text{def}}{=} \langle Q, q_\iota, q_f, \Psi_\Sigma, \Psi_\Gamma, \{Stack\}, \delta \rangle$, where

---

[6] If $\sigma = s_0 \cdot s_1 \cdots s_n$ then $q_0 \xrightarrow{\sigma/\gamma} q$ means that $q_0 \xrightarrow{s_0/f(s_0)} q_1 \xrightarrow{s_1/f(s_1)} \cdots \xrightarrow{s_n/f(s_n)} q$, and $\gamma \stackrel{\text{def}}{=} f(s_0) \cdot f(s_1) \cdots f(s_n) \in \Omega^*$ where $\cdot$ stands for string concatenation.

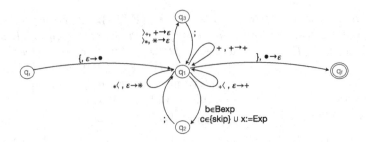

Fig. 3. Parser

- $\mathbb{Q} \stackrel{\text{def}}{=} \{q_i\}_{i \in [1,3]} \cup \{q_\iota, q_f\}$;
- $\Sigma \stackrel{\text{def}}{=} \{ x := \mathsf{e} \,|\, \mathsf{e} \in \mathrm{Exp}, \ x \in Var \} \ \cup \ \{ \mathsf{b} \,|\, \mathsf{b} \in \mathrm{BExp} \} \cup \ \{\mathbf{skip},,\langle,\rangle_*,_+\langle,\rangle_+,$
  $+,;,\{,\}\}$;
- $\Psi_\Sigma \stackrel{\text{def}}{=} \{x := \mathrm{Exp}, \mathrm{BExp}\} \cup \{ \{s\} \,|\, s \in \{\langle,\rangle_*,_+\langle,\rangle_+, +,;, \mathbf{skip}, \{,\}\} \}$;
- $\Gamma \stackrel{\text{def}}{=} \{+,*,\bullet\}$ and $\Psi_\Gamma = \{ \{t\} \,|\, t \in \Gamma \}$[7];
- $\delta : \mathbb{Q} \times \Psi_\Sigma \times \Gamma \to \mathbb{Q} \times \Gamma^*$ is graphically defined in Fig. 3, where each transition is labeled with $(s \in \phi, t \to \gamma)$, meaning that ϕ is a predicate on Σ and $s \in \phi$, while from the stack we pop $t \in \Gamma \cup \{\varepsilon\}$ ($t = \varepsilon$ means that we don't pop anything from the stack) and we push $\gamma \in \Gamma^*$[8].

This parser simply checks brackets balance, where $+$ $(*)$ is pushed whenever a bracket is opened, and the same symbol is popped when it is closed. We can terminate only if the stack is empty (when on the top there is $\bullet$).

4   Program (Re)Interpretation

As usual the interpretation of programs is specified in two phases: The parsing phase of programs, where programs are viewed as sequences of statements, and the semantic interpretation phase, i.e., the corresponding transformation of memories/stores. The first phase is modeled as symbolic Turing Machine reading in input the sequence of symbols corresponding to the program syntax, and providing in output the precise sequences of single statements (skip and assignments) to execute and of guards to evaluate. This resulting set of sequences corresponds indeed to the CFG of the program, and on this structure we can perform the semantic interpretation phase, whose rule definitions are indeed independent from the sequence of statements/guards to execute/evaluate. Indeed, such semantic interpretation phase may be defined on concrete memories, on collecting memories of even on abstract memories, without affecting the computation of the previous interpretation phase.

---

[7] In this case the stack is not really symbolic.

[8] For the sake of readability we write s for singleton predicates $\{s\}$ and the empty updates of the stack, i.e., $\varepsilon \to \varepsilon$, are not depicted.

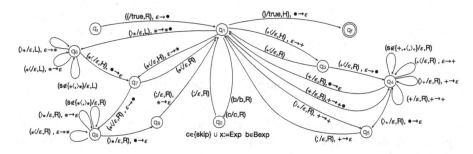

Fig. 4. Execution sequence extractor

4.1 First Phase: The Execution Sequence Extractor

The parsing of the input program, aiming also at extracting the sequence of executed statements and evaluated guards, is modeled as a symbolic Turing machine equipped with a stack. It should be clear that the input language is the language of the parser **pars**, that is indeed embedded in the interpreter. Hence the first component is $\mathtt{cfgEx} \stackrel{\mathrm{def}}{=} \langle \mathbb{Q}, q_\iota, q_f, \Psi_\Sigma, \Psi_\Gamma, \{Stack, Input\}, \tilde{\delta}, \Omega, \mathtt{f} \rangle$

- $\mathbb{Q} \stackrel{\mathrm{def}}{=} \{q_i\}_{i \in [1,9]} \cup \{q_\iota, q_f\}$;
- $\Sigma \stackrel{\mathrm{def}}{=} \{\, x := e \mid e \in Exp, x \in Var \,\} \cup \{\, b \mid b \in BExp \,\} \cup \{\mathbf{skip},_*\langle,\rangle_{*},_+\langle,\rangle_+, +, ;\}$ and $\Psi_\Sigma \stackrel{\mathrm{def}}{=} \{x := Exp, BExp\} \cup \{\, \{s\} \mid s \in \{_*\langle,\rangle_{*},_+\langle,\rangle_+, +, ;, \mathbf{skip}, \{,\}\} \,\}$;
- $\Gamma \stackrel{\mathrm{def}}{=} \{+, *, \bullet\}$ and $\Psi_\Gamma = \{\, \{s\} \mid s \in \Gamma \,\}$;
- $\Omega \stackrel{\mathrm{def}}{=} L_{sp} = \{\, b \mid b \in BExp \,\} \cup \{\, x := e \mid e \in Exp, x \in Var \,\} \cup \{\mathbf{skip}\}$;
- $\delta : \mathbb{Q} \times \Psi_\Sigma \times \Gamma \to \mathbb{Q} \times \{R, L, H\} \times \Gamma^* \times \Omega$ graphically defined in Fig. 4 together with $\mathtt{f} : \Sigma \to \Omega$, where each transition is labeled, as described before, with $((s \in \phi/\mathtt{f}(s), M), t \to \gamma)$.

In particular, q_2 handles the single statement execution or the guard evaluation. q_3 handles the non deterministic choice. In particular it moves to q_1 for executing the statement on the left of + (and when it finds the symbol + it skips, in q_4, what remains up to the closed parenthesis $\rangle_+$). q_3 moves to q_4 if it wants to execute the statements on the right of +. In this case it skips all the statements up to + again in q_4. We use the stack for recognizing nested +. State q_7 handles loops, in particular it moves to q_1 for executing the body (the statements between $_*\langle$ and $\rangle_*$). In this case when we read $\rangle_*$ it moves to q_6 for returning back at the beginning of the loop. q_7 moves to q_8 for skipping the loop, by looking for $\rangle_*$ and continuing the execution.

In this way, if the input is a legal program, then it is accepted and the output sequences are the sequences of statements to execute and of guards to evaluate. We can observe that if we keep also the graph structure of the output (intuitively, ignoring ε-transitions and collapsing states recognizing the same language), then we obtain a graph equivalent to the CFG of the program.

Definition 6 (Partial interpreter evaluation). *The partial interpreter evaluation is the sequence/trace of statements/expressions to actually execute for*

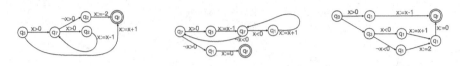

Fig. 5. Examples of interpretation

a given program. Formally, given P ∈ ℒ *and the execution sequence extractor*
cfgEx, $\langle \mathbb{Q}, q_\iota, q_f, \Psi_\Sigma, \Psi_\Gamma \{Stack, Input\}, \tilde{\delta}, \Omega, \mathbf{f} \rangle$ (P ∈ Σ^*), *the partial evaluation*
of P *is* $\mathfrak{T}_{\mathtt{cfgEx}}(P)$.

Let us denote cfgEx[P] the automaton recognizing the output language
$\mathfrak{T}_{\mathtt{cfgEx}}(P)$ of cfgEx transduction of the input sequence P. Then we can observe that
cfgEx[P] corresponds to the CFG (seen as SFSM) of P, i.e., cfgEx[P] ≈ Cfg(P)
(up to label renaming and minimization). Note that cfgEx[P] is a FSM (no more
symbolic), (the one of the statements in P) of the infinite Σ. Let us show this
correspondence on some examples.

Example 1. Consider the program P_1,

$$\{ _+\langle x > 0; _*\langle x > 0; x := x - 1; \rangle_*; \neg x > 0; x := -2; + \neg x > 0; x := x + 1; \rangle_+; \}$$

In the picture we depict the whole path of interpretation by means of
the given interpreter: We obtain so far the automaton cfgEx[P_1] generated
by the transduction of the interpreter on P_1. Each transition is labeled with
$((s/o, M), t \rightarrow \gamma)$ meaning that we read s in input and we pop t from the stack,
while we move M we output ω and we push γ on the stack.

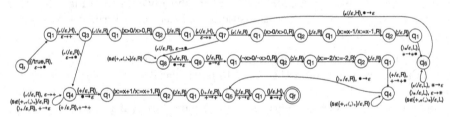

If we transitively collect the transitions with output ε and we collapse states
recognizing the same language, while keeping the branch and the final states, we
obtain the graph on the left of Fig. 5, which corresponds to the CFG of P_1.

Consider now the program P_2

$$\{ _*\langle x > 0; x := x - 1; _*\langle x < 0; x := x + 1; \rangle_*; \neg x < 0 \rangle_*; \neg x > 0; x := 0; \}$$

the graph in the center of Fig. 5 corresponds to the automaton cfgEx[P_2], where
the labels are the output symbols. Finally, consider the program P_3

$$\{ _+\langle x > 0; x := x - 1; + _+\langle x < 0; x := x + 1; + \neg x < 0; x := 2; \rangle_+; x := 0; \rangle_+; \}$$

The graph on the right of Fig. 5 corresponds to cfgEx[P_3], where the labels are
the output symbols.

Table 1. CollR_{sp}: The collecting interpretation rules for L_{sp}.

$$\langle\langle q_0, \textbf{skip}, q_1\rangle, s\rangle \to s \qquad \langle\langle q_0, x := \textbf{e}, q_1\rangle, s\rangle \to s[q_1 \mapsto s^{q_0}[x \mapsto [\![\textbf{e}]\!]_c \, s^{q_0}] \cup s^{q_1}]$$

$$\frac{[\![\textbf{b}]\!]_c \, s^{q_0} \neq \varnothing}{\langle\langle q_0, \textbf{b}, q_1\rangle, s\rangle \to s[q_1 \mapsto [\![\textbf{b}]\!]_c \, s^{q_0} \cup s^{q_1}]}$$

4.2   Second Phase: The Semantic Interpretation

The semantic interpretation is just an interpretation function depending on the domain of denotations, and defined for each element of L_{sp}, the output symbols to interpret. In general, given a graph G, with initial state q_ι whose labels are in the language L_{sp}, and given a semantic rule system SemR_{sp} defining the small-step semantics for L_{sp}, namely determining how semantic denotations in $\mathbb{D}$ (e.g., stores in $\mathbb{S}$) are transformed by the execution of elements in L_{sp}, we can interpret its paths on denotations $\mathbb{D}$ by using the following function on set of graph configurations $\mathbb{C}^G \stackrel{\text{def}}{=} (\mathbb{Q} \times \mathbb{D}) \cup \mathbb{D}$, let $C \subseteq \mathbb{C}^G$, $d, d' \in \mathbb{D}$ and $q_i \in \mathbb{Q}$

$$f^G_{\text{SemR}_{sp}}(q_0, d) \stackrel{\text{def}}{=} \begin{cases} \{d\} & \text{(fix-point)} & \text{if } \nexists\langle q_0, 1, q_1\rangle \in G \\ \{\langle q_1, d'\rangle \mid \exists 1. \ \langle\langle q_0, 1, q_1\rangle, d\rangle \to d' \in \text{SemR}_{sp}\} & & \text{Otherwise} \end{cases}$$

$$f^G_{\text{SemR}_{sp}}(C) \stackrel{\text{def}}{=} \bigcup \left\{ f^G_{\text{SemR}_{sp}}(c) \,\middle|\, c \in C \smallsetminus \mathbb{D} \right\} \cup \left\{ \bigcup \left\{ d \,\middle|\, d \in C \cap \mathbb{D} \right\} \right\}$$

where $\bigcup$ denotes the least upper bound on $\mathbb{D}$. Then, we can compute the fix-point interpretation of the graph G, starting from an initial denotation d_ι as the least fix-point[9] of the extensive version of $f^G_{\text{SemR}_{sp}}$, i.e., $\overline{f}^G_{\text{SemR}_{sp}} \stackrel{\text{def}}{=} \lambda C. \ f^G_{\text{SemR}_{sp}}(C) \cup C$, defined in terms of the semantic rule system SemR_{sp}. This fix-point computes the set of all the reachable configurations, hence in order to extract the final/terminating ones, we have simply to consider, in this fix-point, only the configurations in $\mathbb{D}$.

$$\mathcal{S}[G] \stackrel{\text{def}}{=} \lambda d_\iota. \ (\text{lfp}_{\{\langle q_\iota, d_\iota\rangle\}} \, \overline{f}^G_{\text{SemR}_{sp}}) \cap \mathbb{D}$$

For instance, in order to define a *collecting* small-step semantics we have to define a *collecting* rule system CollR_{sp} interpreting L_{sp} (Table 1) on stores $\mathbb{S}$, where, given the set of initial memories M, the initial store is $s_M \in \mathbb{S}$, $s_M(q) \stackrel{\text{def}}{=} s_\varnothing[q_\iota \mapsto M]$, also denoted $[q_\iota \mapsto M]$, Note that, the interpretation of ε is simply like interpreting *true*, and for this reason it is simply ignored.

Then the graph G collecting semantic interpretation is the following, where being interested only in the memories reached at the end of the program execution, we consider only the store memories at the final point q_f.

$$\forall M \in \wp(\mathbb{M}). \ [\![G]\!]_c M \stackrel{\text{def}}{=} ((\text{lfp}_{\{\langle q_\iota, s_M\rangle\}} \, \overline{f}^G_{\text{CollR}_{sp}}) \cap \mathbb{S})(q_f).$$

---

[9] Given an extensive and monotone function f, its least fix-point computation starting from x is $\text{lfp}_x \, f \stackrel{\text{def}}{=} \bigvee_{n \in \mathbb{N}} f^n(x)$, where $f^0(x) = x$ and $f^{n+1}(x) = f \circ f^n(x)$.

As observed before, when we consider an abstract semantics $\mathcal{A}_\rho{}^{10}$ we obtain an abstract interpreter. The idea is simple, we can define a rule system $\mathtt{AbsR}^\rho_{\mathtt{sp}}$ which is precisely $\mathtt{CollR}_{\mathtt{sp}}$ where the abstract semantics $[\![\cdot]\!]^\rho$ for interpreting expressions is used instead of $[\![\cdot]\!]_c$, and in terms of which we obtain, as before, a corresponding interpretation function $\overline{f}^{\mathtt{G}}_{\mathtt{AbsR}^\rho_{\mathtt{sp}}}$. Then we can define

$$\forall \overline{\mathsf{M}} \in \wp(\mathsf{M}^\rho).\ [\![\mathtt{G}]\!]^\rho \overline{\mathsf{M}} \overset{\mathrm{def}}{=} ((\mathit{lfp}_{\{\langle q_\iota,\, \overline{\mathsf{s}_{\overline{\mathsf{M}}}}\rangle\}}\ \overline{f}^{\mathtt{G}}_{\mathtt{AbsR}^\rho_{\mathtt{sp}}}) \cap \mathbb{S}^\rho)(q_{\mathtt{f}})$$

4.3 Interpreting Programs

Finally we can compose the two phases and obtain the characterization of interpretation for programs $\mathsf{P} \in \mathfrak{L}$. In particular, as observed in the previous section, $\mathtt{cfgEx}[\mathsf{P}]$ returns precisely a graph with $\mathsf{L}_{\mathtt{sp}}$ as label's language, hence we can use the above semantic interpretation on this resulting graph.

Definition 7 (Program interpreter). *Given a semantic rule system* $\mathtt{SemR}_{\mathtt{sp}}$ *for* $\mathsf{L}_{\mathtt{sp}}$ *and* $\mathcal{S}[\mathtt{G}] \overset{\mathrm{def}}{=} \lambda \mathsf{d}_\iota.\ (\mathit{lfp}_{\{\langle q_\iota,\, \mathsf{d}_\iota\rangle\}}\ \overline{f}^{\mathtt{G}}_{\mathtt{SemR}_{\mathtt{sp}}}) \cap \mathbb{D}$ *inductively defined on its labels in* $\mathsf{L}_{\mathtt{sp}}$*. A program interpreter for the language* $\mathfrak{L}$ *is the pair* $\mathtt{int} \overset{\mathrm{def}}{=} \langle \mathtt{cfgEx}, \mathcal{S}[\cdot]\rangle$*. Hence,* $\forall \mathsf{P} \in \mathfrak{L}$ *the program interpretation is* $\mathcal{S}[\mathsf{P}] = \mathcal{S}[\mathtt{int}[\mathsf{P}]] \overset{\mathrm{def}}{=} \mathcal{S}[\mathtt{cfgEx}[\mathsf{P}]]$*.*

For instance, the collecting interpreter for $\mathfrak{L}$ is $\langle \mathtt{cfgEx}, [\![\cdot]\!]_c\rangle$, while an abstract interpreter w.r.t. the variable values abstraction ρ is $\langle \mathtt{cfgEx}, [\![\cdot]\!]^\rho\rangle$.

Combining all together, given $\mathsf{P} = \{\mathsf{C}\} \in \mathfrak{L}$, its collecting semantics starting from initial memories $\mathsf{M} \in \mathsf{M}$ is computed as follows. The following result holds by construction and by the intuitive equivalence between the collecting program semantics and the collecting interpretation of its CFG.

Proposition 1. *Let* $\mathsf{P} = \{\mathsf{C}\} \in \mathfrak{L}$*, then we have* $[\![\mathsf{P}]\!]_c = [\![\mathtt{int}[\mathsf{P}]]\!]_c$*, where by construction* $\forall \mathsf{M} \in \mathsf{M}.\ [\![\mathtt{int}[\mathsf{P}]]\!]_c \mathsf{M} = ((\mathit{lfp}_{\{\langle q_\iota,\, \mathsf{s}_{\mathsf{M}}\rangle\}}\ \overline{f}^{\mathtt{cfgEx}[\mathsf{P}]}_{\mathtt{CollR}_{\mathtt{sp}}}) \cap \mathbb{S})(q_{\mathtt{f}})$*. In the abstract case,* $[\![\mathsf{P}]\!]^\rho = [\![\mathtt{int}[\mathsf{P}]]\!]^\rho$*, where* $\forall \overline{\mathsf{M}} \in \mathsf{M}^\rho.\ [\![\mathtt{int}[\mathsf{P}]]\!]^\rho \overline{\mathsf{M}} \overset{\mathrm{def}}{=} ((\mathit{lfp}_{\{\langle q_\iota,\, \mathsf{s}_{\overline{\mathsf{M}}}\rangle\}}\ \overline{f}^{\mathtt{cfgEx}[\mathsf{P}]}_{\mathtt{AbsR}^\rho_{\mathtt{sp}}}) \cap \mathbb{S}^\rho)(q_{\mathtt{f}})$*.*

4.4 Specializing Interpreters

In classical computational theory [31] the interpreter is indeed a program with two inputs, a fragment of code to execute and the set of initial memories from which to start execution. Our model of program interpretation distinguishes precisely between the application to the first input (the program) and the second input (the initial memories). In particular, the first phase consists precisely in applying the interpreter to the program, and the second phase consists in applying the resulting structure to the set of initial memories. In other words, it should be clear that the simple transduction $\mathtt{cfgEx}[\mathsf{P}]$ is precisely the specialization of the interpreter on the program, precomputing the interpretation computation

---

[10] In this case, we consider directly the semantic abstraction induced by a memory abstraction ρ since we are abstracting in the semantic interpretation phase.

involving only the code, namely the characterization of the sequences of statements to execute and of guards to evaluate. This corresponds precisely to design the program CFG. The only interpretation steps that remain to perform are those concerning the semantic interpretation, depending also on data (formally on initial memories). Hence, we can write

$$spec(\text{int}, \mathsf{P}) = spec(\langle \text{cfgEx}, [\![\cdot]\!]\rangle, \mathsf{P}) \stackrel{\text{def}}{=} \text{cfgEx}[\mathsf{P}]$$

Which is indeed a specializer because by construction we have:

$$\forall \mathsf{M} \in \wp(\mathbb{M}).\ [\![spec(\text{int}, \mathsf{P})]\!]\mathsf{M} = [\![\text{cfgEx}[\mathsf{P}]]\!]\mathsf{M} = [\![\mathsf{P}]\!]\mathsf{M}.$$

5 Specializer (Dis)Optimality

In this section, we formally introduce *specializer optimality*, i.e., the specializer property characterizing the analysis precision.

5.1 Abstract Jones Optimality and Completeness

We consider code specialization in the specific context of the specialization of interpreters and abstract interpretation. Let $\mathcal{A}$ be a semantic abstraction and let int be an interpreter. Note that, given the new definition of interpreter, a semantic abstraction could be both an approximation of the CFG, providing a CFG containing the concrete computations and/or an abstraction of data manipulated by programs. The following definition reinterprets the notion of Jones optimality where computation time is replaced by the precision of an abstract interpreter.

Definition 8 ($\mathcal{A}$-optimality). *A specializer* spec, *implementing the function* spec, *is $\mathcal{A}$-optimal w.r.t the interpreter* int *if it does not lose precision w.r.t. the semantic abstraction $\mathcal{A}$, i.e., if $[\![spec(\text{int}, \mathsf{P})]\!]^{\mathcal{A}} \sqsubseteq [\![\mathsf{P}]\!]^{\mathcal{A}}$.*

Note that, if we replace $[\![P]\!]^{\mathcal{A}}$ with time complexity of P, this definition boils down precisely to Jones-optimality [25,27]. When applied to the case of abstract interpretation, a stronger property is also important, as specified in the following definition.

Definition 9 ($\mathcal{A}$-suboptimality). *A specializer* spec *implementing the function spec is $\mathcal{A}$-suboptimal w.r.t. an interpreter* int *if it does not add precision, i.e., $\forall \mathsf{P} \in \mathfrak{L}.\ [\![spec(\text{int}, \mathsf{P})]\!]^{\mathcal{A}} = [\![\mathsf{P}]\!]^{\mathcal{A}}$.*

While for straightforward abstractions $\mathcal{A}$, such as the identity and the top abstraction, $\mathcal{A}$-suboptimality always holds, for non-straightforward abstractions $\mathcal{A}$, $\mathcal{A}$-suboptimality depends upon the specializer spec and the interpreter int.

Proposition 2. *Given a self-interpreter (written in the interpreted language)* int, *there exists an $\mathcal{A}$-(sub)optimal specializer.*

Proof. The idea is similar to the case of trivial Jones-optimal [25]. Being int a self interpreter, there exists a trivial $\mathcal{A}$-optimal specializer semantics $\overline{spec}$, i.e.,

$$\overline{spec}(\mathsf{P}, x) \stackrel{\text{def}}{=} \begin{cases} x & \text{if } \mathsf{P} = \text{int} \\ spec(\mathsf{P}, x) & \text{otherwise} \end{cases}$$

which is a (computable) specializer semantics, since $[\![\overline{spec}(\text{int}, \mathsf{P})]\!]^{\mathcal{A}} = [\![\mathsf{P}]\!]^{\mathcal{A}}$.

Note that, when spec is not $\mathcal{A}$-optimal, it may happen that we don't have any relation between the original program and the specialized one, or it may happen that the specialized program is indeed less precise. In this case, namely when $\exists \mathsf{P} \in \mathfrak{L}, \exists \mathsf{M} \subseteq \mathsf{M}. [\![spec(\text{int}, \mathsf{P})]\!]^{\mathcal{A}} \mathsf{M} \sqsupset [\![\mathsf{P}]\!]^{\mathcal{A}} \mathsf{M}$, then we say that spec, implementing the function *spec*, is $\mathcal{A}$-*disoptimal* w.r.t. the interpreter int. Note that, both the notions of optimality and disoptimality may happen on a specific program, in particular we can say that spec is ρ-suboptimal/optimal/disoptimal w.r.t. the interpreter int for the program P if the corresponding definition holds for P, i.e., $[\![spec(\text{int}, \mathsf{P})]\!]^{\mathcal{A}} = [\![\mathsf{P}]\!]^{\mathcal{A}}$ (resp. $\sqsubseteq$ or $\sqsupset$).

Let us show the relation of optimality with precision in the abstract analysis, namely w.r.t completeness. Completeness in abstract interpretation means that the abstract computation $[\![\cdot]\!]^{\mathcal{A}}$ is precise as the abstraction of the concrete computation, i.e., $\forall \mathsf{P} \in \mathfrak{L}. [\![\mathsf{P}]\!]^{\mathcal{A}} = \mathcal{A}([\![\mathsf{P}]\!])$ [14,22]. In this case we say that $\mathcal{A}$ is complete, while, if it holds for a program P, we say that $\mathcal{A}$ is complete for P.

Lemma 1. *Let* spec *be a (concrete) specializer implementing spec,* int *a collecting self interpreter and* $\mathcal{A}$ *a semantic abstraction. Let* $\forall \mathsf{P}. \mathsf{P}^s_{\text{int}} \stackrel{\text{def}}{=} spec(\text{int}, \mathsf{P})$, *then we have the following facts:*

1. spec $\mathcal{A}$-*suboptimal w.r.t.* int $\Rightarrow \forall \mathsf{P}. (\mathcal{A}$ *complete for* P $\Leftrightarrow \mathcal{A}$ *complete for* $\mathsf{P}^s_{\text{int}}$*);*
2. $\forall \mathsf{P}. (\mathcal{A}$ *complete for* P *and* $\mathsf{P}^s_{\text{int}} \Rightarrow$ spec $\mathcal{A}$-*suboptimal w.r.t.* int *and* P*);*
3. spec $\mathcal{A}$-*optimal w.r.t.* int $\Rightarrow \forall \mathsf{P}. (\mathcal{A}$ *complete for* P $\Rightarrow \mathcal{A}$ *complete for* $\mathsf{P}^s_{\text{int}}$*);*
4. $\forall \mathsf{P}. (\mathcal{A}$ *complete for* $\mathsf{P}^s_{\text{int}} \Rightarrow$ spec $\mathcal{A}$-*optimal w.r.t.* int *and* P*).*

Proof. Let us recall that, by construction $[\![\mathsf{P}]\!]_c = [\![\mathsf{P}^s_{\text{int}}]\!]_c$.

1. If spec is $\mathcal{A}$-suboptimal then $\forall \mathsf{P}. [\![\mathsf{P}]\!]^{\mathcal{A}} = [\![\mathsf{P}^s_{\text{int}}]\!]^{\mathcal{A}}$. Suppose $\mathcal{A}$ complete for P, then it means that $[\![\mathsf{P}]\!]^{\mathcal{A}} = \mathcal{A}([\![\mathsf{P}]\!])$, therefore we have $[\![\mathsf{P}^s_{\text{int}}]\!]^{\mathcal{A}} = [\![\mathsf{P}]\!]^{\mathcal{A}} = \mathcal{A}([\![\mathsf{P}]\!]_c) = \mathcal{A}([\![\mathsf{P}^s_{\text{int}}]\!]_c)$ hence we have completeness also for $\mathsf{P}^s_{\text{int}}$ Analogously we can prove completeness for Pwhen we have completeness for $\mathsf{P}^s_{\text{int}}$ Intuitively, we have not the inverse implication since when $\mathcal{A}$ is both incomplete for P and $\mathsf{P}^s_{\text{int}}$we cannot imply anything on the optimality of the specializer, while when it is complete for both we can prove the following result.
2. If $\mathcal{A}$is complete for both P and $\mathsf{P}^s_{\text{int}}$then $[\![\mathsf{P}]\!]^{\mathcal{A}} = \mathcal{A}([\![\mathsf{P}]\!])$and $[\![\mathsf{P}^s_{\text{int}}]\!]^{\mathcal{A}} = \mathcal{A}([\![\mathsf{P}^s_{\text{int}}]\!]_c)$ Therefore $[\![\mathsf{P}]\!]^{\mathcal{A}} = \mathcal{A}([\![\mathsf{P}]\!]) = \mathcal{A}([\![\mathsf{P}^s_{\text{int}}]\!]) = [\![\mathsf{P}^s_{\text{int}}]\!]^{\mathcal{A}}$ meaning suboptimality w.r.t. intand P
3. If spec is $\mathcal{A}$-optimal then $\forall \mathsf{P}. [\![\mathsf{P}^s_{\text{int}}]\!]^{\mathcal{A}} \sqsubseteq [\![\mathsf{P}]\!]^{\mathcal{A}}$ Suppose $\mathcal{A}$ complete for P, then it means that $[\![\mathsf{P}]\!]^{\mathcal{A}} = \mathcal{A}([\![\mathsf{P}]\!])$ therefore we have $\mathcal{A}([\![\mathsf{P}^s_{\text{int}}]\!]) \sqsubseteq [\![\mathsf{P}^s_{\text{int}}]\!]^{\mathcal{A}} \sqsubseteq [\![\mathsf{P}]\!]^{\mathcal{A}} = \mathcal{A}([\![\mathsf{P}]\!]) = \mathcal{A}([\![\mathsf{P}^s_{\text{int}}]\!])$ Hence they are all equalities, and therefore we have completeness of $\mathsf{P}^s_{\text{int}}$

4. If, given $P \in \mathfrak{L}$, we have $\mathcal{A}$ complete for P^s_{int} then $[\![P^s_{int}]\!]^{\mathcal{A}} = \mathcal{A}([\![P^s_{int}]\!])$ hence we have $\forall P.\ [\![P^s_{int}]\!]^{\mathcal{A}} = \mathcal{A}([\![P^s_{int}]\!]) = \mathcal{A}([\![P]\!]) \sqsubseteq [\![P]\!]^{\mathcal{A}}$.

Theorem 1. *Let* spec *be a (concrete) specializer implementing* spec, int *a collecting interpreter and $\mathcal{A}$ a semantic abstraction. Let $\forall P.\ P^s_{int} \stackrel{def}{=} spec(int, P)$, then we have that $\forall P \in \mathfrak{L}$ if $\mathcal{A}$ complete for P then: spec $\mathcal{A}$-optimal w.r.t.* int *and $P \Leftrightarrow \mathcal{A}$ complete for $P^s_{int} \Leftrightarrow$ spec $\mathcal{A}$-suboptimal w.r.t.* int *and P.*

Proof. Trivial by Lemma 1. In particular, if *spec* is $\mathcal{A}$-optimal w.r.t. int and P, then by the hypothesis of completeness on P and by Lemma 1(3) we have $\mathcal{A}$ is complete for P^s_{int}, and by Lemma 1(4) we have *spec* $\mathcal{A}$-suboptimal w.r.t. int and P. Finally, by definition *spec* $\mathcal{A}$-suboptimal is also $\mathcal{A}$-optimal.

These results tell us that in order to obtain an obfuscator by specializing an interpreter we have to use a specializer which is not optimal w.r.t. the observation and the interpreter.

We now formalize the relation between the specializer optimality, w.r.t., a given interpreter, and our capability of obfuscating the source program by specializing an interpreter. Our aim is to exploit this relation for driving the distortion of the interpreter by means of the property we have to obfuscate, namely by the property to hide from the analyzer.

Theorem 2. *Given an interpreter* int *and a specializer* spec *(with semantics spec), we define the program transformer $\mathfrak{O}(P) \stackrel{def}{=} spec(int, P)$. For any program P, $\mathfrak{O}(P)$ is an obfuscation of P w.r.t. the semantic abstraction $\mathcal{A}$ iff spec is $\mathcal{A}$-disoptimal w.r.t.* int *on P.*

Proof. If *spec* is $\mathcal{A}$-disoptimal w.r.t. int then $[\![P]\!]^{\mathcal{A}} \sqsubset [\![spec(int, P)]\!]^{\mathcal{A}}$, and therefore we have $[\![P]\!]^{\mathcal{A}} \sqsubset [\![\mathfrak{O}(P)]\!]^{\mathcal{A}}$ by definition of $\mathfrak{O}(P)$, meaning that $\mathfrak{O}(P)$ is an obsfuscator for what we observed in previous sections. On the other hand, if $[\![P]\!]^{\mathcal{A}} \sqsubset [\![\mathfrak{O}(P)]\!]^{\mathcal{A}}$, then surely we have $[\![P]\!]^{\mathcal{A}} \sqsubset [\![spec(int, P)]\!]^{\mathcal{A}}$ (by definition of $\mathfrak{O}(P)$) meaning that the specializer is $\mathcal{A}$-disoptimal.

At this point it should be clear why disoptimality is defined by keeping a (strict) approximation relation and not by losing any relation. Indeed, in this way it guarantees the semantics observed on the obfuscated program to be conservative w.r.t. the original semantics by containing it. In this way, while we force to lose the property we aim at obfuscating, we also partially keep the semantics of the original program by over approximating it.

Finally, since $\mathcal{A}$-disoptimality depends on both the specializer and the interpreter, we can choose to force disoptimality by leaving the specializer unchanged, and by acting only on the interpreter. We characterize a distortion of the interpreter able to make the specializer $\mathcal{A}$-disoptimal. This idea is enforced by two aspects: (1) Due to the construction proposed, the distortion can be simply characterized as a parser inductively transforming the code in a semantically equivalent program[11]; (2) Distortion can be driven by the notion of completeness, which is a semantic property strongly related to optimality as shown before.

---

[11] Note that semantic equivalence on single (atomic) statements is decidable.

5.2 Distorting Interpreters

In order to understand how to distort interpreters for inducing incompleteness we observe the following facts:

- For each (not straightforward) abstraction there always exists a program/code whose abstract semantics is incomplete, hence we can always characterize syntactic elements making an abstract semantics incomplete [23];
- We can think of transforming statements that will be executed in a semantic preserving way, yet including these elements;
- Clearly, it is not decidable to determine which statements will be executed, therefore in order to introduce incomplete syntactic elements in our code that will be surely executed, in general, we need to transform all program statements;
- A language parser transforming each statements by introducing incomplete elements for a fixed abstraction $\mathcal{A}$ produces the required results.
- By composing this parser with the interpreter, we obtain a distorted interpreter for which the control flow graph interpretation, i.e., its specialization w.r.t. the input program, is disoptimal, therefore obtaining an obfuscator obscuring the property expressed by $\mathcal{A}$ on any input program.

We define a module that transforms the interpreter as a SFST accepting in input the language of the parser and in output the required syntactic transformation. This transducer is then composed with the interpreter, forcing the distorter output language to be the input one of the interpreter, hence generating a transformed CFG. This transformed CFG will be the source of interpretation.

Definition 10 (Interpreter Distorter). *Let* $\mathtt{int} = \langle \mathtt{cfgEx}, \mathcal{S}[\cdot] \rangle$ *be an interpreter accepting in input the language* $\mathfrak{L}$. *An interpreter distorter* D *is a SFST whose output language is a (strict) subset of* $\mathfrak{L}$ *and preserving program semantics, i.e.,* $\mathtt{int}^{\mathtt{D}} \stackrel{\mathrm{def}}{=} \langle \mathtt{D} \diamond \mathtt{cfgEx}, \mathcal{S}[\cdot] \rangle$ *is the distorted interpreter if* $\forall \mathsf{P} \in \mathfrak{L}.\mathfrak{T}_{\mathtt{D}}(\mathsf{P}) \in \mathfrak{L}$ *and* $\mathcal{S}[\mathsf{P}] = \mathcal{S}[\mathfrak{T}_{\mathtt{D}}(\mathsf{P})]$.

Note that, if $\mathtt{T}_{\mathtt{pars}}$ is the trivial transducer associated with $\mathtt{pars}$, then $\mathtt{T}_{\mathtt{pars}} \diamond \mathtt{cfgEx} = \mathtt{cfgEx}$.

Example: Trivial Syntactic Distorter. Suppose $\mathtt{f}_{\mathtt{b}}$: BExp $\rightarrow$ BExp and $\mathtt{f}_{\mathtt{c}}$: Stm $\rightarrow$ Stm be semantic preserving transformers, i.e., $\forall \mathtt{b} \in \mathrm{BExp}.\ [\![\mathtt{b}]\!] = [\![\mathtt{f}_{\mathtt{b}}(\mathtt{b})]\!]$ and $\forall \mathtt{c} \in \mathrm{Stm}.\ [\![\mathtt{c}]\!] = [\![\mathtt{f}_{\mathtt{c}}(\mathtt{c})]\!]$, then the distorter in Fig. 6 is a trivial distorter, where the empty stack update $\varepsilon \rightarrow \varepsilon$ and the R moves are omitted in the transitions. As the parser, it is a symbolic pushdown automaton, which transforms the code while parsing it.

Theorem 3. *Let* $\mathtt{int}$ *be a* $\mathfrak{L}$ *interpreter and let* $\mathtt{int}^{\mathtt{D}}$ *be distorted by* D. *Then* $\forall \mathsf{P} = \{\mathtt{C} \in \} \mathfrak{L}$ *we have* $[\![\mathtt{int}[\mathsf{P}]]\!] = [\![\mathtt{int}^{\mathtt{D}}[\mathsf{P}]]\!]$.

This result tells us that the semantics of the program obtained by specializing the distorted interpreter is the same as the semantics of the original program, providing so far a potential obfuscation. Whether it is an obfuscation depends on the property we want to hide, and therefore it depends on the specific distortion and on the specific program semantics.

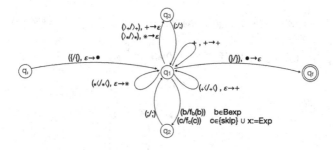

Fig. 6. The trivial distortion

6 Obfuscation by Specializing Distorted Interpreters

In this section we show some examples of interpreter distortion making the CFG specializer disoptimal, therefore producing obfuscated code. As observed before, the first step is to fix the property to hide by obfuscation and a syntactic element making the analysis of this property incomplete. In other words, given a program property $\mathcal{A}$ to hide, we define a $\mathcal{A}$-distorting interpreter, namely an interpreter for which the specializer implementing *spec* is $\mathcal{A}$-disoptimal. This is obtained by isolating a syntactic object producing imprecision and by embedding these objects into the code in such a way the abstract interpretation on $\mathcal{A}$ of the resulting program becomes incomplete.

As an example, in order to obfuscate the program control flow we observe that incompleteness is obtained by injecting opaque predicates in the program [20], hence by using the trivial interpreter distorter we can obfuscate CFG simply by defining the following transformers where $\underline{b} \in$ BExp is an opaque predicate (e.g., an always true predicate), $b' \in$ BExp and $c' \in$ Stms.[12]

$$f_c(c) \overset{\text{def}}{=} {}_+\langle \underline{b}; c + \neg\underline{b}; c'\rangle_+$$
$$f_b(b) \overset{\text{def}}{=} {}_+\langle \underline{b}; b + \neg\underline{b}; b'\rangle_+$$

Data Obfuscation: Parity Obfuscation. Suppose we aim at obfuscating the parity *Par* (formalized as the well-known parity abstraction on numerical values) observation of data [18], i.e., of variable integer values[13]. First of all we provide a general data abstraction distorter, where we define an expression transformers (f_c and f_b) executing a value transformation hiding the property to obfuscate when storing data, and a complementary (i.e., which composed returns the identity) transformation when accessing data [18]. For instance, for obfuscating parity, when we store data we can multiply by 2 (hiding parity),

---

[12] For space reasons, and being quite intuitive, we do not provide the whole formalization of obfuscation by opaque predicates.

[13] For the sake of simplicity we suppose, without losing generality, that variables can only contain integer values, not boolean.

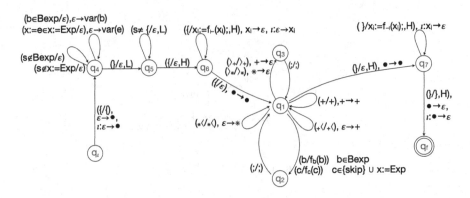

Fig. 7. Data obfuscation interpreter distorter D_{Data}.

and therefore when we access data we have to divide by 2. In order to make everything work, we have to make analogous transformations of variables values at the beginning $(f_\vdash)$ and at the end of the program $(f_\dashv)$. Hence, a simple pushdown automaton is not sufficient since, for these last variables updates, we have to scan the whole program for collecting variable names. In particular, in Fig. 7 we define D_{Data}, where q_4 extracts all the variables accessed in the program and put them on a stack ($var(e)$ and $var(b)$ are sequences of identifiers), q_5 goes back to beginning of the program and q_6 adds, at the beginning, an assignment involving each variable extracted to which we assign its transformation by $f_\vdash$. While creating this assignments we keep in the stack ι the names of all the variables for creating the final assignments at the end of the program (state q_7) assigning to each variable its transformation by $f_\dashv$.

Hence, we define D_{Par} by defining the transformations f_c, f_b, $f_\vdash$ and $f_\dashv$ as follows, where $Var(P) = \{x_i\}_{i \in [1,n]}$

$$f_\vdash(x) \stackrel{\text{def}}{=} 2 * x \qquad\qquad f_\dashv(x) \stackrel{\text{def}}{=} x/2$$

$$f_c(c) \stackrel{\text{def}}{=} \begin{cases} 2 * f_{ex}(a) & \text{if } c = x := a \\ \textbf{skip} & \text{if } c = \textbf{skip} \end{cases} \qquad f_b(b) \stackrel{\text{def}}{=} f_{ex}(b)$$

$$f_{ex}(x) \stackrel{\text{def}}{=} x/2 \qquad\qquad f_{ex}(n) \stackrel{\text{def}}{=} n$$

$$f_{ex}(e \; bop \; e) \stackrel{\text{def}}{=} f_{ex}(e) \; bop \; f_{ex}(e) \qquad f_{ex}(\neg b) \stackrel{\text{def}}{=} \neg f_{ex}(b)$$

In Fig. 8, on the left, we have the parity obfuscation of the program whose CFG is depicted in Fig. 2. The following theorem tells us that the so far designed interpreter distorter provides us with a parity obfuscation technique by specializing the distorted interpreter. Intuitively, at the first access to each variable, by dividing by 2 its value, we lose its parity, adding analysis imprecision and making so far the abstract parity interpreter incomplete, the specializer disoptimal and the resulting program obfuscated w.r.t. parity.

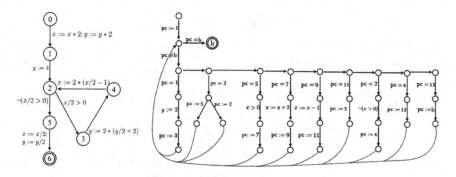

Fig. 8. Obfuscated CFGs.

Theorem 4. *Let* $\text{int}_{Par} \stackrel{\text{def}}{=} \langle D_{Par} \diamond \text{cfgEx}, [\![\cdot]\!]_c \rangle$ *be the distorted interpreter. It is a Par-distorting interpreter, meaning that* $\forall P \in \mathfrak{L}.\ spec(\text{int}_{Par}, P)$ *is an obfuscation of* P *w.r.t* $\mathcal{A}_{Par}$.

Control Obfuscation: CFG Flattening. The last example consists in obfuscating the CFG by flattening its structure [7,36]. For obfuscating programs by flattening the CFG it is sufficient to make the program counter (pc) dynamic, i.e., a variable of the program manipulated during execution. Indeed, in this way the CFG observation (and therefore any CFG property) becomes imprecise [20]. Hence the idea is precisely to provide the transformers distorting the interpreter by handling the program counter while executing the program.

Then, let us consider the new variable pc, we define the distorted parser by inserting each statement in a branch of a non-deterministic choice, whose guard is the value of pc, value that is created and updated during execution. Also this distorter D_{Flat} (Fig. 9) cannot be simply a pushdown automaton for two issues to face. First, we have to *count* the number of deterministic choices we insert, in order to know how many brackets $\rangle_+$ we have to insert at the end (q_4). The stack cl is used precisely with this purpose. The other issue to face, is the fact that when we read $_*\langle$ or $_+\langle$ we cannot know how many statement we will have respectively in the body or in the first branch, hence we cannot predict the value for pc that we can use for skipping the loop or for the other branch. For this reason we use two stacks p (principal) and s (secondary) in order to keep two disjoint chains of values for pc (even and odd values). Finally we have another stack c for keeping trace of the pc of the first statement of a loop and of the final pc of a branch. Moreover, we consider a special value 1_f as final pc.

On the right of Fig. 8 the obfuscation of the program whose CFG is depicted in Fig. 2.

Formally, let us characterize the semantic abstraction made incomplete by flattening the program. Here we can simplify the previous characterization [20] since it is sufficient to find an abstraction made incomplete by a dynamic pc

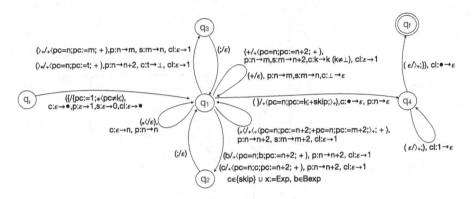

Fig. 9. Flattening obfuscation interpreter distorter D_{Flat}.

(we are not looking for an abstraction incomplete *iff* the *pc* is dynamic), and it should be clear that such an abstraction is precisely the CFG: Let us define

$$\mathcal{A}^{Flat} \stackrel{\text{def}}{=} \lambda[\![P]\!]_c. \ [\![Cfg(P)]\!]_c$$

where it is well known that program collecting semantics is an abstraction of its small-step semantics and

$$[\![Cfg(P)]\!]_c \stackrel{\text{def}}{=} \left\{ \sigma \in S^* \ \middle| \ \begin{array}{l} \forall i \in \mathbb{N}. \ f^{cfgEx[P]}_{CollR_{sp}}(q_i, \sigma_i) \in \{\langle q_{i+1}, \sigma_{i+1}\rangle, \sigma_{i+1}\} \\ q_0 = q_\iota, \ \sigma_0 = [q_\iota \mapsto \mathbb{M}] \end{array} \right\}$$

In this way, it should be clear that $Cfg(P)$ is an abstraction of P, since the set of possible executions contains the set of executions[14].

The following theorem tells us that in order to lose any property of the CFG structure we need to handle the program counter (*pc*) deciding the next statement to execute in the program. Intuitively in this way the semantic abstraction, by abstracting the guards involving the *pc*, loses the CFG structure, and therefore any of its properties.

Theorem 5. *Let* $\text{int}_{Flat} \stackrel{\text{def}}{=} \langle D_{Flat} \diamond cfgEx, [\![\cdot]\!]_c \rangle$ *be the distorted interpreter. It is a $\mathcal{F}$-distorting interpreter, meaning that* $\forall P \in \mathfrak{L}. \ spec(\text{int}_{Flat}, P)$ *is an obfuscation of* P *w.r.t* $\mathcal{A}^{Flat}$.

7   Conclusions

Our paper shows that code transformations for anti reverse engineering, such as code obfuscating transformations, can be designed systematically by specializing distorted interpreters. The idea proposed is to design an obfuscation starting from the static property π to conceal and determining syntactic elements such

---

[14] We can also let the computations start from a subset of initial memories.

that the static analysis of π is imprecise/incomplete. Then we can build a distorter D inductively embedding these elements in single statements of programs without changing their semantics. Finally the distorted interpreter we obtain so far becomes an obfuscator of π when specialized w.r.t. the program to obfuscate, since for the resulting program the static analysis of π is forced to be incomplete. The result is a systematic method for building obfuscating compilers as straight applications of the well known Futamura's projections, therefore going beyond the very first approach [20].

On the Limits of the Approach. The main limit of the proposed approach consists in the fact that it is built on a static model of attacker, namely aiming at defeating reverse engineering techniques based on static program analyses. In particular, on the one hand we believe that it is possible to capture any obfuscation technique where the information to obfuscate is a (static) program property that can be characterized as program/code abstraction, such as slicing obfuscation and opaque predicate obfuscation, on the other hand there probably exist dynamic obfuscation techniques that may not be modeled in the framework as it is, such as self-modifying code and virtualization. Indeed, what we propose is an interpreter distortion based on the distortion of the parser, which is a distortion limited to *obfuscating properties strictly depending on how the code is written*, namely for deceiving static analyses. Nevertheless, the separation of the static and the dynamic phases of the interpreter suggests us that we could try to capture other obfuscation techniques by distorting the semantic interpretation phase, where it is plausible to think of making possible to obfuscate dynamic analyses, but this clearly needs further work.

Another limit of this work is that it is not yet evaluated by means of an implementation. Anyway we believe that this will not represent a problem at least as far as the computational impact is concerned, since once we have built the interpreter depending on the property to obfuscate, then the complexity of the specialization is linear on the length of the program (transformation is performed while parsing the code). While, as far as the computational overhead of the obfuscated program is concerned, it does not depend on the proposed approach but on the way the code is transformed, and therefore on the specific chosen transformation.

Future Works. The notion of Jones optimality can be seen in a wider perspective, not just as a method for removing the overhead in time complexity, but as an universal paradigm to determine when a specializer applied to an interpreter and a program reestablish the initial conditions of the program relatively to some measure [6]. Hence, the existence of Jones optimal specializers is a key aspect in modern PL research (e.g., see the Brown and Palsberg striking result [3]). We believe that widening the range of applicability of the notion of Jones optimality to different (complexity) measures may provide the perfect theoretical framework to understand how the intensional nature of code affects the way we analyze it. Our paper provides a very first application to the case of the precision of an abstract interpreter.

References

1. Arceri, V., Mastroeni, I.: Analyzing dynamic code: a sound abstract interpreter for evil eval. ACM Trans. Priv. Secur. **24**(2), 10:1–10:38 (2021)
2. Barak, B., et al.: On the (im)possibility of obfuscating programs. J. ACM **59**(2), 6 (2012)
3. Brown, M., Palsberg, J.: Jones-optimal partial evaluation by specialization-safe normalization. Proc. ACM Program. Lang. **2**(POPL), 14:1–14:28 (2018). https://doi.org/10.1145/3158102
4. Bruni, R., Giacobazzi, R., Gori, R., Garcia-Contreras, I., Pavlovic, D.: Abstract extensionality: on the properties of incomplete abstract interpretations. Proc. ACM Program. Lang. **4**(POPL), 28:1–28:28 (2020). https://doi.org/10.1145/3371096
5. Bruni, R., Giacobazzi, R., Gori, R., Ranzato, F.: A logic for locally complete abstract interpretations. In: Symposium on Logic in Computer Science, LICS, pp. 1–13. IEEE (2021)
6. Campion, M., Dalla Preda, M., Giacobazzi, R.: Partial (in)completeness in abstract interpretation: limiting the imprecision in program analysis. Proc. ACM Program. Lang. **6**(POPL), 1–31 (2022). https://doi.org/10.1145/3498721
7. Chow, S., Eisen, P., Johnson, H., van Oorschot, P.C.: A white-box DES implementation for DRM applications. In: Feigenbaum, J. (ed.) DRM 2002. LNCS, vol. 2696, pp. 1–15. Springer, Heidelberg (2003). https://doi.org/10.1007/978-3-540-44993-5_1
8. Collberg, C., Herzberg, A., Gu, Y., Giacobazzi, R., Wang, F., Davidson, J.: Toward digital asset protection. IEEE Intell. Syst. **26**(06), 8–13 (2011). https://doi.org/10.1109/MIS.2011.106
9. Collberg, C., Nagra, J.: Surreptitious Software: Obfuscation, Watermarking, and Tamperproofing for Software Protection. Addison-Wesley Professional, Boston (2009)
10. Collberg, C., Thomborson, C.: Watermarking, tamper-proofing, and obduscation-tools for software protection. IEEE Trans. Software Eng. 735–746 (2002)
11. Consel, C., Lawall, J., Meur, A.F.L.: A tour of Tempo: a program specializer for the C language. Sci. Comput. Program. **52**(17(1)), 47–92 (2004)
12. Cousot, P.: Constructive design of a hierarchy of semantics of a transition system by abstract interpretation. Theor. Comput. Sci. **277**(1–2), 47–103 (2002)
13. Cousot, P., Cousot, R.: Abstract interpretation: a unified lattice model for static analysis of programs by construction or approximation of fixpoints. In: Conference Record of the 4th ACM Symposium on Principles of Programming Languages (POPL 1977), pp. 238–252. ACM Press (1977)
14. Cousot, P., Cousot, R.: Systematic design of program analysis frameworks. In: Conference Record of the 6th ACM Symposium on Principles of Programming Languages (POPL 1979), pp. 269–282. ACM Press (1979)
15. Cousot, P., Giacobazzi, R., Ranzato, F.: A^2i: abstract^2 interpretation. Proc. ACM Program. Lang. **3**(POPL), 42:1–42:31 (2019)
16. Dalla Preda, M., Mastroeni, I.: Characterizing a property-driven obfuscation strategy. J. Comput. Secur. **26**(1), 31–69 (2018)
17. D'Antoni, L., Veanes, M.: Minimization of symbolic automata. In: POPL, pp. 541–554 (2014)
18. Drape, S.: Obfuscation of abstract data-types. Ph.D. thesis, University of Oxford (2004)

19. Giacobazzi, R.: Hiding information in completeness holes - new perspectives in code obfuscation and watermarking. In: Proceedings of the 6th IEEE International Conferences on Software Engineering and Formal Methods (SEFM 2008), pp. 7–20. IEEE Press (2008)
20. Giacobazzi, R., Jones, N.D., Mastroeni, I.: Obfuscation by partial evaluation of distorted interpreters. In: Kiselyov, O., Thompson, S. (eds.) Proceedings of the ACM SIGPLAN Symposium on Partial Evaluation and Semantics-Based Program Manipulation (PEPM 2012), pp. 63–72. ACM Press (2012)
21. Giacobazzi, R., Mastroeni, I., Dalla Preda, M.: Maximal incompleteness as obfuscation potency. Formal Asp. Comput. **29**(1), 3–31 (2017)
22. Giacobazzi, R., Ranzato, F., Scozzari., F.: Making abstract interpretation complete. J. ACM **47**(2), 361–416 (2000)
23. Giacobazzi, R., Logozzo, F., Ranzato, F.: Analyzing program analyses. In: Rajamani, S.K., Walker, D. (eds.) Proceedings of the 42nd Annual ACM SIGPLAN-SIGACT Symposium on Principles of Programming Languages, POPL 2015, Mumbai, India, 15–17 January 2015, pp. 261–273. ACM (2015)
24. Giacobazzi, R., Pavlovic, D., Terauchi, T.: Intensional and extensional aspects of computation: From computability and complexity to program analysis and security (NII Shonan Meeting 2018-1). In: NII Shonan Meeting Report 2018 (2018)
25. Glück, R.: Jones optimality, binding-time improvements, and the strength of program specializers. In: Asai, K., Chin, W. (eds.) Proceedings of the ACM SIGPLAN ASIA-PEPM 2002, Asian Symposium on Partial Evaluation and Semantics-Based Program Manipulation, Aizu, Japan, 12–14 September 2002, pp. 9–19. ACM (2002)
26. Jones, N.D.: Transformation by interpreter specialisation. Sci. Comput. Programm. **52**(17(1)), 307–339 (2004)
27. Jones, N.D., Gomard, C.K., Sestoft, P.: Partial Evaluation and Automatic Program Generation. Prentice-Hall, Inc., Upper Saddle River (1993)
28. Jørgensen, J.: Similix: a self-applicable partial evaluator for scheme. In: Hatcliff, J., Mogensen, T.Æ., Thiemann, P. (eds.) DIKU 1998. LNCS, vol. 1706, pp. 83–107. Springer, Heidelberg (1999). https://doi.org/10.1007/3-540-47018-2_3
29. Leuschel, M.: Advanced logic program specialisation. In: Hatcliff, J., Mogensen, T.Æ., Thiemann, P. (eds.) DIKU 1998. LNCS, vol. 1706, pp. 271–292. Springer, Heidelberg (1999). https://doi.org/10.1007/3-540-47018-2_11
30. O'Hearn, P.W.: Incorrectness logic. Proc. ACM Program. Lang. (POPL) **4**(10) (2020)
31. Rogers, H.: Theory of Recursive Functions and Effective Computability. The MIT Press, Cambridge (1992)
32. Romanenko, S.: Unmix, a Specializer for a Subset of Scheme. Keldysh Institute, Moscow (1993–2009). http://code.google.com/p/unmix/
33. Seidl, H., Wilhelm, R., Hack, S.: Compiler Design - Analysis and Transformation. Springer, Heidelberg (2012). https://doi.org/10.1007/978-3-642-17548-0
34. Thiemann, P.: Aspects of the PGG system: specialization for standard scheme. In: Hatcliff, J., Mogensen, T.Æ., Thiemann, P. (eds.) DIKU 1998. LNCS, vol. 1706, pp. 412–432. Springer, Heidelberg (1999). https://doi.org/10.1007/3-540-47018-2_17
35. Veanes, M., Hooimeijer, P., Livshits, B., Molnar, D., Bjørner, N.: Symbolic finite state transducers: algorithms and applications. In: POPL, pp. 137–150 (2012)
36. Wang, C., Davidson, J., Hill, J., Knight, J.: Protection of software-based survivability mechanisms. In: IEEE International Conference of Dependable Systems and Networks, Goteborg, pp. 193–202 (2001)
37. Winskel, G.: The Formal Semantics of Programming Languages: An Introduction. MIT Press, Cambridge (1993)

Bootstrapping Library-Based Synthesis

Kangjing Huang and Xiaokang Qiu

Purdue University, West Lafayette, IN 47907, USA
{huangkangjing,xkqiu}@purdue.edu

Abstract. Constraint-based program synthesis techniques have been widely used in numerous settings. However, synthesizing programs that use libraries remains a major challenge. To handle complex or black-box libraries, the state of the art is to provide carefully crafted mocks or models to the synthesizer, requiring extra manual work. We address this challenge by proposing TOSHOKAN, a new synthesis framework as an alternative approach in which library-using programs can be generated without any user-provided artifacts at the cost of moderate performance overhead. The framework extends the classic counterexample-guided synthesis framework with a bootstrapping, log-based library model. The model collects input-output samples from running failed candidate programs on witness inputs. We prove that the framework is sound when a sound, bounded verifier is available, and also complete if the underlying synthesizer and verifier promise to produce minimal outputs. We implement and incorporate the framework to JSKETCH, a Java sketching tool. Experiments show that TOSHOKAN can successfully synthesize programs that use a variety of libraries, ranging from mathematical functions to data structures. Comparing to state-of-the-art synthesis algorithms which use mocks or models, TOSHOKAN reduces up to 159 lines of code of required manual inputs, at the cost of less than 40 s of performance overheads.

Keywords: Program synthesis · Libraries · Java · Program sketching

1 Introduction

Recent years have seen drastic progress in the development of constraint-based synthesis technology, made possible by the advances in formal methods and automated constraint solvers. The constraint solving based techniques guarantee that the synthesized program satisfies formal specifications and make synthesis algorithms much more scalable, stepping across domain-specific programming

G. Singh and C. Urban (Eds.): SAS 2022, LNCS 13790, pp. 272–298, 2022.
https://doi.org/10.1007/978-3-031-22308-2_13

tasks and applicable to general-purpose software development using practical, real-world languages, such as C/C++ [39,41], Python [34], OCaml [9], Java [14, 20,25,27], or JavaScript [32,37].

Toward using constraint-based synthesis to aid practical software development, a major challenge is synthesizing programs that use libraries, which is common in most real-world software. Note that state-of-the-art programming tools such as those for component-based synthesis [12,14,24,33,43] and unit-test generation [3,29] only need to run candidate programs (including the library) for testing. However, for constraint-based synthesis, the synthesizer has to symbolically reason about and analyze the libraries and generate client code that appropriately exercises library calls. The simplest solution to support libraries would be inlining—concatenate the library source code onto the synthesis problem and handle library methods just like other methods. Unfortunately, in practice, libraries are designed for flexibility and extensibility, making their code large and complex, and hence difficult for the synthesizer to use. For example, the Android platform, which contains more than 12 million lines of code [10], is too big to reason about for any existing synthesizer. Even worse, some libraries may contain native code, which is entirely out of reach of this approach.

To address this issue, a straightforward approach is to manually create *mock libraries*—short pieces of code at the appropriate level of abstraction such that the essential library functionality is implemented in a simple and analyzable way. This approach is adopted by state-of-the-art sketch-based synthesis tools [20,35]. While mocks can be effective, they require extra manual work as balancing the code simplicity and the accuracy of functional equivalence to the authentic implementation. For example, JSKETCH [20] mocks the Java standard library java.util.TreeSet using an object array, whose size can be either bounded or dynamically resizable. The former option is simpler but may fail to mimic the TreeSet's behavior when too many objects are added; the latter option is observably equivalent to the TreeSet container but introduces extra complexity, which makes synthesis performance slow. Researchers have developed techniques to automatically create mock libraries [4,5,16,19] for program analysis or symbolic execution. However, these techniques focus on special classes of libraries and the generated mocks do not aim to aid program synthesis.

Another approach is to use non-executable specifications as *library models*. These models usually capture the essential properties of the library which can be leveraged by the synthesizer. For example, a critical property for a cryptography library is that any decryption after an encryption with the same key is the identity. In [25], this property is described as an algebraic specification: decrypt(encrypt(m, k), k) ⇒ m. Library models are also developed and used in other state-of-the-art synthesis tools, in various novel ways [15,21,23,38,41]. While this approach is promising in both terms of simplicity and performance, it still requires extra manual work in writing the library specifications. This is actually the well-known *specification mining* problem for formal verification, which has been studied for many years [1,2,11,22]. Moreover, these models are hard to reason about automatically and need special treatment when integrated into a synthesis tool. This limits the possible applications their approach may stretch to. For example, The rewriting-based encoding in JLibSketch [25] only handles library models that can be represented as equational axioms.

In this paper, we propose a new synthesis framework called TOSHOKAN ("library" in Japanese) to support constraint-based synthesis algorithms for handling libraries. This framework takes an alternative approach to the problem, extending counterexample-guided inductive synthesis (CEGIS)—a standard inductive synthesis framework [40]—with an automatically built library model from logged behavior of the library. Intuitively, the proposed framework approximates the behavior of the library using a dynamic set of input-output samples, and guesses the output of the library when the input is not covered by any sample. In each CEGIS iteration, when the verifier rejects a candidate program and provides a witness input, a logger runs the failed candidate with the witness input. The witness execution exercises the library on some critical input and the logged input-output pair is added to the library sampling. As the CEGIS loop runs, more and more logs are gained and the sampling eventually becomes precise enough and allows the synthesis problem to be solved or rejected. Comparing with existing library-based synthesis approaches, TOSHOKAN has the following advantages:

1. it does not require any extra manual work (except for the optional query function annotation as discussed in Sect. 4) like writing mock implementation or library models;
2. it synthesizes *provably-correct* programs using real Java libraries, whose correctness is guaranteed by an off-the-shelf verifier (currently JBMC); and
3. it allows the synthesizer to treat the library as a *black box*, making the task solvable using state-of-the-art Java sketching tool through careful encodings.

We give an overview of the TOSHOKAN framework and elaborate how it works through an example in Sect. 2. We then in Sect. 3 formally describe the library-based synthesis problem, the major components of the framework, and the main synthesis algorithm, and prove its soundness and relative completeness. Then in Sect. 4, we embody the framework in the setting of sketch-based synthesis, and present the techniques used in the angelic inductive synthesizer, the centerpiece of the TOSHOKAN framework, including three different library encodings. In Sect. 5, we discuss the design of the library logger, focusing on how we handle references and aliasing, termination and exceptions.

We implemented the TOSHOKAN framework in JSKETCH [20]—a sketch-based Java synthesizer—and compared the new system with standard JSKETCH that supports user-provided models or mocks.[1] The results demonstrate that, TOSHOKAN successfully synthesized correct code for all 11 benchmarks and saves the user from the extra manual work of writing library-abstracting mocks or models. Meanwhile, for most benchmarks, our performance is moderately slower than but still comparable to existing algorithms. More detailed experimental results can be found in Sect. 6.

---

[1] The validated artifact is available via DOI 10.5281/zenodo.7009051.

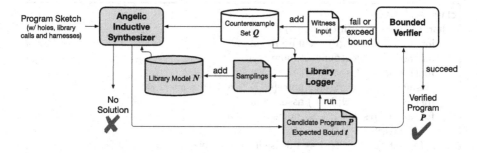

Fig. 1. Overview of the TOSHOKAN framework (distinct components in gray).

2   Overview

Figure 1 gives an overview of the TOSHOKAN framework, with the components distinct from standard CEGIS highlighted in gray. In addition to the standard components from normal CEGIS (verifier, synthesizer, counterexample set, etc.), the proposed framework features a *log-based library model* and a *library logger*. Whenever a candidate program P failed to be verified, the library logger takes P along with the authentic library (either source or binaries), runs the program on all existing counterexample inputs Q, and collects all observed library samplings, i.e., input-output pairs when the library is invoked. These samplings collectively form a library model N, which is an underspecification of the library, i.e., only partially covers the behavior of the library. The angelic inductive synthesizer (AIS) in TOSHOKAN takes N and determines the uncovered behavior of the library *angelically*. In other words, if the model does not cover a particular input, the AIS can determine the corresponding output arbitrarily. In each iteration, the AIS proposes a program P along with an expected bound t under which P should terminate on all inputs from Q; the bounded verifier checks whether P, along with the authentic library, satisfies the specification and terminates in t steps on all inputs. The whole synthesis process terminates when the verifier accepts the proposed program, or when the AIS concludes that there is no solution for the current counterexample set Q and library model N.

TOSHOKAN **by Example** We give a step-by-step illustration of TOSHOKAN's synthesis process through a simple JSKETCH example. Figure 2 shows the *gcd_n_numbers* benchmark (adapted from the Sketch source distribution [36]). The method MultiGCD.main purports to compute the greatest common divider (GCD) of five input integers, using Java standard library java.math.BigInteger.gcd[2] to compute the binary GCD. As a program sketch, the for-loop that calls gcd involves some unknown holes and choices (highlighted in the code) to be filled. Note that the authentic code for gcd is complicated and may even not be available as a black-box library. Hence the user has to provide

---

[2] The actual library operates BigInteger objects; for simplicity, we adapt the signature to handle int's.

```
1  class MultiGCD { /* synthesize algorithm for gcd of N numbers */
2    harness void main(int[] nums) {
3      int n = nums.length; assume n ≥ 2; ...
4      int result = gcd(nums[0], nums[1]);
5      for (int i = ??; i < {| n | n − 1 | n − 2 |}; i++)
6        result = gcd({| result | nums[i] |}, {| result | nums[i] |});
7      for (int i =0; i<N; i++) assert nums[i] % result== 0;
8      for (int i =result+1; i ≤ nums[0]; i++) {
9        bit divisible = 1;
10       for (int j =0; j<N; j++) divisible = divisible && (nums[j] %i == 0);
11       assert !divisible ;
12     }
13  }}
```

Fig. 2. JSKETCH example: *gcd_n_numbers*.

JSKETCH (or the underlying Sketch engine) a mock library or a library model (e.g., see [36]). Both require expertise and extra work from the user (16 and 20 LoC, respectively).

With TOSHOKAN, the user does not need to write mocks or models anymore. Table 1 shows how TOSHOKAN solves this synthesis problem in 4 iterations,[3] *without any user-provided artifacts*. In the initial iteration, the synthesizer proposes a random solution as the candidate program. Then the bounded verifier, which for this example is JBMC [8], checks whether the solution terminates in a fixed number of steps and satisfies all assertions on all inputs nums. The verifier reports a concrete input that violates assertions: num = {3,3,3,1,3}. Besides returning this witness input to the synthesizer, the most noteworthy thing is that TOSHOKAN also runs the failed candidate on the witness input with the authentic gcd implementation, and logs the input-output samples of the all library calls. In this instance, the logger collects a sample gcd(3,3) = 3 and adds it to the library model N. This library model helps the synthesizer understand why the first candidate fails.

With the collected witness input and library sampling, the synthesizer proceeds to the second iteration and proposes a new candidate program. In this iteration, the verifier provides a new witness input num = {2,2,2,2,1}. This time, the logger runs the candidate program with both the current and the previous witness inputs, and collects two samples: gcd(1,3) = 1 and gcd(2,2) = 2. This process continues and collects new witness inputs and library samplings in each iteration, until the synthesizer finds the correct solution in the fourth iteration. The whole synthesis process finishes within 23 s (see full performance data in Sect. 6).

---

[3] TOSHOKAN can actually solve this problem in 1 iteration (see Sect. 6); we use this 4-iteration run for illustration purpose.

Table 1. A TOSHOKAN run for the *gcd_n_numbers* problem in Fig. 2.

Iter#	Candidate Program (filling lines 5–6)	Witness Input	Collected Sampling
1	for(int i = 4; i ¡ n-1; i++) result = gcd(result, result);	nums = {3,3,3,1,3}	gcd(3,3)=3
2	for(int i = 2; i ¡ n-1; i++) result = gcd(num[i], result);	nums = {2,2,2,2,1}	gcd(1,3)=1, gcd(2,2)=2
3	for(int i = 3; i ¡ n; i++) result = gcd(num[i], num[i]);	nums = {3,3,2,3,3}	gcd(1,1)=1
4	for(int i = 1; i ¡ n; i++) result = gcd(num[i], result);	success	N/A

3 The TOSHOKAN Framework

In this section, we formally define the synthesis problem and introduce the main synthesis algorithm in TOSHOKAN. Note that the formalism we give in this section is purely semantical—it is agnostic to the syntax of the program and the implementation of the components it relies on. This allows us to present the key idea of TOSHOKAN framework in a succinct and general way. We will present in the next section more specifically, in the setting of sketch-based synthesis, how the synthesis problem is formulated and solved.

3.1 Libraries

Definition 1 (Library Signature). *A library signature is a pair $\Sigma = (S, \{\Sigma_{w,s}\}_{(w,s)\in S^*\times S})$, where S is a set of sorts, and $\{\Sigma_{w,s}\}_{(w,s)\in S^*\times S}$ is an $S^*\times S$-indexed family of sets of symbols. We denote the set of all symbols by $Funcs(\Sigma)$.*

Definition 2 (Library). *For $\Sigma = (S, \{\Sigma_{w,s}\}_{(w,s)\in S^*\times S})$ a library signature, a Σ-library $L_\Sigma = \{L_f\}_{f\in Funcs(\Sigma)}$ is a family of computable functions $L_f : w \to s$ for each symbol $f \in \Sigma_{w,s}$.*

Example 1. The library signature for the overview example is constituted by a single sort and a single function: $\Sigma = (\{\mathbb{Z}\}, \{\{\mathsf{gcd}\}_{\mathbb{Z}^2\to\mathbb{Z}}\})$. In other words, the signature contains a single symbol gcd, which belongs to $\Sigma_{\mathbb{Z}^2\to\mathbb{Z}}$. We denote the authentic Σ-library as $\mathsf{Real}_\Sigma = \{\mathsf{Real}_{\mathsf{gcd}}\}$, where $\mathsf{Real}_{\mathsf{gcd}} : \mathbb{Z} \times \mathbb{Z} \to \mathbb{Z}$ computes the binary greatest common divider.

Remark: Note that the library functions are defined to be computable and deterministic. This allows us to treat the library as a black box and make queries: providing concrete input values and asking what the output value is.

Handling Side Effect. Definition 2 considers pure library functions without side effects or multiple return values. This restriction does not affect the expressiveness of our framework as the definition is sufficient for encoding more complex libraries in real world. For example, we follow the idea of JLibSketch [25] to handle side effects. Given a Java class which maintains a complex internal state and contains methods that query and update the current internal state, every method in the class can be encoded to a pair of library function: both functions take the current state of the class as an extra argument; one gives the expected return value of the method and one gives the updated state of the class.

Example 2. Consider the class java.util.Stack in Java with an initializer init and two methods void push(int i) and int pop(). This class can be encoded to a library with four functions. The signature of the library is $\Sigma = (\{\mathbb{Z}, \text{Stack}\}, \{\text{pop}\}_{\text{Stack} \to \mathbb{Z}}, \{\text{pop!}\}_{\text{Stack} \to \text{Stack}})$. A function pop : Stack $\to \mathbb{Z}$ captures the value returned from Stack.pop(). In addition, the side effects of the two methods can be represented as library functions push! : Stack $\times \mathbb{Z} \to$ Stack and pop! : Stack $\to$ Stack.

Definition 3 (Sampling). *For Σ a library signature, a Σ-sampling is a family of sets $N_\Sigma = \{N_f\}_{f \in Funcs(\Sigma)}$ in which there is a finite set $N_f \subseteq_{fin} w \times s$ for each $f \in Funcs(\Sigma)$.*

Definition 4 (Consistency). *A Σ-sampling N is consistent with a Σ-library L, denoted as $N \prec_\Sigma L$, if for any $f \in Funcs(\Sigma)$ and any $(t, v) \in N_f$, $L_f(t) = v$.*

Example 3. In the overview example, as shown in Table 1, a Σ-sampling is maintained and expanded in each iteration of the synthesis process. After all four iterations, the sampling is $N = \{N_{\text{gcd}}\}$ where $N_{\text{gcd}} = \{(3,3,3), (1,3,1), (2,2,2), (1,1,1)\}$. By Definition 4, this sampling is consistent with the authentic library defined in Example 1, i.e., $N_{\text{gcd}} \prec_\Sigma \text{Real}_{\text{gcd}}$.

3.2   The Library-Based Synthesis Problem

We next present the library-based synthesis problem, which is essentially tasked to find a correct program interacting with a known library. From the perspective of parametric programming, the space of candidate programs can be encode as a parameter and the underlying library can be given as another parameter. In other words, the synthesis problem can be represented as a parameterized program $\mathcal{P}[c, L](i)$ whose behavior is determined by the input i and two parameters: parameter c controls how to concretize $\mathcal{P}$ to a complete program; and parameter L is the concrete library that $\mathcal{P}$ calls. Once c and L are determined, $\mathcal{P}[c, L]$ becomes a complete program whose behavior is deterministic and verifiable.

The specification of the synthesis problem is also represented semantically by giving a validation condition. In other words, a program satisfies the specification if and only if all concrete runs of the program satisfy the validation condition.

Definition 5 (Validation Condition). *A validation condition for a parameterized program $\mathcal{P}$ is a family of formulae $\phi_\mathcal{P} = \{\phi_\mathcal{P}^t(c, L, i)\}_{t \in \mathbb{N}}$, in which each $\phi_\mathcal{P}^t(c, L, i)$ is satisfied if and only if running $\mathcal{P}[c, L]$ on input i terminates within t steps and satisfies the specification.*

Definition 6 (Library-Based Synthesis Problem). *A library-based synthesis problem is represented as a tuple $(\mathcal{P}, C, L_{Real}, \phi_\mathcal{P})$ where $\mathcal{P}$ is a parameterized program, C is the space of parameters for $\mathcal{P}$, L_{Real} is the library used in $\mathcal{P}$, and $\phi_\mathcal{P}$ is a validation condition for $\mathcal{P}$. The synthesis problem is to find a value $ctr \in C$ and a bound t such that for any input i, $\phi_\mathcal{P}^t(ctr, L_{Real}, i)$ is valid.*

Remark: Note that the synthesis problem only aims to produce programs verifiable in bounded steps (which can be implicitly enforced in $\mathcal{P}$ and/or $\phi_\mathcal{P}$). This is a common practice for modern synthesis tools [7,39,42].

3.3   Inductive Synthesis with Angelic Libraries

We solve the library-based synthesis problem set forth above using TOSHOKAN, an enhanced CEGIS framework as illustrated in Fig. 1. We now formally describe the angelic inductive synthesizer, the key component of the framework.

The Angelic Inductive Synthesizer (AIS), similar to a regular inductive synthesizer in the standard CEGIS loop, maintains a set of sample inputs, finds a candidate program that satisfies the specification at least for the sample set, and gives the candidate to a verification oracle for checking. The salient feature of the AIS is that it also maintains a library sampling N_Σ and ignores the exact behavior of the authentic library not covered by N_Σ. Inspired by angelic programming [6,13], the AIS *divines an angelic library* L_{Ang} that is consistent to N_Σ and guarantees the synthesized program satisfies the specification for L_{Real}. In other words, if executed with the authentic library, the synthesized program does not necessarily satisfy the specification, even if the input is restricted to a sample set. However, the CEGIS loop will collect more counterexamples and samplings in each iteration and guarantees the correctness of the final solution (see our synthesis algorithm later in this section).

Formally, given a validation condition $\phi_{\mathcal{P}}$, let the current input set and library sampling be Q and N, respectively, the synthesis task is to check the following second-order formula:

$$\Phi[\phi_{\mathcal{P}}, Q, N] \equiv \exists \mathsf{ctr}. \exists t. \exists L_{\mathsf{Ang}}. \left(N \prec_\Sigma L_{\mathsf{Ang}} \ \wedge \ \bigwedge_{\mathsf{inp} \in Q} \phi_{\mathcal{P}}^t(\mathsf{ctr}, L_{\mathsf{Ang}}, \mathsf{inp}) \right)$$

where $\phi_{\mathcal{P}}^t$ is the validation condition for the synthesis problem. The following theorem states that any solution to the original library-based synthesis problem is also a solution to the inductive synthesis problem.

Theorem 1. *Given a library-based synthesis problem* $\mathcal{L} = (\mathcal{P}, C, L_{\mathit{Real}}, \phi_{\mathcal{P}})$, *a set of inputs* Q, *and a library sampling* N *such that* $N \prec_\Sigma L_{\mathit{Real}}$, *then if* $\mathcal{L}$ *has a solution* ctr, *it witnesses the validity of* $\Phi[\phi_{\mathcal{P}}, Q, N]$.

Proof. The solution ctr and the authentic library function L_{Real} witness the validity of $\Phi[\phi_{\mathcal{P}}, Q, N]$. First, as N is consistent with L_{Real}, $N \prec_\Sigma L_{\mathsf{Real}}$. Second, as ctr is a solution to $\mathcal{L}$, there is an integer t_0 such that running $\mathcal{P}[\mathsf{ctr}, L_{\mathsf{Real}}]$ on all inputs from Q terminates within t_0 steps, i.e., $\bigwedge_{\mathsf{inp} \in Q} \phi_{\mathcal{P}}^{t_0}[\mathsf{ctr}, L_{\mathsf{Real}}, \mathsf{inp}]$. Therefore $\Phi[\phi_{\mathcal{P}}, Q, N]$ is valid.   □

An AIS just solves $\Phi[\phi_{\mathcal{P}}, Q, N]$ and returns the witnessing solution ctr and bound t. We define it below and discuss our approaches to developing it in Sect. 4.

Definition 7 (Angelic Inductive Synthesizer). *An angelic inductive synthesizer is a procedure that accepts queries of the form* $\mathbf{AIS}(\phi_{\mathcal{P}}, Q, N)$ *where* $\phi_{\mathcal{P}}$ *is a validation condition,* Q *is a finite set of inputs, and* N *is a library sampling. If* $\Phi[\phi_{\mathcal{P}}, Q, N]$ *is valid, the procedure responds with a witnessing solution* (ctr, t); *otherwise it returns* (unsat, 0).

3.4   Verifier and Logger

While the angelic inductive synthesizer presented in Sect. 3.3 is complete (as illustrated in Theorem 1), it is not sufficient to solve the library-based synthesis problem: first, it only guarantees the correctness of the synthesized program on a finite set of inputs Q; second, the correctness of the synthesized program relies on an angelically chosen library L_{Ang}, which is not necessarily consistent with the authentic library L_{Real}. Therefore, our TOSHOKAN framework requires two other components: a bounded verifier and a logger. We define them below.

The bounded verifier is slightly stronger than the standard one in a CEGIS framework: it promises to verify the correctness of the input program and its termination in bounded steps, or provide a counterexample. The logger runs a concrete program and collects the interaction with the underlying library.

Definition 8 (Bounded Verifier).   *A bounded verifier is an oracle that accepts queries of the form* $\mathbf{BV}(\mathcal{P}, c, L, \phi_{\mathcal{P}}, t)$, *where* $(\mathcal{P}, c, L, \phi_{\mathcal{P}})$ *forms a library-based synthesis problem and* $t \in \mathbb{N}$ *is an execution bound, asking "Do all executions of* $\mathcal{P}[c, L]$ *terminate in* t *steps and satisfy the specification* $\phi_{\mathcal{P}}$*?" In other words, it checks the validation condition* $\forall i.\ \phi_{\mathcal{P}}^{t}(c, L, i)$. *If so, the oracle responds with a positive answer* $\top$*; otherwise it responds with a witness input* inp *such that* $\phi_{\mathcal{P}}^{t}(c, L, \text{inp})$ *is invalid, i.e., the concrete execution of* $\mathcal{P}[c, L]$ *on* inp *does not terminate in* t *steps or violates the functional specification.*

Remark: While the **AIS** (cf. Definition 7) treats the library as an absolute black box, it becomes trickier for the bounded verifier—it can treat the library as a black box and do testing only, which can be very slow, or leverage the bytecode (or even source code if available) to make verification more symbolic and efficient.

Definition 9 (Logger).   *A logger is an oracle that accepts queries of the form* $\log(\mathcal{P}, c, L, Q)$, *where* $\mathcal{P}$ *is a parameterized program,* c *is a control parameter, and* L *is a* Σ*-library,* Q *is a finite set of inputs, and runs program* $\mathcal{P}[c, L]$ *with every input from* Q. *The logger returns a library sampling* N *such that for any* $f \in Funcs(\Sigma)$, *a pair* $(t, v) \in N_f$ *if and only if one of the runs involves an invocation* $f(t)$ *to the library and returns value* v.

We will discuss more about the design and implementation of the logger in Sect. 5.

3.5   The Main Synthesis Algorithm

We are now ready to present the main synthesis algorithm for TOSHOKAN, which is shown in Algorithm 1. The algorithm extends the classic CEGIS framework and leverages the three components we described above: **AIS** the angelic inductive synthesizer, **BV** the verifier and **log** the logger. The verifier and the logger repeatedly provide extra counterexamples and library samplings, respectively, to refine the inductive synthesis task.

```
input : A library-based synthesis problem (𝒫, C, L_Real, φ_𝒫)
output: A solution ctr to the input problem, if any; otherwise ⊥
1 def toshokan(𝒫, C, L_Real, φ_𝒫) :
2 |   Q, N, S ← ∅ // cex inputs, library sampling and checked solutions
3 |   ctr ← Init(C) // the control parameter, initially random from C
4 |   t ← Init() // bound of execution steps
5 |   repeat
6 |   |   w ← BV(𝒫, ctr, L_Real, φ_𝒫, t)
7 |   |   if w = ⊤ :
8 |   |   |   break
9 |   |   else:
10 |  |   |   S ← S ∪ {ctr}, Q ← Q ∪ {w} , N ← N∪ log(𝒫, ctr, L_Real, Q)
11 |  |   |   (ctr, t) ← AIS(φ_𝒫, Q, N)
12 |   until ctr = unsat;
13 |   return ctr
```

Algorithm 1: Main synthesis algorithm for TOSHOKAN.

In addition to a set of witness inputs Q, it also maintains a library sampling N as an approximation/model of the authentic library L_{Real}. In other words, N is expanded along the synthesis/verification iterations but always consistent with L_{Real}. The algorithm starts from empty Q, empty N, a random solution ctr and an initial bound t. In each iteration, the **BV** checks whether the current ctr and t lead to a fully correct program $\mathcal{P}[\text{ctr}, L_{Real}]$ terminating in t steps (line 6). if so, the algorithm terminates and returns the solution ctr; otherwise, the failed solution is added to the set of checked solutions C, and the verification result, which is a new witness input w, is added to the set Q (line 10). Note that the **AIS** may not understand why the new witness input w violates the specification, because running $\mathcal{P}[\text{ctr}, L_{Real}]$ on w may involve calls to the library L_{Real} with arguments not covered by the current sampling N. To this end, the algorithm invokes **log** to run the program on all inputs in Q and record the behavior of the library (line 10). The newly generated sampling are added to N. Now with the updated S, Q and N, the algorithm asks the inductive synthesizer to generate a new solution and proceeds to the next iteration (line 11). If the synthesizer cannot find any more solution, the algorithm terminates and concludes that the synthesis problem is unsolvable.

Soundness and Completeness. We now discuss the soundness and completeness of the algorithm.

Theorem 2 (Soundness). *Given an input library-based synthesis problem* $(\mathcal{P}, C, L_{Real}, \phi_{\mathcal{P}})$, *if Algorithm 1 terminates and returns a solution* ctr, *it is a solution to the synthesis problem. If the algorithm returns* unsat, *then the synthesis problem has no solution.*

Proof. If a solution ctr is returned by the algorithm, it must be produced by the **AIS** as a pair (ctr, t) and have passed the checking of the **BV**. Then by Definitions 6 and 8, ctr is indeed a solution to the input problem $(\mathcal{P}, C, L_{Real}, \phi_{\mathcal{P}})$.

If the algorithm returns unsat, the last instance of $\mathbf{AIS}(\phi_{\mathcal{P}}, Q, N)$ has no solution. Then by Theorem 1, the input problem $(\mathcal{P}, C, L_{\mathsf{Real}}, \phi_{\mathcal{P}})$ does not have solution either. $\qquad\square$

The completeness states that if the input synthesis problem is solvable, Algorithm 1 guarantees to produce a solution. We show that algorithm is *relatively complete*: if the underlying **BV** and **AIS** are both enumerative, then the whole algorithm is complete. Intuitively, **BV** and **AIS** are enumerative if they guarantee to provide the "minimal" witness input and candidate program, respectively. We next define the enumerative-ness and prove the relative completeness.

Definition 10. *A bounded verifier **BV** is enumerative if there exists a total ordering assigning a distinct natural number to each possible input of the parameterized program $\mathcal{W} : I \rightarrow \mathbb{N}$, such that for any invocation $\mathbf{BV}(\mathcal{P}, \mathsf{ctr}, L_{\mathsf{Real}}, \phi_{\mathcal{P}}, t)$, it returns a counterexample inp only if for any other input inp' such that $\mathcal{W}(\mathsf{inp}') < \mathcal{W}(\mathsf{inp})$, inp' is not a valid return value.*

Definition 11. *An angelic inductive synthesizer **AIS** is enumerative if there exists a total ordering assigning a distinct natural number to each control value $\mathcal{E} : C \rightarrow \mathbb{N}$, such that for any invocation $\mathbf{AIS}(\phi_{\mathcal{P}}, Q, N)$, it returns ctr only if for any other value ctr' such that $\mathcal{E}(\mathsf{ctr}') < \mathcal{E}(\mathsf{ctr})$, ctr' is not a solution to the AIS problem.*

Theorem 3 (Relative Completeness). *Let **BV** be an enumerative bounded verifier and let **AIS** be an enumerative angelic inductive synthesizer, then running Algorithm 1 with **BV** and **AIS** guarantees to produce a solution if the input library-based synthesis problem is solvable.*

Proof. If the synthesis problem is solvable, there exists a minimal solution ctr. Assume the algorithm does not produce a solution, then due to the soundness, the algorithm will not terminate and **AIS** will produce an infinite sequence of conjectured solution/bound pairs: $(\mathsf{ctr}_0, t_0), (\mathsf{ctr}_1, t_1), \ldots$ such that none of the ctr_i's is a solution. Now as ctr is the minimal solution and **AIS** is enumerative, we have $\mathcal{E}(\mathsf{ctr}_i) < \mathcal{E}(\mathsf{ctr})$ for all $i \geq 0$. Therefore there must exist a solution ctr_R appears in the sequence infinitely often. As ctr_R is not a solution, let inp_R be the minimal counterexample input and running inp_R on $\mathcal{P}[\mathsf{ctr}_R, L_{\mathsf{Real}}]$ terminates in t_R steps. As **BV** is enumerative, it is not hard to prove that there is a infinite subsequence $(\mathsf{ctr}_R, v_0), (\mathsf{ctr}_R, v_1), \ldots$ where $v_0, v_1, \ldots$ is strictly increasing. In other words, there must be a pair (ctr_R, v_m) proposed by the **AIS** and $v_m > t_R$. Therefore v_m is sufficiently large for **AIS** to know that ctr_R terminates and fails to satisfy the specification, then ctr_R will not be proposed again after (ctr_R, v_m). The contradiction concludes the proof. $\qquad\square$

Remark: Note that enumerative verifiers and synthesizers are not uncommon in practice. For example, in Sketch, one can use the minimize keyword to enforce the synthesizer to fill holes with values as small as possible. Moreover, an enumerative verifier can be constructed from a regular verifier: once a witness input $i = \mathsf{inp}$

is found by the regular verifier, add an assumption $i <$ inp to the program and rerun the regular verifier to find a smaller witness input; repeat the process until no more witness input can be found. The last found witness input in the process should be the minimal one.

4 Angelic Inductive Synthesis

So far we have overviewed the TOSHOKAN framework with the general library-based synthesis problem defined in a semantical way. In this section, we present our approaches to developing the angelic inductive synthesizer in depth, in the setting of program sketching. In other words, the representation of parameterized program and specification is concretized to a sketched program, and the synthesis task is to fill holes of a sketched program such that all assertions are satisfied. We first present a simple language for program sketching, then discuss three different ways to encode and solve the angelic inductive synthesis problem.

The TOSHOKAN **Core Language.** We instantiate the library-based synthesis problem (Definition 6) to JSKETCH, a Java sketching language [20]. Below we show how the **AIS** problem can be encoded for a TOSHOKAN core language. The language is similar to Sketch and allows us to reuse the JSKETCH-to-Sketch compilation [20] and the Sketch synthesis engine [39].

The syntax of the TOSHOKAN core language is presented in Fig. 3. Besides standard programming constructs covered by Sketch (e.g., assignments, conditionals and loops), this language also supports library function definitions and calls, which are shown as the highlighted portion of the syntax. The language describes a program sketch which begins with a list of library functions (the $\mathcal{L}$ part). A library function may take primitive or composite values as arguments and return an primitive or composite value. For each library function f used in the program, there exists a corresponding full, authentic implementation f_{Real}, which does not include any holes, assumptions or assertions, or calls to other library functions.[4] The second part of the sketch is the harness functions (or the $\mathcal{H}$ part). It may include constant holes of the form ??, choice of expressions of the form $\{|\ \cdot\ |\ \cdot\ |\}$, assumptions, assertions, and arbitrary calls to the library functions.

Intuitively, the synthesis task is to fill the unknown constants with values (assumed to be naturals) such that running the harness functions will not trigger any assertion failure before any assumption violation. Formally, let $\mathcal{P} = \mathcal{L}; \mathcal{H}$ be a program sketch in the TOSHOKAN core language, and let the number of holes in $\mathcal{H}$ be m, then this sketch characterizes a library-based synthesis problem as per Definition 6:

$$\left(\mathcal{H}, \mathbb{N}^m, \{f_{\text{Real}}\}_{f_{\text{Real}}\in\mathcal{L}}, \phi_{\mathcal{P}}\right)$$

---

[4] This limitation is not fundamental and can be generalized in the future. Without calls between library functions, the implementation of library logger becomes easier since logging instrumentation would only need to be done on client code.

z, z_1, z_2 : integer variable y, y_1, y_2 : composite variable
$k \in \mathbb{Z}$: int const f, g : lib function h : harness function
$\mathcal{P} ::= \mathcal{L}; \mathcal{H}$
$\mathcal{L} ::=$ library $f_{\mathsf{Real}}(\bar{z})\ S \mid \mathcal{L}; \mathcal{L}$
$\mathcal{H} ::=$ harness $h(\bar{z})\ S' \mid \mathcal{H}; \mathcal{H}$
$S ::=$ skip $\mid z = E \mid S; S \mid$ if B then S else $S \mid$ while B do S
$S' ::=$ skip $\mid z = E' \mid$ assume$(B) \mid$ assert$(B) \mid z = f(\bar{V})$
$\qquad \mid y = g(\bar{V}) \mid S'; S' \mid$ if B then S' else $S' \mid$ while B do S'
$E ::= k \mid z \mid E + E \mid E - E$
$E' ::= E \mid ?? \mid \{| E' \mid E' |\}$
$B ::=$ true $\mid z_1 < z_2 \mid y_1 = y_2 \mid B \wedge B \mid \neg B$
$V ::= z \mid y$

Fig. 3. Syntax of the TOSHOKAN core language (the library-related part is highlighted).

where $\phi_{\mathcal{P}}$ generates bounded validation conditions from a concrete program and a concrete input, checking that the execution terminates (in a bounded number of steps) and satisfies all assertions. Formally, let ctr be the values filled to holes and let inp be the input to the harness, the validation condition can be formulated in the following form:

$$\phi_{\mathcal{P}}^t(\mathsf{ctr}, \mathsf{inp}) \equiv \exists S_0 \ldots S_t . \exists Z_0 \ldots Z_t . \Big($$
$$\forall 0 \le j \le t . Follow(S_j, Z_{j+1}, S_{j+1}) \wedge Exec(Z_j, S_j, Z_{j+1}) \Big)$$

The formula guesses a t-step run of the program, including the executed statement S_j and the valuation Z_j of the variables before the statement, for each step j. The predicate *Follow* checks that statement S_{j+1} follows statement S_j given the current valuation Z_{j+1}. The predicate *Exec* checks that running S_j with the current valuation Z_j will successfully yield the next valuation Z_{j+1}.

Direct Encoding for Libraries of Primitive Type. Now we have a library-based synthesis problem represented by the input sketch in the TOSHOKAN core language. Recall that a key step of our main synthesis algorithm is to solve the angelic inductive synthesis problem **AIS**$(\phi_{\mathcal{P}}, Q, N)$ as described in Definition 7: given a library sampling N, guess an angelic library consistent with N and generate a candidate program that satisfies the specification $\phi_{\mathcal{P}}$ on the sample input set Q. Our approach is to represent this problem as another sketched program which does not contain library calls. As our core language is consistent with Sketch both in syntax and semantics, the problem can be directly solved by Sketch [39] or other synthesis engines.

We start from the simplest case: the library functions all take primitive arguments only and return primitive values—this is already sufficient for the overview example gcd_n_numbers. In this case, the angelic choices can be simply represented as uninterpreted functions. Assuming $\mathcal{P}$ contains a library function int f(int u_1, ..., int u_m) among others, we encode the problem $\mathbf{AIS}(\phi_\mathcal{P}, Q, N)$ to a program sketch as shown in Fig. 4. The function h is copied from the harness function in the original $\mathcal{P}$ which may involves unknown control holes to be synthesized, assumptions and assertions delimiting the behavior of the program, and calls to the library functions. The new harness function test simply takes the input for h and makes sure the input matches one of the sample inputs in set Q, then calls the real harness h. The library function f is implemented as follows: if the input $(u_1, ..., u_m)$ matches the one sample input $(s_1, ..., s_m)$ from the library sampling N, then return the corresponding output t; otherwise, return an angelic value from an uninterpreted function f_{Ang}. The uninterpreted function is arbitrary but guarantees the functionality, i.e., L_{Ang} always returns the same output with the same input.

```
int  f_Ang(int u); // uninterpreted func for angelic choices, for each library   func f
...
int  f(int u_1, ..., int u_m) { //guessed angelic model, for each library func f
  if  (u_1 = s_1 ∧ ··· ∧ u_m = s_m) return t; // for every sample input—output pair
      (s_1, ..., s_m, t) ∈ N_f
  ... return f_Ang(u); // if the input is not covered by N, make an angelic choice
} ...
void h(int i_1, ..., int i_n) { /* the original harness func */ }
harness test (int i_1, ..., int i_n) {
  assume  ⋁ i == inp; //assume i is from the current witness input set
         inp∈Q
  h(i_1, ..., i_n); //run the original harness on i and check all assertions
}
```

Fig. 4. Direct encoding of $\mathbf{AIS}(\phi_\mathcal{P}, Q, N)$.

Note that Fig. 4 assumes that function f takes integer parameter and returns integer values, but the encoding can be easily generalized to more primitive types supported by modern synthesizers. For example, Sketch has native support of synthesizing control parameters and uninterpreted functions of int and bit, as well as constant-sized arrays or nested arrays of primitive values.

Call-Tree-Based Encoding for Libraries of Composite Type. Now let us consider encoding libraries of composite type, i.e., the library function may take as argument or return values from user-defined, variable-size types, e.g., records, variable-size arrays, algebraic data types. While the direct encoding presented in Fig. 4 is straightforward and efficient and Sketch has native support for arrays, structs and algebraic data types, naturally extending this encoding to support composite types is not practically feasible for two reasons: first, for many real-world libraries (e.g., for encryption/decryption), the source code is not available and internal data is unknown; second, some libraries are implemented with

```
class Stack { ...
  public Stack() {...}
  public void push(int i) {...}
  public int pop() {...}
}
public class Main {
  static Stack main() {
    s = new Stack();
    s.push(1); s.push(2);
    int i = s.pop();
    assert i == 2; return s;
} }
```

```
int E_Stack = −1, E_push! = −2, E_pop! = −3;
int pop_Ang(int[] call_tree);
int pop(int[] call_tree) {
  ... return f_Ang(u); //direct encoding for
                          primitive type
} ...
int[] main() {
  int[] s_tree = [E_Stack]; //s = new Stack()
  s_tree = [E_push!] + s_tree + [1]; //s.push(1)
  s_tree = [E_push!] + s_tree + [2]; //s.push(2)
  int i = pop(s_tree); //i = s.pop()
  assert i = 2; return s_tree; }
```

(a) Java program manipulating Stack.

(b) Encoded program.

Fig. 5. Example: call-tree-based encoding for Stack.

complex data structures (e.g., java.util.Stack is implemented as a dynamically resizable array), making the direct encoding inefficient.

To this end, we use a different, call-based encoding for libraries with composite type. The idea is to characterize the library's internal state using the call tree that creates the current value. We illustrate the call tree representation through the following example.

Consider a Java program that uses the Stack library (see Example 2), which is shown in Fig. 5a. The main function creates a Stack object s, computes an integer i through a sequence of method calls to s, and returns the updated s. While the exact representation of the returned object is hard/impossible to obtain, the object can be determined by an expression new Stack().push(1).push(2).pop(). This expression can be uniquely represented as a call tree as shown in Fig. 6. Furthermore, one can assign a unique number to every Stack-valued method. For example, in Fig. 6, init, push! and pop! are assigned −1, −2, −3, respectively. Then the call tree's Polish notation can be uniquely represented as an array (see the right hand side of Fig. 6).[5]

Based on this array representation of call trees, we encode library-using programs to array-manipulating programs. Intuitively, we maintain an array s_tree for each non-primitive value s used in the program, and every method call or object initialization m is simulated by a corresponding manipulation to the array: if a m updates s, then expand the call tree by extending s_tree accordingly; if m computes a primitive value from s, then follow the direct encoding and use an uninterpreted function m_Ang to make an angelic choice. Figure 5b shows the encoding of Fig. 5a: we use $[E_m]$ to represent the integer value encoding a method

---

[5] Here we assume all integer arguments are positive and use negative integers to represent methods. If negative integers are involved in the program, the array encoding has to have an extra bit to indicate a leaf node is a primitive value or a method call.

m, and the function main is generated by a line-by-line translation from the original Main method. Note that s.pop() returns a primitive value and hence is translated using the direct encoding as shown in Fig. 4. Figure 7 formally presents the call-tree-based encoding of method declarations calls, assuming there is a single composite type C and a single primitive type int.

Query-Based Encoding for Libraries with Query Functions. The call-tree-based encoding for composite type presented above has a potential scalability issue: the call tree grows unboundedly when more and more library calls are made. Therefore, the size of the corresponding array representation will quickly become larger than synthesis engines can handle, especially when library calls are involved in a loop.

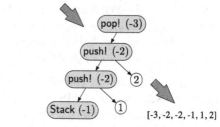

Fig. 6. Example: Polish notation of call tree.

We address this problem by using another query-based encoding when the library admits *query functions*, which are inspired by the state query methods proposed by Pei *et al.* [30]. Intuitively, query methods have no side effects and can be used to characterize the library class' internal mutable state. For example, consider a non-naive Java class SortedList defining a linked list data structure that would sort itself as new elements are added into it, as shown in Fig. 8a. The SortedList class contains two methods: insert and search. The search method is actually a query function—the internal sate and behavior of a SortedList object I is unique determined by I.search(i) for all possible input i. We

$$
\begin{aligned}
&[\![C(\mathbf{int}\ \bar{z})\{\dots\};]\!] = \mathbf{int}\ E_C =< \text{fresh\_int} >; \\
&[\![\mathbf{int}\ f(\mathbf{int}\ \bar{z})\{\dots\};]\!] = \mathbf{int}\ E_{f!} =< \text{fresh\_int} >;\quad \mathbf{int}\ f_{\mathsf{Ang}}(\mathbf{int}[]\ call\_tree, \mathbf{int}\ \bar{z}); \\
&\qquad\qquad\qquad\qquad\quad \mathbf{int}\ f(\mathbf{int}[]\ call\_tree, \mathbf{int}\ \bar{z})\{< \text{direct encoding} >\} \\
&[\![C\ g(\mathbf{int}\ \bar{z})\{\dots\};]\!] = \mathbf{int}\ E_{g!} =< \text{fresh\_int} >;\quad \mathbf{int}\ E_g =< \text{fresh\_int} >; \\
&[\![\mathbf{void}\ u(\mathbf{int}\ \bar{z})\{\dots\};]\!] = \mathbf{int}\ E_{u!} =< \text{fresh\_int} >; \\
&\qquad [\![y := o.f(\bar{z});]\!] = o_{tree} = [E_{f!}] + o_{tree} + \bar{z};\quad y = f(o_{tree}, \bar{z}); \\
&\qquad [\![q := o.g(\bar{z});]\!] = o_{tree} = [E_{g!}] + o_{tree} + \bar{z};\quad q_{tree} = [E_g] + o_{tree} + \bar{z}; \\
&\qquad\qquad [\![o.u(\bar{z});]\!] = o_{tree} = [E_{u!}] + o_{tree} + \bar{z}; \\
&[\![C\ o := \mathbf{new}\ C(\bar{z})]\!] = \mathbf{int}[]\ o_{tree} = [E_C] + \bar{z} \\
&\qquad\qquad [\![\text{skip}]\!] = \text{skip} \\
&\qquad\qquad [\![S; S]\!] = [\![S]\!]; [\![S]\!]
\end{aligned}
$$

Fig. 7. Call-tree-based encoding.

ignore the detection of query functions and assume the programmer manually marks query functions, using the @query keyword.

Given a library with query functions, we can solve the angelic inductive synthesis problem using a query-based encoding. We formally define query functions below:

Definition 12 (Query Function). *Let Σ be a library signature containing two sorts $\{P, C\}$ where P is primitive and C is composite. Then a Σ-library L_Σ admits a set of query functions $\mathcal{Q}$ if: 1) $\mathcal{Q} \subseteq \Sigma_{C \times P^* \to \{true, false\}}$; and 2) For every non-query function $f \in \Sigma_{C \times \cdots \to C}$, and every $a, a' \in C$, if $f(a, \bar{b}) \neq f(a', \bar{b})$, a and a' are distinguishable by query functions, i.e., there exists a $g \in \mathcal{Q}$ and $\bar{e} \in P^*$ such that $g(a, \bar{e}) \neq g(a', \bar{e})$.*

Continuing on the SortedList example, Fig. 8b shows how this program is encoded. Note that the AIS is based on a finite set of inputs Q. Therefore, we can approximate the internal state of a SortedList object lst using a bit vector lst_query, which contains values search(inp) for every inp $\in Q$. When a new SortedList is created, the bit vector is initialized with all 0's as the search function always returns false. To update the bit vector, we expect the logger to invoke the query function search before and after each non-query function call, namely insert and insert!, and collect the inputs/outputs as a library sampling N. Based on N, all library functions are directly encoded in a way similar to Fig. 4.

In addition, for the search function itself, we encode it to an extra function search$_Q$. When search$_Q$ is called for lst_query with input u, it essentially retrieves whether u matches any sample input covered by Q; if so, it simply returns the corresponding value in lst_query; otherwise it proceeds to the directly encoded search function.

5   The Logger

In this section, we discuss another major component of the TOSHOKAN framework: the logger **log**, whose definitions have been given (in Definition 9). We discuss our design in the setting of program sketching to match the **AIS** design we described in Sect. 4. The design is mostly straightforward—simply run the candidate program with the current set of counterexample inputs Q, and for every library call it encounters, log the input and the corresponding output. Below we discuss some issues we identified and addressed in the design and implementation of the logger.

References and Aliasing. Real world libraries manipulate dynamically allocated structs and objects using references (pointers), which may be aliased or overlapped (e.g., two List references a and b such that a $\neq$ b but a.next == b.next). Therefore, a library function call will not only affect the references explicitly passed in as arguments, but also those aliased or overlapped with these arguments, which can be unboundedly many and cannot be tracked using library sampling.

```
public class SortedList {
  int value;
  SortedList next;
  SortedList ()
    { ... }
  @query public boolean
  /* query func annotation */
    search (int u)
    { ... }
  public boolean insert (int i )
    { ... }
  ...
}
public class Main {
  static void main(int i ) {
    SortedList lst =
        new SortedList();
    assert ! lst . search ( i );
    lst . insert ( i );
    assert lst . search ( i );
  }
}
```

```
// direct  encoding for all  library  functions
bit searchAng(int u); bit insertAng(bit[n]
    q_result, int u);
bit [n] insert!Ang(bit[n] q_result, int u);
bit search (bit [n] q_result , int u) { ... }
bit insert (bit [n] q_result , int u) { ... }
bit [n] insert!(bit[n] q_result, int u) { ... } ...
// query−based encoding for query functions
int [n] lStack = { 0, ..., 0 }
int [n] Q = { <current sample input set> }
bit searchQ(bit[n] q_result, int u) {
// if  u is covered by Q return query result
  if  (u == Q[0]) return q_result[0]; ...
  if  (u == Q[n − 1]) return q_result[n − 1];
  return search (u);
//otherwise, use model from direct  encoding
} ...
void main(int i ) {
  bit [n] lst_query = lStack;
  assert !searchQ(lst_query, i);
  lst_query = insert!(lst_query, i);
  assert searchQ(lst_query, i);
}
```

(a) Example: SortedList with query
function annotated.

(b) Query-based encoding for example SortedList.

Fig. 8. Example of SortedList and its corresponding query-based encoding.

To this end, we track library calls with arguments that are *aliased or disjoint only*. More concretely, we first extend the definition of library sampling (see Definition 3) and the logger in the following way. Assume Σ is a library signature containing a reference sort Ref and L is a Σ-library containing a function f : $\mathsf{Ref}^n \to \mathsf{Ref}$. Then an extended library sampling of f is a finite set of

$$N_f \subseteq_{\mathrm{fin}} \mathcal{B}(n) \times \mathsf{Ref}^n \times \mathsf{Ref} \times 3^{\{0,1,\ldots,n\}}$$

where $\mathcal{B}(n)$ is the set of partitions of the set $\{1, \ldots, n\}$. The first element is a partition of the references into aliased equivalence classes; references from different equivalence classes must be disjoint. The second and the third elements are simply the input and output of the function. The last element indicates whether the output reference is aliased, overlapped, or disjoint with the n arguments.

Next, we also adapt the call-tree-based encoding for libraries. In addition to the encoding we presented in Fig. 7, the encoded program explicitly maintains the relationship between all references: aliased, disjoint, or overlapped. Whenever a reference is updated (via either an assignment or a library call), all aliased references will be updated in the same way and all disjoint references will be kept unchanged. For other overlapped references, as we don't track precise information to updated them, they will be havoced, i.e., they will be updated arbitrarily, being disjoint or still overlapped with the updated reference.

Termination and Exceptions. Termination is a tricky issue for program analysis and verification, and also for our synthesis framework. Note that the input program to the logger is not necessarily terminating: it may invoke library calls infinitely often and the logger may not terminate either. In this case, the logger can set an execution limit T: if the execution reaches T steps, the logger just halts and returns the samples collected thus far. The limit T can be simply set as the integer t_0 found by the **AIS**—according to Definition 7 and the formula $\Phi[\phi_\mathcal{P}, Q, N]$ **AIS** solves, all sample runs of the synthesized program with the conjectured angelic library L_{Ang} guarantee to terminate within t_0 steps. In other words, if the real execution with the authentic library L_{Real} does not terminate within t_0 steps, the library behavior collected by the logger is already enough to distinguish L_{Real} and L_{Ang}.

Another similar issue is about the exceptions. While the TOSHOKAN core language is simple, it may present exceptions such as division-by-zero and array index out-of-bound. More importantly, the library calls made by the candidate program also might be invalid and throw exceptions from running the authentic implementation of the library. In these cases, our logger simply returns the library samplings collected thus far and input to the last library call that causes the exception. These samplings will let the **AIS** know how the witness input leads to the exception so that the next candidate can avoid this scenario.

6   Evaluation

We implemented the TOSHOKAN framework in JSKETCH [20]—a sketch-based Java synthesizer—and conducted experimental evaluation. It takes a JSKETCH file (intuitively a Java program with unknown constants, expressions, etc.) as input and produces a concrete Java program satisfying user-provided specification. Note that our goal is not outperforming vanilla JSKETCH using models and mocks [25]: the primary goal of TOSHOKAN is to reduce the extra LoC that other methods require the user to write. Therefore, our evaluation attempts to answer the following research questions: **RQ1:** *Can* TOSHOKAN *synthesize programs interacting with a wide variety of libraries?* **RQ2:** *Does* TOSHOKAN *reduce the LoC that the synthesizer user needs to write with acceptable performance?* In this section, we first describe our implementation and benchmarks, then report the experimental results which answer the two research questions.

Implementation. The implementation was written in Rust and C++ with around 10k total LoC. We leverage the current frontend of JSKETCH to encode most Java-specific features to Sketch, and encode the angelic inductive synthesis problem as described in Sect. 4. Once a Sketch solution is obtained, we further leverage the decoder of JSKETCH to generate a concrete Java program candidate for verification and logging.

We employ JBMC [8] as the bounded verifier. Note that JBMC verifies compiled Java bytecode, i.e., it does not rely on the availability of the library's source code. JBMC also serves as the logger: if a candidate program failed verification, we build a Java program that explicitly runs the failed program with all witness inputs and finishes with assert false. JBMC will claim that the program is wrong and provide the trace of execution. We implemented a data extractor to collect input-output samples for the library calls involved in the trace. We remark that the JBMC-based logger is potentially unsound as JBMC uses its own library models.

Benchmarks. To evaluate TOSHOKAN, we have adopted and converted a number of synthesis benchmarks from various sources, including Sketch modular synthesis benchmarks using function models [35], JDIAL benchmark using external libraries [17] and our own benchmarks using composite-type libraries. We also write some benchmarks ourselves by converting some well-known, widely used algorithms and data structures into sketch format with holes added, so that the benchmark set could be more diversified. We hope the wide range of the benchmarks adopted could help demonstrate the wide variety of libraries upon which our methods could be applied to.

Sketch modular synthesis [35] benchmarks are obtained from Sketch source repository as part of the project's experimental feature benchmarks [36]. These benchmarks come with two versions: one model version and one mock version for each synthesis task. The model version utilizes the function model features of Sketch to solve synthesis tasks with unknown library functions, as long as models of the functions are provided. The mock versions are effectively the same synthesis tasks, but with concrete implementations of the library functions. We excluded some benchmarks that are not legit (e.g., no synthesis task or no argument for the library function). This ends up in a total of 4 benchmarks adapted from this benchmark set. JDIAL [17] benchmarks are obtained from JDIAL-Debugger's Github repository [18]. Among the JDIAL direct manipulation benchmarks, we picked two out of three benchmarks that use external libraries (excluding *evalPoly_3* which seems to be identical to *evalPoly_2*). We also combined them into a larger one, *evalPoly_combined*.

Up to this point, all the benchmarks we adopted are using libraries of primitive types. To demonstrate the effectiveness of our methods handling libraries of composite types, we converted a number of well-known, widely used algorithms and data structures into sketch formats with added holes. This creates 4 new benchmarks, namely *stack_match*, *set_match*, *arraylist_match*, and *heap_sort*, all in encoding for libraries of composite types.

It ends up in a total of 11 benchmarks to be evaluated in experiments. Whereas the sizes of the client-code sketches are relatively small, the authentic libraries involved in these benchmarks are not small. E.g., the ArrayList from OpenJDK8 [28] contains 1.4kLOC. Moreover, the authentic versions of the libraries contain Java features like reflection and lambda expression that JSKETCH does not support yet; some of them also invoke native code. There-

Table 2. Description of benchmarks and experimental results.

Benchmark						TOSHOKAN		JSKETCH (Model)		JSKETCH (Mock)	
Name	LoC	#C	Lib Data Type	Lib Func(s)	Enc	Time(s)	#I	Model LoC	Time(s)	Mock LoC	Time(s)
gcd_n_numbers	70	12	int	gcd	D	22.44	1	20(29%)	4.8	16(23%)	5.96
lcm_n_numbers	74	12	int	lcm	D	25.91	3	21(28%)	3.92	17(23%)	4.11
powerroot_sqrt	65	15	int	sqrt	D	15.40	1	14(22%)	3.81	19(29%)	3.84
primality_sqrt	56	12	int	sqrt	D	32.89	4	14(25%)	3.76	19(34%)	3.75
evalPoly_1	61	15	int	pow	D	22.77	3	30(49%)	3.91	11(18%)	4.32
evalPoly_2	59	15	int	pow	D	6.86	1	30(51%)	3.78	11(19%)	3.74
evalPoly_combined	97	30	int	pow	D	15.52	2	30(31%)	3.99	11(11%)	4.31
stack_match	24	8	Stack	push,pop	C	39.18	5	N/A	N/A	22(92%)	3.86
set_match	26	8	HashSet	add,contains	C,Q	8.76	1	29(112%)	4.02	32(123%)	4.01
arraylist_match	26	8	ArrayList	push_back,get	C,Q	41.75	5	29(112%)	4.1	22(85%)	3.8
heap_sort	72	20	Heap	insert,pop_min	C	32.56	4	N/A	N/A	159(221%)	4.44

Enc–Encoding(s) used in benchmark for TOSHOKAN

D–Direct encoding of primitive types, C–Call-tree based encoding, Q–Query based encoding

#C–number of control bits in the sketch after preprocessing. #I–number of iterations TOSHOKAN runs.

fore inlining these libraries is beyond the capacities of JSKETCH as currently implemented.

For each benchmark, we list the size of the program sketch, the number of control bits in the sketch, and the library's signature (see Table 2). Note that the "#C" column of the table describes the numbers of bits needed to represent a solution candidate for the synthesis task in the benchmark, i.e. a number of N control bits of the benchmark indicates that the search space of its solution is 2^N. Additionally, the LoC sizes of the model and mock code which JSKETCH uses for the respective benchmark are shown in the table, as well as their relative sizes to the benchmark per se.

Experimental Results. The experiments were conducted on a server with 2 Intel(R) Xeon(R) E5-2630 v4 10-core CPUs, with each core having 2 threads, at main frequency of 2.20 GHz, with 128 GB of memory. The experiments were run as 10 independent parallel tasks, and the whole process terminates once any of the 10 simultaneously running tasks returns with a correct synthesized solution.

Since the solving process of Sketch synthesis engine involves nondeterministic algorithms presenting nondeterministic intermediate results and performance, as well as having a large range of different configuration parameters that could be potentially optimized, the parallelism described above could be a great help in increasing overall performance for both our methods and our comparing methods, as long as parallel computing resources are available. Experiments were run on all 11 benchmarks with a timeout of 1 h. Performance of sketch with appropriate models and/or mocks on these same benchmarks are also collected whenever possible using the same parallel methods described above, as baseline of performance for the effectiveness evaluation.

TOSHOKAN successfully solved all benchmarks within the timeout. Our experimental results, including the solving time and number of iterations taken by TOSHOKAN to find the solution, are shown in Table 2. The results give an **answer to RQ1**: TOSHOKAN was able to effectively handle synthesis tasks that interact with a wide range of different libraries and library functions, including advanced arithmetic operations, as well as complex composite data structures. This indicates a good variety of our methods' possible applications.

Now let us proceed to the second research question. We take the mock/model LoC as a measure of the extra code needed for the synthesizer user to write which TOSHOKAN managed to save, and the extra time TOSHOKAN takes to solve the benchmark comparing to mock/model as measures of performance overhead. We believe the measures allow us to reasonably indicate the benefit/cost ratio of our approach.

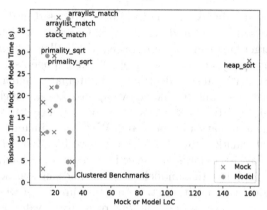

Figure 9 compares the absolute amount of extra LoC against extra time by TOSHOKAN. This figure indicates how TOSHOKAN trades extra synthesis time for saving the programmer's effort (in terms of LoC). For example, by adopting TOSHOKAN, a programmer who wants to write the *set_match* program could save 32 LoC writing at the cost of waiting for only 4 extra seconds. This figure would paint a picture from a potential user's perspective on the performance numbers.

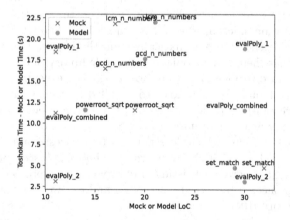

Fig. 9. Experimental results: saved LoC vs. extra time, absolute amount (above for all benchmarks and below for clustered benchmarks).

Observing Table 2 and the figures, we are encouraged toward an **answer to RQ2**: On one hand, TOSHOKAN saves the user some work from writing various kinds of mocks and models. Depending on the actual complexities of the underlying library and synthesis task, the Mock/Model LoC ranges from 11 to 159, and could be as high as 2.21× of the original sketch LoC. On the other hand, the performance slowdown is moderate. All benchmarks on TOSHOKAN showed a slowdown of less than 40 s. Given the extra LoC of code writing TOSHOKAN managed to eliminate, we consider this performance as acceptable in proving the effectiveness of our methods.

7   Related Work

Several library models have been proposed in different settings and handled by the synthesizer in different ways. Gascon *et al.* [15] model each component of the target language as a proof rule, which allows the synthesizer to symbolically execute programs consisting of these components. JLibSketch [25] model libraries as equational specifications and automate the reasoning about library models by term rewriting. Unlike above approaches in which the rules/equations are manually written by experts, the model in TOSHOKAN is simply a partial function and automatically generated. We tried to include the JLibSketch on the reported benchmarks [25]. Unfortunately, we found the Java programs produced for all these benchmarks are flawed and cannot be handled by our implementation.[6]

The function models used in modular synthesis [35] are more flexible. The model can be either strong (deterministic) or weak (nondeterministic). In other words, there can be a unique or multiple valid outputs for the same input. The key contribution of their work is a CEGIS+ algorithm which handles both strong and weak models efficiently. However, the functional models and the canonicalization functions they rely on are still manually written, while our library models are generated automatically from the logger. This is made possible by the fact that there is a canonical, executable library in our setting. In contrast, the original functions in [35] are not necessarily executable—these functions per se can be templates with holes to be filled by the synthesizer. The JSKETCH (Model version) which we have compared with implements the CEGIS+ algorithm (see experimental results in Sect. 6). The idea of angelic synthesis is also used by BURST [26], which does not aim to synthesize and handle library models.

There is a rich literature in *component-based synthesis*, which aims to generate a program consisting of library calls to a provided API. This line of work was pioneered by PROSPECTOR [24] and followed by many synthesis tools including CODEHINT [14], SYPET [12], EDSYNTH [43] and FRANGEL [33]. These systems typically synthesize code making library calls by actually executing the candidate program on a set of test cases. Our approach also treats the library as a black box but not for testing. We synthesize provably-correct, library-using programs by incorporating inductive synthesis (using JSKETCH) and bounded verification (using JBMC).

Unit-test generation is another related research area. The task is to generate sequences of method calls to exercise the library to be tested. For example,

---

[6] As a limitation of current JSKETCH, when generators are involved, the raw output of JSKETCH is not compilable and some manual adaptation is needed. This is impossible for TOSHOKAN because the CEGIS loop must compile JSKETCH output every iteration.

Pacheco *et al.* [29] generate method calls randomly and guide the generation with feedback from executing the generated sequences. FUDGE [3] extracts code snippets from corpus code and mutate them to generate fuzz drivers. Instead of testing libraries, our purpose is to synthesize client code of libraries that satisfies formal specifications.

The idea of delegating complex verification tasks to external oracles is also explored by SyMO [31], but the main distinction is about the synthesizer's side. SyMO (and all existing SyGuS solvers) treat libraries as a white-box, defined function. In other words, when library call f(x) is part of the grammar, SyGuS solvers need access to the implementation of f(x) as a defined function. In contrast, our angelic inductive synthesizer treats the library as a black box. Moreover, many libraries are not pure-functional (e.g. Stack.push), with side effects updating the internal composite data structure, which cannot be handled by SyMO.

External function handling in direct manipulation. The most related work to this paper is JDIAL [17], which performs direct manipulation, a special form of program repair. In each iteration of the synthesis procedure, JDIAL leverages Sketch to guess a *single input-output pair* of the library function which is not covered by the current program's execution, then runs the library function with the guessed input to check whether the guessed output is correct. While JDIAL and TOSHOKAN share the same idea of dynamically expanding the library model, they are different in several aspects. First, JDIAL supports interactive program repair, while TOSHOKAN, for the first time, integrates the dynamic library model into a fully-automatic sketch-based synthesis procedure. Second, JDIAL only handles simple mathematical functions such as Math.pow or Math.max, and it is not clear how their approach can be extended to support libraries manipulating objects, with internal states and references, etc., and how scalable their approach toward more sophisticated libraries. Third, JDIAL runs authentic libraries eagerly and not guided by counterexamples, e.g., its Math.max example takes more than 90 iterations. By contrast, TOSHOKAN runs the whole rejected program and only logs those library calls witness the failure, making the generated library model smaller and more helpful for the synthesizer.

8 Conclusion

We proposed TOSHOKAN, a new program synthesis framework in which programs that use external libraries could be synthesized without any mock or model from the user. TOSHOKAN extends the classic counterexample-guided inductive synthesis framework with a bootstrapping, log-based library model. We found that, comparing to existing synthesis techniques that are able to handle external libraries through user-provided models or mocks, our methods save the user from the extra manual work, at the cost of moderate performance overhead.

Acknowledgments. This research was supported in part by the National Science Foundation under Grant Nos. CCF-1919197 and CCF-2046071.

References

1. Ammons, G., Bodík, R., Larus, J.R.: Mining specifications. In: Proceedings of the 29th ACM SIGPLAN-SIGACT Symposium on Principles of Programming Languages. POPL 2002. ACM (2002). https://doi.org/10.1145/503272.503275
2. Astorga, A., Madhusudan, P., Saha, S., Wang, S., Xie, T.: Learning stateful preconditions modulo a test generator. In: Proceedings of the 40th ACM SIGPLAN Conference on Programming Language Design and Implementation. PLDI 2019. ACM (2019). https://doi.org/10.1145/3314221.3314641
3. Babić, D., et al.: Fudge: fuzz driver generation at scale. In: Proceedings of the 2019 27th ACM Joint Meeting on European Software Engineering Conference and Symposium on the Foundations of Software Engineering. ESEC/FSE 2019. ACM (2019). https://doi.org/10.1145/3338906.3340456
4. Bastani, O., Anand, S., Aiken, A.: Specification inference using context-free language reachability. In: Proceedings of the 42nd Annual ACM SIGPLAN-SIGACT Symposium on Principles of Programming Languages. POPL 2015. ACM (2015). https://doi.org/10.1145/2676726.2676977
5. Bastani, O., Sharma, R., Aiken, A., Liang, P.: Active learning of points-to specifications. In: Proceedings of the 39th ACM SIGPLAN Conference on Programming Language Design and Implementation. PLDI 2018. ACM (2018). https://doi.org/10.1145/3192366.3192383
6. Bodik, R., Chandra, S., Galenson, J., Kimelman, D., Tung, N., Barman, S., Rodarmor, C.: Programming with angelic nondeterminism. In: Proceedings of the 37th annual ACM SIGPLAN-SIGACT symposium on Principles of programming languages. POPL 2010. ACM (2010). https://doi.org/10.1145/1706299.1706339
7. Bornholt, J., Torlak, E.: Finding code that explodes under symbolic evaluation. In: Proc. of the ACM on Programming Languages. OOPSLA 2018, vol. 2. ACM, October 2018. https://doi.org/10.1145/3276519
8. Cordeiro, L., Kesseli, P., Kroening, D., Schrammel, P., Trtik, M.: JBMC: a bounded model checking tool for verifying Java bytecode. In: Chockler, H., Weissenbacher, G. (eds.) CAV 2018. LNCS, vol. 10981, pp. 183–190. Springer, Cham (2018). https://doi.org/10.1007/978-3-319-96145-3_10
9. Delaware, B., Pit-Claudel, C., Gross, J., Chlipala, A.: Fiat: deductive synthesis of abstract data types in a proof assistant. In: Proceedings of the 42nd Annual ACM SIGPLAN-SIGACT Symposium on Principles of Programming Languages. POPL 2015. ACM (2015). https://doi.org/10.1145/2676726.2677006
10. Doughty-White, P., Quick, M.: Codebases: millions of lines of code (2015). https://informationisbeautiful.net/visualizations/million-lines-of-code/
11. Ernst, M.D., et al.: The daikon system for dynamic detection of likely invariants. Science of Computer Programming 69(1), 35–45 (2007). https://doi.org/10.1016/j.scico.2007.01.015, special issue on Experimental Software and Toolkits
12. Feng, Y., Martins, R., Wang, Y., Dillig, I., Reps, T.W.: Component-based synthesis for complex APIs. In: Proceedings of the 44th ACM SIGPLAN Symposium on Principles of Programming Languages. POPL 2017. ACM (2017). https://doi.org/10.1145/3009837.3009851
13. Floyd, R.W.: Nondeterministic algorithms. J. ACM (JACM) **14**(4), 636–644 (1967). https://doi.org/10.1145/321420.321422
14. Galenson, J., Reames, P., Bodik, R., Hartmann, B., Sen, K.: CodeHint: dynamic and interactive synthesis of code snippets. In: Proceedings of the 36th International Conference on Software Engineering. ICSE 2014. ACM (2014). https://doi.org/10.1145/2568225.2568250

15. Gascón, A., Tiwari, A., Carmer, B., Mathur, U.: Look for the proof to find the program: decorated-component-based program synthesis. In: Majumdar, R., Kunčak, V. (eds.) CAV 2017. LNCS, vol. 10427, pp. 86–103. Springer, Cham (2017). https://doi.org/10.1007/978-3-319-63390-9_5
16. Heule, S., Sridharan, M., Chandra, S.: Mimic: computing models for opaque code. In: Proceedings of the 2015 10th Joint Meeting on Foundations of Software Engineering - ESEC/FSE 2015 (2015). https://doi.org/10.1145/2786805.2786875
17. Hu, Q., Samanta, R., Singh, R., D'Antoni, L.: Direct manipulation for imperative programs. In: Chang, B.-Y.E. (ed.) SAS 2019. LNCS, vol. 11822, pp. 347–367. Springer, Cham (2019). https://doi.org/10.1007/978-3-030-32304-2_17
18. JDial Debugger (2021). https://github.com/JDial-Debugger/backend/tree/master/SkechObject/benchmarks
19. Jeon, J., Qiu, X., Fetter-Degges, J., Foster, J.S., Solar-Lezama, A.: Synthesizing framework models for symbolic execution. In: ICSE 2016. ACM (2016). https://doi.org/10.1145/2884781.2884856
20. Jeon, J., Qiu, X., Foster, J.S., Solar-Lezama, A.: Jsketch: sketching for Java. In: Proceedings of the 2015 10th Joint Meeting on Foundations of Software Engineering. ESEC/FSE 2015. ACM (2015). https://doi.org/10.1145/2786805.2803189
21. Jha, S., Gulwani, S., Seshia, S.A., Tiwari, A.: Oracle-guided component-based program synthesis. In: Proceedings of the 32nd ACM/IEEE International Conf. on Software Engineering. ICSE 2010, vol. 1. ACM (2010). https://doi.org/10.1145/1806799.1806833
22. Li, W., Seshia, S.A.: Sparse coding for specification mining and error localization. In: Qadeer, S., Tasiran, S. (eds.) RV 2012. LNCS, vol. 7687, pp. 64–81. Springer, Heidelberg (2013). https://doi.org/10.1007/978-3-642-35632-2_9
23. Lustig, Y., Vardi, M.Y.: Synthesis from component libraries. Int. J. Softw. Tools Technol. Transf. 603–618 (2012). https://doi.org/10.1007/s10009-012-0236-z
24. Mandelin, D., Xu, L., Bodík, R., Kimelman, D.: Jungloid mining: helping to navigate the API jungle. In: Proceedings of the 2005 ACM SIGPLAN Conference on Programming Language Design and Implementation. PLDI 2005. ACM (2005). https://doi.org/10.1145/1065010.1065018
25. Mariano, B., et al.: Program synthesis with algebraic library specifications. In: Proceedings of the ACM on Programming Languages. OOPSLA 2019, vol. 3. ACM (Oct 2019). https://doi.org/10.1145/3360558
26. Miltner, A., Nuñez, A.T., Brendel, A., Chaudhuri, S., Dillig, I.: Bottom-up synthesis of recursive functional programs using angelic execution. In: Proceedings of the ACM on Programming Languages. POPL 2022, vol. 6. ACM, January 2022. https://doi.org/10.1145/3498682
27. Murali, V., Qi, L., Chaudhuri, S., Jermaine, C.: Neural sketch learning for conditional program generation. In: International Conference on Learning Representations (2018). https://openreview.net/forum?id=HkfXMz-Ab
28. OpenJDK (2014). https://hg.openjdk.java.net/jdk8/jdk8/jdk/file/tip/src/share/classes/java/util/ArrayList.java
29. Pacheco, C., Lahiri, S.K., Ernst, M.D., Ball, T.: Feedback-directed random test generation. In: 29th International Conference on Software Engineering (ICSE 2007), May 2007. https://doi.org/10.1109/ICSE.2007.37
30. Pei, Y., Furia, C.A., Nordio, M., Wei, Y., Meyer, B., Zeller, A.: Automated fixing of programs with contracts. IEEE Trans. Softw. Eng. 40(5), 427–449 (2014). https://doi.org/10.1109/TSE.2014.2312918

31. Polgreen, E., Reynolds, A., Seshia, S.A.: Satisfiability and synthesis modulo oracles. In: Finkbeiner, B., Wies, T. (eds.) VMCAI 2022. LNCS, vol. 13182, pp. 263–284. Springer, Cham (2022). https://doi.org/10.1007/978-3-030-94583-1_13

32. Raychev, V., Bielik, P., Vechev, M., Krause, A.: Learning programs from noisy data. In: Proceedings of the 43rd Annual ACM SIGPLAN-SIGACT Symposium on Principles of Programming Languages. POPL 2016. ACM (2016). https://doi.org/10.1145/2837614.2837671

33. Shi, K., Steinhardt, J., Liang, P.: Frangel: component-based synthesis with control structures. In: Proceedings of the ACM on Programming Languages. POPL 2019, vol. 3. ACM, January 2019. https://doi.org/10.1145/3290386

34. Singh, R., Gulwani, S., Solar-Lezama, A.: Automated feedback generation for introductory programming assignments. In: Proceedings of the 34th ACM SIGPLAN Conference on Programming Language Design and Implementation. PLDI 2013. ACM (2013). https://doi.org/10.1145/2491956.2462195

35. Singh, R., Singh, R., Xu, Z., Krosnick, R., Solar-Lezama, A.: Modular synthesis of sketches using models. In: McMillan, K.L., Rival, X. (eds.) VMCAI 2014. LNCS, vol. 8318, pp. 395–414. Springer, Heidelberg (2014). https://doi.org/10.1007/978-3-642-54013-4_22

36. Sketch (2021). https://github.com/asolarlez/sketch-frontend/blob/master/src/experiments/sk/models/

37. Skrupsky, N., Monshizadeh, M., Bisht, P., Hinrichs, T., Venkatakrishnan, V.N., Zuck, L.: Waves: automatic synthesis of client-side validation code for web applications. In: 2012 International Conference on Cyber Security, December 2012. https://doi.org/10.1109/CyberSecurity.2012.13

38. Smith, C., Albarghouthi, A.: Program synthesis with equivalence reduction. In: Enea, C., Piskac, R. (eds.) VMCAI 2019. LNCS, vol. 11388, pp. 24–47. Springer, Cham (2019). https://doi.org/10.1007/978-3-030-11245-5_2

39. Solar-Lezama, A.: The sketch programmers manual (2020). https://people.csail.mit.edu/asolar/manual.pdf, version 1.7.6

40. Solar-Lezama, A., Tancau, L., Bodik, R., Seshia, S., Saraswat, V.: Combinatorial sketching for finite programs. In: Proceedings of the 12th International Conference on Architectural Support for Programming Languages and Operating Systems. ACM (2006). https://doi.org/10.1145/1168857.1168907

41. Srivastava, S., Gulwani, S., Chaudhuri, S., Foster, J.S.: Path-based inductive synthesis for program inversion. In: Proceedings of the 32nd ACM SIGPLAN Conference on Programming Language Design and Implementation. PLDI 2011. ACM (2011). https://doi.org/10.1145/1993498.1993557

42. Torlak, E., Bodik, R.: A lightweight symbolic virtual machine for solver-aided host languages. In: Proceedings of the 35th ACM SIGPLAN Conference on Programming Language Design and Implementation. PLDI 2014. ACM (2014). https://doi.org/10.1145/2594291.2594340

43. Yang, Z., Hua, J., Wang, K., Khurshid, S.: EdSynth: synthesizing API sequences with conditionals and loops. In: 2018 IEEE 11th International Conference on Software Testing, Verification and Validation. ICST 2018, April 2018. https://doi.org/10.1109/ICST.2018.00025

Boosting Robustness Verification
of Semantic Feature Neighborhoods

Anan Kabaha$^{(\boxtimes)}$ⓘ and Dana Drachsler-Cohenⓘ

Technion, Haifa, Israel
anan.kabaha@campus.technion.ac.il, ddana@ee.technion.ac.il

Abstract. Deep neural networks have been shown to be vulnerable to adversarial attacks that perturb inputs based on semantic features. Existing robustness analyzers can reason about semantic feature neighborhoods to increase the networks' reliability. However, despite the significant progress in these techniques, they still struggle to scale to deep networks and large neighborhoods. In this work, we introduce VeeP, an active learning approach that splits the verification process into a series of smaller verification steps, each is submitted to an existing robustness analyzer. The key idea is to build on prior steps to predict the next optimal step. The optimal step is predicted by estimating the robustness analyzer's *velocity* and *sensitivity* via parametric regression. We evaluate VeeP on MNIST, Fashion-MNIST, CIFAR-10 and ImageNet and show that it can analyze neighborhoods of various features: brightness, contrast, hue, saturation, and lightness. We show that, on average, given a 90 minute timeout, VeeP verifies 96% of the maximally certifiable neighborhoods within 29 minutes, while existing splitting approaches verify, on average, 73% of the maximally certifiable neighborhoods within 58 minutes.

1 Introduction

The reliability of deep neural networks (DNNs) has been undermined by adversarial examples: perturbations to inputs that deceive the network. Many adversarial attacks perturb an input image by perturbing each pixel independently by up to a small constant ϵ [14,27,36,45,46]. To understand the local robustness of a DNN in ϵ-balls around given images, many analysis techniques have been proposed [12,13,16,24,34,38,42,47,48,52,54]. In parallel, semantic adversarial attacks have been introduced, such as HSV transformations [21] and colorization and texture attacks [5]. Figure 1 illustrates some of these transformations. Unlike ϵ-ball adversarial attacks which are not visible, feature adversarial attacks can be visible, because the assumption is that humans and networks should not misclassify an image due to perturbations of semantic features. Reasoning about networks' robustness to semantic feature perturbations introduces new challenges to robustness analyzers. The main challenge is that unlike ϵ-ball attacks, where pixels can be perturbed independently, feature attacks impose dependencies on the pixels. Abstracting a feature neighborhood to its smallest bounding ϵ-ball

G. Singh and C. Urban (Eds.): SAS 2022, LNCS 13790, pp. 299–324, 2022.
https://doi.org/10.1007/978-3-031-22308-2_14

will lead to too many false alarms. Thus, existing robustness analyzers designed for ϵ-ball neighborhoods perform very poorly on feature neighborhoods.

This gave rise to several works on analyzing the robustness of feature neighborhoods [3,32,42]. These works rely on existing ϵ-ball robustness analyzers and employ two main techniques to reduce the loss of precision. First, they encode the pixels' dependencies imposed by the features by adding layers to the network [32] or by computing a tight linear abstraction of the feature neighborhood [3]. Second, they split the input range into smaller parts, each is verified independently, e.g., using uniform splitting [3,32,42]. Despite of these techniques, for deep networks and large neighborhoods, existing works either lose too much precision and fail to verify or split the neighborhoods into too many parts. In the latter case, approaches must choose between a very long execution time (several hours for deep networks and a single neighborhood) or forcing the analysis to terminate within a certain timeout, leading to certification of neighborhoods that are significantly smaller than the maximal certifiable neighborhoods. These inherent limitations diminish the ability to understand how vulnerable a network is to feature attacks.

Our work: splitting of feature neighborhoods via active learning. We address the following problem: given a set of features, each with a target perturbation diameter, find a maximally robust neighborhood defined by these features. We propose a dynamic close-to-optimal input splitting to boost the robustness certification of feature neighborhoods. Unlike previous splitting techniques, which perform uniform splitting [3,32] or branch-and-bound [6,7,19,30,35,48,52], our splitting relies on active learning: the success or failure of previous splits determines the size of future splits. The key idea is to phrase the verification task as a process, where each step picks an unproven part of the neighborhood and submits it to a robustness analyzer. The analyzer either succeeds in proving robustness or fails. Our goal is to compute the optimal split. An optimal split is one where the number of failed steps is minimal, the size of each proven part is maximal, and the execution time is minimal. Predicting an optimal split requires estimating the exact robustness boundary of the neighborhood, which is challenging.

Splitting by predicting the analyzer's velocity and sensitivity. We present VeeP (for **ve**rification **p**redictor), a learning algorithm, treating the robustness analyzer as the oracle, which dynamically defines the splitting. VeeP defines the next step by predicting the next optimal diameters. To this end, it approximates the analyzer's *sensitivity* and *velocity* for the unproven part. Informally, the sensitivity is a function of the diameters quantifying how certain the robustness analyzer is that the neighborhood is robust. A positive sensitivity means the analyzer determines the neighborhood is robust, while a non-positive sensitivity means the analyzer fails. The velocity is a function of the diameters quantifying the speed of the robustness analyzer. VeeP predicts the diameters of the next step by solving a constrained optimization problem: it looks for the diameters maximizing the velocity such that its sensitivity is positive. VeeP relies on parametric regression to approximate the velocity and sensitivity functions of the current step. It terminates either when it succeeds verifying robustness for the given

Hue

Saturation

Lightness

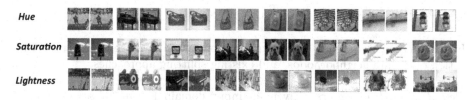

Fig. 1. Examples of ImageNet images and maximally perturbed images in the neighborhoods that VeeP verified robust, for an AlexNet model.

target diameters or when it fails to prove robustness for too small parts. It is thus a sound and precise verifier, up to a tunable precision level.

We implemented VeeP in a system, which relies on GPUPoly [34] as the robustness analyzer (the oracle). We evaluate VeeP on different kinds of architectures, including ResNet models for CIFAR-10 and AlexNet models for ImageNet. Our experiments focus on several semantic features: brightness, contrast, and HSL (hue, saturation, lightness). Results show that, when given a 90 minute timeout, VeeP almost perfectly closes the gap between the maximal certified feature neighborhoods and the minimal feature adversarial examples: the verified diameters that VeeP computes are, on average, at least 96% of the maximal certifiable diameter. On average, VeeP completes in 29 minutes. We compare to branch-and-bound, which computes 74% of the maximal diameters in 54 minutes, and to uniform splitting, which computes 73% of the maximal diameters in 62 minutes. We study the acceleration rate of VeeP over branch-and-bound and uniform splitting by running an experiment without a timeout. Results show that VeeP reduces the execution time of branch-and-bound by 4.4x and of uniform splitting by 10.2x. We also compare to the theoretical optimal greedy baseline that "knows" the optimal diameter of every step. We show that VeeP's time overhead is only 1.2x more than this theoretical optimal baseline. Figure 1 illustrates how large the neighborhoods that VeeP verifies. It shows pairs of original ImageNet images and the maximally perturbed image in the neighborhood that VeeP verified robust, for an AlexNet model. In these examples, every neighborhood is defined by a different feature (hue, saturation, and lightness), and the target diameter submitted to VeeP is determined by computing a minimal adversarial feature example along the corresponding feature.

To conclude, our main contributions are:

- A learning algorithm, called VeeP, to verify robustness of feature neighborhoods. VeeP computes an optimal split of the neighborhood, each part is verified by a robustness analyzer. To predict the next split, VeeP approximates the analyzer's velocity and sensitivity using parametric regression.
- An evaluation of VeeP on MNIST, Fashion MNIST, CIFAR-10 and ImageNet over fully-connected, convolutional, ResNet, and AlexNet models. Our evaluation focuses on neighborhoods defined using brightness, contrast, and HSL. Results show that VeeP provides a significant acceleration over branch-and-bound and uniform splitting.

2   Preliminaries

In this section, we provide the background on neural network classifiers, verification of feature neighborhoods, and existing splitting approaches.

Neural network classifiers. Given an input domain $\mathbb{R}^d$ and a set of classes $C = \{1, \ldots, c\}$, a classifier is a function mapping inputs to a score vector over the possible classes $D : \mathbb{R}^d \to \mathbb{R}^c$. A fully-connected network consists of L layers. The first layer takes as input a vector from $\mathbb{R}^d$, denoted i, and it passes the input as is to the next layer. The last layer outputs a vector, denoted $o^D(i)$, consisting of a score for each class in C. The classification of the network for input i is the class with the highest score, $c' = \mathrm{argmax}(o^D(i))$. When it is clear from the context, we omit the superscript D. The layers are functions, denoted $h_1, h_2, \ldots, h_L$, each takes as input the output of the preceding layer. The network's function is the composition of the layers: $o(i) = D(i) = h_L(h_{L-1}(\cdots (h_1(i))))$. The function of layer m is defined by a set of processing units called neurons, denoted $n_{m,1}, \ldots, n_{m,k_m}$. Each neuron takes as input the outputs of all neurons in the preceding layer and outputs a real number. The output of the layer m is the vector $(n_{m,1}, \ldots, n_{m,k_m})^T$ consisting of all its neurons' outputs. A neuron $n_{m,k}$ has a weight for each input $w_{m,k,k'}$ and a single bias $b_{m,k}$. Its function is computed by first computing the sum of the bias and the multiplication of every input by its respective weight: $\hat{n}_{m,k} = b_{m,k} + \sum_{k'=1}^{k_{m-1}} w_{m,k',k} \cdot n_{m-1,k'}$. This output is then passed to an activation function φ to produce the output $n_{m,k} = \varphi(\hat{n}_{m,k})$. Activation functions are typically non-linear functions. In this work, we focus on the ReLU activation function, $\mathrm{ReLU}(x) = \max(0, x)$. We note that, for simplicity's sake, we explain our approach for fully-connected networks, but it extends to other architectures, e.g., convolutional and residual networks.

Local robustness. A safety property for neural networks that has drawn a lot of interest is *local robustness*. Its meaning is that a network does not change its classification for a given input under a given type of perturbation. Formally, given an input x, a neighborhood containing x, $I(x) \subseteq \mathbb{R}^d$, and a classifier D, we say D is robust in $I(x)$ if $\forall x' \in I(x)$, $\mathrm{argmax}(D(x')) = \mathrm{argmax}(D(x))$. We focus on feature neighborhoods, consisting of perturbations of an input x along a set of features $f_1, \ldots, f_T$. The perturbation of an input along a feature f is a function $f : \mathbb{R}^d \times \mathbb{R} \to \mathbb{R}^d$, mapping an input x and a diameter δ to the perturbation of x along the feature f by δ. To abbreviate, we call the perturbation function the feature f, similarly to [32]. For all features f and inputs x, we assume $f(x, 0) = x$. Given a feature f, a diameter $\bar{\delta}$, and an input x, the feature neighborhood $I_{f, \bar{\delta}}(x)$ is the set of all perturbations of x along f by up to diameter $\bar{\delta}$: $I_{f, \bar{\delta}}(x) = \{f(x, \delta) \mid 0 \le \delta \le \bar{\delta}\}$. We extend this definition to a set of features by considering a diameter for every feature. Given a set of features $f_1, \ldots, f_T$, their diameters $\bar{\delta}_1, \ldots, \bar{\delta}_T$, and an input x, we define:

$$I_{f_1, \bar{\delta}_1, \ldots, f_T, \bar{\delta}_T}(x) = \{f_T(\ldots f_2(f_1(x, \delta_1), \delta_2)\ldots, \delta_T) \mid 0 \le \delta_1 \le \bar{\delta}_1, \ldots, 0 \le \delta_T \le \bar{\delta}_T\}$$

3 Verification of Feature Neighborhoods: Motivation

There are many verifiers for analyzing robustness of neural networks [12,13, 16,24,34,38,42,47,48,52,54]. Most of them analyze box neighborhoods, where each input entry is bounded by an interval $[l, u]$ (for $l, u \in \mathbb{R}$). In particular, they can technically reason about feature neighborhoods: first, one has to over-approximate a feature neighborhood $I_{f_1, \bar{\delta}_1, ..., f_T, \bar{\delta}_t}(x)$ to a bounding box neighborhood, and then pass the box neighborhood to any of these verifiers. However, this approach loses the dependency between the input entries, imposed by the features, and may result in spurious counterexamples. To capture the dependencies, a recent work proposes to encode features as a layer and add it to the network as the first layer [32]. This has been shown to be effective for various features, such as brightness, hue, saturation, and lightness. However, for deep networks and large feature neighborhoods, encoding the dependency is not enough to prove robustness: either the analysis time is too long or the analyzer loses too much precision and fails. Because feature neighborhoods have low dimensionality (every feature introduces a single dimension), divide-and-conquer is a natural choice for scaling the analysis [3,32,42].

Divide-and-conquer for feature neighborhoods. Divide-and-conquer is highly effective for scaling the analysis of feature neighborhoods. The key challenge is computing a useful split. A branch-and-bound approach (BaB) computes the split lazily [6,7,19,30,35,48,52]. To illustrate, consider a single feature neighborhood $I_{f,\bar{\delta}}(x)$. A BaB approach begins by analyzing $I_{f,\bar{\delta}}(x)$. If the analysis fails, it splits the neighborhood into two neighborhoods, $I_{f,\delta}(x)$ and $I_{f,\bar{\delta}-\delta}(f(x,\delta))$. Then, it analyzes each neighborhood separately and continues to split neighborhoods upon failures. As a result, it tends to waste a lot of time on analyzing too large neighborhoods until reaching to suitable-sized neighborhoods. A uniform splitting approach determines a number m and splits the neighborhood into $I_{f,\bar{\delta}/m}(x), \ldots, I_{f,\bar{\delta}/m}(f(x,\bar{\delta}\cdot(m-1)/m))$ [3,32,42]. This approach may still fail for some neighborhoods, due to timeouts or loss in precision, or waste too much time on verifying too small neighborhoods. This raises the question: *can we dynamically determine a split that minimizes the execution time of the verification?*

4 Problem Definition: Time-Optimal Feature Verification

In this section, we define the problem of robustness verification of feature neighborhoods minimizing the execution time. To simplify notation, the definitions assume a single feature, but they easily extend to multiple features.

We view the robustness analysis of feature neighborhoods as a process. Given a feature neighborhood, the verifier executes a series of steps, dynamically constructed, until reaching the maximal diameter for which the network is robust. Our verification process relies on a box analyzer $\mathcal{A}$, which can determine the robustness of box neighborhoods. Every verification step determines the next (sub)neighborhood to verify and invokes the analyzer. The analyzer $\mathcal{A}$ need not be complete and may fail due to overapproximation error. That is, given a network and a box neighborhood, A returns *robust*, *non-robust*, or *unknown*. Since the goal of the feature verifier is to compute a maximal neighborhood, if A returns *unknown*, it splits the last neighborhood into smaller neighborhoods. To guarantee that the verification process terminates, if A fails to verify a feature neighborhood with a diameter up to a predetermined threshold δ_{MIN}, we assume that this neighborhood is not robust. Because the feature verifier terminates when reaching the maximal diameter, the challenge is not to improve its precision but rather to keep its execution time minimal. We next provide formal definitions.

Definition 1 (Verification Step). *Given a box analyzer A, a classifier D, and a feature neighborhood defined by f, $\bar{\delta}$ and x, a verification step is a pair (δ_x, δ), such that $0 \leq \delta_x < \bar{\delta}$ and $0 < \delta \leq \bar{\delta}$. The result of a verification step (δ_x, δ) is A's result for D and $I_{f,\delta}(f(x, \delta_x))$, which is* robust, *not* robust *or* unknown.

We next define feature verification sequence, consisting of verification steps.

Definition 2 (Feature Verification Sequence). *Given a box analyzer A, a precision level δ_{MIN}, a classifier D, and a feature neighborhood defined by f, $\bar{\delta}$, and x, a feature verification sequence is a sequence of verification steps $s_1, \ldots, s_m$ that verify the maximally robust neighborhood up to $\bar{\delta}$, i.e., either:*

- *there is no step whose result is not* robust *and, for every $\delta_y \in [0, \bar{\delta}]$, there is a step $s = (\delta_x, \delta)$, where $\delta_x \leq \delta_y \leq \delta_x + \delta$, for which A returns* robust. *That is, the verification steps cover all inputs in $I_{f,\bar{\delta}}(x)$, or*
- *there is no step whose result is not* robust, *except perhaps the last step $s_m = (\delta_{m,x}, \delta_m)$ whose result is* unknown *or not* robust *and $\delta_m = \delta_{MIN}$. For every $\delta_y \in [0, \delta_{m,x}]$, there is a step $s = (\delta_x, \delta)$, where $\delta_x \leq \delta_y \leq \delta_x + \delta$, for which A returns* robust. *That is, the verification steps cover all inputs in $I_{f,\delta_{m,x}}(x)$ and we assume there is an adversarial example in $I_{f,\delta_{MIN}}(f(x, \delta_{m,x}))$.*

Finally, we define the problem of time-optimal feature verification. To this end, we introduce a notation. Given a verification step s, we denote by $t(s)$ the execution time of the analyzer A on the neighborhood defined by step s. We note that we assume that the time to define a verification step $s = (\delta_x, \delta)$ is negligible with respect to $t(s)$. Given a feature verification sequence $S = (s_1, \ldots, s_m)$, its execution time is the sum of its steps' execution times: $t(S) = \Sigma_{i=1}^{m} t(s_i)$. Our goal is to compute a feature verification sequence minimizing the execution time.

Definition 3 (Time-Optimal Feature Verification). *Given a box analyzer A and a feature neighborhood defined by f, $\bar{\delta}$ and x, a time-optimal feature verification sequence S is one that minimizes the execution time: $argmin_S t(S)$.*

This problem is challenging because divide-and-conquer algorithms have the execution time of a verification step only *after* they invoke A on that step's neighborhood. Thus, constructing a verification sequence is bound to involve suboptimal choices. However, we show that it is possible to *predict* the execution time of a (new) verification step based on the execution times of the previous steps. We note that although we focus on analysis of deep neural networks, we believe that predicting verification steps based on prior steps is a more general concept which is applicable to analysis of other machine learning models.

5 Prediction by Proof Velocity and Sensitivity

In this section, we present the key concepts on which we build to predict the verification steps: proof velocity and sensitivity. We show that these can be modeled by parametric functions. We then explain how these functions can be used to predict optimal steps by solving a constrained optimization problem.

Proof velocity. To minimize the execution time of the verification process, we wish to maximize the *proof velocity*. Proof velocity is the ratio of the neighborhood's *certified diameter* and the time to verify it by the box analyzer $\mathcal{A}$. In the following, we denote the execution time of step $s = (\delta_x, \delta)$ by $t(s) = t_{\mathcal{A}}(I_{f,\delta}(f(x, \delta_x)))$. The certified diameter of this step's neighborhood, denoted $\delta_{\mathcal{A}}^s$, is equal to δ, if $\mathcal{A}$ returns *robust*, and 0, if $\mathcal{A}$ returns *non-robust* or *unknown*.

Definition 4 (Proof Velocity). *Given a box analyzer $\mathcal{A}$, a classifier D, a feature neighborhood defined by f, $\bar{\delta}$, and x, and a verification step $s = (\delta_x, \delta)$, the proof velocity of s is:* $V_{\mathcal{A}}(I_{f,\delta}(f(x, \delta_x))) = \frac{\delta_{\mathcal{A}}^s}{t(I_{f,\delta}(f(x, \delta_x)))}.$

The velocity is either a positive number, if $\mathcal{A}$ returns *robust*, and 0 otherwise. A zero velocity means that the feature verifier has to split this neighborhood and that we have not gained from this analysis. Empirically, we observe that if $\mathcal{A}$ relies on linear approximations to analyze the network robustness, the proof velocity can be modeled as a function of the certified diameter. For small networks or neighborhoods, the velocity is approximately a linear function of the diameter, because the analysis time is, in practice, constant. The larger the network or the neighborhood, the longer the analysis time because the overapproximation error increases, and thus the analyzer $\mathcal{A}$ executes more refinement steps (e.g., back-substitution [42] or solving linear programs [48]). We empirically observe that when the network or the neighborhood are large enough to trigger refinement steps, the execution time is approximately exponentially related to the diameter: $t(\delta) \propto exp(\beta \cdot \delta)$, for some parameter β. Consequently, $V(\delta) \propto \delta \cdot exp(-\beta \cdot \delta)$. Note that, for $\beta = 0$, the proof velocity is linear in δ. Thus, this function captures both cases of small network/neighborhood and large network/neighborhood. We illustrate this relation in Fig. 2, showing the measured proof velocity (the blue dots) as a function of the diameter δ, across different models and three box analyzers relying on different linear approximations. The figure also shows the function we use to approximate the proof velocity (the red curve). The figure shows how close the approximation is. We next summarize this observation.

Observation 1. *For every verification step $s = (\delta_x, \delta)$, if $\delta_{\mathcal{A}}^s > 0$, the velocity can be approximated by:* $V(\delta) = \alpha_V \cdot \delta \cdot exp(-\beta_V \cdot \delta)$ *for $\beta_V \geq 0$ and $\alpha_V \in \mathbb{R}$.*

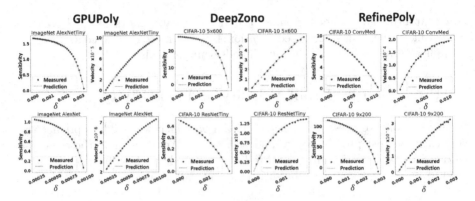

Fig. 2. Velocity and sensitivity as functions of the diameter δ, for different models and three box analyzers: GPUPoly [34], DeepZono [41], and RefinePoly [40]. Blue dots show the measured values and red curves show our function approximations.

We can use this observation to predict time-optimal verification steps. To this end, at the beginning of every verification step, we require to (1) estimate the parameters of the velocity's function and (2) predict the maximal δ^s_{MAX} for which the analyzer $\mathcal{A}$ returns *robust*. With these values, we can define the next step by computing $\delta \in (0, \delta^s_{\text{MAX}}]$ maximizing the proof velocity. In order to predict the maximal value δ^s_{MAX}, we define the concept of *neighborhood sensitivity*.

Neighborhood sensitivity. The *sensitivity* concept builds on the commonly known concept *network confidence*. Given a classifier D and an input x, the confidence of the classifier in class j is the output $o^D_j(x)$, i.e., the score that D assigns for j on input x. Based on this term, we define the *sensitivity* of x as the difference between the confidence in j and the highest confidence in a class different from j:

$$S^D(x, j) = o^D_j(x) - \text{argmax}_{j' \neq j}(o^D_{j'}(x))$$

If $S^D(x, j) > 0$, then D classifies x as j, and the higher $S^D(x, j)$ the more certain the classifier is in its classification of x as j. We extend this term to neighborhoods. We define the neighborhood sensitivity as the minimal sensitivity of its inputs: $S^D(I, j) = \min\{S^D(x', j) \mid x' \in I\}$. From this definition, we get few observations. First, for any $I \subseteq I'$, we have $S^D(I', j) \leq S^D(I, j)$. That is, extending a neighborhood with more inputs may decrease the neighborhood sensitivity in j. Second, if $S^D(I, j) \leq 0$, then I is not robust to j. Third, if $\mathcal{A}$ is precise, then for every verification step $s = (\delta_x, \delta)$, we have $\delta^s_{\mathcal{A}} = \delta$ if and only if the sensitivity $S^D(I_{f,\delta}(f(x, \delta_x)), j)$ is positive. In practice, we rely on an imprecise analyzer $\mathcal{A}$ and we cannot compute the exact neighborhood sensitivity. However, we can approximate a neighborhood's sensitivity by relying on the analysis of $\mathcal{A}$. Since most incomplete analyzers compute, for every output neuron k, real-valued bounds $[l_k, u_k]$, we can approximate the neighborhood sensitivity:

$$S^D_{\mathcal{A}}(I_{f,\delta}(f(x, \delta_x)), j) = l_j - \max_{j' \neq j} u_{j'}$$

Thus, to compute the maximal δ_{MAX}^s whose neighborhood can be proven robust by $\mathcal{A}$, we can compute the maximal δ_{MAX}^s for which $S_{\mathcal{A}}^D(I_{f,\delta_{\text{MAX}}^s}(f(x,\delta_x)), j) > 0$. The remaining question is how to approximate the sensitivity function. Empirically, we observe that if $\mathcal{A}$ relies on linear approximations to analyze the network robustness, the neighborhood sensitivity has an exponential relation to the diameter. This is demonstrated in Fig. 2, for different models and linear approximations. The figure shows how close the approximation is (red curves) to the measured sensitivity (the blue dots). We next summarize this observation.

Observation 2. *For every verification step, the neighborhood sensitivity can be approximated by:* $S_{\mathcal{A}}(\delta) = \alpha_S + \beta_S \cdot exp(\gamma_S \cdot \delta)$, *where* $\alpha_S, \beta_S, \gamma_S \in \mathbb{R}$.

This exponential relation can be explained by considering the effect of linear approximations on non-linear computations. At a high-level, the exponential relation is linked to the number of non-linear neurons being approximated. We exemplify this relation in the extended version of this paper [23, Appendix A].

Time-optimal feature verification via proof velocity and sensitivity. Given the functions of the velocity and sensitivity, we can state our problem as a constrained optimization. Given an analyzer $\mathcal{A}$, a feature neighborhood defined by f, $\bar{\delta}$ and x, and the currently maximal certified diameter δ_x, the δ of the optimal verification step $s = (\delta_x, \delta)$ is a solution to the following optimization problem:

$$\max V^D(I_{f,\delta}(f(x,\delta_x))) \text{ such that } S_{\mathcal{A}}^D(I_{f,\delta}(f(x,\delta_x)), c_x) > 0$$

Here, c_x is the classification of x. Because both functions are convex, the global maximum can be computed as standard. First, we compute the feasible region of δ by comparing $S^D(I_{f,\delta}(f(x,\delta_x)), c_x)$ to zero. Second, we compute the derivative of $V^D(I_{f,\delta}(f(x,\delta_x)))$, compare to zero, and compute the optimal δ. If the optimal δ is not feasible, we take the closest feasible value. Therefore, if we know the parameters of the velocity and sensitivity functions, we can compute an optimal verification step. The challenge is to approximate these parameters, for every step. In the next section, we explain how to predict them from the previous steps.

6   VeeP: A System for Time-Optimal Feature Verification

In this section, we present our system, called VeeP, for computing time-optimal verification steps. VeeP builds on the ideas presented in Sect. 5 and dynamically constructs the verification steps by solving the constrained optimization problem. The challenge is predicting the parameters of the velocity and sensitivity functions. The key idea is to treat the analyzer as an *oracle*, whose responses to previous verification steps are used to define the next step. Conceptually, VeeP builds on active learning, where it acts as the learner for optimal verification steps and the analyzer acts as the oracle. Throughout execution, VeeP tracks the accumulated verified diameters of the robust neighborhood. If a verification step succeeds, the robust neighborhood is extended and the verified diameters increase. If a step fails, the next predicted diameters will be smaller, up to a minimal value δ_{MIN}. Thus, although VeeP predicts the diameters, which may be too small or large, its overall analysis is sound and precise up to δ_{MIN}. It is sound because it employs divide-and-conquer and relies on a sound analyzer. It is precise because if a step fails for diameters greater than δ_{MIN}, then VeeP attempts again to extend the robust neighborhood by predicting smaller diameters. We begin this section by explaining how VeeP reasons about neighborhoods defined by a single feature and then extend it to general feature neighborhoods.

6.1 VeeP for Single Feature Neighborhoods

In this section, we describe VeeP for analyzing neighborhoods defined by a single feature. VeeP takes as inputs a classifier D, a feature f, a diameter $\bar{\delta}$, and an input x. During its execution, it maintains in δ_x the sum of the certified diameters. It returns the maximal $\delta_x \leq \bar{\delta}$ for which the neighborhood is robust, up to precision δ_{MIN}. VeeP operates iteratively, where the main computation of every iteration is determining a verification step $s_k = (\delta_x, \delta_k)$ to submit to the analyzer $\mathcal{A}$.

Defining a verification step. The goal of a verification step is to increase the accumulated certified diameter δ_x by a diameter δ_k. VeeP aims at choosing δ_k such that (1) the sensitivity of $I_{f,\delta_k}(f(x,\delta_x))$, as determined by the box analyzer $\mathcal{A}$, is positive, and (2) $I_{f,\delta_k}(f(x,\delta_x))$ maximizes the proof velocity. VeeP leverages Observation 1 and 2 and approximates them as $S_k(\delta) = \alpha_S + \beta_S \cdot exp(\gamma_S \cdot \delta)$ and $V_k(\delta) = \alpha_V \cdot \delta \cdot exp(-\beta_V \cdot \delta)$. It solves two parametric regression problems to determine $\theta_S^k = (\alpha_S, \beta_S, \gamma_S)$ and $\theta_V^k = (\alpha_V, \beta_V)$. This requires to obtain examples: $e_S^1 = (\delta^1, S(\delta^1)), ..., e_S^M = (\delta^M, S(\delta^M))$ and $e_V^1 = (\delta^1, V(\delta^1)), ..., e_V^M = (\delta^M, V(\delta^M))$. The minimal number of examples is three for $S_k(\delta)$ and two for $V_k(\delta)$. Given the examples, the parameters are determined by minimizing a loss:

$$\theta_S^k = \underset{\alpha_S,\beta_S,\gamma_S}{\operatorname{argmin}} L(\alpha_S, \beta_S, \gamma_S, e_S^1, \ldots, e_S^M) \qquad \theta_V^k = \underset{\alpha_V,\beta_V}{\operatorname{argmin}} L(\alpha_V, \beta_V, e_V^1, \ldots, e_V^M)$$

For the loss, VeeP uses the least squares error. Given the parameters, VeeP solves the optimization problem (Sect. 5) to approximate the optimal value of δ_k:

$$\max V_{\theta_V^k}(\delta) \text{ such that } S_{\theta_S^k}(\delta) > 0$$

The remaining question is how to obtain examples. A naive approach is to randomly select $\delta^1, \ldots, \delta^M$ and for each δ^i run the analyzer $\mathcal{A}$ on $I_{f,\delta^i}(f(x,\delta_x))$, to find the sensitivity and velocity. However, these M calls to $\mathcal{A}$ are highly time consuming, especially because their only goal is to predict the next diameter to analyze. Instead, VeeP relies on previous steps to estimate examples by leveraging two empirical observations. First, the function $V_k(\delta)$ is similar to previous $V_{k-i}(\delta)$, for small values of i. Thus, VeeP can use as examples $(\delta_{k-i}, V_{k-i}(\delta_{k-i}))$, for small values of i. Second, the function $S_k(\delta)$ is similar to $S_{k-i}(\delta)$, for small values of i, up to a small alignment term: $S_k(0) - S_{k-i}(0)$. Thus, VeeP can use as examples $(\delta_{k-i}, S_{k-i}(\delta_{k-i}) + S_k(0) - S_{k-i}(0))$, for small values of i. Note that computing $S_k(0)$ does not require to run $\mathcal{A}$, because the sensitivity of $I_{f,0}(f(x,\delta_x))$ is

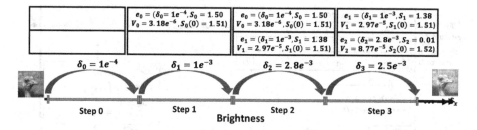

Fig. 3. Analysis for the brightness feature, an ImageNet image, and AlexNetTiny.

exactly the sensitivity of the input $f(x, \delta_x)$, which can be computed by running it through the classifier D. Based on these observations, VeeP obtains examples as follows. Its first example is $(0, S_k(0))$. Since the velocity of this step's neighborhood is zero, it is not used to approximate $V_k(\delta)$. The next $M-1$ examples are defined as described by the previous $M-1$ predicted diameters, which have already been submitted to $\mathcal{A}$. Note that the examples are defined from previous steps regardless of whether their neighborhoods have been proven robust or not. When VeeP begins its computation and has no previous steps, it executes $M-1$ steps whose diameters are some small predetermined values.

Example. Figure 3 shows an example of VeeP's analysis for a brightness neighborhood with $\bar{\delta} = 0.2$, an ImageNet image x (the image on the left) and an AlexNet-Tiny classifier D. We assume $M = 3$. The first two steps rely on predetermined small diameters $\delta_0 = 10^{-4}$ and $\delta_1 = 10^{-3}$. VeeP begins by submitting to $\mathcal{A}$ the neighborhood $I_{f,\delta_0}(x)$ and $\mathcal{A}$ returns *robust*. VeeP thus updates the accumulated diameter $\delta_x = 10^{-4}$ and constructs the example e_0. The example consists of the sensitivity S_0 and velocity V_0 (computed from $\mathcal{A}$'s analysis), and the sensitivity $S_0(0)$ at $\delta_x = 0$ (computed by running x through D). The next verification step submits to $\mathcal{A}$ the neighborhood $I_{f,\delta_1}(f(x, 10^{-4}))$ and $\mathcal{A}$ returns *robust*. VeeP thus updates $\delta_x = 1.1 \cdot 10^{-3}$ and constructs the example e_1, consisting of the sensitivity S_1 and velocity V_1 (computed from $\mathcal{A}$'s analysis) and the sensitivity $S_1(0)$ (computed by running $f(x, 10^{-4})$ through D). To predict the next diameter δ_2, VeeP relies on e_0, e_1 and $S_2(0)$ (computed by running $f(x, 1.1 \cdot 10^{-3})$ through D). Its examples are: $e_S^0 = (0, 1.52)$, $e_S^1 = (10^{-4}, S_0 + S_2(0) - S_0(0))$, $e_S^2 = (10^{-3}, S_1 + S_2(0) - S_1(0))$, and $e_V^0 = (10^{-4}, V_0)$, $e_V^1 = (10^{-3}, V_1)$. Given the examples, it minimizes the MSE loss to compute the parameters θ_S^2 and θ_V^2. Afterwards, it solves the constrained optimization function to compute δ_2. The result is $\delta_2 = 2.8 \cdot 10^{-3}$. VeeP submits to $\mathcal{A}$ the neighborhood $I_{f,\delta_2}(f(x, 1.1 \cdot 10^{-3}))$ and $\mathcal{A}$ returns *robust*. VeeP updates δ_x and constructs the example e_2, as described before. VeeP predicts the next diameter δ_3, by repeating this process using the examples e_1 and e_2. It continues until reaching the target diameter $\bar{\delta} = 0.2$. The most perturbed image in this neighborhood is shown on the right of Fig. 3.

Overall operation. The operation of VeeP is summarized in Fig. 4 and mostly follows the description above, up to few modifications to guarantee termination.

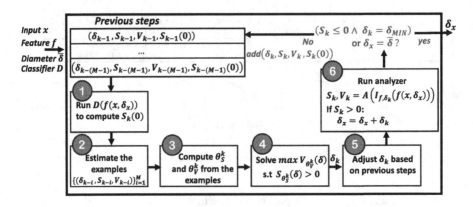

Fig. 4. The VeeP System.

Initially, VeeP sets $\delta_x = 0$ and generates the first $M - 1$ steps using predetermined diameters. Every verification step predicts the next diameter based on previous iterations, as described before (steps 1–4 in Fig. 4). Then, to avoid certification failures and guarantee termination, VeeP performs three corrections to the predicted diameter δ_k (step 5). First, it checks whether in the last M steps, there has been a step i with a smaller predicted diameter, $\delta_i < \delta_k$, that failed. If so, VeeP sets δ_k to the minimal value between the last verified diameter (if exists) and the last failed one from the last M steps. Second, it subtracts a small constant from δ_k. Third, it guarantees that δ_k is not below the precision level by setting $\delta_k = \max(\delta_k, \delta_{\text{MIN}})$. These refinements, along with the prediction based on recent examples, aim at mitigating predicting too large or too small diameters. The neighborhood defined by (δ_x, δ_k) is submitted to the analyzer $\mathcal{A}$ (step 6), which returns the real-valued bounds of the output neurons. Accordingly, VeeP computes the sensitivity S_k and velocity V_k. If $S_k > 0$, then the neighborhood is robust and thus δ_x is increased by δ_k. Afterwards, VeeP checks the termination conditions. The first condition is $S_k \leq 0$ and $\delta_k = \delta_{\text{MIN}}$, indicating that the neighborhood is maximal. The second condition is $\delta_x = \bar{\delta}$, indicating that VeeP certified the target diameter. If the conditions are not met, VeeP constructs the example of this step and continues to another iteration.

Correctness analysis. We next discuss the time overhead of VeeP and its correctness. The first lemma analyzes the time overhead of VeeP. The overhead is the additional time that VeeP requires compared to an oblivious splitting approach. The overhead of every step consists of the call to the classifier D (to compute $S_k(0)$) and the time to solve the regression problems (to approximate S_k and V_k). The time overhead also includes the $M - 1$ initial calls to the analyzer $\mathcal{A}$.

Lemma 1. *The total overhead is $n \cdot (T_D + T_R) + \Sigma_{i=1}^{M-1} T_{\mathcal{A},i}$, where T_D is the time to run a single input in the classifier D, T_R is the time to solve a regression problem from M examples, n is the number of verification steps and $T_{\mathcal{A},i}$ is the execution time of $\mathcal{A}$ on the ith initial step.*

In practice, T_D and T_R are significantly shorter than the time to run the analyzer $\mathcal{A}$. Since the value of M is small (we pick $M = 3$ or $M = 4$), the overhead of the initial queries to the analyzer is negligible when compared to the total execution time of VeeP. As a result, we observe that the execution time of VeeP is very close to the optimal greedy baseline that "knows" the optimal diameter of every step. We continue with a lemma guaranteeing termination and a theorem guaranteeing soundness and precision (up to δ_{MIN}). Proofs are provided in the extended version of this paper [23, Appendix B].

Lemma 2. *Given a classifier D, an input x, a feature f and a diameter $\bar{\delta}$, if $\mathcal{A}$ is guaranteed to terminate, then VeeP is guaranteed to terminate.*

Theorem 1. *Given a classifier D, an input x, a feature f, a diameter $\bar{\delta}$, and a precision level δ_{MIN}, if $\mathcal{A}$ is sound (but may be incomplete), then VeeP is:*

- *sound: if it returns $I_{f,\delta_x}(x)$, then this neighborhood is robust, and*
- *precise up to δ_{MIN}: if it returns δ_x smaller than $\bar{\delta}$, then we assume there is $\hat{\delta} \in (\delta_x, \delta_x + \delta_{MIN}]$ such that $x' = f(x, \hat{\delta})$ is an adversarial example.*

6.2   VeeP for Multi-feature Neighborhoods

In this section, we present VeeP's algorithm to verify neighborhoods defined by multiple features $f_1, f_2, \ldots, f_T$. VeeP computes a sequence of verification steps that cover the maximal robust T-dimensional hyper-rectangle neighborhood. The sequence is constructed such that VeeP computes the maximal diameters feature-by-feature. To compute the maximal diameter of the ith feature, VeeP computes the maximal robust i-dimensional neighborhood of the first i features. Similarly to Sect. 6.1, a verification step is a pair of an offset vector $(\delta_1, \ldots, \delta_T)$ (instead of δ_x) and a diameter δ. A verification step thus corresponds to a hyper-cube neighborhood $I_{f_1, \delta, \ldots, f_T, \delta}(x_0)$, where x_0 is the perturbation of x as determined by the features and offsets $(x_0 = f_T(\ldots (f_2(f_1(x, \delta_1), \delta_2), \ldots), \delta_T))$. While VeeP could predict a different diameter for each feature, this would increase the prediction's complexity by a factor of T. Besides this, the analysis is similar to Sect. 6.1 but generalizes it to high dimension, resulting in few differences. First, computing the offsets is more subtle than computing δ_x. Second, the examples used for prediction also leverage the *closest* examples. Third, computing the accumulated verified diameters, required for checking the termination conditions, involves obtaining the *vertices* of the certified region. We next explain all these differences, then exemplify VeeP's operation, and finally present the algorithm.

Offsets. Initially, all offsets are zero. Recall that VeeP computes the maximal diameters feature-by-feature, and, for every f_i, it computes the maximal robust i-dimensional neighborhood of $f_1, \ldots, f_i$. After every verification step, VeeP computes the next offsets. Assume VeeP is currently at feature f_i. If a step fails for $\delta > \delta_{\text{MIN}}$, the offsets of the next step are identical. If a step fails for $\delta = \delta_{\text{MIN}}$ or reaches $\bar{\delta}_i$, VeeP computes the initial offsets of f_{i+1}, as shortly described. Otherwise, VeeP computes the next offsets based on a feature-by-feature order (from 1 to i). The order, defined in [23, Appendix C], guarantees that VeeP covers the entire i-dimensional neighborhood. We later exemplify it on a running example. Upon starting a feature f_j, VeeP computes the initial offsets based on the already certified neighborhoods. This is obtained by finding the earliest step forming a vertex on the j-dimensional boundary of the certified region, such that the vertex's j^{th} offset is within $(0, \bar{\delta}_j)$. This leverages the already certified neighborhoods: since the steps define hyper-cube neighborhoods, as a byproduct of their analysis, there is also progress in the direction of the succeeding, not yet analyzed, features. The complete computation is provided in [23, Appendix C].

Examples. The diameter of a verification step is predicted by $M + 1$ examples: $(0, S_k(0))$, $M - 1$ (adapted) recent examples and, to increase the prediction accuracy, the *closest* example, with respect to the Euclidean distance. The $M - 1$ recent examples are used only if they (aim to) advance the diameter of the same feature as the current step does. If not all of them advance the same feature, VeeP completes the missing examples with closest examples or initialization examples.

Termination. VeeP terminates when it reaches all target diameters or all maximal diameters. These conditions generalize the termination conditions presented in Sect. 6.1. To check the first condition, VeeP maintains an array ds of the certified diameters, which are updated after every verification step. The diameters are computed from the vertices bounding the certified region. Although the region induced by the maximal diameters is a hyper-rectangle, the certified region may form other shapes. During the analysis, VeeP computes the vertices of the certified region. To update ds, it selects the maximal bounded hyper-rectangle, with respect to the Euclidean norm. To check the second condition, VeeP checks whether it has failed for T consecutive iterations for a neighborhood whose diameter is δ_{MIN}. Correctness follows from the the operation of VeeP: upon failure of a neighborhood with diameter δ_{MIN}, it proceeds to the next feature. Thus, T consecutive failures imply that VeeP has reached all maximal diameters.

Example. We next exemplify VeeP for a neighborhood defined by brightness and contrast, where $\bar{\delta}_1 = \bar{\delta}_2 = 0.08$ and $M = 3$ (Fig. 5). VeeP computes the maximal diameters one by one: first the brightness's diameter and then the contrast's diameter. Figure 5(a) visualizes the verification steps that compute the maximal diameter of brightness. The sequence begins from the offset $(0, 0)$ (i.e., $x_0 = x$), and the computation is similar to Sect. 6.1. When VeeP reaches $\bar{\delta}_1$, it continues to the contrast feature. It begins by finding the earliest verification step forming a vertex on the 2-dimensional boundary of the certified region, such that the vertex's second offset is within $(0, \bar{\delta}_2)$. This is the first step and the vertex is $(0, 0.018)$ (since this step's diameter is 0.018). Thus, the initial offset of contrast is $(0, 0.018)$. During the analysis of the contrast feature, VeeP computes verification steps feature-by-feature. Thus, after initializing the offsets, VeeP advances the brightness's offset, until reaching its maximal certified diameter (rightmost square, top row, Fig. 5(b)). Then, by the order VeeP follows for the verification steps, it (again) looks for the earliest step forming a vertex on the 2-dimensional boundary

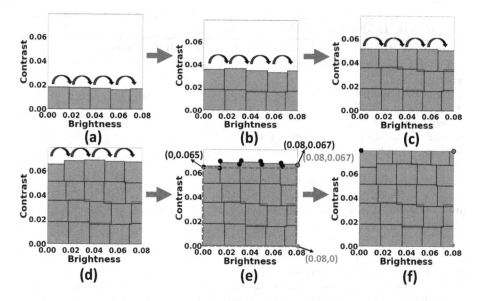

Fig. 5. Example of VeeP's analysis to certify a neighborhood defined by brightness and contrast, for an MNIST image, on a fully-connected network.

of the certified region, such that the vertex's second offset is within $(0, \bar{\delta}_2)$. This is the leftmost square, top row, Fig. 5(b). Thus, it sets the next offset (i.e., of the leftmost square, top row, Fig. 5(c)) to that vertex's offsets. The rest of the computation continues similarly (Fig. 5(c), (d), and (f)). We next illustrate the different sets of examples used for the prediction (besides $(0, S_k(0))$). Consider Fig. 5(b). The examples used by the middle step at the top row are the two leftmost squares at the top row and the middle square at the row below. The examples used by the leftmost square at the top row are the three closest examples – the three leftmost squares at the bottom row – since there are no steps advancing the contrast's diameter. After every verification step, VeeP constructs for each feature the vertices of the certified neighborhood. Figure 5(e) shows the vertices after completing the verification steps of Fig. 5(d): ten red vertices for contrast and two yellow vertices for brightness. Figure 5(f) shows the vertices after completing all verification steps. Given the vertices, VeeP computes the accumulated verified diameter of each feature, which is the minimum coordinate of its vertices. For example, in Fig. 5(e), the verified diameter of brightness is 0.08, which is the minimum of the first coordinates of $(0.08, 0)$ and $(0.08, 0.067)$, and similarly, the verified diameter of contrast is 0.065. VeeP updates the current maximal diameters to these diameters if they form a larger hyper-rectangle than the current ones. Note that if VeeP terminates after reaching all target diameters (e.g., Fig. 5(f)), the certified region is a hyper-rectangle and is thus returned.

Overall operation. Algorithm 1 summarizes the operation of VeeP. VeeP begins by initializing ds, the maximal diameters array, the first $M - 1$ examples (as

---

Algorithm 1: Multi-feature-VeeP $(D, x, f_1, \bar{\delta}_1, \ldots, f_T, \bar{\delta}_T)$

Input: A classifier D, input x, features $f_1, \ldots, f_T$ and diameters $\bar{\delta}_1, \ldots, \bar{\delta}_T$.
Output: Diameter array ds s.t. $I_{f_1,ds[1],\ldots,f_T,ds[T]}(x)$ is maximally robust.

1 $ds = [0, \ldots, 0]$
2 $Ex = \text{InitExamples}(M)$
3 $\text{offsets} = [0, \ldots, 0]$
4 $\text{count\_min} = 0$
5 **while** $\exists ds[i] < \bar{\delta}_i \wedge count\_min < T$ **do**
6       $x_0 = perturb(x, f_1, \ldots, f_T, \text{offsets})$
7       $S_0 = D(x_0)$
8       $\delta = \text{predict}(Ex, x_0, S_0)$
9       $t_0 = time()$
10      $\{l_{o,j}, u_{o,j}\}_{j=1}^{c} = \mathcal{A}(D, I_{f_1,\delta,\ldots,f_T,\delta}(x_0))$
11      $t_1 = time()$
12      $S = l_{c_x} - \max_{j \neq c_x} u_j$
13      $V = S > 0$? $\frac{\delta}{t_1 - t_0}$: 0
14      $Ex = Ex \cup \{(\delta, S, V, S_0, \text{offsets})\}$
15      $\text{offsets} = \text{compute\_next\_offsets}(Ex, \bar{\delta}_1, \ldots, \bar{\delta}_T)$
16      $BV_1, \ldots, BV_T = \text{compute\_certified\_neighborhood\_vertices}(Ex)$
17      $ds\_curr = [0, \ldots, 0]$
18   **for** $i = 1; i \leq T; i{+}{+}$ **do**
19          $ds\_curr[i] = min\{v_i \mid v \in BV_i\}$
20   **if** *vectorNorm(ds_curr)* > *vectorNorm(ds)* **then** $ds = ds\_curr$
21      $count\_min = (S \leq 0 \wedge \delta == \delta_{\text{MIN}})$? $count\_min + 1 : 0$
22 **return** ds

---

described in Sect. 6.1), the `offset` array and a counter `count_min`, tracking the number of consecutive failures. Then, it enters a loop, where each iteration computes a single verification step. An iteration of the loop begins by determining x_0 from the offsets (Line 6). Then, it progresses as described in Sect. 6.1 (Lines 7–14): it computes x_0's sensitivity, predicts δ, submits to $\mathcal{A}$, computes the velocity and sensitivity, and adds this verification step as a new example. After that, it computes the new offsets (Line 15). Next, the maximal diameters are computed. To this end, VeeP constructs, for each feature, the vertices of the certified region (Line 16). Computing the vertices is a technical computation determined from the set of examples. We omit the exact computation. Given the vertices, VeeP computes the current verified diameters `ds_curr`. The current verified diameter of feature i is the minimum i^{th} coordinate of its vertices (Lines 17–19). Then, if the Euclidean norm of `ds_curr` is greater than that of `ds`, it updates `ds` (Line 20). Lastly, the counter `count_min` is increased, if $\mathcal{A}$ failed, or resets, otherwise (Line 21). The loop continues as long as VeeP has not reached all target diameters and has not failed during the last T iterations (Line 5).

Correctness. We next present the correctness guarantees of Algorithm 1. Proofs are provided in the extended version of this paper [23, Appendix B].

Lemma 3. *Given a classifier D, an input x, features $f_1, \ldots, f_T$ and diameters $\bar{\delta}_1, \ldots, \bar{\delta}_T$, if $\mathcal{A}$ is guaranteed to terminate, then VeeP is guaranteed to terminate.*

Lastly, we show that VeeP is sound and precise, up to precision of δ_{MIN} for each feature's maximal diameter.

Theorem 2. *Given a classifier D, an input x, features $f_1, \ldots, f_T$ and diameters $\bar{\delta}_1, \ldots, \bar{\delta}_T$, if $\mathcal{A}$ is sound (but may be incomplete), then:*

– *VeeP is sound: at the end of the algorithm $I_{f_1, ds[1], \ldots, f_T, ds[T]}(x)$ is robust.*
– *VeeP is precise up to δ_{MIN} for each feature's maximal diameter.*

7 Evaluation

In this section, we evaluate VeeP. We begin with implementation aspects and optimizations and then present our experiments.

Implementation. We implemented VeeP in Python[1]. It currently supports neighborhoods defined by one or two features. For the analyzer, it relies on GPUPoly [34]. It further builds on the idea of Semantify-NN [32] that encodes features as input layers with the goal of encoding pixel relations to reduce overapproximation errors. Semantify-NN encodes features using fully-connected and convolutional layers. For some features, this approach is infeasible for high-dimensional datasets because of the high memory overhead. To illustrate, denote the input dimension by $h \times w \times 3$. The HSL input layers, as defined in Semantify-NN, map an (R,G,B) triple into a single value in the feature domain, resulting in a perturbed output of $h \times w$. This output is then translated back to the input domain. Namely, a fully-connected layer requires $(h \times w) \times (h \times w \times 3)$ weights. For ImageNet, where $h = w = 224$, this layer becomes too large to fit into a standard memory (over 60GB). Instead, we observe that for some features the feature layer's weights are mostly zeros and thus this layer can be implemented using sparse layers [2,37]. Our implementation sets $\delta_{\text{MIN}} = 10^{-5}$ and $M = 3$. As optimization, it does not keep all previous examples, but only the required ones, which are dynamically determined. For example, for the neighborhood in Fig. 5, VeeP keeps only the examples at the top two rows.

Evaluation setup. We trained models and ran the experiments on a dual AMD EPYC 7742 server with 1TB RAM and eight NVIDIA A100 GPUs. We evaluated VeeP on four image datasets: MNIST [28] and Fashion-MNIST [53], with images of size 28×28, CIFAR-10 [25], with images of size $32 \times 32 \times 3$, and ImageNet [11], with images of size $224 \times 224 \times 3$. We considered fully-connected, convolutional [29], ResNet [18], and AlexNet [26] models. For MNIST and Fashion-MNIST, we used FC-5000 $\times$ 10, a fully-connected network with 50k neurons. For MNIST, we also used a convolutional network SuperConv with 88k neurons (from ERAN's repository[2]). For CIFAR-10, we used ResNetTiny with 311k neurons (from ERAN) and

---

[1] https://github.com/ananmkabaha/VeeP.
[2] https://github.com/eth-sri/eran.

ResNet18 with 558k neurons. For ImageNet, we used AlexNetTiny with 444k and AlexNet with 600k neurons. The last four models were trained with PGD [31]. Since GPUPoly currently does not support MaxPool layers, we replaced them in AlexNet with convolutional ones (justified by [44]). The CIFAR-10 models were taken from ERAN's repository, and we trained the other models.

Baseline approaches. We compare VeeP to popular splitting approaches: branch-and-bound (BaB) [6,7,19,30,35,48,52] and uniform splitting [3,32,42]. Any BaB technique starts by attempting to certify the robustness of the given neighborhood. If it fails, it splits the verification task into two parts and attempts to certify the robustness of each separately. If the certification fails again, BaB repeats the splitting process until all parts certify the original neighborhood. The difference between BaB techniques is what neurons they can split and how they choose what to split. For example, some rely on heavy computations, such as solving a linear program [6,35]. For our setting, where the split focuses on the input neurons and the input has low dimensionality, the *long-edge* approach, which splits the input neuron with the largest interval, has been shown to be efficient [6]. We thus compare to this approach. Uniform splitting splits a neighborhood into smaller neighborhoods of the same size, sufficiently small so the analyzer can certify them. Thus, it requires a pre-determined split size (unlike VeeP and BaB which adapt it during the execution). For a fair comparison, we need to carefully determine this size: providing a too small size will result in too long execution times (biasing our results), while providing a too large size will result in certification failures. Thus, we estimate the maximal split size which will enable the uniform splitting to certify successfully. To this end, before running the experiments, we run the following computation. For each neighborhood, we define several smaller neighborhoods. For each, we look for the maximal ϵ which can be verified by GPUPoly without splitting. Finally, we determine the split size of the uniform splitting to be the minimal value of ϵ across all these smaller neighborhoods. For a fair comparison, both baseline approaches were integrated in our system, i.e., they rely on GPUPoly and the feature layers described before.

Experiments. We run two experiments: one limits the execution time with a timeout and measures the maximal certified diameter, and the other one measures execution time as a function of the certified diameter. In each experiment, we run multiple problem instances. In each instance, we provide each approach a network, an image, one or two features, and a target diameter (if there are two features, both have the same target diameter). We define the target diameter to be the diameter of the minimal feature adversarial example δ_{adv} (computed by a grid search). That is, we provide each approach an upper bound on the maximal certified diameter. We measure how close is the returned certified diameter to δ_{adv}. Note that our problem instances are challenging because the feature neighborhoods we consider are the largest possible.

Maximal certified diameter given a timeout. In the first experiment, we evaluate the maximal certified diameter of all approaches, given a timeout. The evaluated

Table 1. VeeP vs. branch-and-bound and uniform splitting over brightness, contrast, hue, saturation, and lightness neighborhoods, averaged over 50 images.

Dataset	Model			VeeP		BaB		Uniform	
			δ_{adv}	$\delta_f\%$	$t[m]$	$\delta_f\%$	t [m]	$\delta_f\%$	t [m]
MNIST	SuperConv	Brightness	0.61	100	0.5	100	1.16	98	4.1
MNIST	SuperConv	B&C	0.56	99	26.1	98	35.2	81	77.3
MNIST	FC 5000 × 10	Brightness	0.15	100	1.9	100	11.5	100	13.4
MNIST	FC 5000 × 10	B&C	0.134	94	54.5	59	86.4	62	81.8
F-MNIST	FC 5000 × 10	Brightness	0.3	100	3.5	100	15.5	100	27.9
CIFAR-10	ResNetTiny	Brightness	0.42	100	7.9	100	32.1	89	60.6
CIFAR-10	ResNetTiny	B&C	0.3	96	73.4	49	144.6	30	164.1
CIFAR-10	ResNetTiny	Hue	3.36	99	27.5	62	59.1	77	48.94
CIFAR-10	ResNetTiny	Saturation	0.83	98	5.6	100	21.0	96	68.8
CIFAR-10	ResNetTiny	Lightness	0.39	100	10.8	100	45.9	76	32.6
ImageNet	AlexNetTiny	Brightness	0.22	95	68.8	59	87.6	59	82.7
ImageNet	AlexNetTiny	Hue	0.99	78	40.6	25	67.4	37	68.1
ImageNet	AlexNetTiny	Saturation	0.39	97	27.7	79	69.0	71	74.9
ImageNet	AlexNetTiny	Lightness	0.16	93	64.8	17	83.4	52	71.4

feature neighborhoods are defined by brightness (a linear feature) and contrast and HSL (non-linear features). The contrast feature defines the brightness difference between light and dark areas of the image, and the HSL features are color space transformations, where hue defines the position in the color wheel, saturation controls the image's colorfulness and lightness the perceived brightness. We run VeeP, BaB, and uniform splitting over the different models. For most networks and neighborhoods, we let each splitting approach run on a single GPU for 1.5 hours. For ResNet18, AlexNet, and the brightness and contrast (B&C) neighborhoods of TinyResNet, we let each splitting approach run on eight GPUs for 3 hours. We measure the execution time in minutes $t[m]$ and the maximal certifiable diameter δ_f. We compare δ_f to the diameter of the closest adversarial example in the feature domain δ_{adv} (for B&C, we compare to $(\delta_{adv}, \delta_{adv})$). Table 1 reports our results for the smaller models. Each result is averaged on 50 images. The results indicate that VeeP proves on average at least 96% of the maximal certifiable diameters in 29 minutes. The maximal diameters computed by the baselines are 74%, for BaB, and 73%, for uniform splitting. Their execution times are 54 minutes, for BaB, and 62 minutes, for uniform splitting. Table 2 reports our results for the two largest models, ResNet18 and AlexNet. Because of the long timeout, we focus on ten images and compare only to BaB. Our results show that VeeP proves at least 96% of the maximal diameters, while BaB proves 44%. VeeP's execution time is 98 minutes, whereas BaB is 160 minutes.

318   A. Kabaha and D. Drachsler-Cohen

Table 2. VeeP vs. branch-and-bound over large models, averaged over 10 images.

Dataset	Model		δ_{adv}	VeeP		BaB	
				$\delta_f\%$	t [m]	$\delta_f\%$	t [m]
CIFAR-10	ResNet18	Brightness	0.41	100	88.4	58	150
CIFAR-10	ResNet18	Saturation	0.85	98	45.2	98	123
ImageNet	AlexNet	Brightness	0.42	92	130	6	180
ImageNet	AlexNet	Saturation	0.56	100	67.3	52	165
ImageNet	AlexNet	Lightness	0.32	93	162	3	180

Execution time as a function of the certified diameter. In the second experiment, we measure the execution time of every approach as a function of the certified diameter. In this experiment, there is no timeout and thus we focus on two models, ResNetTiny and AlexNetTiny, and two features: brightness and saturation. For each network and a feature, we consider 50 images. For each network, image, and a feature, the target diameter is the diameter of the closest adversarial example δ_{adv}. We run all approaches until completion. During the execution of each approach, we record the intermediate progress, that is, the required time for certifying $r \cdot \delta_{adv}$ of the neighborhood, for ratio $r \in \{0.1, 0.2, \ldots, 0.8, 0.9, 0.95, 0.98\}$.

Figure 6 shows the results of this experiment. It depicts the execution time in minutes of each approach as a function of r, i.e., the ratio of the certified diameter and the target diameter δ_{adv}. Our results indicate that VeeP provides acceleration of 4.4x compared to BaB and acceleration of 10.2x compared to uniform splitting. The figure demonstrates the main drawbacks of uniform splitting and branch-and-bound. On the one hand, choosing a large step size for uniform splitting can certify smaller ratios of the target diameter more quickly. On the other hand, for larger ratios, uniform splitting must use a smaller step size, which significantly increases the execution time. The results also show that BaB wastes a lot of time on attempts to certify too large neighborhood until converging to a certifiable split size. We note that both baseline approaches are sub-optimal since they do not attempt to compute the optimal split size. In contrast, VeeP predicts the split sizes that minimize the execution time and thus performs better than the baselines. We validate VeeP's optimality by comparing it to a theoretical greedy optimal baseline. The theoretical baseline "knows" (without any computation) the optimal step size for every verification step. To simulate it, before every verification step of the optimal baseline, we compute the optimal step size by running a grid search over the remaining diameter (i.e., $\bar{\delta} - \delta_x$). We then let the optimal baseline pick the diameter determined by the grid search. Note that this baseline is purely theoretical: we do not consider the execution time of running the grid searches as part of its execution time. Our results indicate that VeeP's performance is very close to the theoretical baseline's performance, VeeP is slower by only a factor of 1.2x. The additional overhead of VeeP stems from several factors: (1) the time to estimate the predictors, (2) the

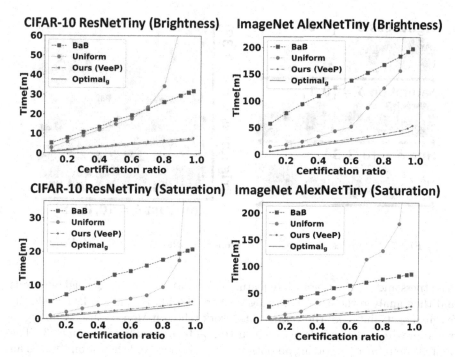

Fig. 6. Comparison of VeeP to uniform splitting, branch-and-bound, and a greedy optimal baseline, averaged over 50 images.

time to run the network on $f(x, \delta_x)$, and (3) the inaccuracies of our predictors and correction steps.

Lastly, we exemplify how large the feature neighborhoods that VeeP certifies are. Figure 7 shows four certified neighborhoods, defined by different features. For each, the figure shows the features, the range of the certified diameters, and several images generated by uniformly sampling from the certified range. The images are organized across the diameter axis, where the original image x is at the origin. These examples demonstrate that the certified feature neighborhoods contain images that are visually different compared to the original image. Being able to certify large feature neighborhoods allows network designers understand the robustness level of their networks to feature perturbations.

8   Related Work

In this section, we discuss the most closely related work to VeeP.

Network robustness and feature verification. Many works introduce verifiers analyzing the robustness of L_∞-balls, where each pixel is bounded by an interval [12,13,16,24,34,38,42,47,48,52,54]. Other works consider feature verification [3,32,42,49]. Earlier works on feature verification, focusing on rotations,

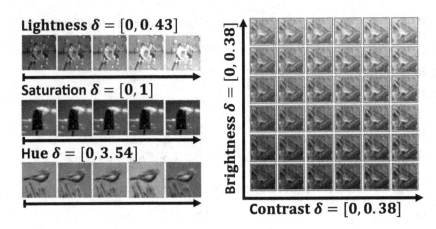

Fig. 7. Examples of images in feature neighborhoods, certified by VeeP.

brightness and contrast, translate feature neighborhoods into L_∞ neighborhoods and then analyze them with existing verifiers [42,49]. Recent works encode the feature constraints into the verifier. One work relies on Monte Carlo sampling to overapproximate geometric feature constraints by convex linear bounds [3]. The bounds are refined by solving an optimization problem and then submitted to an existing verifier. Other work proposes an input layer that encodes the feature and is added to the original network [32]. All works also employ uniform splitting.

Splitting techniques. To increase precision and scalability, many verifiers rely on uniform splitting [3,32,42] or branch-and-bound (BaB) [6,7,19,30,35,48,52]. Long-edge is a common BaB technique that splits the input with the largest interval [7,52]. Smart-Branching (BaBSB) [7] and Smart-ReLU (BaBSR) [6,48] rely on a fast computation to estimate the expected improvement of splitting an input or a neuron and then split the one maximizing the improvement. Filtered Smart Branching (FSB) extends BaBSR by bound propagation to estimate multiple candidates of BaBSR [35,48]. Another work relies on an indirect effect analysis to estimate the neuron splitting gain [19]. Others suggest to train GNNs via supervised learning to obtain a splitting strategy [30]. However, building the dataset and training the GNNs can be time consuming. In contrast to BaB, which lazily splits inputs or neurons, VeeP dynamically predicts the optimal split.

Feature attacks. Several adversarial attacks rely on semantic feature perturbations. One work relies on HSV color transformations (which is close to HSL) [21]. Other works link adversarial examples to PCA features [4,8,56]. Other feature attacks include facial feature perturbations [15], colorization and texture attacks [5], features obtained using scale-invariant feature transform (SIFT) [51], and semantic attribute perturbations using multi-attribute transformation models [22].

Learning. Our approach is related to several learning techniques. It is mainly related to active learning, where a learner learns a concept by querying an oracle [1]. Active learning is suitable for tasks in which labeling a dataset is expensive [55], for example real-life object detection [17], crowd counting [57], and image segmentation [39]. Similarly, in our setting, querying the analyzer to obtain examples is expensive. Our setting is also related to online learning, where new data gradually becomes available. Online learning typically addresses tasks with time-dependent data [20], e.g., visual tracking [33], stock price prediction [50], and recommendation systems [9]. In contrast, VeeP's examples are not time-dependent. Our approach is also related to CEGIS and CEGAR. Counterexample-guided inductive synthesis (CEGIS) synthesizes a program by iteratively proposing candidate solutions to an oracle [43]. The oracle either confirms or returns a counterexample. Counterexample-guided abstraction-refinement (CEGAR) is a program verification technique for dynamically computing abstractions capable of verifying a given property [10]. It begins from some abstraction to the program and iteratively refines it as long as there are spurious counterexamples. In contrast, VeeP relies on recent examples, not necessarily counterexamples.

9   Conclusion

We presented VeeP, a system for verifying the robustness of deep networks in neighborhoods defined by a set of features. Given a neighborhood, VeeP splits the verification process into a series of verification steps, each aiming to verify a maximal part of the given neighborhood in a minimal execution time. VeeP defines the next verification step by constructing velocity and sensitivity predictors from previous steps and by considering recent failures. VeeP is guaranteed to terminate and is sound and precise up to a parametric constant. We evaluate VeeP over challenging experiments: deep models for MNIST, Fashion-MNIST, CIFAR-10 and ImageNet, and large feature neighborhoods, defined by the closest feature adversarial example. Results show that the average diameter of the neighborhoods that VeeP verifies is at least 96% of the maximal certifiable diameter. Additionally, VeeP provides a significant acceleration compared to existing splitting approaches: up to 10.2x compared to uniform splitting and 4.4x compared to branch-and-bound.

Acknowledgements. We thank the reviewers for their feedback. This research was supported by the Israel Science Foundation (grant No. 2605/20).

References

1. Angluin, D.: Learning regular sets from queries and counterexamples. In: Informaion and Computation (1987)
2. Ardakani, A., Condo, C., Gross, W.J.: Sparsely-connected neural networks: towards efficient VLSI implementation of deep neural networks. In: ICLR (2017)
3. Balunovic, M., Baader, M., Singh, G., Gehr, T., Vechev, M.T.: Certifying geometric robustness of neural networks. In: NeurIPS (2019)

4. Bhagoji, A.N., Cullina, D., Sitawarin, C., Mittal, P.: Enhancing robustness of machine learning systems via data transformations. In: CISS (2018)
5. Bhattad, A., Chong, M.J., Liang, K., Li, B., Forsyt, D.A.: Unrestricted adversarial examples via semantic manipulation. In: ICLR (2020)
6. Bunel, R., Lu, J., Turkaslan, I., Torr, P.H.S., Kohli, P., Kumar, M.P.: Branch and bound for piecewise linear neural network verification. J. Mach. Learn. Res. (2020)
7. Bunel, R., Turkaslan, I., Torr, P.H.S., Kohli, P., Mudigonda, P.K.: A unified view of piecewise linear neural network verification. In: NeurIPS (2018)
8. Carlini, N., Wagner., D.A.: Adversarial examples are not easily detected: bypassing ten detection methods. In: AISec (2017)
9. Chen, N., Hoi, S.C.H., Li, S., Xiao, X.: Mobile app tagging. In: WSDM (2016)
10. Clarke, E.M., Grumberg, O., Jha, S., Lu, Y., Veith, H.: Counterexample-guided abstraction refinement. In: CAV (2000)
11. Deng, J., Dong, W., Socher, R., Li, L.J., Li, K., Fei-Fei, L.: ImageNet: a large-scale hierarchical image database. In: CVPR (2009)
12. Elboher, Y.Y., Gottschlich, J., Katz, G.: An abstraction-based framework for neural network verification. In: CAV (2020)
13. Gehr, T., Mirman, M., Drachsler-Cohen, D., Tsankov, P., Chaudhuri, S., Vechev, M.T.: AI2: safety and robustness certification of neural networks with abstract interpretation. In: SP (2018)
14. Goodfellow, I.J., Shlens, J., Szegedy., C.: Explaining and harnessing adversarial examples. In: ICLR (2015)
15. Goswami, G., Ratha, N.K., Agarwal, A., Singh, R., Vatsa., M.: Unravelling robustness of deep learning based face recognition against adversarial attacks. In: AAAI (2018)
16. Gowal, S., et al.: Scalable verified training for provably robust image classification. In: ICCV (2019)
17. Haussmann, E., et al.: Scalable active learning for object detection. In: IV (2020)
18. He, K., Zhang, X., Ren, S., Sun., J.: Deep residual learning for image recognition. In: CVPR (2016)
19. Henriksen, P., Lomuscio, A.: DEEPSPLIT: an efficient splitting method for neural network verification via indirect effect analysis. In: IJCAI (2021)
20. Hoi, S.C., Sahoo, D., Lu, J., Zhao, P.: Online learning: a comprehensive survey. In: Neurocomputing (2021)
21. Hosseini, H., Poovendran, R.: Semantic adversarial examples. In: CVPR Workshops (2018)
22. Joshi, A., Mukherjee, A., Sarkar, S., Hegde, C.: Semantic adversarial attacks: parametric transformations that fool deep classifiers. In: ICCV (2019)
23. Kabaha, A., Drachsler-Cohen, D.: Boosting robustness verification of semantic feature neighborhoods. In: https://arxiv.org/abs/2209.05446 (2022)
24. Katz, G., Barrett, C.W., Dill, D.L., Julian, K., Kochenderfer., M.J.: Reluplex: an efficient SMT solver for verifying deep neural networks. In: CAV (2017)
25. Krizhevsky, A.: Learning multiple layers of features from tiny images (2009)
26. Krizhevsky, A., Sutskever, I., Hinton, G.E.: ImageNet classification with deep convolutional neural networks. In: NeurIPS (2012)
27. Kurakin, A., Goodfellow, I.J., Bengio, S.: Adversarial machine learning at scale. In: ICLR (2017)
28. Lecun, Y., Bottou, L., Bengio, Y., Haffner, P.: Gradient-based learning applied to document recognition. Proc. IEEE **86**(11), 2278–2324 (1998)
29. LeCun, Y., et al.: Backpropagation applied to handwritten zip code recognition. Neural Comput. **1**, 541–551 (1989)

30. Lu, J., Kumar, M.P.: Neural network branching for neural network verification. In: ICLR (2020)
31. Madry, A., Makelov, A., Schmidt, L., Tsipras, D., Vladu, A.: Towards deep learning models resistant to adversarial attacks. In: ICLR (2018)
32. Mohapatra, J., Weng, T., Chen, P., Liu, S., Daniel, L.: Towards verifying robustness of neural networks against A family of semantic perturbations. In: CVPR (2020)
33. Abbass, M.Y., et al.: A survey on online learning for visual tracking. Vis. Comput. **37**(5), 993–1014 (2020). https://doi.org/10.1007/s00371-020-01848-y
34. Müller, C., Serre, F., Singh, G., Püschel, M., Vechev, M.: Scaling polyhedral neural network verification on GPUs. In: MLSYS (2021)
35. Palma, A.D., et al.: Improved branch and bound for neural network verification via Lagrangian decomposition. arXiv:2104.06718 (2021)
36. Papernot, N., McDaniel, P.D., Goodfellow, I.J., Jha, S., Celik, Z.B., Swami, A.: Practical black-box attacks against machine learning. In: AsiaCCS (2017)
37. Richter, O., Wattenhofer, R.: TreeConnect: a sparse alternative to fully connected layers. In: ICTAI (2018)
38. Ryou, W., Chen, J., Balunovic, M., Singh, G., Dan, A.M., Vechev, M.T.: Scalable polyhedral verification of recurrent neural networks. In: CAV (2021)
39. Saidu, I.C., Csató, L.: Active learning with Bayesian UNet for efficient semantic image segmentation. J. Imaging (2021)
40. Singh, G., Ganvir, R., Püschel, M., Vechev., M.T.: Beyond the single neuron convex barrier for neural network certification. In: NeurIPS (2019)
41. Singh, G., Gehr, T., Mirman, M., Püschel, M., Vechev, M.T.: Fast and effective robustness certification. In: NeurIPS (2018)
42. Singh, G., Gehr, T., Püschel, M., Vechev, M.: An abstract domain for certifying neural networks. Proc. ACM Program. Lang. **3**, 1–30 (2019)
43. Solar-Lezama, A., Tancau, L., Bodík, R., Seshia, S.A., Saraswat, V.A.: Combinatorial sketching for finite programs. In: ASPLOS (2006)
44. Springenberg, J.T., Dosovitskiy, A., Brox, T., Riedmiller, M.A.: Striving for simplicity: the all convolutional net. In: ICLR Workshop (2015)
45. Szegedy, C., Zaremba, W., Sutskever, I., Bruna, J., Erhan, D., Goodfellow, I.J., Fergus., R.: Intriguing properties of neural networks. In: ICLR (2014)
46. Tramèr, F., Kurakin, A., Papernot, N., Goodfellow, I.J., Boneh, D., D., P.: Ensemble adversarial training: attacks and defenses. In: ICLR (2018)
47. Tran, H., Bak, S., Xiang, W., Johnson, T.T.: Verification of deep convolutional neural networks using image stars. In: CAV (2020)
48. Wang, S., et al.: Beta-crown: efficient bound propagation with per-neuron split constraints for neural network robustness verification. In: NeurIPS (2021)
49. Wang, S., Pei, K., Whitehouse, J., Yang, J., Jana, S.: Efficient formal safety analysis of neural networks. In: NeurIPS (2018)
50. Wang, X., Yang, K., Liu, T.: Stock price prediction based on morphological similarity clustering and hierarchical temporal memory. In: IEEE Access (2021). https://doi.org/10.1109/ACCESS.2021.3077004
51. Wicker, M., Huang, X., Kwiatkowska., M.: Feature-guided black-box safety testing of deep neural networks. In: TACAS (2018)
52. Wu, H., et al.: Parallelization techniques for verifying neural networks. In: FMCAD (2020)
53. Xiao, H., Rasul, K., Vollgraf, R.: Fashion-MNIST: a novel image dataset for benchmarking machine learning algorithms. CoRR, abs/1708.07747 (2017)
54. Xu, K., et al.: Automatic perturbation analysis for scalable certified robustness and beyond. In: NeurIPS (2020)

55. Zhan, X., Wang, Q., Huang, K., Xiong, H., Dou, D., Chan, A.B.: A comparative survey of deep active learning. CoRR abs/2203.13450 (2022)
56. Zhang, Y., Tian, X., Li, Y., Wang, X., Tao, D.: Principal component adversarial example. IEEE Trans. Image Process. **29**, 4804–4815 (2020)
57. Zhao, Z., Shi, M., Zhao, X., Li, L.: Active crowd counting with limited supervision. In: ECCV (2020)

Fast and Incremental Computation of Weak Control Closure

Abu Naser Masud[✉][ID]

School of Innovation, Design and Engineering Mälardalen University,
Västerås, Sweden
abu.naser.masud@mdu.se

Abstract. Control dependence is a fundamental concept used in many program analysis techniques such as program slicing, program debugging, program parallelization, and detecting security leaks. Since the introduction of this concept in the late eighties, numerous definitions of control dependencies and their computation methods have been developed. The later definitions are progressively more generalized covering a wide spectrum of modern programming language constructs. The most generalized concepts are the weak and strong control closure (WCC and SCC) that capture the nontermination (in)sensitive control dependencies of a given program. In this paper, we have developed a novel method to compute WCC incrementally. Any client application of WCC such as program slicing requires computing the WCC repeatedly in a fixpoint computation. An incremental algorithm to compute WCC will improve the performance of the client application significantly. We have provided the proof of correctness and the theoretical worst-case complexity of our algorithm. We have performed an experimental evaluation on well-known benchmarks, and our experiments reveal that we have significantly improved the practical efficiency in computing WCC incrementally. We have obtained an average speedup of 31.03 in all benchmarks and a maximum speedup of 35.29 than the best state-of-the-art algorithm computing WCC.

Keywords: Control dependence · Weak control closure · Strong control closure · Program slicing · Nontermination insensitive · Nontermination sensitive

1 Introduction

Control dependence is a fundamental concept used in many program analyses techniques such as compiler optimization and debugging [6], program slicing [7,11,22], and information flow security [5]. It expresses a relation between two program instructions stating that one controls the execution of another. The state-of-the-art control dependence computation is based on computing postdominator relations [6]. It is the fastest algorithm which is applicable for programs that must exit from a single program point. However, modern software systems such as nonterminating reactive systems or distributed web

G. Singh and C. Urban (Eds.): SAS 2022, LNCS 13790, pp. 325–349, 2022.
https://doi.org/10.1007/978-3-031-22308-2_15

services do not have any exit point and postdominator-based control dependence computation algorithms are not applicable for such systems [1,20].

Danicic et al. [4] introduced the concept of weak and strong control closure (WCC and SCC) that capture weak and strong forms of control dependencies from (non)terminating systems that are nontermination insensitive and nontermination sensitive respectively. These are the most general form of the closure relation of control dependencies. Program transformation technique such as program slicing may require preserving nontermination in the sliced program if the original program is nonterminating. Slicing based on SCC preserves nontermination and produces larger slices which may be useful for program verification. On the other hand, slicing based on WCC may not preserve nontermination and produces smaller slices. There exist numerous definitions of control dependencies in the literature [2,6,19,21,22]. All such dependencies are the special cases of control dependencies captured by WCC and SCC. Thus, WCC and SCC have a wider applicability than the control dependencies based on computing postdominator relations.

Let us illustrate these concepts and their relations by the program P in Fig. 1. Suppose we are interested to detect program statements that affect the value of x at Statement 8. The assignment to x at Statements 1 and 4 directly affect the value of x at Statement 8. We can obtain these direct influences by computing data dependencies. Moreover, the boolean expression $i > 0$ at Statement 2 indirectly affects the value of x at Statement 8 as it decides whether Statement 4 will be executed or not. We can obtain these indirect influences by computing control dependencies. Furthermore, Statement 6 directly affects the boolean

```
1:  x=5;
2:  while(i>0)
3:  {
4:      x=x+i;
5:      y=y−i;
6:      i=i−1;
7:  }
8:  print(x)
```

Fig. 1. Programs P

expression at Statement 2 due to data dependence, and thus statements 1, 2, 4, and 6 affect the value of x at Statement 8. Statement 4 is control dependent on Statement 2 as it decides whether statement 4 will be executed or not. The standard control dependence computation method identifies this control dependence as follows: there exist two paths from Statement 2 to the end of this program in which Statement 4 always executes in one path and Statement 4 may not execute in the other path. This proves that Statement 2 controls the execution of Statement 4. This method only works if the program has a single exit point. However, if the whole program is under an infinite loop such as the following:

$$\text{Program } Q: \textbf{while}(\textit{true})\{S_1, \dots, S_8\}$$

where $S_1, \dots, S_8$ refers to statements 1 to 8 in Program P, then the above method for computing the control dependencies will not work since there is no exit point to this code. WCC (see Definition 4 in Sect. 2) is the generalization of the standard control dependencies that also works for nonterminating programs and computes the closure relation of control dependencies. For example, if we would like to know what affects the computation of x at Statement 8 in Program Q, we see that there are two paths from Statement 2 to statements 4 and 8. This is enough to say that a control closure of a set S of program statements including statements 8 and 4 must include Statement 2 (provided that Statement 2 is reachable from S) as it decides which one (Statement 4 or Statement 8) will be executed next. One difference between SCC and WCC is that the SCC of S will also include the **while(true)** statement as it preserves the nontermination. Statement 2 is nontermination sensitively control dependent on the **while(true)** statement and thus SCC will include this statement.

1 Let C be the the the slicing criterion, and let $S = C$.
2 **repeat**
3 $\quad\Big|\quad S' := \bigcup_{n \in S} \{m : m \xrightarrow{dd}{}^* n\}$
4 $\quad\Big|\quad S := cl(S')$
5 **until** $S = S'$

Algorithm 1: SLICING

Danicic et al.'s original algorithms to compute WCC and SCC are expensive. Most recent works [12,14,18] on computing WCC and SCC have shown performance improvements in these algorithms. These improvements are mostly on the one-time application of these algorithms. However, client applications such as program slicing require computing WCC/SCC incrementally. Existing algorithms lose performance due to repeated computation of unnecessary information. To illustrate this fact, we recall Algorithm 1 from [12,14][1] which is the static backward slicing algorithm computing the slice set S from the given slicing criterion C. Given any control flow graph (CFG) representation of a program and the slicing criterion C which is a subset of the CFG nodes, Algorithm 1 computes S until a fixpoint is reached. The relation $\xrightarrow{dd}{}^*$ denotes the transitive-reflexive closure of the data dependence relation $\xrightarrow{dd}$. The function $cl(.)$ computes WCC or SCC in each fixpoint iteration. It is obvious that an incremental computation of this function will improve the overall performance of the program slicing algorithm.

In this paper, we have developed a novel algorithm that is able to compute WCC incrementally. We proved the correctness of our algorithm theoretically and experimentally, provided the theoretical worst-case time complexity of our method which is quadratic in the size of the CFG, implemented our algorithm in the Clang/LLVM compiler framework, and compared our results with the best state-of-the-art method by performing experimental evaluation on SPEC CPU 2017 benchmarks. Our experiments reveal that the algorithm developed in this paper is the fastest among all algorithms computing WCC reported in the literature if WCC needs to be computed incrementally. We have obtained the maximum

---

[1] We replaced the **goto** statement in [12,14] by the **repeat..until** loop.

speedup of 35.29 on our largest benchmark and an average speedup of 31.03 on all benchmarks with respect to the best baseline approach computing WCC.

The remainder of this paper is organized as follows. Section 2 brings some relevant concepts and notations from the literature on control dependence and WCC, Sect. 3 provides the details of our algorithm developed in this paper, the proof of correctness, and its theoretical worst-case time complexity, Sect. 4 explains the experimental evaluation, Sect. 5 discusses the works that are related to ours, and Sect. 6 concludes the paper.

2   Background

In this section, we recall definitions of CFG, control dependence, WCC, and other related concepts from the relevant literature [4,14]. The definitions of Control dependence and WCC are provided at the level of CFG representation of programs. First, we recall the formal definition of a control flow graph (CFG) from our earlier study [12,14].

Definition 1 (CFG). *A CFG is a directed graph* (N, E) *where*

1. *N is the set of nodes that includes a* Start *node from where the execution starts, at most one* End *node where the execution terminates normally,* Cond *nodes representing boolean conditions, and* nonCond *nodes; and*
2. *$E \subseteq N \times N$ is the relation describing the possible flow of execution in the graph. An* End *node has no successor, a* Cond *node has at most one true successor and at most one false successor, and all other nodes have at most one successor.*

Applications like program slicing may remove part of the code and we may obtain a CFG from such code in which a Cond node has either or both of the successors missing. Other kinds of nodes may have a missing successor as well. An execution that reaches such nodes may be silently nonterminating because an execution may not proceed and the control is not returned to the operating system. Moreover, a CFG may not have an End node and the execution of its code may possibly be nonterminating. Thus, our definition of CFG can represent a wide range of practical programs. Note that our CFGs are deterministic according to the definition.

The functions $succ_G(n)$ and $pred_G(n)$ denote the set of successors and predecessors of the CFG node n in the graph G. We sometimes drop the subscript G if it is understood from the context. A path in a graph G is the sequence of CFG nodes $n_1, \ldots, n_k$ such that $n_{i+1} \in succ_G(n_i)$ (also $n_i \in pred_G(n_{i+1})$) for all $1 \le i \le k - 1$. We use the notation $[n_1..n_k]$ to denote such a path. A *nontrivial* path contains more than one node; otherwise, the path is a *trivial* path. A path is *proper* if its initial and final vertices are distinct. Two paths $[n_1..n_k]$ and $[m_1..m_l]$ are *disjoint* if $n_i \ne m_j$ for any $k, l > 0$, $1 \le i \le k$, and $1 \le j \le l$. If $[n_2..n_k]$ and $[m_2..m_l]$ are *disjoint* paths and $n_1 = m_1$, then we say that $[n_1..n_k]$

and $[m_1..m_l]$ are *disjoint* paths from n_1. We use the notation $n \in \pi$ to denote that the CFG node n belongs to the path π, and use the notation $n \in \pi - S$ to indicate that n is any node in the path π that does not belong to the set of CFG nodes S.

We now recall the definition of WCC from Danicic et al. [4] with some auxiliary relevant definitions. In what follows, let $G = (N, E)$ be a CFG, and let $N' \subseteq N$.

Definition 2 (N'-Path). *An N'-path is a finite path $[n_1..n_k]$ in a CFG G where $k > 1, n_k \in N'$ and $n_i \notin N'$ for all $1 < i < k$.*

Intuitively, an N'-path must end at a node in N', the first node in this path can be any node from N (or N'), and no intermediate node in this path must be from N'. With this definition, we can now define an N'-weakly committing node as follows:

Definition 3 (N'-Weakly Committing). *A node $n \in N$ is N'-weakly committing in a CFG G if all N'-paths from n have the same endpoint. In other words, there is at most one element of N' that is 'first- reachable' from n.*

The following definition states whether a given subset of CFG nodes N' is N'-weakly control-closed.

Definition 4 (Weak Control Closure). *N' is weakly control-closed in G if and only if all nodes $n \notin N'$ that are reachable from N' are N'-weakly committing in G.*

Given any subset N' of CFG nodes, if N' is not weakly control-closed in the CFG G according to Definition 4, then we compute the WCC set of N' denoted $WCC(N')$ (or WCC for brevity) such that $N' \subseteq WCC(N') \subseteq N$. The definition of weak control closure captures the control dependencies obtained from postdominator relations. To illustrate this relation, we now bring the definition of postdominator relation and the control dependencies based on this relation.

A CFG node n *postdominates* another CFG node m if and only if every path from m to the *End* node must go through n. If $n \neq m$ in this definition, then we say that n *strictly postdominates* m. Note that this definition relies on the fact that the CFG must have a unique End node. The standard definition of postdominator-based control dependencies was first introduced by Ferrante et al. [6] as follows:

Definition 5 (Control Dependence [6,12,21]). *Node n is control dependent on node m (written $m \xrightarrow{cd} n$) in the CFG G if (1) there exists a nontrivial path π in G from m to n such that every node $m' \in \pi - \{m, n\}$ is postdominated by n, and (2) m is not strictly postdominated by n.*

Since the definition of postdominator relies on the existence of a unique *End* node, the above definition of control dependence is applicable when this restriction holds. Intuitively, the relation $m \xrightarrow{cd} n$ holds when there exist two branches of m such that n is always executed in one branch and may not execute in the other branch. To illustrate this relationship with WCC, let us assume that N' includes n, the unique End node n_e, and the Start node $n_\triangleright$. Also, assume that all nodes are reachable from node $n_\triangleright$. Then, $[m..n]$ is an N'-path. Since m is not strictly postdominated by n, there must be another path $[m..n_e]$ which is also an N'-path. Then, node m is not N'-weakly committing due to having two N'-paths with different endpoint. Thus, N' is not a WCC due to not capturing the control dependence relation $m \xrightarrow{cd} n$, and a WCC of N' must include m.

The concept of N'-weakly deciding nodes are introduced by Danicic et al. [4] to provide an algorithm to compute the WCC of N'.

Definition 6 (Weakly Deciding Vertices). *A node $n \in N$ is N'-weakly deciding in G if and only if there exist two finite proper N'-paths in G such that both start at n and have no other common vertices. $WD_G(N')$ denotes the set of all N'-weakly deciding vertices in G.*

Thus, if there exists an N'-weakly deciding vertex n, then n is not N'-weakly committing. The WCC of a subset $N' \subseteq N$ of CFG nodes in a CFG G can be computed according to the following equation:

$$WCC(N') = N' \cup \{n : n \in WD_G(N'), n \text{ is reachable from } N' \text{ in } G\} \quad (1)$$

Example 1. Consider the CFG in Fig. 2. Let $N' = \{n_0, n_1, n_5, n_{11}\}$. Here are some examples of N'-paths in this CFG:

$$\pi_0 = n_1, n_0$$
$$\pi_1 = n_3, n_1$$
$$\pi_2 = n_3, n_2, n_1$$
$$\pi_3 = n_6, n_4, n_3, n_1$$
$$\pi_4 = n_6, n_5$$
$$\pi_5 = n_{10}, n_1$$
$$\pi_6 = n_{10}, n_9, n_6, n_4, n_3, n_2$$

The path $[n_3..n_0]$ is not an N'-path as it includes the node $n_1 \in N'$. The CFG node n_1 is N'-weakly committing since there exists a single N'-path π_0. Also, node n_3 is N'-weakly committing as both π_1 and π_2 have the same endpoint n_1. However, node n_6 is not N'-weakly committing due to the paths π_3 and π_4. It is an N'-weakly deciding node. Thus, N' is not weakly control closed. Similarly, nodes $n_7, \ldots, n_{10}$ are N'-weakly deciding due to having two disjoint N'-paths from these nodes. As all these nodes are reachable from $n_{11} \in N'$, the WCC of N' must include these nodes according to Eq. 1.

Regarding the program semantics of the client application of WCC or SCC such as program slicing or information flow security, the execution semantics of programs are captured/preserved through computing the additional dependencies such as data dependencies as shown in Algorithm 1. However, the data dependencies are not enough to capture the indirect influences of conditional statements or boolean instructions in loop statements. Thus, WCC/SCC is applied on top of data dependencies to capture these indirect influences.

3   Incremental Computation of WCC

We compute WCC in two steps. First, we generate an *influencer graph* $\mathcal{G} = (\mathcal{N}, \mathcal{E})$ from the CFG $G = (N, E)$ such that $\mathcal{N} = N$, and $\mathcal{G}$ is a directed graph that encodes direct influences to all CFG nodes by the Cond nodes. We say that a Cond node n influences the execution of a node m if there exists a path $[n..m]$ in the CFG G which does not include any other Cond node. The *influencer graph* $\mathcal{G}$ is thus a program representation encoding all direct influences in the source code. This simplistic informal definition of influence is extended in the following section to construct the influencer graph $\mathcal{G}$. In the second step, given any set $N' \subseteq N$, we traverse $\mathcal{G}$ from the nodes in N' to detect all Cond nodes that are weakly deciding and are reachable from the nodes in N' in G. We compute the graph $\mathcal{G}$ only once. But, we traverse it incrementally to compute WCC and avoid recomputing decisions taken earlier.

3.1   Generating the Influencer Graph

The intuitive idea of having an influencer graph is the following. Given any CFG node n, we should immediately recognize which Cond node m controls the execution of n (if any). Usually, m is the last Cond node in any path from the Start node to n. Subsequently, there may be other Cond nodes preceding m that control the execution of m. Let π be any path from the Start node to n, and let $m_1, \ldots, m_k$ be the subsequence of Cond nodes in π. We intend to obtain the edges (n, m_k) and (m_{i+1}, m_i) for all $1 \le i \le k - 1$ in the influencer graph. Then, given any CFG node $n \in N'$, any path $[n..m_i]$ in the influencer graph indicates that there may be an N'-path $[m_i..n]$ in the CFG if no node in this path is in N' except n. After obtaining the influencer graph of any CFG, we can limit our search space to verify which Cond nodes should belong to the WCC. We perform the search in the influencer graph in a way, as explained in the next section, that ensures that the paths in the influencer graph correspond to N'-paths in the CFG. Since any Cond node m which is N'-weakly deciding and thus has two disjoint N'-paths may belong to the WCC of N', we assign each edge in the influence graph by a branch number to identify the disjointness of the N'-paths. In order to generate the influencer graph, we consider a distinct branch number for each branch of a Cond node. A CFG node is called a Join node if it has multiple predecessors. A Join node is also a Cond node when it has two successors. We assign a default label to the branch emerging from a Join but nonCond node. The influencer graph $\mathcal{G} = (\mathcal{N}, \mathcal{E})$ is a directed graph with edge labels that can be obtained from the CFG $G = (N, E)$. Any edge $(n, m, l) \in \mathcal{E}$ in $\mathcal{G}$ implies that there exists a path $[m..n]$ in the CFG G, m is a Cond or a Join node, and the edge label l can take any value from the set $\{0, 1, 2, 3\}$ to represent the branch number. The semantics of the encoding of edge label l is the following:

- l=0 represents the default branch number emerging from the Join node m,

- $l = 1$ or $l = 2$ implies that m is a Cond node which usually has at most two branches and n can be reached from m in the CFG by traversing the branch marked by l,
- $l = 3$ implies that m is a Cond node and n can be reached from m by traversing any of the two branches of m.

Since any CFG node can have at most two branches according to the definition of CFG (Definition 1), we need at most four unique branch numbers. In the practical implementation of our approach, we handle more than four branch labels to handle *switch* statements. However, we restrict ourselves to four unique branch numbers for the brevity of our presentation.

In the following, we provide the formal definition of an influencer graph $\mathcal{G}$.

Definition 7. (Influencer Graph). *Let $G = (N, E)$ be a CFG. An influencer graph $\mathcal{G} = (\mathcal{N}, \mathcal{E})$ of a CFG G consists of the set of CFG nodes $\mathcal{N} = N$, and the set of edges $\mathcal{E}$ containing all edges (n, m, l) such that m is either a Join or a Cond node, and there exists a CFG path $[m..n]$ such that no node $n' \in [m..n] - \{n, m\}$ is a Cond or a Join node. The edge label l can take any value as follows:*

1. *$l = 0$ if m is a Join node*
2. *$l = 3$ if m is a Cond node, n is a Join node, and no disjoint path exists from m to n in the CFG, and*
3. *$l \in \{1, 2\}$ if m is a Cond node, n is not a Join node, and for all edges $(n, m', l') \in \mathcal{E}$ such that $[m..n]$ and $[m'..n]$ are disjoint paths in G, we must have that $l' \neq l$.*

Any edge (n, m, l) in $\mathcal{G}$ implies that m may affect the execution of n if $l \neq 0$. Thus, m may influence the execution of n, and the graph $\mathcal{G}$ encodes all such influences in the CFG G. When $l = 0$, m will not directly influence n, but n may be influenced by another node m' if there exists an edge (m, m', l') in $\mathcal{G}$ such that $l' \neq 0$. In fact, for all sequences of edges $(n, m, 0)$ and (m, m', l') in $\mathcal{G}$, we can remove the edge $(n, m, 0)$ and add a new edge (n, m', l') in $\mathcal{G}$ in a post-processing phase of generating $\mathcal{G}$. This compact representation will only encode all direct influences in $\mathcal{G}$. However, we consider it as a syntactic sugar and keep the edge $(n, m, 0)$ in $\mathcal{G}$ to simplify its generation. Since any CFG node has at most two successors according to the definition of CFG, we need at most four unique labels for the influencer graph $\mathcal{G}$.

Figure 2(a) presents the CFG of a function taken from the Perlebench benchmark obtained from the well-known SPEC CPU2017 [3] benchmark suite. This CFG is generated by the Clang frontend [9], and each node in this CFG represents a basic block containing the straight-line sequence of instructions written in C language. All Cond nodes (e.g., n_9, n_8, n_3, etc.) in this CFG have two successors, all Join nodes (e.g., n_1, n_6, n_3, etc.) have multiple predecessors, and there exist nodes that are both Cond and Join nodes (e.g. n_6, n_3, etc.). Figure 2(b) presents the influencer graph that is obtained from the CFG in (a) according to Definition 7.

Algorithm 2 generates the influencer graph $\mathcal{G}$ of a given CFG G. It uses the following notations/functions:

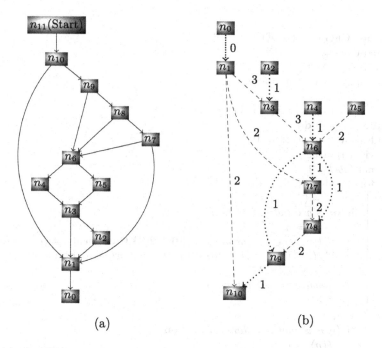

(a)   (b)

Fig. 2. (a) The CFG generated by the Clang frontend for the "Perl_do_open_raw" function taken from the Perlbench benchmark in SPEC CPU2017 [3] (we omit the program instructions for simplicity), (b) The *influencer graph* $\mathcal{G}$ generated by Algorithm 2 in which edge styles are differed by their edge labels

- The function $\mathcal{I} : N \to N \cup \{\bot, \iota\}$ records the direct influence of a given CFG node. For example, $\mathcal{I}(n) = m$ implies that m may be a Cond node (or a Join node) which may influence the execution of n directly (resp. indirectly). Initially, $\mathcal{I}(n) = \bot$ for all CFG nodes n representing that an influencer node of n is yet to be recognized. Also, we initially set $\mathcal{I}(n_\triangleright) = \iota$ to denote that the execution of the Start node $n_\triangleright$ is not influenced by any other node.
- The function $\mathcal{E}_m$ denotes the set of all edges from the node m in the influencer graph $\mathcal{G}$. In particular, any $(n, l) \in \mathcal{E}_m$ implies that (m, n, l) is an edge in $\mathcal{G}$.
- The function $\mathcal{D}ist(n, m)$ denotes the minimum distance of node n from either m if m is a Cond node or a Cond node immediately before m in the CFG if m is a Join node. We compute this function during the generation of the influencer graph and use this function to traverse correct N'-paths during the computation of WCC which is explained in the next section.

Algorithm 2 is a worklist-based algorithm that visits each edge (n, m) in the CFG exactly once, detects and includes an edge (m, n', l) in the influencer graph $\mathcal{G}$ for any $l \in \{0, 1, 2, 3\}$ and $n' \in N$ that may influence m where $n' = n$ or $n' = \mathcal{I}(n)$ (see Lines 13, 14, 21, 27, 31, 36). It also computes the minimum distance $\mathcal{D}ist(m, n')$ from n' to m or a Cond node immediately before m in the

Input: CFG $G = (N, E)$
Output: $\mathcal{G} = (\mathcal{N}, \mathcal{E})$, $\mathcal{D}ist$

```
1  forall (n ∈ N do
2  |    I(n) = ⊥, visit(n)=false
3  end
4  W = {(n▷, 0, 0)} and I(n▷) = ι
5  while (W ≠ ∅) do
6  |    Remove (n, l, d) from W
7  |    visit(n)=true
8  |    newlabel = 1
9  |    forall (m ∈ succ(n)) do
10 |    |    nedge = (⊥, ⊥)
11 |    |    if (n is a Cond node) then
12 |    |    |    I(m) = n
13 |    |    |    if ((n, X) ∉ Eₘ for any X ∈ {0, 1, 2, 3}) then  nedge = (n, newlabel)
14 |    |    |    if ((n, l') ∈ Eₘ ∧ l' > 0 such that l' ≠ newlabel) then
                        nedge = (n, 3)
15 |    |    |    newlabel = newlabel + 1
16 |    |    |    dist = 1
17 |    |    end
18 |    |    if (n is a nonCond Join node) then
19 |    |    |    I(n) = n
20 |    |    |    I(m) = n
21 |    |    |    nedge = (n, 0)
22 |    |    |    dist = d + 1
23 |    |    end
24 |    |    if (n is not a Cond and Join node) then
25 |    |    |    I(m) = I(n)
26 |    |    |    if (I(n) ≠ ι ∧ ¬(I(n), X) ∈ Eₘ for any X ∈ {0, 1, 2, 3}) then
27 |    |    |    |    nedge = (I(n), l)
28 |    |    |    |    dist = d + 1
29 |    |    |    end
30 |    |    |    if (I(n) ≠ ι ∧ (I(n), l') ∈ Eₘ ∧ l' > 0 ∧ l' ≠ l) then
31 |    |    |    |    nedge = (I(n), 3)
32 |    |    |    |    dist = min(d + 1, Dist(m, I(n))
33 |    |    |    end
34 |    |    end
35 |    |    if (nedge = (m', l') ≠ (⊥, ⊥)) then
36 |    |    |    Eₘ = Eₘ ∪ {nedge}
37 |    |    |    Dist(m, m') = dist
38 |    |    end
39 |    |    if (¬visit(m) ∧ nedge = (m', l')) then  W = W ∪ {(m, l', dist)}
40 |    |    else if (¬visit(m)) then  W = W ∪ {(m, l, dist)}
41 |    end
42 end
```

Algorithm 2: GENINFLUENCERGRAPH

CFG. The choice of n' depends on the kind of visited node n. If n is a Cond node or a Join node, then $n' = n$ as n is recognized to be the new influencer of m, and $n' = \mathcal{I}(n)$ otherwise to interpret the fact that the influencer of n becomes the influencer of m. The choice of l depends on the following facts:

- If n is a Cond node, then the first and the second visited successors m_1 and m_2 of n introduce the edges $(m_1, n, 1)$ and $(m_2, n, 2)$ in $\mathcal{G}$. However, we include the edge $(m_i, n, 3)$ instead of (m_i, n, l) for $l = 1$ or $l = 2$ if there already exists an edge (m_i, n, l') in $\mathcal{G}$ for any $i = 1, 2$, $l' > 0$, and $l' \neq l$ since m_i can be reached from n through either of the two branches.
- If n is a Join node and not a Cond node, we include the edge $(m, n, 0)$ in $\mathcal{G}$ to represent the fact that m is not influenced by n, but there possibly be a successor of n in $\mathcal{G}$ that may influence m.
- If n is neither a Join node nor a Cond node, then we include the edge $(m, \mathcal{I}(n), l)$ in $\mathcal{G}$ where the edge-label l may be the continuation of the previously selected edge-label or $l = 3$ if $\mathcal{G}$ already includes an edge $(m, \mathcal{I}(n), l')$ for any $l' > 0$ and $l' \neq l$.

3.2   An Incremental Algorithm to Compute WCC

Once we obtain the influencer graph $\mathcal{G}$ as explained in the previous section, we perform a search for disjoint N'-paths in $\mathcal{G}$ to detect all N'-weakly deciding nodes. Then, the WCC of N' includes N' and all N'-weakly deciding nodes that are reachable from N' in the CFG. Before we provide a systematic search in graph $\mathcal{G}$, we provide a few details on $\mathcal{G}$.

There may have multiple edges (n_1, n, l) and (n_2, n, l) to the node n in $\mathcal{G}$ with the same edge label. This is due to the sequence of CFG nodes n, n_1, n_2 in the CFG such that n is a Cond or Join node, and n_i is neither a Cond nor a Join node for $i = 1, 2$. Thus, both n_1 and n_2 belong to the same branch of n and both are predecessor nodes of n in $\mathcal{G}$. If either n_1 or n_2 belongs to N', then the edge (n_i, n, l) represents the N'-path $[n..n_i]$ for any $i \in \{1, 2\}$. However, if both n_1 and n_2 are in N', then only $[n..n_1]$ is an N'-path, but $[n..n_2]$ is not. Our systematic search in $\mathcal{G}$ incorporates this fact by looking into the distance $\mathcal{D}ist(n_i, n)$ computed in Algorithm 2 and considers the N'-path $[n..n_1]$ as $\mathcal{D}ist(n_1, n) < \mathcal{D}ist(n_2, n)$.

We compute the set of N'-weakly deciding vertices by traversing the graph $\mathcal{G}$ from the nodes in N' in the forward direction according to Algorithm 4. We maintain the following functions as invariant during the fixpoint iteration of the algorithm:

- The function $\mathcal{E}nd : N \to N$ records the end element of a potential N'-path from the given node. For example, $\mathcal{E}nd(n) = m$ implies that $[m..n]$ is a potential N'-path in the CFG. Initially, we set $\mathcal{E}nd(n) = \bot$ for each CFG node n to represent the fact that an N'-path from n is yet to be traversed (if exists).
- For all CFG nodes n such that either $n \in N'$ or n is identified as an N'-weakly deciding node, we set $wdVec(n) = true$; $wdVec(n) = false$ otherwise.

- The function $\mathcal{L} : N \rightarrow \mathcal{P}(\{1, 2, 3\})$ records the set of non-zero edge-labels of a given node n, and any $l \in \mathcal{L}(n)$ indicates that an N'-path exists from n in the branch of the CFG marked by l. For example, $\mathcal{L}(n) = \{1, 3\}$ indicates that an N'-path exists from node n in the CFG which can be visited by traversing any of the two branches of n in the CFG.
- The function $\mathcal{M} : N \times \{0, 1, 2, 3\} \rightarrow N \times \mathbb{N}$ represents the pair of a CFG node and a nonnegative integer number in relation to a given pair of a CFG node and an edge label. Given any CFG node m and the edge label $l \in \{0, 1, 2, 3\}$, $\mathcal{M}(m, l) = (n, d)$ represents the fact that (n, m, l) is an edge in the influencer graph $\mathcal{G}$ with distance $d = \mathcal{D}ist(n, m)$ such that the path $[m..n]$ is either an N'-path or a prefix of an N'-path. If there exist multiple edges (n', m, l) and (n, m, l) in $\mathcal{G}$ such that both represent N'-paths (or a prefix of N'-paths) $[m..n]$ and $[m..n']$, we set $\mathcal{M}(m, l) = (n, d)$ if $d = \mathcal{D}ist(n, m) < \mathcal{D}ist(n', m)$. We set $\mathcal{M}(m, l) = (\bot, \bot)$ when no N'-path exists from m in the CFG. If $\mathcal{M}(m, l) = (n, d)$, we use the functions $first$ and $second$ to denote the equality $first(\mathcal{M}(m, l)) = n$ and $second(\mathcal{M}(m, l)) = d$ respectively.

Given the CFG G, a subset of CFG nodes N', and the boolean variable *initialize?*, Algorithm 3 computes the WCC of N'. If *initialize?* is *true*, the functions $\mathcal{E}nd, \mathcal{L}, wdVec$, and $\mathcal{M}$ are initialized, and the influencer graph $\mathcal{G}$ and the function $\mathcal{D}ist$ are computed by applying Algorithm 2. Algorithm 4 is applied to compute the set of N'-weakly deciding nodes WD followed by computing the reachability of the nodes in WD from N' in the CFG G. We omit the details of the CHECKREACHABILITY function as it is a simple graph reachability algorithm visiting each edge in the CFG exactly once starting from N' and return the set of all nodes in WD that are reachable from N'.

For the subsequent application of Algorithm 3 in computing the WCC of a superset of N' (after the first computation of WCC set), Algorithm 3 is called with the boolean variable *initialize?* set to *false* . Algorithm 4 is applied with the previously computed values of the functions $\mathcal{E}nd, \mathcal{L}, wdVec$, and $\mathcal{M}$. These functions are considered as the internal states of the algorithm which are initialized only once and the WCC set is computed incrementally if the input set N' grows incrementally in the consecutive calls of Algorithm 3.

Algorithm 4 computes the set of N'-weakly deciding nodes from the influencer graph $\mathcal{G}$ and the set N'. We assume that the functions $\mathcal{E}nd, \mathcal{L}, wdVec, \mathcal{M}$, and $\mathcal{D}ist$ are globally available to Algorithms 3 - 5. Algorithm 4 systematically traverses the graph $\mathcal{G}$ from the nodes in N' in the forward direction and updates the functions $\mathcal{E}nd, \mathcal{L}, wdVec, \mathcal{M}$ to record the visit of N'-paths and their disjointedness. While visiting an edge (n, m, l) in $\mathcal{G}$, $\mathcal{L}(m)$ is updated to record the visit of the node m through the branch $l \neq 0$, $\mathcal{M}(m, l)$ is updated to record the predecessor node n of m providing the N'-path through the branch l and the distance from n (or the nearest Cond node of n) to m. A CFG node m is included in the set of N'-weakly deciding vertices WD if the following constraints are satisfied:

$$|\mathcal{L}(m)| > 1 \tag{2}$$

$$|\{\mathcal{E}nd(p) : l' \in \mathcal{L}(m), p = first(\mathcal{M}(m, l')), \mathcal{E}nd(p) \neq \bot\}| > 1 \tag{3}$$

Input: $G, N', initialize?$
Output: WCC
1 **if** $(initialize?)$ **then**
2   **forall** $(n \in N)$ **do**
3        $\mathcal{E}nd(n) = \bot,\ \mathcal{L}(n) = \emptyset,\ wdVec(n) = false$
4   **forall** $l \in \{0, \dots, 3\}$ **do** $\mathcal{M}(n,l) = (\bot, \bot)$
5   **end**
6     $(\mathcal{G}, \mathcal{D}ist) =$ GENINFLUENCERGRAPH(G)
7 **end**
8 $WD =$ COMPUTEWD$(\mathcal{G}, N')$
9 $WCC = N' \cup$ CHECKREACHABILITY(G, WD, N')

Algorithm 3: COMPUTEWCC

Input: $\mathcal{G} = (N, \mathcal{E}), N'$
Output: WD
1 $WD = \emptyset$
2 **forall** $(n \in N')$ **do**
3     $wdVec(n) = true,\ \mathcal{E}nd(n) = n$
4 **end**
5 $W = N'$
6 **while** $(W \neq \emptyset)$ **do**
7   Remove n from W
8   **forall** $((m,l) \in \mathcal{E}_n)$ **do**
9   **if** $(wdVec(m))$ **then** continue
10   **if** $(l \neq 0)$ **then** $\mathcal{L}(m) = \mathcal{L}(m) \cup \{l\}$
11   **if** $(\mathcal{M}(m,l) = (\bot, \bot) \vee second(\mathcal{M}(m,l)) > \mathcal{D}ist(n,m))$ **then**
12           $\mathcal{M}(m,l) = (n, \mathcal{D}ist(n,m))$
13   **end**
14        $changed = false$
15        $S = \{\mathcal{E}nd(p) : l' \in \mathcal{L}(m), p = first(\mathcal{M}(m,l')), \mathcal{E}nd(p) \neq \bot\}$
16   **if** $(|S| > 1)$ **then**
17           $errorEnd = \mathcal{E}nd(m)$
18           $\mathcal{E}nd(m) = m$
19           $WD = WD \cup \{m\}$
20           $wdVec(m) = true$
21           $changed = true$
22   **if** $(errorEnd \neq \bot \wedge errorEnd \neq m)$ **then**
23   propagateToReplace$(m, errorEnd)$
24   **end**
25   **end**
26   **else**
27           $changed = (\mathcal{E}nd(m)! = \mathcal{E}nd(first(\mathcal{M}(m,l))))$
28           $\mathcal{E}nd(m) = \mathcal{E}nd(first(\mathcal{M}(m,l)))$
29   **end**
30   **if** $(changed)$ **then** $W = W \cup \{m\}$
31   **end**
32 **end**

Algorithm 4: COMPUTEWD

Input: $m, errorEnd$

1 $W_q = \{m\}$
2 **while** $(W_q \neq \emptyset)$ **do**
3 | Remove n from W_q
4 | **for** $(m \in succ_{\mathcal{G}}(n))$ **do**
5 | | **if** $(\mathcal{E}nd(m) == errorEnd \wedge wdVec(m) == false)$ **then**
6 | | | $\mathcal{E}nd(m) = \bot$
7 | | | $W_q = W_q \cup \{m\};$
8 | | **end**
9 | **end**
10 **end**

Algorithm 5: propagateToReplace

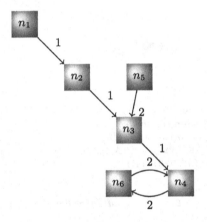

Fig. 3. An example influencer graph

Equation 2 implies that m is a Cond node in the CFG having two branches and multiple N'-paths exit from m in the CFG. Equation 3 implies that there exist two predecessors m_1 and m_2 of m in $\mathcal{G}$ such that $\mathcal{E}nd(m_1) \neq \mathcal{E}nd(m_2)$ and $\mathcal{E}nd(m_i) \neq \bot$ for $i = 1, 2$. Thus, there exist two disjoint N'-paths from m in the CFG, and m is included in the set of an N'-weakly deciding vertices WD. We provide the theoretical proof of the correctness of our approach in the next section.

While visiting the graph $\mathcal{G}$, it may happen that the update of the function $\mathcal{E}nd$ is based on partial information that may lead to error if proper actions are not taken. We illustrate this scenario by an example in Fig. 3. Let n_1 and n_5 belong to N' and $\mathcal{E}nd(n_i) = \bot$ for all $1 \leq i \leq 6$ initially. During the visit of this graph from n_5, Algorithm 4 updates $\mathcal{E}nd(n_i) = n_5$ for all $i \in \{3, \dots, 6\}$. While visiting the graph from n_1, eventually node n_3 is included in WD due to visiting two disjoint paths $[n_3..n_5]$ and $[n_3..n_1]$, and $\mathcal{E}nd$ is updated by $\mathcal{E}nd(n_3) = n_3$. Next, if node n_4 is visited without taking any action, Eqs. 2 and 3 are satisfied for node n_4 since $\mathcal{E}nd(n_6) = n_5$ and $\mathcal{E}nd(n_3) = n_3$, and node n_4 will be included in WD imprecisely. Even though two N'-paths exist from n_4, the paths are not disjoint. We resolve this imprecision in our algorithm as follows. If a CFG node m is included in WD, we set $\mathcal{E}nd(m) = m$ due to our choice of invariant during the fixpoint computation. Moreover, node m should be the end element for all nodes $n \notin WD$ and that belong to a path π from m in $\mathcal{G}$. However, if we had $\mathcal{E}nd(m) = m' \neq \bot$ before we set $\mathcal{E}nd(m) = m$, and if we have $\mathcal{E}nd(n) = m'$, we reset $\mathcal{E}nd(n) = \bot$ so that $\mathcal{E}nd(n)$ can be set to m in a later visit to n from m. For example, for the influencer graph in Fig. 3, we reset $\mathcal{E}nd(n) = \bot$ and later set $\mathcal{E}nd(n) = n_3$ for $n \in \{n_4, n_6\}$ after we set $\mathcal{E}nd(n_3) = n_3$. This action will not include n_4 in WD as Eq. 3 will not be satisfied for node n_4 due to resetting $\mathcal{E}nd(n_6)$. Algorithm 4 performs this reset by calling the $propagateToReplace$ procedure in Algorithm 5.

3.3   Proof of Correctness

In this section, we provide a number of lemmas to justify that Algorithm 4 correctly discovers all N'-weakly deciding nodes. Finally, we provide Theorem 1 to prove that Algorithm 3 correctly computes the WCC of N'.

Lemma 1. *Any path $[n_1..n_k]$ in the influencer graph $\mathcal{G}$ implies that there exists a path $[n_k..n_1]$ in the CFG.*

Proof. Let $n \in N$ be a CFG node such that $n_i \in succ(n)$ for any $1 \leq i \leq k-1$. Algorithm 2 includes the edge (n_i, n_{i+1}) in $\mathcal{G}$ while visiting the CFG node n due to one of the following cases:

1. If n is a Cond node or a Join node, then $n_{i+1} = n$ and n_{i+1}, n_i is a path in the CFG,
2. Otherwise, $n_{i+1} = \mathcal{I}(n)$.

Let $\mathcal{I}(n) = m_1$ for any $m_1 \in N$. According to Algorithm 2, m_1 can only be a Join or a Cond node (see Lines 12, 19, 20). Then, $\mathcal{I}(n) = m_1$ is obtained due to traversing a CFG path $m_1, \ldots, m_l = n$ such that no m_j is a Cond or Join node and $\mathcal{I}(m_j) = m_1$ (Line 25) for $2 \leq j \leq l$. Thus, there exists CFG paths $[m_1..n]$, and consequently, $[m_1..n_i]$ is a CFG path with $n_{i+1} = m_1$ being a Cond node. Thus, any path $[n_1..n_k]$ in the influencer graph $\mathcal{G}$ is obtained due to the existence of a CFG path $[n_k..n_1]$ such that $n_2, \ldots, n_k$ are all Cond or Join nodes. $\qquad\square$

Note. *While constructing the graph $\mathcal{G}$, an edge (n,m) is included in this graph if either m is a Cond or Join node, or $m = I(n')$ for some node n' such that $I(n') \neq \bot$. If $I(n') = \bot$, we would not have an edge (n,m) in this graph (see the conditions at lines 26, 30, and 35 in Algorithm 2).*

Lemma 2. *Let $N' \subseteq N$, let $[n_1..n_k]$ be any path in the influencer graph $\mathcal{G}$, let $n_1 \in N'$, and let $n_i \notin N'$ for all $2 \leq i \leq k$. Then, either $\pi = [n_k..n_1]$ is an N'-path or there exists another N'-path which is a prefix of π in the CFG G.*

Proof. According to Lemma 1, there exists a path $[n_k..n_1]$ in the CFG G. If no node in this path is in N' except n_1, then $[n_k..n_1]$ is an N' path. However, if the path $[n_k..n_1]$ includes multiple nodes from N', then there exists a node $m \in [n_k..n_1]$ which is in N' and the closest node to n_k. Thus, $[n_k..m]$ is an N'-path in the CFG which is the prefix of $[n_k..n_1]$. □

Lemma 3. *Let $\mathcal{E}nd(n) = m$ for any $n, m \in N$ computed in Algorithm 4. Then, there exists a path $\pi = [m..n]$ in the influencer graph $\mathcal{G}$ such that either $m \in N'$ or $m \in WD$.*

Proof. Algorithm 4 assigns $\mathcal{E}nd(n) = m$ while traversing an edge (n', n, l) in $\mathcal{G}$ for any $n' \in N$. Either (i) $\mathcal{E}nd(n) = n$ (Line 18) or (ii) $\mathcal{E}nd(n) = \mathcal{E}nd(n_1) = m$ for any predecessor $n_1 = first(\mathcal{M}(n, l)$ of n (Line 28). In the first case, $n = m$ and $n \in WD$. Thus, π is a trivial path containing only the node n, and the lemma trivially holds. In the second case, we use the inductive reasoning to show that there exists a path $n_k, \ldots, n_1$ in $\mathcal{G}$ such that $\mathcal{E}nd(n_i) = \mathcal{E}nd(n_{i+1})$ for all $1 \leq i \leq k - 1$ due to the update in Line 28, and eventually we must have $n_k = m$ and $\mathcal{E}nd(m) = m$ since $\mathcal{G}$ is a finite graph. Algorithm 4 assigns $\mathcal{E}nd(m) = m$ if $m \in N'$ (Line 3) or $m \in WD$ (Line 18) during traversing $\mathcal{G}$, and consequently, the lemma holds. □

Lemma 4. *Let $\mathcal{E}nd(n) \neq \bot$ for any $n \in N$ computed in Algorithm 4. Then, there exists an N'-path from n in the CFG.*

Proof. Let $n = n_0$, and let $\mathcal{E}nd(n_0) = n_1$ for any $n_1 \in N$. According to Lemma 3, there exists a path $[n_1..n_0]$ in the influencer graph $\mathcal{G}$ such that either $n_1 \in N'$ or $n_1 \in WD$. If $n_1 \in N'$, then according to Lemma 2, there exists an N'-path from n in the CFG G. However, if $n_1 \in WD$, there exists a predecessor m_1 of n_1 in $\mathcal{G}$ such that $\mathcal{E}nd(m_1) \neq \bot$. Let $\mathcal{E}nd(m_1) = n_2$. We apply the inductive reasoning to infer that there exists a sequence of paths $[n_k..n_{k-1}], \ldots, [n_1..n_0]$ in $\mathcal{G}$ such that $n_i \in WD$ for $0 \leq i \leq k - 1$, and eventually $n_k \in N'$ since $\mathcal{G}$ is finite, $\mathcal{E}nd(m) = m$ for all $m \in N'$ due to initialization (Line 3 in Algorithm 4), and $\mathcal{E}nd(m')$ for all $m' \notin N'$ are updated from $\mathcal{E}nd(m)$ by traversing $\mathcal{G}$ from N'. Thus, according to Lemma 2, there exists an N'-path from n in the CFG. □

Lemma 5. *Let $n \in N$ be a CFG node satisfying Eq. 2 and Eq. 3. Then, there exist two edges (n_1, n, l_1) and (n_2, n, l_2) in $\mathcal{G}$ such that $l_1 \neq l_2$, $\mathcal{E}nd(n_1) \neq \mathcal{E}nd(n_2)$, $\mathcal{E}nd(n_i) \neq \bot$ and $l_i > 0$ for $i = 1, 2$.*

Proof. Since $|\mathcal{L}(n)| > 1$, there exist two edges (n_1, n, l_1) and (n_2, n, l_2) in $\mathcal{G}$ for any $n_1, n_2 \in N$ such that $l_1 \neq l_2$ and $l_i > 0$ for $i = 1, 2$. The conditions $l_1 \neq l_2$ and $l_i > 0$ for $i = 1, 2$ imply that node n is a Cond node having two successors in the CFG.

Since Eq. 3 is satisfied for the node n, either $\mathcal{E}nd(n_1) \neq \mathcal{E}nd(n_2)$ and the lemma holds consequently, or $\mathcal{E}nd(n_1) = \mathcal{E}nd(n_2)$. In the second case, there exists another edge (n_3, n, l_3) such that $\mathcal{E}nd(n_3) \neq \mathcal{E}nd(n_i)$ for $i = 1, 2$. As n is a Cond node, $l_3 \neq 0$ according to Algorithm 2 (see Lines 13 and 14 in Algorithm 2). So, we have one of the following possibilities: (i) $l_3 \neq l_1$ and

$l_3 \neq l_2$, (ii) $l_3 = l_1$, but $l_3 \neq l_2$, or (iii) $l_3 = l_2$, but $l_3 \neq l_1$. Consequently, we have the CFG nodes n_3 and either n_2 due to Case (i) or (ii) or n_1 due to Case (iii) such that the conditions in the lemma are satisfied. $\qquad\square$

Lemma 6. *Let $\pi = [n..m]$ be a CFG path such that n is reachable from the Start node. Then, there exists a subsequence of CFG nodes $n_1,\ldots,n_k = m$ of π such that $[n_k..n_1]$ is a path in $\mathcal{G}$.*

Proof. We consider the subsequence of CFG nodes $n_1,\ldots,n_k = m$ of π such that each n_i is a Cond or Join node for $1 \leq i \leq k-1$. Let $m_0^i = n_i,\ldots,m_{i_k}^i = n_{i+1}$ be the sequence of nodes from n_i to n_{i+1} in π for all $1 \leq i \leq k-1$ and $i_k \geq 0$. Algorithm 2 traverses the path π as it is reachable from the Start node. At each visit to the node m_j^i for any $1 \leq j \leq i_k$, Algorithm 2 inserts the edge (m_j^i, n_i, l) for any $l \in \{0,\ldots,3\}$. Thus, (n_{i+1}, n_i, l) is an edge in $\mathcal{G}$ for all $1 \leq i \leq k-1$, and $[n_k..n_1]$ is a path in $\mathcal{G}$. $\qquad\square$

Lemma 7. *Let $n \in N$ be a CFG node such that there exist two disjoint N'-paths from n in the CFG. Then, Eqs. 2 and 3 are satisfied for n in Algorithm 4.*

Proof. Let π_1 and π_2 be two disjoint N'-paths from n in the CFG. According to Lemma 6, there exist two paths $[n_k..n_1]$ and $[m_l..m_1]$ in $\mathcal{G}$ which are subsequences of nodes in π_1 and π_2 respectively. Also, $n_k, m_l \in N'$ since π_1 and π_2 are N'-paths in the CFG.

Node n is a Cond node having two distinct branches in the CFG, and thus we must have $n_1 = n$ and $m_1 = n$. So, there exist two edges (n_2, n, l_1) and (m_2, n, l_2) in the influencer graph $\mathcal{G}$ such that $l_1 \neq l_2$ since n_2 and m_2 are at different branches of n. Also, since n is a Cond node, $l_i > 0$ for $i = 1, 2$. Thus, Eq. 2 is satisfied for n.

Since π_1 and π_2 are disjoint paths that only meet at the CFG node n, $[n_k..n_1]$ and $[m_l..m_1]$ are also disjoint paths that only meet at $n_1 = m_1$. We must have $\mathcal{E}nd(n_k) = n_k$ and $\mathcal{E}nd(m_l) = m_l$ since $n_k, m_l \in N'$. While visiting the influencer graph $\mathcal{G}$ in Algorithm 4, $\mathcal{E}nd(n_2)$ and $\mathcal{E}nd(m_2)$ may take any value from the sets $\{n_2,\ldots,n_k\}$ and $\{m_2,\ldots,m_l\}$ respectively, which are disjoint sets. Thus, Eq. 3 is satisfied for n. $\qquad\square$

Lemma 8. *Let $n \in N$ be a CFG node satisfying Eqs. 2 and 3. Then, n is an N'-weakly deciding node.*

Proof. According to Lemma 5, there exist two edges (n_1, n, l_1) and (m_1, n, l_2) in $\mathcal{G}$ such that $l_1 \neq l_2$, $\mathcal{E}nd(n_1) \neq \mathcal{E}nd(m_1)$, $\mathcal{E}nd(n_1) \neq \bot, \mathcal{E}nd(m_1) \neq \bot$ and $l_i > 0$ for $i = 1, 2$.

For any $m \in N'$, $\mathcal{E}nd(m) = m$ due to initialization, and $\mathcal{E}nd(m') \neq \bot$ is derived from this initial values of $\mathcal{E}nd(m)$ for all other $m' \notin N'$. Let $\mathcal{E}nd(n_1) = n_2$. There exists a path $[n_2..n_1]$ in $\mathcal{G}$ such that either $n_2 \in N'$ or $n_2 \in WD$ (Lemma 3). If $n_2 \in WD$, there exist a predecessor n_2' of n_2 such that $\mathcal{E}nd(n_2') \neq \bot$ according to Algorithm 4 (see Lines 15–18 in Algorithm 4). Let $\mathcal{E}nd(n_2') = n_3$. Since $\mathcal{G}$ is finite, we apply inductive reasoning to infer that there exists a path $[n_k..n_1]$ in $\mathcal{G}$ such that $n_k \in N'$, $[n_{i+1}..n_i]$ is a path in $\mathcal{G}$ and $n_i \in WD$ for all

$1 \leq i \leq k - 1$. Similarly, there exists a path $[m_l..m_1]$ in $\mathcal{G}$ such that $m_l \in N'$, $[m_{i+1}..m_i]$ is a path in $\mathcal{G}$ and $m_i \in WD$ for all $1 \leq i \leq l - 1$.

In what follows, we show that the paths $\pi_1 = [m_l..m_1, n]$ and $\pi_2 = [n_k..n_1, n]$ are disjoint by contradiction. Suppose there exist no such disjoint paths to n. Thus, they meet at the first common node $n_i = m_j$ in π_1 and π_2 for any $1 \leq i \leq k$ and $1 \leq j \leq l$. So, the paths $[n_k..n_{i+1}]$ and $[m_l..m_{j+1}]$ are disjoint.

Now, if there exists a node $m \in [n_i..n]$ which is in WD and thus $\mathcal{E}nd(m) \neq \perp$, we can apply inductive reasoning as before to show that there exists a path $[m^p..m^1]$ for any $p \geq 1$ such that $m_p \in N'$. This path does not meet any of the paths $[n_k..n_{i+1}]$ and $[m_l..m_{j+1}]$ as they are disjoint. This implies that we can always have two disjoint paths from n regardless of whether $[m^p..m^1]$ meet with $[n_i..n]$ and/or $[m_j..n]$:

1. the path $[n_k..n]$ if $[m^p..m^1]$ meet with both $[n_i..n]$ and $[m_j..n]$ or only with $[m_j..n]$, and
2. another path $[m^p..m^t]$ followed by $[m^t..n]$ where m^t meet at $[m_j..n]$.

This contradicts our assumption that no paths like π_1 and π_2 to n are disjoint. So, our assumption about the existence of the node $m \in WD$ is not correct. Thus, no node in the paths $[n_i..n]$ and $[m_j..n]$ are in WD. We must have $\mathcal{E}nd(n_i) \neq \perp$ due to the path $[n_k..n_i]$ such that $\mathcal{E}nd(n_k) = n_k$. Algorithm 4 then traverses the paths $[n_i..n]$ and $[m_j..n]$ and set $\mathcal{E}nd(m) = \mathcal{E}nd(n_i)$ for all $m \in [n_i..n]$ and $m \in [m_j..n]$ (see conditions at Line 16 and the update at Line 28 in Algorithm 4). This contradicts the assumption of the lemma that $\mathcal{E}nd(n_1) \neq \mathcal{E}nd(n_2)$. Thus, our only assumption that π_1 and π_2 are not disjoint cannot be true.

Then, π_1 and π_2 lead to two N'-paths π_3 and π_4 from n in the CFG G according to Lemma 4. These paths are disjoint as all Cond and Join nodes in these paths are disjoint. Node n is thus an N'-weakly deciding vertex. □

Theorem 1. *Algorithm 3 correctly and precisely computes the WCC of a subset N' of CFG nodes.*

Proof. For all N'-weakly deciding node n in the CFG, Eqs. 2 and 3 are satisfied for n in Algorithm 4 according to Lemma 7. Moreover, for all CFG nodes n satisfying Eqs. 2 and 3 in Algorithm 4, n is an N'-weakly deciding node according to Lemma 8. Since Algorithm 4 includes all CFG nodes n in WD if Eqs. 2 and 3 are satisfied for n, Algorithm 4 includes a CFG node n in WD if and only if n is an N'-weakly deciding node. Algorithm 3 then computes the set WCC that includes N' and a subset of WD that are reachable from N' in the CFG. □

3.4   Worst-Case Time Complexity

In this section, we provide a number of lemmas to state the theoretical worst-case time complexity of our algorithms.

Lemma 9. *Let $\mathcal{G} = (\mathcal{N}, \mathcal{E})$ be the influencer graph generated from a CFG $G = (N, E)$ such that $|\mathcal{G}| = |\mathcal{N}| + |\mathcal{E}|$ and $|G| = |N| + |E|$. Then, it holds that $O(|\mathcal{G}|) = O(|G|)$.*

Proof. For each visit to a CFG edge, Algorithm 2 inserts at most one edge in $\mathcal{G}$. Moreover, since $N = \mathcal{N}$, we must have $O(|\mathcal{G}|) = O(|G|)$.   □

Lemma 10. *The worst-case time complexity of Algorithm 2 is $O(|N|log_2|N|)$.*

Proof. The worst-case time complexity of Algorithm 2 is dominated by the **while** loop (line 5–42). The **while** loop visits each CFG node exactly once. For each visited node n, the **forall** loop (line 9–41) visits each edge from n exactly once. Thus, the **while** and the **forall** loop collectively iterates $|N| + |E|$ times. The worst-case cost of each basic operation inside the **while** and the **forall** loop is constant except for the costs of the operations $(n, X) \in \mathcal{E}_m$ and $(\mathcal{I}(n), X) \in \mathcal{E}_m$ at Lines 13, 14, 26, and 30, the cost of inserting the edge $\{nedge\}$ in $\mathcal{E}_m$ at Line 36, and the cost of accessing and updating $Dist(m, .)$ at Lines 32 and 37. All these data structures can contain at most $|N|$ elements, and the worst-case cost for insertion, search, and update operations are $O(log_2|N|)$ as practical implementation of these data structures use red-black trees. Thus, the worst-case cost of the entire loop (Line 5–42) is $O((|N| + |E|) * log_2|N|)$. Since any CFG node has at most two outgoing edges according to the definition of CFG, we have $O(|N|) = O(|E|)$, and the worst-case time complexity of Algorithm 2 is $O(|N|log_2|N|)$.   □

Lemma 11. *The worst-case time complexity of Algorithm 4 is $O(|N|^2)$.*

Proof. The worst-case cost of Algorithm 4 is dominated by the **while** loop (Line 6–32). This loop iterates as long as there exist elements in the worklist W. While visiting an edge (n, m, l) in the influencer graph $\mathcal{G}$, m is included in W if $\mathcal{E}nd(m)$ is changed (see Lines 18, 21, 27–30). The function $\mathcal{E}nd(m)$ may change its value $\perp$ to some other value $n \in N$ for the first time. If $\mathcal{E}nd(m) = m$ is set once, its value will never be changed and it will never be included in W. Also, $\mathcal{E}nd(m) = n$ may change to $\mathcal{E}nd(m) = n'$ if there exists a path $[n..m]$ in the influencer graph such that $n' \in [n..m]$ and n' is included in WD, or $n' \in N'$ is an immediate predecessor of m. Thus, if $\mathcal{E}nd(m)$ is changed $|N|$ times, it implies that $|N|$ nodes are in $WD \cup N'$ and thus no new node can be included in W as $\mathcal{E}nd$ will then never be changed, and the *changed* variable will always be false afterward. So, we can safely consider that for each node m in the influencer graph, $\mathcal{E}nd(m)$ may change two times (from $\perp$ to some value $n \in N$, and n to m if $m \in WD$). Each additional change will be due to including a node in WD. Since at most $|N|$ node can be included in WD, the **while** and the loop **forall** loop (Lines 8–31) will iterate at most $2 * |N| + 2 * |\mathcal{E}|$ times in total.

By choosing suitable data structures, all other operations in the **while** and **forall** loops can be performed at constant time except for the operation of the *propagateToReplace* procedure in Algorithm 5. Algorithm 5 requires visiting each node and edge in the graph $\mathcal{G}$ at most once with all other operations in the **while** loop at constant cost. Thus, the worst-case cost of Algorithm 5 is $O(|\mathcal{N}| + |\mathcal{E}|)$ which is effectively $O(|N|)$ due to Lemma 9. Thus, the worst-case cost of the **while** loop in Algorithm 4 is $O((2 * |N| + 2 * |\mathcal{E}|) * |N|)$ which is equivalent to $O(|N|^2)$. This is also the worst-case cost of Algorithm 4.   □

Theorem 2. *The worst-case time complexity of Algorithm 3 computing the WCC set is $O(|N|^2)$.*

Proof. The worst-case cost of the CHECKREACHABILITY procedure can be at most $O(|N|)$ times as it requires visiting each node and edge at most once in a loop with all other operations in the loop at a constant cost. Thus, the worst-case cost of Algorithm 3 is dominated by the worst-case cost of the COMPUTEWD procedure which is $O(|N|^2)$ according to Lemma 11.

Note that even though the worst-case cost of Algorithm 3 is quadratic in the size of the CFG, we believe that the amortized complexity of this algorithm is much better as indicated by our experimental evaluation in the next section.

4   Experimental Evaluation

The main objectives of our experimental evaluation include measuring the correctness of our algorithm and comparing its practical efficiency with the state-of-the-art approaches. In doing so, we have implemented our algorithms in the Clang/LLVM compiler framework [9]. We have compared our approach with the state-of-the-art WCC computation algorithm developed earlier [12,14] which is currently the best-known algorithm for computing WCC with an average speedup of 10.6 compared to the algorithm of Danicic et al. [4]. This state-of-the-art algorithm is also implemented in the Clang/LLVM compiler framework and released as open-source in a GitHub repository[2].

All experiments are performed in an Intel(R) Core(TM) i7-7567U 3.50GHz CPU with 16 GB of RAM memory and all implementations are compiled using the LLVM version 11.0.0. We have used seven benchmarks from the SPEC CPU 2017 benchmark suite consisting of approximately 2081 KLOC. These benchmarks are written in C language and were also used in the experimental evaluation of the state-of-the-art approaches. Note that the SPEC CPU 2017 benchmark suite contains other benchmarks. However, they are not written solely in the C language. Since our implementation can only handle C code, these other benchmarks are thus excluded from the experiments.

In order to perform experiments for the incremental computation of WCC, we choose the set N' of CFG nodes randomly. This choice of randomness is due to the fact that N' should be provided by the client application of WCC such as program slicing as illustrated in Algorithm 1. This choice of randomness neither affects the generality of our algorithm nor affects our experiment in any way. We run each experiment 10 times. The number 10 is selected due to the fact that earlier experimental evaluation [12,14] ran each experiment 10 times as well. For the client applications like slicing or information flow control, this number will depend on the size of the CFG, the maximal number of Cond nodes in a maximal path, and the point of interest such as the nodes in the slicing criterion, etc. Usually, this number should be the maximum number of iterations to reach

---

[2] https://github.com/anm-spa/CDA.

Table 1. Execution times of computing WCC incrementally on seven selected benchmarks from SPEC CPU 2017 [3]

#	Benchmarks	KLOC	#proc	T_ω	T_M	Speedup
1	Mcf	3	40	17728.4	52010.9	2.93
2	Nab	24	327	121747.7	430778.8	3.54
3	Xz	33	465	66832.0	147705.6	2.21
4	X264	96	1449	60603.5	208273.6	3.44
5	Imagick	259	2586	56359.8	225375.0	4.0
6	Perlbench	362	2460	2006511.4	18762418.0	9.35
7	GCC	1304	17827	12317538.2	434684910.3	35.29
	Total/Average	2081	25154	14647321.0	454511472.2	31.03

fixed-point in Algorithm 1. However, since this number is unknown, 10 is a good number for the experiments to get an indication of whether we can obtain a significant speedup or not. Each experiment took the Z number of randomly selected N' sets where Z is a random number between 1 and 15.

We computed the influencer graph only once and apply our WCC computation algorithm (Algorithm 3) Z times consecutively for each experiment. On the other hand, we apply the state-of-the-art algorithm [12,14] Z times consecutively to compute the WCC set for each experiment. In order to verify the correctness of our method, we compare the WCC sets computed by our incremental algorithm and the best baseline algorithm in [12,14] computed for the same N' set. We obtained exactly the same WCC sets for all experiments in each benchmark computed by both methods. This provides us the empirical proof of the correctness of our method.

For each experiment, we recorded the time in milliseconds taken by both methods. The results are presented in Table 1 in which T_ω denotes the execution time of our algorithm, T_M denotes the execution time of the best baseline algorithm, and #proc is the number of procedures in each benchmark. The *speedup* column indicates the speedup of our method which is computed as T_M/T_ω. In the final row, all numbers in each column are the sum of the numbers in 7 benchmarks except the final number in the *speedup* column. The speedup in the final row is obtained from the values of T_M and T_ω in the final row which gives us the average speedup for the entire experiment.

Table 1 illustrates that we improved the performance in the incremental computation of WCC significantly. The performance improvements are between 2 to 4 times for smaller benchmarks compared to the best baseline approach. However, for larger benchmarks like *Perlbench* or *GCC*, the performance improvements are significant. We obtained a speedup of 9.35 and 35.29 times for *Perlbench* and *GCC* respectively. On average, we obtained a speedup of 31.03 for the entire experiment. This proves that our approach can be the best alternative to compute WCC over the state-of-the-art algorithms.

As seen in Table 1, the performance improvement results are skewed towards larger benchmarks such as *GCC* and *Perlbench*. We bring our discussion of these skewed results from our earlier results on non-incremental WCC computation methods [14]. The higher gain for GCC is due to the fact that GCC is the largest benchmark in the benchmark suite, the size of CFGs for the procedures in this benchmark is much bigger than the size of the CFGs in the benchmarks like *Mcf*, *Xz*, or *Nab*. The *Xz* benchmark (for example) provides the lowest speedup due to the fact that it has fewer procedures than *GCC* and the sizes of the CFGs for most procedures in this benchmark are very small; the average size of a CFG (i.e. number of CFG nodes) is only 8 per procedure. *GCC* has 38 times more procedures than Xz and the average size of a CFG per procedure is 20. Also, greater speedups are obtained in larger CFGs. There are 171 and 55 procedures in *GCC* with the size of the CFGs greater than 200 and 500 respectively and the maximum CFG size is 15912, whereas the maximum CFG size in *Xz* is 87. The *Perlbench* is the second largest benchmark in our experiments in terms of the CFG size and the number of procedures. We obtained the second highest speedup (9.35) for this benchmark. Our results would have been less skewed if we would consider other benchmarks similar to *GCC* or *Perlbench* that have more procedures and the CFG sizes are larger, unlike *Xz* or *Mcf*.

5   Related Work

The concept of control dependence was first introduced by Denning and Denning [5] in analyzing the information-flow security of programs. He used the dominator-based (inverse of postdominator) approach to identify program instructions influenced by the conditional instructions in the program. Weiser [22] shown how to use this concept in program slicing. This concept was first formalized by Ferrante et al. [6] and used it to compute the program dependence graph (PDG). PDG is a program representation that can be used for program slicing and program optimization techniques. This formal definition of control dependence was based on computing postdominator relation which is still being used in modern compilers such as LLVM or GCC for program transformation and program optimization techniques.

Several alternatives to this standard definition are introduced in the literature. The earliest of these alternatives is the work of Podgurski and Clarke [19]. They provided the concept of weak and strong syntactic dependence where strong syntactic dependence is the standard control dependence relation of Ferrante et al. and the weak syntactic dependence is the nontermination sensitive control dependence relation. Bilardi and Pingali [2] provided a generalized framework of Podgurski and Clarke which is parameterized with respect to a set of CFG paths providing different control dependence relations. The above control dependences were extended by Ranganath et al. [20,21] to deal with programs containing exceptions or nonterminating programs. Modern software such as web services, distributed systems, or robot control software may be nonterminating and it may be desirable to compute control dependence from such systems. The authors in Reference [20, 21] introduced control dependencies that are applicable to these modern programming language constructs. They defined the nontermination insensitive and nontermination sensitive control dependencies in the opposite sense of Podgurski and Clarke, and provided algorithms to compute these control dependence relations.

Danicic et al. [4] provided the concept of weak and strong control closure that are nontermination insensitive and nontermination sensitive respectively. These definitions are the most general and unifying definitions capturing a wide variety of programming language constructs. They have shown that all previously defined control dependence relations are the special case of these two generalized concepts. They have provided algorithms to compute WCC and SCC and the worst-case time complexity of these algorithms are $O(|N|^3)$ and $O(|N|^4)$ where $|N|$ is the number of vertices of the CFG.

More recently, a number of works extending and improving various concepts of Danicic et al. have been introduced. Our earlier works in [12, 14] provided algorithms to compute WCC and SCC that improved the theoretical worst-case time complexity by an order of the size of the CFG as well as the practical efficiency. We have extended the definitions of WCC and SCC for interprocedural programs in order to prove the semantic correctness of dependence-based program slicing in [17], and provided an algorithm to compute the WCC for interprocedural programs in [18]. However, none of these improvements considered the incremental computation of WCC.

Léchenet et al. [10] provided an improvement of Danicic et al. by applying various optimizations and demonstrated the efficiency improvements in practical evaluation. The theoretical complexity of their algorithm is not provided and the algorithm is not incremental in nature. Khanfar et al. [8] developed a demand-driven algorithm to compute direct control dependencies to a particular program statement which requires that the program must have a unique exit point. This algorithm is not incremental in nature and their algorithm does not compute WCC.

Recently, we have shown an interesting duality relationship between computing the SSA program and the WCC relation [13]. Our incremental algorithm may provide an improved algorithm to compute the SSA program without computing the standard dominance frontier-based SSA construction as done in [15, 16].

6   Conclusion and Future Works

Numerous definitions of control dependence relations are introduced in the literature to handle a wide spectrum of programming language constructs. The weak and strong control closures are the most generalized definitions capturing nontermination (in)sensitive control dependencies. Since the introduction of these concepts, a series of works have been published to provide an improved algorithm computing WCC and SCC and extend them to handle interprocedural programs. However, there exists no effort that provides an incremental computation of WCC. Incremental computation of WCC is especially important for the client application of WCC such as program slicing since it requires the repeated computation of WCC in a fixpoint iteration. A non-incremental algorithm loses performance by repeatedly computing unnecessary information. In this paper, we have developed a novel algorithm to compute WCC incrementally which is also the fastest algorithm among all the existing approaches to computing WCC. We have provided the proof of correctness of our method and analyzed its worst-case time complexity which is quadratic in terms of the size of the CFG. We have implemented our algorithm in the Clang/LLVM compiler framework and compared it with the best baseline approach by running experiments on well-known benchmarks. We have obtained an average speedup of 31.03 in all benchmarks and a maximum speedup of 35.29 in the largest benchmark. This gives us an indication that the amortized complexity of our algorithm is much better than the theoretical worst-case complexity.

The future direction of this work includes developing a method that also computes SCC and is applicable to interprocedural programs. The further extension will be to develop definitions and algorithms to handle time-sensitive weak and strong control closure that will be beneficial to detect timing leaks in security-critical software.

Acknowledgment. This research is supported by the Swedish Knowledge Foundation via the HERO project.

References

1. Amtoft, T.: Correctness of practical slicing for modern program structures. Department of Computing and Information Sciences, Kansas State University, Tech. rep. (2007)
2. Bilardi, G., Pingali, K.: A framework for generalized control dependence. SIGPLAN Not. **31**(5), 291–300 (1996). https://doi.org/10.1145/249069.231435
3. Bucek, J., Lange, K.D., v. Kistowski, J.: Spec CPU2017: next-generation compute benchmark. In: Companion of the 2018 ACM/SPEC International Conference on Performance Engineering, pp. 41–42. ICPE '18, ACM, New York, NY, USA (2018). https://doi.org/10.1145/3185768.3185771
4. Danicic, S., Barraclough, R., Harman, M., Howroyd, J.D., Kiss, Á., Laurence, M.: A unifying theory of control dependence and its application to arbitrary program structures. Theor. Comput. Sci. **412**(49), 6809–6842 (2011). https://doi.org/10.1016/j.tcs.2011.08.033
5. Denning, D.E., Denning, P.J.: Certification of programs for secure information flow. Commun. ACM **20**(7), 504–513 (1977). https://doi.org/10.1145/359636.359712
6. Ferrante, J., Ottenstein, K.J., Warren, J.D.: Dependence graph and its use in optimization. ACM Trans. Program. Lang. Syst. **9**(3), 319–349 (1987). https://doi.org/10.1145/24039.24041
7. Khanfar, H., Lisper, B., Masud, A.N.: Static backward program slicing for safety-critical systems. In: de la Puente, J.A., Vardanega, T. (eds.) Ada-Europe 2015. LNCS, vol. 9111, pp. 50–65. Springer, Cham (2015). https://doi.org/10.1007/978-3-319-19584-1_4

8. Khanfar, H., Lisper, B., Mubeen, S.: Demand-driven static backward slicing for unstructured programs. Tech. rep. (2019). http://www.es.mdh.se/publications/5511-

9. Lattner, C., Adve, V.: The LLVM compiler framework and infrastructure tutorial. In: LCPC'04 Mini Workshop on Compiler Research Infrastructures. West Lafayette, Indiana (2004). https://doi.org/10.1007/11532378_2

10. Léchenet, J.-C., Kosmatov, N., Le Gall, P.: Fast computation of arbitrary control dependencies. In: Russo, A., Schürr, A. (eds.) FASE 2018. LNCS, vol. 10802, pp. 207–224. Springer, Cham (2018). https://doi.org/10.1007/978-3-319-89363-1_12

11. Lisper, B., Masud, A.N., Khanfar, H.: Static backward demand-driven slicing. In: Proceedings of the 2015 Workshop on Partial Evaluation and Program Manipulation, pp. 115–126. PEPM '15, ACM, New York, NY, USA (2015). https://doi.org/10.1145/2678015.2682538

12. Masud, A.N.: Simple and efficient computation of minimal weak control closure. In: Pichardie, D., Sighireanu, M. (eds.) SAS 2020. LNCS, vol. 12389, pp. 200–222. Springer, Cham (2020). https://doi.org/10.1007/978-3-030-65474-0_10

13. Masud, A.N.: The duality in computing SSA programs and control dependency. IEEE Trans. Softw. Eng., pp. 1–16 (2022). https://doi.org/10.1109/TSE.2022.3192249

14. Masud, A.N.: Efficient computation of minimal weak and strong control closure. J. Syst. Softw. **184**, 111140 (2022). https://doi.org/10.1016/j.jss.2021.111140

15. Masud, A.N., Ciccozzi, F.: Towards constructing the SSA form using reaching definitions over dominance frontiers. In: 19th International Working Conference on Source Code Analysis and Manipulation, SCAM 2019, Cleveland, OH, USA, September 30 - October 1, 2019, pp. 23–33. IEEE (2019). https://doi.org/10.1109/SCAM.2019.00012

16. Masud, A.N., Ciccozzi, F.: More precise construction of static single assignment programs using reaching definitions. J. Syst. Softw. **166**, 110590 (2020). https://doi.org/10.1016/j.jss.2020.110590

17. Masud, A.N., Lisper, B.: Semantic correctness of dependence-based slicing for interprocedural, possibly nonterminating programs. ACM Trans. Program. Lang. Syst. **42**(4), 1–56 (2021). https://doi.org/10.1145/3434489

18. Masud, A.N., Lisper, B.: On the computation of interprocedural weak control closure. In: Proceedings of the 31st ACM SIGPLAN International Conference on Compiler Construction, pp. 65–76. CC 2022, Association for Computing Machinery, New York, NY, USA (2022). https://doi.org/10.1145/3497776.3517782

19. Podgurski, A., Clarke, L.A.: A formal model of program dependences and its implications for software testing, debugging, and maintenance. IEEE Trans. Softw. Eng. **16**(9), 965–979 (1990). https://doi.org/10.1109/32.58784

20. Ranganath, V.P., Amtoft, T., Banerjee, A., Dwyer, M.B., Hatcliff, J.: A new foundation for control-dependence and slicing for modern program structures. In: Sagiv, M. (ed.) ESOP 2005. LNCS, vol. 3444, pp. 77–93. Springer, Heidelberg (2005). https://doi.org/10.1007/978-3-540-31987-0_7

21. Ranganath, V.P., Amtoft, T., Banerjee, A., Hatcliff, J., Dwyer, M.B.: A new foundation for control dependence and slicing for modern program structures. ACM Trans. Program. Lang. Syst. 29(5) (2007). https://doi.org/10.1145/1275497.1275502

22. Weiser, M.: Program slicing. In: Proc. 5th International Conference on Software Engineering, pp. 439–449. ICSE '81, IEEE Press, Piscataway, NJ, USA (1981). http://dl.acm.org/citation.cfm?id=800078.802557

Local Completeness Logic on Kleene Algebra with Tests

Marco Milanese[ID] and Francesco Ranzato[(⊠)][ID]

Dipartimento di Matematica, University of Padova, Padova, Italy
`francesco.ranzato@unipd.it`

Abstract. Local Completeness Logic (LCL) has been put forward as a program logic for proving both the correctness and incorrectness of program specifications. LCL is an abstract logic, parameterized by an abstract domain that allows combining over- and under-approximations of program behaviors. It turns out that LCL instantiated to the trivial singleton abstraction boils down to O'Hearn incorrectness logic, which allows us to prove the presence of program bugs. It has been recently proved that suitable extensions of Kleene algebra with tests (KAT) allow representing both O'Hearn incorrectness and Hoare correctness program logics within the same equational framework. In this work, we generalize this result by showing how KATs extended either with a modal diamond operator or with a top element are able to represent the local completeness logic LCL. This is achieved by studying how these extended KATs can be endowed with an abstract domain so as to define the validity of correctness/incorrectness LCL triples and to show that the LCL proof system is logically sound and, under some hypotheses, complete.

Keywords: Local completeness logic · Incorrectness logic · Complete abstract interpretation · Kleene algebra with tests

1 Introduction

Kleene algebra [7] with tests (KAT) [17] allows an equational reasoning on programs and their properties. Programs are modeled as elements of a KAT, so that their properties can be algebraically derived through the general equational theory of KATs. KATs feature sound, complete, and decidable equational theories and have found successful applications in several different contexts, most notably in network programming [1,2,12,30,31]. The foundational study of Kozen [18] has shown that the reasoning of Hoare correctness logic [16] can be encoded and formulated equationally within a KAT. Later work by Desharnais, Möller and Struth [10,24] extended KAT with a domain (KAD) to express the modal operators of propositional dynamic logic [11], thus enabling a more natural way of reasoning through a map from actions to propositions. The expressive power of KAD has been recently substantiated by Möller, O'Hearn and Hoare [23], who have shown how to encode both Hoare [16] correctness and O'Hearn [25] incorrectness program logics in a unique class of KAD where a backward diamond modality is exploited to encode strongest postconditions. Furthermore, very recently, Zhang, De Amorim and Gaboardi [33, Theorem 1] have shown that O'Hearn incorrectness logic cannot be formulated within a conventional KAT, but, at the same time, a full fledged

G. Singh and C. Urban (Eds.): SAS 2022, LNCS 13790, pp. 350–371, 2022.
https://doi.org/10.1007/978-3-031-22308-2_16

modal KAT is not needed. In fact, [33] proves that a KAT including a greatest element, called TopKAT, is capable to encode both Hoare and O'Hearn logic in a purely equational fashion. Moreover, [33] provides a PSPACE algorithm to decide TopKAT equality, based on a reduction to Cohen et al. [6]'s algorithm for KAT.

This stream of works made it possible to reason equationally on both program correctness and incorrectness in the same algebraic framework. For example, in the KAD framework where a backward diamond modality $\langle a|p$ plays the role of strongest postcondition of a KAT element a (viz., a program) for a KAT test p (viz., a precondition), the validity of a Hoare correctness triple $\{p\}\, a\, \{q\}$ is determined by the inequality $\langle a|p \leq q$, while the validity of an O'Hearn incorrectness triple $[p]\, a\, [q]$ boils down to $q \leq \langle a|p$. Moreover, if a KAT test s plays the role of specification for a program a and a Hoare triple $\{p\}\, a\, \{q\}$ is provable, then a can be proved correct through the inequality $q \leq s$. Vice versa, if $[p]\, a\, [q]$ is a provable incorrectness triple, then incorrectness of a can be verified as $q \leq \neg s$.

The Problem. Recently, Bruni et al. [4] put forward a novel program logic, called local completeness logic LCL, which is parameterized by an abstract domain [8,9] of program stores and simultaneously combines over- and under-approximations of program behaviours. This program logic leverages the notion of *locally complete* abstract interpretation, meaning that the abstract interpretation of atomic program commands, such as variable assignments and Boolean guards, is complete (i.e. with no false alarm) *locally* on the preconditions, as opposed to standard completeness [13,29] which must be satisfied *globally* for all the preconditions. While a global completeness program logic was proposed in [14], Bruni et al. [4] design a proof system for inferring that a program analysis is locally complete. It turns out [4, Section VI] that the instantiation of this LCL program logic to the trivial store abstraction with a unique "don't know" value abstracting any concrete store property, boils down to O'Hearn incorrectness logic [25]. Moreover, Bruni et al. [5] also show that abstract interpretations can be made locally complete through minimal domain refinements that repair the lack of local completeness in a given program analysis.

In the original definition of LCL in [4] program properties are represented as elements of a concrete domain C and program semantics as functions of type $C \to C$. Although straightforward, this approach determines a specific type of program semantics. Vice versa, by exploiting a KAT, program properties are represented as tests and programs as generic elements of the KAT. Hence, a KAT based formulation becomes agnostic w.r.t. the underlying semantics and can therefore admit multiple different models of computation (e.g., trace-based semantics, or even models not related to program semantics as shown by the language-theoretic example in Sect. 3.5). Furthermore, KAT is a particularly suitable formalism for compositionally reasoning on programs as all its basic composition operations on programs (concatenation, choice and Kleene iteration) are directly modeled within the algebra: this allows us to represent composite programs and tests as elements of the KAT and, in particular, to check for their equality and inclusion directly in the algebra. Thus, following the KAT-based model of incorrectness logic advocated by Möller, O'Hearn and Hoare [23], this paper pushes forward this line of work by studying an algebraic formulation of LCL program logic, with the objective of showing that there is no need to leverage particular semantic properties of programs to reason on their local completeness.

Contributions. In this work, we show that the local completeness logic LCL can be made fully algebraic in a suitable KAT, yet preserving all its noteworthy logical properties proved in [4]. For this purpose we show that:

- Our proof systems are logically sound and complete (likewise [4], completeness needs some additional hypotheses).
- By instantiating the algebraic version of the LCL logic to the trivial domain abstracting any concrete value to "don't know" we exactly obtain O'Hearn incorrectness program logic [25], thus retrieving its logical soundness and completeness as consequences of our results.
- Triples of O'Hearn incorrectness logic carry two postconditions, corresponding to normal and erroneous program termination. While the original local completeness logic LCL in [4] only considers normal termination, we propose a generalization that also supports erroneous termination. Moreover, we use the KAD construction of [23] to generalize our logical soundness and completeness results to incorrectness triples.

In particular, we study two different formulations of LCL given: (1) in a KAD, the KAT model used in [23], and (2) in a TopKAT, the KAT model employed in [33]. In both frameworks, we put forward a suitable notion of abstract domain of KAT that, correspondingly, induces a sound abstract semantics for KAT programs (i.e., KAT terms). Our local completeness logic on KAT, called LCK, turns out to be logically sound w.r.t. this abstract semantics, meaning that a provable LCK triple $[p] \ a \ [q]$ for an abstract domain A on a KAT K satisfies:

(i) q is below the strongest postcondition in K of the program term a for the precondition p;
(ii) the program term a is locally complete for the precondition p in the abstract domain A;
(iii) the approximations in A of q and of the strongest postcondition of a for p coincide.

The proofs of all the results have been omitted and can be found in the full version of the paper [22].

2   Background on Kleene Algebra with Tests

A Kleene algebra with tests (KAT) is a purely algebraic structure that provides an elegant equational framework for program reasoning. A KAT consists of actions, playing the role of programs, and tests, interpreted as pre/postconditions and Boolean guards. KAT elements can be combined with three basic operations: nondeterministic choice $a_1 + a_2$, sequential composition $a_1; a_2$, and Kleene iteration a^*. A standard model of KAT used to represent computations is the relational model, in which KAT elements are binary relations on some set, thus modeling programs as a relation between input and output states. Further models of KAT include regular languages over a finite alphabet, square matrices over another Kleene algebra, and Kleene algebra modulo theories [15]. In the following, we briefly recall some basics of KAT. For more details, the reader is referred to [7, 10, 17].

An *idempotent-semiring* (*i-semiring*) is a tuple $(A, +, \cdot, 0, 1)$ where: (1) $(A, +, 0)$ is a commutative monoid with an idempotent addition, i.e., for all $a \in A$, $a + a = a$; (2) $(A, \cdot, 1)$ is a monoid, where the multiplication symbol $\cdot$ is often omitted, such that, for any $a \in A$, $0 \cdot a = a \cdot 0$; (3) multiplication distributes over addition (in both arguments). In an i-semiring A, the relation $a \leq b \overset{\triangle}{\Leftrightarrow} a + b = b$ is a partial order, referred to as the natural ordering, that we will implicitly use throughout the paper. Note that the addition $+$ is the join w.r.t. this natural ordering.

A *test-semiring* is a tuple $(A, \text{test}(A), +, \cdot, \neg, 0, 1)$ where: (1) $(A, +, \cdot, 0, 1)$ is an i-semiring; (2) $\text{test}(A) \subseteq A$, and $(\text{test}(A), \vee, \wedge, \neg, 0, 1)$ is a Boolean subalgebra of A with greatest element 1 and least element 0, complement $\neg$, where the meet $\wedge$ and join $\vee$ of the Boolean algebra $\text{test}(A)$ coincide, resp., with multiplication $\cdot$ and addition $+$.

A *Kleene algebra* is a tuple $(K, +, \cdot, {}^*, 0, 1)$ where: (1) $(K, +, \cdot, 0, 1)$ is an i-semiring; (2) $(\cdot)^* : K \to K$ is a unary operation, called Kleene star or iteration, satisfying the following conditions:

$$1 + aa^* \leq a^* \qquad\qquad 1 + a^*a \leq a^* \qquad\qquad (*\text{-unfold})$$
$$b + ac \leq c \Rightarrow a^*b \leq c \qquad b + ca \leq c \Rightarrow ba^* \leq c \qquad (*\text{-induction})$$

Definition 2.1 (KAT [17]). A *Kleene algebra with tests* (*KAT*) is a two-sorted algebra $(K, \text{test}(K), +, \cdot, {}^*, \neg, 0, 1)$ such that $(K, \text{test}(K), +, \cdot, \neg, 0, 1)$ is a test-semiring and $(K, +, \cdot, {}^*, 0, 1)$ is a Kleene algebra.

A KAT K is *countably-test-complete* (*CTC*) if any countable subset of $\text{test}(K)$ admits least upper bound (lub).

A KAT is *$*$-continuous*, referred to as KAT^*, if it satisfies the following condition: for all $a, b, c \in K$, $ab^*c = \bigvee_{n \in \mathbb{N}} ab^nc$ (this equation implicitly assumes that the lub $\bigvee_{n \in \mathbb{N}} ab^nc$, w.r.t. the natural ordering of K, exists).

A *relational KAT* [19] on a carrier set X is determined by a set $K \subseteq \wp(X \times X)$ of binary relations on X with tests $\text{test}(K) \subseteq \wp(\{(x, x) \mid x \in X\})$, where addition is union, multiplication is composition of relations, the additive identity is the empty relation, the multiplicative identity is $\{(x, x) \mid x \in X\}$, the Kleene star is the reflexive-transitive closure, and test complement is set complementation w.r.t. the multiplicative identity.

Informally, a backward diamond $\langle \cdot | \cdot$ on a KAT allows us to compute strongest postconditions of programs, that is, $\langle a|p$ can be interpreted as $\text{post}[a]p$.

Definition 2.2 (bdKAT [23]). A *backward-diamond KAT* (*bdKAT*) is a two-sorted algebra $(K, \text{test}(K), +, \cdot, {}^*, \neg, 0, 1, \langle|)$ such that:

(1) $(K, \text{test}(K), +, \cdot, {}^*, \neg, 0, 1)$ is a KAT;
(2) $\langle \cdot | \cdot : K \to (\text{test}(K) \to \text{test}(K))$ is a *backward-diamond* operator satisfying the following conditions: for all $a, b \in K$ and $p, q \in \text{test}(K)$,

$$\langle a|p \leq q \Leftrightarrow pa \leq aq \qquad\qquad (\text{bd1})$$
$$\langle ab|p = \langle b|(\langle a|p) \qquad\qquad (\text{bd2})$$

$\square$

The axiom (bd1) is equivalent to requiring that $\langle a|p$ is the least test in K satisfying $pa \leq aq$ (the original definition of Kleene algebra with domain in [10] is of this form). Moreover, $pa \leq aq$ in (bd1) is equivalent to $pa = paq$ (see [10, Lemma 3.4]).

Definition 2.3 (TopKAT [21]). A *KAT with top* (*TopKAT*) is a KAT K that contains a largest element $\top \in K$, that is, for all $a \in K$, $a \leq \top$.   □

3   Local Completeness Logic in KAT

We investigate how the local completeness program logic LCL [4] can be interpreted on a KAT. To achieve this, we need to address the following tasks:

- To define a notion of abstract domain of a KAT, with the aim of abstracting the set of program predicates, namely tests of a KAT;
- To establish a concrete semantics and a corresponding sound abstract semantics of programs on KATs;
- To adapt the local completeness proof system to attain valid triples on a KAT;
- To prove logical soundness and completeness w.r.t. a KAT of this new proof system.

3.1   Program Properties in KAT

Program properties can be broadly classified as intensional and extensional. The former relate to how programs are written, while the latter concern the input-output relation of a program, i.e., its strongest postcondition denotational semantics. Local completeness logic LCL relies on an abstract interpretation of programs which crucially depends on intensional properties of programs, meaning that even if two programs share the same denotation, they could well have different abstract semantics. Thus, we expect that an appropriate definition of abstract semantics based on a KAT model should also be intensional. Given two elements a and b of a modal bdKAT playing the role of programs, we therefore expect that their backward diamond functions might coincide, i.e. $\langle a| = \langle b|$, even if a and b encode different programs, i.e. $a \neq b$. However, as shown by the following remark for the basic relational model of KAT, it might happen that for certain classes of KAT models the backward diamond interpretation is injective.

Proposition 3.1. *Let K be a relational KAT on a set X where* $\text{test}(K) = \wp(\{(x, x) \mid x \in X\})$. *Then, for all $a, b \in K$,* $\langle a| = \langle b| \Leftrightarrow a = b$.

This means that, at least for some fundamental KAT models, KAT elements are equal iff they are extensionally equal, or, equivalently, they carry exclusively extensional program properties. In this case, when a program is encoded with a KAT element all the intensional properties are lost and it is indistinguishable from any other program with the same denotational semantics. Therefore, an abstract interpretation-based semantics can not be defined directly on KAT elements.

3.2 KAT Language

As a consequence of the discussion in Sect. 3.1, the concrete semantics cannot be directly defined on KAT elements. A solution is to define it on an inductive language. Actually, in a language of programs, two elements are equal iff they are syntactically equal, or, in other terms, if the corresponding programs are written in the same way. This property makes a language an ideal basis upon which a semantics can be defined, because this brings the chance of depending on intensional properties.

A natural choice for defining this language of programs is the so-called *KAT language*, as originally defined by Kozen and Smith [19, Section 2.3], because it contains all and only the operators of a KAT, so that the interpretation of language terms as KAT elements is the most natural one. This language is inductively defined from two disjoint sets of primitive actions and tests through the basic elements/operations $0, 1, +, \cdot, ^*$ of KATs. More precisely, given a set Σ of *primitive actions* and a set B of *primitive tests* such that $\Sigma \cap B = \varnothing$, the corresponding *KAT language* $T_{\Sigma,B}$ of terms is defined as follows:

$$\text{Atom} \ni \mathsf{a} ::= a \in \Sigma \mid p \in B$$

$$T_{\Sigma,B} \ni \mathsf{t} ::= \mathsf{a} \mid 0 \mid 1 \mid \mathsf{t_1} + \mathsf{t_2} \mid \mathsf{t_1} \cdot \mathsf{t_2} \mid \mathsf{t}^*$$

For simplicity, we assume that 0 and 1 are primitive tests in B, so that $0, 1 \in \text{Atom}$. The notation $\text{Atom}(\mathsf{t}) \subseteq \text{Atom}$ will denote the set of atoms occurring in a term $\mathsf{t} \in T_{\Sigma,B}$. Notice that a KAT language $T_{\Sigma,B}$ is an equivalent representation of the language of regular commands used in [4,25] for their program logics.

Given a KAT K, an evaluation of atoms in K is a mapping $u : \text{Atom} \to K$ such that $p \in B \Rightarrow u(p) \in \text{test}(K)$. An evaluation u induces an interpretation of terms $[\![\cdot]\!]_u : T_{\Sigma,B} \to K$, which is inductively defined as expected:

$$[\![\mathsf{a}]\!]_u \triangleq u(\mathsf{a}) \qquad\qquad [\![\mathsf{t_1} + \mathsf{t_2}]\!]_u \triangleq [\![\mathsf{t_1}]\!]_u + [\![\mathsf{t_2}]\!]_u$$

$$[\![\mathsf{t_1} \cdot \mathsf{t_2}]\!]_u \triangleq [\![\mathsf{t_1}]\!]_u \cdot [\![\mathsf{t_2}]\!]_u \qquad\qquad [\![\mathsf{t}^*]\!]_u \triangleq [\![\mathsf{t}]\!]_u^*$$

In turn, the concrete semantic function

$$[\![\cdot]\!]^K : T_{\Sigma,B} \to \big(\text{test}(K) \to \text{test}(K)\big)$$

models the strongest postcondition of a program, i.e. of a language term, for a given precondition, i.e. a KAT test. This is therefore defined in terms of the backward diamond of a bdKAT as follows:

$$[\![\mathsf{t}]\!]^K p \triangleq \langle [\![\mathsf{t}]\!]_u | p. \tag{1}$$

We will often use $[\![\mathsf{t}]\!]$ to denote a concrete semantics, by omitting the superscript K when it is clear from the context.

3.3 Kleene Abstractions

An abstract domain is used in abstract interpretation for approximating store properties, i.e., sets of program stores form the concrete domain, likewise in our KAT model, the role of concrete domain is played by the set of tests $\text{test}(K)$ of a KAT K, ordered by the natural ordering induced by K.

Definition 3.2 (Kleene Abstract Domain). A poset $(A, \leq_A)$ is a *Kleene abstract domain* of a bdKAT K if:

(i) There exists a Galois insertion, defined by a concretization map $\gamma : A \to \text{test}(K)$ and an abstraction map $\alpha : \text{test}(K) \to A$, of the poset $(A, \leq_A)$ into the poset $(\text{test}(K), \leq_K)$;

(ii) A is countably-complete, i.e., any countable subset of A admits a lub. □

The abstract semantic function $[\![\cdot]\!]_A^\sharp : T_{\Sigma,B} \to (A \to A)$ defines how abstract preconditions are transformed into abstract postconditions. Likewise store-based abstract interpretation, this abstract semantics is inductively defined as follows:

$$[\![\mathsf{a}]\!]_A^\sharp p^\sharp \triangleq \alpha([\![\mathsf{a}]\!]^K \gamma(p^\sharp)) \qquad [\![\mathsf{t}_1 + \mathsf{t}_2]\!]_A^\sharp p^\sharp \triangleq [\![\mathsf{t}_1]\!]_A^\sharp p^\sharp + [\![\mathsf{t}_2]\!]_A^\sharp p^\sharp$$
$$[\![\mathsf{t}_1 \cdot \mathsf{t}_2]\!]_A^\sharp p^\sharp \triangleq [\![\mathsf{t}_2]\!]_A^\sharp ([\![\mathsf{t}_1]\!]_A^\sharp p^\sharp) \qquad [\![\mathsf{t}^*]\!]_A^\sharp p^\sharp \triangleq \bigvee_{n \in \mathbb{N}} ([\![\mathsf{t}]\!]_A^\sharp)^n p^\sharp \qquad (2)$$

It is worth remarking that condition (ii) of Definition 3.2 ensures that the abstract semantics of the Kleene star in (2) is well defined. It turns out that $[\![\cdot]\!]_A^\sharp$ is a sound (and monotonic) abstract semantics.

Theorem 3.3 (Soundness of bdKAT Abstract Semantics). *Let A be a Kleene abstraction of a CTC bdKAT K and $T_{\Sigma,B}$ be a language interpreted on K. For all $p^\sharp, q^\sharp \in A$, $p \in \text{test}(K)$, and $\mathsf{t} \in T_{\Sigma,B}$:*

$$p^\sharp \leq_A q^\sharp \Rightarrow [\![\mathsf{t}]\!]_A^\sharp p^\sharp \leq_A [\![\mathsf{t}]\!]_A^\sharp q^\sharp \qquad \text{(monotonicity)}$$
$$\alpha([\![\mathsf{t}]\!]^K p) \leq_A [\![\mathsf{t}]\!]_A^\sharp \alpha(p) \qquad \text{(soundness)}$$

3.4 Local Completeness Logic on BdKAT

Given a Kleene abstract domain A, we will slightly abuse notation by using

$$A \triangleq \gamma \circ \alpha : \text{test}(K) \to \text{test}(K)$$

as a function (indeed, this is the upper closure operator on tests induced by the Galois insertion defining A). Let us recall the notions of global vs. local completeness. If $f : \text{test}(K) \to \text{test}(K)$ is any test transformer then:

- A is *globally complete* for f, denoted $\mathbb{C}^A(f)$, iff $A \circ f = A \circ f \circ A$;
- A is *locally complete* for f on a concrete test $p \in \text{test}(K)$, denoted $\mathbb{C}_p^A(f)$, iff $A \circ f(p) = A \circ f \circ A(p)$.

It is known [14] that global completeness is hard to achieve in practice, even for simple programs. Moreover, a complete and compositional (i.e., inductively defined on program structure) abstract interpretation is even harder to design [3]. This motivated to study a local notion of completeness in abstract interpretation [4] as a pragmatic and more attainable weakening of standard global completeness.

In our local completeness logic on a Kleene algebra, a triple $[p]\ \mathsf{t}\ [q]$, where p and q are tests and t is a language term, will be valid when:

$$\frac{a \in \Sigma \cup B \qquad \mathcal{C}_p^A([\![a]\!])}{\vdash_A^K [p] \, a \, [[\![a]\!]p]} \text{ (transfer)}$$

$$\frac{p' \le p \le A(p') \qquad \vdash_A^K [p'] \, t \, [q'] \qquad q \le q' \le A(q')}{\vdash_A^K [p] \, t \, [q]} \text{ (relax)}$$

$$\frac{\vdash_A^K [p] \, t_1 \, [r] \qquad \vdash_A^K [r] \, t_2 \, [q]}{\vdash_A^K [p] \, t_1 \cdot t_2 \, [q]} \text{ (seq)} \qquad \frac{\vdash_A^K [p] \, t_1 \, [q_1] \qquad \vdash_A^K [p] \, t_2 \, [q_2]}{\vdash_A^K [p] \, t_1 + t_2 \, [q_1 + q_2]} \text{ (join)}$$

$$\frac{\vdash_A^K [p] \, t \, [r] \qquad \vdash_A^K [p+r] \, t^* \, [q]}{\vdash_A^K [p] \, t^* \, [q]} \text{ (rec)} \qquad \frac{\vdash_A^K [p] \, t \, [q] \qquad q \le A(p)}{\vdash_A^K [p] \, t^* \, [p+q]} \text{ (iterate)}$$

Fig. 1. Proof system LCK$_A$.

(1) q is an under-approximation of the concrete semantics of t from a precondition p;
(2) A is locally complete for $[\![t]\!]$ on the precondition p;
(3) q and $[\![t]\!]p$ have the same over-approximation in A.

Definition 3.4 (Triple Validity). Let K a CTC bdKAT, A be a Kleene abstraction of K, and $T_{\Sigma,B}$ be a KAT language interpreted on K. For all $p, q \in \text{test}(K)$ and $t \in T_{\Sigma,B}$, a triple $[p]$ t $[q]$ is valid in A, denoted by $\models_A^K [p]$ t $[q]$, if

(i) $q \le_K [\![t]\!]^K p$;
(ii) $[\![t]\!]_A^\sharp \alpha(p) = \alpha(q) = \alpha([\![t]\!]^K p)$. $\qquad\qquad\qquad\qquad\qquad\square$

The local completeness proof system in [4] can be adapted to our algebraic framework, yielding the set of rules denoted by LCK$_A$ in Fig. 1. The only syntactic difference concerns the usage of elements of test(K) as pre/postconditions and the language of terms $T_{\Sigma,B}$ playing the role of programs.

It turns out that the logic LCK$_A$ is logically sound (we use "logical" soundness to avoid overloading the soundness of abstract semantics).

Theorem 3.5 (Logical Soundness of $\vdash_A^K$). *If* $\vdash_A^K [p]$ t $[q]$ *then*

(i) $q \le_K [\![t]\!]p$;
(ii) $[\![t]\!]_A^\sharp \alpha(p) = \alpha(q) = \alpha([\![t]\!]p)$.

Analogously to what happens for LCL, we can prove that LCK$_A$ is logically complete under these two additional hypotheses:

(A) The following infinitary rule is added to LCK$_A$:

$$\frac{\forall n \in \mathbb{N}. \ \vdash_A^K [p_n] \, t \, [p_{n+1}]}{\vdash_A^K [p_0] \, t^* \, [\bigvee_{n \in \mathbb{N}} p_n]} \text{ (limit)}$$

Let us point out that the lub $\bigvee_{n \in \mathbb{N}} p_n$ always exists in K, as a consequence of the CTC requirement on K.

(B) The concrete semantics of the primitive actions and tests occurring in the program are globally complete.

It can be proved that the rule (limit) preserves logical soundness (see the full version [22]).

Theorem 3.6 (Logical Completeness of $\vdash_A^K$). *Assume that conditions (A) and (B) hold. If $\models_A^K [p] \, t \, [q]$ then $\vdash_A^K [p] \, t \, [q]$.*

Summing up, this shows that the local completeness logic LCL introduced in [4] can be made *fully algebraic* by means of a natural interpretation on modal KATs with a backward diamond operator, still preserving its logical soundness and completeness, which are proved by using just the algebraic axioms of this class of KATs. Hence, this shows that there is no need to leverage particular semantic properties of programs to reason on their local completeness.

3.5   An Example of a Language-Theoretic KAT

To give an example digressing from programs and showing the generality of the KAT-based approach, we describe a language-theoretic model of Kleene algebra, early introduced by Kozen and Smith [19, Section 3].

Let $\Sigma = \{u\}$ and $B = \{b_1, b_2\}$ be, resp., the sets of primitive actions and tests. An *atom* is a string $c_1 c_2$, where $c_i \in \{b_i, \overline{b}_i\}$. If $c_i = b_i$, where $i \in \{1, 2\}$, then b_i appears positively in the atom $c_1 c_2$, while if $c_i = \overline{b}_i$ it appears negatively. A *guarded string* is either a single atom or a string $\alpha_0 a_1 \alpha_1 ... a_n \alpha_n$, where α_i are atoms and $a_i \in \Sigma$. If we are only interested in the first (last) atom of a guarded string $\alpha a_1 \alpha_1 ... a_n \beta$, we may refer to it through the syntax αx ($x\beta$). Concatenation of guarded strings is given by a coalesced product operation $\diamond$, which is partially defined as follows:

$$x\alpha \diamond \beta y \triangleq \begin{cases} x\alpha y & \text{if } \alpha = \beta \\ \text{undefined} & \text{otherwise} \end{cases}$$

The elements of this KAT $\mathcal{G}$ are sets of guarded strings. Thus, $+$ is set union, the product is defined as pointwise coalesced product:

$$A \cdot B \triangleq \{x \diamond y \mid x \in A, y \in B\},$$

while the Kleene iteration is: $A^* \triangleq \bigcup_{n \in \mathbb{N}} A^n$. The product identity corresponds to the whole set of atoms $1_\mathcal{G} \triangleq \{b_1 b_2, b_1 \overline{b}_2, \overline{b}_1 b_2, \overline{b}_1 \overline{b}_2\}$, while $0_\mathcal{G}$ is the empty set. The set of tests is $\text{test}(\mathcal{G}) \triangleq \wp(1_\mathcal{G})$.

It turns out that $\mathcal{G}$ is a bdKAT, whose backward diamond is as follows: for all $a \in \mathcal{G}$ and $p \in \text{test}(\mathcal{G})$,

$$\langle a|p = \{\beta \mid x\beta \in pa\}. \tag{3}$$

Proof. Let $r = \{\beta \mid x\beta \in pa\}$. It can be proved (see the full version [22]) that in a bdKAT K, for all $p \in \text{test}(K)$ and $a \in K$, (bd1) holds iff $\langle a|p$ is the least (w.r.t. the natural ordering) $q \in \text{test}(K)$ such that $pa = paq$. Therefore, it is enough to show that r is the least $q \in \text{test}(\mathcal{G})$ satisfying $pa = paq$.

Let $x\beta \in pa$. By definition, $\beta \in r$ means that $x\beta \diamond \beta = x\beta$ is contained in par. This therefore means that $pa \leq par$. The opposite inequality is trivial since r is a test, hence $r \leq 1_{\mathcal{G}}$, and by monotonicity of $\cdot$, we have that $pa \geq par$, thus implying $pa = par$. Assume now, by contradiction, that there exists $t \in \text{test}(\mathcal{G})$ such that $pa = pat$, $t \leq r$ and $t \neq r$. This means that there is at least an atom β in r which is not in t. By definition of r, there is a guarded string $x\beta \in pa$. Since $pa = pat$, the last atom of all the guarded strings in pa must be in t, but this does not hold for $x\beta$ as $\beta \notin t$. $\qquad\square$

Let us consider the evaluation function $G : \text{Atom} \to \mathcal{G}$ as defined in [19]:

$$G(\mathsf{a}) \triangleq \{\alpha\mathsf{a}\beta \mid \alpha, \beta \in 1_{\mathcal{G}}\},$$

$$G(\mathsf{b}) \triangleq \{\alpha \in 1_{\mathcal{G}} \mid \mathsf{b} \text{ appears positively in } \alpha\}.$$

We consider the abstract domain $A \triangleq \{\top, e, o, \bot\}$ determined by the following abstraction $\alpha : \text{test}(\mathcal{G}) \to A$ and concretization $\gamma : A \to \text{test}(\mathcal{G})$ maps:

$$\alpha(p) \triangleq \begin{cases} \bot & \text{if } p = \emptyset \\ e & \text{if } \emptyset \subsetneq p \subseteq \{\mathsf{b}_1\mathsf{b}_2, \overline{\mathsf{b}}_1\overline{\mathsf{b}}_2\} \\ o & \text{if } \emptyset \subsetneq p \subseteq \{\overline{\mathsf{b}}_1\mathsf{b}_2, \mathsf{b}_1\overline{\mathsf{b}}_2\} \\ \top & \text{otherwise} \end{cases} \qquad \gamma(p^\sharp) \triangleq \begin{cases} \emptyset & \text{if } p^\sharp = \bot \\ \{\mathsf{b}_1\mathsf{b}_2, \overline{\mathsf{b}}_1\overline{\mathsf{b}}_2\} & \text{if } p^\sharp = e \\ \{\overline{\mathsf{b}}_1\mathsf{b}_2, \mathsf{b}_1\overline{\mathsf{b}}_2\} & \text{if } p^\sharp = o \\ 1_{\mathcal{G}} & \text{if } p^\sharp = \top \end{cases}$$

By counting, in an atom, the number of primitive tests that appear positively we obtain an integer that may be even or odd. Hence, this abstract domain A represents the property of being even e or odd o of all the atoms occurring in a test $p \in \text{test}(\mathcal{G})$.

By using our logic LCK, we study the correctness of the program $\mathsf{r} \triangleq (\mathsf{u} \cdot \mathsf{b}_1)^* \in \mathcal{G}$, assuming a precondition $p \triangleq \{\mathsf{b}_1\mathsf{b}_2, \overline{\mathsf{b}}_1\overline{\mathsf{b}}_2\} \in \text{test}(\mathcal{G})$ and a specification $\text{Spec} \triangleq p = \gamma(e)$. Let us define two auxiliary tests: $q \triangleq \{\mathsf{b}_1\mathsf{b}_2, \mathsf{b}_1\overline{\mathsf{b}}_2\}$, $s \triangleq \{\mathsf{b}_1\mathsf{b}_2, \mathsf{b}_1\overline{\mathsf{b}}_2, \overline{\mathsf{b}}_1\overline{\mathsf{b}}_2\}$. Using the equation (3), we can easily check the following local completeness equations:

$$\alpha(\llbracket\mathsf{u}\rrbracket A(s)) = \alpha(\llbracket\mathsf{u}\rrbracket 1_{\mathcal{G}}) = \alpha(1_{\mathcal{G}}) = \top = \alpha(1_{\mathcal{G}}) = \alpha(\llbracket\mathsf{u}\rrbracket s) \qquad \Rightarrow \quad \mathbb{C}_s^A(\llbracket\mathsf{u}\rrbracket)$$

$$\alpha(\llbracket\mathsf{u}\rrbracket A(p)) = \alpha(\llbracket\mathsf{u}\rrbracket p) = \alpha(1_{\mathcal{G}}) = \top = \alpha(1_{\mathcal{G}}) = \alpha(\llbracket\mathsf{u}\rrbracket p) \qquad \Rightarrow \quad \mathbb{C}_p^A(\llbracket\mathsf{u}\rrbracket)$$

$$\alpha(\llbracket\mathsf{b}_1\rrbracket A(1_{\mathcal{G}})) = \alpha(\llbracket\mathsf{b}_1\rrbracket 1_{\mathcal{G}}) = \alpha(q) = \top = \alpha(q) = \alpha(\llbracket\mathsf{b}_1\rrbracket 1_{\mathcal{G}}) \qquad \Rightarrow \quad \mathbb{C}_{1_{\mathcal{G}}}^A(\llbracket\mathsf{b}_1\rrbracket)$$

Therefore, we have the following derivation in LCK_A of the triple $[p]\ \mathsf{r}\ [s]$:

$$\cfrac{\cfrac{\cfrac{\mathbb{C}_p^A(\llbracket\mathsf{u}\rrbracket)}{\vdash_A^\kappa [p]\ \mathsf{u}\ [1_{\mathcal{G}}]}\text{(transfer)} \quad \cfrac{\mathbb{C}_{1_{\mathcal{G}}}^A(\llbracket\mathsf{b}_1\rrbracket)}{\vdash_A^\kappa [1_{\mathcal{G}}]\ \mathsf{b}_1\ [q]}\text{(transfer)}}{\vdash_A^\kappa [p]\ \mathsf{u}\cdot\mathsf{b}_1\ [q]}\text{(seq)} \quad \cfrac{\cfrac{\cfrac{\mathbb{C}_s^A(\llbracket\mathsf{u}\rrbracket)}{\vdash_A^\kappa [s]\ \mathsf{u}\ [1_{\mathcal{G}}]}\text{(transfer)} \quad \cfrac{\mathbb{C}_{1_{\mathcal{G}}}^A(\llbracket\mathsf{b}_1\rrbracket)}{\vdash_A^\kappa [1_{\mathcal{G}}]\ \mathsf{b}_1\ [q]}\text{(transfer)}}{\vdash_A^\kappa [s]\ \mathsf{u}\cdot\mathsf{b}_1\ [q]}\text{(seq)} \quad q \leq A(s)}{\vdash_A^\kappa [s]\ (\mathsf{u}\cdot\mathsf{b}_1)^*\ [s]}\text{(iterate)}}{\vdash_A^\kappa [p]\ (\mathsf{u}\cdot\mathsf{b}_1)^*\ [s]}\text{(rec)}$$

Here, in accordance with the soundness Theorem 3.5, we have that $s \subseteq \llbracket\mathsf{r}\rrbracket p \subseteq A(s)$. Observe that $A(s) \nsubseteq \text{Spec}$ holds, meaning that an abstract interpretation-based analysis fails to prove that the program r is correct for Spec. However, unlike conventional abstract interpretation, LCK_A is capable to show that $s \setminus \text{Spec} = \{\mathsf{b}_1\overline{\mathsf{b}}_2\}$ is indeed a true alert, meaning that the program r is really incorrect and the failure to prove its correctness was not due to a false alarm.

$$\frac{\mathbf{a} \in \text{Atom}}{\vdash_{\text{UL}} [p] \, \mathbf{a} \, [[\![\mathbf{a}]\!]p]} \ \text{(transfer)}$$

$$\frac{}{\vdash_{\text{UL}} [p] \, \mathbf{t} \, [0]} \ \text{(empty)} \qquad \frac{p' \leq p \quad \vdash_{\text{UL}} [p'] \, \mathbf{t} \, [q'] \quad q \leq q'}{\vdash_{\text{UL}} [p] \, \mathbf{t} \, [q]} \ \text{(consequence)}$$

$$\frac{\vdash_{\text{UL}} [p_1] \, \mathbf{t} \, [q_1] \quad \vdash_{\text{UL}} [p_2] \, \mathbf{t} \, [q_2]}{\vdash_{\text{UL}} [p_1 + p_2] \, \mathbf{t} \, [q_1 + q_2]} \ \text{(disj)} \qquad \frac{\vdash_{\text{UL}} [p] \, \mathbf{t}_1 \, [r] \quad \vdash_{\text{UL}} [r] \, \mathbf{t}_2 \, [q]}{\vdash_{\text{UL}} [p] \, \mathbf{t}_1 \cdot \mathbf{t}_2 \, [q]} \ \text{(seq)}$$

$$\frac{}{\vdash_{\text{UL}} [p] \, \mathbf{t}^* \, [p]} \ \text{(iterate zero)} \qquad \frac{\vdash_{\text{UL}} [p] \, \mathbf{t}^* \cdot \mathbf{t} \, [q]}{\vdash_{\text{UL}} [p] \, \mathbf{t}^* \, [q]} \ \text{(iterate non-zero)}$$

$$\frac{\forall n \in \mathbb{N}. \ \vdash_{\text{UL}} [p_n] \, \mathbf{t} \, [p_{n+1}]}{\vdash_{\text{UL}} [p_0] \, \mathbf{t}^* \, [\bigvee_{n \in \mathbb{N}} p_n]} \ \text{(back-v)} \qquad \frac{\vdash_{\text{UL}} [p] \, \mathbf{t}_i \, [q], \text{ with } i = 1 \text{ or } i = 2}{\vdash_{\text{UL}} [p] \, \mathbf{t}_1 + \mathbf{t}_2 \, [q]} \ \text{(choice)}$$

Fig. 2. Proof System UL.

3.6 Under-Approximation Logic

O'Hearn [25] incorrectness logic (IL) establishes two main novelties w.r.t. the seminal Hoare logic of program correctness [16]: (1) a valid postcondition of an incorrectness triple for a program P is an *under-approximation* of the strongest postcondition of P, rather than an over-approximation of Hoare logic; (2) incorrectness triples feature two postconditions: one corresponding to a "normal" program termination and one corresponding to an erroneous termination. Even if IL was originally defined with both those features, we first neglect the second one — i.e., we consider "normal" termination only — and we refer to the resulting program logic as Under-approximation Logic, denoted by UL. For the sake of clarity, Fig. 2 recalls the UL proof system, adapted to our algebraic framework. We only focus on the "propositional" fragment of this logic, meaning that the roles of all the special program commands (i.e., error, assume, skip, nondet used in [25]) and variable manipulations commands of incorrectness logic are played by some corresponding elements in Atom. Hence, for all of them, the single rule (transfer) is unifying and enough for our purposes.

Analogously to what has been proved in [4, Section 6] for LCL, it turns out that the trivial abstraction, i.e., the abstract domain $A_{tr} \triangleq \{\top\}$ that approximates all the concrete elements to a single abstract element $\top$, allows us to show that the instantiation $\text{LCK}_{A_{tr}}$, with the additional rule (limit), boils down to UL, namely, our LCK logic generalizes UL, even when both are interpreted on KATs.

Theorem 3.7 ($\text{LCK}_{A_{tr}} \equiv \text{UL}$). *Let K be a CTC bdKAT. Assume that $\text{LCK}_{A_{tr}}$ includes the rule* (limit). *For any $p, q \in \text{test}(K)$ and $\mathbf{t} \in T_{\Sigma, B}$:*

$$\vdash^{K}_{A_{tr}} [p] \, \mathbf{t} \, [q] \quad \Leftrightarrow \quad \vdash_{\text{UL}} [p] \, \mathbf{t} \, [q].$$

Moreover, since the abstraction map defining A_{tr} is $\alpha_{A_{tr}} = \lambda x. \top$, we have that condition (ii) of Definition 3.4 for the validity of a LCK triple trivially holds, that is,

$[\![t]\!]^{\sharp}_A \alpha(p) = \top = \alpha(q) = \alpha([\![t]\!]^K p)$. This therefore entails that

$$\models^K_{A_{tr}} [p] \, t \, [q] \quad \Leftrightarrow \quad \models_{\mathrm{UL}} [p] \, t \, [q]. \tag{4}$$

This allows us to retrieve the soundness and completeness results of incorrectness logic [25] as a consequence of those for LCK.

Corollary 3.8. *Under the same hypotheses of Theorem 3.7, the proof system* UL *is sound and complete, that is,* $\vdash_{\mathrm{UL}} [p] \, t \, [q] \Leftrightarrow \models_{\mathrm{UL}} [p] \, t \, [q]$.

4 Incorrectness Logic in KAT

Incorrectness logic IL has been introduced by O'Hearn [25] as a natural under-approximating counterpart of the pivotal Hoare correctness logic [16], and quickly attracted a lot of research interest [20,26–28,32]. Incorrectness logic distinguishes two postconditions corresponding to normal and erroneous/abnormal program termination. Here, we generalize the algebraic formulation of our LCK logic to support abnormal termination. We follow the approach of Möller, O'Hearn and Hoare [23], namely, each language term is interpreted as a pair of KAT elements which model the normal and abnormal execution. The evaluation function has type $u : \mathrm{Atom} \to (K \times K)$, while the interpretation function has type $[\![\cdot]\!]_u : T_{\Sigma,B} \to (K \times K)$. As a shorthand $[\![\cdot]\!]_u$ can be subscripted with **ok** or **err** to denote, resp., its first normal and second erroneous component. The definition is as follows:

$$\begin{aligned}
[\![a]\!]_u &\triangleq u(a) \\
[\![t_1 + t_2]\!]_u &\triangleq ([\![t_1]\!]_{u_{\mathrm{ok}}} + [\![t_2]\!]_{u_{\mathrm{ok}}}, [\![t_1]\!]_{u_{\mathrm{err}}} + [\![t_2]\!]_{u_{\mathrm{err}}}) \\
[\![t_1 \cdot t_2]\!]_u &\triangleq ([\![t_1]\!]_{u_{\mathrm{ok}}} \cdot [\![t_2]\!]_{u_{\mathrm{ok}}}, [\![t_1]\!]_{u_{\mathrm{err}}} + [\![t_1]\!]_{u_{\mathrm{ok}}} \cdot [\![t_2]\!]_{u_{\mathrm{err}}}) \\
[\![t^*]\!]_u &\triangleq ([\![t]\!]^*_{u_{\mathrm{ok}}}, [\![t]\!]^*_{u_{\mathrm{ok}}} \cdot [\![t]\!]_{u_{\mathrm{err}}})
\end{aligned} \tag{5}$$

Following the original definition of IL, the precondition encodes an **ok** condition only, while the postcondition contains both an **ok** and an **err** component. Hence, the latter is given by a pair $(p, q) \in \mathrm{test}(K) \times \mathrm{test}(K)$, typically denoted by **ok** : p, **err** : q. The concrete semantics $[\![\cdot]\!] : T_{\Sigma,B} \to (\mathrm{test}(K) \to (\mathrm{test}(K) \times \mathrm{test}(K)))$ is defined as

$$[\![t]\!]p \triangleq \mathbf{ok} : \langle [\![t]\!]_{u_{\mathrm{ok}}} | p, \mathbf{err} : \langle [\![t]\!]_{u_{\mathrm{err}}} | p$$

To refer to one of its components, $[\![\cdot]\!]$ can be subscripted with **ok** or **err**, e.g., $[\![t]\!]_{\mathrm{ok}} \, p$.

Given a Kleene abstract domain A on K, the corresponding abstract semantics $[\![\cdot]\!]^{\sharp}_A : T_{\Sigma,B} \to (A \to (A \times A))$ is defined as follows:

$$\begin{aligned}
[\![a]\!]^{\sharp}_A p^{\sharp} &\triangleq \mathbf{ok} : \alpha([\![a]\!]_{\mathrm{ok}} \, \gamma(p^{\sharp})), \mathbf{err} : \alpha([\![a]\!]_{\mathrm{err}} \, \gamma(p^{\sharp})) \\
[\![t_1 + t_2]\!]^{\sharp}_A p^{\sharp} &\triangleq \mathbf{ok} : [\![t_1]\!]^{\sharp}_{A_{\mathrm{ok}}} p^{\sharp} + [\![t_2]\!]^{\sharp}_{A_{\mathrm{ok}}} p^{\sharp}, \mathbf{err} : [\![t_1]\!]^{\sharp}_{A_{\mathrm{err}}} p^{\sharp} + [\![t_2]\!]^{\sharp}_{A_{\mathrm{err}}} p^{\sharp} \\
[\![t_1 \cdot t_2]\!]^{\sharp}_A p^{\sharp} &\triangleq \mathbf{ok} : [\![t_2]\!]^{\sharp}_{A_{\mathrm{ok}}} ([\![t_1]\!]^{\sharp}_{A_{\mathrm{ok}}} p^{\sharp}), \mathbf{err} : [\![t_1]\!]^{\sharp}_{A_{\mathrm{err}}} p^{\sharp} + [\![t_2]\!]^{\sharp}_{A_{\mathrm{err}}} ([\![t_1]\!]^{\sharp}_{A_{\mathrm{ok}}} p^{\sharp}) \\
[\![t^*]\!]^{\sharp}_A p^{\sharp} &\triangleq \mathbf{ok} : \bigvee_{n \in \mathbb{N}} ([\![t]\!]^{\sharp}_{A_{\mathrm{ok}}})^n p^{\sharp}, \mathbf{err} : [\![t]\!]^{\sharp}_{A_{\mathrm{err}}} \bigvee_{n \in \mathbb{N}} ([\![t]\!]^{\sharp}_{A_{\mathrm{ok}}})^n p^{\sharp}
\end{aligned} \tag{6}$$

The ok part coincides with the semantics of LCK, while the err component puts in place some differences. In particular, the composition exhibits a short-circuiting behavior, meaning that an error in the first command aborts the execution without executing the second one, while the Kleene star allows an error to occur after some error-free iterations. It is straightforward to check that this definition of abstract semantics is monotonic and sound.

The proof system LCK can be extended with incorrectness triples. In particular, a triple $[p]$ t $[\text{ok} : q][\text{err} : r]$ is valid if the standard validity conditions hold for both ok and err.

Definition 4.1 (Incorrectness Triple). Let K be a CTC bdKAT K and $T_{\Sigma,B}$ be a language interpreted on K. An *incorrectness triple* is either $[p]$ t $[\text{ok} : q]$ or $[p]$ t $[\text{err} : r]$, where $p, q, r \in \text{test}(K)$ and t $\in T_{\Sigma,B}$.
Let A be a Kleene abstract domain on K with abstraction map $\alpha : \text{test}(K) \to A$.

- The triple $[p]$ t $[\text{ok} : q]$ is valid if: (1) $q \leq [\![t]\!]_{\text{ok}}\, p$, and (2) $[\![t]\!]^{\sharp}_{A_{\text{ok}}}\, \alpha(p) = \alpha(q) = \alpha([\![t]\!]_{\text{ok}}\, p)$.
- The triple $[p]$ t $[\text{err} : r]$ is valid if: (1) $r \leq [\![t]\!]_{\text{err}}\, p$, and (2) $[\![t]\!]^{\sharp}_{A_{\text{err}}}\, \alpha(p) = \alpha(r) = \alpha([\![t]\!]_{\text{err}}\, p)$.
- A triple $[p]$ t $[\text{ok} : q][\text{err} : r]$ is valid when both $[p]$ t $[\text{ok} : q]$ and $[p]$ t $[\text{err} : r]$ are valid. In particular, if $q = r$ then the triple $[p]$ t $[\epsilon : q]$ is valid. $\square$

The proof system LCIL_A defining the local completeness incorrectness logic is given in Fig. 3.

Theorem 4.2 (Logical Soundness of LCIL_A). *The triples provable in LCIL_A are valid.*

Furthermore, it turns out that LCIL_A is logically complete.

Theorem 4.3 (Logical Completeness of LCIL_A). *Let A be a Kleene abstract domain on a CTC bdKAT K and $T_{\Sigma,B}$ be a language interpreted on K. Assume that the atoms in t $\in T_{\Sigma,B}$ are globally complete, i.e., for all $\mathbf{a} \in \text{Atom}(t)$, $\mathbb{C}^A([\![\mathbf{a}]\!]_{\text{ok}})$ and $\mathbb{C}^A([\![\mathbf{a}]\!]_{\text{err}})$ hold. If $[p]$ t $[\text{ok} : q][\text{err} : r]$ is valid, then it is provable in LCIL_A.*

Example 4.4. Consider a relational bdKAT $K \triangleq \wp(\mathbb{Z} \times \mathbb{Z})$ on the set of integers $\mathbb{Z}$, where $\mathbf{1}_K \triangleq \{\langle z, z \rangle \mid z \in \mathbb{Z}\}$ and $\mathbf{0}_K \triangleq \varnothing$, and the standard integer interval abstraction Int [8,9]. Let us consider a language with primitive actions $\Sigma \triangleq \{\mathbf{x} := \mathbf{x} + 1, \text{err}\}$. The evaluation function $u : \Sigma \cup B \to K_{\text{ok}} \times K_{\text{err}}$ is defined as expected:

$$u(\mathbf{x} := \mathbf{x} + 1) = (\{\langle z, z + 1 \rangle \mid z \in \mathbb{Z}\}, \mathbf{0}_K), \qquad u(\text{err}) = (\mathbf{0}_K, \mathbf{1}_K).$$

We study the correctness of the program $\mathbf{r} \equiv ((\mathbf{x} := \mathbf{x} + 1) + \text{err})^{*}$, for the precondition $p \triangleq \{\langle 0, 0 \rangle, \langle 2, 2 \rangle\}$ and the specification $\text{Spec} \triangleq (\text{ok} : \{\langle z, z \rangle \mid z \geq 0\}, \text{err} : \mathbf{0}_K)$. Let us define an auxiliary sequence of tests $p_n \triangleq \{\langle n, n \rangle, \langle n + 2, n + 2 \rangle\}$ and $s \triangleq \{\langle z, z \rangle \mid z \geq 0\}$.

$$\frac{\mathbf{a} \in \mathrm{Atom} \qquad \mathbb{C}_p^A(\llbracket \mathbf{a} \rrbracket_{\mathrm{ok}}) \qquad \mathbb{C}_p^A(\llbracket \mathbf{a} \rrbracket_{\mathrm{err}})}{\vdash_A^K [p]\, \mathbf{a}\, [\mathrm{ok}: \llbracket \mathbf{a} \rrbracket_{\mathrm{ok}}\, p][\mathrm{err}: \llbracket \mathbf{a} \rrbracket_{\mathrm{err}}\, p]} \text{ (transfer)}$$

$$\frac{p' \leq p \leq A(p') \qquad \vdash_A^K [p']\, \mathbf{t}\, [\epsilon: q'] \qquad q \leq q' \leq A(q)}{\vdash_A^K [p]\, \mathbf{t}\, [\epsilon: q]} \text{ (relax)}$$

$$\frac{\vdash_A^K [p]\, \mathbf{t}_1\, [\mathrm{ok}: r] \qquad \vdash_A^K [r]\, \mathbf{t}_2\, [\mathrm{ok}: q]}{\vdash_A^K [p]\, \mathbf{t}_1 \cdot \mathbf{t}_2\, [\mathrm{ok}: q]} \text{ (seq-ok)}$$

$$\frac{\vdash_A^K [p]\, \mathbf{t}_1\, [\mathrm{ok}: q][\mathrm{err}: r] \qquad \vdash_A^K [q]\, \mathbf{t}_2\, [\mathrm{err}: s]}{\vdash_A^K [p]\, \mathbf{t}_1 \cdot \mathbf{t}_2\, [\mathrm{err}: r + s]} \text{ (seq-err)}$$

$$\frac{\vdash_A^K [p]\, \mathbf{t}^*\, [\mathrm{ok}: q] \qquad \vdash_A^K [q]\, \mathbf{t}\, [\mathrm{err}: r]}{\vdash_A^K [p]\, \mathbf{t}^*\, [\mathrm{err}: r]} \text{ (rec-err)}$$

$$\frac{\vdash_A^K [p]\, \mathbf{t}_1\, [\epsilon: q_1] \qquad \vdash_A^K [p]\, \mathbf{t}_2\, [\epsilon: q_2]}{\vdash_A^K [p]\, \mathbf{t}_1 + \mathbf{t}_2\, [\epsilon: q_1 + q_2]} \text{ (join)}$$

$$\frac{\forall n \in \mathbb{N}.\ \vdash_A^K [p_n]\, \mathbf{t}\, [\mathrm{ok}: p_{n+1}]}{\vdash_A^K [p_0]\, \mathbf{t}^*\, [\mathrm{ok}: \bigvee_{n \in \mathbb{N}} p_n]} \text{ (limit)}$$

Fig. 3. Proof system LCIL$_A$.

We can easily check the local completeness of the atoms by exploiting the following characterization (see the full version [22]) of the backward diamond operator in a relational KAT K on a set X where $\mathrm{test}(K) = \wp(\{(x,x) \mid x \in X\})$: for all $a \in K$ and $p \in \mathrm{test}(K)$,

$$\langle a|p = \{(y,y) \mid \exists x \in X.\ (x,x) \in p, (x,y) \in a\}.$$

We therefore have the following derivation in LCIL$_{\mathrm{Int}}$ for $\mathbf{r}$:

$$\frac{\dfrac{\mathbb{C}_{p_n}^{\mathrm{Int}}(\llbracket \mathbf{x} := \mathbf{x} + 1 \rrbracket_{\mathrm{ok}}) \qquad \mathbb{C}_{p_n}^{\mathrm{Int}}(\llbracket \mathbf{x} := \mathbf{x} + 1 \rrbracket_{\mathrm{err}})}{\vdash_{\mathrm{Int}}^K [p_n]\, \mathbf{x} := \mathbf{x} + 1\, [\mathrm{ok}: p_{n+1}]} \text{(transfer)} \qquad \dfrac{\mathbb{C}_{p_n}^{\mathrm{Int}}(\llbracket \mathbf{err} \rrbracket_{\mathrm{ok}}) \qquad \mathbb{C}_{p_n}^{\mathrm{Int}}(\llbracket \mathbf{err} \rrbracket_{\mathrm{err}})}{\vdash_{\mathrm{Int}}^K [p_n]\, \mathbf{err}\, [\mathrm{ok}: 0]} \text{(transfer)}}{\vdash_{\mathrm{Int}}^K [p_n]\, (\mathbf{x} := \mathbf{x} + 1) + \mathbf{err}\, [\mathrm{ok}: p_{n+1}] \quad \dagger} \text{(choice)}$$
$$\text{(limit)}$$

$$\frac{\dfrac{\mathbb{C}_{s}^{\mathrm{Int}}(\llbracket \mathbf{x} := \mathbf{x} + 1 \rrbracket_{\mathrm{ok}}) \qquad \mathbb{C}_{s}^{\mathrm{Int}}(\llbracket \mathbf{x} := \mathbf{x} + 1 \rrbracket_{\mathrm{err}})}{\vdash_{\mathrm{Int}}^K [s]\, \mathbf{x} := \mathbf{x} + 1\, [\mathrm{err}: 0]} \text{(transfer)} \qquad \dfrac{\mathbb{C}_{s}^{\mathrm{Int}}(\llbracket \mathbf{err} \rrbracket_{\mathrm{ok}}) \qquad \mathbb{C}_{s}^{\mathrm{Int}}(\llbracket \mathbf{err} \rrbracket_{\mathrm{err}})}{\vdash_{\mathrm{Int}}^K [s]\, \mathbf{err}\, [\mathrm{err}: s]} \text{(transfer)}}{\vdash_{\mathrm{Int}}^K [s]\, (\mathbf{x} := \mathbf{x} + 1) + \mathbf{err}\, [\mathrm{err}: s] \quad \ddagger} \text{(choice)}$$

$$\frac{\dfrac{\dagger}{\vdash_{\mathrm{Int}}^K [p_0]\, ((\mathbf{x} := \mathbf{x} + 1) + \mathbf{err})^*\, [\mathrm{ok}: s]} \text{(limit)} \qquad \dfrac{\ddagger}{\vdash_{\mathrm{Int}}^K [s]\, (\mathbf{x} := \mathbf{x} + 1) + \mathbf{err}\, [\mathrm{err}: s]} \text{(choice)}}{\vdash_{\mathrm{Int}}^K [p_0]\, ((\mathbf{x} := \mathbf{x} + 1) + \mathbf{err})^*\, [\mathrm{err}: s]} \text{(rec-err)}$$

By soundness of LCIL$_{\mathrm{Int}}$ in Theorem 4.2, the program $\mathbf{r}$ satisfies the ok part of Spec because

$$\llbracket \mathbf{r} \rrbracket_{\mathrm{ok}}\, p \subseteq \mathrm{Int}(s) = s \subseteq s = \mathrm{Spec}_{\mathrm{ok}}.$$

However, the err part is not satisfied as $\mathrm{Int}(s) = s \not\subseteq \varnothing = \mathbf{0}_K = \mathrm{Spec}_{\mathrm{err}}$. Moreover, LCIL$_{\mathrm{Int}}$ also catches true alerts as $s \smallsetminus \mathrm{Spec}_{\mathrm{err}} = s$. □

$$\frac{a \in \text{Atom}}{\vdash_{\text{IL}} [p] \ \mathbf{a} \ [\text{ok} : [\![a]\!]_{\text{ok}} \, p][\text{err} : [\![a]\!]_{\text{err}} \, p]} \ (\text{transfer}) \qquad \frac{}{\vdash_{\text{IL}} [p] \ \mathbf{t} \ [\epsilon : 0]} \ (\text{empty})$$

$$\frac{p' \leq p \qquad \vdash_{\text{IL}} [p'] \ \mathbf{t} \ [\epsilon : q'] \qquad q \leq q'}{\vdash_{\text{IL}} [p] \ \mathbf{t} \ [\epsilon : q]} \ (\text{consequence})$$

$$\frac{\vdash_{\text{IL}} [p_1] \ \mathbf{t} \ [\epsilon : q_1] \qquad \vdash_{\text{IL}} [p_2] \ \mathbf{t} \ [\epsilon : q_2]}{\vdash_{\text{IL}} [p_1 + p_2] \ \mathbf{t} \ [\epsilon : q_1 + q_2]} \ (\text{disj}) \qquad \frac{\vdash_{\text{IL}} [p] \ \mathbf{t}_1 \ [\text{err} : q]}{\vdash_{\text{IL}} [p] \ \mathbf{t}_1 \cdot \mathbf{t}_2 \ [\text{err} : q]} \ (\text{short-circuit})$$

$$\frac{\vdash_{\text{IL}} [p] \ \mathbf{t}_1 \ [\text{ok} : r] \qquad \vdash_{\text{IL}} [r] \ \mathbf{t}_2 \ [\epsilon : q]}{\vdash_{\text{IL}} [p] \ \mathbf{t}_1 \cdot \mathbf{t}_2 \ [\epsilon : q]} \ (\text{seq-normal}) \qquad \frac{}{\vdash_{\text{IL}} [p] \ \mathbf{t}^* \ [\text{ok} : p]} \ (\text{iterate zero})$$

$$\frac{\forall n \in \mathbb{N}. \ \vdash_{\text{IL}} [p_n] \ \mathbf{t} \ [\text{ok} : p_{n+1}]}{\vdash_{\text{IL}} [p_0] \ \mathbf{t}^* \ [\text{ok} : \bigvee_{n \in \mathbb{N}} p_n]} \ (\text{back-v}) \qquad \frac{\vdash_{\text{IL}} [p] \ \mathbf{t}^* \cdot \mathbf{t} \ [\epsilon : q]}{\vdash_{\text{IL}} [p] \ \mathbf{t}^* \ [\epsilon : q]} \ (\text{iterate non-zero})$$

$$\frac{\vdash_{\text{IL}} [p] \ \mathbf{t}_i \ [\epsilon : q], \ \text{with } i \in \{1, 2\}}{\vdash_{\text{IL}} [p] \ \mathbf{t}_1 + \mathbf{t}_2 \ [\epsilon : q]} \ (\text{choice})$$

Fig. 4. Proof system IL.

4.1 Relationship with Incorrectness Logic

Section 3.6 has shown that LCK yields a generalization of UL. The same can be done for IL, i.e., we prove that LCIL_A with incorrectness triples generalizes the incorrectness logic of [25]. For the sake of clarity, we recall in Fig. 4 an algebraic version of IL. Analogously to the reduction of Theorem 3.7, this generalization is obtained by letting $A = A_{tr}$, where A_{tr} is the trivial abstract domain.

Theorem 4.5. *Let K be a CTC bdKAT and $T_{\Sigma, B}$ a language interpreted on K. For any $p, q \in \text{test}(K)$, $\mathbf{t} \in T_{\Sigma, B}$,*

$$\vdash^{K}_{A_{tr}} [p] \ \mathbf{t} \ [\text{ok} : q][\text{err} : r] \quad \Leftrightarrow \quad \vdash_{\text{IL}} [p] \ \mathbf{t} \ [\text{ok} : q][\text{err} : r].$$

The abstraction map $\alpha = \lambda x. \top$ of A_{tr} makes the validity of a triple trivially true. In particular, $[\![\mathbf{t}]\!]^{\sharp}_{A_{tr \, \text{ok}}} \alpha(p) = \top = \alpha(q) = \alpha([\![\mathbf{t}]\!]_{\text{ok}} \, p)$ and $[\![\mathbf{t}]\!]^{\sharp}_{A_{tr \, \text{err}}} \alpha(p) = \top = \alpha(q) = \alpha([\![\mathbf{t}]\!]_{\text{err}} \, p)$ hold. As a consequence, we obtain that

$$\vDash^{K}_{A_{tr}} [p] \ \mathbf{t} \ [\text{ok} : q][\text{err} : r] \quad \Leftrightarrow \quad \vDash_{\text{IL}} [p] \ \mathbf{t} \ [\text{ok} : q][\text{err} : r] \qquad (7)$$

By this equivalence (7) and Theorems 4.2 and 4.3, we can thus retrieve the logical soundness and completeness of IL as a consequence of the one of $\text{LCIL}_{A_{tr}}$.

Corollary 4.6. *Let K be a CTC bdKAT and $T_{\Sigma, B}$ a language interpreted on K. For any $p, q \in \text{test}(K)$, $\mathbf{t} \in T_{\Sigma, B}$, $\vdash_{\text{IL}} [p] \ \mathbf{t} \ [\text{ok} : q][\text{err} : r] \Leftrightarrow \vDash_{\text{IL}} [p] \ \mathbf{t} \ [\text{ok} : q][\text{err} : r]$.*

5 Local Completeness Logic in TopKAT

We have shown in Sect. 3 how KAT extended with a modal backward-diamond operator allows us to interpret and represent the local completeness program logic. This result follows the approach by Moller, O'Hearn and Hoare [23], who leverage a backward-diamond operator in their KAT interpretation of correctness/incorrectness logics. On the other hand, Zhang, de Amorim and Gaboardi [33] have recently shown that incorrectness logic can be formulated for a standard KAT, provided that it contains a top element, thus giving rise to a so-called TopKAT. In particular, [33] observed that a Top-KAT is enough to express the codomain of relational KATs. In this section, we take a similar path in studying an alternative formulation of local completeness logic based on a TopKAT.

5.1 Abstracting TopKATs

We expect that the base case of abstract semantics $[\![a]\!]_A^\sharp p^\sharp$ for a basic action $a \in \text{Atom}$ is defined as best correct approximation in A of the concrete semantics of a on the concretization of $p^\sharp$. In a bdKAT this is achieved in definition (2) through its backward-diamond operator, which is crucially used in (1) to define the strongest postcondition as $[\![a]\!]^K \gamma(p^\sharp) = \langle [\![a]\!]_u | \gamma(p^\sharp)$. Zhang et al. [33] observed that in a relational model of KAT, the codomain inclusion $\text{cod}(q) \subseteq \text{cod}(pa)$ defining the meaning of an under-approximation triple $[p]\, a\, [q]$ can be expressed in a TopKAT as the inequality $\top q \leq \top pa$, thus hinting that this latter condition could be taken as definition of validity of incorrectness triples in a TopKAT. We follow here a similar approach by considering the element $\top p[\![a]\!]_u$ as a proxy for strongest postconditions in a TopKAT. It is worth noticing that while in a bdKAT a strongest postcondition $\langle [\![a]\!]_u | p$ is always a test, in a TopKAT K, given $p \in \text{test}(K)$ and a term $t \in T_{\Sigma,B}$, it is not guaranteed that there exists a test $q \in \text{test}(K)$ such that $\top p[\![t]\!]_u = \top q$, as shown by the following example.

Example 5.1 (Strongest Postconditions in TopKAT). Consider the Kleene algebra $A_3 = \{0, 1, a\}$ consisting of 3 elements and characterized by Conway [7, Chapter 12]. This algebra can be lifted to a KAT by letting $\text{test}(A_3) \triangleq \{0, 1\}$ and defining the KAT operators as follows:

+	0	1	a
0	0	1	a
1	1	1	1
a	a	1	a

·	0	1	a
0	0	0	0
1	0	1	a
a	0	a	0

$0^* \triangleq 1$	$1^* \triangleq 1$	$a^* \triangleq 1$

We have that $1 \geq a$ and $1 \geq 0$, because $1 + a = 1$ and $1 + 0 = 1$, so that A_3 is a TopKAT with $\top = 1$. Moreover, $\top \cdot 1 \cdot a = 1 \cdot 1 \cdot a = a$, whereas there exists no $q \in \text{test}(A_3)$ satisfying $\top \cdot q = a$. Indeed, $\top \cdot 1 = 1 \cdot 1 = 1 \neq a$ and $\top \cdot 0 = 0 \neq a$. □

In general, the lack of such a $q \in \text{test}(K)$ implies that the abstract domain cannot be defined as an abstraction of the set of topped-tests $\{\top p \mid p \in \text{test}(K)\}$, because in this case we could miss the abstraction $\alpha(\top p[\![a]\!]_u)$. To settle this issue, an abstract domain must provide an approximation of the larger set

$$\text{top}(K) \triangleq \{\top a \mid a \in K\}$$

which contains all the multiplicative elements of type $\top a$.

Definition 5.2 (Top Kleene Abstract Domain). A poset $(A, \leq)$ is a *top Kleene abstract domain* of a TopKAT K if:

(i) There exists a Galois insertion, defined by $\gamma : A \to \text{top}(K)$ and $\alpha : \text{top}(K) \to A$, of the poset $(A, \leq_A)$ into the poset $(\text{top}(K), \leq_K)$;
(ii) A is countably-complete. □

The abstract semantic function $\llbracket \cdot \rrbracket_A^\sharp : T_{\Sigma,B} \to (A \to A)$ on a top Kleene abstraction A can be therefore defined for the base case $\mathbf{a} \in \text{Atom}$ as

$$\llbracket \mathbf{a} \rrbracket_A^\sharp p^\sharp \triangleq \alpha(\gamma(p^\sharp) \llbracket \mathbf{a} \rrbracket_u),$$

while the remaining inductive cases are defined as in (2) for Kleene abstractions. The monotonicity and soundness properties of this abstract semantics hold, provided that the TopKAT is *-continuous[1], which is referred to as TopKAT*.

Theorem 5.3 (Soundness of TopKAT Abstract Semantics). *Let A be a Kleene abstraction of a TopKAT* K and $T_{\Sigma,B}$ be a language interpreted on K. For all $p^\sharp, q^\sharp \in A$, $a \in K$ and $\mathbf{t} \in T_{\Sigma,B}$:*

$$p^\sharp \leq_A q^\sharp \Rightarrow \llbracket \mathbf{t} \rrbracket_A^\sharp p^\sharp \leq_A \llbracket \mathbf{t} \rrbracket_A^\sharp q^\sharp \qquad \text{(monotonicity)}$$

$$\alpha(\top a \llbracket \mathbf{t} \rrbracket_u) \leq_A \llbracket \mathbf{t} \rrbracket_A^\sharp \alpha(\top a) \qquad \text{(soundness)}$$

5.2 Local Completeness Logic on TopKAT

Completeness and triple validity are adapted to the TopKAT framework as follows. Given a Top Kleene abstract domain A on a TopKAT* K, A is defined to be locally complete for $a \in K$ on an element $b \in K$, denoted by $\mathbb{C}_b^A(a)$, when

$$A(\top ba) = A(A(\top b)a)$$

holds. Moreover, A is globally complete for a, denoted by $\mathbb{C}^A(a)$, when it is locally complete for any $b \in K$.

Likewise, a triple $[a] \, \mathbf{t} \, [b]$, with $a, b \in K$ and $\mathbf{t} \in T_{\Sigma,B}$, is valid, denoted by $\models_A^{\text{TK}} [a] \, \mathbf{t} \, [b]$, when:

(1) $\top b \leq \top a \llbracket \mathbf{t} \rrbracket_u$;   (2) $\llbracket \mathbf{t} \rrbracket_A^\sharp \alpha(\top a) = \alpha(\top b) = \alpha(\top a \llbracket \mathbf{t} \rrbracket_u)$.

The corresponding proof system, denoted by LCTK_A, has the same rules of LCK_A in Fig. 1 except (transfer), (relax) and (iterate) which are modified as follows:

$$\frac{c \in \text{Atom} \qquad \mathbb{C}_a^A(\llbracket c \rrbracket_u)}{\vdash_A^{\text{TK}} [a] \, c \, [a \llbracket c \rrbracket_u]} \text{(transfer)}$$

---

[1] This condition plays a role similar to the CTC condition for bdKATs.

$$\frac{\mathsf{T}a' \leq \mathsf{T}a \leq A(\mathsf{T}a') \qquad \vdash_A^{\mathrm{TK}} [a'] \; \mathbf{t} \; [b'] \qquad \mathsf{T}b \leq \mathsf{T}b' \leq A(\mathsf{T}b)}{\vdash_A^{\mathrm{TK}} [a] \; \mathbf{t} \; [b]} \; \text{(relax)}$$

$$\frac{\vdash_A^{\mathrm{TK}} [a] \; \mathbf{t} \; [b] \qquad \mathsf{T}b \leq A(\mathsf{T}a)}{\vdash_A^{\mathrm{TK}} [a] \; \mathbf{t}^* \; [a + b]} \; \text{(iterate)}$$

This incarnation LCTK_A of local completeness logic for TopKAT* turns out to be logically sound and, under additional hypotheses, complete.

Theorem 5.4 (Logical Soundness of $\vdash_A^{\mathrm{TK}}$). *If* $\vdash_A^{\mathrm{TK}} [a] \; \mathbf{t} \; [b]$ *then*

(i) $\mathsf{T}b \leq \mathsf{T}a[\![\mathbf{t}]\!]_u$;
(ii) $[\![\mathbf{t}]\!]_A^\sharp \alpha(\mathsf{T}a) = \alpha(\mathsf{T}b) = \alpha(\mathsf{T}a[\![\mathbf{t}]\!]_u)$.

Logical completeness needs the following additional conditions:

(a) Likewise LCK_A, the same infinitary rule for Kleene star:

$$\frac{\forall n \in \mathbb{N}. \; \vdash_A^{\mathrm{TK}} [a_n] \; \mathbf{t} \; [a_{n+1}]}{\vdash_A^{\mathrm{TK}} [a_0] \; \mathbf{t}^* \; [\bigvee_{n \in \mathbb{N}} a_n]} \; \text{(limit)}$$

where we assume that:
  – $\bigvee_{n \in \mathbb{N}} a_n$ always exists. Let us remark that for bdKAT, such explicit condition was not needed, as it was entailed by the CTC requirement on the KAT.
  – T distributes over $\bigvee_{n \in \mathbb{N}} a_n$, i.e., $\mathsf{T} \bigvee_{n \in \mathbb{N}} a_n = \bigvee_{n \in \mathbb{N}} \mathsf{T}a_n$.
  It turns out that this additional rule (limit) is sound (see the full version [22]).
(b) Global completeness of all the primitive actions and tests occurring in the program.

Theorem 5.5 (Logical Completeness of $\vdash_A^{\mathrm{TK}}$). *Assume that conditions (a) and (b) hold. If* $\models_A^{\mathrm{TK}} [a] \; \mathbf{t} \; [b]$ *then* $\vdash_A^{\mathrm{TK}} [a] \; \mathbf{t} \; [b]$.

Let us describe an example of derivation in LCTK_A.

Example 5.6. Consider a relational KAT $K = \wp(\mathbb{Z} \times \mathbb{Z})$ on the set of integers $\mathbb{Z}$, where $1_K \triangleq \{(z, z) \mid z \in \mathbb{Z}\}$ and $0_K \triangleq \varnothing$. Notice that $\mathbb{Z} \times \mathbb{Z} \in K$ is the top element T of K, meaning that K is a TopKAT. Let us consider a language with primitive actions $\Sigma = \{\mathbf{x} := \mathbf{x} + 1\}$ and primitive tests $B = \{\mathbf{x} \geq 0, \mathbf{x} < 0\}$. The evaluation function $u : \Sigma \cup B \to K$ is defined as expected by the following relations:

$$u(\mathbf{x} := \mathbf{x} + 1) \triangleq \{(z, z + 1) \mid z \in \mathbb{Z}\},$$
$$u(\mathbf{x} \geq 0) \triangleq \{(z, z) \mid z \in \mathbb{Z}, z \geq 0\},$$
$$u(\mathbf{x} < 0) \triangleq \{(z, z) \mid z \in \mathbb{Z}, z < 0\}.$$

Consider the following sign abstraction Sign $\triangleq \{\mathbb{Z}, \mathbb{Z}_{\leq 0}, \mathbb{Z}_{\neq 0}, \mathbb{Z}_{\geq 0}, \mathbb{Z}_{< 0}, \mathbb{Z}_{= 0}, \mathbb{Z}_{> 0}, \varnothing\}$ of $\wp(\mathbb{Z})$, whose abstraction and concretization maps are straightforward. Let us verify that the program

$$r \equiv \left((\mathbf{x} \geq 0) \cdot (\mathbf{x} := \mathbf{x} + 1)\right)^* \cdot (\mathbf{x} < 0)$$

does not terminate with precondition $p \triangleq \{(0,0),(10,10)\}$, i.e., we prove the specification Spec $\triangleq \varnothing$. Let us define the following auxiliary elements: $q \triangleq \{(1,1),(11,11)\}$, $s \triangleq p+q$, $t_{\geq 0} \triangleq \{(x,z) \mid x \in \mathbb{Z}, z \in \mathbb{Z}_{\geq 0}\}$, and observe that $\mathrm{Sign}(t_{\geq 0}) = t_{\geq 0}$. The following local completeness conditions for the atoms hold:

$$\alpha(\mathrm{Sign}(\top p)[\![x \geq 0]\!]_u) = \alpha(t_{\geq 0}[\![x \geq 0]\!]_u) = \mathbb{Z}_{\geq 0} = \alpha(\top p[\![x \geq 0]\!]_u),$$

$$\alpha(\mathrm{Sign}(\top p)[\![x := x+1]\!]_u) = \alpha(t_{\geq 0}[\![x := x+1]\!]_u) = \mathbb{Z}_{>0} = \alpha(\top p[\![x := x+1]\!]_u),$$

$$\alpha(\mathrm{Sign}(\top s)[\![x < 0]\!]_u) = \alpha(t_{\geq 0}[\![x < 0]\!]_u) = \varnothing = \alpha(\top s[\![x < 0]\!]_u).$$

Moreover, we also have that:

$$\top q = \{(x,z) \mid x \in \mathbb{Z}, z \in \{1,11\}\} \leq t_{\geq 0} = \mathrm{Sign}(\top p).$$

The following derivation shows that the triple $[p]\ r\ [\mathbf{0}_K]$ is provable in $\mathrm{LCTK}_{\mathrm{Sign}}$:

$$
\cfrac{
  \cfrac{
    \cfrac{
      \cfrac{C^{\mathrm{Sign}}_p([\![x \geq 0]\!]_u)}{\vdash^{\mathrm{TK}}_{\mathrm{Sign}} [p]\ x \geq 0\ [p]}\text{(transfer)} \quad
      \cfrac{C^{\mathrm{Sign}}_p([\![x := x+1]\!]_u)}{\vdash^{\mathrm{TK}}_{\mathrm{Sign}} [p]\ x := x+1\ [q]}\text{(transfer)}
    }{\vdash^{\mathrm{TK}}_{\mathrm{Sign}} [p]\ (x \geq 0)\cdot(x := x+1)\ [q]}\text{(seq)} \quad \top q \leq \mathrm{Sign}(\top p)
  }{\vdash^{\mathrm{TK}}_{\mathrm{Sign}} [p]\ ((x \geq 0)\cdot(x := x+1))^*\ [s]}\text{(iterate)} \quad
  \cfrac{C^{\mathrm{Sign}}_s([\![x < 0]\!]_u)}{\vdash^{\mathrm{TK}}_{\mathrm{Sign}} [s]\ x < 0\ [\mathbf{0}_K]}\text{(transfer)}
}{\vdash^{\mathrm{TK}}_{\mathrm{Sign}} [p]\ ((x \geq 0)\cdot(x := x+1))^*\cdot(x < 0)\ [\mathbf{0}_K]}\text{(seq)}
$$

By Theorem 5.4, we have that $\top \mathbf{0}_K \subseteq \top p[\![r]\!]_u \subseteq \mathrm{Sign}(\top \mathbf{0}_K) = \varnothing$, meaning that the program does not terminate, and Spec is satisfied as $\top p[\![r]\!]_u = \varnothing = \top \text{Spec}$. $\qquad\square$

5.3 Relationship with Under-Approximation Logic

We have shown in Sect. 3.6 that the backward-diamond formulation of LCK generalizes UL. The same can be done for the TopKAT formulation. A TopKAT version of the UL proof system has been already proposed in [33, Figure 6]. The reduction here considered refers to such system, with the following minor differences:

- We consider only propositional fragments of the logic, meaning that the rules (assume) and (identity) are replaced by the following single (transfer) rule:

$$\cfrac{c \in \mathrm{Atom}}{\vdash_{\mathrm{UL}} [a]\ c\ [a[\![c]\!]_u]}\text{(transfer)}$$

- The premises of the (consequence) rule in [33, Figure 6], $b \leq b'$ and $c' \leq c$, are relaxed to $\top b \leq \top b'$ and $\top c' \leq \top c$. Notice that the former implies the latter. Furthermore, the soundness proof of [33, Theorem 4] is not affected by this change, because $(\top b' \geq \top b \wedge \top c \geq \top c' \wedge \top bp \geq c) \Rightarrow \top b'p \geq \top bp \geq \top c \geq \top c'$, and, by [33, Theorem 3], it holds that $\top b'p \geq \top c'$ entails $\top b'p \geq c'$.
- The (limit) rules of LCTK_A and UL differ on the distributivity condition. We assume that distributivity also holds in UL.

By instantiating to the trivial abstract domain A_{tr}, it turns out that the two proof systems become equivalent.

Theorem 5.7 (LCTK$_{A_{tr}}$ $\equiv$ UL). *Let K be a TopKAT*. For any $a, b \in K$, $\mathsf{t} \in T_{\Sigma,B}$:*

$$\vdash^{\mathrm{TK}}_{A_{tr}} [a] \; \mathsf{t} \; [b] \quad \Leftrightarrow \quad \vdash_{\mathrm{UL}} [a] \; \mathsf{t} \; [b].$$

In turn, the logical soundness and completeness of UL can be retrieved as a consequence of those of LCTK.

Corollary 5.8. *Under the same hypotheses of Theorem 5.7, the proof system UL is sound and complete, that is, $\vdash_{\mathrm{UL}} [p] \; \mathsf{t} \; [q] \Leftrightarrow \models_{\mathrm{UL}} [p] \; \mathsf{t} \; [q]$.*

Finally, let us mention that the full version [22] also shows how to define an incorrectness logic in TopKAT.

6 Conclusion

This work has shown that the abstract interpretation-based local completeness logic introduced in [4] can be generalized to and interpreted in Kleene algebra with tests. In particular, we proved that this can be achieved both for KATs extended with a modal backward diamond operator playing the role of strongest postcondition, and for KATs endowed with a top element. Our results generalize both the modal [23] and top [33] KAT approaches that encode Hoare correctness and O'Hearn incorrectness logic using different classes of KATs. In particular, our KAT-based logic leverages an abstract interpretation of KAT, a problem that was not studied so far.

Our plan for future work includes, but is not limited to, the following questions.

- For a KAT with top $\top$, following the technical idea underlying the approach by Zhang et al. [33], we defined an abstract domain as an approximation of all the algebraic elements of type $\top \cdot a$, where a is any element of the KAT (cf. Definition 5.2). Although this definition technically works, it is somehow artificial, because the elements $\top \cdot a$ do not carry a clear intuitive meaning. As an interesting future task, we would like to characterize under which conditions an element $\top \cdot a$ coincides with $\top \cdot p$ for some test $p \in \text{test}(K)$, and if such test p is unique.
- This work is a first step towards an *algebraic and equational approach to abstract interpretation*. We envisage that the reasoning made by an abstract interpreter of programs could be made purely equational within a KAT equipped with a suitable collection of axioms. The ambition would be to conceive a notion of *abstract Kleene algebra* (AKA) making this slogan true: *AKA is for the abstract interpretation of programs what KAT is for concrete interpretation of programs*.

Acknowledgements. Francesco Ranzato has been partially funded by the *Italian Ministry of University and Research*, under the PRIN 2017 project no. 201784YSZ5 "AnalysiS of PRogram Analyses (ASPRA)", by *Facebook Research*, under a "Probability and Programming Research Award", and by an *Amazon Research Award* for "AWS Automated Reasoning".

References

1. Anderson, C.J., et al.: NetKAT: Semantic foundations for networks. In: Proceedings of the 41st ACM SIGPLAN-SIGACT Symposium on Principles of Programming Languages, pp. 113–126. POPL 2014, ACM (2014). https://doi.org/10.1145/2535838.2535862

2. Beckett, R., Greenberg, M., Walker, D.: Temporal NetKAT. In: Proceedings of the 37th ACM SIGPLAN Conference on Programming Language Design and Implementation, PLDI 2016, pp. 386–401. ACM (2016). https://doi.org/10.1145/2908080.2908108

3. Bruni, R., Giacobazzi, R., Gori, R., Garcia-Contreras, I., Pavlovic, D.: Abstract extensionality: on the properties of incomplete abstract interpretations. Proc. ACM Program. Lang. 4(POPL), 28:1–28:28 (2020). https://doi.org/10.1145/3371096

4. Bruni, R., Giacobazzi, R., Gori, R., Ranzato, F.: A Logic for locally complete abstract interpretations. In: Proceedings 36th ACM/IEEE Symposium on Logic in Computer Science (LICS 2021), pp. 1–13. IEEE (2021). https://doi.org/10.1109/LICS52264.2021.9470608

5. Bruni, R., Giacobazzi, R., Gori, R., Ranzato, F.: Abstract interpretation repair. In: Proceedings of the 43rd ACM SIGPLAN International Conference on Programming Language Design and Implementation, pp. 426–441. PLDI 2022, Association for Computing Machinery, New York, NY, USA (2022). https://doi.org/10.1145/3519939.3523453

6. Cohen, E., Kozen, D., Smith, F.: The complexity of Kleene algebra with tests. Tech. rep., Cornell University, USA (1996). https://www.cs.cornell.edu/kozen/Papers/ckat

7. Conway, J.: Regular Algebra and Finite Machines. Dover Publications, Chapman and Hall Mathematics Series (2012)

8. Cousot, P., Cousot, R.: Abstract interpretation: a unified lattice model for static analysis of programs by construction or approximation of fixpoints. In: Proceedings of the 4th ACM SIGACT-SIGPLAN Symposium on Principles of Programming Languages (POPL 1977), pp. 238–252. ACM (1977). https://doi.org/10.1145/512950.512973

9. Cousot, P., Cousot, R.: Systematic design of program analysis frameworks. In: Proceedings of the 6th ACM SIGACT-SIGPLAN Symposium on Principles of Programming Languages (POPL 1979), pp. 269–282. ACM (1979). https://doi.org/10.1145/567752.567778

10. Desharnais, J., Möller, B., Struth, G.: Kleene algebra with domain. ACM Trans. Comput. Logic 7(4), 798–833 (2006). https://doi.org/10.1145/1183278.1183285

11. Fischer, M.J., Ladner, R.E.: Propositional dynamic logic of regular programs. J. Comput. Syst. Sci. 18(2), 194–211 (1979). https://doi.org/10.1016/0022-0000(79)90046-1

12. Foster, N., Kozen, D., Milano, M., Silva, A., Thompson, L.: A coalgebraic decision procedure for NetKAT. In: Proceedings of the 42nd Annual ACM SIGPLAN-SIGACT Symposium on Principles of Programming Languages, POPL 2015, pp. 343–355. ACM (2015). https://doi.org/10.1145/2676726.2677011

13. Giacobazzi, R., Ranzato, F., Scozzari, F.: Making abstract interpretation complete. J. ACM 47(2), 361–416 (2000). https://doi.org/10.1145/333979.333989

14. Giacobazzi, R., Logozzo, F., Ranzato, F.: Analyzing program analyses. In: Proceedings of the 42nd Annual ACM SIGPLAN-SIGACT Symposium on Principles of Programming Languages, POPL 2015, pp. 261–273 (2015). https://doi.org/10.1145/2676726.2676987

15. Greenberg, M., Beckett, R., Campbell, E.: Kleene algebra modulo theories: a framework for concrete KATs. In: Proceedings of the 43rd ACM SIGPLAN International Conference on Programming Language Design and Implementation, pp. 594–608. PLDI 2022, Association for Computing Machinery, New York, NY, USA (2022). https://doi.org/10.1145/3519939.3523722

16. Hoare, C.A.R.: An axiomatic basis for computer programming. Commun. ACM 12(10), 576–580 (1969). https://doi.org/10.1145/363235.363259

17. Kozen, D.: Kleene algebra with tests. ACM Trans. Program. Lang. Syst. **19**(3), 427–443 (1997). https://doi.org/10.1145/256167.256195

18. Kozen, D.: On Hoare logic and Kleene algebra with tests. ACM Trans. Comput. Logic **1**(1), 60–76 (2000). https://doi.org/10.1145/343369.343378

19. Kozen, D., Smith, F.: Kleene algebra with tests: completeness and decidability. In: van Dalen, D., Bezem, M. (eds.) CSL 1996. LNCS, vol. 1258, pp. 244–259. Springer, Heidelberg (1997). https://doi.org/10.1007/3-540-63172-0_43

20. Le, Q.L., Raad, A., Villard, J., Berdine, J., Dreyer, D., O'Hearn, P.W.: Finding real bugs in big programs with incorrectness logic. Proc. ACM Program. Lang. **6**(OOPSLA1) (2022). https://doi.org/10.1145/3527325

21. Mamouras, K.: Equational theories of abnormal termination based on kleene algebra. In: Proceedings 20th International Conference on Foundations of Software Science and Computation Structures, FOSSACS 2017. Lecture Notes in Computer Science, vol. 10203, pp. 88–105 (2017). https://doi.org/10.1007/978-3-662-54458-7_6

22. Milanese, M., Ranzato, F.: Local completeness logic on Kleene algebra with tests. arXiv e-prints arXiv:2205.08128 (2022)

23. Möller, B., O'Hearn, P., Hoare, T.: On algebra of program correctness and incorrectness. In: Fahrenberg, U., Gehrke, M., Santocanale, L., Winter, M. (eds.) RAMiCS 2021. LNCS, vol. 13027, pp. 325–343. Springer, Cham (2021). https://doi.org/10.1007/978-3-030-88701-8_20

24. Möller, B., Struth, G.: Algebras of modal operators and partial correctness. Theor. Comput. Sci. **351**(2), 221–239 (2006). https://doi.org/10.1016/j.tcs.2005.09.069

25. O'Hearn, P.W.: Incorrectness logic. Proc. ACM Program. Lang. **4**(POPL), 1–32 (2020). https://doi.org/10.1145/3371078

26. Poskitt, C.M.: Incorrectness logic for graph programs. In: Gadducci, F., Kehrer, T. (eds.) ICGT 2021. LNCS, vol. 12741, pp. 81–101. Springer, Cham (2021). https://doi.org/10.1007/978-3-030-78946-6_5

27. Raad, A., Berdine, J., Dang, H.-H., Dreyer, D., O'Hearn, P., Villard, J.: Local reasoning about the presence of bugs: incorrectness separation logic. In: Lahiri, S.K., Wang, C. (eds.) CAV 2020. LNCS, vol. 12225, pp. 225–252. Springer, Cham (2020). https://doi.org/10.1007/978-3-030-53291-8_14

28. Raad, A., Berdine, J., Dreyer, D., O'Hearn, P.W.: Concurrent incorrectness separation logic. Proc. ACM Program. Lang. **6**(POPL), 1–29 (2022). https://doi.org/10.1145/3498695

29. Ranzato, F.: Complete abstractions everywhere. In: Giacobazzi, R., Berdine, J., Mastroeni, I. (eds.) VMCAI 2013. LNCS, vol. 7737, pp. 15–26. Springer, Heidelberg (2013). https://doi.org/10.1007/978-3-642-35873-9_3

30. Smolka, S., Eliopoulos, S.A., Foster, N., Guha, A.: A fast compiler for NetKAT. In: Proceedings of the 20th ACM SIGPLAN International Conference on Functional Programming, ICFP 2015, pp. 328–341. ACM (2015). https://doi.org/10.1145/2784731.2784761

31. Smolka, S., Kumar, P., Foster, N., Kozen, D., Silva, A.: Cantor meets Scott: semantic foundations for probabilistic networks. In: Proceedings of the 44th ACM SIGPLAN Symposium on Principles of Programming Languages, pp. 557–571. POPL 2017, ACM (2017). https://doi.org/10.1145/3009837.3009843

32. Yan, P., Jiang, H., Yu, N.: On incorrectness logic for quantum programs. Proc. ACM Program. Lang. **6**(OOPSLA1) (2022). https://doi.org/10.1145/3527316

33. Zhang, C., de Amorim, A.A., Gaboardi, M.: On incorrectness logic and Kleene algebra with top and tests. Proc. ACM Program. Lang. **6**(POPL), 1–30 (2022). https://doi.org/10.1145/3498690

Semantic Foundations for Cost Analysis of Pipeline-Optimized Programs

Gilles Barthe[1], Adrien Koutsos[2], Solène Mirliaz[3], David Pichardie[4(✉)], and Peter Schwabe[5]

[1] MPI-SP & IMDEA Software Institute, Bochum, Germany
[2] Inria Paris, Paris, France
[3] Univ Rennes, CNRS, IRISA, Rennes, France
[4] Meta, Paris, France
`david.pichardie@ens-rennes.fr`
[5] MPI-SP, Bochum, Germany

Abstract. In this paper, we develop semantic foundations for precise cost analyses of programs running on architectures with multi-scalar pipelines and in-order execution with branch prediction. This model is then used to prove the correction of an automatic cost analysis we designed. The analysis is implemented and evaluated in an extant framework for high-assurance cryptography. In this field, developers aggressively hand-optimize their code to take maximal advantage of micro-architectural features while looking for provable semantic guarantees.

1 Introduction

Provable cost analysis, such as [22,28], provides a rich palette of methods and tools for estimating (generally in the form of upper bounds) execution time with respect to a mathematical operational and cost model. However, operational and cost models commonly used in provable cost analysis elude micro-architectural features, such as caches, predictors, and pipelines, which are performance-critical and carefully exploited in high-performance implementations. As a consequence, the upper bounds computed by existing cost analyses are overly coarse. In particular, they cannot be used to guide carefully crafted manual optimizations, for instance the instruction scheduling of the program, since a typical provable cost analysis will be oblivious to instruction scheduling.

Specific areas of computer science require high-performance and maximal reliability. It is for example the case of cryptographic engineers who develop high-speed implementations of common cryptographic algorithms. Increasingly, cryptographic engineering is adopting high-assurance techniques [5] to deliver provable guarantees that implementations are correct with respect to their high-level specification (expressed mathematically or as pseudo-code), cryptographically secure, and protected against side-channels. Unfortunately, high-assurance cryptography still relies on simulation or benchmarking for measuring the efficiency of implementations, largely ignoring the line of work in provable cost analysis.

G. Singh and C. Urban (Eds.): SAS 2022, LNCS 13790, pp. 372–396, 2022.
https://doi.org/10.1007/978-3-031-22308-2_17

```
 1   r = 0;           //1          r0 = 0;              //1
 2   t = [A +   0];   //1          r1 = 0;              //1
 3   r += t;          //3          t0 = [A +   0];      //1
 4   t = [A +   4];   //3          t1 = [A +   4];      //2
 5   r += t;          //5          t2 = [A +   8];      //2
 6   t = [A +   8];   //5          r0 += t0;            //3
 7   r += t;          //7          t0 = [A + 12];       //3
 8   t = [A + 12];    //7          r1 += t1;            //4
 9   r += t;          //9          t1 = [A + 16];       //4
10   t = [A + 16];    //9          r0 += t2;            //4
11   r += t;          //11         t2 = [A + 20];       //5
12   t = [A + 20];    //11         r1 += t0;            //5
13   r += t;          //13         t0 = [A + 24];       //5
14   t = [A + 24];    //13         r0 += t1;            //6
15   r += t;          //15         t1 = [A + 28];       //6
16   t = [A + 28];    //15         r1 += t2;            //7
17   r += t;          //17         r0 += t0;            //7
18                                 r1 += t1;            //8
19                                 r = r0+r1;           //9
```

Listing 1.1: Straightforward   Listing 1.2: Optimized

Fig. 1. Two different approaches to scheduling instructions for code that accumulates 8 consecutive 32-bit integers from memory. Comments indicate execution cycles on the microarchitecture described in Fig. 2.

Listing 1.1 provide a classic example of an array sum program that can be aggressively optimized in order to take advantage of modern micro-architectural mechanisms. The program computes (in variable r) the sum of the elements of an array A. An optimized version of this program is given in Listing 1.2, which exploits the architecture capability to perform loads in parallel, avoiding the two cycles penalty for each element occurring in Listing 1.1. It thus uses more registers to store the pending results. A standard cost analysis would conclude, wrongly, that the optimized program has a worst execution time than the original: indeed, both programs executed the same amount of loads, but the optimized program performs an additional assignment and addition. Summing the delay of each instruction, as a naive cost analysis would do, concludes that the optimized version is worse than the original. To understand the benefit of this optimization, the programmer has to reason on the model of instruction parallelism.

This paper develops semantic foundations for cost analysis of pipelined-optimized programs. We focus on the instruction pipeline mechanism and do not model caches in this work. Our work is intended for the programmer who wants to formally check the cost impact of manual optimizations. Such programmers are usually happy to assume that all program code and all data is in L1 cache, in order to focus on careful instruction selection, scheduling, and register allocation. Cryptographic primitives fall into this case. We focus on in-order processors, as out-of-order processors will change the scheduling imagined by the programmer. Although out-of-order processors are more common due to their efficiency, manual optimizations are still particularly relevant for in-order embedded systems. Indeed, embedded systems cannot handle the complexity and energy cost of out-of-order processors.

Our work makes the following contributions.

- We provide a detailed semantic model, presented in Sect. 3, which is a small-step semantics precisely modeling the execution cost (in processor cycles) of instruction parallelism and branch prediction inside an in-order processor.
- We then design in Sect. 4 a provably correct static analysis that computes safe relational bounds on this cost. The analysis is a mix of a standard relational numerical analysis, a standard may/must static analysis and a new block symbolic execution that extracts a tight range for the execution time of an instruction block. The static analysis is proven sound with respect to the small-step semantics (Theorem 3). The full proof of correctness is given in the companion report [1].
- We have implemented our approach into Jasmin [3,4], an existing framework for high-performance and high-assurance cryptography. We use our analysis to obtain relational cost bounds for scalar and vectorized implementations of popular cryptographic algorithms. These experiments show that our estimates are precise (in particular the difference between the upper and lower bounds is tight), and significantly improve on the bounds delivered by traditional cost analyses which ignore instruction parallelism.

2 Processor Behavior on an Example

We consider a low-level language (inspired from Jasmin [3,4] internal representation), with memory load/store, and scalar operations. Programs in our language are executed on a *multi-scalar pipelined processor*. A *pipelined processor* decomposes the execution of an atomic instruction into several stages such that the next instruction can enter the first stage as soon as the previous instruction leaves it. A sequence of stages constitutes a pipeline, and the latency of a pipeline is the number of stages it comprises. A multi-scalar pipelined processor has several pipelines in parallel, allowing it to execute simultaneously several instructions, by loading them into different pipelines. All pipelines are not identical: each pipeline can have a different latency, and supports a different set of instructions. The latency of a pipeline depends on the instructions supported, where basic instructions, such as additions, will be executed quickly, while more complex operations (e.g. multiplications and floating-point operations) will take a longer time.

Figure 2 describes an example of a processor with five pipelines (A, L, S, M and J) and the instructions each pipeline can handle: for example, multiplication has a latency of 5, and is only supported by the pipeline M. This is a

	A	L	S	M	J ǎ
Add/Sub (1)	✓	✓			
Comp (1)	✓	✓	✓		
Load (2)		✓	✓		
Store (2)			✓		
Mult (5)				✓	
Jump (4)					✓

Fig. 2. Instructions handled by each pipeline of our processor, with their latencies in parenthesis

simple processor, real processors have more pipelines and can handle a larger instruction set. Note that the method presented in this paper is not specific to this processor: the number of pipelines, the instructions supported and their latencies are parameters of the cost semantics and of the analysis.

Instruction Fetching. We now give a high-level overview of how a processor fetches an instruction, which is done in three steps. First, the processor checks that the instruction has no data-dependency conflict with other instructions already in the pipelines. Then, the processor resolves the instruction by evaluating the registers read by the instruction into values – which are either integers or memory addresses. Finally, the resolved instruction, called a *transient* instruction, is placed in a pipeline supporting it.

Data-Dependencies. Before starting executing an instruction – i.e. loading it in the first stage of a pipeline – the processor must check that this instruction has no conflict with other instructions being currently executed. For example, consider the execution of lines 1 through 3 of Listing 1.1 on the processor of Fig. 2. The resulting state of the processor can be found in Fig. 3a. The first instruction can be placed in stage A_1 (the first stage of the A pipeline), while simultaneously loading the second instruction into stage L_1. However, the instruction of the third line cannot be loaded during the same cycle, because it depends on the values of registers r and t, which will be written by the previous instructions: the processor must wait for their executions to finish before fetching l.3.

Essentially, an instruction can be executed if: i) there is a pipeline available (i.e. whose first stage is empty) supporting it; and ii), none of its variables (a.k.a. registers or memory locations such as @A) have *data-dependencies* with instructions currently in the pipelines. More precisely, an instruction atom cannot be executed if:

- any variable it reads is written by another instruction currently in a pipeline (*read-after-write* dependency);
- any variable it writes is read or written by another instruction in the pipeline (*write-after-read* and *write-after-write*).

We refer to these dependencies using the acronyms RaW, WaR and WaW. Coming back to our example, the instruction 1.3 needs to wait for two cycles – the latency of the load – to be fetched after 1.2 because of a RaW dependency on t.

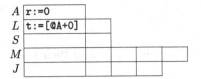

(a) State of the pipelines after line 5 and 6 of the first iteration of Listing 1.1

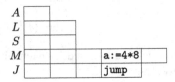

(b) State of the pipelines after fetching a jump

Fig. 3. Example of pipeline states for the processor of Fig. 2. Each cell represents a pipeline stage, e.g. stage J_4 in the second state contains a jump.

Instruction Resolution. Before being placed in the first stage of a pipeline supporting it, the instruction is *resolved*, by replacing the registers it reads by their current value. We illustrate this mechanism on the array sum (Listing 1.1). Let us suppose that the first cell of A contains value 32, stored in t after the execution of 1.2. The instruction 1.3 r := r + t is resolved into the transient instruction r := 0 + 32. Note that a transient instruction no longer reads any register, which allows to avoid some data-dependency conflicts. After the instruction 1.2 has been fetched, we can expect the pipelines to be in the state of Fig. 3a, where @A designates the address stored in A.

Branch Prediction. When the processor executes a sequence, it simply increments its program counter to find the next instruction to execute. But in the case of a conditional jump, the next instruction to execute is harder to infer. In that case, a jump must be resolved: if the jump is taken, then its destination is computed and used to update the program counter. Otherwise, the processor continues its execution with an incremented program pointer. The jump must go through all the stages of its pipeline to affect the program counter. Not fetching any instruction during its processing would severely impact the performances of the processor. It is more interesting to start fetching and executing one of the two branches as soon as a jump is encountered, without waiting for the jump to be fully processed. The branch predictor (BP) is in charge of deciding which branch will be speculatively executed. It typically uses a history, usually in the form of a buffer, to remember the previous branches taken and bases its decisions upon it. When the jump has been fully processed, the prediction is checked. In case of a correct prediction, the execution of the speculated branch continues. Otherwise, all the modifications made by the speculated branch must be roll backed, and the correct branch starts its execution. The roll-back requires to buffer the speculated instructions when they are retired from their pipeline and to identify which instructions in the pipelines are speculation.

The content of the pipelines, i.e. the instructions already loaded, is not sufficient to roll back the pipelines. For example, consider the following two code snippets. The instruction $jmp(c) : T$ is a conditional jump: the program continues with the instruction at address T – further in the code – if c holds, or goes to the next instruction otherwise. So the *then* branch of this conditional is not displayed here, only its *else* branch. In the first code snippet, the *else* branch contains only l.3, while it contains l.2-3 in the second.

```
1 a := 4 * 8;          1 jump (c) : T;
2 jump (c) : T;        2 a := 4 * 8;
3 b := 2 + 6;          3 b := 2 + 6;
```

These two programs are executed from empty pipelines and we assume here that the *else* branch is speculatively executed. Let us take a snapshot of the processor state after the three instructions have been fetched and after the processor has executed three cycles to make the instructions progress in their pipelines. For both executions, the pipelines should be in the state of Fig. 3b. Notice that the speculated addition `b := 2 + 6` has been fully executed and has left the pipeline. Also, in both cases, the multiplication is at the same depth (4) as the jump, and there is no way of telling if it was speculatively executed, or if it was fetched before the jump. Hence it is not possible to determine if the multiplication must be removed simply by inspecting the pipelines.

Therefore, to be able to perform roll backs, the processor: (i) buffers the effects of the retired instructions (here the addition); and (ii), timestamps the instructions to track their dependencies. Any instruction that has been fully executed is placed into a buffer, called the *speculation buffer*, before acting on the memory. Once it is guaranteed that no previous jump can roll it back, it is *committed*, effectively modifying the memory. When a roll back is performed, any instruction in the buffer or the pipelines with an higher timestamp than the jump is removed. These mechanisms are inspired from [10].

3   Concrete Small-Step Pipeline Semantics

In this section we define the concrete small-step semantics of a multi-pipelined processor where the cost in cycles is tracked. This semantics precisely models a pipelined processor with branch prediction. It includes a speculation buffer in order to model the roll back mechanism used after branch misprediction. In the next section, we will present an approximation of this semantics w.r.t. the cost, which we use to build a sound static analysis. Figure 5 summarizes the notations used by our semantics rules in Fig. 7, 8 and 9.

Language. The syntax of our language is given in Fig. 4. Atomic instructions $atom \in Atoms$ can be basic arithmetic operations, memory loads/stores and jump instructions. The instructions operate on registers in Reg, which can contain integer values in $\mathbb{Z}$ or memory locations in $MemLocs$. Finally, programs are built using sequential composition of atomic instructions, conditionals and while loops.

Operands: Labels:
    o $::= r \in$ Reg   Register ℓ $\in \mathcal{L}$
             $\mid n \in \mathbb{Z}$ Integer

                                              Statements:
Atomic instructions Atoms: s $::=$ **atom**   Atomic
    atom $::= r := o_1 + o_2$ Addition $\mid s_1; s_2$ Sequence
             $\mid r := o_1 - o_2$ Subtraction $\mid \ell :$ **if** o
             $\mid r := o_1 \leq o_2$ Comparison   **then** s_1
             $\mid r := o_1 \times o_2$ Multiplication   **else** s_2 Conditional
             $\mid r_1 := [r_2 + o]$ Load $\mid \ell :$ **while** o
             $\mid [r + o_1] := o_2$ Store   **do** s
             $\mid$ **jmp**(o) Conditional jump   **done**   Loop
                                                       $\mid$ **skip**   Skip

Fig. 4. Syntax of the language

The jump instruction is not meant to be directly written by the programmer. Its role will be explained in the semantic rules for conditionals. Conditionals and loops are annotated with distinct labels ℓ in the set of labels $\mathcal{L}$. The branch predictor uses them to distinguish the different conditional jumps and to build its history of past jumps.

The syntax is inspired from the Jasmin language [3,4], which features precisely such a combination of low-level atomic instructions that translate directly to assembly and high-level structures consisting of while loops and conditionals.

Memory State. Values are stored at locations, Location = Reg $\cup$ MemLocs, comprising registers and memory locations. A memory state $\sigma :$ Location $\mapsto$ Val is a map from locations to values, which are either integers or memory locations (see Fig. 5). For any atomic instruction **atom** and memory state σ, we let $\mathbb{S}[\![\text{atom}]\!]\sigma$ be the memory state obtained when evaluating **atom** in σ. This atomic instruction semantics is defined as usual—we omit the details.

Pipeline State. Our semantics is parametric in the processor's architecture, i.e. the number of pipelines, the instructions they support, and the instructions' latencies. For simplicity, the jump instruction is handled by a single pipeline J. This is the usual settings for branch predictors as it simplifies the design of the processor. Formally, we assume a fixed set of pipelines Pips. For every pipeline $X \in$ Pips, we note X_i the i-th stage of X. For any atomic instruction **atom**, its latency characterizes the number of stages required to execute the instruction before it can leave the pipeline. We note $|\text{atom}|$ its latency, and we write $X \in$ **atom** if the pipeline X handles the instruction **atom**. We also confuse **atom** with the set of *all* pipelines that handle **atom**. Then, the latency of a pipeline $|X|$ is the maximal latency of the instructions it supports. The pipelines are ordered so that given an instruction handled by several pipelines, these pipelines will be checked in a fixed order. For instance on our processor, for a comparison, the

Latency
$\quad$ |atom| $\qquad \in \mathbb{N}$

Values (Val) :
$\quad$ $v \qquad ::= l \in$ MemLocs $\qquad\qquad$ Memory location
$\qquad\qquad | \ n \in \mathbb{Z} \qquad\qquad\qquad$ Number

Locations (Location):
$\quad$ $x \qquad ::= l \in$ MemLocs $\qquad\qquad$ Memory location
$\qquad\qquad | \ r \in$ Reg $\qquad\qquad\qquad$ Register

Memory state (S):
$\quad$ $\sigma \qquad\qquad \in$ Location $\rightarrow$ Val

Pipelines:
$\quad$ $X \qquad\qquad \in$ Pips $\qquad\qquad\qquad$ Pipeline
$\quad$ $X_1, X_2, \ldots \quad \in$ Stages $\qquad\qquad$ Stage
$\quad$ $\epsilon \qquad\qquad\qquad\qquad\qquad\qquad\quad$ Empty stage content

Transient instructions (Atoms$_t$):
$\quad$ atom$_t \qquad ::= r := v_1 \bowtie v_2 \qquad$ Scalar operations ($\bowtie \in \{+, -, \times, \leq\}$)
$\qquad\qquad\quad | \ r := [l + n] \qquad\qquad$ Load
$\qquad\qquad\quad | \ [l + n] := v \qquad\qquad$ Store
$\qquad\qquad\quad | \ \mathtt{jmp}(v) \qquad\qquad\qquad$ Jump

Pipeline state:
$\quad$ Cells $\qquad = ((\mathbb{N} \times$ Atoms$_t) \cup \epsilon) \quad$ Cells
$\quad$ $\pi \qquad\qquad \in$ Stages $\rightarrow$ Cells $\qquad$ Pipeline state
$\quad$ $\pi[j : j \leq i] \qquad\qquad\qquad\qquad$ Roll back of instructions older than i

Branch prediction (BP):
$\quad$ $h \qquad\qquad\qquad\qquad\qquad\qquad$ Branch prediction history
$\quad$ BP-predict $(h, \ell) \qquad\qquad\quad$ BP prediction on jump ℓ
$\quad$ BP-update $(h, \ell, taken) \qquad$ Update the BP history with jump
$\qquad\qquad\qquad\qquad\qquad\qquad\qquad$ results

Speculation buffer:
$\quad$ $\beta \qquad\qquad \in \mathcal{P}(\mathbb{N} \times$ Atoms$_t) \quad$ Speculation buffer
$\quad$ $\min(\beta, \pi) \quad \in \mathbb{N} \qquad\qquad\qquad$ Minimal index in β and π
$\qquad\qquad\qquad\qquad\qquad\qquad\qquad$ ($= 0$ if empty)
$\quad$ $\max(\beta, \pi) \quad \in \mathbb{N} \qquad\qquad\qquad$ Maximal index in β and π
$\qquad\qquad\qquad\qquad\qquad\qquad\qquad$ ($= 0$ if empty)
$\quad$ $\beta(\sigma) \qquad = (\bigcirc_{(j, \mathtt{atom}_t) \in \beta} \mathbb{S}[\![\mathtt{atom}_t]\!])(\sigma) \quad$ Application of all instructions of β
$\quad$ $\beta[j : j \leq i] \ \in \mathcal{P}(\mathbb{N} \times$ Atoms$_t) \quad$ All instructions more recent than i

Processor state:
$\quad$ $\omega \qquad\qquad = \langle \sigma, \pi, h, \beta \rangle \qquad\qquad$ Processor state

Fig. 5. Concrete pipelined processor

pipelines will be checked in the order A, then L, then S. As a shorthand, we write $X = \min\{Y \in$ atom$\}$ to get the first pipeline handling atom.

$\quad$ Each stage of a pipeline is either empty (denoted ϵ), or contains a transient instruction – obtained by resolving an atomic instruction – ready to be processed.

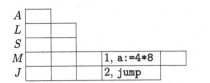

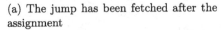

(a) The jump has been fetched after the assignment

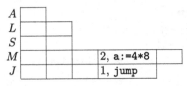

(b) The jump has been fetched before the assignment, and thus depends on its prediction

Fig. 6. The timestamps associated to the instructions records prediction dependencies, and allow to perform roll backs if necessary.

The set of transient instructions is denoted $\mathsf{Atoms_t}$. As explained in Sect. 2, we need to annotate the instructions in the pipelines to know if they are speculation and depend on a jump retiring. Each transient instruction in a pipeline stage is associated to a timestamp, which orders it w.r.t. the other instructions in the pipelines. A smaller timestamp denotes an older instruction. The timestamp is incremented each time we fetch a new instruction. Therefore, a pipeline state π is a function from pipeline stages Stages to pairs of an integer and a transient instruction $((i, \mathsf{atom_t}) \in (\mathbb{N} \times \mathsf{Atoms_t}))$, or to the empty slot ϵ. To be able to roll back a jump with index i, we use the pipeline state $\pi[j : j \leq i]$, which is the state π where only instructions older than i in π have been kept. Newer instructions of π (i.e. such that $\pi(X_k) = (j, \mathsf{atom_t})$ with $j > i$) are replaced with ϵ. We illustrate this in Fig. 6, using the branch prediction example of Sect. 2. Recall that the two programs had the same pipelines state (described in Fig. 3b). But when adding the timestamps, we obtain two distinct states. In the first case (Fig. 6a), the multiplication has been fetched before the jump, and thus its timestamps (1) is smaller than the one of the jump (2). Hence, in case of rollback due to a misprediction of the jump, the multiplication will not be evinced. In the second case (Fig. 6b), the multiplication is speculatively executed, and fetched after the jump: its timestamps (2) is greater than the one of the jump (1), and will thus be evinced if the jump destination was mispredicted.

Speculation Buffer. After it has been executed, an instruction is stored in the speculation buffer β. The instruction will be committed, i.e. its effect will be applied on the memory σ, only when the processor is guaranteed that it was not an incorrect speculation. Similarly to the pipeline state π, the speculation buffer β keeps track of the index of the instructions to check the sequential dependencies. Hence β is a set of pairs $(i, \mathsf{atom_t}) \in (\mathbb{N} \times \mathsf{Atoms_t})$. We let $\min(\beta, \pi)$ be the minimal index associated to an instruction in β and π (we define similarly $\max(\beta, \pi)$). Similarly to π, $\beta[j : j \leq i]$ is the buffer β where only the instructions older than i in β have been kept. The effect of the instructions in the speculation buffer should be taken into account as if it was already applied on

LOCK RAW
$$\frac{x \in \text{read}(\textbf{atom}, \sigma) \qquad x \in \text{write}(\textbf{atom}')}{\text{locks}(\textbf{atom}, \textbf{atom}', \sigma)}$$

LOCK WAW
$$\frac{x \in \text{write}(\textbf{atom}, \sigma) \qquad x \in \text{write}(\textbf{atom}')}{\text{locks}(\textbf{atom}, \textbf{atom}', \sigma)}$$

LOCK WAR
$$\frac{x \in \text{write}(\textbf{atom}, \sigma) \qquad x \in \text{read}(\textbf{atom}')}{\text{locks}(\textbf{atom}, \textbf{atom}', \sigma)}$$

JUMP LOCK
$$\frac{}{\text{locks}(\textbf{jmp}(\_), \textbf{jmp}(\_), \_)}$$

Fig. 7. Rules of data dependency locks

the memory state σ. The notation $\beta(\sigma)$ corresponds to the application on σ of these instructions, from the oldest to the most recent.

Branch Prediction History. The branch predictor is guided by a history of previous jumps. Usually, it is a buffer associating a boolean *taken* or *not taken* to each jump label ℓ, but this can change depending on the processor. Therefore, we chose to keep its precise implementation abstract in our model. We note h this history and assume two operators: BP-predict(h, ℓ) holds if the BP predicts that the jump at ℓ will be taken; and $h' = \text{BP-update}(h, \ell, taken)$ updates the history depending on whether or not the jump was actually taken. We suppose that these operations are deterministic and that the history is not modified by external sources. However, we make no assumption on the quality of the prediction: it can mispredict every time for instance.

Directives. The processor behaves greedily, and tries to fetch as many instructions as possible per cycle. If no pipeline is available for the next instruction **atom**, or if **atom** has a data-dependency conflict with the instructions already in the pipelines, then the processor cannot fetch the instruction **atom** and must execute a cycle. Executing a cycle makes all instructions progress one stage further in their pipeline. When an instruction **atom** has been through $|\textbf{atom}|$ stages, then it is retired and it is placed in the speculation buffer β. At each cycle, β tries to commit its oldest instructions.

These three actions, fetching an instruction, executing a cycle and committing from the speculation buffer, are called *directives*. The fetch **atom** directive loads the instruction **atom** in the first stage of an available pipeline. The commit directive removes the oldest instruction of the speculation buffer if it does not depend on a jump in π. Finally the cycle directive executes a processor cycle, which makes instructions progress in their pipelines, then calls directive commit. All those directives are defined by the rules in Fig. 8, and described below. Notice that the fetch directive does no need the speculation buffer β because it will always be applied on a memory state $\beta(\sigma)$.

Data-Dependencies. An instruction is fetched only if the variables it reads or writes are available. This is checked by the locks(**atom**, **atom**', σ) statement

$$\text{next}(\pi, X_i) = \begin{cases} \epsilon & \text{if } i = 1 \text{ or } |\pi(X_{i-1})| = i - 1 \\ \pi(X_{i-1}) & \text{otherwise} \end{cases}$$

$$\text{retired}(\pi) = \{(k, \text{atom}_t) \mid \exists X_i \in \text{Stages}, \pi(X_i) = (k, \text{atom}_t) \wedge |\text{atom}_t| = i\}$$

FETCH
$$\frac{\begin{array}{c} X = \min\{Y \in \text{atom} \mid \pi(Y_1) = \epsilon\} \\ \pi' = \pi[X_1 \mapsto (i, \text{resolve}(\text{atom}, \sigma))] \end{array}}{(\sigma, \pi) \xrightarrow[\text{fetch } (i, \text{atom})]{} \pi'}$$

READY
$$\frac{\begin{array}{c} \forall Y_i, \pi(Y_i) \neq \epsilon \Rightarrow \neg \text{locks}(\text{atom}, \pi(Y_i), \sigma) \\ X \in \text{atom} \qquad \pi(X_1) = \epsilon \end{array}}{\text{ready}(\text{atom}, \sigma, \pi)}$$

COMMIT
$$\frac{i = \min(\beta, \pi) \\ (i, \text{atom}_t) \in \beta \qquad \beta' = \beta \setminus (i, \text{atom}_t)}{(\sigma, \pi, \beta) \xrightarrow[\text{commit}]{} (\mathbb{S}[\![\text{atom}_t]\!]\sigma, \beta')}$$

ONE-CYCLE
$$\frac{\begin{array}{c} \pi' = \pi[\forall X_i, X_i \mapsto \text{next}(\pi, X_i)] \\ (\sigma, \pi', \beta \cup \text{retired}(\pi)) \xrightarrow[\text{commit}]{}{}^* (\sigma', \beta') \\ i = \min(\beta', \pi') \qquad \min(\beta') \neq i \end{array}}{(\sigma, \pi, \beta) \hookrightarrow (\sigma', \pi', \beta')}$$

Fig. 8. Directives in a speculative context

(defined in Fig. 7), which holds whenever the instruction atom *has* a data dependency with the transient instruction atom' in the memory state σ. There are three rules—for the WaW, WaR and RaW dependencies—which are defined using the variables used by atom. These rules rely on the auxiliary functions read(atom, σ) and write(atom, σ) which return, respectively, the variables read and written by atom in σ—the state σ is used to check if memory accesses are in conflict. For instance, the atomic instruction $a := [b + n]$ reads the value in the memory location pointed by $b + n$, that is the memory location $\sigma(b) + n$. The functions read and write are overloaded to also compute the variables read and written by transient instructions such as atom': read(atom'). In that case, we do not need the memory state because transient instructions have already been resolved.

Jumps are interdependent, and we cannot fetch a jump if one is already being processed. This is captured by the JUMP LOCK rule.

Fetch. The FETCH rule in Fig. 8 defines the judgment $(\sigma, \pi) \xrightarrow[\text{fetch } (i, \text{atom})]{} \pi'$, which places an instruction in the pipelines. First, it resolves the instruction using resolve(atom, σ), and then places it into the first stage of a pipeline supporting it. This fetch directive will only be applied on a state (σ, π) which does not violate the data-dependencies. This condition will be checked using the statement ready(atom, σ, π) defined by the READY rule, which verifies that: 1) the state (σ, π) is ready to fetch the instruction atom, by checking that $\neg \text{locks}(\text{atom}, \text{atom}', \sigma)$ for any atom' in the pipelines (i.e. there are no data-dependencies); and 2), that there is an available pipeline X supporting the instruction. Notice that the fetch directive does not check ready itself.

Commit. The buffer β prevents mis-speculated instructions from being applied on the memory state σ. Instructions in β are committed only if they are the oldest, *i.e.* have the smallest timestamp, ensuring that they do not depend on a jump, which would then have a smaller timestamp while still being in π. This is captured by the judgment $(\sigma, \pi, \beta) \xrightarrow[\text{commit}]{} (\sigma', \beta')$, which is defined by the COMMIT rule. This rule allows to commit an instruction (i, atom_t) in the speculation buffer β if it is the oldest instruction in both the buffer and the pipeline state. Since timestamps record how old instructions are – where smaller indices denote older instructions – and since all instructions have distinct timestamps, we check that (i, atom_t) is the oldest instruction by verifying that i is the smallest timestamp in both β and π.

Executing Cycles. $(\sigma, \pi, \beta) \hookrightarrow (\sigma', \pi', \beta')$ represents the execution of one cycle and is defined by the ONE-CYCLE rule. It makes all the instructions progress one stage further in their pipeline, and relies on $\text{next}(\pi, X_i)$ to get the new content of the stage X_i, according to the previous stage X_{i-1}. The operator next makes all instructions advance by one stage if they have not yet reached the end of their executions. Then, all the instructions that are retired, obtained by the operator retired, are added to β to be validated. Finally, we commit as many instructions from β as possible—we check that we no longer commit any instructions by verifying that the oldest instruction, with timestamp i, is not in the new speculation buffer β'.

Small-Step. Given a statement s and an initial processor state ω, the judgment $(s, \omega) \rightarrow^t (s', \omega')$ states that after t cycles of fetching and executing instructions from s, the processor ends in state ω', and it still has to fetch and execute s'. The statements s is always a sequence of the form $s_1; s_2$, and our rules are defined inductively on the syntax of s_1—s_2 is the continuation, which is essential for the branch predictor. We describe the most important rules below, which are given in Fig. 9—the full semantics is in the companion report [1].

Atomic. The rules for $s_1 = \text{atom}$ are ATOMIC and CYCLE. In the ATOMIC rule, we test whether the current state of the processor is ready to fetch atom using $\text{ready}(\text{atom}, \beta(\sigma), \pi)$. We use the state $\beta(\sigma)$, since an instruction to be fetched must consider the pending instructions in the speculation buffer β for its memory state, to be consistent with the speculation it might be in. The fetched instruction atom is timestamped using a timestamp greater than all the timestamps in both β and π. Finally, the fetch (i, atom) directive places the instruction in the pipelines. Here, no new cycle is necessary, hence $t = 0$, and the continuation s remains to be fetched and executed. The second rule, CYCLE, is used when the state is not ready for atom. In that case, a cycle is executed, and the processor still has to fetch and execute $\text{atom}; s$.

Conditional. The rules SPEC-COND-TRUE-CORRECT and SPEC-COND-TRUE-INCORRECT define the behavior of the processor when encountering a conditional

$$\boxed{\begin{array}{c} (s,\omega) \to^t (s',\omega') \\ \text{execute } t \text{ cycles and fetch} \\ \text{as much instructions of} \\ s \neq \texttt{skip as possible before} \\ \text{each cycle} \end{array}}$$

ATOMIC
$$\dfrac{i = \max(\beta,\pi)+1 \qquad \text{ready}(\texttt{atom},\beta(\sigma),\pi) \qquad (\beta(\sigma),\pi) \xrightarrow[\text{fetch }(i,\texttt{atom})]{} \pi'}{(\texttt{atom}; s, \langle \sigma,\pi,h,\beta\rangle) \to^0 (s, \langle \sigma,\pi',h,\beta\rangle)}$$

CYCLE
$$\dfrac{\neg\,\text{ready}(\texttt{atom},\beta(\sigma),\pi) \qquad (\sigma,\pi,\beta) \hookrightarrow (\sigma',\pi',\beta')}{(\texttt{atom}; s, \langle \sigma,\pi,h,\beta\rangle) \to^1 (\texttt{atom}; s, \langle \sigma',\pi',h,\beta'\rangle)}$$

SPEC-COND-TRUE-CORRECT
$$\dfrac{\begin{array}{c}(\texttt{jmp}(b);\texttt{skip},\omega) \to^t (\texttt{skip}, \langle \sigma_2,\pi_2,h,\beta_2\rangle) \qquad \pi_2(J_1) = (\_,\texttt{jmp}:v) \qquad v \neq 0 \\ \neg\,\text{BP-predict}(\ell,h) \qquad h' = \text{BP-update}(\ell,h,\mathit{false}) \\ (s_1;s_3, \langle \sigma_2,\pi_2,h,\beta_2\rangle) \xrightarrow{=} ^{|\texttt{jmp}|} (s', \langle \sigma_3,\pi_3,h,\beta_3\rangle)\end{array}}{(\ell: \texttt{if } b \texttt{ then } s_1 \texttt{ else } s_2; s_3,\omega) \to^{t+|\texttt{jmp}|} (s', \langle \sigma_3,\pi_3,h',\beta_3\rangle)}$$

SPEC-COND-TRUE-INCORRECT
$$\dfrac{\begin{array}{c}(\texttt{jmp}(b);\texttt{skip},\omega) \to^t (\texttt{skip}, \langle \sigma_2,\pi_2,h,\beta_2\rangle) \qquad \pi_2(J_1) = (k,\texttt{jmp}:v) \qquad v \neq 0 \\ \text{BP-predict}(\ell,h) \qquad h' = \text{BP-update}(\ell,h,\mathit{false}) \\ (s_2;s_3, \langle \sigma_2,\pi_2,h,\beta_2\rangle) \xrightarrow{=} ^{|\texttt{jmp}|} (\_, \langle \sigma_3,\pi_3,h,\beta_3\rangle)\end{array}}{(\ell: \texttt{if } b \texttt{ then } s_1 \texttt{ else } s_2; s_3,\omega) \to^{t+|\texttt{jmp}|} (s_1;s_3, \langle \sigma_3,\pi_3[j:j\le k],h',\beta_3[j:j\le k]\rangle)}$$

Fig. 9. Selected small-step semantics rules with explicit speculation

and the then-branch must be taken (i.e. when $b \neq 0$ in our language). The two rules presented can be decomposed into three steps: first the processor fetches the jmp; then executes it with the speculative execution of one of the branches; and finally, either continues normally the execution if the speculation was correct, or it rolls back if it mis-speculated.

The cost t is exactly the number of cycles needed to fetch the atomic jump (since the continuation is skip). Because the continuation is skip, no more rules can be applied, and the last rule applied is ATOMIC to fetch $\texttt{jmp}(b)$. Hence the jump is now in stage J_1, and we can consult the pipeline state to find which branch to take. We also obtain the timestamp k of the jump for the roll back.

In both rules, the predicted branch is then executed. The speculation lasts exactly $|\texttt{jmp}|$ cycles, which is checked by the ENFORCE-CYCLE-* rules defined in Fig. 10: in case the branch and continuation are too short, we let the processor execute cycles on an empty program with judgment $(s,\omega) \xrightarrow{=}^t (s',\omega')$. After processing the jump, the history h is updated. The processor behavior after the speculation ends depends on the correctness of the prediction. If the processor correctly predicted the branch, then the continuation s' obtained after the speculation is used (rule SPEC-COND-TRUE-CORRECT). Otherwise, the continuation and all instructions in π and β that were speculated are discarded (rule SPEC-COND-TRUE-INCORRECT). We keep the state σ_3 since committed instructions

$$\frac{(s,\omega) \overset{=}{\longrightarrow}{}^{t} (s',\omega')}{\text{execute } t \text{ cycles and fetch}}$$

execute t cycles and fetch
as much instructions of s as
possible before each cycle

ENFORCE-CYCLE
$$\frac{(s,\omega) \to^{t} (s',\omega')}{(s,\omega) \overset{=}{\longrightarrow}{}^{t} (s',\omega')}$$

ENFORCE-CYCLE-EXACT
$$\frac{(s,\omega) \to^{k} (\texttt{skip},\omega'') \qquad \omega'' \hookrightarrow^{t-k} \omega'}{(s,\omega) \overset{=}{\longrightarrow}{}^{t} (\texttt{skip},\omega')}$$

Fig. 10. Small-step semantics to enforce arbitrary cycle execution

$(p,\sigma,h) \Downarrow_t \sigma'$

executes the program p
from σ in t cycles

DONE
$$\frac{(p;\texttt{skip}, \langle \sigma, \pi_\epsilon, h, \emptyset \rangle) \to^{t} (\texttt{skip}, \langle \sigma'', \pi, \_, \beta \rangle) \qquad (\sigma'',\pi,\beta) \hookrightarrow^{t'} (\sigma',\pi_\epsilon,\emptyset)}{(p,\sigma,h) \Downarrow_{t+t'} \sigma'}$$

Fig. 11. Execution cost for small-step semantics

were necessarily older than the jump which was in J during the speculation. Finally, the processor restarts its execution from the correct branch s_1.

Remark that the history h does not change during the speculation. This is because the processor does not fetch another jump while there is already a jump in the pipeline. Therefore, two predictions cannot be interlaced: the branch history cannot change between the prediction of rule SPEC-COND-* and its update at the end of the rule.

Fetch and Execution Cost. For any program p and processor state ω, the judgment $(p;\texttt{skip},\omega) \to^{t} (\texttt{skip},\omega')$ states that all instructions of p have been fetched in t cycles. If ω has empty an pipeline state π_ϵ and an empty speculation buffer, then t is the *fetch cost* of p. But not all instructions have been executed and committed after t cycles: some instructions may still be in π or β. To obtain the full execution cost, we need to keep executing cycles until we reach a pipeline state π_ϵ, where all the stages are empty (i.e. $\forall X_i, \pi_\epsilon(X_i) = \epsilon$), and an empty speculation buffer. This is captured by the judgment $(p,\sigma,h) \Downarrow_t \sigma'$, which gives the *execution cost* t of a program p starting with memory state σ and a branch predictor history h—see the DONE rule in Fig. 11.

4   Static Analysis

We now present the static analysis technique we designed, which allows to obtain provable relational bounds of the execution cost of a program. To do this, we first instrument the original program s by adding a cost variable cost, such that the set of possible run-time values of cost in the instrumented program contains the exact value of the execution cost of s. We then perform a standard relational numerical static analysis on this instrumented program to obtain rela-

Alias analysis notations:

$\sigma^\sharp$	$\in S_a^\sharp$	Abstract alias memory states
$[\![atom]\!]_a^\sharp$	$\in S_a^\sharp \to S_a^\sharp$	Abstract alias semantics for an atomic instruction
$\bowtie_{May}^\sharp, \bowtie_{Must}^\sharp$	$\in Atoms \times Atoms \times S_a^\sharp \to bool$	No data-dependency test
$\iota_a^\sharp[s]$	$\in S_a^\sharp$	Initial abstract alias memory state for the given statement s
γ_a	$\in S_a^\sharp \to \mathcal{P}(S)$	Concretization function

Abstract states:

$\pi^\sharp$	$\in P^\sharp = Stages \to (Atoms \cup \epsilon)$	Abstract pipeline state
$\pi_\epsilon^\sharp$	$\in P^\sharp$	The empty abstract pipeline state

Numerical analysis notations:

$\sigma^\sharp$	$\in S_n^\sharp$	Abstract numerical memory states
$[\![s]\!]_n^\sharp$	$\in S_n^\sharp \to S_n^\sharp$	Abstract numerical analysis of statement s
$\iota_n^\sharp[s]$	$\in S_n^\sharp$	Initial abstract memory state for the given statement s
γ_n	$\in S_n^\sharp \to \mathcal{P}(S \times S)$	Concretization function returning pre and post states
proj_R	$\in S_n^\sharp \to S_n^\sharp$	Projects an invariant on registers R

Instrumentation notations:

$(\pi^\sharp, \sigma^\sharp, n)$	$\in I^\sharp = P^\sharp \times S_a^\sharp \times \mathbb{N}$	Abstract processor state
$[\![s]\!]_{\bowtie^\sharp}$	$\in I^\sharp \to I^\sharp$	Abstract semantics of a statement s (parameterized by a no data-dependency test $\bowtie^\sharp$)
$\mathbb{T}$	$\in (Stmt \times S_a^\sharp) \to (Stmt \times S_a^\sharp)$	Instrumentation of a statement
$[\![blk]\!]^\sharp$	$\in S_a^\sharp \to (\mathbb{N} \times \mathbb{N} \times S_a^\sharp)$	Cost analysis (lower and upper bounds) of a block with alias information

Fig. 12. Static analysis notation

tional bounds between the original program cost and input variables (for instance the length of an input array). The instrumentation is performed using a standard may/must static analysis and a symbolic execution of instruction blocks.

The analysis algorithm is presented in Sect. 4.1, illustrated on an example and with the soundness theorem guaranteed. The soundness proof is detailed in Sect. 4.2.

4.1 Instrumentation for a Numerical Analysis

The instrumentation of each statement is defined by induction in Fig. 13 and the notations of the analyses are summarized in Fig. 12. For blocks—a sequence of atomic instructions $atom_1; \ldots; atom_n$ without control-flow structure—the instrumentation relies on a block cost approximations $[\![blk]\!]^\sharp$ which outputs the bounds $[u, o]$ of the cost to execute blk. The instrumentation relies on an alias analysis—whose purpose is explained later—and is thus parameterized by an

Block Instrumentation:

$$[\![a]\!]_{\bowtie^\sharp}(\pi^\sharp, \sigma^\sharp, n) = \begin{cases} (\pi^\sharp[X_1 \mapsto a], [\![a]\!]^\sharp \sigma^\sharp, n) & \text{If } \exists X \in \min\{Y \in a \mid Y_1 = \epsilon\} \\ & \text{and } \forall a', \bowtie^\sharp (a, a', \sigma^\sharp) \text{ holds} \\ (cycle(\pi^\sharp), \sigma^\sharp, n+1) & \text{Otherwise} \end{cases}$$

$$[\![a_1; \ldots; a_n]\!]_{\bowtie^\sharp} \sigma^\sharp = [\![a_n]\!]_{\bowtie^\sharp} \circ \ldots \circ [\![a_1]\!]_{\bowtie^\sharp} (\pi_\epsilon^\sharp, \sigma^\sharp, 0)$$

$$[\![\text{blk}]\!]^\sharp \sigma_1^\sharp = (u, o + \max(\pi^\sharp), \sigma_2^\sharp) \quad \text{with} \quad \begin{array}{l} [\![\text{blk}]\!]_{\bowtie^\sharp_{\text{Must}}} \sigma_1^\sharp = (\_, \sigma_2^\sharp, u) \\ [\![\text{blk}]\!]_{\bowtie^\sharp_{\text{May}}} \sigma_1^\sharp = (\pi^\sharp, \_, o) \end{array}$$

Program Instrumentation:

$$\mathbb{T}(\text{blk}, \sigma_1^\sharp) = (\text{blk; cost += } [u, o], \sigma_2^\sharp) \qquad \text{if } [\![\text{blk}]\!]^\sharp \sigma_1^\sharp = (u, o, \sigma_2^\sharp)$$

$$\mathbb{T}(s_1; s_2, \sigma_1^\sharp) = (s_1'; s_2', \sigma_3^\sharp) \qquad \text{if } (s_1', \sigma_2^\sharp) = \mathbb{T}(s_1, \sigma_1^\sharp) \text{ and } (s_2', \sigma_3^\sharp) = \mathbb{T}(s_2, \sigma_2^\sharp)$$

If $(s_1', \sigma_2^\sharp) = \mathbb{T}(s_1, [\![b]\!]_a^\sharp \sigma_1^\sharp)$ and $(s_2', \sigma_2^\sharp) = \mathbb{T}(s_2, [\![\neg b]\!]_a^\sharp \sigma_1^\sharp)$:

$$\mathbb{T}(\text{if } b \text{ then } s_1 \text{ else } s_2, \sigma_1^\sharp) = (\text{cost += } [0, L]; \text{if } b \text{ then } s_1' \text{ else } s_2', \sigma_2^\sharp \sqcup \sigma_3^\sharp)$$

If $\sigma^\sharp = \text{lfp}(\lambda \Sigma \to \sigma_0^\sharp \sqcup [\![s]\!]_a^\sharp \circ [\![b]\!]_a^\sharp \Sigma)$ and $\mathbb{T}(s, [\![b]\!]_a^\sharp \sigma^\sharp) = (s', \_)$:

$$\mathbb{T}(\text{while } b \text{ do } s \text{ done}, \sigma_0^\sharp) =$$
$$(\text{while } b \text{ do } (\text{cost += } [0, L]; \ s') \text{ done; cost += } [0, L], [\![\neg b]\!]_a^\sharp \sigma^\sharp)$$

Fig. 13. Instrumentation of a program $(L = |\text{jmp}|)$

abstract memory state $\sigma^\sharp$ from the alias analysis. The instrumentation adds non-deterministic increment cost += $[u, o]$ to the cost variable.

Instrumented programs are analyzed using a numerical analysis $[\![\cdot]\!]_n^\sharp$. We let R_0 be the input registers of our programs, and denote by $\iota_n^\sharp[s]$ the initial abstract memory state of the program s. Let s' be the instrumentation of a program s. To obtain the cost (invariant) $\mathbb{C}$ of s, we project the abstract numerical invariant of s' on the input registers R_0 and the cost variable:

$$\mathbb{C}(s) = \text{proj}_{R_0 \cup \{\text{cost}\}}([\![s']\!]_n^\sharp(\iota_n^\sharp[s])) \quad \text{where} \quad (s', \_) = \mathbb{T}(s, \iota_a^\sharp[s]))$$

Block Instrumentation. The block instrumentation computes the cost with $[\![\text{blk}]\!]^\sharp$. It performs two simulations $[\![\text{blk}]\!]_{\bowtie^\sharp_{\text{Must}}}$ and $[\![\text{blk}]\!]_{\bowtie^\sharp_{\text{May}}}$ of the block to obtain under and over approximations of the execution cost. To simulate the execution of a block, the analysis takes the instructions of the block in order and tries to fetch them. If no instruction can be fetched, e.g. because the first stage of all pipelines are full, or because of a data-dependency, it increments its cycle counter and updates its abstract pipeline state $\pi^\sharp$ with a function *cycle*—which makes instructions advance on stage forward in their pipelines. In these simulations, the pipeline abstract state $\pi^\sharp$ is a function from stages to unresolved instructions (the abstract simulation cannot resolve instructions, as this require a concrete memory state).

The simulation relies on an abstract memory state $\sigma^\sharp$ from an auxiliary alias analysis conducted in parallel to the instrumentation. This alias analysis is used to determine if there may be data-dependencies between the current instruction and any instruction in the pipelines, using an alias operator $\bowtie^\sharp$. The alias operator $\bowtie^\sharp$ used depends on how data-dependencies should be handled, which depends on whether we are computing the lower or upper-bound. When computing the lower bound, we are in the best-case scenario, and assume that there is a data-dependency—hence a delay—only if the memory location *must* always alias. Hence we require that the must-alias operator $\bowtie^\sharp_{\text{Must}}$ satisfies:

$$\neg \bowtie^\sharp_{\text{Must}} (\text{atom}, \text{atom}', \sigma^\sharp) \implies \forall \sigma \in \gamma(\sigma^\sharp), \text{locks}(\text{atom}, \text{atom}', \sigma)$$

On the other hand, the upper bound corresponds to the worst-case scenario, and relies on a *may* alias analysis to detect instructions that may induce a delay: if an instruction is known never to alias with any instruction already in the pipeline, no data-dependency delay needs to be added. We require that the may-alias operator $\bowtie^\sharp_{\text{May}}$ satisfies:

$$\bowtie^\sharp_{\text{May}} (\text{atom}, \text{atom}', \sigma^\sharp) \implies \forall \sigma \in \gamma(\sigma^\sharp), \neg \text{locks}(\text{atom}, \text{atom}', \sigma)$$

If there is no data-dependency, then the simulation finds an empty stage for atom and updates the alias analysis.

Example. Consider the instrumentation of the program below. This program computes in register p the scalar product of two vectors stored in arrays A and B. We suppose that A and B do not alias at the beginning, and that the may and must alias analyses are able to determine that there is no aliasing between the address read l.14 and l.18. Each instruction is commented with the cycle at which it is fetched in its block, starting from an empty pipeline.

```
 1  // Initialization              17      r2  := i*8;         // 6
 2  cost := 0;                      18      b   := [B + r2];    // 11
 3  p    := 0;      // 1            19      c   := a*b;         // 13
 4  i    := 0;      // 1            20      p   := p+c;         // 18
 5  r0   := n-i;    // 2            21      i   := i+1;         // 18
 6  // Block's cost                 22      r0  := n-i;         // 19
 7  cost += [1, 2] ;                23      // Block's cost
 8  while (r0 > 0) do               24      cost += [18, 19];
 9      // Backtrack penalty        25  done;
10      cost += [0, 4];             26  // Backtrack penalty
11      r1 := i*8;        // 1      27  cost += [0, 4];
12      a  := [A + r1]; // 6
```

Finally, we use a numerical static analysis to obtain the final value of the cost variable. On the example above, we assume that the inputs A and B are of size $n \geq 0$, and we select $R_0 = \{n\}$ as input register. Once projected, the relation between cost and the initial value of n gives a cost of the program in the interval $[1 + 18n; 6 + 23n]$.

The soundness of the static analysis is formalized in the following theorem where we used the concretization function γ_n to link the initial and final states.

Definition 1 (Initial states). *A memory state σ_0 is initial if it satisfies*

$$(\sigma_0, \sigma_0) \in \gamma_n(\iota_n^\sharp[s]) \ \wedge \ \sigma_0 \in \gamma_a(\iota_a^\sharp[s])$$

Theorem 1 (Static analysis soundness). *Let s be a program and σ_0 an initial state. Then, the computed numerical relation is a sound approximation of the execution cost of s from σ_0:*

$$\forall h, t, (s, \sigma_0, h) \Downarrow_t \_ \implies (\sigma_0, \{\mathsf{cost} \mapsto t\}) \in \gamma_n \circ \mathbb{C}(s)$$

4.2 Proof of Soundness

To prove Theorem 1, we need to prove that: (i) the block approximation is sound; and (ii), the program instrumentation is sound.

The following theorem states the soundness of our block instrumentation.

Theorem 2 (Block approximation correction). *For any block blk and abstract memory state $\sigma^\sharp$:*

$$[\![blk]\!]^\sharp \sigma^\sharp = (u, o, \_) \ \Rightarrow \ \forall \sigma \in \gamma(\sigma^\sharp), t, h, \ ((blk, \sigma, h) \Downarrow_t \_ \Rightarrow t \in [u, o])$$

The theorem is proved by bi-simulation, by induction on the number of instructions of blk. For the lower bound, if the concrete semantics fetches an instruction, the correction of the must analysis ensures that the simulation will fetch it too. However, the abstract simulation of the pipeline state may fetch instruction earlier than the concrete semantics, e.g. when the must alias analysis does not detect that an aliasing always occurs. Thus the under-approximation cost is smaller or equal to the concrete cost.

For the upper bound, the converse reasoning applies. If the concrete semantics executes a cycle, because of a conflict, then the correction of the may alias analysis guarantees that the over-approximation also executes a cycle. The may analysis may not be able to statically prove that some instruction cannot alias with an instruction already in the pipeline, which can result in more cycles in the abstract semantics. Thus the over-approximation cost is larger or equal to the concrete cost.

Soundness of the Program Instrumentation. We rely on an approximate program semantics to prove the soundness of our program instrumentation. This big-step semantics is defined inductively on the syntax, with a special case for blocks, and computes bounds for each statement. It abstracts away the reorder buffer and the branch prediction history, keeping only the memory state σ and the abstract state $\sigma^\sharp$ computed by the alias analyses. Its rules are in Fig. 14 and follows the scheme of the instrumentation. It is straightforward to show that the cost-approximate semantics computes the same bounds than the ones of the cost variable in the instrumented program.

The cost-approximate semantics is sound w.r.t. the small-step semantics.

$$\text{SEQ-NO-BLOCK}$$

BLOCK

$$\frac{s_1; s_2 \text{ not a block}}{\begin{array}{c} (s_1, \sigma_1, \sigma_1^\sharp) \Downarrow_{[u,o]} (\sigma_2, {\sigma_2}^\sharp) \\ (s_2, \sigma_2, {\sigma_2}^\sharp) \Downarrow_{[u',o']} (\sigma_3, {\sigma_3}^\sharp) \end{array}}{(s_1; s_2, \sigma_1, \sigma_1^\sharp) \Downarrow_{[u+u', o+o']} (\sigma_3, {\sigma_3}^\sharp)}$$

$$\frac{s \text{ a block}}{[\![\text{blk}]\!]^\sharp \sigma_1^\sharp = (u, o, {\sigma_2}^\sharp) \qquad \sigma_2 \in \mathbb{S}[\![s]\!]\sigma_1}{(s, \sigma_1, \sigma_1^\sharp) \Downarrow_{[u,o]} (\sigma_2, {\sigma_2}^\sharp)}$$

COND-TRUE

$$\frac{[\![b]\!]\sigma_1 \neq 0 \qquad (\mathtt{jmp}(b); s_1, \sigma_1, \sigma_1^\sharp) \Downarrow_{[u,\_]} (\sigma_2, {\sigma_2}^\sharp) \qquad (s_1, \sigma_1, \sigma_1^\sharp) \Downarrow_{[\_,o]} (\sigma_2, \sigma_2^\sharp)}{(\text{if } b \text{ then } s_1 \text{ else } s_2, \sigma_1, \sigma_1^\sharp) \Downarrow_{[u, o+|\mathtt{jmp}|]} (\sigma_2, {\sigma_2}^\sharp)}$$

COND-TRUE

$$\frac{[\![b]\!]\sigma_1 = 0 \qquad (\mathtt{jmp}(b); s_2, \sigma_1, \sigma_1^\sharp) \Downarrow_{[u,\_]} (\sigma_2, {\sigma_2}^\sharp) \qquad (s_1, \sigma_2, \sigma_1^\sharp) \Downarrow_{[\_,o]} (\sigma_2, \sigma_2^\sharp)}{(\text{if } b \text{ then } s_1 \text{ else } s_2, \sigma_1, \sigma_1^\sharp) \Downarrow_{[u, o+|\mathtt{jmp}|]} (\sigma_2, {\sigma_2}^\sharp)}$$

WHILE

$$\frac{(\text{if } b \text{ then } (s; \mathtt{while} \ b \ \mathtt{do} \ s \ \mathtt{done}), \sigma_1, \sigma_1^\sharp) \Downarrow_{[u,o]} (\sigma_2, {\sigma_2}^\sharp)}{(\mathtt{while} \ b \ \mathtt{do} \ s \ \mathtt{done}, \sigma, \sigma^\sharp) \Downarrow_{[u,o]} (\sigma_2, {\sigma_2}^\sharp)}$$

Fig. 14. The big-step approximate semantics computes the cost bounds of statements, with the help of an alias abstract memory state $\sigma^\sharp$

Theorem 3 (Cost-approximate soundness). *Let s be a program, σ_1 a memory state, $\sigma_1^\sharp$ an abstract alias state such that $\sigma_1 \in \gamma_a(\sigma_1^\sharp)$, and s' the instrumentation of s (i.e. $(s', \_) = \mathbb{T}(s, \sigma_1^\sharp))$, then*

$$\forall t, h, u, o, \sigma_2, \ \left(\begin{array}{c} (s, \sigma_1, h) \Downarrow_t \sigma_2 \\ \wedge (s, \sigma_1, \sigma_1^\sharp) \Downarrow_{[u,o]} (\sigma_2, \_) \end{array} \right) \implies \left(\begin{array}{c} \sigma_2[\text{cost} \mapsto t] \in \mathbb{S}[\![s']\!]\sigma_1 \\ \wedge u \leq t \leq o \end{array} \right)$$

Also, the existence of an execution in the small-step semantics is enough to guarantee the existence of bounds for the cost-approximate semantics.

Theorem 4 (Cost-approximate existence). *Let s be a program and σ_1 a memory state and $\sigma_1^\sharp$ an abstract alias state such that $\sigma_1 \in \gamma_a(\sigma_1^\sharp)$*

$$\forall t, h, \sigma_2, \ (s, \sigma_1, h) \Downarrow_t \sigma_2 \implies \left(\exists o, u, (s, \sigma_1, \sigma_1^\sharp) \Downarrow_{[u,o]} (\sigma_2, \_) \right)$$

For Theorem 3, only the second component of the conjunction requires a detailed proof—the other is a trivial property of the instrumentation. The proof of this theorem is given in the companion report [1], and relies on several intermediate semantics, until we obtain a big-step semantics with immediate application of instructions on the memory state (i.e. where the effects of an instruction are applied immediately, and not when it is committed) and with approximations due to dropping the branch prediction history and concrete memory state in the block analysis.

Cost from a Non-empty Pipeline State. The difficulty of Theorem 3's proof is that the intermediate processor states in the small-step semantics do not necessarily have an empty pipeline state and empty speculation buffer, while Theorem 2 consider the execution cost of a block from an *empty pipeline state*.

Assume that we have two blocks blk_1 and blk_2 that are executed one after the other (e.g. blk_1 and blk_2 can be the body of a while loop). Then, blk_2 is executed starting from the processor state ω_1 resulting from blk_1's execution.

$$(\mathsf{blk}_1, \langle \sigma_1, \pi_\epsilon, h, \emptyset \rangle) \to^{t_1} \omega_1, \quad (\mathsf{blk}_2, \omega_1) \to^{t_2} (\mathtt{skip}, \omega_2) \text{ and } \omega_2 \hookrightarrow^{t_2'} \langle \sigma', \pi_\epsilon, h', \emptyset \rangle$$

Here, we need to show that $t_1 + t_2 + t_2' \leq o_1 + o_2$, where:

$$(\mathsf{blk}_1, \sigma_1, \sigma_1^\sharp) \Downarrow_{[\_, o_1]} (\sigma_2, \sigma_2^\sharp) \quad \text{and} \quad (\mathsf{blk}_2, \sigma_2, \sigma_2^\sharp) \Downarrow_{[\_, o_2]} (\sigma', \sigma'^\sharp)$$

The fetch cost t_1 of blk_1 is smaller than its execution cost t_1'. Hence using Theorem 2:

$$(\mathsf{blk}_1, \sigma_1, h) \Downarrow_{t_1'} \sigma_2 \quad \text{and} \quad t_1 \leq t_1' \leq o_1$$

But we cannot bound the execution cost of blk_2 by o_2, because Theorem 2 only bounds the cost of executing blk_2 starting from an *empty pipeline and speculation buffer state*. Since it starts from a (potentially) non-empty state ω_1, t_2 may be strictly larger than o_2.

Intuitively, the cost approximation $t_1 + t_2 + t_2' \leq o_1 + o_2$ holds because the additional cost incurred when starting from an non-empty pipeline state has already been accounted by the *previous* block, i.e. in o_1. To formalize this, let $\max(\pi)$ be the maximum delay of all resources in π:

$$\max(\pi) = \max \left(\underbrace{\max_{X_i \in \mathsf{Stages}, \pi(X_i) \neq \emptyset} (|\pi(X)| - i + 1)}_{\text{delays on locations}}, \underbrace{\max_{X \in \mathsf{Pips}} \mathbb{1}_{X_1 \neq \emptyset}}_{\text{delay for first stages}} \right)$$

where $\mathbb{1}_C$ evaluates to 1 if the predicate C is true, 0 otherwise.

The following lemma guarantees that we do bound the cost of a statement by computing its cost from an empty pipeline.

Lemma 1. *Let $\langle \sigma, \pi, h, \beta \rangle$ be a processor state and s a program. Consider the following two executions starting from the pipeline and buffer states, resp., π, β and $\pi_\epsilon, \emptyset$.*

$$(s; \mathit{skip}, \langle \sigma, \pi, h, \beta \rangle) \to^t (\mathit{skip}, \langle \_, \pi', \_, \_ \rangle)$$
$$\text{and } (s; \mathit{skip}, \langle \sigma, \pi_\epsilon, h, \emptyset \rangle) \to^{t'} (\mathit{skip}, \langle \_, \pi'', \_, \_ \rangle)$$

Then $t' \leq t$ and $t + \max(\pi') \leq \max(\pi) + t' + \max(\pi'')$

The proof, given in the companion report [1], is not straightforward, and requires some care. Indeed, the two executions may not execute cycles synchronously: there is no guarantee that the execution which started with non-empty pipelines will execute a cycle when the other execution, which started from π_ϵ, does. To tackle this issue, we introduce the notion of *lateness*, a partial order relation on pipeline states that captures the fact that a pipeline state has already executed more cycles than another one. We prove that this partial ordering is preserved by our semantics.

Proof of Theorem 1. To conclude the proof of Theorem 1, let us take s a program, σ_0 an initial memory state, h a branch predictor history, such that the execution cost of s is t in the small-step semantics: $(s, \sigma_0, h) \Downarrow_t \sigma_1$. Recall that $\mathbb{C}(s) = \text{proj}_{R_0 \cup \{\text{cost}\}}([\![s']\!]_n^\sharp(\iota_n^\sharp[s]))$ with $\mathbb{T}(s, \iota_a^\sharp[s]) = (s', \_)$. By Theorem 4, there exists o and u such that $(s, \sigma_0, \sigma_0^\sharp) \Downarrow_{[u,o]} (\sigma_1, \_)$. By Theorem 3, $\sigma_1[\text{cost} \mapsto t] \in \mathbb{S}[\![s']\!](\sigma_0)$.

Using the soundness of the numerical abstraction $[\![\cdot]\!]_n^\sharp$, we have

$$\forall \sigma^\sharp, \forall (\sigma_0, \sigma) \in \gamma_n(\sigma^\sharp), \ \{\sigma_0\} \times \mathbb{S}[\![s]\!]\sigma \subseteq \gamma_n([\![s]\!]_n^\sharp \sigma^\sharp)$$

and in particular $\{\sigma_0\} \times \mathbb{S}[\![s']\!]\sigma_0 \subseteq \gamma_n([\![s']\!]_n^\sharp \iota_n^\sharp[s])$. After projecting on R_0 and cost, we obtain $(\sigma_0, \{\text{cost} \mapsto t\}) \in \gamma_n \circ \mathbb{C}(s)$ which concludes this proof.

5 Implementation

We implemented our instrumentation technique on top of Jasmin [3,4]. This framework allows to build high-assurance and high-speed cryptographic implementations by: i) combining low-level assembly instructions (e.g. flags and vectorized instructions) and high-level structured control flow; ii) using a verified compiler, with a mechanized Coq proof of behavior preservation; iii) verification tools for proving properties of Jasmin programs, including an embedding of Jasmin in the Easycrypt proof assistant [6], and a static analyzer to check the memory safety of Jasmin programs. The Jasmin compiler performs several compilation passes, such as dead-code elimination, function call inlining, and sharing of stack variables. All these compilation passes are proven correct in Coq (i.e. they preserve the semantics of programs)[1].

We have integrated our cost analysis late enough in the compilation chain in order to avoid change of the cost between the intermediate representation that is analyzed and the final assembly code that is generated by the compiler. Our analysis is implemented in OCaml and currently not verified in Coq. The analysis is parameterized by a user-given processor specification file, listing the instructions, their latency and the pipelines supporting them.

By default, the instrumentation respects the approximation semantics by making no assumption on the branch predictor. In the worst-case scenario the instrumentation thus considers that the branching always mis-predicts. We also provide an option that lets the user assume a basic branch predictor for the processor, which always tries to take the same branch as previously taken. Such a branch predictor can only mis-predict twice on a given while loop execution: when it enters and when it leaves.

The alias and numerical static analyzer (mentioned in Sect. 4) have been obtained by modifying the Jasmin static analyzer. This analyzer, which uses

---

[1] Currently, Jasmin only supports x86 architectures. Note however that our method is not specific to x86, and can be applied to other architectures.

Programs	Lower bound	Upper bound	Naive upper bound
scalar prod (ref)	44 len	44 len + 8	46 len + 11
scalar prod (opt)	17.5 len - 23.5	17.5 len + 33	20 len + 39
poly1305 (ref)	7 len + 25	7.1 len + 150	7.5 len + 177
poly1305 (opt)	2.1 len + 25	2.2 len + 1410	3.9 len + 1098
aes	44.8 len + 446	44.9 len + 1115	50.7 len + 1946
chacha (ref)	16.2 len + 23	16.4 len + 1052	17.6 len + 1040
chacha (opt)	4 len + 27	4.1 len + 2130	5.7 len + 3035
fe25519_mul	427	427	464

Fig. 15. Experimental results.

abstract interpretation techniques [12], was initially introduced in [4] to prove safety, and was executed before any compilation pass. Our cost analysis is run later in the compilation chain and it has been necessary to enhance the Jasmin relational numerical analysis with a *dynamic packing* technique, which handles the same variable with different degrees of precision at different program points. This a slight variation of the *packing* technique introduced in [13] where packs of variable where fixed at the level of block/function.

6 Experiments

We evaluate our cost analysis on different implementations of cryptographic primitives written in Jasmin. Examples include Poly1305 [7], a lookup-table-based implementation of AES [15], ChaCha20 [9] and multiplication in the finite field $\mathbb{F}_p$ with $p = 2^{255} - 19$. The latter is a core routine of the Curve25519 key exchange [8]. We report our experiments in Fig. 15. For some examples we report results for both a reference ("ref") and a hand-optimized ("opt") implementation. When cost depends on the (length of) inputs, our tool computes a symbolic cost w.r.t. to a variable len; for AES and ChaCha encryption and Poly1305 authentication this variable is the length of the input message. In the invariant computed by the numerical analysis, we only keep the best asymptotic constraint when several bounds were available. The tests were done assuming a basic branch predictor. The only target architecture currently supported by Jasmin is AMD64 (also known as x86-64 or x64). There are only very few in-order AMD64 CPUs; for our experiments we decided to approximate one of them, namely the Intel Atom 330. The pipeline structure and instruction latencies are modeled according to the documentation in Fog's CPU manuals [17,18].

We compare our results with a reference naive analysis (last column in Fig. 15) that over-approximates the cost of any block of atomic instructions by the sum of the latencies of each instruction. This approach hence coincides with state-of-the-art cost analyzer that do not take into account instruction pipelining. We also compare the reference programs to their hand-optimized variant, if available. For all programs we obtain a smaller upper-bound than the naive analysis. It shows that our bound computation is likely to improve precision over cost analyzers that ignore instruction pipelining. Our lower and upper-bounds are asymptotically very close, which shows that our cost analysis is asymptotically precise. For programs with hand-optimized version, the upper bound of the optimized program is asymptotically smaller than the lower bound of the original program. This shows our tool usefulness in proving the impact of programmer optimizations.

7 Related Work

Starting from the seminal work of Wegbreit [28], there has been a large body of work for analyzing the cost of programs using recurrence relations [2], program logics [25], type systems [14, 21, 23, 26], and static analysis [19]. These approaches rely on sophisticated methods for computing numerical invariants and inferring iterations bounds for loops or recursive computations. Our method allows to leverage these powerful methods in a more realistic cost model that accommodates cost-critical micro-architectural features.

Cost analysis is also useful for reasoning about side-channel leakage. Ngo *et al.* [24] define the constant-resource policy, an observational information flow policy which guarantees that the execution cost of a program does not depend on its secret inputs. Their analysis is an instance of a relational cost analysis [11], a variant of cost analysis that computes lower and upper bounds for the relative cost of two programs. These works are carried in the setting of a simple cost model; applying our cost model and methodology to side-channel analysis is an interesting direction for future work.

An alternative is to carry dynamic analyses with cycle-accurate cost models. For instance, Yourst [30] develops a model for a x86-64 processor. Dynamic approaches trade off precision for generality—bounds are for specific inputs. However, it would be interesting to explore if cycle-accurate cost models could be used for refining instrumentation.

An even simpler approach is to measure execution time for a large number of inputs. When combined with a statistical analysis, this approach yields a useful heuristic for analyzing if cryptographic implementations leak [27]. However, this approach does not provide any guarantee.

Worst Case Execution Time (WCET) analysis is a well-known industrial success in cost analysis. Using Abstract Interpretation, state-of-the-art analyzers are able to predict a safe upper-bound for embedded micro-architectures with strict real-time constraints. They take into account several advanced architectural optimizations, including pipelines and caches [16, 20, 29]. Our approach differs in scope, precision and semantic foundations. We focus our reasoning on instruction scheduling and provide feedback to programmer who want to hand-optimize their program, like in cryptographic implementation. Our abstraction is more coarse (e.g., we do not try to merge symbolic pipelines on junction points), but already precise enough for the cryptographic application area. WCET tools are clearly more ambitious in term of cost model and precision but they do not ground their work on a semantic model with the same level of mathematical rigour than us. We consider our work as an attempt to reconcile cost precision and rigorous semantic proofs. We also believe that our instrumentation approach can be more easily connected to previous foundational cost analysis works [22] by reusing off-the-shelf cost analyzers.

8 Conclusion

We developed a precise cost semantics for pipelined-optimized softwares executed on in-order processors. The semantics is suitable for automatic cost analysis and formal semantic proofs of soundness. Preliminary experiments demonstrate that our automatic analysis is more accurate than a naive cost analysis.

One direction for future work would be to extend our cost semantics with a cache model and extend our analysis with a may/must tracking of cache misses. An other perspective is to formalize in Coq the soundness of our cost analysis in order to integrate it with the Jasmin high-assurance Coq framework.

References

1. Companion report. https://hal.inria.fr/hal-03779257
2. Albert, E., Arenas, P., Genaim, S., Puebla, G.: Closed-form upper bounds in static cost analysis. J. Autom. Reason. **46**, 161–203 (2011)
3. Almeida, J.B., et al.: Jasmin: high-assurance and high-speed cryptography. In: Proceedings of CCS'2017, pp. 1807–1823. ACM (2017)
4. Almeida, J.B., et al.: The last mile: high-assurance and high-speed cryptographic implementations. In: Proceedings of S&P'2020, pp. 965–982. IEEE (2020)
5. Barbosa, M., et al.: SoK: computer-aided cryptography. In: Proceedings of S&P 2021, pp. 777–795. IEEE (2021)
6. Barthe, G., Dupressoir, F., Grégoire, B., Kunz, C., Schmidt, B., Strub, P.-Y.: EasyCrypt: a tutorial. In: Aldini, A., Lopez, J., Martinelli, F. (eds.) FOSAD 2012-2013. LNCS, vol. 8604, pp. 146–166. Springer, Cham (2014). https://doi.org/10.1007/978-3-319-10082-1_6
7. Bernstein, D.J.: The Poly1305-AES message-authentication code. In: Gilbert, H., Handschuh, H. (eds.) FSE 2005. LNCS, vol. 3557, pp. 32–49. Springer, Heidelberg (2005). https://doi.org/10.1007/11502760_3
8. Bernstein, D.J.: Curve25519: new Diffie-Hellman speed records. In: Yung, M., Dodis, Y., Kiayias, A., Malkin, T. (eds.) PKC 2006. LNCS, vol. 3958, pp. 207–228. Springer, Heidelberg (2006). https://doi.org/10.1007/11745853_14
9. Bernstein, D.J.: ChaCha, a variant of Salsa20. In: Workshop Record of SASC 2008: The State of the Art of Stream Ciphers (2008)
10. Cauligi, S., et al.: Constant-time foundations for the new spectre era. In: Proceedings of PLDI'2020, pp. 913–926. ACM (2020)
11. Çiçek, E., Barthe, G., Gaboardi, M., Garg, D., Hoffmann, J.: Relational cost analysis. In: Proceedings of POPL 2017, pp. 316–329. ACM (2017)
12. Cousot, P., Cousot, R.: Abstract interpretation: a unified lattice model for static analysis of programs by construction or approximation of fixpoints. In: Proceedings of POPL 1977, pp. 238–252. ACM (1977)
13. Cousot, P., et al.: The ASTRÉE analyzer. In: Sagiv, M. (ed.) ESOP 2005. LNCS, vol. 3444, pp. 21–30. Springer, Heidelberg (2005). https://doi.org/10.1007/978-3-540-31987-0_3

396   G. Barthe et al.

14. Crary, K., Weirich, S.: Resource bound certification. In: Proceedings of POPL 2000, pp. 184–198. ACM (2000)
15. Daemen, J., Rijmen, V.: AES proposal: Rijndael, version 2 (1999). http://csrc.nist.gov/archive/aes/rijndael/Rijndael-ammended.pdf
16. Ferdinand, C., et al.: Reliable and precise WCET determination for a real-life processor. In: Henzinger, T.A., Kirsch, C.M. (eds.) EMSOFT 2001. LNCS, vol. 2211, pp. 469–485. Springer, Heidelberg (2001). https://doi.org/10.1007/3-540-45449-7_32
17. Fog, A.: The microarchitecture of Intel, AMD and VIA CPUs - An optimization guide for assembly programmers and compiler makers (2020). https://www.agner.org/optimize/microarchitecture.pdf
18. Fog, A.: The microarchitecture of Intel, AMD and VIA CPUs - instruction tables (2020). https://www.agner.org/optimize/instruction_tables.pdf
19. Gulwani, S., Mehra, K.K., Chilimbi, T.M.: SPEED: precise and efficient static estimation of program computational complexity. In: Proceedings of POPL 2009, pp. 127–139. ACM (2009)
20. Hahn, S., Reineke, J.: Design and analysis of SIC: a provably timing-predictable pipelined processor core. In: Proceedings of RTSS 2018, pp. 469–481. IEEE (2018)
21. Hughes, J., Pareto, L.: Recursion and dynamic data-structures in bounded space: towards embedded ML programming. In: Proceedings of ICFP 1999. pp. 70–81. ACM (1999)
22. Knoth, T., Wang, D., Polikarpova, N., Hoffmann, J.: Resource-guided program synthesis. In: Proceedings of PLDI 2019, pp. 253–268. ACM (2019)
23. Knoth, T., Wang, D., Reynolds, A., Hoffmann, J., Polikarpova, N.: Liquid resource types. In: Proceedings of ICFP 2020, pp. 106:1–106:29 (2020)
24. Ngo, V.C., Dehesa-Azuara, M., Fredrikson, M., Hoffmann, J.: Verifying and synthesizing constant-resource implementations with types. In: Proceedings of SP 2017, pp. 710–728. IEEE Computer Society (2017)
25. Nielson, H.R.: A Hoare-like proof system for analysing the computation time of programs. Sci. Comput. Program. 9(2), 107–136 (1987)
26. Reistad, B., Gifford, D.K.: Static dependent costs for estimating execution time. In: Proceedings of LFP1994, pp. 65–78. ACM (1994)
27. Reparaz, O., Balasch, J., Verbauwhede, I.: Dude, is my code constant time? In: Proceedings of DATE 2017, pp. 1697–1702. IEEE (2017)
28. Wegbreit, B.: Verifying program performance. J. ACM 23(4), 691–699 (1976)
29. Wilhelm, R., Grund, D., Reineke, J., Schlickling, M., Pister, M., Ferdinand, C.: Memory hierarchies, pipelines, and buses for future architectures in time-critical embedded systems. IEEE Trans. Comput. Aided Des. Integr. Circuits Syst. 28(7), 966–978 (2009)
30. Yourst, M.T.: PTLsim: a cycle accurate full system x86-64 microarchitectural simulator. In: Proceedings of ISPASS 2019, pp. 23–34. IEEE Computer Society (2007)

Parameterized Recursive Refinement Types for Automated Program Verification

Ryoya Mukai, Naoki Kobayashi[(✉)] [iD], and Ryosuke Sato

The University of Tokyo, Tokyo, Japan
koba@is.s.u-tokyo.ac.jp

Abstract. Refinement types have recently been applied to program verification, where program verification problems are reduced to type checking or inference problems. For fully automated verification of programs with recursive data structures, however, previous refinement type systems have not been satisfactory: they were not expressive enough to state complex properties of data, such as the length and monotonicity of a list, or required explicit declarations of precise types by users. To address the problem above, we introduce *parameterized recursive refinement types* (PRRT), which are recursive datatypes parameterized by integer parameters and refinement predicates; those parameters can be used to express various properties of data structures such as the length/sortedness of a list and the depth/size of a tree. We propose an automated type inference algorithm for PRRT, by a reduction to the satisfiability problem for CHCs (Constrained Horn Clauses). We have implemented a prototype verification tool and evaluated the effectiveness of the proposed method through experiments.

1 Introduction

There has been a lot of progress on automated/semi-automated verification techniques for functional programs, such as those based on higher-order model checking [6,14,16] and refinement types [2,15,17,18,20–22,24,25]. Fully automated verification of functional programs using recursive data structures, however, still remains a challenge. In the present paper, we follow the approach using refinement types, and introduce *parameterized recursive refinement types* and a type inference procedure for them.

Refinement types can be used to express various properties of recursive data types. For example, if we are interested in the length of an integer list, we can prepare a type of the form $\mathtt{ilistL}[n]$, which describes a list of *length* n, and assign the following types to constructors:

$$\mathtt{Nil} : \mathtt{ilistL}[0]$$

$$\mathtt{Cons} : \forall n.\mathtt{int} \times \mathtt{ilistL}[n] \to \mathtt{ilistL}[n+1]$$

© The Author(s), under exclusive license to Springer Nature Switzerland AG 2022
G. Singh and C. Urban (Eds.): SAS 2022, LNCS 13790, pp. 397–421, 2022.
https://doi.org/10.1007/978-3-031-22308-2_18

The type of Cons indicates that Cons takes a pair consisting of an integer and a list of length n as an argument, and returns a list of length $n + 1$. If we are interested in the sortedness of a list (in the ascending order) instead, we may prepare a type of the form ilistS$[b, x]$, which describes a list consisting of elements no less than x, where the additional Boolean parameter b denotes whether the list is null (thus, if b is true, the value of x should be ignored). The following types can then be assigned to the constructors. (Actually, the second parameter 0 of the type of Nil does not matter and may be any other value.)

Nil : ilistS[true, 0]

Cons : $\forall b, x, y.\ x : \text{int} \times \{\text{ilistS}[b, y] \mid \neg b \Rightarrow x \leq y\} \rightarrow \text{ilistS}[\text{false}, x]$

Once an appropriate refinement type is assigned to each occurrence of a constructor, a standard procedure for automated/semi-automated refinement type inference (e.g., based on a reduction to the CHC solving problem [2, 15, 18, 25]) is applicable.

A main problem in applying the refinement type approach above to the *fully-automated* verification is that each constructor has more than one refinement type, and it is unclear which type should be used for each occurrence of the constructor (unless a programmer explicitly declares it). For example, for a sorting function sort, an input list is a plain, unsorted list, while the output list should be sorted; hence the latter should have type ilistS$[b, x]$ for some b, x. In the context of fully automated verification, we cannot expect a programmer to declare the types like ilistL$[n]$ and ilistS$[b, x]$ above. Thus, an automated verification tool should choose appropriate refinements of recursive data types from infinitely many candidates.

To address the problem above, we parameterize recursive types with integers and predicates, and assign generic types to data type constructors. For example, for integer lists, we prepare a parameterized type ilist$\langle n; e_{\text{Nil}}, (\varphi_{\text{Cons}}, e_{\text{Cons}})\rangle$, where n is an integer denoting the number of integer parameters, φ_{Cons} is a predicate on integers, and e_{Nil} and e_{Cons} are functions on integer tuples, and we assign the following types to constructors:

$$\text{Nil} : \forall k, P_{\text{Cons}}, f_{\text{Nil}}, f_{\text{Cons}}.\text{ilist}\langle k; f_{\text{Nil}}, (P_{\text{Cons}}, f_{\text{Cons}})\rangle[f_{\text{Nil}}()]$$

$$\text{Cons} : \forall k, P_{\text{Cons}}, f_{\text{Nil}}, f_{\text{Cons}}.\forall \widetilde{y}.$$
$$\{x : \text{int} \times \text{ilist}\langle k; f_{\text{Nil}}, (P_{\text{Cons}}, f_{\text{Cons}})\rangle[\widetilde{y}] \mid P_{\text{Cons}}(x, \widetilde{y})\}$$
$$\rightarrow \text{ilist}\langle k; f_{\text{Nil}}, (P_{\text{Cons}}, f_{\text{Cons}})\rangle[f_{\text{Cons}}(x, \widetilde{y})]$$

Here, (i) P_{Cons} is a predicate variable, (ii) f_{Nil} and f_{Cons} are functions of types unit $\rightarrow \text{int}^k$ and $\text{int}^{k+1} \rightarrow \text{int}^k$ respectively, and (iii) $\widetilde{y}$ is a sequence of k integer variables (where k is the first parameter of ilist). By changing the part $\langle k; f_{\text{Nil}}, (P_{\text{Cons}}, f_{\text{Cons}})\rangle$, we can express various list properties. For example, list type constructors ilistL and ilistS can be defined as follows:

$$\text{ilistL} := \text{ilist}\langle 1; \lambda().0, (\lambda(x, y).\text{true}, \lambda(x, y).y + 1)\rangle$$

$$\text{ilistS} := \text{ilist}\langle 2; \lambda().(0, 0), (\lambda(x, y_1, y_2).y_1 > 0 \Rightarrow x \leq y_2, \lambda(x, y_1, y_2).(1, x))\rangle.$$

In fact, by instantiating the parameters k, $P_{\mathtt{Cons}}$, $f_{\mathtt{Nil}}$ and $f_{\mathtt{Cons}}$ to 1, $\lambda(x, y).\mathtt{true}$, $\lambda().0$, and $\lambda(x, y).y + 1$ respectively, we obtain the following types for $\mathtt{Nil}$ and $\mathtt{Cons}$:

$$\mathtt{Nil} : \mathtt{ilistL}[0]$$
$$\mathtt{Cons} : \forall y.\{x : \mathtt{int} \times \mathtt{ilistL}[y] \mid \mathtt{true}\} \to \mathtt{ilistL}[y + 1],$$

which corresponds to the types of $\mathtt{Nil}$ and $\mathtt{Cons}$ given for $\mathtt{ilistL}$. Similarly, by instantiating the parameters k, $P_{\mathtt{Cons}}$, $f_{\mathtt{Nil}}$ and $f_{\mathtt{Cons}}$ to 2, $\lambda(x, y_1, y_2).y_1 > 0 \Rightarrow x \leq y_2$, $\lambda().(0, 0)$, and $\lambda(x, y_1, y_2).(1, x)$ respectively, we obtain the types of $\mathtt{Nil}$ and $\mathtt{Cons}$ given for $\mathtt{ilistS}$.

The remaining question is how to automatically assign an appropriate instantiation of parameterized recursive types to each occurrence of a constructor. To this end, we first pick the values of k, $f_{\mathtt{Nil}}$, $f_{\mathtt{Cons}}$ (in the case of lists; we will deal with more general recursive data types in the following sections) in a certain heuristic manner, and prepare a predicate variable for $P_{\mathtt{Cons}}$. We can then reduce the problem of refinement type inference to the CHC satisfiability problem [1] in a standard manner [2,18], and use an automated CHC solver [2,4,7]. If the refinement type inference fails, that may be due to the lack of sufficient parameters; thus, we increase the value of k and accordingly update the guess for $f_{\mathtt{Nil}}$ and $f_{\mathtt{Cons}}$ so that the resulting refinement types are strictly more expressive. This refinement loop may not terminate due to the incompleteness of the type system discussed later in Sect. 3, but we can guarantee a weak form of relative completeness, that if a program is typable, then the type inference procedure terminates eventually under the hypothetical completeness assumption of the underlying CHC solver, as discussed later in Sect. 4.

We have implemented the procedure sketched above, and succeeded in fully automatic verification of several small but challenging programs using lists and trees. Our contributions are summarized as follows.

– The design of parameterized recursive refinement types (PRRT): the idea of parameterizing recursive types with some indices goes back at least to Xi and Pfenning's work [24], and that of parameterization of types with refinement predicates has also been proposed by Vazou et al. [21]. We believe, however, that the specific combination of the parameterizations, specifically designed with fully automated verification in mind, is new.
– An inference procedure for PRRTs, its implementation and experiments.

The rest of this paper is structured as follows. Section 2 introduces the target language of our verification method based on parameterized recursive refinement types. Section 3 proposes a new refinement type system, and Sect. 4 explains a type inference procedure, which serves as a program verification procedure. Section 5 reports an implementation and experimental results. Section 6 discusses related work, and Sect. 7 concludes the paper.

2   Target Language

We consider a first-order[1] call-by-value functional language as the target of our refinement type inference.

2.1   Syntax

We assume a finite set of data constructors, ranged over by L. The set of *expressions*, ranged over by e, is defined by:

$$e \text{ (expressions)} ::= s \mid f(\widetilde{s}) \mid \texttt{fail} \mid \texttt{if } s \texttt{ then } e_1 \texttt{ else } e_2$$
$$\mid \texttt{let } x = e_1 \texttt{ in } e_2$$
$$\mid \texttt{match } s \texttt{ with } \{L_1(\widetilde{x}_1) \rightarrow e_1, \ldots, L_k(\widetilde{x}_k) \rightarrow e_k\}$$
$$s \text{ (simple expressions)} ::= x \mid n \mid s_1 + s_2 \mid L(s_1, \ldots, s_k)$$
$$D \text{ (programs)} ::= \{f_1(\widetilde{x}_1) = e_1, \ldots, f_k(\widetilde{x}_k) = e_k\}$$

The syntax of expressions above is fairly standard. A simple expression denotes an integer or a recursive data structure; we represent Booleans as integers, where non-zero integers are considered $\texttt{true}$ and 0 is considered $\texttt{false}$. We write $\widetilde{\cdot}$ for a sequence; for example, $\widetilde{s}$ denotes a sequence of simple expressions $s_1, \ldots, s_k$. For a technical convenience, the arguments of a function call $f(\widetilde{s})$ are restricted to simple expressions; this is not a fundamental restriction, $f\ e$ can be expressed by $\texttt{let } x = e \texttt{ in } f\ x$. The expression $\texttt{fail}$ is a special command to indicate an error; the purpose of our refinement type system introduced later is to guarantee that $\texttt{fail}$ does not occur during the execution of any well-typed program. As demonstrated in the examples below, the expression $\texttt{fail}$ is often used to express the specification of a program. The conditional expression $\texttt{if } s \texttt{ then } e_1 \texttt{ else } e_2$ evaluates e_2 if the value of s is 0 and evaluates e_1 otherwise. The match expression $\texttt{match } s \texttt{ with } \{L_1(\widetilde{x}_1) \rightarrow e_1, \ldots, L_k(\widetilde{x}_k) \rightarrow e_k\}$ evaluates $[\widetilde{v}_i/\widetilde{x}_i]e_i$ if the value of s is $L_i(\widetilde{v}_i)$. For the sake of simplicity, we have only $+$ as an operator on integers, but other standard primitives $(-, \times, <, =, \ldots)$ can be incorporated with no difficulty, and used in examples.

A program D is a set of (mutually recursive) function definitions. We assume that the set $\{f_1, \ldots, f_k\}$ of function names contains $\texttt{main}$, the name of the "main" function.

2.2   Typing

We introduce a simple (monomorphic) type system, and require that programs and expressions are well-typed in the type system.

---

[1] The restriction to first-order programs is just for the sake of simplicity; our refinement type system can be easily extended for higher-order functions in a standard manner.

We assume a finite set $\mathcal{D}$ of (names of) recursive data types, ranged over by d. The set of (simple) types, ranged over by κ, is defined by:

$$\kappa \ (\text{simple types}) ::= b \mid (b_1, \ldots, b_k) \to b$$
$$b \ (\text{base types}) ::= \text{int} \mid \text{d}$$

Here, a type of the form $(b_1, \ldots, b_k) \to \text{d}$ is called a constructor type. When $k = 1$, we just write $b \to \text{d}$ for $(b) \to \text{d}$. To distinguish simple types from refinement types introduced later, we sometimes call simple types *sorts*.

A *constructor environment*, written $\mathcal{C}$, is a map from the set of data constructor to the set of constructor types. A (simple) type environment, written $\mathcal{K}$, is a map from a finite set of variables to types. The type judgment relations $\mathcal{C}; \mathcal{K} \vdash_{\text{ST}} e : \kappa$ and $\mathcal{C} \vdash_{\text{ST}} D : \mathcal{K}$ are defined by the typing rules in Fig. 1.

Henceforth, we consider only expressions e and programs D such that $\mathcal{C}; \mathcal{K} \vdash_{\text{ST}} e : \kappa$ and $\mathcal{C} \vdash_{\text{ST}} D : \mathcal{K}$ for some $\mathcal{C}, \mathcal{K}$. As usual, programs well-typed in the simple type system do not get stuck; however, they may be reduced to the error state fail.

In the rest of this paper, we further impose the following restriction on constructor types: for each constructor type $\mathcal{C}(L) = (b_1, \ldots, b_k) \to \text{d}$, we require that $\{b_1, \ldots, b_k\} \subseteq \{\text{int}, \text{d}\}$. Thus, we forbid a constructor type like $(\text{int}, \text{d}_1) \to \text{d}_2$ with $\text{d}_1 \neq \text{d}_2$. We permute argument types and normalize each constructor type to the form $(\text{int}^k, \text{d}^\ell) \to \text{d}$. Again, the restriction is just for the sake of simplicity of the discussions in later sections. We write $\mathcal{C}_\text{d}$ for the restriction of $\mathcal{C}$ on type d, $\{L : \kappa \in \mathcal{C} \mid \kappa \text{ is of the form } (\widetilde{b}) \to \text{d}\}$. Note that $\mathcal{C}$ can be decomposed to the disjoint union of maps $\mathcal{C}_{\text{d}_1} \uplus \cdots \uplus \mathcal{C}_{\text{d}_k}$. For the integer list type ilist discussed in Sect. 1, $\mathcal{C}_{\text{ilist}} = \{\text{Nil} \mapsto (\,) \to \text{ilist}, \text{Cons} \mapsto (\text{int}, \text{ilist}) \to \text{ilist}\}$.

2.3 Operational Semantics

We define a small-step semantics of the language. The sets of evaluation contexts and values, respectively ranged over by E and v, are defined by:

$$E ::= [\,] \mid E + s \mid n + E \mid L(\widetilde{v}, E, \widetilde{s}) \mid f(\widetilde{v}, E, \widetilde{s}) \mid \text{if } E \text{ then } e_1 \text{ else } e_2$$
$$\mid \text{let } x = E \text{ in } e \mid \text{match } E \text{ with } \{L_1(\widetilde{x}_1) \to e_1, \ldots, L_k(\widetilde{x}_k) \to e_k\}$$
$$v ::= n \mid L(v_1, \ldots, v_k)$$

The reduction relation $e \longrightarrow_D e'$ on (closed) expressions is defined by the rules in Fig. 2. The expression $[\widetilde{v}/\widetilde{x}]e$ (which is an abbreviated form of $[v_1/x_1, \ldots, v_k/x_k]e$) denotes the expression obtained from e by substituting $\widetilde{v}$ for $\widetilde{x}$. We write $\longrightarrow_D^*$ for the reflexive and transitive closure of $\longrightarrow_D$. We sometimes omit the subscript D and just write $\longrightarrow$ and $\longrightarrow^*$ for $\longrightarrow_D$ and $\longrightarrow_D^*$ respectively.

For a program D such that $\mathcal{C} \vdash_{\text{ST}} D : \mathcal{K}$ and $\mathcal{K}(\text{main}) = (b_1, \ldots, b_k) \to \text{int}$, we say D is *safe* if there exist no $v_1 : b_1, \ldots, v_k : b_k$ and E such that $\text{main}(v_1, \ldots, v_k) \longrightarrow_D^* E[\text{fail}]$. In the rest of this paper, we shall develop a

$$\frac{\mathcal{K}(x) = \kappa}{\mathcal{C}; \mathcal{K} \vdash_{\mathrm{ST}} x : \kappa} \tag{ST-Var}$$

$$\frac{}{\mathcal{C}; \mathcal{K} \vdash_{\mathrm{ST}} n : \mathtt{int}} \tag{ST-Int}$$

$$\frac{\mathcal{C}; \mathcal{K} \vdash_{\mathrm{ST}} s_1 : \mathtt{int} \quad \mathcal{C}; \mathcal{K} \vdash_{\mathrm{ST}} s_2 : \mathtt{int}}{\mathcal{C}; \mathcal{K} \vdash_{\mathrm{ST}} s_1 + s_2 : \mathtt{int}} \tag{ST-Plus}$$

$$\frac{\mathcal{C}(L) = (b_1, \ldots, b_k) \to \mathtt{d} \quad \mathcal{C}; \mathcal{K} \vdash_{\mathrm{ST}} s_i : b_i \text{ for each } i \in \{1, \ldots, k\}}{\mathcal{C}; \mathcal{K} \vdash_{\mathrm{ST}} L(s_1, \ldots, s_k) : \mathtt{d}} \tag{ST-DC}$$

$$\frac{\mathcal{K}(f) = (b_1, \ldots, b_k) \to b \quad \mathcal{C}; \mathcal{K} \vdash_{\mathrm{ST}} s_i : b_i \text{ for each } i \in \{1, \ldots, k\}}{\mathcal{C}; \mathcal{K} \vdash_{\mathrm{ST}} f(s_1, \ldots, s_k) : b} \tag{ST-App}$$

$$\frac{}{\mathcal{C}; \mathcal{K} \vdash_{\mathrm{ST}} \mathtt{fail} : \mathtt{int}} \tag{ST-Fail}$$

$$\frac{\mathcal{C}; \mathcal{K} \vdash_{\mathrm{ST}} s : \mathtt{int} \quad \mathcal{C}; \mathcal{K} \vdash_{\mathrm{ST}} e_1 : b \quad \mathcal{C}; \mathcal{K} \vdash_{\mathrm{ST}} e_2 : b}{\mathcal{C}; \mathcal{K} \vdash_{\mathrm{ST}} \mathtt{if}\ s\ \mathtt{then}\ e_1\ \mathtt{else}\ e_2 : b} \tag{ST-If}$$

$$\frac{\mathcal{C}; \mathcal{K} \vdash_{\mathrm{ST}} e_1 : b_1 \quad \mathcal{C}; \mathcal{K}, x : b_1 \vdash_{\mathrm{ST}} e_2 : b}{\mathcal{C}; \mathcal{K} \vdash_{\mathrm{ST}} \mathtt{let}\ x = e_1\ \mathtt{in}\ e_2 : b} \tag{ST-Let}$$

$$\frac{\mathcal{C}; \mathcal{K} \vdash_{\mathrm{ST}} s : \mathtt{d} \quad \mathcal{C}(L_i) = (\widetilde{b_i}) \to \mathtt{d} \quad \mathcal{C}; \mathcal{K}, \widetilde{x}_i : \widetilde{b}_i \vdash_{\mathrm{ST}} e_i : b \text{ for each } i \in \{1, \ldots, k\}}{\mathcal{C}; \mathcal{K} \vdash_{\mathrm{ST}} \mathtt{match}\ s\ \mathtt{with}\ \{L_1(\widetilde{x}_1) \to e_1, \ldots, L_k(\widetilde{x}_k) \to e_k\} : b} \tag{ST-Match}$$

$$\frac{\mathcal{K} = (f_1 : (\widetilde{b}_1) \to b'_1, \ldots, f_k : (\widetilde{b}_k) \to b'_k) \quad \mathcal{C}; \mathcal{K}, \widetilde{x}_i : \widetilde{b}_i \vdash_{\mathrm{ST}} e_i : b'_i \text{ for each } i \in \{1, \ldots, k\}}{\mathcal{C} \vdash_{\mathrm{ST}} \{f_1(\widetilde{x}_1) = e_1, \ldots, f_k(\widetilde{x}_k) = e_k\} : \mathcal{K}} \tag{ST-Prog}$$

Fig. 1. Simple Type System

$$E[n_1 + n_2] \longrightarrow_D E[n] \text{ (if } n \text{ is the sum of } n_1 \text{ and } n_2) \tag{E-Plus}$$
$$E[f(\widetilde{v})] \longrightarrow_D E[[\widetilde{v}/\widetilde{x}]e] \text{ (if } f(\widetilde{x}) = e \in D) \tag{E-Call}$$
$$E[\mathtt{if}\ n\ \mathtt{then}\ e_1\ \mathtt{else}\ e_2] \longrightarrow_D E[e_1] \text{ (if } n \neq 0) \tag{E-IfT}$$
$$E[\mathtt{if}\ 0\ \mathtt{then}\ e_1\ \mathtt{else}\ e_2] \longrightarrow_D E[e_2] \tag{E-IfF}$$
$$E[\mathtt{match}\ L_i(\widetilde{v})\ \mathtt{with}\ \{L_1(\widetilde{x}_1) \to e_1, \ldots, L_k(\widetilde{x}_k) \to e_k\}] \longrightarrow_D E[[\widetilde{v}/\widetilde{x}_i]e_i] \tag{E-Match}$$

Fig. 2. Reduction Rules

refinement type system that guarantees the safety of any well-typed program, and an automated procedure for proving the well-typedness, hence the safety of a given program. Note that the safety of a program does not imply the termination of the program; termination verification, for which various techniques [8,9] are available, is outside the scope of this paper.

Example 1. The program D_1 defined below declares function **range**, which takes an integer n and returns the list $[n, n-1, \ldots, 1]$, and checks that the length of **range**(n) equals its argument n.

$$D_1 = \{\mathtt{range}(n) = \mathtt{if}\ n\ \mathtt{then\ let}\ r = \mathtt{range}(n-1)\ \mathtt{in}\ \mathtt{Cons}(n, r)$$
$$\mathtt{else}\ \mathtt{Nil}(),$$
$$\mathtt{len}(l) = \mathtt{match}\ l\ \mathtt{with}\ \{\mathtt{Nil}() \rightarrow 0,\ \mathtt{Cons}(n, l') \rightarrow 1 + \mathtt{len}(l')\},$$
$$\mathtt{main}(n) = \mathtt{let}\ r = \mathtt{range}(n)\ \mathtt{in\ let}\ l = \mathtt{len}(r)\ \mathtt{in}$$
$$\mathtt{if}\ n \neq l\ \mathtt{then\ fail\ else}\ 0\}$$

The evaluation of $\mathtt{main}(n)$ terminates without failure if $n \geq 0$, and falls into an infinite loop if $n < 0$. □

Example 2. The following program D_2 focuses on function $\mathtt{isort}$, which sorts a list in the ascending order by the insertion sort algorithm, and checks that its return value is sorted.

$$D_2 = \{\mathtt{gen}(n) = \mathtt{if}\ n\ \mathtt{then}\ \mathtt{Cons}(*, \mathtt{gen}(n-1))\ \mathtt{else}\ \mathtt{Nil}(),$$
$$\quad \mathtt{insert}(x, l) = \mathtt{match}\ l\ \mathtt{with}\ \{$$
$$\quad\quad \mathtt{Nil}() \rightarrow \mathtt{Cons}(x, \mathtt{Nil}()),$$
$$\quad\quad \mathtt{Cons}(y, l') \rightarrow \mathtt{if}\ x < y\ \mathtt{then}\ \mathtt{Cons}(x, l)\ \mathtt{else}\ \mathtt{Cons}(y, \mathtt{insert}(x, l'))$$
$$\quad \},$$
$$\quad \mathtt{isort}(l) = \mathtt{match}\ l\ \mathtt{with}\ \{$$
$$\quad\quad \mathtt{Nil}() \rightarrow \mathtt{Nil}(),\ \mathtt{Cons}(n, l') \rightarrow \mathtt{insert}(n, \mathtt{isort}(l'))$$
$$\quad \},$$
$$\quad \mathtt{is\_sorted\_rec}(x, l) = \mathtt{match}\ l\ \mathtt{with}\ \{$$
$$\quad\quad \mathtt{Nil}() \rightarrow 1,$$
$$\quad\quad \mathtt{Cons}(y, l') \rightarrow \mathtt{if}\ x \leq y\ \mathtt{then}\ \mathtt{is\_sorted\_rec}(y, l')\ \mathtt{else}\ 0$$
$$\quad \},$$
$$\quad \mathtt{is\_sorted}(l) = \mathtt{match}\ l\ \mathtt{with}\ \{$$
$$\quad\quad \mathtt{Nil}() \rightarrow 1,\ \mathtt{Cons}(n, l') \rightarrow \mathtt{is\_sorted\_rec}(n, l')$$
$$\quad \},$$
$$\quad \mathtt{main}(n) = \mathtt{let}\ s = \mathtt{is\_sorted}(\mathtt{isort}(\mathtt{gen}(n)))\ \mathtt{in}$$
$$\quad\quad\quad \mathtt{if}\ s\ \mathtt{then}\ 0\ \mathtt{else\ fail}$$
$$\}$$

The term $*$ indicates a non-deterministic integer value, omitted in the formal syntax for the sake of simplicity. The function $\mathtt{insert}$ constitutes a part of the insertion sort, which takes x and a sorted list l and returns a sorted list that consists of x and the elements of l. The function $\mathtt{is\_sorted}$ returns 1 if the given list is sorted in the ascending order, and 0 otherwise. □

Example 3. The type $\mathtt{itree}$ for binary trees with integer values is defined with $\mathcal{C}_{\mathtt{itree}} = \{\mathtt{Leaf} \mapsto () \rightarrow \mathtt{itree}, \mathtt{Node} \mapsto (\mathtt{int}, \mathtt{itree}, \mathtt{itree}) \rightarrow \mathtt{itree}\}$. The following program D_3 generates a random tree with a given size, and verifies that the generated tree has the given size as expected.

$$D_3 = \{\, \mathtt{gen\_tree}(n) =$$
$$\quad \mathtt{if}\ n\ \mathtt{then}$$
$$\qquad \mathtt{let}\ m = *\ \mathtt{in\ let}\ \ell = \mathtt{gen\_tree}(m)\ \mathtt{in}$$
$$\qquad \mathtt{let}\ r = \mathtt{gen\_tree}(n-1-m)\ \mathtt{in}\ \mathtt{Node}(*, l, r)$$
$$\qquad \mathtt{else}\ \mathtt{Nil}(),$$
$$\quad size(t) = \mathtt{match}\ t\ \mathtt{with}\ \{$$
$$\qquad \mathtt{Leaf}() \to 0,$$
$$\qquad \mathtt{Node}(\_, \ell, r) \to 1 + size(\ell) + size(r)$$
$$\quad \},$$
$$\quad main(n) = \mathtt{let}\ s = size(\mathtt{gen\_tree}(n))\ \mathtt{in}$$
$$\qquad \mathtt{if}\ s \neq n\ \mathtt{then}\ \mathtt{fail}\ \mathtt{else}\ 0$$
$$\}.$$

If $n \neq 0$,[2] $\mathtt{gen\_tree}(n)$ picks a number m, and returns a tree of size n, consisting of the left child of size m and the right child of size $n - 1 - m$. Function $\mathtt{size}$ calculates the tree size (the number of nodes except leaves). $\qquad\square$

3   A Parameterized Refinement Type System

This section introduces a refinement type system that guarantees the safety of well-typed programs.

3.1   Refinement Types

The syntax of *parameterized recursive refinement types*, ranged over by τ, is defined by:

$$\tau\ \text{(types)} ::= \{\beta \mid \varphi\} \mid \{(\beta_1, \ldots, \beta_k) \mid \varphi'\} \to \{\beta \mid \varphi\}$$
$$\beta\ \text{(type patterns)} ::= \delta[y_1, \ldots, y_n]$$
$$\delta\ \text{(raw types)} ::= \mathtt{int} \mid \mathrm{d}\langle n; (P_1, F_1), \ldots, (P_k, F_k)\rangle$$
$$P\ \text{(predicates)} ::= \lambda(\widetilde{y}).\varphi$$

Here, φ denotes a formula over integer arithmetic, and F denotes a function on integer tuples; we do not fix the precise syntax of φ and F, but assume that standard arithmetic and logical operators are available. In $\delta[y_1, \ldots, y_n]$, (i) $n = 1$ if the *raw type* δ is $\mathtt{int}$, and (ii) $n = m$ if $\delta = \mathrm{d}\langle m; (P_1, F_1), \ldots, (P_k, F_k)\rangle$. Intuitively, $\{\mathtt{int}[x] \mid \varphi\}$ is the type of an integer x that satisfies φ. The type $\{(\beta_1, \ldots, \beta_k) \mid \varphi'\} \to \{\beta \mid \varphi\}$ describes a function or a constructor that takes arguments of types $\beta_1, \ldots, \beta_k$ that satisfy φ', and returns a value of type $\{\beta \mid \varphi\}$. For example, $\{(\mathtt{int}[x]) \mid x > 0\} \to \{\mathtt{int}[y] \mid y > x\}$ describes a function that takes a positive integer x as an argument and returns an integer greater than

---

[2] Actually, $\mathtt{gen\_tree}(n)$ will not terminate if $n < 0$, but that does not concern us here since we are interested in only the safety property.

x. As this example indicates, the variables occurring in the part $(\beta_1, \ldots, \beta_k)$ are bound in $\{(\beta_1, \ldots, \beta_k) \mid \varphi'\} \rightarrow \{\beta \mid \varphi\}$, and may occur in φ' and φ. As usual, we allow implicit renaming of bound variables. We often write $\delta^!{[s_1, \ldots, s_n]}$ for $\{\delta[y_1, \ldots, y_n] \mid y_1 = s_1 \wedge \cdots \wedge y_n = s_n\}$; we sometimes omit the superscript ! when there is no danger of confusion.

Refinement types for datatypes are more involved. For each (simple) datatype d with $\mathcal{C}_\mathsf{d} = \{L_1 : (\mathsf{int}^{\ell_1}, \mathsf{d}^{m_1}) \rightarrow \mathsf{d}, \ldots, L_k : (\mathsf{int}^{\ell_k}, \mathsf{d}^{m_k}) \rightarrow \mathsf{d}\}$, we consider refinement types of the form:

$$\{\mathsf{d}\langle n; (P_1, F_1), \ldots, (P_k, F_k)\rangle[y_1, \ldots, y_n] \mid \varphi\}.$$

Here, n denotes the number of integer parameters $y_1, \ldots, y_n$, and (P_i, F_i) is a pair of a predicate and a function corresponding to the constructor L_i. The above type denotes a data structure constructed from $L_1, \ldots, L_k$, by assigning the following type to L_i.

$$\{(\mathsf{int}[x_1], \ldots, \mathsf{int}[x_{\ell_i}], \delta[\widetilde{y}_1], \ldots, \delta[\widetilde{y}_{m_i}]) \mid P_i(\widetilde{x}, \widetilde{y}_1, \ldots, \widetilde{y}_{m_i})\}$$
$$\rightarrow \delta^![F_i(\widetilde{x}, \widetilde{y}_1, \ldots, \widetilde{y}_{m_i})]$$

Here, δ denotes $\mathsf{d}\langle n; (P_1, F_1), \ldots, (P_k, F_k)\rangle$, $\widetilde{x} = x_1, \ldots, x_{\ell_i}$, and $\widetilde{y}_i = y_{i,1}, \ldots, y_{i,n}$. Thus, the arity of the predicate P_i and the function F_i is $\ell_i + m_i n$, and F_i returns an n-tuple of integers. Recall that the part $\delta^![F_i(\widetilde{x}, \widetilde{y}_1, \ldots, \widetilde{y}_{m_i})]$ should be considered an abbreviated form of $\{\delta[z_1, \ldots, z_n] \mid (z_1, \ldots, z_n) = F_i(\widetilde{x}, \widetilde{y}_1, \ldots, \widetilde{y}_{m_i})\}$. Note that P_i and F_i take only integers as their arguments; thus information about recursive data structures is abstracted to integers by the type system.

For example, ilistL in Sect. 1 is expressed as

$$\mathsf{ilist}\langle 1; (\lambda().\mathsf{true}, \lambda().0), (\lambda(x, y).\mathsf{true}, \lambda(x, y).y + 1)\rangle,$$

and the constructors Nil and Cons are given the following types:

$$\mathsf{Nil} : () \rightarrow \mathsf{ilistL}^![0]$$
$$\mathsf{Cons} : (\mathsf{int}[x], \mathsf{ilistL}[y]) \rightarrow \mathsf{ilistL}^![y + 1].$$

Note that the argument type of Cons is

$$\{(\mathsf{int}[x], \mathsf{ilistL}[y]) \mid (\lambda(x, y).\mathsf{true})(x, y)\} \equiv \{(\mathsf{int}[x], \mathsf{ilistL}[y]) \mid \mathsf{true}\},$$

which has been abbreviated to $(\mathsf{int}[x], \mathsf{ilistL}[y])$.

As another example, recall ilistS in Sect. 1. It is expressed as:

$$\mathsf{ilist}\langle 2; (\lambda().\mathsf{true}, \lambda().(0, 0)),$$
$$(\lambda(x, y_1, y_2).(y_1 > 0 \Rightarrow x \leq y_2), \lambda(x, y_1, y_2).(1, x))\rangle,$$

and the constructors are given the following types:

$$\mathsf{Nil} : () \rightarrow \mathsf{ilistS}^![0, 0]$$
$$\mathsf{Cons} : \{(\mathsf{int}[x], \mathsf{ilistS}[y_1, y_2]) \mid y_1 > 0 \Rightarrow x \leq y_2\} \rightarrow \mathsf{ilistS}^![1, x].$$

Remark 1. If we are interested in proving that a sorting function takes an integer list as an argument and returns a sorted list that is a *permutation* of the argument, we need to parameterize the list type also with information about the elements of a list. One way to do so would be to introduce the type ilistP$[y_1, y_2, y_3]$ of a list of length y_1 that contains y_3 occurrences of the element y_2, and the type ilistSP$[y_1, y_2, y_3, y_4]$ of a sorted list (of type ilistS$[y_1, y_2]$) containing y_4 occurrences of the element y_3. Then the type of a sorting function can be expressed as: $\{\text{ilistP}[y_1, y_2, y_3] \mid \text{true}\} \to \{\text{ilistSP}[y_1, z, y_2, y_3] \mid \text{true}\}$. □

3.2 Typing

We define the type judgment relations $\mathcal{C}; \Gamma; \varphi \vdash e : \tau$ and $\mathcal{C} \vdash D : \Gamma$ for expressions and programs by the typing rules in Fig. 3. Here, $\mathcal{C}$ is a constructor type environment as before, and Γ maps each variable (including a function name) to its type. The type bindings on integer types and datatypes are restricted to the form $x : \{\beta \mid \text{true}\}$, so we just write $x : \beta$. The conditions on variables of integer types and datatypes are instead accumulated in the part φ of the type environment. Type bindings on integer types are further restricted to $x : \text{int}[x]$; hence we sometimes just write $x : \text{int}$. In a type judgment $\mathcal{C}; \Gamma; \varphi \vdash e : \tau$, we implicitly require that all the types are well-formed; for example, φ and τ may contain only integer variables occurring in Γ (including those in the part β) as free variables. The definition of well-formedness is given in the longer version of this paper [13].

The type judgment $\mathcal{C}; \Gamma; \varphi \vdash e : \tau$ intuitively means that if each free variable in e has type $\Gamma(x)$ and satisfies the condition described by φ, then e is safely executed (without reaching fail), and either e diverges or evaluates to a value of type τ. In Fig. 3, $\models \varphi$ means that the formula φ is a valid formula of integer arithmetic.

We explain some key rules. The typing rules for expressions are fairly standard, except T-DC and T-SUB for datatypes. In T-APP, we require that the β-part of the argument types matches between the function and actual arguments. The condition $\models \varphi \wedge (\bigwedge_{i=1}^{l_k} \varphi_i) \Rightarrow \varphi'$ requires that the condition φ' required by the function is met by the actual arguments. In rule T-FAIL, the condition $\models \neg\varphi$ ensures that there exists no environment that makes φ hold, so that fail is unreachable. In T-IF, the branching condition is accumulated in the conditions for the then- and else-branches. In T-LET, the condition φ_1 on the value of e_1 is accumulated in the condition for e_2.

In rule T-DC, the third and fourth conditions require that the arguments of the constructor L_i has an appropriate type, and the fifth condition requires that they also satisfy the precondition P_i. The last premise ensures the post condition (represented by the function F_i) of the data constructor implies the condition φ' on the constructed data. Note that the "δ-part" may be locally chosen in the rule (thus, the constructor L_i is polymorphic on $\langle n; (P_1, F_1), \ldots, (P_k, F_k) \rangle$, and that part may be instantiated for each occurrence of the constructor), but that the same δ must be used among $L_i(s_1, \ldots, s_{\ell_i + m_i})$ and the components $s_{\ell_i + 1}, \ldots, s_{\ell_i + m_i}$.

$$\frac{\Gamma(x) = \beta \qquad \models \varphi \Rightarrow \varphi'}{\mathcal{C}; \Gamma; \varphi \vdash x : \{\beta \mid \varphi'\}} \qquad \text{(T-VAR)}$$

$$\frac{\mathcal{C}; \mathtt{ST}(\Gamma) \vdash_{\mathtt{ST}} s : \mathtt{int}}{\mathcal{C}; \Gamma; \varphi \vdash s : \{\mathtt{int}[x] \mid x = s\}} \qquad \text{(T-INT)}$$

$$\frac{\begin{array}{c} \Gamma(f) = \{(\beta_1, \ldots, \beta_k) \mid \varphi'\} \rightarrow \{\beta \mid \varphi_r\} \\ \mathcal{C}; \Gamma; \varphi \vdash s_i : \{\beta_i \mid \varphi_i\} \text{ for each } i \in \{1, \ldots, k\} \\ \models \varphi \wedge (\bigwedge_{i=1}^{k} \varphi_i) \Rightarrow \varphi' \\ \models \varphi \wedge (\bigwedge_{i=1}^{k} \varphi_i) \wedge \varphi_r \Rightarrow \varphi'_r \end{array}}{\mathcal{C}; \Gamma; \varphi \vdash f(s_1, \ldots, s_k) : \{\beta \mid \varphi'_r\}} \qquad \text{(T-APP)}$$

$$\frac{\models \neg\varphi}{\mathcal{C}; \Gamma; \varphi \vdash \mathtt{fail} : \mathtt{int}} \qquad \text{(T-FAIL)}$$

$$\frac{\mathcal{C}; \Gamma; \varphi \vdash s : \mathtt{int} \qquad \mathcal{C}; \Gamma; \varphi \wedge s \neq 0 \vdash e_1 : \tau \qquad \mathcal{C}; \Gamma; \varphi \wedge s = 0 \vdash e_2 : \tau}{\mathcal{C}; \Gamma; \varphi \vdash \mathtt{if} \; s \; \mathtt{then} \; e_1 \; \mathtt{else} \; e_2 : \tau} \qquad \text{(T-IF)}$$

$$\frac{\mathcal{C}; \Gamma; \varphi \vdash e_1 : \{\beta \mid \varphi_1\} \qquad \mathcal{C}; \Gamma, x : \beta; \varphi \wedge \varphi_1 \vdash e_2 : \tau}{\mathcal{C}; \Gamma; \varphi \vdash \mathtt{let} \; x = e_1 \; \mathtt{in} \; e_2 : \tau} \qquad \text{(T-LET)}$$

$$\frac{\begin{array}{c} \mathcal{C}_{\mathtt{d}} = \{L_1 : (\mathtt{int}^{\ell_1}, \mathtt{d}^{m_1}) \rightarrow \mathtt{d}, \ldots, L_k : (\mathtt{int}^{\ell_k}, \mathtt{d}^{m_k}) \rightarrow \mathtt{d}\} \\ \delta = \mathtt{d}\langle n; (P_1, F_1), \ldots, (P_k, F_k) \rangle \\ \mathcal{C}; \Gamma; \varphi \vdash s_j : \{\mathtt{int}[x_j] \mid \varphi_j\} \text{ for each } j \in \{1, \ldots, \ell_i\} \\ \mathcal{C}; \Gamma; \varphi \vdash s_{\ell_i + j} : \{\delta[\widetilde{y}_j] \mid \varphi_{\ell_i + j}\} \text{ for each } j \in \{1, \ldots, m_i\} \\ \models \varphi \wedge (\bigwedge_{j=1}^{\ell_i + m_i} \varphi_j) \Rightarrow P_i(x_1, \ldots, x_{\ell_i}, \widetilde{y}_1, \ldots, \widetilde{y}_{m_i}) \\ \models \varphi \wedge (\bigwedge_{j=1}^{\ell_i + m_i} \varphi_j) \wedge (\widetilde{y}) = F_i(x_1, \ldots, x_{\ell_i}, \widetilde{y}_1, \ldots, \widetilde{y}_{m_i}) \Rightarrow \varphi' \end{array}}{\mathcal{C}; \Gamma; \varphi \vdash L_i(s_1, \ldots, s_{\ell_i + m_i}) : \{\delta[\widetilde{y}] \mid \varphi'\}} \qquad \text{(T-DC)}$$

$$\frac{\begin{array}{c} \mathcal{C}_{\mathtt{d}} = \{L_1 : (\mathtt{int}^{\ell_1}, \mathtt{d}^{m_1}) \rightarrow \mathtt{d}, \ldots, L_k : (\mathtt{int}^{\ell_k}, \mathtt{d}^{m_k}) \rightarrow \mathtt{d}\} \\ \delta = \mathtt{d}\langle n; (P_1, F_1), \ldots, (P_k, F_k) \rangle \\ \mathcal{C}; \Gamma; \varphi \vdash s : \{\delta[\widetilde{y}] \mid \varphi_0\} \\ \Gamma'_i = \Gamma, x_1 : \mathtt{int}[x_1], \ldots, x_{\ell_i} : \mathtt{int}[x_{\ell_i}], x_{\ell_i + 1} : \delta[\widetilde{y}_1], \ldots, x_{\ell_i + m_i} : \delta[\widetilde{y}_{m_i}] \\ \varphi'_i = \varphi \wedge P_i(x_1, \ldots, x_{\ell_i}, \widetilde{y}_1, \ldots, \widetilde{y}_{m_i}) \wedge [F_i(x_1, \ldots, x_{\ell_i}, \widetilde{y}_1, \ldots, \widetilde{y}_{m_i})/\widetilde{y}]\varphi_0 \\ \mathcal{C}; \Gamma'_i; \varphi'_i \vdash e_i : \tau \text{ for each } i \in \{1, \ldots, k\} \end{array}}{\mathcal{C}; \Gamma; \varphi \vdash \mathtt{match} \; s \; \mathtt{with} \; \{L_1(\widetilde{x}_1) \rightarrow e_1, \ldots, L_k(\widetilde{x}_k) \rightarrow e_k\} : \tau} \qquad \text{(T-MATCH)}$$

$$\frac{\mathcal{C}; \Gamma; \varphi \vdash e : \{\beta \mid \varphi_1\} \qquad \models \varphi \wedge \varphi_1 \Rightarrow \varphi_2}{\mathcal{C}; \Gamma; \varphi \vdash e : \{\beta \mid \varphi_2\}} \qquad \text{(T-SUB)}$$

$$\frac{\begin{array}{c} \Gamma = (f_1 : \{(\widetilde{\beta}_1) \mid \varphi_1\} \rightarrow \{\beta'_1 \mid \varphi'_1\}, \ldots, f_k : \{(\widetilde{\beta}_k) \mid \varphi_k\} \rightarrow \{\beta'_k \mid \varphi'_k\}) \\ \mathcal{C}; \Gamma, \widetilde{x}_i : \widetilde{\beta}_i; \varphi_i \vdash e_i : \{\beta'_i \mid \varphi'_i\} \text{ for each } i \in \{1, \ldots, k\} \end{array}}{\mathcal{C} \vdash \{f_1(\widetilde{x}_1) = e_1, \ldots, f_k(\widetilde{x}_k) = e_k\} : \Gamma} \qquad \text{(T-PROG)}$$

Fig. 3. Refinement Type System

In rule T-MATCH, the type environment Γ'_i for the subexpression e_i is obtained from Γ by adding type bindings for the variables $\widetilde{x}_i$ (see the fourth line of the premises). The condition φ'_i (defined on the fifth line) is obtained by strengthening the condition φ with information that s matches $L_i(\widetilde{x}_i)$. Note that as in rule T-DC, the "δ-part" is shared among s and decomposed elements (bound to) $x_{\ell_i+1}, \ldots, x_{\ell_i+m_i}$. The rule T-SUB is for subsumption. We allow only the refinement condition to be weakened; for datatypes, the β-part (of the form $d\langle n; (P_1, F_1), \ldots, (P_k, F_k) \rangle [\tilde{y}])$ is fixed.

Example 4. Let us recall the program D_1 defined in Example 1. It is typed as $C \vdash D_1 : \Gamma_0$, where Γ_0 consists of:

$$\text{range}: \text{int}[n] \to \text{ilistL}^!{[n]},$$
$$\text{len}: \text{ilistL}[n] \to \text{int}^!{[n]},$$
$$\text{main}: \text{int}[n] \to \{\text{int}[x] \mid \text{true}\}.$$

Below we focus on the definition of the function **range**, and show how to derive $C; \Gamma_1; \text{true} \vdash \text{if } n \text{ then } e_2 \text{ else } \text{Nil}() : \text{ilistL}^!{[n]}$ (which is required for deriving $C \vdash D_1 : \Gamma_0$), where

$$\Gamma_1 = (\Gamma_0, n : \text{int})$$
$$e_2 = (\text{let } r = \text{range}(n-1) \text{ in } \text{Cons}(n, r))$$
$$\text{ilistL} = \text{ilist}\langle 1; (\lambda().\text{true}, \lambda().0), (\lambda(x, y).\text{true}, \lambda(x, y).y + 1)\rangle.$$

First, the type of $\text{range}(n-1)$ in the body is derived as follows.

$$\frac{\begin{array}{c} \Gamma_1(\text{range}) = \{\text{int}[m] \mid \text{true}\} \to \{\text{ilistL}[y] \mid y = m\} \\ C; \Gamma_1; n \neq 0 \vdash n - 1 : \{\text{int}[m] \mid m = n - 1\} \\ \models m = n - 1 \Rightarrow \text{true} \\ \models m = n - 1 \wedge y = m \Rightarrow y = n - 1 \end{array}}{C; \Gamma_1; n \neq 0 \vdash \text{range}(n-1) : \{\text{ilistL}[y] \mid y = n - 1\}.} \text{ (T-APP)}$$

Second, the expression $\text{Cons}(n, r)$ is typed as:

$$\frac{\begin{array}{c} C; \Gamma_2; \varphi_2 \vdash n : \{\text{int}[x_1] \mid \text{true}\} \\ C; \Gamma_2; \varphi_2 \vdash r : \{\text{ilistL}[y_1] \mid y_1 = n - 1\} \\ \models \varphi_2 \Rightarrow (\lambda(x, y).\text{true})(x_1, y_1) \\ \models \varphi_2 \wedge y_1 = n - 1 \wedge z = (\lambda(x, y).y + 1)(x_1, y_1) \Rightarrow z = n \end{array}}{C; \Gamma_2; \varphi_2 \vdash \text{Cons}(n, r) : \{\text{ilistL}[z] \mid z = n\},} \text{ (T-DC)}$$

where $\Gamma_2 = (\Gamma_1, r : \text{ilistL}[q])$ and $\varphi_2 = (n \neq 0 \wedge q = n - 1)$. Finally, using the judgments above, we obtain:

$$\frac{\begin{array}{cc} \begin{array}{c} C; \Gamma_1; n \neq 0 \vdash \text{range}(n-1) : \text{ilistL}^!{[n-1]} \\ C; \Gamma_2; \varphi_2 \vdash \text{Cons}(n, r) : \text{ilistL}^!{[n]} \\ \hline C; \Gamma_1; n \neq 0 \vdash e_2 : \text{ilistL}^!{[n]} \end{array} & \begin{array}{c} \models n = 0 \Rightarrow (\lambda().\text{true})() \\ \models n = 0 \wedge y = (\lambda().0)() \Rightarrow y = n \\ \hline C; \Gamma_1; n = 0 \vdash \text{Nil}() : \text{ilistL}^!{[n]} \end{array} \end{array}}{C; \Gamma_1; \text{true} \vdash \text{if } n \text{ then } e_2 \text{ else } \text{Nil}() : \text{ilistL}^!{[n]}.}$$

$\square$

Our type system can also deal with properties on trees, as demonstrated in the following example.

Example 5. Recall the program D_3 given in Example 3. It is typed as $\mathcal{C} \vdash D_3 : \Gamma_0$, where Γ_0 is:

$$\Gamma_0 = \{\texttt{gen\_tree}: \texttt{int}[n] \to \texttt{itreeZ}^!\![n],$$
$$\texttt{size}: \texttt{itreeZ}[n] \to \texttt{int}^!\![n],$$
$$\texttt{main}: \texttt{int}[n] \to \{\texttt{int}[x] \mid \texttt{true}\}\}.$$

Here, $\texttt{itreeZ} = \texttt{itree}\langle 1; (\lambda().\texttt{true}, \lambda().0), (\lambda(x,y_1,y_2).\texttt{true}, \lambda(x,y_1,y_2).y_1 + y_2 + 1)\rangle$. Intuitively, $\texttt{itreeZ}[n]$ is the type of trees with n nodes. The expression $\texttt{Node}(*, \ell, r)$ in the definition of the function $\texttt{gen\_tree}$ is typed by:

$$\frac{\begin{array}{c}\mathcal{C}; \Gamma_1; \varphi_1 \vdash * : \{\texttt{int}[x_1] \mid \texttt{true}\} \\ \mathcal{C}; \Gamma_1; \varphi_1 \vdash \ell : \{\texttt{itreeZ}[y_1] \mid y_1 = m\} \\ \mathcal{C}; \Gamma_1; \varphi_1 \vdash r : \{\texttt{itreeZ}[y_2] \mid y_2 = n - 1 - m\} \\ \models \varphi_1 \Rightarrow (\lambda(x,y_1,y_2).\texttt{true})(x_1,y_1,y_2) \\ \models \varphi_1 \wedge y_1 = m \wedge y_2 = n - 1 - m \wedge z = y_1 + y_2 + 1 \Rightarrow z = n\end{array}}{\mathcal{C}; \Gamma_1; \varphi_1 \vdash \texttt{Node}(*, \ell, r) : \{\texttt{itreeZ}[z] \mid z = n\},} \text{(T-DC)}$$

where

$$\Gamma_1 = (\Gamma_0, n : \texttt{int}, m : \texttt{int}, \ell : \texttt{itreeZ}[m], r : \texttt{itreeZ}[n - 1 - m])$$
$$\varphi_1 = (n \neq 0).$$

The last premise $(\models \varphi_1 \wedge y_1 = m \wedge y_2 = n - 1 - m \wedge z = y_1 + y_2 + 1 \Rightarrow z = n)$ uses the function $\lambda(x,y_1,y_2).y_1 + y_2 + 1$ in $\texttt{itreeZ}$ to obtain an accumulated value for the tree size.

The $\texttt{match}$ expression in function $\texttt{size}$ is typed by:

$$\frac{\dfrac{\mathcal{C}; \Gamma_2; \varphi_1' \vdash 0 : \texttt{int}^!\![0]}{\mathcal{C}; \Gamma_2; \varphi_1' \vdash 0 : \texttt{int}^!\![n]} \text{(T-Sub)} \qquad \dfrac{\mathcal{C}; \Gamma_2'; \varphi_2' \vdash e_3 : \texttt{int}^!\![1 + y_1 + y_2]}{\mathcal{C}; \Gamma_2'; \varphi_2' \vdash e_3 : \texttt{int}^!\![n]} \text{(T-Sub)}}{\mathcal{C}; \Gamma_2; \texttt{true} \vdash e_2 : \texttt{int}^!\![n],} \text{(T-Match)}$$

where

$$\Gamma_2 = (\Gamma_0, t : \texttt{itreeZ}[n])$$
$$\Gamma_2' = (\Gamma_2, \_ : \texttt{int}, \ell : \texttt{itreeZ}[y_1], r : \texttt{itreeZ}[y_2])$$
$$e_2 = (\texttt{match } t \texttt{ with } \{\texttt{Leaf}() \to 0, \texttt{Node}(\_, \ell, r) \to e_3\})$$
$$e_3 = 1 + \texttt{size}(\ell) + \texttt{size}(r)$$
$$\varphi_1' = (n = 0)$$
$$\varphi_2' = (n = 1 + y_1 + y_2).$$

□

Remark 2. It is sometimes too restrictive to fix the β-part in rule T-SUB. For example, the function `isort` of the program D_2 (defined in Example 2) is equivalent to the function `isort'` defined below, which is obtained by substituting `Nil()` in the match body of D_2 with l.

$$\texttt{isort}'(l) = \texttt{match } l \texttt{ with } \{$$
$$\texttt{Nil()} \rightarrow l, \ \texttt{Cons}(n, l') \rightarrow \texttt{insert}(n, \texttt{isort}'(l'))$$
$$\}.$$

However, since l is returned directly, the argument and return types of `isort'` share the same β-part. Therefore, our type system cannot express that `isort'` converts an unsorted list to a sorted one. To relax the restriction, we need a more sophisticated version of the subtyping rule T-SUB, which would cause too much burden for the type inference procedure discussed in the next section. It is left for future work to overcome the problem above without incurring too much overhead for type inference. $\square$

The following proposition states the soundness of the type system (recall the definition of safety in Sect. 2.3).

Proposition 1 (soundness). *Suppose $C \vdash D : \Gamma$, with $\Gamma(\texttt{main}) = \{(\beta_1, \ldots, \beta_k) \mid \texttt{true}\} \rightarrow \{\beta \mid \texttt{true}\}$. Then, the program D is safe.*

The proposition follows from the soundness of a standard refinement type system without parameterization $\langle n; (P_1, F_1), \ldots, (P_k, F_k) \rangle$, as follows. Because only constructors are polymorphic on the part $\langle n; (P_1, F_1), \ldots, (P_k, F_k) \rangle$, if a program D is well-typed, then by annotating each occurrence of constructor L_i with the parameter $\langle n; (P_1, F_1), \ldots, (P_k, F_k) \rangle$, and treating the annotated constructor $L_i^{(\langle n; (P_1, F_1), \ldots, (P_k, F_k) \rangle)}$ as a new constructor, and the δ-part $\texttt{d} \langle n; (P_1, F_1), \ldots, (P_k, F_k) \rangle$ as the name of a new datatype, we can obtain a program D' that is well-typed without the parameterization. The safety of D' follows from the soundness of a standard refinement type system (without parameterization); hence D is also safe.

Note that the completeness does not hold: there exists a program that is safe but not typable in our refinement type system. Beside the issue discussed in Remark 2, the sources of incompleteness include the restriction of the parameters of data types to integers. For example, consider the property of the append function: "a function takes two lists and returns the list obtained by appending two lists." In theory, it is possible to encode all the information of a list by using Gödel encoding, but that is not possible in practice, where we have to restrict the underlying integer arithmetic, e.g., to linear integer arithmetic.

4 Inferring Parameterized Refinement Types

This section describes a type inference procedure, which takes a program (without type annotations) and a constructor type environment as input, and checks whether the program is well-typed. The overall flow of the type inference procedure is shown in Fig. 4.

In Step 1, we first determine the raw type of each expression, with the values of the part $[n; \widetilde{(P, F)}]$ kept unknown. For example, given the program D_2 in Example 2, we infer:

$$\texttt{gen}: \texttt{int} \rightarrow \texttt{ilist}[\rho_1], \texttt{isort}: \texttt{ilist}[\rho_1] \rightarrow \texttt{ilist}[\rho_2],$$

where ρ_1 and ρ_2 are variables representing the part $[n; \widetilde{(P, F)}]$. (Note that the same variable ρ_1 is assigned to the return type of gen and the argument type of isort, since the return value of gen is passed to isort.) This is performed by using an ordinary unification-based type inference algorithm.

In Step 2, the part n and $\widetilde{F}$ of each raw type variable ρ_i is chosen, while the predicates $\widetilde{P}$ are kept unknown. In Step 3, we prepare predicate variables for the unknown predicates in raw types and refinement predicates, and reduce the typability problem to the satisfiability problem for constrained Horn clauses (CHCs) [1]. We then invoke an off-the-shelf CHC solver [2,4,7] to check whether the obtained CHCs are satisfiable. If so, we can conclude that the program is well-typed (and outputs inferred types); otherwise, we go back to Step 2 and refine the F-part of raw types, with an increased value of n.

In the rest of this section, we explain more details of Steps 2 and 3.

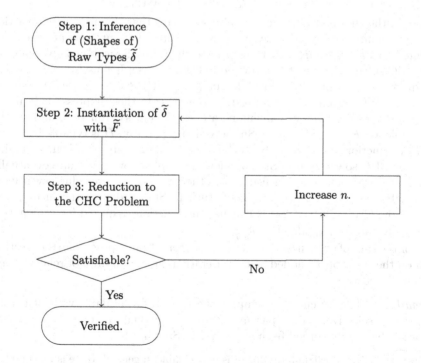

Fig. 4. The flow of type inference

4.1   Step 2: Instantiation of Raw Types with $\widetilde{F}$

In Step 2, we determine the components n and $\widetilde{F}$ of δ.

For the sake of simplicity, the number of integer parameters n is shared by all types, and the functions $\widetilde{F}$ do not depend on δ but on d. On the other hand, the predicate variables $\widetilde{P}$ are specific to δ. Thus, we explicitly write $\delta = \mathsf{d}\langle n; (P_{\delta,1}, F_{\mathsf{d},1}), \ldots, (P_{\delta,k}, F_{\mathsf{d},k})\rangle$ here.

We choose n and $F_{\mathsf{d},j}$ as follows, to ensure that the precision of type inference is monotonically improved at each iteration. Suppose $\mathcal{C}_{\mathsf{d}} = \{L_1 : (\mathtt{int}^{\ell_1}, \mathtt{d}^{m_1}) \rightarrow \mathsf{d}, \ldots, L_k : (\mathtt{int}^{\ell_k}, \mathtt{d}^{m_k}) \rightarrow \mathsf{d}\}$. Let us write $n^{(i)}$ and $F_{\mathsf{d},j}^{(i)}$ for the values of n and $F_{\mathsf{d},j}$ at the i-th iteration of the refinement loop in Fig. 4. At the $(i+1)$-th iteration, we pick $n' > 0$ and a tuple of functions $(F_1', \ldots, F_k')$ with $F_j' \in \mathtt{int}^{\ell_j + m_j n'} \rightarrow \mathtt{int}^{n'}$ (that has not been chosen before) and set $n^{(i+1)}$ and $F_{\mathsf{d},j}^{(i+1)}$ as follows.

$$n^{(i+1)} := n^{(i)} + n'$$

$$F_{\mathsf{d},j}^{(i+1)} := \lambda(\widetilde{x}, \widetilde{y}_1, \ldots, \widetilde{y}_{m_j}).(F^{(i)}(\widetilde{x}, \widetilde{y}_1', \ldots, \widetilde{y}_{m_j}'), F_j'(\widetilde{x}, \widetilde{y}_1'', \ldots, \widetilde{y}_{m_j}'')).$$

Here, $\widetilde{x}$ and $\widetilde{y}_j$ are sequences of variables of length ℓ_k and $n^{(i+1)}$ respectively, and $\widetilde{y}_j = \widetilde{y}_j', \widetilde{y}_j''$ with $|\widetilde{y}_j'| = n^{(i)}$ and $|\widetilde{y}_i''| = n'$. For example, if $n^{(i)} = 1$ and $F_j^{(i)}(x, y_1, y_2) = x + y_1 + y_2$ with $n' = 1$ and $F_j'(x, y_1, y_2) = 1 + \max(y_1, y_2)$, then $F_j^{(i+1)}(x, y_{11}, y_{12}, y_{21}, y_{22}) = (x + y_{11} + y_{21}, 1 + \max(y_{12}, y_{22}))$.

Since the choice of $n^{(i)}$ and $F_{\mathsf{d},j}^{(i)}$ above ensures that the information carried by types monotonically increases, we can guarantee that our type inference procedure is *relatively complete* with respect to the (hypothetical[3]) completeness of the CHC solver used in Step 3, in the following sense. Let us assume that the language for describing functions of type $\bigcup_{j=1}^{\omega} \mathtt{int}^{l_i + m_i j} \rightarrow \mathtt{int}^j$ is recursively enumerable; for example, we can restrict functions to those expressible in linear integer arithmetic. Then we can enumerate all the tuples of functions and use the i-th tuple as $(F_1', \ldots, F_k')$ above. Suppose that a program D is typable by using, as $F_{\mathsf{d},j}$, functions belonging to the language assumed above. Then, assuming that the CHC solver used in Step 3 below is complete, our procedure eventually terminates and outputs "Verified". (In other words, our procedure eventually terminates output "Verified", or gets stuck in Step 3 due to the incompleteness of the CHC solver.) This is because the functions required for typing D is eventually chosen and added to $F_{\mathsf{d},j}^{(i)}$.

For the sake of efficiency, the actual implementation imposes a further restriction on the function F_j' added at each iteration, at the sacrifice of relative completeness; see Sect. 5.1.

Remark 3. While we currently employ the same n for all data types, it can be effective to selectively add a parameter to an individual raw type, based on the unsatisfiable core returned from the solver in Step 3.

---

[3] Since the CHC satisfiability problem is undecidable in general, there is no complete CHC solver.

4.2   Step 3: Reduction to CHC Solving

In this step, we prepare predicate variables for the P-part of raw types and unknown refinement predicates φ, and construct a template of a type derivation tree. We then extract constraints on the predicate variables based on the typing rules. The extracted constraints consists of *constrained Horn clauses* (CHCs), of the following form:

$$\forall \widetilde{x}.(H \Leftarrow B_1 \wedge \cdots \wedge B_k),$$

where B_i and H are atomic constraints of the form $p(s_1, \ldots, s_\ell)$ or integer constraints ($s_1 \leq s_2$, $s_1 = s_2, \ldots$). The program is well-typed (with the choice of n and $\widetilde{F}$ in the previous step), just if the CHCs are satisfiable, i.e., if there exists an assignment of predicates to predicate variables that make all the clauses valid. The latter problem (of CHC satisfiability) is undecidable in general, but there are various efficient solvers that work well for many inputs [2,4,7].

Since the reduction from refinement type inference to the CHC satisfiability problem is fairly standard (see, e.g., [2,18]), we sketch the reduction only informally, through an example.

Example 6. Let us recall the program D_1 in Example 1, and focus on the function range. When $n = 1$, we need to derive $\mathcal{C}; \Gamma_1; p_1(h) \vdash \texttt{if } h \texttt{ then } e_2 \texttt{ else Nil}() : \tau_0$ (which is required in T-PROG for proving $\mathcal{C} \vdash D_1 : \Gamma_0$), where

- $\Gamma_0 = (\texttt{range} : \{\texttt{int}[h] \mid p_1(h)\} \rightarrow \{\texttt{ilistL}[i] \mid p_2(h, i)\}, \ldots)$,
- $\Gamma_1 = (\Gamma_0, h : \texttt{int})$,
- $e_2 = (\texttt{let } r = \texttt{range}(h - 1) \texttt{ in Cons}(h, r))$,
- $\tau_0 = \{\texttt{ilist}_1[i] \mid p_2(h, i)\}$, and
- $\texttt{ilist}_1 := \texttt{ilist}\langle 1; (p_3, \lambda().0), (p_4, \lambda(x, y).y + 1)\rangle$.

The derivation for the judgment is of the form:

$$
\frac{
\begin{array}{cc}
\vdots & \\
\dfrac{\mathcal{C}; \Gamma_1; p_1(h) \wedge h \neq 0 \vdash \texttt{range}(h-1) : \tau_3}{\mathcal{C}; \Gamma_1, r : \tau_3; \varphi_2 \vdash \texttt{Cons}(h, r) : \tau_0} & \models p_1(h) \wedge h = 0 \Rightarrow p_3() \\
& \models p_1(h) \wedge h = 0 \wedge i = 0 \Rightarrow p_2(h, i) \\
\mathcal{C}; \Gamma_1; p_1(h) \wedge h \neq 0 \vdash e_2 : \tau_0 & \mathcal{C}; \Gamma_1; p_1(h) \wedge h = 0 \vdash \texttt{Nil}() : \tau_0
\end{array}
}{\mathcal{C}; \Gamma_1; p_1(h) \vdash \texttt{if } h \texttt{ then } e_2 \texttt{ else Nil}() : \tau_0.}
$$

where $\varphi_2 = (p_1(h) \wedge h \neq 0 \wedge p_5(h, j))$ and $\tau_3 = \{\texttt{ilistL}[j] \mid p_5(h, j)\}$. From the side conditions of the subderivation on the righthand side, the following CHCs are obtained:

$$p_3() \Leftarrow p_1(h) \wedge h = 0,$$
$$p_2(h, i) \Leftarrow p_1(h) \wedge h = 0 \wedge i = 0.$$

CHCs are also obtained from the other subderivation in a similar manner.   □

5   Implementation and Experiments

This section reports an implementation and experimental results.

5.1   Implementation

We have implemented a prototype program verifier for a subset of OCaml, which supports first-order functions, integers, and recursive data structures, based on the type inference procedure described above. As the backend CHC solvers, we employed multiple solvers: Z3 [12] ver. 4.8.12, HoIce [2] ver. 1.9.0, and Eldarica [4] ver. 2.0.7; that is because these solvers have pros and cons, and their running times vary depending on problem instances, as we report in Sect. 5.2.

As for the function F' in Sect. 4.1, the current implementation supports only the following functions $f_{i,\diamond} \in \mathtt{int}^{\ell_k + m_k} \to \mathtt{int}$ with $i \in \{1, 2, 3\}$ and $\diamond \in \{+, \max, \min\}$ (where n' in Sect. 4.1 is set to 1).

$$f_{1,\diamond}(x_1, \ldots, x_{\ell_k}, y_1, \ldots, y_{m_k}) = \begin{cases} 1 + (y_1 \diamond \cdots \diamond y_{m_k}) & \text{if } m_k > 0 \\ 0 & \text{otherwise} \end{cases}$$

$$f_{2,\diamond}(x_1, \ldots, x_{\ell_k}, y_1, \ldots, y_{m_k}) = x_1 \diamond \cdots \diamond x_{\ell_k} \diamond y_1 \diamond \cdots \diamond y_{m_k}$$

$$f_{3,\diamond}(x_1, \ldots, x_{\ell_k}, y_1, \ldots, y_{m_k}) = x_1 \diamond \cdots \diamond x_{\ell_k},$$

and chooses $f_{1,+}, f_{2,+}, f_{3,+}, f_{1,\max}, f_{2,\max}, f_{3,\max}, f_{1,\min}, f_{2,\min}, f_{3,\min}$ in this order, at each iteration. (Here, max and min are operations over integers extended with $-\infty$ and ∞.) In the case of lists, $f_{1,+}$, $f_{2,+}$, $f_{3,+}$, $f_{2,\max}$, and $f_{2,\min}$ can be used for computing the length, the sum of elements, the head element, the maximal element, and the minimal element of a list, respectively; since $f_{1,\max}$ and $f_{1,\min}$ coincide with $f_{1,+}$ for lists, it will be excluded out. Since the set of functions added as F' is finite, the current implementation obviously does not satisfy the relative completeness discussed in Sect. 4.1. Supporting more functions is not difficult in theory, but because the current implementation seemed to have already hit a certain limitation of the state-of-the-art CHC solvers (as reported in the next subsection), we plan to add more functions only after more efficient CHC solvers become available.

5.2   Experiments and Results

To evaluate the effectiveness of our approach, we have tested our prototype tool for several list/tree-processing programs. The experiments were conducted on a machine with Ubuntu 20.04.1 on Windows Subsystem for Linux 2, AMD Ryzen 7 3700X 8-Core Processor, and 16GB RAM.

Table 1. The experimental results

Program	#Lines	n	Time [s]	CHC solver	#clauses	#pvars
List-sum	17	2	2.25	HoICE	25	12
List-max	20	2	2.33	Z3	26	12
List-sorted	19	3	3.08	Z3	46	22
Range-basic	12	1	1.52	HoICE	16	8
Range-len (Ex. 1)	15	1	1.81	HoICE	25	12
Range-concat-len	21	1	2.61	HoICE	58	22
Isort-len	28	1	2.39	HoICE	66	27
Isort-is-sorted (Ex. 2)	30	3	4.32	Z3	79	33
Msort-len	45	—	—	—	145	49
Msort-is-sorted	52	—	—	—	161	54
Tree-size (Ex. 3)	15	1	1.95	HoICE	32	14
Tree-depth	21	1	2.07	HoICE	34	15
Bst-size	20	1	2.65	HoICE	64	28
Bst-sorted	51	—	—	—	148	74

Table 1 summarizes the experimental results. The benchmark set consists of the following programs.

- "list-sum" takes an integer m as an input, randomly generates a list so that the sum of elements is m, and then checks that the sum of elements is indeed m. Similarly, "list-max" generates a list so that the maximum element is m, and checks that the maximum element is indeed m, and "list-sorted" randomly generates a sorted list and checks that the list is indeed sorted.
- "range-X" generates a list $[m; m-1; \cdots ; 1]$ using the function range in Example 1, and checks its properties, where the property is "$n = 0$ if the generated list is null, and $m > 0$ otherwise" for X=basic, "the length is m" for X=len. The program "range-concat-len" calls gen(m) twice, concatenates the two lists, and check that the length of the resulting list is $2m$.
- "isort-X" takes an integer m as an input, generates a list of length m, sorts it with isort in Example 2, and checks properties of the resulting list, where the property is "the length of the list is m" for X=len, and "the list is sorted" for X=sorted.
- "msort-X" is a variation of "isort-X", where isort is replaced with a function for the merge sort.
- "tree-size" ("tree-depth", resp.) takes an integer m as an input, generates a tree of size (depth, resp.) m, and checks that the size (depth, resp.) of the tree is indeed m (for X=size).
- "bst-X" generates a binary search tree of a given size, and checks that the tree has the expected size (for X=size) or that the tree is a valid binary search tree (for X=sorted).

Appendix A shows some of the concrete programs used in the experiments.

In the table, the column "#Lines" shows the number of lines of the program (excluding empty and comment lines), and the column "n" shows the final value of n in Fig. 4, when the verification succeeded; the cell filled with "—" indicates a timeout (due to the backend CHC solver), where the time limit was set to 300 s. The columns "Time" and "CHC solver" show the running time and the backend CHC solver. Actually, we have run our tool for each of the three CHC solvers: Z3 [12] ver. 4.8.12, HoIce [2] ver. 1.9.0, and Eldarica [4] ver. 2.0.7, and the table shows only the best result. The result for other solvers are reported in Appendix A. The columns "#clauses" and "#pvars" show the numbers of output clauses and predicate variables, respectively (which do not depend on the value of n).

The results show that our tool works reasonably well: we are not aware of *fully automated* tools that can verify most of those programs. Our tool failed, however, to verify "msort-len", "msort-is-sorted", and "bst-sorted". To analyze the reason, we have manually prepared an optimal choice of functions $\widetilde{F}$ for those problems, and run the CHC solvers for the resulting CHC problems. None of the CHC solvers could solve the problems in time. This indicates that the main bottleneck in the current tool is not the choice of functions $\widetilde{F}$ discussed in Sects. 4.1 and 5.1, but rather the backend CHC solver. We expect that "msort-len", "msort-is-sorted", and "bst-sorted" can be automatically verified by our method if a more efficient CHC solver becomes available. It would be, however, important also to improve the heuristics for choosing n and $\widetilde{F}$, as briefly discussed in Remark 3.

6   Related Work

As already mentioned in Sect. 1, the idea of parameterizing recursive types with indices to represent various properties goes back at least to Xi and Pfenning's work on dependent ML [23,24]. In their system, however, explicit declarations of refinement types are required for data constructors and recursive functions. Kawaguchi et al. [5] introduced recursive refinement types, which allows a restricted form of parameterization of datatypes with predicates, and Vazou et al. [21] have introduced abstract refinement types, which are refinement types parameterized with predicates. Like Xi and Pfenning's system (and unlike ours), those systems also require explicit declarations of abstract refinement types for datatype constructors and/or functions, although refinement parameters in the code part can be omitted and automatically inferred (cf. [21], Sect. 3.4). The type system of Vazou et al. [21] supports polymorphism on predicates, unlike our type system.

The reduction from (ordinary) refinement types to the CHC satisfiability problem has been well studied [2,3,19]; we used that technique in Step 3 of our type inference procedure. The problem of inferring parameterized recursive refinement types appears to be related with that of inferring implicit parameters in refinement type systems [17,20]. In fact, Tondwalkar et al. [17] reduced the inference problem to the problem of solving existential CHCs, an extension of the CHC problem, and our problem of inferring P and F can also be reduced to that problem. We, however decided not to take that approach, because efficient solvers for existential CHCs are not available.[4] We instead designed a heuristic procedure to construct F, and reduced the rest of the inference problem to the satisfiability problem for ordinary CHCs.

There have been other (non-type-based) approaches to verification of programs manipulating recursive data structures. The series of work on TVLA [10, 11] targets programs with destructive updates, and infers the shape of data structures by using a 3-valued logic. Besides the difference in the target programs, to our knowledge, their analysis fixes predicates used for abstraction a priori (e.g., in [10], "instrumentation predicates" are specified by a user of the tool), whereas our tool fixes only the set of functions F_j's for mapping data structures to integers, and leaves it to the underlying CHC solver to find appropriate predicates. Thanks to the type-based approach, our approach can also be naturally extended to deal with higher-order programs.

7 Conclusion

We have introduced *parameterized recursive refinement types* (PRRT) that can express various properties of recursive data structures in a uniform manner, and proposed a type inference procedure for PRRT, to enable fully automatic verification of functional programs that use recursive data structures. We have implemented a prototype automated verification tool, and confirmed that the tool can automatically verify small but non-trivial programs. Future work includes an extension of the verification tool for a full-scale functional language, and a further refinement of the type inference procedure to improve the efficiency of the tool.

Acknowledgments. We would like to thank anonymous referees for useful comments. This work was supported by JSPS KAKENHI Grant Number JP20H05703.

Appendix

A   Details of Experiments

Table 2 presents the experimental results for each backend CHC solver. The columns "n" and "Time" for each solver have the same meaning as Sect. 5.2.

---

[4] The work of Tondwalkar et al. [17] does not suffer from this problem, since the existential CHCs obtained in their work is acyclic, while the existential CHCs generated from our inference problem would be cyclic.

Table 2. The results of verification with three solvers

Program	Z3		HoICE		Eldarica	
	n	Time [s]	n	Time [s]	n	Time [s]
List-sum	2	2.34	2	2.25	2	4.26
List-max	2	2.33	2	2.39	2	6.79
List-sorted	3	3.08	—	—	3	23.07
Range-basic	1	1.60	1	1.52	1	1.80
Range-len	—	—	1	1.81	1	2.92
Range-concat-len	—	—	1	2.61	—	—
Isort-len	—	—	1	2.39	—	—
Isort-is-sorted	3	4.32	—	—	—	—
Msort-len	—	—	—	—	—	—
Msort-is-sorted	—	—	—	—	—	—
Tree-size	—	—	1	1.95	1	8.73
Tree-depth	—	—	1	2.07	—	—
Bst-size	—	—	1	2.65	—	—
Bst-sorted	—	—	—	—	—	—

As examples of the benchmark programs, Listings 18.1 and 18.2 respectively show the programs named "list-sum" and "bst-size" in Sect. 5.2.

Listing 18.1. Program list-sum

```
type list = Nil | Cons of int * list

let rec gen n =
  if n = 0 then Nil
  else
    let x = Random.int (n + 1) in
    Cons(x, gen (n - x))

let rec sum xs =
  match xs with
  | Nil -> 0
  | Cons(x, xs) -> x + sum xs

let rec main n =
  if n >= 0 then
    let s = sum (gen n) in
    assert (s = n)
  else
    0
```

Listing 18.2. Program bst-size

```
type bst = Leaf | Node of int * bst * bst

let rec insert t x =
  match t with
    | Leaf             -> Node(x, Leaf, Leaf)
    | Node(y, l, r) ->
      if x < y then Node(y, insert l x, r)
      else Node(y, l, insert r x)

let rec gen n =
  if n = 0 then Leaf
  else insert (gen (n - 1)) (Random.int 10000)

let rec size t =
  match t with
    | Leaf             -> 0
    | Node(_, l, r) -> 1 + size l + size r

let rec main n =
  if n >= 0 then
    let g = size (gen n) in
    assert (g = n)
  else
    0
```

References

1. Bjørner, N., Gurfinkel, A., McMillan, K., Rybalchenko, A.: Horn clause solvers for program verification. In: Beklemishev, L.D., Blass, A., Dershowitz, N., Finkbeiner, B., Schulte, W. (eds.) Fields of Logic and Computation II. LNCS, vol. 9300, pp. 24–51. Springer, Cham (2015). https://doi.org/10.1007/978-3-319-23534-9_2
2. Champion, A., Chiba, T., Kobayashi, N., Sato, R.: ICE-based refinement type discovery for higher-order functional programs. J. Autom. Reason. **64**(7), 1393–1418 (2020). https://doi.org/10.1007/s10817-020-09571-y
3. Hashimoto, K., Unno, H.: Refinement type inference via horn constraint optimization. In: Blazy, S., Jensen, T. (eds.) SAS 2015. LNCS, vol. 9291, pp. 199–216. Springer, Heidelberg (2015). https://doi.org/10.1007/978-3-662-48288-9_12
4. Hojjat, H., Rümmer, P.: The ELDARICA horn solver. In: 2018 Formal Methods in Computer Aided Design (FMCAD), pp. 1–7 (2018)
5. Kawaguchi, M., Rondon, P.M., Jhala, R.: Type-based data structure verification. In: Hind, M., Diwan, A. (eds.) Proceedings of the 2009 ACM SIGPLAN Conference on Programming Language Design and Implementation, PLDI 2009, Dublin, Ireland, June 15–21, 2009, pp. 304–315. ACM (2009). https://doi.org/10.1145/1542476.1542510
6. Kobayashi, N., Sato, R., Unno, H.: Predicate abstraction and CEGAR for higher-order model checking. In: PLDI 2011, pp. 222–233. ACM Press (2011)

7. Komuravelli, A., Gurfinkel, A., Chaki, S.: SMT-based model checking for recursive programs. Formal Methods Syst. Design **48**(3), 175–205 (2016). https://doi.org/10.1007/s10703-016-0249-4

8. Kuwahara, T., Terauchi, T., Unno, H., Kobayashi, N.: Automatic termination verification for higher-order functional programs. In: Shao, Z. (ed.) ESOP 2014. LNCS, vol. 8410, pp. 392–411. Springer, Heidelberg (2014). https://doi.org/10.1007/978-3-642-54833-8_21

9. Lee, C.S., Jones, N.D., Ben-Amram, A.M.: The size-change principle for program termination. In: Hankin, C., Schmidt, D. (eds.) Conference Record of POPL 2001: The 28th ACM SIGPLAN-SIGACT Symposium on Principles of Programming Languages, London, UK, January 17–19, 2001, pp. 81–92. ACM (2001). https://doi.org/10.1145/360204.360210

10. Lev-Ami, T., Sagiv, M.: TVLA: a system for implementing static analyses. In: Palsberg, J. (ed.) SAS 2000. LNCS, vol. 1824, pp. 280–301. Springer, Heidelberg (2000). https://doi.org/10.1007/978-3-540-45099-3_15

11. Manevich, R., Yahav, E., Ramalingam, G., Sagiv, M.: Predicate abstraction and canonical abstraction for singly-linked lists. In: Cousot, R. (ed.) VMCAI 2005. LNCS, vol. 3385, pp. 181–198. Springer, Heidelberg (2005). https://doi.org/10.1007/978-3-540-30579-8_13

12. de Moura, L., Bjørner, N.: Z3: an efficient SMT solver. In: Ramakrishnan, C.R., Rehof, J. (eds.) TACAS 2008. LNCS, vol. 4963, pp. 337–340. Springer, Heidelberg (2008). https://doi.org/10.1007/978-3-540-78800-3_24

13. Mukai, R., Kobayashi, N., Sato, R.: Parameterized recursive refinement types for automated program verification (2022), a longer version of this paper, available from http://www.kb.is.s.u-tokyo.ac.jp/~koba/

14. Ong, C.H.L., Ramsay, S.: Verifying higher-order programs with pattern-matching algebraic data types. In: Proceedings of POPL, pp. 587–598. ACM Press (2011)

15. Rondon, P.M., Kawaguchi, M., Jhala, R.: Liquid types. In: PLDI 2008, pp. 159–169 (2008)

16. Sato, R., Unno, H., Kobayashi, N.: Towards a scalable software model checker for higher-order programs. In: Proceedings of PEPM 2013, pp. 53–62. ACM Press (2013)

17. Tondwalkar, A., Kolosick, M., Jhala, R.: Refinements of futures past: Higher-order specification with implicit refinement types. In: Møller, A., Sridharan, M. (eds.) 35th European Conference on Object-Oriented Programming, ECOOP 2021, July 11–17, 2021, Aarhus, Denmark (Virtual Conference). LIPIcs, vol. 194, pp. 18:1–18:29. Schloss Dagstuhl - Leibniz-Zentrum für Informatik (2021). https://doi.org/10.4230/LIPIcs.ECOOP.2021.18

18. Unno, H., Kobayashi, N.: On-Demand refinement of dependent types. In: Garrigue, J., Hermenegildo, M.V. (eds.) FLOPS 2008. LNCS, vol. 4989, pp. 81–96. Springer, Heidelberg (2008). https://doi.org/10.1007/978-3-540-78969-7_8

19. Unno, H., Kobayashi, N.: Dependent type inference with interpolants. In: Proceedings of the 11th International ACM SIGPLAN Conference on Principles and Practice of Declarative Programming, September 7–9, 2009, Coimbra, Portugal, pp. 277–288. ACM (2009)

20. Unno, H., Terauchi, T., Kobayashi, N.: Automating relatively complete verification of higher-order functional programs. In: The 40th Annual ACM SIGPLAN-SIGACT Symposium on Principles of Programming Languages, POPL 2013, pp. 75–86. ACM (2013)

21. Vazou, N., Rondon, P.M., Jhala, R.: Abstract refinement types. In: Felleisen, M., Gardner, P. (eds.) ESOP 2013. LNCS, vol. 7792, pp. 209–228. Springer, Heidelberg (2013). https://doi.org/10.1007/978-3-642-37036-6_13

22. Vazou, N., Seidel, E.L., Jhala, R., Vytiniotis, D., Jones, S.L.P.: Refinement types for haskell. In: Proceedings of the 19th ACM SIGPLAN international conference on Functional programming, Gothenburg, Sweden, September 1–3, 2014, pp. 269–282. ACM (2014)

23. Xi, H., Pfenning, F.: Eliminating array bound checking through dependent types. In: Davidson, J.W., Cooper, K.D., Berman, A.M. (eds.) Proceedings of the ACM SIGPLAN '98 Conference on Programming Language Design and Implementation (PLDI), Montreal, Canada, June 17–19, 1998, pp. 249–257. ACM (1998). https://doi.org/10.1145/277650.277732

24. Xi, H., Pfenning, F.: Dependent types in practical programming. In: Proceedings of POPL, pp. 214–227 (1999)

25. Zhu, H., Nori, A.V., Jagannathan, S.: Learning refinement types. In: Proceedings of ICFP 2015, pp. 400–411. ACM (2015). https://doi.org/10.1145/2784731.2784766

Adversarial Logic

Julien Vanegue[(✉)]

Bloomberg, New York, USA
jvanegue@bloomberg.net

Abstract. We introduce *Adversarial Logic*, an extension of Incorrectness Logic [1] with an explicit Dolev-Yao [2] adversary to statically analyze the severity of security vulnerabilities in the under-approximate setting. Adversarial logic is built on the ability to separate logical facts known to the adversary from facts solely known to the program under analysis. This flavor of program incorrectness can be used to analyze software in which error behavior occurs at deeper levels of interaction between the program and its environment, such as subtle cases of information disclosure requiring multiple program executions to be uncovered. We introduce the *Oscillating Bit Protocol*, an example algorithm where such a vulnerability can be detected using adversarial logic while remaining elusive to other frameworks. We define a flavor of symbolic execution in which the adversary guides the introduction of symbolic variables and the checking of attack assertions. Additionally, we introduce *equivalence testing*, an under-approximate version of program equivalence only proven on specific program paths and used to extract differences between comparable implementations. We provide a denotational semantics for adversarial logic and prove its soundness, thereby guaranteeing that extracted attack paths are true positives.

1 Introduction

The ever growing volume of software developed over the last several decades has led to a situation where software vendors and open source projects are unable to keep up with the sheer number of vulnerabilities found and disclosed by the community every year. In just the Linux kernel, a single testing tool [3] identified more than 3,000 bugs in two years, and thousands of others are regularly found in mainstream projects [4]. A crucial problem in the presence of such large numbers of bugs is to determine the practical security implications of each bug to inform which bugs must get fixed first.

Particularly dangerous software attacks attempt to elevate privileges [5] or steal secrets [6] using an adversarial program (or *exploit*) manually written by a security expert. Determining the potential for compromise of a vulnerable program is a time-consuming task of paramount importance, that has received surprisingly little attention from the formal verification community. This is especially critical as (a) known bugs are left unremediated for a long time, (b) security compromises are increasingly costly and (c) existing tools keep finding hundreds of new bugs every month.

G. Singh and C. Urban (Eds.): SAS 2022, LNCS 13790, pp. 422–448, 2022.
https://doi.org/10.1007/978-3-031-22308-2_19

This paper provides a logical foundation for *exploit programming* [7] dedicated to the static *exploitability* analysis of program bugs. Not all bugs are considered equal from an exploitability perspective: Can it be used to divert the program's control flow or corrupt data [8]? Does it allow information disclosure leading to password or private key compromise [6]? Does it allow untrusted code execution as root, or other remote user [5]? Elaborate exploits often require multiple stages of probing the target for reconnaissance [9] or leverage several weak bugs to build a complete attack. For example, an exploit may first attempt to guess internal program addresses using an information disclosure vulnerability to infer the location of sensitive data [10], and then use a subsequent array out of bound access to tamper with said data. Analyzing such bug chaining currently remains out of reach for existing program analysis frameworks.

Historically, program verification has focused on sound and over-approximate analysis guaranteeing the absence of entire classes of bugs in analyzed software [11,12] at the expense of false positives. To work around program analysis undecidability, recent trends are focusing on under-approximate and complete analyses in which findings are guaranteed to uncover real issues. Theoretical underpinning of bug finding now enjoys a foundational theory of incorrectness logic [1] (IL), a new logic focusing on uncovering true bugs rather than proving the absence of bugs. Fuzz testers [3,4] and other complete tools are indeed immediately actionable in the software development life-cycle of large software organizations, where the absence of false positives is critical to developer adoption. Incorrectness logic was recently extended to include heap reasoning [13] and concurrency checking [14] demonstrating its versatile nature. Adding an explicit attack program to reason about adversarial behaviors of incorrectness is a fundamentally under-approximate problem, and naturally extends IL.

We introduce adversarial logic (AL), a new under-approximate logic extending incorrectness logic (IL) to determine bug exploitability by leveraging accumulated error in software programs. Adversarial reasoning can be used as a theoretical basis to determine the existence of true attacks in buggy software. The resulting logic gives rise to a notion of *attack soundness* that captures sufficient conditions for an attack to be guaranteed satisfiable by an adversary. To prove soundness, it is sufficient to demonstrate that some execution paths of the program are exploitable. This differs from typical verification frameworks which attempt to prove statements about all possible program paths. We prove the main attack soundness result of this paper in Sect. 5. AL extends IL in the following ways:

- We consider the system under analysis to be a parallel composition of the analyzed program and an explicit adversarial program attempting to falsify the program specification.
- We focus on proving the satisfiability of an *attack contract* rather than following the usual methodology of checking code contracts in the program itself.
- We introduce adversarial preconditions, which allows for program errors to accumulate transitively. IL has no error preconditions and only error postconditions.

- We add channel communication rules to model that only explicitly shared program output is visible to an external adversary.
- We introduce a new *adversarial consequence* rule to derive additional adversarial knowledge otherwise remaining unobserved in program output.
- We generalize the backward variant rule of IL to the parallel case, so that AL can determine the existence of attacks in interactive protocol loops without unrolling the entire attack path.

The new adversarial consequence rule is of particular importance to the discovery of indirect information disclosure attacks, as AL can model leaking of internal program state without assuming its direct observability by the adversary.

It is worth noting that adversarial logic does not encode *root cause analysis* [15] as it does not attempt winding back to the source of bugs. Rather, it provides a framework to analyze *bug effects* by considering unintended computations as first-class primitives, allowing the transitive tracking of error conditions through the adversarial interpretation of the program.

The rest of the paper is organized as follow: we introduce a motivating example of an information disclosure attack in the *Oscillating Bit Protocol* in Sect. 2. We introduce the rules of Adversarial Logic in Sect. 3. We explore additional examples demonstrating the usage of AL in Sect. 4. Among these new examples is a technique to under-approximate program equivalence we call *equivalence testing*. We give the denotational semantics of AL and prove soundness of AL rules with respect to its semantics in Sect. 5. We briefly provide alternative presentations to adversarial logic based on the formalism of dynamic logic [16] and information systems [17] in Sect. 6. Finally, we cover related work in Sect. 7 and conclude on future work.

2   Motivation

Let us start with an example in Table 1 where an information disclosure attack is performed in $\mathcal{O}(n)$ interactions with the program. Note how the value of the *secret* variable is used to grant access to the function *do_serve*. Due to a discrepancy in the return value of the *server* function, it is possible for an adversary to determine the secret without reading it directly. The server's observable return value will be 0 (the adversary's goal encoded in *adv_assert* on line 14), or 1 (the provided value was too big) or 2 (the provided value was too small). Therefore, an adaptive search can guess the secret value in a maximum attempts of $\mathcal{O}(n)$ instead of the naive brute-force algorithm in $\mathcal{O}(2^n)$ where n is the size of the secret in bits. The oscillating nature of checking the adversarial assertion is represented as a finite state automaton in Table 2.

Table 1. Oscillating bit protocol: target program (Left) and adversary (Right)

```
// pre: client socket established
1. uint8 secret = rand8();             // pre: socket established to server
2.                                     1. int client(int sock)
3. void server(int sock)               2. {
4. {                                    3.   uint8 ret = 1 in
5.   uint8  err  = 0 in                 4.   uint8 guess = UINT8_MAX in
6.   uint8  cred = 0 in                 5.   uint8 step = (UINT8_MAX / 2) + 1 in
7.   while (true) do                    6.   while (true) do
8.     read(sock, cred);                7.     write(sock, guess);
9.     if (secret == cred)              8.     read(sock, ret);
10.        err = 0;                      9.     if (ret == 1)
11.    else if (secret < cred)          10.       guess = guess - step;
12.        err = 1;                      11.    else if (ret == 2)
13.    else if (secret > cred)          12.       guess = guess + step;
14.        err = 2;                      13.    step = (step / 2) + 1;
15.    if (!err) do_serve(sock);        14.    adv_assert(ret == 0);
16.    write(sock, err);                15.  done
17.  done                               16.}
18.}
```

Table 2. OBT attack has initial state (I) and started state (S) then oscillates between high (H) and low (L) before terminating in success (T) or failure (F).

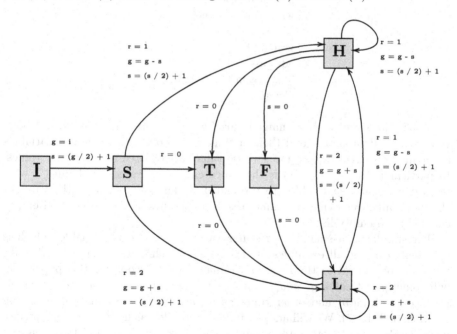

Since integer are represented with 8-bits in this example, the adversary would need to consider only $8 + 1 = 9$ values before it can successfully guess the secret and satisfy the adversarial assertion. Note that width 8 is chosen for simplicity, and this class of *linear-complexity attacks* scales very well when x grows to 16, 32, 64, etc. Not all attacks are that simple in practice, and one can imagine polynomial or more complex attack strategies up to infinite ones. The full sequence of interactions in the oscillating bit protocol is given in appendix.

3   Adversarial Logic

Adversarial Logic (AL) marries under-approximate reasoning [1,18] with an adversarial model [2] suitable for the study of complex software implementation attacks. We will work with this toy imperative language made of variables, expressions, channels, predicates and commands.

Variables	V ::= x | n | α
Expressions	E ::= V | rand() | E + E | E - E | ...
Channels	L ::= s | $\emptyset$ | (V::L) | (L::V) | (s \ V)
Predicates	B ::= B $\wedge$ B | B $\vee$ B | $\neg$B | E == E | E $\leq$ E | ...
Data types	T ::= uint8 | uint32 | float
Commands	C ::= skip | x := E | s := L | C_1; C_2 | C_1 || C_2
	| if B then C_1 else C_2
	| while B do C done
	| read(s, x)
	| write(s, E)
	| adv_assert(B)
	| T x = E in C
	| Com(C_1,C_2)

Expressions are made of named variables x, concrete integers n, symbolic values α, random values, and their arithmetic combinations. Channel variables are named resources (s_1, s_2, etc.) whose values are ordered lists of scalar values In particular, the value $(s::x)$ is the concatenation of values in channel s with the value of variable x added to the end of s. The value $(s \backslash x)$ is the value of channel s after removing the value of x from the head. The value of an empty channel is an empty list.

For simplicity, a small set of scalar variable types T is available, which is sufficient to cover all examples of this paper. Machine encoding of such data types is not central to the logic and remains out of scope for this paper. We will sometimes treat the *rand()* value as an *uint8* (such as the oscillating bit protocol in Table 5) and other times as a *float* (as in the equivalence testing example of Table 7). We will adopt *rand8()* or *randf()* as needed to make precise which version is used, or simply *rand()* when the version is obvious from context.

Predicates are built from the usual logical *and, or, not,* as well as equality and inequality tests. All commands can be used in program or adversarial terms, except assertions which are limited to the adversary. The communication primitive *Com* is distinct from read and write, and *Com* can be applied at any time after the corresponding write is completed and before the corresponding read is performed. This flexibility makes AL able to encode any desired caching strategy. Although studies of specific caching strategies are out of scope for this paper, attacks leveraging caching behavior are now mainstream [19, 20] and it is critical to allow a spectrum of possibilities as to when communication effectively happens on channels. As such, we leave *Com* implicit in our examples and apply the corresponding proof rule when required to make progress.

Although AL can reason about the full adversarial term when available, it is not required to be the case and a minimal template is often sufficient. Example 2 and 3 of Sect. 4 show how such templates can be leveraged to build attack proofs. Additional syntactic sugar is defined for convenience purpose:

$$\text{if } P \ c \stackrel{\text{def}}{=} \text{if } P \text{ then } c \text{ else } skip$$
$$\text{T } x = E_1, y = E_2 \text{ in } C \stackrel{\text{def}}{=} \text{T } x = E_1 \text{ in } (\text{T } y = E_2 \text{ in } C)$$
$$\text{if } P \ c_1 \text{ else if } Q \ c_2 \text{ else } c_3 \stackrel{\text{def}}{=} \text{if } P \text{ then } c_1 \text{ else } (\text{if } Q \text{ then } c_2 \text{ else } c_3)$$

AL inherits from incorrectness logic in that its semantics is defined using a couple of relations *ok* and *ad* where *ok* is the program interpretation and *ad* is the adversarial interpretation. We recall that inference triples in incorrectness logic are written as:

$$[ok: P] \ c \ [ok: Q][er: R]$$
$$\stackrel{\text{def}}{=}$$
$$[ok: P]c[ok: Q] \text{ and } [ok: P]c[er: R].$$

Each code fragment *c* lifts precondition *P* to postcondition *Q* and error post-condition *R*. We generalize *er* by *ad* so that inference triples are written as:

$$[ok: P_1][ad: P_2] \ c \ [ok: Q_1][ad: Q_2]$$
$$\stackrel{\text{def}}{=}$$
$$[ok: P_1]c[ok: Q_1] \text{ and } [ad: P_2]c[ad: Q_2].$$

Program interpretation and adversarial interpretation are compositional and allow independent reasoning over *ok* and *ad*. A novelty of adversarial logic is that assertions are solely checked by the adversary. Rules **Success** and **Failure** check the satisfiability of an *attack contract* rather than a *program contract*. Checking of assertions augment adversarial knowledge, as both outcomes may inform the choice of subsequent interactions with the program.

$$\textbf{Success} \ \frac{}{[ad: Q \wedge (Q \Rightarrow B)] \ \text{adv\_assert(B)} \ [ad: Q \wedge true]}$$

$$\textbf{Failure} \ \frac{}{[ad: Q \wedge (Q \Rightarrow \neg B)] \ \text{adv\_assert(B)} \ [ad: Q \wedge \neg B]}$$

More succinctly, rules in AL are written as:

$$[\epsilon: P] \ c \ [\epsilon: Q]$$

where $\epsilon \in \{ok, ad\}$ is a short notation to write two rules $[ok: P]$ c $[ok: Q]$ and $[ad: P]$ c $[ad: Q]$ as one when the rule is valid in both program and adversarial interpretations. This allows a much more succinct representation of adversarial logic proof rules.

Basic operations such as reading and writing on channels require the use of new **Read** and **Write** rules. I/O rules are defined as synchronous primitives, where a read (resp. write) happens immediately if data is available on the (potentially infinite) channel.

$$\textbf{Read} \ \frac{s \in Chan(P)}{[\epsilon: P] \ read(s, x) \ [\epsilon: \exists v \exists x' \exists s'.P(s'/s, x'/x) \wedge s = (s' \backslash v) \wedge x = v]}$$

$$\textbf{Write} \ \frac{s \in Chan(P)}{[\epsilon: \exists v.P \wedge x = v] \ write(s, x) \ [\epsilon: \exists s'.P(s'/s) \wedge s = (s'::v)]}$$

Access to channel are implemented using Floyd's axiom of assignment as applied to channel values (lists). Channels in AL are accessed *first-in / first-out* and can be used to represent files, sockets, and other inter-process communication primitive of real systems. If an attempt is made to read data on an empty channel, the **Skip** rule can be used to simulate a blocking read. Reads and writes are performed one datum at a time. Operations on bigger data length can easily be encoded using repetition of these base rules.

Parallel composition of a program c_p and an adversary c_a is constructed from a program interpretation and an adversarial interpretation of parallel terms:

$$[ok: P_1][ad: P_2] \ c_p \ || \ c_a \ [ok: Q_1][ad: Q_2]$$

Two parallel terms may either be an adversarial term and a program term, or two independent program terms, with $\epsilon_1, \epsilon_2 \in \{ok, ad\}$:

$$\textbf{Par} \ \frac{[\epsilon_1: P_1]c_1[\epsilon_1: Q_1] \qquad [\epsilon_2: P_2]c_2[\epsilon_2: Q_2]}{[\epsilon_1: P_1][\epsilon_2: P_2] \ c_1 \ || \ c_2 \ [\epsilon_1: Q_1][\epsilon_2: Q_2]} \ \epsilon_1, \epsilon_2 \in \{ok, ad\}$$

The **Par** rule does not permit communication in itself. This follows from the adversarial logic principle that no information is shared unless explicitly revealed. This parallel rule is unusual as it uses two pre-conditions and two post-conditions, enforcing variable separation without requiring an extra conjunctive connector as done in separation logic [21].

When two parallel terms need to share information, AL requires to use the communication rule **Com** on channel s. While program and adversary share no local or free variables, shared channels are required for communication. To preserve uniqueness of names, we may use s_a in the adversarial interpretation, and s_p in the program interpretation to refer to channel s, although we will just use s when the meaning is clear from context. Examples of **Com** usage can be found in the simplest example of next section in Table 3.

$$\textbf{Com} \ \frac{s \in Chan(P) \cap Chan(A) \qquad \epsilon_1, \epsilon_2 \in \{ok, ad\}}{[\epsilon_1: P][\epsilon_2: A] \ c_1 \ || \ c_2 \ [\epsilon_1: \exists v \exists s'.P(s'/s) \wedge s = (s' \backslash v)][\epsilon_2: \exists v \exists s'.A(s'/s) \wedge s = (s'::v)]}$$

Applications of adversarial logic include cases where the adversary wishes to infer hidden values of variables and predicates that have not been communicated. In these cases, the **Adversarial Consequence** rule can augment the adversarial postcondition A' if observable values communicated by the program are consequences of hidden program conditions, represented as program predicate Q). We require that $Free(Q) = \emptyset$ as free variables in Q are not defined in the adversarial term. This can be guaranteed by creating fresh names during the introduction of Q in the adversarial context, so that no names are shared. It is assumed that $s \in Chan(A) \cap Chan(P)$. Basic usage of this rule can be found in all examples of Sect. 4.

$$\textbf{Adv.Cons.} \quad \frac{[ok: P : \exists w.v_1 = w]c_p : if(Q)write(s, v_1)[ok: P' : Q \wedge \exists w.s = (l_s :: w)]}{[ad: A : \exists w.s = (w :: l_a)]c_a : read(s, v_2)[ad: A' : \exists w.s = l_a \wedge v_2 = w]} \\ \overline{[ok: P][ad: A] \; c_p \; || \; c_a \; [ok: P'][ad: A' \wedge \exists v_1.Q \wedge v_1 = v_2]}$$

Adversarial logic generalizes the **Backward variant** rule of incorrectness logic [1] for parallel composition of program and adversarial terms, which we name the Parallel Backward Variant, or **PBV**.

$$\textbf{PBV} \quad \frac{[ok: P(n)][ad: A(m)] \; c_p \; || \; c_a \; [ok: P(n+i)][ad: A(m+j)]}{[ok: P(0)][ad: A(0)] \; c_p^n \; || \; c_a^m \; [ok: \exists n.P(n)][ad: \exists m.A(m)]} \quad i, j \in \{0, 1\} \wedge i+j \geq 1$$

AL's backward variant rule is a parallel composition of a program fragment c_p repeated n times with an adversarial code fragment c_a repeated m times. It is not required for the number of program steps n and adversarial steps m to be the same, as long as at least one step is taken at each iteration ($i, j \in \{0, 1\} \wedge i+j \geq 1$). This condition enforces that every extracted attack trace is finite. Examples in this article show cases where $n = m$ (the oscillating bit protocol), and others where $n \neq m$ (equivalence testing).

The PBV rule cannot be expressed using two instances of IL's original BV rule, as PBV can express conditions where adversarial and program conditions are subject to communication. It may also be useful to apply the original sequential BV rule in parallel when program and adversarial terms are independently reducible, however this does not equate to using the parallel version of the rule which can provide synchronization across terms. A practical example of PBV usage is demonstrated in Table 5 of Sect. 4.

One notable incorrectness rule absent from AL is the sequential short-circuit. In this rule, execution of the second term of a sequence is avoided if the first term terminates by an error. As adversarial logic is meant to analyze consequences of erroneous program executions, short-circuiting serves no benefit. This highlights a key difference between IL's original error relation er and AL's adversarial relation ad. All other rules of adversarial logic are similar to incorrectness logic with the difference that either ok or ad can be used in the precondition, therefore restoring a lost symmetry in incorrectness logic while preserving its meaning.

(a) Adversarial logic core rules with restored symmetry from IL : $\epsilon \in \{ok, ad\}$

$$\text{Unit} \frac{}{[\epsilon\colon P] \text{ skip } [\epsilon\colon P]} \qquad \text{Constancy} \frac{[\epsilon\colon P]c[\epsilon : Q]}{[\epsilon : P \wedge F]c[\epsilon\colon Q \wedge F]} \; Mod(c) \cap Free(F) = \emptyset$$

$$\text{Consequence} \frac{[\epsilon\colon P \Rightarrow P'] \qquad [\epsilon\colon P]c[\epsilon\colon Q] \qquad [\epsilon\colon Q' \Rightarrow Q]}{[\epsilon\colon P']c[\epsilon\colon Q']}$$

$$\text{Assume} \frac{}{[\epsilon\colon P] \text{ assume(B) } [\epsilon\colon P \wedge B]} \qquad \text{Rand} \frac{}{[\epsilon\colon P] \; x = \text{rand}() \; [\epsilon\colon \exists x'.P(x'/x) \wedge x = v]}$$

$$\text{Assign} \frac{}{[\epsilon\colon P] \; x = e \; [\epsilon\colon \exists x'.P(x'/x) \wedge x = e(x'/x)]}$$

$$\text{Disj} \frac{[\epsilon\colon P_1]c[\epsilon\colon Q_1] \qquad [\epsilon\colon P_2]c[\epsilon\colon Q_2]}{[\epsilon\colon P_1 \vee P_2]c[\epsilon\colon Q_1 \vee Q_2]} \qquad \text{Local} \frac{[\epsilon\colon P \wedge x = e]c[\epsilon\colon Q] \qquad x \notin Free(P)}{[\epsilon\colon P] \; T \; x = e \text{ in } c \; [\epsilon\colon \exists x \in T.Q]}$$

$$\text{Seq} \frac{[\epsilon\colon P]c_1[\epsilon\colon Q] \qquad [\epsilon\colon Q]c_2[\epsilon\colon R]}{[\epsilon\colon P]c_1;c_2[\epsilon\colon R]} \qquad \text{Choice} \frac{[\epsilon\colon P]c_i[\epsilon\colon Q]}{[\epsilon\colon P]c_1 + c_2[\epsilon\colon Q]} \; i \in [1,2]$$

$$\text{Iterate Zero} \frac{}{[\epsilon\colon P]c^*[\epsilon\colon P]} \qquad \text{Iterate non-zero} \frac{[\epsilon\colon P]c^*;c[\epsilon\colon Q]}{[\epsilon\colon P]c^*[\epsilon\colon Q]}$$

$$\text{while } B \text{ do } C \text{ done} \triangleq (\text{assume}(B); C)^*; \text{assume}(\neg B)$$
$$\text{if } B \text{ then } C \text{ else } C' \triangleq (\text{assume}(B); C) + (\text{assume}(\neg B); C')$$

(b) Adversarial Logic : communication rules between program and adversary

$$\text{Read} \frac{s \in Chan(P)}{[\epsilon\colon P] \text{ read(s, x) } [\epsilon\colon \exists v \exists x' \exists s'.P(s'/s, x'/x) \wedge s = (s'\backslash v) \wedge x = v]}$$

$$\text{Write} \frac{s \in Chan(P)}{[\epsilon\colon \exists v.P \wedge x = v] \text{ write(s, x) } [\epsilon\colon \exists v \exists s'.P(s'/s) \wedge s = (s'::v)]}$$

$$\text{Par} \frac{[\epsilon_1\colon P_1]c_1[\epsilon_1\colon Q_1] \qquad [\epsilon_2\colon P_2]c_2[\epsilon_2\colon Q_2]}{[\epsilon_1\colon P_1][\epsilon_2\colon P_2] \; c_1 \parallel c_2 \; [\epsilon_1\colon Q_1][\epsilon_2\colon Q_2]} \; \epsilon_1, \epsilon_2 \in \{ok, ad\}$$

$$\text{Com} \frac{s \in Chan(P) \cap Chan(A) \qquad \epsilon_1, \epsilon_2 \in \{ok, ad\}}{[\epsilon_1\colon P][\epsilon_2\colon A] \; c_1 \parallel c_2 \; [\epsilon_1\colon \exists v \exists s'.P(s'/s) \wedge s = (s'\backslash v)][\epsilon_2\colon \exists v \exists s'.A(s'/s) \wedge s = (s'::v)]}$$

(c) Adversarial Logic: knowledge rules between program and adversary

$$\text{PBV} \frac{[ok\colon P(n)][ad\colon A(m)] \; c_p \parallel c_a \; [ok\colon P(n+i)][ad\colon A(m+j)]}{[ok\colon P(0)][ad\colon A(0)] \; c_p^n \parallel c_a^m \; [ok\colon \exists n.P(n)][ad\colon \exists m.A(m)]} \; i, j \in \{0,1\} \wedge i + j \geq 1$$

$$\text{Adv.Cons.} \frac{[ok\colon P : \exists w.v_1 = w]c_p : if(Q)write(s, v_1)[ok\colon P' : Q \wedge \exists w.s = (l_s::w)]}{[ad\colon A : \exists w.s = (w::l_a)]c_a : read(s, v_2)[ad\colon A' : \exists w.s = l_a \wedge v_2 = w]}{[ok\colon P][ad\colon A] \; c_p \parallel c_a \; [ok\colon P'][ad\colon A' \wedge \exists v_1.Q \wedge v_1 = v_2]}$$

$$\text{Success} \frac{}{[ad\colon Q \wedge (Q \Rightarrow B)] \text{ adv\_assert(B) } [ad\colon Q \wedge true]}$$

$$\text{Failure} \frac{}{[ad\colon Q \wedge (Q \Rightarrow \neg B)] \text{ adv\_assert(B) } [ad\colon Q \wedge \neg B]}$$

4   Reasoning with Adversarial Logic

In this section, we put AL to work with three distinct examples. The simplest example of Table 3 is sufficient to explain symbolic variable introduction, adversarial consequence and assertion checking by the adversary. The oscillating bit protocol example from Table 1 of Sect. 2 is then proved step-by-step, including a proof showing the use of the parallel backward variant (PBV) rule for the determination of the existence of attacks. In example 3, two pricing functions are under-approximated to find common price boundaries through adversarial assertions and combines usage of the PBV rule and the adversarial consequence rule to perform equivalence testing.

4.1   Example 1: Trivial Case

Let us consider the example in Table 3 where an adversary wants to capture a flag *win* with an input value n reaching value 10 million (10M for short).

Table 3. Simple example implementation. The adversary wishes to discover conditions on symbolic variable *val* to satisfy assertion (res $==$ 1)

```
// Precond: s channel established   // Precond: s channel established
program(int s)                      adversary(int s)
{                                   {
   uint32 n, win in                    uint32 val = α in
   read(s, n);                         uint32 res = 0 in
   if (n > 10M) win = 1;               write(s, val);
   else win = 0;                       read(s, res);
   write(s, win);                      adv_assert(res == 1);
}                                   }
```

An adversarial proof such as the one in Table 4 may contain several *proof phases* corresponding to non-blocking subsequences of program or adversarial derivations. A proof is typically divided into the following phases:

1. The bootstrap phase (P_0 to P_3 and A_0 to A_3) where program and adversary have yet to be composed.
2. The initial phase (P_3, A_3) to (P_9, A_9) typically starts with application of the **Par** rule until composed terms fail to make more progress other than **Skip**
3. Optionally, one or more intermediate phases separated by applications of the **Com** rule used to communicate and unblock stuck terms, interleaved with calls to **AdvAssert** failing to satisfy the attack contract.
4. The final phase ends with a call to **Success** where the adversarial assertion is satisfied (A_{12}), or when the adversarial program terminate otherwise.

432   J. Vanegue

Table 4. Simplest example in Adversarial Logic. Unlike traditional program symbolic execution, assertions and symbolic variables can only be introduced in the adversarial part of the system.

	Program(int s) {	Adversary(int s) {	
→ Local	$P_0 = \{ok: \exists s_p.s_p = \emptyset\}$	$A_0 = \{ad: \exists s_a.s_a = \emptyset\}$	
→ Local	uint32 n in	uint32 val $= \alpha$ in	→ Local
	$P_1 = \{ok: P_0 \wedge \exists u.n = u\}$	$A_1 = \{ad: A_0 \wedge \exists \alpha.val = \alpha\}$	
→ Local	uint32 win in	uint32 res $= 0$ in	→ Local
	$P_2 = \{ok: P_1 \wedge \exists v.win = v\}$	$A_2 = \{ad: A_1 \wedge res = 0\}$	
→ Skip	read(s, n);	write(s,val);	→ Write
	$P_3 = \{ok: P_2\}$	$A_3 = \{ad: \exists s_a^2.A_2(s_a^2/s_a) \wedge s_a = (s_a^2::\alpha)\}$	

→ Par	$(P_3, A_3) = \{ok: P_3\}\{ad: A_3\}$
→ Com	read(s,n) || read(s,res)
	$(P_4, A_4) = \{ok: \exists \alpha \exists s_p^2.P_3(s_p^2/s_p) \wedge s_p = (s_p^2::\alpha)\}\{ad: \exists s_a^2.A_3(s_a^2/s_a) \wedge s_a = (s_a^2\backslash\alpha)\}$
→ Read	read(s,n) || read(s, res)
	$(P_5, A_5) = \{ok: \exists \alpha \exists s_p^3 \exists n_2.P_4(s_p^3/s_p, n_2/n) \wedge s_p = (s_p^3\backslash\alpha) \wedge n = \alpha\}\{ad: A_4\}$
→ If, Assn	if (n > 10M) win = 1 || read(s, res)
	$(P_6, A_6) = \{ok: \exists w_2.P_5(w_2/win) \wedge n > 10M \wedge win = 1\}\{ad: A_5\}$
→ If, Assn	else win = 0 || read(s, res)
	$(P_7, A_7) = \{ok: \exists w_3.P_5(w_3/win) \wedge n \leq 10M \wedge win = 0\}\{ad: A_6\}$
→ Disj	$(P_8, A_8) = \{ok: P_6 \vee P_7\}\{ad: A_7\}$
→ Write	write(s, win) || read(s, res)
	$(P_9, A_9) = \{ok: \exists w \exists s_p^4.P_8(s_p^4/s_p) \wedge s_p = (s_p^4::w) \wedge win = w\}\{ad: A_8\}$
→ Com	skip || read(s,res)
	$(P_{10}, A_{10}) = \{ok: \exists s_p^5.P_9(s_p^5/s_p) \wedge s_p = (s_p^5\backslash w)\}$
	$\{ad: \exists w \exists s_a^3.A_9(s_a^3/s_a) \wedge s_a = (s_a^3::w)\}$
→ Read	skip || read(s, res)
	$(P_{11}, A_{11}) = \{ok: P_{10}\}\{ad: \exists s_a^4 \exists r_2 \exists w.A_{10}(s_a^4/s_a, r_2/res) \wedge s_a = (s_a^4\backslash w) \wedge res = w\}$
→ Adv.C.	skip || adv_assert(res == 1)
	$(P_{12}, A_{12}) = \{ok: P_{11}\}\{ad: A_{11} \wedge \exists n \exists x.((n > 10M \wedge x = 1) \vee (n \leq 10M \wedge x = 0))$
	$\wedge\, n = \alpha \wedge res = x\}$
→ Success	skip || adv_assert(res == 1)

Note how symbolic variable α is introduced by the adversarial interpretation (A_1) and propagated to the program's logic (P_4) using the communication rule. Program and adversarial interpretations remain independent until the parallel rule is used to compose terms. Note how P_9 in insufficient to prove the assertion $res == 1$ thus requiring the application of the adversarial consequence rule to obtain additional knowledge $(n = \alpha) \wedge (n > 10M)$.

4.2 Example 2: Oscillating Bit Protocol

We now analyze the motivating example presented in Sect. 2. It is possible to prove existence of an information disclosure attack in the oscillating bit protocol with or without the parallel backward variant rule. As we will show, use of the PBV rule allows to significantly shorten the proof. Without it, the adversarial interpretation goes through several instances of adversarial failures where $adv\_assert(retcode == 0)$ cannot be satisfied. After a sufficient number of guesses are performed and constraints over the secret are learned, the adversary finally provides a value that matches the secret. In the OBP example, $cred == 160$ is the secret value which cannot be inferred without performing $\mathcal{O}(n)$ steps.

Table 5. Oscillating Bit Protocol (OBT) in AL using disjunction and parallel backward variant rules. Introduction of the PBV rule cut the number of needed steps and can be used to deduce the existence of an attack without guessing the secret.

	$P_1 = \{ok:\ \emptyset\}$	$A_1 = \{ad:\ \emptyset\}$	
$\to Rand$	uint8 secret = rand8() in	uint8 ret = 1 in	$\to Loc$
	$P_2 = \{ok:\ \exists s.secret == s\}$	$A_2 = \{ad:\ A_1 \wedge ret = 1\}$	
$\to Loc$	uint8 err = 0 in	uint8 guess = UINT8_MAX in	$\to Loc$
	$P_3 = \{ok:\ P_2 \wedge err = 0\}$	$A_3 = \{ad:\ A_2 \wedge guess = UINT8\_MAX\}$	
$\to Loc$	uint8 cred = 0 in	uint8 step = (guess / 2) + 1 in	$\to Loc$
	$P_4 = \{ok:\ P_3 \wedge cred = 0\}$	$A_4 = \{ad:\ A_3 \wedge step = (guess/2) + 1\}$	
$\to Wh$	while (true) do	while (true) do	$\to Wh$
	$P_5 = \{ok:\ true \wedge P_4\}$	$A_5 = \{ad:\ true \wedge A_4\}$	
$\to Skip$	read(sock, cred);	write(sock,guess);	$\to Wr$
	$P_6 = \{ok:\ P_5\}$	$A_6 = \{ad:\ \exists s_a^1 \exists g.A_5(s_a^1/s_a) \wedge guess = g$	
		$\qquad\qquad \wedge s_a = (s_a^1::g)\}$	

$\to Par$ $\quad (P_7, A_7) = \{ok:\ P_6\}\{ad:\ A_6\}$

$\to Com$ $\quad$ read(sock, cred) || read(sock,ret)

$\qquad (P_8, A_8) = \{ok:\ \exists w \exists s_p^1.P_7(s_p^1/s_p) \wedge s_p = (s_p^1 \backslash w)\}$

$\qquad\qquad \{ad:\ \exists w \exists s_a^1.A_7(s_a^1/s_a) \wedge s_a = (s_a^1::w)\}$

$\to Read$ $\quad$ read(sock, cred) || read(sock,ret)

$\qquad (P_9, A_9) = \{ok:\ \exists c \exists s_p^2.P_8(s_p^2/s_p, c/cred) \wedge s_p = (s_p^2 \backslash c) \wedge cred = c\}\{ad:\ A_8\}$

$\to If, Disj$ $\quad$ if (secret == cred) err = 0 || read(sock,ret)

$\qquad (P_{10}, A_{10}) = \{ok:\ P_9 \vee (secret = cred \wedge \exists e.P_9(e/err) \wedge err = 0)\}\{ad:\ A_9\}$

$\to If, Disj$ $\quad$ else if (secret < cred) err = 1 || read(sock,ret)

$\qquad (P_{11}, A_{11}) = \{ok:\ P_{10} \vee (secret < cred \wedge \exists e.P_{10}(e/err) \wedge err = 1)\}\{ad:\ A_{10}\}$

$\to If, Fra.$ $\quad$ if (err == 0) do_serve(sock) || read(sock,ret)

$\qquad (P_{12}, A_{12}) = \{ok:\ (P_{11} \wedge err \neq 0) \vee (P_{11} \wedge err = 0)\}\{ad:\ A_{11}\}$

$\to Write$ $\quad$ write(sock, err) || read(sock, ret)

$\qquad (P_{13}, A_{13}) = \{ok:\ \exists e \exists s_p^3.P_{12}(s_p^3/s_p) \wedge err = e \wedge s_p = (s_p^3::e)\}\{ad:\ A_{12}\}$

- -

$\to Com$ $\quad$ read(sock, cred) || read(sock, ret)

$\qquad (P_{14}, A_{14}) = \{ok:\ \exists w \exists s_p^4.P_{13}(s_p^4/s_p) \wedge s_p = (s_p^4 \backslash w)\}$

$\qquad\qquad \{ad:\ \exists w \exists s_a^2.A_{13}(s_a^2/s_a) \wedge s_a = (s_a^2::w)\}$

$\to Read$ $\quad$ read(sock, cred) || read(sock, ret)

$\qquad (P_{15}, A_{15}) = \{ok:\ P_{14}\}\{ad:\ \exists r \exists r_2 \exists s_a^3.A_{14}(s_a^3/s_a, r_2/ret) \wedge s_a = (s_a^3 \backslash r) \wedge ret = r\}$

$\to If, Disj$ $\quad$ read(sock, cred) || if (ret == 1) guess = guess - step

$\qquad (P_{16}, A_{16}) = \{ok:\ P_{15}\}$

$\qquad\qquad \{ad:\ (ret = 1 \wedge \exists g.A_{15}(g/guess) \wedge guess = g - step) \vee (ret \neq 1 \wedge A_{15})\}$

$\to If, Disj$ $\quad$ read(sock, cred) || if (ret == 1) guess = guess - step

$\qquad (P_{17}, A_{17}) = \{ok:\ P_{16}\}$

$\qquad\qquad \{ad:\ (ret = 2 \wedge \exists g.A_{16}(g/guess) \wedge guess = g + step) \vee (ret \neq 2 \wedge A_{16})\}$

$\to Assn$ $\quad$ read(sock, cred) || step = (step / 2) + 1

$\qquad (P_{18}, A_{18}) = \{ok:\ P_{17}\}\{ad:\ \exists s.A_{17}(s/step) \wedge step = s/2 + 1)\}$

$\to Fail$ $\quad$ read(sock, cred) || attack_assert(ret == 0)

$\qquad (P_{19}, A_{19}) = \{ok:\ P_{18}\}\{ad:\ A_{18} \wedge ret \neq 0)\}$

$\to PBV$ $\quad (P_{20}, A_{20}) = \{ok:\ \exists n.P_n : (secret = cred) \wedge (err = 0)\}\{ad:\ \exists n.A_n : (ret = 0)\}$

$\to Succ$ $\quad$ read(sock, cred) || attack_assert(ret == 0)

For brevity, we provide analysis of the example using PBV rule in Table 5, while the version without PBV is given in appendix. A combination of PBV and disjunction rules allows the adversary to find an iteration where the secret is correctly guessed without executing the loop $\mathcal{O}(n)$ times. Recall the form of the PBV rule with c_p the program term and c_a the adversarial term:

$$\frac{[\textit{ok}: P(n)][\textit{ad}: A(m)] \ c_p \ || \ c_a \ [\textit{ok}: P(n+i)][\textit{ad}: A(m+j)]}{[\textit{ok}: P(0)][\textit{ad}: A(0)] \ c_p^n \ || \ c_a^m \ [\textit{ok}: \exists n.P(n)][\textit{ad}: \exists m.A(m)]} \ \ i, j \in \{0, 1\} \wedge i+j \geq 1$$

In the oscillating bit protocol example, the PBV rule takes a simpler form where $n = m$ and $i = j = 1$ for all values of (n, m). Applying the PBV rule for this example proceeds as such: $P(0)$ is $secret = v_1$, $A(0)$ is $guess = v_2$, $P(n)$ is $secret = v_1$, $A(n)$ is $guess = v_1$, $P(n+1)$ is $secret = cred$ and $A(n+1)$ is $ret = 0$. Note how $P(0)$ and $P(n)$ are both $s == v_1$ as the secret value does not change across iterations. This condition is not strictly required and may not be guaranteed in more complex examples, such as if the secret variable value changes over time.

$$\frac{[\textit{ok}: secret = v_1][\textit{ad}: guess = v_1] \ c_p \ || \ c_a \ [\textit{ok}: secret = cred][\textit{ad}: ret = 0]}{[\textit{ok}: secret = v_1][\textit{ad}: guess = v_2] \ c_p^n \ || \ c_a^n \ [\textit{ok}: \exists P_n.secret = v_1][\textit{ad}: \exists A_n.guess = v_1]}$$

We distinguish adversarial proofs which do not appeal to the parallel backward variant rule from those using PBV since the use of PBV allows to reach adversarial success without guessing the secret. Adversarial proofs with PBV are not sufficient to build a concrete attack, but they are sufficient to prove that an attack exists.

4.3 Example 3: Equivalence Testing

Equivalence properties are relevant to security to prove compatibility or indistinguishability of two programs. For example, comparing multiple parsing implementations of a given input language (network headers, ASN.1, etc.) can uncover subtle program behaviors allowing exploitation or fingerprinting of systems [22].

Equivalence results are generally established by showing that the labeled transition system of a program implementation is equivalent to the LTS of its specification [23]. Bisimulation requires two LTS to be observationally equivalent for all transitions. Proving such equivalence is out of reach in the underapproximate framework, in which only some program executions must be analyzed. Take for example the *epsilon-delta* definition of the limit of a function:

$$\forall \epsilon > 0 \exists \delta > 0 : |x - c| < \delta \implies |f(x) - L| < \epsilon$$

Universary quantified propositions like this one are unprovable in IL and AL, which restricts us to under-approximate equivalence testing for certain inputs. This is useful to prove that two programs are equivalent *sometimes*, and find values for which programs agree. For f_1 and $f_2 : \exists x : f_1(x) = f_2(x)$. Let us assume that $f_1(x)$ and $f_2(x)$ can be written as:

$$f_1(x) = \exists x.(P_1(x) \Rightarrow Q_1(x)) \wedge ... \wedge (P_n(x) \Rightarrow Q_n(x))$$
$$f_2(x) = \exists x.(R_1(x) \Rightarrow T_1(x)) \wedge ... \wedge (R_m(x) \Rightarrow T_m(x))$$

We use this general form where P_1 to P_n (resp. R_1 to R_m) represent the path conditions associated to output values Q_1 to Q_n (resp. T_1 to T_m). Existence of a crossing point between f_1 and f_2 can now be written as:

$$EquTst(f_1, f_2) = \exists x \exists i \exists j : (P_i(x) \Rightarrow Q_i(x)) \wedge (R_j(x) \Rightarrow T_j(x)) \wedge (Q_i(x) \Leftrightarrow T_j(x))$$

Testing equivalence of f_1 and f_2 is computable in adversarial logic even when internal program variables (possibly random ones) are involved in the calculation of f_1 or f_2. Equivalence testing does not require proving $P_i \Leftrightarrow R_j$ (as required in bisimulation) as internal computations P_i and R_j may be hidden to the adversary. Hence equivalence testing is neither a bisimulation nor a simulation.

Table 6. Two pricing functions with user-supplied order number and random initial price.

```
                              // Client: Adversarial software
                              // Precond: chan s1 and s2 established
                              1.  void       Adv(int s1, int s2)
                              2.  {
// Preprocessor definitions   3.     float   guess = 0 in
 1. define V1MIL 1000000      4.     float   guess2 = 0 in
 2. define V9MIL (V1MIL*9)    5.     uint32 num = α in // Sym
 3. define V18MIL (V1MIL*18)  6.     write(s1, num); // Test GP1
 4. define V10MIL (V1MIL*10)  7.     read(s1, guess1);
 5. define V20MIL (V1MIL*20)  8.     write(s2, num); // Test GP2
 // Shared initial service state 9.  read(s2, guess2);
 // Between GetPrice and GetPrice2 10. adv_assert(guess1 == guess2);
 6. float initp = rand();     11. }


// Precond: chan s1 established  // Precond: channel s2 established
 7. void GetPrice(int s1)       22. void GetPrice2(int s2)
 8. {                           23. {
 9.    float curp in            24.    float curp2 in
10.    uint32 ord in            25.    uint32 ord2 in
11.    float dec in             26.    float dec2 in
12.    while (true) do          27.    while (true) do
13.      read(s1, ord);         28.      read(s2, ord2);
14       dec = ord / V10MIL;    29.      dec2 = ord2 / V20MIL;
15.      if (ord <= V9MIL)      30.      if (ord2 <= V18MIL)
16.        curp = initp * (1 - dec); 31.   curp2 = initp * (1 - dec2);
17.      else                   32.      else
18.        curp = initp / 10;   33.        curp2 = initp / 10;
19.      write(s1, curp);       34.      write(s2, curp2);
20.    done                     35.    done
21. }                           36. }
```

Consider the code in Table 6 where a pricing service contains two functions *GetPrice* and *GetPrice2* reading on channels s_1 and s_2 to compute market price based on a globally initialized random market value *initp* and ordered quantities *num*. The first function converges faster than the other due to a different current price calculation.

Adversarial logic can be used to prove that functions *GetPrice* and *GetPrice2* meet at the same limit price (a tenth of the initial price) for certain input order

Table 7. Equivalence testing: PBV and adversarial consequence rules are combined to find an input for which two pricing functions have the same output.

	$A_0 = \{ok: \emptyset\}$
$P_0 = \{ok: \emptyset\}$	float guess1
	$A_1 = \{ok: \exists c_1.guess1 = v_1 \wedge A_0\}$ $\rightarrow Loc$
$\rightarrow Rand$ float initp = read();	float guess2
$P_1 = \{ok: \exists f.initp = f \wedge P_0\}$	$A_2 = \{ok: \exists c_2.guess2 = v_2 \wedge A_1\}$ $\rightarrow Loc$

$\rightarrow Par$ $(P_2, A_2) = \{ok: P_1\}\{ad: A_2\}$

$\rightarrow Dup$ float curp $\parallel$ uint32 num $= \alpha$

$(P_2, A_2, Q_2) = \{ok: P_2\}\{ad: A_2\}\{ok: P_2\}$

$\rightarrow Loc(\times 3)$ float curp $\parallel$ uint32 num $= \alpha$ $\parallel$ float curp2

$(P_3, A_3, Q_3) = \{ok: \exists c.curp = c \wedge P_2\}\{ad: \exists a.num = \alpha \wedge A_2\}\{ok: \exists w.curp2 = w \wedge Q_2\}$

$\rightarrow Loc, Wri, Loc$ uint32 ord $\parallel$ write(s1, num) $\parallel$ uint32 ord2

$(P_4, A_4, Q_4) = \{ok: \exists o.ord = o \wedge P_3\}$
$\{ad: \exists a \exists s1_a^2.A_3(s1_a^2/s1_a) \wedge num = \alpha \wedge s1_a = (s1_a^2::\alpha)\}$
$\{ok: \exists o'.ord = o' \wedge Q_3\}$

$\rightarrow Loc, Loc$ float dec $\parallel$ read(s1,guess1) $\parallel$ float dec2 {

$(P_5, A_5, Q_5) = \{ok: \exists d.dec = d \wedge P_4\}\{ad: A_4\}\{ok: \exists d^2.dec2 = d^2 \wedge Q_4\}$

$\rightarrow Whi, Whi$ while (true) do $\parallel$ read(s1,guess1) $\parallel$ while (true) do

$(P_6, A_6, Q_6) = \{ok: true \wedge P_5\}\{ad: A_5\}\{ok: true \wedge Q_5\}$

$\rightarrow Com$ read(s1, ord) $\parallel$ read(s1, guess1) { $\parallel$ read(s1, ord2)}

$(P_7, A_7, Q_7) = \{ok: \exists \alpha \exists s1_p^2.P_6(s1_p^2/s1_p) \wedge s1_p = (s1_p^2::\alpha)\}$
$\{ad: \exists \alpha \exists s1_a^5.A_6(s1_a^5/s1_a) \wedge s1_a = (s1_a^5\backslash \alpha)\}\{ok: Q_6\}$

$\rightarrow Read$ read(s1, ord) $\parallel$ read(s1, guess1) $\parallel$ read(s2, ord2)

$(P_8, A_8, Q_8) = \{ok: \exists \alpha \exists x \exists s1_p^3.P_7(x/ord, s1_p^3/s1_p) \wedge s1_p = (s1_p^3\backslash \alpha) \wedge ord = \alpha\}$
$\{ad: A_7\}\{ok: Q_7\}$

$\rightarrow Assn$ dec = ord / V10MIL $\parallel$ read(s1, guess1) $\parallel$ read(s2, ord2)

$(P_9, A_9, Q_9) = \{ok: \exists d^2.P_8(d^2/dec) \wedge dec = ord/V10M\}\{ad: A_8\}\{ok: Q_8\}$

$\rightarrow If$ if (ord <= 9MIL) curp = initp * (1 - dec) $\parallel$ read(s1, guess) $\parallel$ read(s2, ord2)

$(P_{10}, A_{10}, Q_{10}) = \{ok: \exists c^3.P_9(c^3/curp| \wedge ord \leq V9M \wedge curp = initp * (1 - dec)\}$
$\{ad: A_9\}\{ok: Q_9\}$

$\rightarrow If$ else curp = initp / 10 $\parallel$ read(s1, guess1) $\parallel$ read(s2, ord2)

$(P_{11}, A_{11}, Q_{11}) = \{ok: \exists c^2.P_{10}(c^3/curp| \wedge ord > V9M \wedge curp = initp/10)\}\{ad: A_9\}\{ok: Q_9\}$

$\rightarrow Disj$ write(s1,curp) $\parallel$ read(s1, guess1) $\parallel$ read(s2, ord2)

$(P_{12}, A_{12}, Q_{12}) = \{ok: P_{11} \vee P_{10}\}\{ad: A_9\}\{ok: Q_9\}$

$\rightarrow Wri$ write(s1,curp) $\parallel$ read(s1, guess1) $\parallel$ read(s2, ord2)

$(P_{13}, A_{13}, Q_{13}) = \{ok: \exists u \exists s1_p^4.P_{12}(s1_p^4/s1_p) \wedge curp = u \wedge s1_p = (s1_p^4::u)\}$
$\{ad: A_{12}\}\{ok: Q_{12}\}$

- -

$\rightarrow Com$ read(s1, guess1) $\parallel$ read(s1, guess1) $\parallel$ read(s2, ord2)

$(P_{14}, A_{14}, Q_{14}) = \{ok: \exists u \exists s1_p^5.P_{13}(s1_p^5/s1_p) \wedge s1_p = (s1_p^5\backslash u)\}$
$\{ad: \exists u \exists s1_a^4.A_{13}(s1_a^4/s1_a) \wedge s1_a = (s1_a^4::u)\}\{ok: Q_{13}\}$

$\rightarrow Read$ read(s1, ord) $\parallel$ read(s1, guess1) $\parallel$ read(s2, ord2)

$(P_{15}, A_{15}, Q_{15}) = \{ok: P_{14}\}\{ok: Q_{14}\}$
$\{ad: \exists g \exists u \exists s1_a^5.A_{14}(g/guess1, s1_a^5/s1_a) \wedge s1_a = (s1_a^5\backslash u) \wedge guess1 = u\}$

$\rightarrow PBV$ read(s1, ord) $\parallel$ read(s1,guess1) $\parallel$ read(s2, ord2)

$(P_{16}, A_{16}, Q_{16}) = \{ok: \exists f.\alpha > V9M \wedge initp = f \wedge (curp = initp/10)\}$
$\{ad: \exists u.guess1 = u\}\{ok: Q_{15}\}$

$\rightarrow Adv.Cons.$ read(s1, ord) $\parallel$ read(s1,guess1) $\parallel$ read(s2, ord2)

$(P_{17}, A_{17}, Q_{17}) = \{ok: P_{16}\}\{ad: \exists \alpha \exists f \exists u.guess1 = u \wedge u = f/10 \wedge \alpha > V9M\}\{ok: Q_{16}\}$

$\rightarrow Wri$ read(s1, ord) $\parallel$ write(s2,num) $\parallel$ read(s2, ord2)

$(P_{18}, A_{18}, Q_{18}) = \{ok: P_{17}\}\{ad: \exists \alpha \exists s2_a^2.A_{17}[s2_a^2/s2_a] \wedge num = \alpha \wedge s2_a = (s2_a^2::\alpha)\}$
$\{ok: Q_{17}\}$

- -

$\rightarrow Com$ read(s1, ord) $\parallel$ read(s2,guess2) $\parallel$ read(s2, ord2)

$(P_{19}, A_{19}, Q_{19}) = \{ok: P_{18}\}\{ad: \exists \alpha \exists s2_a^3.A_{18}[s2_a^3/s2_a] \wedge s2_a = (s2_a^3\backslash \alpha)\}$
$\{ok: \exists \alpha \exists s2_q^2.Q_{18}[s2_q^2/s2_q] \wedge s2_q = (s2_q^2::\alpha)\}$

$\rightarrow Read$ read(s1, ord) $\parallel$ read(s2,guess2) $\parallel$ read(s2, ord2)

$(P_{20}, A_{20}, Q_{20}) = \{ok: P_{19}\}\{ad: A_{19}\}$
$\{ok: \exists \alpha \exists o2 \exists s2_q^2.Q_{19}[s2_q^2/s2_q, o2/ord2] \wedge s2_q = (s2_q^2\backslash \alpha) \wedge ord2 = \alpha\}$

$\rightarrow Assn$ read(s1, ord) $\parallel$ read(s2,guess2) $\parallel$ dec2 = ord2 / V20MIL

$(P_{21}, A_{21}, Q_{21}) = \{ok: P_{20}\}\{ad: A_{20}\}\{ok: \exists d2.Q_{20}[d2/dec2] \wedge dec2 = ord2/V20M\}$

$\rightarrow If$ read(s1, ord) $\parallel$ read(s2,guess2) $\parallel$ if (ord2 $\leq$ V18M) curp2 = initp * (1 - dec2)

$(P_{22}, A_{22}, Q_{22}) = \{ok: P_{21}\}\{ad: A_{21}\}$
$\{ok: \exists c2.Q_{21}[c2/curp2] \wedge (ord2 \leq V18M) \wedge curp2 = initp * (1 - dec2)\}$

$\rightarrow If$ read(s1, ord) $\parallel$ read(s2,guess2) $\parallel$ else curp2 = initp / 10

$(P_{23}, A_{23}, Q_{23}) = \{ok: P_{22}\}\{ad: A_{22}\}$
$\{ok: \exists c2.Q_{21}[c2/curp2] \wedge (ord2 > V18M) \wedge (curp2 = initp/10)\}$

$\rightarrow Disj$ read(s1, ord) $\parallel$ read(s2,guess2) $\parallel$ else curp2 = initp / 10

$(P_{24}, A_{24}, Q_{24}) = \{ok: P_{23}\}\{ad: A_{23}\}\{ok: Q_{22} \vee Q_{23}\}$

$\rightarrow Wri$ read(s1, ord) $\parallel$ read(s2,guess2) $\parallel$ write(s2,curp2)

$(P_{25}, A_{25}, Q_{25}) = \{ok: P_{24}\}\{ad: A_{24}\}$
$\{ok: \exists c \exists s2_q^2.Q_{24}[s2_q^2/s2_q] \wedge (curp2 = c) \wedge s2_q = (s2_q^2::c)\}$

- -

$\rightarrow Com$ read(s1, ord) $\parallel$ read(s2,guess2) $\parallel$ read(s2, ord2)

$(P_{26}, A_{26}, Q_{26}) = \{ok: P_{25}\}\{ad: \exists c \exists s2_a^4.A_{25}[s2_a^4/s2_a] \wedge s2_a = (s2_a^4::c)\}$
$\{ok: \exists c \exists s2_q^5.Q_{25}[s2_q^5/s2_q] \wedge s2_q = (s2_q^5\backslash c)\}$

$\rightarrow Read$ read(s1, ord) $\parallel$ read(s2, guess2) $\parallel$ read(s2, ord2)

$(P_{27}, A_{27}, Q_{27}) = \{ok: P_{26}\}\{ok: Q_{26}\}$
$\{ad: \exists g^2 \exists u^2 \exists s2_a^5.A_{26}(g^2/guess2, s2_a^5/s2_a) \wedge s2_a = (s2_a^5\backslash u^2) \wedge guess2 = u^2\}$

$\rightarrow PBV$ read(s1, ord) $\parallel$ read(s2,guess2) $\parallel$ read(s2, ord2)

$(P_{28}, A_{28}, Q_{28}) = \{ok: P_{27}\}\{ad: \exists u^2.guess2 = u^2\}$
$\{ok: \exists f.(\alpha > V18M) \wedge (initp = f) \wedge (curp2 = initp/10)\}$

$\rightarrow Adv.Cons.$ read(s1, ord) $\parallel$ read(s2,guess2) $\parallel$ read(s2, ord2)

$(P_{29}, A_{29}, Q_{29}) = \{ok: P_{28}\}\{ad: \exists \alpha \exists f \exists u^2.(guess2 = u^2) \wedge (u = f/10) \wedge (\alpha > V18M)\}$
$\{ok: Q_{28}\}$

$\rightarrow Succ$ read(s1, ord) $\parallel$ adv_assert(guess1 == guess2) $\parallel$ read(s2, ord2) quantities above which the price does not decrease anymore. In order to model this example in adversarial logic, we define and use a derived rule *Dup* at step (P_2, A_2) in Table 7. The *Dup* rule can be expressed solely based on the parallel rule with parameters $\epsilon_1 = \epsilon_2 = ok$ and $P_1 = P_2$ and $Q_1 = Q_2$ and $c_1 = c_2$.

$$\mathbf{Dup} \; \frac{[ok : P_1]c_1[ok : Q_1] \qquad [ok : P_1]c_1[ok : Q_1]}{[ok : P_1][ok : P_1] \, c_1 \parallel c_1 \, [ok : Q_1][ok : Q_1]}$$

The proof exhibits loop iterations at which the price converges, and symbolically compares return values in the adversary. Combining the parallel backward variant rule at (P_{16}, A_{16}, Q_{16}) followed by the adversarial consequence rule at (P_{17}, A_{17}, Q_{17}) gather *GetPrice* conditions, while this happens at (P_{28}, A_{28}, Q_{28}) and (P_{29}, A_{29}, Q_{29}) for function *GetPrice2*. This is possible without the adversary having preliminary knowledge of internal program values and state (such as the initial price), as long as the target program code is known.

5 Semantics

In this section, we develop a denotational semantics for adversarial logic. This semantics is defined compositionally for each of the rules of AL (Table 8).

Table 8. Relational denotational semantics for AL with transitions from state pairs (σ_p, σ_a) to (σ_q, σ_b) with $\epsilon, \epsilon_1, \epsilon_2 \in \{ok, ad\}$ and $\Sigma_x \in \{\Sigma_a, \Sigma_p\}$

$$
\begin{aligned}
[\![x = e]\!]ok &= \{(\sigma, ((\sigma_p \mid x \mapsto [\![e]\!]_{\sigma_p}), \sigma_a))\} \\
[\![x = e]\!]ad &= \{(\sigma, (\sigma_p, (\sigma_a \mid x \mapsto [\![e]\!]_{\sigma_a})))\} \\
[\![x = \mathbf{rand}()]\!]ok &= \{(\sigma, ((\sigma_p \mid x \mapsto v), \sigma_a))\} \\
[\![x = \mathbf{rand}()]\!]ad &= \{(\sigma, (\sigma_p, (\sigma_a \mid x \mapsto v)))\} \\
[\![\mathbf{adv\_assert\ B}]\!]ok &= \emptyset \\
[\![\mathbf{adv\_assert\ B}]\!]ad &= \{((\sigma_p, \sigma_a), \sigma) \mid [\![B]\!]\sigma_a = \text{true}\} \uplus \{((\sigma_p, \sigma_a), \sigma) \mid [\![B]\!]\sigma_a = \text{false}\} \\
[\![\mathbf{skip}]\!]\epsilon &= \{(\sigma, \sigma) \mid \sigma \in \Pi\} \\
[\![\mathbf{assume\ B}]\!]\epsilon &= \{(\sigma, \sigma) \mid [\![B]\!]\sigma = \text{true}\} \\
[\![C^*]\!]\epsilon &= \cup_{i \in \mathbb{N}} [\![C_i]\!]\epsilon \\
[\![C_1 + C_2]\!]\epsilon &= [\![C_1]\!]\epsilon + [\![C_2]\!]\epsilon \\
[\![\mathbf{local}\ x = e\ \mathbf{in}\ C]\!]ok &= \{(((\sigma_p \mid x \mapsto [\![e]\!]_{\sigma_p}), \sigma_a), ((\sigma_q \mid x \mapsto v), \sigma_a)) \mid x \in Var, e \in Expr\} \\
[\![\mathbf{local}\ x = e\ \mathbf{in}\ C]\!]ad &= \{((\sigma_p, (\sigma_a \mid x \mapsto [\![e]\!]_{\sigma_a})), (\sigma_p, (\sigma_b \mid x \mapsto v))) \mid x \in Var, e \in Expr\} \\
[\![C_1; C_2]\!]\epsilon &= \{(\sigma_1, \sigma_3) \mid (\sigma_1, \sigma_2) \in [\![C_1]\!]\epsilon \text{ and } (\sigma_2, \sigma_3) \in [\![C_2]\!]\epsilon\} \\
[\![C_1 \| C_2]\!](\epsilon_1, \epsilon_2) &= \{(\sigma_1, \sigma_1') \mid (\sigma_1, \sigma_1') \in [\![C_1]\!]\epsilon_1\} \cup \{(\sigma_2, \sigma_2') \mid (\sigma_2, \sigma_2') \in [\![C_2]\!]\epsilon_2\} \\
[\![\mathbf{read(s,x)}]\!]\epsilon &= \{((\sigma \mid s \mapsto (l::v)), (\sigma \mid x \mapsto v, s \mapsto l)) \mid s \in Chan, x \in Var\} \\
[\![\mathbf{write(s,x)}]\!]\epsilon &= \{((\sigma \mid s \mapsto l, x \mapsto v), (\sigma \mid s \mapsto (l::v))) \mid s \in Chan, x \in Var\} \\
[\![\mathbf{Com}(C_1, C_2)]\!](\epsilon_1, \epsilon_2) &= \{(((\sigma_1 \mid s \mapsto (v::l_1)), (\sigma_2 \mid s \mapsto l_2)), \\
&\quad ((\sigma_1 \mid s \mapsto l_1), (\sigma_2 \mid s \mapsto (l_2::v)))) \mid s \in Chan\}
\end{aligned}
$$

$$
\begin{aligned}
\Sigma_a &: [Variables \rightarrow Values] \\
\Sigma_p &: [Variables \rightarrow Values] \\
\Pi &= \Sigma_p \times \Sigma_a \\
[\![B]\!] &: \Sigma_x \rightarrow Bool \\
\sigma &= (\sigma_p, \sigma_a) : \Pi \\
[\![C]\!] &\subset \Pi \times \Pi
\end{aligned}
$$

We lay the groundwork to prove soundness of the logic and semantics by reminding some standard definitions.

Definition 1 (Post Image and Semantic Triples). *For any relation $r \in \Sigma \times \Sigma$ and predicate $p \subseteq \Sigma$:*

- *The post-image of r, $post(r) \in P(\Sigma) \to P(\Sigma)$: $post(r)p = \{(\sigma' \mid \exists \sigma \in p. (\sigma, \sigma') \in r\}$*
- *The over-approximate Hoare triple: $\{p\}r\{q\}$ iff $post(r)p \subseteq q$*
- *The under-approximate incorrectness triple: $[p]r[q]$ is true iff $post(r)p \supseteq q$*

We then introduce adversarial semantic triples, which can be understood as a composition of semantic relation between program states Σ_p and adversarial states Σ_a where $\Pi = \Sigma_p \times \Sigma_a$ is the decomposed view of the state space.

Definition 2 (Adversarial Triples). *For any composed relation $(ok, ad) \in \Pi \times \Pi$ and predicates $(p, a) \subseteq \Pi$ with p the program predicate and a the adversarial predicate:*

- *The post-image of (ok, ad) noted $post((ok, ad)) \in P(\Pi) \to P(\Pi)$:*

$$post((ok, ad))(p, a) = \{(\sigma_q, \sigma_b) \mid \exists (\sigma_p, \sigma_a) \in (p, a). ((\sigma_p, \sigma_a), (\sigma_q, \sigma_b)) \in (ok, ad)\}$$

- *The under-approximate adversarial triple:*

$$[p][a](ok, ad)[q][b] \text{ is true iff } post((ok, ad))(p, a) \supseteq (q, b)$$

Conditions for membership $((\sigma_p, \sigma_a), (\sigma_q, \sigma_b)) \in (ok, ad)$ are defined as:

1. $(\sigma_p, \sigma_q) \in ok$ and $(\sigma_a, \sigma_b) \in ad$ if $VAR(\sigma_p) \cap VAR(\sigma_a) = \emptyset$
2. $(ok, ad)((\sigma_p, \sigma_a)) = (\sigma_q, \sigma_b)$ otherwise.

The first formulation of membership is enough for the **Par** rule and all rules where program and adversary are reduced independently. The second formulation is needed for the **Com, Backward variant** and **Adversarial consequence** rules as a channel s may ve involved to share information between program and adversary.

Definition 3 (Incorrectness Principles in Adversarial Logic). *Adversarial logic preserves the symmetries of incorrectness logic:*

- $\wedge\vee$ *symmetry:* $[\epsilon: p]c[\epsilon: q_1] \wedge [\epsilon: p]c[\epsilon: q_2] \iff [\epsilon: p]c[\epsilon: q_1 \vee q_2]$
- $\Uparrow\Downarrow$ *symmetry:* $[\epsilon: p \Rightarrow p'] \wedge [\epsilon: p]c[\epsilon: q] \wedge [\epsilon: q' \Rightarrow q] \iff [\epsilon: p']c[\epsilon: q']$

Adversarial logic inherits the consequence and disjunction rules of incorrectness logic, and therefore preserves incorrectness symmetries. Under-approximate reasoning is similarly unchanged, preserving principles of agreement and denial [1]. The central tool for soundness proof is the characterization lemma, which relates the state transition system of the denotational semantics to the inference system of adversarial logic.

Lemma 1 (Characterization). *The following statements are equivalent:*

1. $[pre\_ok: p][pre\_ad: a]\, C_1 \parallel C_2\, [post\_ok: q][post\_ad: b]$ *is true.*
2. *Every state in the conclusion is reachable from a state in the premises:*
   $$\forall(\sigma_q, \sigma_b) \in (q, b)\, \exists\sigma_p \in p\, \exists\sigma_a \in a : ((\sigma_p, \sigma_a), (\sigma_q, \sigma_b)) \in (ok, ad)$$

The characterization lemma in Adversarial Logic extends the one of Reverse Hoare Logic of de Vries and Koutavas [18] as inherited by Incorrectness Logic [1]. Sufficient conditions for the characterization lemma to hold can be decomposed into three subcases:

1. if $\sigma_a = \sigma_b : \forall(\sigma_q, \sigma_b) \in (q, b)\, \exists\sigma_p \in p : (\sigma_p, \sigma_q) \in ok$
2. if $\sigma_p = \sigma_q : \forall(\sigma_q, \sigma_b) \in (q, b)\, \exists\sigma_a \in a : (\sigma_a, \sigma_b) \in ad$
3. Otherwise: $\forall(\sigma_q, \sigma_b) \in (q, b)\, \exists(\sigma_p, \sigma_a) \in (p, a) : ((\sigma_p, \sigma_a), (\sigma_q, \sigma_b)) \in (ok, ad)$

Cases (1) and (2) yield from the fact that core incorrectness rules of adversarial logic are the same as incorrectness logic. We shall provide additional proofs for rules **Read**, **Write**, **Success** and **Failure** which are new to AL. Case (3) is necessary when both program and adversary take steps together, as done in parallel composition, communication, backward variant and adversarial consequence rules.

Definition 4 (Interpretation of Specifications). $[ok: p][ad: a](C_1 \| C_2)[ok: q][ad: b]$ *is true iff the adversarial triple* $[p][a](\llbracket C_1 \| C_2 \rrbracket_{(ok, ad)})[q][b]$ *holds.*

Proving that this equivalence holds for AL requires proving the soundness theorem of adversarial logic.

Theorem 1 (Soundness). *Every adversarial logic proof is validated by the rules of adversarial denotational semantics.*

To prove soundness, we appeal to the following substitution lemma generalized from reverse hoare logic [18], which we hold true without proving it.

Lemma 2 (Substitution). $\sigma \in P(n/x) \iff (\sigma|x \to n) \in P$. *That is:*

- $\sigma_p \in P(n/x) \iff (\sigma_p|x \to n) \in P$ *if* $x \in \sigma_p$
- $\sigma_a \in A(n/x) \iff (\sigma_a|x \to n) \in A$ *if* $x \in \sigma_a$

The substitution lemma can be instantiated for the program relation as well as the adversarial relation when $x \in Vars$. There is no ambiguity allowed since AL forbids variable sharing. We also follow de Vries and Koutavas [18] by managing local variables using alpha-renaming, rather than using explicit substitution like O'Hearn [1]. This changes the soundness proof for the local variable rule and the assignment rule. For all symmetric cases involving ϵ, we may give the proof one of these two cases and omit the identical proof for the other side.

Proof. We prove soundness for each rule of Adversarial logic. For most cases, we appeal to the characterization lemma of adversarial logic semantics to show that for all post-states of semantic triples, there is a pre-state that satisfies the adversarial precondition of the corresponding rule.

Proof (Unit). Assume (σ_p, σ_a) skip (σ_q, σ_b) and $[\epsilon\colon P]$ skip $[\epsilon\colon Q]$. Show that $\forall(\sigma_q, \sigma_b) \in [\epsilon\colon Q] \ \exists(\sigma_a, \sigma_p) \in [\epsilon\colon P]$. By skip rule, $P = Q$, so $[\epsilon\colon P]$ skip $[\epsilon\colon P]$ is true and $(\sigma_p, \sigma_a) = (\sigma_q, \sigma_b)$. Since $(\sigma_q, \sigma_b) \in [\epsilon\colon P]$ and $(\sigma_p, \sigma_a) = (\sigma_q, \sigma_b)$ then $(\sigma_p, \sigma_a) \in [\epsilon\colon P]$.

Proof (Constancy). Show that $\forall \sigma' \in [\epsilon\colon Q \wedge F] \ \exists \sigma \in [\epsilon\colon P \wedge F]$. By induction hypothesis, $\exists \sigma \in [\epsilon\colon P]$ such that $\sigma \to \sigma'$ and $[\epsilon\colon \sigma' \in Q]$. Since $Mod(c) \cap Free(F) = \emptyset$, $\sigma \to \sigma'$ preserves F. Therefore $\sigma \in [\epsilon\colon P \wedge F]$.

Proof (Assume). Let (σ_p, σ_a) assume B (σ_p, σ_a) and $[\epsilon\colon P]$ assume(B) $[\epsilon\colon P \wedge B]$. Show that $\forall(\sigma_q, \sigma_b) \in [\epsilon\colon P \wedge B] \ \exists(\sigma_p, \sigma_a) \in [\epsilon\colon P]$. Since $(\sigma_p, \sigma_a) = (\sigma_q, \sigma_b)$ by assume rule, $(\sigma_p, \sigma_a) \in P \wedge B$. By consequence rule, $(\sigma_p, \sigma_a) \in [\epsilon\colon P]$.

Proof (Rand). Assume (σ_p, σ_a) x = rand() (σ_q, σ_b) with $(\sigma_q, \sigma_b) = (\sigma_p \mid x \mapsto r, \sigma_a)$. Let $(\sigma_q, \sigma_b) \in [\epsilon\colon P(x/x') \wedge x = r]$ and show that $\forall(\sigma_q, \sigma_b) \ \exists(\sigma_p, \sigma_a) \in [\epsilon\colon P]$. Let us first cover the subcase where $x \in \sigma_p$ and $\epsilon = ok$ Take $(\sigma_p \mid x \mapsto n) \in [ok\colon P]$. By the substitution lemma, $\sigma_p \in [ok\colon P(n/x)]$. By assign rule, $\sigma_q \in [ok\colon P(r/x)]$. That is, $\sigma_p \in [ok\colon \exists x'.P(x'/x) \wedge x' = r]$. The second subcase where $x \in \sigma_a$ and $\epsilon = ad$ can be proved similarly.

Proof (Assign). Take (σ_p, σ_a) x = e (σ_q, σ_b) with $(\sigma_q, \sigma_b) = (\sigma_p \mid x \mapsto \llbracket e \rrbracket_{\sigma_p}, \sigma_a)$. Let $(\sigma_q, \sigma_b) \in [\epsilon\colon P(x/x') \wedge x = e(x'/x)]$ and show that $\forall(\sigma_q, \sigma_b) \ \exists(\sigma_p, \sigma_a) \in [\epsilon\colon P]$. Let us first cover the subcase where $x \in \sigma_p$. Take $(\sigma_p \mid x \mapsto n) \in [ok\colon P]$. By the substitution lemma, $\sigma_p \in [ok\colon P(n/x)]$. By assign rule, $\sigma_q \in [ok\colon P(\llbracket e \rrbracket_{\sigma_p \mid x \mapsto n}/x)]$. Taking $\llbracket e \rrbracket_{\sigma_p \mid x \mapsto n} = m$ we obtain that $\sigma_p \in [ok\colon \exists x'.P(x'/x) \wedge x' = m]$. The second subcase where $x \in \sigma_a$ and $\epsilon = ad$ can be proved similarly.

Proof (Local). Let us first take the case where $x \in \sigma_q$. Show that $\forall(\sigma_q \mid x \mapsto v, \sigma_a) \in [ok\colon \exists x.Q]$ there is $(\sigma_p \mid x \mapsto \llbracket e \rrbracket_{\sigma_p}, \sigma_a) \in [ok\colon P]$. By the substitution lemma, $\sigma_q \in [ok\colon \exists x.Q(v/x)]$, that is $\sigma_q \in [ok\colon \exists x.Q]$ since x is bound. By induction hypothesis and executing backward, we obtain $\sigma_p \in [ok\colon P \wedge x = e]$. By the substitution lemma, we have $(\sigma_p \mid x \mapsto \llbracket e \rrbracket_{\sigma_p}) \in [ok\colon P(e/x)]$. Since $x \notin Free(P)$, we conclude $(\sigma_p \mid x \mapsto \llbracket e \rrbracket_{\sigma_p}) \in [ok\colon P]$. The second subcase where $x \in \sigma_b$ can be proved similarly.

Proof (Read). We first define $\sigma' = (\sigma \mid x \mapsto v, s \mapsto l)$ and prove that for all $\sigma' \in [\epsilon\colon \exists x' \exists s'.P(s'/s, x'/x) \wedge (s = s' \backslash v) \wedge x = v]$ there is $(\sigma \mid s \mapsto (l\colon\colon v)) \in [\epsilon\colon P]$. By the substitution lemma: $\sigma \in [\epsilon\colon \exists x' \exists s'.P(s'/s, x'/x) \wedge (s = s' \backslash v) \wedge x = v)(v/x)(l/s)]$ That is: $\sigma \in [\epsilon\colon \exists x'.\exists s'.P(s'/s, x'/x) \wedge (l = (s' \backslash v))]$. By rewriting s', we obtain $\sigma \in [\epsilon\colon \exists x.P((l\colon\colon v)/s, x'/x)]$. Executing read backward, we get $(\sigma \mid s \mapsto (l\colon\colon v), x \mapsto x') \in [\epsilon\colon P]$. We can conclude since $\{\sigma \mid s \mapsto (l\colon\colon v), x \mapsto x'\} \subseteq \{\sigma \mid s \mapsto (l\colon\colon v)\}$

Proof (Write). Let $[\![write(s,x)]\!]\epsilon = \{((\sigma \mid s \mapsto l, x \mapsto v), (\sigma \mid s \mapsto (l::v)))\}$ and $[\epsilon: P \wedge x = y \wedge s = l]$ write(s,x) $[\epsilon: \exists s'.P(s'/s) \wedge s = (s'::v)]$. Define $\sigma' = (\sigma \mid s \mapsto (l::v))$ and show that $\forall \sigma' \in [\epsilon: \exists s'.P(s'/s) \wedge s = (s'::v)]$ there is a $(\sigma \mid s \mapsto l, x \mapsto v) \in [\epsilon: P \wedge x = v \wedge s = l]$. By the substitution lemma, $\sigma \in [\epsilon: \exists s'.P(s'/s)((l::v)/s) \wedge (l::v) = (s'::v)]$. That is, $\sigma \in [\epsilon: P(s'/s) \wedge s' = l]$. By inlining s' we get $\sigma \in [\epsilon: P(l/s) \wedge s = (l::v)]$. By executing write backward, we obtain $\sigma \in [\epsilon: P \wedge x = v \wedge s = l]$.

Proof (Com). Assume $[\![Com(C_1, C_2)]\!]_{\epsilon_1, \epsilon_2} = \{(((\sigma_1 \mid s \mapsto (v::l_1)), (\sigma_2 \mid s \mapsto l_2)), (\sigma'_1, \sigma'_2))\}$ with $\epsilon_1, \epsilon_2 \in \{ok, ad\}$ and $\sigma'_1 = (\sigma_1 \mid s \mapsto l_1)$ and $\sigma'_2 = (\sigma_2 \mid s \mapsto (l_2::v))$. Prove for all $(\sigma'_1, \sigma'_2) \in [\epsilon_1 : \exists s'.P(s'/s) \wedge s = (s'\backslash v)][\epsilon_2 : \exists s'.A(s'/s) \wedge s = (s'::v)]$ there exists $((\sigma_1 \mid s \mapsto (v::l_1)), (\sigma_2 \mid s \mapsto l_2)) \in [\epsilon_1 : P][\epsilon_2 : A]$. By the substitution lemma, $((\sigma_1 \mid s \mapsto (v::l_1)), (\sigma_2 \mid s \mapsto l_2)) \in [\epsilon_1 : P((v::l_1)/s)][\epsilon_2 : A(l_2/s)]$. Introducing s', we have $((\sigma_1 \mid s \mapsto (v::l_1)), (\sigma_2 \mid s \mapsto l_2)) \in [\epsilon_1 : \exists s'.P(s'/s) \wedge s' = (v::l_1)][\epsilon_2 : \exists s'.A(s'/s) \wedge s' = l_2]$. By $[\![Com(C_1, C_2)]\!]$ rule, $(\sigma'_1, \sigma'_2) \in [\epsilon_1 : \exists s'.P(s'/s) \wedge s' = (v::l_1) \wedge s = l_1] [\epsilon_2 : \exists s'.A(s'/s) \wedge s' = l_2 \wedge s = (l_2::v)]$. Rewriting s using s' we now have: $(\sigma'_1, \sigma'_2) \in [\epsilon_1 : \exists s'.P(s'/s) \wedge s = (s'\backslash v)][\epsilon_2 : \exists s'.A(s'/s) \wedge s = (s'::v)]$.

Proof (Iterate). Immediate by semantic definitions and *Iterate* rules.

Proof (Sequencing). Immediate by semantic definition and induction hypotheses.

Proof (Choice). Immediate by semantic definition and induction hypotheses.

Proof (Disjunction). Immediate by logical definition and $\wedge \vee$ symmetry [1] of AL.

Proof (Consequence). Immediate by logical definition and $\Uparrow\Downarrow$ symmetry [1] of AL.

Proof (Par). Immediate by semantic definitions and induction hypotheses.

Proof (Success). Assume (σ_p, σ_a) adv_assert(B) $\{(\sigma_q, \sigma_b) \mid [\![B]\!]_{\sigma_a} = true\}$ by $\uplus$ left subset. Success rule gives us that $[ad : P \wedge (P \Rightarrow B)]$ adv_assert(B) $[ad : P \wedge true]$. Show that $\forall(\sigma_q, \sigma_b) \in P \wedge true \, \exists(\sigma_p, \sigma_a) \in P \wedge (P \Rightarrow B)$. Success rule does not modify any variable of (σ_p, σ_a), therefore $(\sigma_p, \sigma_a) = (\sigma_q, \sigma_b)$ and $(\sigma_p, \sigma_a) \in P \wedge B$. Since $(P \wedge B) \Longleftrightarrow P \wedge (P \Rightarrow B)$, we conclude that $(\sigma_p, \sigma_a) \in P \wedge (P \Rightarrow B)$.

Proof (Failure). Assume (σ_p, σ_a) adv_assert(B) $\{(\sigma_q, \sigma_b) \mid [\![B]\!]_{\sigma_a} = false\}$ by $\uplus$ right subset. Failure rule gives us that $[ad: P \wedge (P \Rightarrow \neg B)]$ adv_assert(B) $[ad: P \wedge \neg B]$. Show that $\forall(\sigma_q, \sigma_b) \in P \wedge \neg B \, \exists(\sigma_p, \sigma_a) \in P \wedge (P \Rightarrow \neg B)$. Failure rule does not modify any variable of (σ_p, σ_a), therefore $(\sigma_p, \sigma_a) = (\sigma_q, \sigma_b)$ and $(\sigma_p, \sigma_a) \in P \wedge \neg B$. Since $(P \wedge \neg B) \Longleftrightarrow P \wedge (P \Rightarrow \neg B)$, we conclude that $(\sigma_p, \sigma_a) \in P \wedge (P \Rightarrow \neg B)$.

Proof (Adversarial Consequence). We know that $(A' \wedge \exists v1.Q \wedge v1 = v2) \Rightarrow A'$. Applying the consequence rule backwards, $\sigma_b \in [ad\colon A' \wedge \exists v1.Q \wedge v1 = v2]$ implies $\sigma_b \in [ad\colon A']$. Therefore by induction hypothesis, we know $\exists \sigma_a \in [ad\colon A]$. By the second induction hypothesis, we also know that $\forall \sigma_q \in [ok\colon P'] \, \exists \sigma_p \in [ok\colon P]$. Applying the parallel rule backward, we obtain that $\forall(\sigma_q, \sigma_b) \in [ok\colon P'][ad\colon A'] \, \exists(\sigma_p, \sigma_a) \in [ok\colon P][ad\colon A]$.

Proof (Parallel Backward Variant). We show that $\forall(\sigma_q, \sigma_b) \in [ok\colon \exists n.P(n)][ad\colon \exists m.A(m)]$ there exists (σ_p, σ_a) such as $(\sigma_p, \sigma_a) \rightarrow (\sigma_q, \sigma_b)$ and $(\sigma_p, \sigma_a) \in [ok\colon P(0)][ad\colon A(0)]$.

Proof (Case $n = m = 0$). Immediate by definition of **Iterate Zero** rule, with $(\sigma_p, \sigma_a) = (\sigma_q, \sigma_b)$.

Proof (Case $n = m$ and $i = j = 1$). By inductive hypothesis, it holds that $[ok\colon P(n-1)][ad\colon A(m-1)]c_1 || c_2 [ok\colon P(n)][ad\colon A(m)]$ and there is a $(\sigma_{p(n-1)}, \sigma_{a(m-1)}) \in [ok\colon P(n-1)][ad\colon A(m-1)]$. We reuse the induction hypothesis several times going backward until we reach $(\sigma_{p0}, \sigma_{a0}) \in [ok\colon P(0)][ad\colon A(0)]$

Proof (Case $n \neq m$). By inductive hypothesis, it holds that $[ok\colon P(n)][ad\colon A(m)]c_1 || c_2 [ok\colon P(n+i)][ad\colon A(m+j)]$. Therefore, $\exists(\sigma_{q(n-i)}, \sigma_{b(m-j)}) \in [ok\colon P(n-i)][ad\colon A(m-j)]$. Define $\delta(n, m) : (\mathbb{N} \times \mathbb{N}) \rightarrow (\mathbb{B} \times \mathbb{B})$ the function mapping values of (n, m) to their corresponding values (i_n, j_m) where $i, j \in \{0, 1\}$. We have three subcases:

- $\delta(n, m) = (0, 1)$ and $\exists(\sigma_{q(n)}, \sigma_{b(m-1)}) \in [ok\colon P(n)][ad\colon A(m-1)]$.
- $\delta(n, m) = (1, 0)$ and $\exists(\sigma_{q(n-1)}, \sigma_{b(m)}) \in [ok\colon P(n-1)][ad\colon A(m)]$.
- $\delta(n, m) = (1, 1)$ and $\exists(\sigma_{q(n-1)}, \sigma_{b(m-1)}) \in [ok\colon P(n-1)][ad\colon A(m-1)]$.

Recursively going backward using one of the three subcases, we eventually reach one of the two following termination conditions:

- The program reaches its initial condition before the adversary:
    - $(\sigma_{q0}, \sigma_{b(m-j)}) \in [ok\colon P(0)][ad\colon A(m-j)]$.
    - For all remaining $(m-j)$ steps, we have $\delta(0, m) = (0, 1)$
    - $(\sigma_{p0}, \sigma_{a0}) \xrightarrow{m-j} (\sigma_{p0}, \sigma_{b(m-j)}) \in [ok\colon P(0)][ad\colon A(m-j)]$
- The adversary reaches its initial condition before the program:
    - $(\sigma_{q(n-i)}, \sigma_{b0}) \in [ok\colon P(n-i)][ad\colon A(0)]$.
    - For all remaining $n-i$ steps, we have $\delta(n, 0) = (1, 0)$
    - $(\sigma_{p0}, \sigma_{a0}) \xrightarrow{n-i} (\sigma_{q(n-i)}, \sigma_{a0}) \in [ok\colon P(n-i)][ad\colon A(0)]$

6   Alternative Presentation

Different representations of program semantics can encode much of the same concepts as adversarial logic, albeit at different levels of abstractions. We briefly mention a couple of such representations without deep-diving into their respective theory.

6.1 Dynamic Logic

Many of the concepts put forward in this article can be expressed using the
dynamic logic of Harel [16]. Let an adversarial system $S = (W, m, \pi)$ and its
specification $A\$ = [f_{s_0}, f_{s_1}, ..., f_{s_n}]$ with $\mathbb{F} \in A\$$ a list of formulae to be satisfied
in order. A structure S can be defined as a triple (W, m, π) where W is a non-
empty set of states, m is the state transition function, and π is a labeling function
indicating in which state formulae in $\mathbb{F}$ hold.

$$S = (W, m, \pi) \hat{=} \begin{cases} W = P \times A \\ m : W \to 2^{W \times W} \\ \pi : F \to 2^W \end{cases} \tag{1}$$

Satisfiability $S \vdash A\$$ can then be defined as conditions on the structure S.

$$\exists z s_0, s_1, ..., s_n z \hat{=} \begin{cases} s_0 = (\sigma_{p_0}, \sigma_{a_0}) \in \pi(f_{s_0}) \\ s_n = (\sigma_{p_n}, \sigma_{a_n}) \in \pi(f_{s_n}) \\ \forall j < n : ((\sigma_{p_j}, \sigma_{a_j}), (\sigma_{p_{j+1}}, \sigma_{a_{j+1}})) \in m(p, a) \\ \forall f_k \in A\$: \exists j_1 < j_2 < n : \\ \quad -\sigma_{j_1} \notin \pi(f_k) \wedge \sigma_{j_1+1} \in \pi(f_k) \\ \quad -\sigma_{j_2} \notin \pi(f_{k+1}) \wedge \sigma_{j_2+1} \in \pi(f_{k+1}) \end{cases} \tag{2}$$

The correspondence between dynamic logic [18] and incorrectness reasoning
was remarked by O'Hearn [1]. This correspondence is preserved in adversarial
logic with the change that every states is a couple (p, a) representing the product
of the program state and the adversary state.

6.2 Information Systems

We now express adversarial logic concepts in the framework of domain theory [17]. In this formalism, we understand *adversarial systems* as a special kind
of Scott's information system. We define an adversarial system $\mathbb{E} = \{\mathcal{D}, Con_\mathcal{D}, \vdash$
$, \bot\}$ where $\mathcal{D} = \Psi_a \times \Sigma \times \Delta \times \Psi_p$ is the adversarial domain, $Con_\mathcal{D}$ is the set
of all finite subsets of $\mathcal{D}$, $\bot$ is the least informative element of $\mathcal{D}$ and $\vdash$ is an
entailment relation on $\mathcal{D}$. The entailment relation operates on a set of contexts
Ψ_a, Ψ_p, Δ, and Σ, where (Fig. 1 and 2):

- Σ is the program input to execute the program with adversarial conditions.
- Ψ_p is the program context holding the symbolic program P.
- Δ is the program output produced by interpreting P with program input.
- Ψ_a is the adversarial context containing facts known by the adversary.

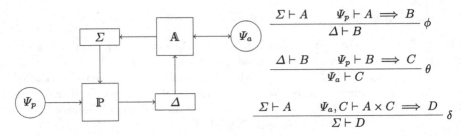

Fig. 1. Entailment relations for adversarial systems with $\mathbb{P}$ the program and $\mathbb{A}$ the adversary. Σ is the program input, Δ is the program output, Ψ_a is the adversarial context and Ψ_p is the program context.

$$\dfrac{\Sigma \vdash A \qquad \Psi_p \vdash A \Longrightarrow B}{\Delta \vdash B} \phi \qquad \dfrac{\Psi_p \vdash B \Longrightarrow C}{\Psi_a \vdash C} \theta \qquad \dfrac{\Sigma \vdash A \qquad \Psi_a \vdash A \times C \Longrightarrow D}{\Sigma \vdash D} \delta$$

Fig. 2. Expected shape of proof tree in adversarial systems

We distinguish Ψ_a and Ψ_p to enforce that program knowledge is not shared to the adversary unless explicitly done so through the Ψ_a context. Entailment relation $\vdash$ is further partitioned into three sub-relations to distinguish each case of inference:

- $\vdash_\delta$: $\Sigma \times \Psi_a \to \Sigma$ is the adversarial entailment relation.
- $\vdash_\phi$: $\Sigma \times \Psi_p \to \Delta$ is the program entailment relation.
- $\vdash_\theta$: $\Delta \times \Psi_p \to \Psi_a$ is the knowledge entailment relation.

Adversarial entailment $\Sigma \times \Psi_a \vdash_\delta \Sigma$ derives next symbolic program input based on the previous input and the adversarial knowledge in context Ψ_a. Program entailment $\Sigma \times \Psi_p \vdash_\phi \Delta$ allows the program to compute an output value based on adversarial input (or from the program itself in case of recursive or internal procedures). Knowledge entailment $\Delta \times \Psi_p \vdash_\theta \Psi_a$ is the only rule which can increase adversarial knowledge Ψ_a. For example, adversarial knowledge of predicate $P(A, B)$ can be obtained based on an observable program output $C \in \Delta$ where $\vdash_\theta C \Longrightarrow P(A, B)$ holds with $P(A, B) \in \Psi_p$, $A \in \Sigma$ and $B \in \Psi_p$. Reachability on $\mathbb{E}$ is defined as computing the least fixed point of the transitive closure of $\vdash$ to discover if the adversarial specification $\mathbb{A}\$$ is satisfiable. Formally, $\mathcal{D} \vdash \mathbb{A}\$ \iff \exists\, g \in \mathcal{D}$ such as $\{g\} \subseteq \mathit{lfp}_\mathcal{D}(\bot_\mathcal{D})$ and $g \vdash \mathbb{A}\$$. The oscillating bit protocol logic can be encoded in formula P as:

$$P = (s = 160) \wedge ((r^n = 0) \Rightarrow (v^n = s)) \wedge ((r^n = 1) \Rightarrow (v^n < s))$$
$$\wedge\, ((r^n = 2) \Rightarrow (v^n > s))$$

The initial adversarial term can be encoded in formula A_0 as:

$$A_0 = (o = 0128) \wedge (s < v^n \Rightarrow (v^{n+1} = v^n - o^n \wedge o^{n+1} = o^n/2))$$
$$\wedge\, (s > v^n \Rightarrow (v^{n+1} = v^n + o^n \wedge o^{n+1} = o^n/2))$$

Modeling the oscillating bit protocol in this framework is done in appendix.

7 Related Work

Related work in extended static checking and formal verification of software comes with a dense prior art, We enumerate a small fraction of the literature which directly influenced our thinking behind adversarial logic.

Incorrectness logic [1] is used as the starting point to formalize adversarial reasoning. In particular, AL borrows the backward variant rule of incorrectness logic and extend it to the parallel setting, a feature left out of scope of concurrent separation incorrectness logic by Raad et al. [14]. In the other hand, AL drops short-circuiting rules of IL, as program errors in AL must be carried transitively to determine the existence of attack paths. The characterization lemma used in under-approximate reasoning in IL and AL was introduced in reverse Hoare logic [18] and take its root in dynamic Logic [16].

Abstract Interpretation is a program analysis framework pioneered by Cousot and Cousot [12] and considered a reference technique in the verification of the absence of bugs. Abstract interpretation is practical [24] and comes with a rich legacy of applications including the creation of abstractions for theorem proving [25], model checking [26], worst-case execution time analysis [27], thread-modular analysis for concurrent programs [28], and input data tracking [29]. In comparison, adversarial logic (and incorrectness logic before it) cannot guarantee the absence of bugs due to its fundamentally under-approximate nature focused on eliminating false positives at the expense of false negatives. Incorrectness principles have been captured in the abstract interpretation framework by the local completeness logic LCL [30], and algebras of correctness and incorrectness can provide a unified formalism to connect both approaches [31].

Process calculus [23] is a well-established formalism to reason about parallel communicating programs and program equivalence using bisimulation. Abadi and Blanchet [32] designed the spi-calculus to verify secrecy properties of cryptographic protocols in the symbolic model. To the same goal, the proverif [33] tool by Blanchet et al. implements the Dolev-Yao model [2] with explicit attacker. It may be possible to extend proverif to include arithmetic in its specifications language, which is required to implement the examples of this paper.

Separation logic is a well-established logic to encode heap reasoning in program analysis. Separation logic comes in both over-approximate [21] and under-approximate [13] flavors. Combined with parallel constructs, separation logic leads to concurrent separation logics [34] and concurrent incorrectness separation logic [14]. Adversarial Logic provides a limited kind of separation between variables of parallel processes without requiring an explicit separating conjunction. Encoding separation expressiveness without the star operator is not unseen, and was previously implemented in the framework of linear maps [35]. Adding support for heap reasoning is a natural next step for adversarial logic.

Automated bug finding by symbolic execution [36,37], white-box fuzz testing [38], and extended static checkers [39] using SMT solvers [40] are often used to maximize code coverage in static and dynamic program analysis. These tools typically focus on checking sequential properties of non-interactive parser-like code [41], leaving concurrency out of scope. Symbolic execution using SMT solvers have known scalability issues with path explosions in loops and constraint tracking in deep paths. Adversarial logic addresses these issues by only requiring a subset of paths to be analyzed sufficient to prove the presence of exploitable bugs. AL implements a flavor of concurrent symbolic execution where symbolic variables are introduced by the adversary to drive attack search without requiring knowledge of internal program state. As such, AL can express adversarial symbolic execution [42] as used to detect concurrency-related cache timing leaks.

Automated exploit generation (AEG [43]) leverages preconditioned symbolic execution to craft a sufficient program condition to exploit stack-based buffer overflow security vulnerabilities. Specific domains of heap vulnerabilities for interpreted languages have been demonstrated practical to attack by Heelan et al. [44]. Concepts of adversarial logic could possibly be added to extend AEG, such as for tackling information disclosure vulnerabilities as illustrated by the Oscillating Bit Protocol example in Sect. 2.

8   Conclusion and Future Work

Adversarial logic (AL) is a new under-approximate logic extending incorrectness logic [1] to perform exploitability analysis of software bugs. Reasoning about accumulated error in programs is critical to understand the severity of security issues and prioritize bug fixing accordingly. This new logic can be used to discover attacks which require a deeper level of interaction with the program, such as subtle information disclosure attacks in interactive protocol loops. We provided a denotational semantics and proved the soundness of adversarial logic showing that all exhibited attack traces in AL are true positives. In the future, embedding adversarial logic principles in concurrent incorrectness separation logic [14] will extend adversarial logic with heap reasoning, so AL can also be used to perform exploitability analysis of pointer bugs.

Acknowledgments. The author thanks Peter O'Hearn, Azalea Raad and Samantha Gottlieb for their useful reviews of this paper.

References

1. O'Hearn, P.W.: Incorrectness logic. Proc. ACM Program. Lang. **4**(POPL), 1–32 (2019)
2. Dolev, D., Yao, A.: On the security of public key protocols. IEEE Trans. Inf. Theory **29**(2), 198–208 (1983)
3. Vyukov, D.: Syzkaller (2015)
4. Serebryany, K.:Continuous fuzzing with libfuzzer and addresssanitizer. In: 2016 IEEE Cybersecurity Development (SecDev), pp. 157–157. IEEE (2016)
5. Project, T.A.: Apache log4j security vulnerabilities (2022)
6. Durumeric, Z., et al.: The matter of heartbleed, pp. 475–488 (2014)
7. Bratus, S., Locasto, M.E., Patterson, M.L., Sassaman, L., Shubina, A.: Exploit programming: from buffer overflows to weird machines and theory of computation. USENIX; Login **36**(6), 13–21 (2011)

8. Dowd, M.: Sendmail release notes for the crackaddr vulnerability (2003)
9. Sotirov, A.: Apache OpenSSL heap overflow exploit (2002)
10. Gruss, D., Lipp, M., Schwarz, M., Fellner, R., Maurice, C., Mangard, S.: KASLR is dead: long live KASLR. In: Bodden, E., Payer, M., Athanasopoulos, E. (eds.) ESSoS 2017. LNCS, vol. 10379, pp. 161–176. Springer, Cham (2017). https://doi.org/10.1007/978-3-319-62105-0_11
11. Hoare, C.A.R.: An axiomatic basis for computer programming. Commun. ACM **12**(10), 576–580 (1969)
12. Cousot, P., Cousot, R.: Abstract interpretation: a unified lattice model for static analysis of programs by construction or approximation of fixpoints. In: Proceedings of the 4th ACM SIGACT-SIGPLAN Symposium on Principles of Programming Languages, pp. 238–252 (1977)
13. Raad, A., Berdine, J., Dang, H.-H., Dreyer, D., O'Hearn, P., Villard, J.: Local reasoning about the presence of bugs: incorrectness separation logic. In: Lahiri, S.K., Wang, C. (eds.) CAV 2020. LNCS, vol. 12225, pp. 225–252. Springer, Cham (2020). https://doi.org/10.1007/978-3-030-53291-8_14
14. Raad, A., Berdine, J., Dreyer, D., O'Hearn, P.W.: Concurrent incorrectness separation logic (2022)
15. Blazytko, T., et al.: {AURORA}: Statistical crash analysis for automated root cause explanation. In: 29th {USENIX} Security Symposium ({USENIX} Security 2020), pp. 235–252 (2020)
16. Harel, D., et al.: First-order dynamic logic (1979)
17. Scott, D.S.: Domains for denotational semantics. In: Nielsen, M., Schmidt, E.M. (eds.) ICALP 1982. LNCS, vol. 140, pp. 577–610. Springer, Heidelberg (1982). https://doi.org/10.1007/BFb0012801
18. de Vries, E., Koutavas, V.: Reverse Hoare logic. In: Barthe, G., Pardo, A., Schneider, G. (eds.) SEFM 2011. LNCS, vol. 7041, pp. 155–171. Springer, Heidelberg (2011). https://doi.org/10.1007/978-3-642-24690-6_12
19. Kocher, P., et al.: Spectre attacks: exploiting speculative execution. In: 2019 IEEE Symposium on Security and Privacy (SP), pp. 1–19. IEEE (2019)
20. Lipp, M., et al.: Meltdown. arXiv preprint arXiv:1801.01207 (2018)
21. Reynolds, J.C.: Separation logic: a logic for shared mutable data structures. In: Proceedings 17th Annual IEEE Symposium on Logic in Computer Science, pp. 55–74. IEEE (2002)
22. Cardwell, J.R.: Ipv6 security issues in Linux and FreeBSD kernels: a 20-year retrospective (2018)
23. Milner, R.: Communicating and Mobile Systems: The PI Calculus. Cambridge University Press, Cambridge (1999)
24. Blanchet, B., et al.: A static analyzer for large safety-critical software. In: Proceedings of the ACM SIGPLAN 2003 Conference on Programming Language Design and Implementation, pp. 196–207 (2003)
25. Cousot, P., Cousot, R.: Abstract interpretation and application to logic programs. J. Logic Program. **13**(2–3), 103–179 (1992)
26. Cousot, P., Cousot, R.: Refining model checking by abstract interpretation. Autom. Softw. Eng. **6**(1), 69–95 (1999)
27. Wilhelm, R., et al.: The worst-case execution-time problem-overview of methods and survey of tools. ACM Trans. Embed. Comput. Syst. (TECS) **7**(3), 1–53 (2008)
28. Miné, A.: Relational thread-modular static value analysis by abstract interpretation. In: McMillan, K.L., Rival, X. (eds.) VMCAI 2014. LNCS, vol. 8318, pp. 39–58. Springer, Heidelberg (2014). https://doi.org/10.1007/978-3-642-54013-4_3

29. Urban, C., Müller, P.: An abstract interpretation framework for input data usage. In: Ahmed, A. (ed.) ESOP 2018. LNCS, vol. 10801, pp. 683–710. Springer, Cham (2018). https://doi.org/10.1007/978-3-319-89884-1_24

30. Bruni, R., Giacobazzi, R., Gori, R., Ranzato, F.: A logic for locally complete abstract interpretations. In: 2021 36th Annual ACM/IEEE Symposium on Logic in Computer Science (LICS), pp. 1–13. IEEE (2021)

31. Möller, B., O'Hearn, P., Hoare, T.: On algebra of program correctness and incorrectness. In: Fahrenberg, U., Gehrke, M., Santocanale, L., Winter, M. (eds.) RAMiCS 2021. LNCS, vol. 13027, pp. 325–343. Springer, Cham (2021). https://doi.org/10.1007/978-3-030-88701-8_20

32. Abadi, M., Gordon, A.D.: A calculus for cryptographic protocols: the SPI calculus. Inf. Comput. **148**(1), 1–70 (1999)

33. Blanchet, B., Smyth, B., Cheval, V., Sylvestre, M.: Proverif 2.00: automatic cryptographic protocol verifier, user manual and tutorial, pp. 05–16 (2018)

34. Brookes, S., O'Hearn, P.W.: Concurrent separation logic. ACM SIGLOG News **3**(3), 47–65 (2016)

35. Lahiri, S.K., Qadeer, S., Walker, D.: Linear maps. In: Proceedings of the 5th ACM Workshop on Programming Languages Meets Program Verification, pp. 3–14 (2011)

36. Cadar, C., Ganesh, V., Pawlowski, P.M., Dill, D.L., Engler, D.R.: Exe: automatically generating inputs of death. ACM Trans. Inf. Syst. Secur. (TISSEC) **12**(2), 1–38 (2008)

37. Cadar, C., Dunbar, D., Engler, D.R., et al.: Klee: unassisted and automatic generation of high-coverage tests for complex systems programs. In: OSDI, vol. 8, pp. 209–224 (2008)

38. Godefroid, P., Levin, M.Y., Molnar, D.: Sage: whitebox fuzzing for security testing. Queue **10**(1), 20:20–20:27 (2012)

39. Ball, T., Hackett, B., Lahiri, S.K., Qadeer, S., Vanegue, J.: Towards scalable modular checking of user-defined properties. In: Leavens, G.T., O'Hearn, P., Rajamani, S.K. (eds.) VSTTE 2010. LNCS, vol. 6217, pp. 1–24. Springer, Heidelberg (2010). https://doi.org/10.1007/978-3-642-15057-9_1

40. de Moura, L., Bjørner, N.: Z3: an efficient SMT solver. In: Ramakrishnan, C.R., Rehof, J. (eds.) TACAS 2008. LNCS, vol. 4963, pp. 337–340. Springer, Heidelberg (2008). https://doi.org/10.1007/978-3-540-78800-3_24

41. Vanegue, J., Lahiri, S.K.: Towards practical reactive security audit using extended static checkers. In: 2013 IEEE Symposium on Security and Privacy, pp. 33–47. IEEE (2013)

42. Guo, S., Wu, M., Wang, C.: Adversarial symbolic execution for detecting concurrency-related cache timing leaks. In: Proceedings of the 2018 26th ACM Joint Meeting on European Software Engineering Conference and Symposium on the Foundations of Software Engineering, pp. 377–388 (2018)

43. Brumley, D., Cha, S.K., Avgerinos, T.: Automated exploit generation. US Patent App. 13/481,248 (2012)

44. Heelan, S., Melham, T., Kroening, D.: Automatic heap layout manipulation for exploitation, pp. 763–779 (2018)

CLEVEREST: Accelerating CEGAR-based Neural Network Verification via Adversarial Attacks

Zhe Zhao[1], Yedi Zhang[1], Guangke Chen[1], Fu Song[1(✉)], Taolue Chen[2], and Jiaxiang Liu[3]

[1] ShanghaiTech University, Shanghai, China
{zhaozhe1,zhangyd1,chengk,songfu}@shanghaitech.edu.cn
[2] Birkbeck, University of London, London, UK
t.chen@bbk.ac.uk
[3] Shenzhen University, Shenzhen, China
jiaxiang.liu@szu.edu.cn

Abstract. Deep neural networks (DNNs) have achieved remarkable performance in a myriad of complex tasks. However, lacking of robustness and black-box nature hinder their deployment in safety-critical systems. A large number of testing and formal verification techniques have been proposed recently, aiming to provide quality assurance for DNNs. Generally speaking, testing is a fast and simple way to disprove—but not to prove—certain properties of DNNs, while formal verification can provide correctness guarantees but often suffers from scalability and efficiency issues. In this work, we present a novel methodology, CLEVEREST, to accelerate formal verification of DNNs by synergistically combining testing and formal verification techniques based on the counterexample guided abstraction refinement (CEGAR) framework. We instantiate our methodology by leveraging CEGAR-NN, a CEGAR-based neural network verification method, and a representative adversarial attack method for testing. We conduct extensive experiments on the widely-used ACAS Xu DNN benchmark. The experimental results show that the testing can effectively reduce the usage of formal verification in the check-refine loop, hence significantly improves the efficiency.

1 Introduction

As a new programming paradigm, deep learning has achieved incredible performance in a large number of complex tasks such as computer vision [31], autonomous driving [1] and cyber-security [7,8,51]. Nevertheless, deep neural networks (DNNs) have shown to be intrinsically vulnerable to perturbations [54],

This work is supported by the National Natural Science Foundation of China (62072309 and 62272397), an oversea grant from the State Key Laboratory of Novel Software Technology, Nanjing University (KFKT2022A03), Birkbeck BEI School Project (EFFECT) and the Natural Science Foundation of Guangdong Province (2022A1515011458).

G. Singh and C. Urban (Eds.): SAS 2022, LNCS 13790, pp. 449–473, 2022.
https://doi.org/10.1007/978-3-031-22308-2_20

which significantly hinders their applications in safety-critical domains. Insofar approaches on quality assurance of DNNs can be roughly classified into two (complementary) categories: testing (e.g., [4,6,20,32,38,41,45,54,69]) and formal verification (e.g. [15,18,21,23,24,26,28,33,35,39,40,49,50,59,60,67]). The purpose of testing is to disprove the robustness of DNNs by providing adversarial examples (i.e., counterexamples). In contrast, formal verification is often used to provide theoretical guarantees of DNNs, and, once violated, counterexamples may be provided. Computationally, testing is able to scale up to large DNN models, whereas formal verification is currently limited in scalability.

Early efforts on robustness verification reduce the problem to constraint solving (e.g., SMT [15,24,28,29,48], LP and MILP [5,14,34,55,61,68]). Such techniques are often both sound (i.e., no false negative) and complete (i.e., no false positive), but are limited in scalability. To improve the scalability, abstraction techniques have been proposed including abstract interpretation [18,49,50,56,60, 63,65] and network abstraction [2,16,19,47,52]. Abstract interpretation approximates the output ranges of neurons for a given input region while network structure abstraction approximates the network via a smaller network which could be verified using existing verification approaches. Unfortunately, abstraction techniques often compromise accuracy. Refinement techniques thus have been adopted which, guided by counterexamples, refine either the estimated output ranges [50,60,63,65] or the abstract network [16,44]. Despite these advances, scalability remains a major challenge in formal verification of DNNs.

In this work, we propose CLEVEREST (CEGAR neural network verification adversarial attacks), a novel methodology to accelerate robustness verification of DNNs by synergistically combining robustness testing and formal verification in the celebrated counterexample guided abstraction refinement (CEGAR) framework [10]. To the best of our knowledge, this is the first attempt to synergistically integrate efficient testing with formal verification for DNN quality assurance. We note that prior work [66] only utilizes testing methods to find adversarial examples before the complete verification, which is to reduce time overhead, but is simply a sequential composition of testing and verification and cannot improve the verification itself.

The methodology of CEGAR follows an abstract-check-refine paradigm. To verify a DNN N against a property, an over-approximation $\widehat{N}$ of N is built and then the check-refine loop is executed. First, we check if the property holds for $\widehat{N}$. If $\widehat{N}$ satisfies the property, we can conclude that N satisfies the property as well (because $\widehat{N}$ is an over-approximation) and stop. Otherwise a counterexample x is found on $\widehat{N}$. We check if x is also a counterexample for N. If it is, we conclude that N does not satisfy the property and stop. Otherwise, the counterexample is spurious and $\widehat{N}$ is refined to exclude the counterexample x. Note that the existing CEGAR-based DNN verification utilizes computational expensive verification techniques to check the abstract systems and to obtain counterexamples in the check-refine loop [16,44].

Our insight of CEGAR in DNN verification is that the abstract systems in early stages of the check-refine loop are often coarse-grained where counterexamples could be easily found by existing robustness testing techniques. Based on this observation, we propose to verify the robustness of DNNs by applying an *abstract-test-refine* paradigm. The abstract-test-refine paradigm is similar to the standard abstract-check-refine paradigm, except that the abstract systems are to be checked by testing. If the testing fails to find a counterexample, the check-refine is leveraged after which the test-refine loop is applied again.

Our framework can be instantiated by any robustness testing and CEGAR-based verification technique. To evaluate its effectiveness, we implement a verification tool, named CLEVEREST-NN, by leveraging the preprocessing, abstraction, refinement and verification procedures from the CEGAR-NN framework [16] and the PGD adversarial attack [38] for testing. In particular, we show how to encode properties as loss functions so that an adversarial attack could be leveraged. We also propose an attack guided abstraction which allows us to avoid too coarse abstract systems by leveraging an adversarial attack during the iterative abstraction. We thoroughly conduct experiments on the widely used ACAS Xu benchmark [27,28], an airborne collision avoidance system built for unmanned aircraft. The experimental results based on 45 DNNs show that our tool is very promising. For instance, compared with CEGAR-NN, CLEVEREST-NN solved 21 more (62 vs. 41 out of 90) clear-of-conflict related verification instances within the same time limit. Furthermore, on the verification instances solved by both tools, the average execution time (per verification instance) is reduced by 42% (from 3,584s to 2,076s).

To summarize, our main contributions are as follows.

- We propose CLEVEREST, a methodology to accelerate DNN verification by synergistically combining robustness testing and CEGAR-based verification.
- We implement our methodology based on CEGAR-NN and PGD adversarial attack, giving rise to a new DNN verification tool CLEVEREST-NN.
- We conduct extensive experiments on ACAS Xu. The experimental results show that our method significantly improve the performance of CEGAR-NN.

Outline. Section 2 presents the background for DNNs, their verification and adversarial attacks. We propose our methodology in Sect. 3 and instantiate the methodology for DNN verification in Sect. 4. Section 5 reports experimental results. Section 6 discusses related work. We conclude this work in Sect. 7.

2   Background

In this section, we introduce the background of DNNs as well as their verification and adversarial attacks.

Deep Neural Networks. An ℓ-layer ($\ell \geq 2$) deep neural network (DNN) N is a graph structured in layers (cf. Figure 1), where the first layer is called an *input layer*, the last layer is called an *output layer*, and the $\ell - 2$ intermediate layers are called *hidden layers*. All the nodes in these layers are called *neurons* and neurons in hidden layers are called *hidden neurons*. Each neuron in a non-input layer is associated with a *bias* and could be pointed to by other neurons via

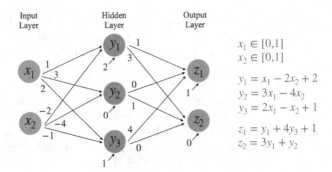

Fig. 1. A fully connected FNN with 2 input nodes (x_1, x_2), 2 output nodes (z_1, z_2) and 1 hidden layers, the activation function is not included. Each edge is associated with a weight value and each node except for inputs is associated with a bias.

weighted, directed edges. The DNN is called a *feed-forward* deep neural network (FNN) if all the weighted, directed edges are from the i-th layer to the $(i+1)$-th layer. An FNN is *fully connected* if each neuron in the i-th layer is connected from all the neurons in the $(i-1)$-th layer. Given an input, the DNN propagates it through the network layer by layer and computes an output. In this work, we consider (fully connected) FNNs, though our methodology is generic.

Formally, an ℓ-layer FNN N is a function $N : X \rightarrow Y$, which maps an input vector $\vec{x} \in X$ to an output vector $\vec{y} = N(\vec{x}) \in Y$. Here, $N(\vec{x}) = \vec{W}_\ell \vec{v}_{\ell-1} + \vec{b}_\ell$, and the output vector $\vec{v}_i$ of the i-th layer is recursively defined as follows:

$$\vec{v}_1 = \vec{x}, \quad \vec{v}_i = \sigma(\vec{W}_i \vec{v}_{i-1} + \vec{b}_i) \text{ for } i = 2, \cdots, \ell - 1,$$

where $\vec{W}_i$ and $\vec{b}_i$ (for $2 \le i \le \ell$) are the weight matrix and bias vector of the i-th layer respectively, and σ is an activation function (e.g., ReLU, sigmoid, tanh) applied to the input vector entrywise. For classification tasks, the output *class* of a given input $\vec{x}$ is the first index i such that $N(\vec{x})$ at the index i is of the highest value. In this work, we denote by $N_c(\vec{x})$ the output class.

Neural Network Verification. The (neural network) *verification query* for a given FNN N is often formalized as a triple $\langle P, N, Q \rangle$, where the pre-condition P is a property on inputs and the post-condition Q is a property on outputs. The verification query amounts to checking if $N(\vec{x})$ satisfies the post-condition Q for all inputs $\vec{x} \in X$ that fulfil the pre-condition P. A *counterexample* of the verification query $\langle P, N, Q \rangle$ is an input $\vec{x} \in X$ such that $\vec{x}$ satisfies the pre-condition P but $N(\vec{x})$ does not satisfy the post-condition Q. In practice, pre-conditions (resp. post-conditions) are often given as conjunctions of linear constraints on the input values (resp. output values).

Robustness, originated with the study of adversarial attacks [54], is a typical property of DNNs which requires a DNN to produce the same classification result for an input when a small perturbation is added. The perturbation range of an input is usually represented as a ball centered at the input under the L-norm distance. There are three widely-used L-norms: L_0, L_2 and L_∞ norms [6].

Given two inputs $\vec{x}, \vec{x}'$, the L_0 norm distance $\|\vec{x} - \vec{x}'\|_0$ is the number of non-zero elements in the vector $\vec{x} - \vec{x}'$, the L_2 norm distance $\|\vec{x} - \vec{x}'\|_2$ is the Euclidean distance between $\vec{x}$ and $\vec{x}'$, and the L_∞ norm distance $\|\vec{x} - \vec{x}'\|_\infty$ is the maximal entry in the vector $|\vec{x} - \vec{x}'|$. A DNN is (local) *robust* w.r.t. an input $\vec{x} \in X$ and a threshold $\epsilon > 0$ if $N_c(\vec{x}) = N_c(\vec{x}')$ for any $\vec{x}' \in X$ such that $\|\vec{x} - \vec{x}'\|_p \le \epsilon$. Counterexamples in this setting are often called *adversarial examples*. The robustness property for any L-norm could be expressed as a neural network verification query, where the constraints $\|\vec{x} - \vec{x}'\|_p \le \epsilon$ for $p = 0, \infty$ and $N_c(\vec{x}) = N_c(\vec{x}')$ for any $\vec{x}' \in X$ can be encoded as conjunctions of linear constraints. Therefore, we define a robustness property as a verification query $\langle P, N, Q \rangle$, where P is given by an input $\vec{x}$ and a threshold $\epsilon > 0$, and Q is given by a conjunction of linear constraints on the output. Towards robustness of DNNs, instead of qualitatively verifying if a given robustness property holds or not, one may have an interest in computing a *maximum robustness radius* ϵ such that $\langle (\vec{x}, \epsilon), N, Q \rangle$ holds but $\langle (\vec{x}, \epsilon'), N, Q \rangle$ does not hold for any $\epsilon' > \epsilon$.

Reachability is another property of DNNs which specifies that inputs from a given input region must produce outputs that lie in a given output region. For example, a DNN model controlling the velocity of an autonomous vehicle may have a safety property specifying that the model never produces a desired velocity value greater than the vehicle's maximum physical speed for any input.

As a convention in neural network verification [16], we say the verification query $\langle P, N, Q \rangle$ is satisfiable (SAT) if it *has* a counterexample, otherwise $\langle P, N, Q \rangle$ is unsatisfiable (UNSAT) indicating no counterexample can be found.

Adversarial Attacks. Consider a DNN N, an input $\vec{x} \in X$ and a distance threshold ϵ (based on L_p norms), an adversarial attack task is to find an adversarial example $\vec{x}' \in X$ such that $N_c(\vec{x}) \ne N_c(\vec{x}')$ and $\|\vec{x} - \vec{x}'\|_p \le \epsilon$. Note that it is the same as finding a counterexample that violates the corresponding robustness property. Since the discovery of adversarial examples [54], many adversarial attacks have been invented as efficient methods for testing the robustness of DNNs [4,6,20,32,38,41,45]. We only briefly recap one representative and promising attack, Project Gradient Descent (PGD) adversarial attack [38], which will be used in our implementation.

The PGD adversarial attack is an iterative attack with a randomized start seed. It first adds a Gaussian noise to the input $\vec{x}$, resulting in a randomized seed $\vec{x}_0 \in X$ such that $\|\vec{x} - \vec{x}_0\|_\infty \le \epsilon$. After that, it iteratively computes a sequence of input samples $\vec{x}_1, \vec{x}_2, \cdots, \vec{x}_m$ until an adversarial example is successfully found or the number of iterations exceeds a given threshold m. Namely, $\vec{x}_{i+1} = \mathtt{clip}_{\epsilon, \vec{x}}(\vec{x}_i + \alpha \cdot \mathtt{sign}(\nabla_{\vec{x}} J(\vec{x}_i, y)))$ where

- $0 < \alpha < \epsilon$ is a small step size;
- y is the ground-truth class $N_c(\vec{x})$ of the input $\vec{x}$;
- $\mathtt{sign}(\cdot)$ is a sign function such that $\mathtt{sign}(z)$ is $+1$ if $z > 0$, -1 if $z < 0$ and 0 if $z = 0$; (it is used in the entry-wise way.)
- $\mathtt{clip}_{\epsilon, \vec{x}}(\vec{x}')$ is a clip function which performs per-entry clipping of the sample $\vec{x}'$ to ensure that $\|\vec{x} - \vec{x}'\|_\infty \le \epsilon$;

– $J(\vec{x}, y)$ is a loss function (e.g., the mean-squared error or the categorical cross-entropy of the DNN);
– $\nabla_{\vec{x}}$ is the partial derivative of the loss function $J(\vec{x}, y)$ at $\vec{x}$.

Intuitively, the attack is to search an input sample $\vec{x}' \in X$ to maximize the loss function. To prevent the attack from trapping in local optima, the above search of an adversarial example is often repeated multiple times. The details of the PGD adversarial attack algorithm are given in Appendix A.1.

Example 1. Consider the illustrative example shown in Fig. 1. we can obtain the computational flow of the neural network in terms of the specific weights and biases. Suppose we want to verify if $z_1 > z_2$, from the neural network verification point of view, we can treat these equations and properties as constraints for SMT solving [28], or perform symbolic interval analysis from the input layer-by-layer [59], etc. From the adversarial attack point of view, we simply need to find a counterexample in the input interval to disprove $z_1 > z_2$. When this problem is easy to disprove, the use of attack algorithm saves substantial time over formal verification. We explore how to synergistically combine SMT-based formal verification and adversarial attacks in this work.

3   Methodology

In this section, we present our methodology based on counterexample-guided abstraction refinement (CEGAR). We start by presenting the standard CEGAR in literature, and then explain how to integrate it with testing.

3.1   The Standard CEGAR Framework

The standard CEGAR framework based on the abstract-check-refine paradigm is shown in Algorithm 1 (*without* the blue-colored code at lines 3–9). Given a verification query $\langle P, N, Q \rangle$, upon termination Algorithm 1 returns either UNSAT indicating that the verification query $\langle P, N, Q \rangle$ holds, or (SAT,*cex*) indicating that the query $\langle P, N, Q \rangle$ does not hold where *cex* is a counterexample. In detail, Algorithm 1 first builds an initial abstract model $\widehat{N}$ via invoking the procedure abstract (line 1). It then iteratively verifies and refines $\widehat{N}$ until the verification query is proved UNSAT or a genuine counterexample *cex* in the target system N is found (lines 10–15). In each iteration, the verification query $\langle P, \widehat{N}, Q \rangle$ with the up-to-date abstract system $\widehat{N}$ is verified by invoking the underlying verification engine verify (line 10). If it is proved UNSAT, Algorithm 1 returns UNSAT and the verification query $\langle P, N, Q \rangle$ holds. In case $\langle P, \widehat{N}, Q \rangle$ is proved SAT, a counterexample *cex* is returned by verify whose feasibility in the target system N is checked (line 12). If *cex* is a genuine counterexample in the target system N, Algorithm 1 returns (SAT,*cex*) (line 13); otherwise the abstract system $\widehat{N}$ is refined via invoking the refinement procedure refine (line 14).

Remark that it is implicitly assumed that the abstraction abstract and the refinement refine procedures only generate over-approximations of the target

---

Algorithm 1: Our CEGAR framework

Input : a verification query $\langle P, N, Q \rangle$
Output: verification result UNSAT, or SAT with a counterexample cex

1 $\widehat{N} \leftarrow$ abstract(P,N,Q);   /* Generate an initial abstract system */
2 **while** True **do**
3     $cex \leftarrow$ test$(P, \widehat{N}, Q)$;   /* Test the abstract system */
4   **if** $cex \neq$ NULL **then**   /* Find a counterexample by testing */
5   **if** cex is a counterexample of $\langle P, N, Q \rangle$ **then**
6   **return** (SAT, cex);   /* Find a genuine counterexample */
7   **else**
8           $\widehat{N} \leftarrow$ refine$(\widehat{N}, cex)$;   /* Refine the abstract system */
9   **continue**;   /* Skip verify and back to test */
10   $cex \leftarrow$ verify$(P, \widehat{N}, Q)$;   /* Verify the abstract system */
11   **if** $cex \neq$ NULL **then**   /* Find a counterexample by verification */
12   **if** cex is a counterexample of $\langle P, N, Q \rangle$ **then**
13   **return** (SAT, cex);   /* Find a genuine counterexample */
14   **else** $\widehat{N} \leftarrow$ refine$(\widehat{N}, cex)$;   /* Refine the abstract system */
15   **else return** UNSAT

---

system N and the underlying verification engine verify is sound. Otherwise, one cannot conclude that verification query $\langle P, N, Q \rangle$ holds even if Algorithm 1 returns UNSAT. Furthermore, the underlying verification engine is often required to be complete and has the capability for producing a counterexample if the verification query is SAT, namely, the verification of $\langle P, \widehat{N}, Q \rangle$ returns either UNSAT or a counterexample cex if SAT.

3.2 Our CEGAR Framework

Our CEGAR framework is based on the key observation that it is fast to find counterexamples in the coarse-grained, abstract systems via testing techniques. As a result, we propose an *abstract-test-refine* paradigm, where check-refine is applied *only* when the testing fails to find a counterexample. Our CEGAR framework is shown in Algorithm 1, where the blue-colored code (lines 3–9) follows the abstract-test-refine paradigm while the other code is the same as in the standard CEGAR framework.

Given a verification query $\langle P, N, Q \rangle$, after building the initial abstract system $\widehat{N}$ (line 1), Algorithm 1 first repeatedly tests and refines the abstract system $\widehat{N}$ until either a counterexample found in the abstract system $\widehat{N}$ is genuine in the target system N; or the procedure test fails to find a counterexample in the abstract system $\widehat{N}$ (within a given test budget) (lines 3–9). It is easy to see that the test-refine (lines 3–9) is the same as the original check-refine (lines 10–15), except that the verify procedure is replaced by the test procedure. When the testing fails to found an adversarial example, check-refine is applied as in the de facto CEGAR scheme except that the refined system $\widehat{N}$ is retested again in the test-refine loop. At this moment, the abstract system $\widehat{N}$ may have already been significantly refined by the test-refine loop so that computational expensive verification of many coarse-grained abstract systems could be avoided. Ideally, if the testing method is powerful enough, it would be able to find a counterexample in most cases. Consequently, for the verification query that does not hold, the test-refine loop could more likely find a genuine counterexample and avoid calls to verification, thus, the `verify` procedure would be rarely invoked. We note that for the verification query that holds, `verify` would be invoked at least once.

Proposition 1. *If Algorithm 1 returns (*SAT*,cex), then cex is a counterexample of the verification query* $\langle P, N, Q \rangle$. *If Algorithm 1 returns* UNSAT, *then the verification query* $\langle P, N, Q \rangle$ *holds.*   □

Remark that, the new CEGAR scheme may not be effective in verifying general software/hardware systems, as finding counterexamples is still non-trivial via testing. However, for neural networks, counterexamples (adversarial attacks) are pervasive and there have been advanced techniques to find them (cf. Sect. 2).

4   DNN Verification in Our CEGAR Scheme

In this section, we first recall the preprocessing, abstraction and refinement procedures provided in CEGAR-NN based on which we show how to instantiate our CEGAR framework by leveraging the PGD adversarial attack [38] for testing due to its effectiveness and efficiency. We should emphasize that our CEGAR scheme can be used on any de facto CEGAR-based DNN verification approaches and leverage any promising testing methods such as BIM [32], DeepFool [41], C&W [6] and DeepXplore [46].

4.1   CEGAR-NN

CEGAR-NN instantiates the `abstract`, `verify` and `refine` procedures in CEGAR, where `verify` is implemented by the Marabou DNN verification engine [29].

Preprocessing. CEGAR-NN first preprocesses a verification query $\langle P, N, Q \rangle$, by transforming it into an equivalent verification query $\langle P, N', Q' \rangle$ such that the post-condition Q' is a conjunction of linear inequalities of form $y > c$ for some constant c. Furthermore, each hidden neuron should be classified as a `pos`/`neg` neuron, and a `dec`/`inc` neuron. A hidden neuron is `pos` (resp. `neg`) if all the weights on its outgoing edges are positive (resp. negative), while a hidden neuron is `inc` (resp. `dec`) if increasing the value of this neuron while keeping all the inputs unchanged increases (resp. decreases) the values of the output neurons. As stated by Elboher et al. [16], these restrictions are for the sake of simplicity, and can be achieved by adding a few neurons (at most 4× increase in network size) during preprocessing. From now on, we assume the verification query $\langle P, N, Q \rangle$ has already been preprocessed and satisfies the above assumptions.

The abstract and refine Procedures. CEGAR-NN has two abstraction strategies, called *abstraction-to-saturation* and *indicator-guided abstraction*. Both strategies are based on the `merge` operator, which merges a pair of hidden neurons in a same layer that share the same `pos/neg` and `inc/dec` attributes, resulting in an over-approximated DNN. The abstraction-to-saturation strategy iteratively applies the `merge` operator, producing the smallest abstract DNN. However, this strategy may obtain DNNs that are too coarse so that multiple rounds of refinement are required. The indicator-guided abstraction strategy is proposed to address this issue by estimating when the abstraction has become too coarse using a finite set of chosen inputs X_I. After each abstraction step, the post-condition Q is checked in the abstract DNN using the chosen inputs. If the post-condition Q is violated by some input in X_I, the abstraction is then stopped.

Generally speaking, the `refine` procedure is the inverse of `abstract`, which refines an abstract DNN by iteratively recovering two merged neurons from the corresponding abstract neuron until the counterexample is excluded.

4.2 Instantiating Our CEGAR Scheme

To instantiate our CEGAR framework, we show how to disprove a verification query $\langle P, N, Q \rangle$ and improve the `abstract` procedure, both via an adversarial attack based testing.

Disproving Verification Query. Given a verification query $\langle P, N, Q \rangle$, we assume that P is a conjunction of linear constraints $\bigwedge_{i=1}^{m} lp_i \leq x_i \leq up_i$ on the input values and Q is a conjunction of linear inequalities of $\bigwedge_{i=1}^{n} y_i > c_i$, where the variables x_i's and y_i's correspond to the values of input neurons and output neurons respectively, and lp_i's, up_i's and c_i's are constants. Such properties are widely considered in the DNN verification community, e.g., [18,28,58,66]. To leverage an adversarial attack for testing, we encode the pre-condition P by transforming a conjunction of linear constraints $\bigwedge_{i=1}^{m} lp_i \leq x_i \leq up_i$ into a non-standard L_∞ epsilon ball, and encode the post-condition Q in a loss function J which is maximized by the adversarial attack to find a counterexample.

- **Encoding the pre-condition P.** From the pre-condition P, we let $\vec{\bar{x}}$ be an input such that for every $1 \leq i \leq m$, $\vec{\bar{x}}[i] = \frac{up_i+lp_i}{2}$, and $\vec{\epsilon}$ be a vector such that $\vec{\epsilon}[i] = \frac{up_i-lp_i}{2}$ for every $1 \leq i \leq m$. Clearly, for each $\vec{x}' \in X$, $|\vec{\bar{x}}-\vec{x}'| \leq \vec{\epsilon}$ iff $\vec{x}'$ satisfies P. We denote by `encode(P)` the pair $(\vec{\bar{x}}, \vec{\epsilon})$. For example, suppose $m = 2$ and the constraints lp_i and up_i are $[0, 0.5]$ and $[1, 1]$ for $i = 1, 2$, respectively, then we can obtain $\vec{\bar{x}} = [0.5, 0.75]$, $\vec{\epsilon} = [0.5, 0.25]$.
- **Encoding the post-condition Q.** From the post-condition Q, we define the loss function J as

$$J(\vec{x}) := -\prod_{i=1}^{n} \Big(\max(N(\vec{x})[i] - c_i, 0) \Big)$$

where $N(\vec{x})[i]$ denotes the value of the output neuron y_i. The output property Q in general can be an arbitrary Boolean structure and involve multiple

---

Algorithm 2: PGD adversarial attack based testing

Input : a verification query $\langle P, N, Q\rangle$, restart times n, number of steps per
        time m, a small step size α
Output: an adversarial example cex or NULL

1   $(\vec{\hat{x}}, \vec{\epsilon}) \leftarrow \texttt{encode}(P)$;
2   $J \leftarrow \texttt{encode}(Q)$;
3   **for** $i \leftarrow 1$ **to** n **do**
4   Generate a vector of Gaussian noises $\vec{\delta}$ such that $|\vec{\delta}| \leq \vec{\epsilon}$;
5      $\vec{x}' \leftarrow \vec{\hat{x}} + \vec{\delta}$;   /* Create a randomized seed */
6   **for** $j \leftarrow 1$ **to** m **do**
7          $\vec{y} \leftarrow N(\vec{x}')$;   /* Get the output */
8   **if** $\vec{y}$ *does not satisfy the post-condition* Q **then**
9   **return** $\vec{x}'$;   /* Find a counterexample */
10   **else**
11             $\nabla \leftarrow \texttt{back\_propagate}(N, J(\vec{x}'))$;   /* Get gradient of $J(\vec{x}')$ */
12             $\vec{x}' \leftarrow \texttt{clip}_{\vec{\epsilon},\vec{\hat{x}}}(\vec{x}' + \alpha \times \text{sign}(\nabla))$;   /* Compute a new sample */
13 **return** NULL;

---

neurons which can be transformed into a conjunction of linear inequalities (cf. [16]). Recall that an adversarial attack attempts to maximize $J(\vec{x})$, hence to minimize each term $\max(N(\vec{x})[i] - c_i, 0)$ until it is 0. When $J(\vec{x}')$ is 0 for some input $\vec{x}'$, there exists some i such that $N(\vec{x}')[i] > c_i$ does not hold, hence the output $N(\vec{x}')$ does not satisfy Q. This input $\vec{x}'$ is a counterexample. We denote by $\texttt{encode}(Q)$ the loss function J. We should emphasize that our loss function J is different from the cross-entropy loss function used in the PGD adversarial attack [38], which is not applicable when the output property involves lower or upper bounds. Our loss function is constructed for each output property given as a conjunction of linear inequalities, and can be applied in a variety of verification problems [18,28,58,66].

Based on the above encodings, we implement the test procedure for Algorithm 1 via a PGD adversarial attack based testing (cf. Algorithm 2). Given a verification query $\langle P, N, Q\rangle$, the number of restart times n, the number of iteration steps per time m, a small step size α, Algorithm 2 returns either a counterexample $\vec{x}'$ that satisfies the pre-condition P but violates the post-condition Q, or NULL indicating that no counterexample can be found. Note that the pair of the parameters (n, m) is regarded as the test budget.

In detail, Algorithm 2 first computes the pair $(\vec{\hat{x}}, \vec{\epsilon})$ that encodes the inputs fulfilling the pre-condition P (line 1) and the loss function J that encodes the post-condition Q (line 2). Then, it iteratively executes the outer for-loop (lines 3–12) up to n times. During each iteration, a randomized seed $\vec{x}'$ is obtained by adding Gaussian noises $\vec{\delta}$ to $\vec{\hat{x}}$ (lines 4–5) and then the inner for-loop (lines 6–12) is executed, which iteratively computes a series of new samples (up to m samples) starting from the randomized seed $\vec{x}'$.

During each iteration of the inner for-loop (lines 6–12), Algorithm 2 first computes the output $\vec{y} = N(\vec{x}')$ of the DNN N by forward propagating the input $\vec{x}'$. If $\vec{y}$ does not satisfy the post-condition Q, then $\vec{x}'$ is a counterexample and Algorithm 2 returns $\vec{x}'$. Otherwise, Algorithm 2 performs a backward propagation to get the gradient ∇ of J using $J(\vec{x}')$ (line 11) from which a new sample $\vec{x}'$ is created (line 12), where the clip function $\text{clip}_{\vec{\epsilon},\widehat{x}}$ ensures that $|\widehat{\vec{x}} - \vec{x}'| \leq \vec{\epsilon}$ after updating, hence the new sample $\vec{x}'$ still satisfies the pre-condition P.

Lemma 1. *If Algorithm 2 returns cex for the verification query $\langle P, N, Q \rangle$, then cex is a counterexample of the verification query $\langle P, N, Q \rangle$.*

One may be wondering how to choose hyper-parameters such as restart times n, number of steps per time m, and step size α, and how to handle non-differentiable layers when leveraging adversarial attacks. According to our experiments, the time consumed by attacks is marginal compared to that used in the complete verification method, and the parameters can be selected as in the prior work [32,38]. For non-differentiable layers, gradient estimation methods (e.g. [9]) can be used to approximate the gradient of J.

Improving abstract via Attacks. We exploit the adversarial attack based testing in the building of the initial abstract system, i.e., the abstract procedure in Algorithm 1.

Recall that Elboher et al. [16] proposed two abstraction strategies in CEGAR-NN: abstraction-to-saturation and indicator-guided abstraction, where the former may produce DNNs that are too coarse so that multiple rounds of refinement are required, while the latter is proposed to address this issue by checking if the abstraction has become too coarse using a finite set of chosen inputs X_I, all of which satisfy the pre-condition P. It was mentioned that the set X_I can be generated randomly (adopted in their tool), or according to some coverage criterion of the input region. In this work, we present a more effective way, i.e., *attack-guided abstraction*, to generate the set X_I via an adversarial attack based testing which are more likely to be counterexamples in abstract systems.

We first adjust Algorithm 2 to return all generated $n \times m$ samples, named Algorithm 2*. Our attack-guided abstraction is formalized in Algorithm 3. Given a verification query $\langle P, N, Q \rangle$, and the parameters (restart times n, number of steps per time m, step size α) for the adversarial attack (cf. Algorithm 2*), Algorithm 3 returns an abstract DNN $\widehat{N}$.

In detail, the abstract DNN $\widehat{N}$ is initialized with the given DNN N (line 1) and a set X_I of samples is created by applying Algorithm 2* to $\langle P, \widehat{N}, Q \rangle$ (line 2). After that, we check if the post-condition Q holds using the samples from X_I (line 3). If Q is violated by some sample $\vec{x} \in X_I$, Algorithm 3 returns $\widehat{N}$ (line 4). Otherwise, it iteratively performs the merge operation to compute a less accurate abstract DNN $\widehat{N}'$ and tests $\widehat{N}'$ against Q until either no neurons that can be merged or $\langle P, \widehat{N}', Q \rangle$ becomes SAT, i.e., a counterexample is found (lines 5–15).

During each iteration of the while-loop (lines 5–15), Algorithm 3 first chooses a mergeable pair (v_i, v_j) of neurons (line 6), for which we adopt an approach

---

Algorithm 3: Attack-guided abstraction

    Input   : a verification query $\langle P, N, Q \rangle$, restart times n, number of steps per
                 time m, step size α
    Output: an abstract DNN $\widehat{N}$

1 $\widehat{N} \leftarrow N$;
2 $X_I \leftarrow$ the set of samples created by applying Algorithm 2* to $\langle P, \widehat{N}, Q \rangle$;
3 **if** $\exists \vec{x} \in X_I . \widehat{N}(\vec{x})$ *does not satisfy* Q **then**
4 | return $\widehat{N}$;
5 **while** $\exists$ *a pair of neurons that can be merged* **do**
6 | $(v_i, v_j) \leftarrow$ ChooseBestMergeablePair$(\widehat{N})$;
7 | $\widehat{N}' \leftarrow$ merge$(\widehat{N}, v_i, v_j)$;
8 | **if** $\exists \vec{x} \in X_I . \widehat{N}'(\vec{x})$ *does not satisfy* Q **then**
9 | | return $\widehat{N}$;
10 | **else**
11 | | $X' \leftarrow$ the set of samples created by applying Algorithm 2* to $\langle P, \widehat{N}', Q \rangle$;
12 | | **if** $\exists \vec{x} \in X' . \widehat{N}'(\vec{x})$ *does not satisfy* Q **then**
13 | | | return $\widehat{N}$;
14 | | **else** $X_I \leftarrow X_I \cup X'$
15 | $\widehat{N} \leftarrow \widehat{N}'$;
16 **return** $\widehat{N}$;

---

by Elboher et al. [16]. Next, we build a less accurate abstract DNN $\widehat{N}'$ by
merging (v_i, v_j) in $\widehat{N}$ (line 7) and test if there exists some counterexample $\vec{x} \in X_I$
for $\langle P, \widehat{N}', Q \rangle$ (line 8). If so, we return the previous abstract DNN $\widehat{N}$ (line 9).
Otherwise, we create a new set X' of samples by applying Algorithm 2* to the
query $\langle P, \widehat{N}', Q \rangle$ (line 11). After that, the query $\langle P, \widehat{N}', Q \rangle$ is tested again using
the new samples from X' (line 12). If a counterexample $\vec{x} \in X'$ for $\langle P, \widehat{N}', Q \rangle$
exists, we return the previous abstract DNN $\widehat{N}$ (line 13); otherwise the set X_I
and the abstract DNN $\widehat{N}$ are updated accordingly for the next iteration.

Lemma 2. *For any verification query* $\langle P, N, Q \rangle$, *if Algorithm 3 returns an
abstract DNN* $\widehat{N}$, *then either* $\langle P, \widehat{N}, Q \rangle$ *or* $\langle P, \widehat{N}', Q \rangle$ *has a counterexample, where*
$\widehat{N}'$ *is the abstract DNN obtained from* $\widehat{N}$ *by merging a pair of neurons in the
while-loop of Algorithm 3. Furthermore,* $\widehat{N}$ *is an over-approximation of the DNN
N according to soundness of the* merge *operator [16].*

CLEVEREST-NN. By instantiating the **abstract** and **test** procedures in Algorithm 3 and Algorithm 2 respectively, as well as the **refine** and **verify** procedures implemented as in CEGAR-NN, we obtain a concrete CEGAR-based neural network verification algorithm, named CLEVEREST-NN. Thanks to the completeness of **verify** in CEGAR-NN and the termination guarantee of the refinement, CLEVEREST-NN is both sound and complete.

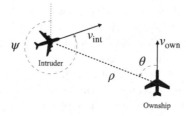

Fig. 2. An illustrating scenario of the ACAS Xu system

   In addition to solving verification queries, CLEVEREST-NN also features a binary-search based approach to approximate the maximum robustness radius ϵ such that $\langle (\vec{x}, \epsilon), N, Q \rangle$ holds for a given DNN N, an input $\vec{x} \in X$ and a post-condition Q. To this end, for each candidate ϵ, we leverage the CEGAR-based approach to verify $\langle (\vec{x}, \epsilon), N, Q \rangle$.

5   Implementation and Evaluation

We have implemented our method in the tool CLEVEREST-NN, where the verify and refine modules are the same as CEGAR-NN [16]. (Indeed, verify is the Marabou DNN verification engine [29].) The input of CLEVEREST-NN is a DNN in the NNet format, pre- and post-conditions, forming a verification query, and the parameters (n, m, α) for adversarial attack based testing. When computing a maximal robustness radius, the pre-condition should be an input sample, the lower bound and upper bound of the radius, instead of a linear constraint.
   We conduct experiments on 45 ACAS Xu DNNs for airborne collision avoidance [27,28]. ACAS Xu is a system (cf. Figure 2) designed for an unmanned aircraft (called Ownship) to produce horizontal turning advisories in order to prevent a collision with another nearby aircraft (called Intruder). Each ACAS Xu DNN has 310 neurons, 5 inputs, 6 hidden layers and 5 outputs. The five inputs are normalized data from airborne sensors, indicating the distance ρ between Intruder and Ownship, the relative angles θ, ψ between Ownship and Intruder, the speeds v_{own} and v_{int} of Ownship and Intruder. The five outputs represent turning advisories: strong left, weak left, strong right, weak right, or clear-of-conflict (i.e., safe to continue along the current trajectory). The ACAS Xu system selects one of 45 DNNs according to the data reading from the airborne sensors and the turning advisory of the selected DNN with the lowest score is the final turning advisory of the system.
   In our experiments, we consider two groups of verification queries and one group of queries for computing maximal robustness radii, where the former two groups are provided by CEGAR-NN and the latter one is obtained from Reluplex [28]. The first group, called COC-queries, consists of 2 verification queries for each ACAS Xu DNN, which ensure that the DNN always advises clear-of-conflict for distant intruders, i.e., the output of clear-of-conflict is always smaller than the other labels (e.g., the previous runner-up operation). The second group,

called ROB-queries, consists of 20 robustness properties with $\epsilon = 0.1$ which ensure that the DNN is robust against small input perturbations.

The third group, called MR-queries, consists of 5 queries for one chosen ACAS Xu DNN, which are used to compute maximal robustness radii, where the five inputs are Points 1–5 of Reluplex [28].

We first evaluate the effectiveness of our attack-guided abstraction strategy (i.e., Algorithm 3), and then evaluate the effectiveness of our CEGAR scheme (cf. Sect. 3.2) using the PGD adversarial attack based testing (i.e., Algorithm 2) both for solving verification queries, and finally evaluate the performance of the overall framework for computing maximal robustness radii. For the sake of presentation, we refer to the different CEGAR schemes with two different abstraction strategies as follows.

– SAT-CLEVEREST-NN = CLEVEREST-NN + abstraction-to-saturation,
– SAT-CEGAR-NN = CEGAR-NN + abstraction-to-saturation,
– ATT-CLEVEREST-NN = CLEVEREST-NN + attack-guided abstraction,
– ATT-CEGAR-NN = CEGAR-NN + attack-guided abstraction.

The experiments were conducted on a machine with Intel Xeon CPU E5-2690 2.60GHz CPU, 64-bit Ubuntu 18.04 LTS operating systems, 256G RAM, with a 3 h timeout per query unless stated explicitly. Note that all experiments were performed on the CPU only for a fair comparison with CEGAR-NN. We remark that the adversarial attack in our CLEVEREST-NN could be accelerated using GPU. The restart times n, number of steps per time m and step size α of the PGD adversarial attack based testing are 10, 10 and $\frac{up-lp}{4}$, respectively, where up and lp are the upper bound and lower bound of the inputs. Note that we compare with [16] only because it is the only publicly available CEGAR-based tool that abstracts/refines network structures. We expect to verify more properties and datasets in the future, with the development and implementation of the CEGAR-based neural network verification framework.

5.1 Performance of Our Attack-guided Abstraction

To evaluate the effectiveness of our attack-guided abstraction strategy, we compare it with the abstraction-to-saturation strategy in both the CEGAR-NN and CLEVEREST-NN frameworks (i.e., ATT-CEGAR-NN vs. SAT-CEGAR-NN and ATT-CLEVEREST-NN vs. SAT-CLEVEREST-NN) for solving 90 (2 × 45) COC-queries. We exclude the indicator-guided abstraction strategy, as it was shown in [16] that the indicator-guided abstraction strategy is significantly worse than the abstraction-to-saturation strategy in the CEGAR-NN framework.

SAT-CEGAR-NN vs. ATT-CEGAR-NN. Figure 3(a) depicts a comparison between ATT-CEGAR-NN and SAT-CEGAR-NN. The blue marks above the red dashed line are the verification queries where ATT-CEGAR-NN (i.e., the attack-guided abstraction strategy) is faster. The red marks on the top are the verification queries where SAT-CEGAR-NN time-outs, while those on the right

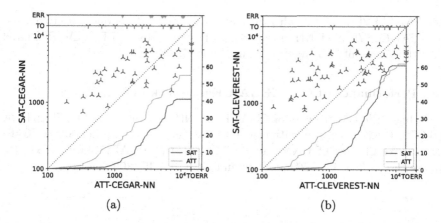

Fig. 3. (a) Comparison between SAT-CEGAR-NN and ATT-CEGAR-NN and (b) comparison between SAT-CLEVEREST-NN and ATT-CLEVEREST-NN, for solving the 90 COC-queries, where the scatter plots compare execution time (log-scale, in seconds); TO denotes timeout; ERR denotes erroneous results on abstract DNNs; the curve plots the number of solved queries with the increased time limit per query.

are where ATT-CEGAR-NN time-outs. The yellow marks on the top are verification queries where SAT-CEGAR-NN reported incorrect results on abstract DNNs. SAT-CEGAR-NN reported UNSAT on 28 abstract DNNs that are indeed SAT.[1]

In summary, ATT-CEGAR-NN solved 55 out of 90 verification queries while SAT-CEGAR-NN solved 41. On those solved by both tools, ATT-CEGAR-NN is faster than SAT-CEGAR-NN on 75.68% verification queries and the average speed-up is 2.23×. From the curve plot in Fig. 3(a), we can observe that ATT-CEGAR-NN constantly solve more verification queries than SAT-CEGAR-NN with the increased time limit per query. We conclude that our attack-guided abstraction strategy outperforms the abstraction-to-saturation strategy in CEGAR-NN.

SAT-CLEVEREST-NN vs. ATT-CLEVEREST-NN. Figure 3(b) depicts a comparison between ATT-CLEVEREST-NN and SAT-CLEVEREST-NN on solving the 90 COC-queries.

In summary, ATT-CLEVEREST-NN solved 62 out of 90 verification queries while SAT-CLEVEREST-NN solved 61. On those solved by both tools, ATT-CLEVEREST-NN is faster than SAT-CLEVEREST-NN on 76.92% of the verification queries and the average speed-up is 2.17×. From the curve plot in Fig. 3(b), we can observe that ATT-CLEVEREST-NN can solve more verification queries

---

[1] This issue has been reported to and confirmed by some authors of Marabou and CEGAR-NN; they replied that this problem is triggered by networks having both very small and very large weights. ATT-CEGAR-NN avoided these errors because these abstract DNNs were proved SAT via our adversarial attack based testing. We have performed differential verification using another sound and complete tool on all intermediate abstract DNNs to confirm our findings.

than SAT-CLEVEREST-NN with the increased time limit per query up to 5,500 s, while SAT-CLEVEREST-NN becomes slightly better than ATT-CLEVEREST-NN when the time limit per query is greater than 5,500 s.

5.2 Performance of Our CEGAR Framework CLEVEREST-NN

To evaluate the effectiveness of CLEVEREST-NN, we compare CLEVEREST-NN and CEGAR-NN configured with the same abstraction strategy, i.e., SAT-CEGAR-NN vs. SAT-CLEVEREST-NN and ATT-CEGAR-NN vs. ATT-CLEVEREST-NN. We use the 90 (2×45) COC-queries and 900 (20×45) ROB-queries.

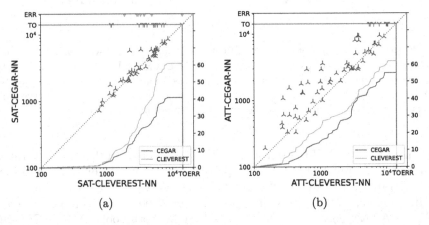

(a)   (b)

Fig. 4. (a) Comparison between SAT-CEGAR-NN and SAT-CLEVEREST-NN and (b) comparison between ATT-CEGAR-NN and ATT-CLEVEREST-NN, for solving the 90 COC-queries.

SAT-CEGAR-NN vs. SAT-CLEVEREST-NN on COC-queries. Figure 4(a) depicts a comparison between SAT-CEGAR-NN and SAT-CLEVEREST-NN for solving the 90 COC-queries.

In summary, SAT-CLEVEREST-NN solved 61 out of 90 verification queries, while SAT-CEGAR-NN solved 41 and reported erroneous results on abstract DNNs for 28 verification queries. On those solved by both tools, SAT-CLEVEREST-NN is faster than SAT-CEGAR-NN on 53.66% verification queries and the average speed-up is 1.09×.

ATT-CEGAR-NN vs. ATT-CLEVEREST-NN on COC-queries. Figure 4(b) depicts a comparison between ATT-CEGAR-NN and ATT-CLEVEREST-NN for solving the 90 COC-queries. ATT-CLEVEREST-NN solved 62 out of 90 verification queries, while ATT-CEGAR-NN solved only 55 verification queries without reporting erroneous results on abstract DNNs. On those solved by both tools, ATT-CLEVEREST-NN is faster than SAT-CEGAR-NN on 74.54% verification queries and the average speed-up is 1.64×. From the curve plot in Fig. 4(a) (resp. Figure 4(b)), we can observe that SAT-CLEVEREST-NN (resp. ATT-CLEVEREST-NN) constantly solved more verification queries than SAT-CEGAR-NN (resp. ATT-CEGAR-NN) with the increased the time limit per query with just a handful of exceptions. These results suggest that our CEGAR framework CLEVEREST-NN is more effective than CEGAR-NN for both the abstraction-to-saturation and attack-guided-saturation strategies.

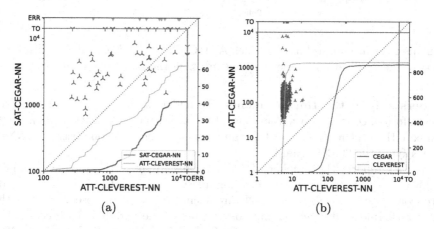

(a)   (b)

Fig. 5. (a) Comparison between SAT-CEGAR-NN and ATT-CLEVEREST-NN for solving the 90 COC-queries, and (b) Comparison between ATT-CEGAR-NN and ATT-CLEVEREST-NN, for solving the 900 (20 × 45) ROB-queries.

SAT-CEGAR-NN vs. ATT-CLEVEREST-NN on COC-queries. Figure 5(a) depicts a comparison between SAT-CEGAR-NN and ATT-CLEVEREST-NN for solving the 90 COC-queries. ATT-CLEVEREST-NN solved 62 out of 90 verification queries, while SAT-CEGAR-NN solved only 41 verification queries and reported erroneous results on abstract DNNs for 28 verification queries. On those solved by both tools, ATT-CLEVEREST-NN is faster than SAT-CEGAR-NN on 81.58% verification queries and the average speed-up is 3.75×. From the curve plot in Fig. 5(a), we can observe that ATT-CLEVEREST-NN solved more verification queries than SAT-CEGAR-NN with the increased time limit per query. These results reveal the improvement brought by this work over CEGAR-NN.

ATT-CEGAR-NN vs. ATT-CLEVEREST-NN on ROB-queries. Figure 5(b) depicts a comparison of between ATT-CEGAR-NN and ATT-CLEVEREST-NN for solving the 900 (20 × 45) ROB-queries.

ATT-CLEVEREST-NN solved 877 out of 900 verification queries, while ATT-CEGAR-NN solved 860 verification queries without reporting any incorrect results on the abstract DNNs. On those solved by both tools, ATT-CLEVEREST-NN is faster than SAT-CEGAR-NN on all the verification queries and the average speed-up is 29.52×. These results indicate that our CEGAR framework is significantly more efficient in verifying robustness properties. We found that almost all

Table 1. #Call per query to the verification engine

Tool	#Call
SAT-CEGAR-NN	2.24
SAT-CLEVEREST-NN	1.09
ATT-CEGAR-NN	2.49
ATT-CLEVEREST-NN	1.00

Table 2. #Binary search step

	Index 1		Index 2		Index 3		Index 4		Average	
	No_c	No_a	No_c	No_a	No_c	No_a	No_c	No_a	No_c	No_a
Point 1	1	3	1	8	4	9	2	2	2.0	5.5
Point 2	1	2	1	3	1	3	1	3	1.0	2.75
Point 3	1	3	1	2	1	1	1	1	1.0	1.75
Point 4	1	5	1	6	1	6	1	6	1.0	5.75
Point 5	1	1	1	1	1	1	1	1	1.0	1.0

`ROB-queries` are non-robust on which `ATT-CLEVEREST-NN` is able to disprove most of the verification queries without invoking the verification engine.

Understanding the Improvements. To understand why ours can improve the performance, we analyze the usage of the underlying verification engine and compare the execution time of `test` and `verify` operations on abstract DNNs, for verifying the 90 `COC-queries`.

Table 1 reports the number of average calls to the verification engine per verification query (where the verification queries on which `CEGAR-NN` reported erroneous results on abstract DNNs are excluded). We can observe that both our attack-guided abstraction and abstract-test-refine paradigm can reduce the usage of formal verification (except for `SAT-CEGAR-NN` vs. `ATT-CEGAR-NN`), which play a major role in improving the efficiency. When `ATT-CLEVEREST-NN` is used, the verification engine is invoked only once per verification query. (Note that the only verification is unavoidable, because all the 90 `COC-queries` are `UNSAT`, so the verification engine has to be used to prove `UNSAT`.) The number of calls to the verification engine for `SAT-CEGAR-NN` and `ATT-CEGAR-NN` is somehow counter-intuitive. We found it is because `SAT-CEGAR-NN` often performs a large number of `merge` operations in one refinement step to exclude a counterexample, while `ATT-CEGAR-NN` only performs few `merge` operations in one refinement step to exclude a counterexample. The execution time is improved by reducing the number `merge` operations.

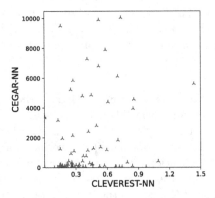

Fig. 6. Comparison of `test` and `verify` operations on abstract DNNs between CLEVEREST-NN and CEGAR-NN.

Figure 6 depicts the execution time of `test` and `verify` operations on abstract DNNs between CLEVEREST-NN and CEGAR-NN using both abstraction strategies, where the last calls to the verification engine are executed. We can observe that testing is significantly faster than formal verification. Indeed, the average testing time used by CLEVEREST-NN is 0.26s while the average verification time used by CEGAR-NN is 1006.94s, with average speed-up 31,513× per verification query.

5.3 Approximating Maximum Robustness Radii

To evaluate CLEVEREST-NN for approximating maximum robustness radii, we compare the number of binary-search steps of ATT-CLEVEREST-NN and ATT-CEGAR-NN within 6 h on the 20 `MR-queries`, where the larger number indicates better capability for approximating maximum robustness radii. The 20 `MR-queries` are obtained from the Points 1–5 of Reluplex [28] each of which has four queries (named Index 1–4) for approximating maximum robustness radii without changing the *clear-of-conflict* output advisory.

The results are shown in Table 2, where columns (No_c) and (No_a) give the number of binary search steps of ATT-CEGAR-NN and ATT-CLEVEREST-NN respectively. We can observe that ATT-CLEVEREST-NN excels in this case.

6 Related Work

CLEVEREST proposes a synergy between testing and CEGAR-based formal verification for neural networks. As there is a vast amount of literature regarding these topics, we discuss here the most relevant ones.

Robustness Testing. The robustness of neural networks have received extensive attention over the past few years. Many adversarial attacks under the white-box setting have been proposed [6, 12, 20, 32, 38, 45], where white-box means that all information about the network is available. White-box adversarial attacks often find counterexamples by leverage gradient information, therefore are highly efficient. There also exist black-box adversarial attacks [4, 9] that use only the inputs and outputs of the network to find counterexamples. We instantiate our methodology by leveraging the PGD adversarial attack which is a white-box one, as it is generally assumed that all network details are known during network verification. Remarkably, both black-box and white-box adversarial attacks could be leveraged in our CEGAR scheme thanks to the generality of our methodology.

Neural networks have also received attention from the perspective of traditional software testing. For example, DeepXplore [46] proposes the notion of neuron coverage to guide the testing process. Following their idea, a series of coverage criteria have been suggested for neural network testing [30, 36]. Conventional testing techniques have also been adapted to test neural networks, such as concolic testing [53] and mutation testing [37]. We did not use neuron coverage to guide testing in this work, as several coverage metrics are not related to robustness [13] and coverage-guided testing is mainly used to improve the coverage, instead of quickly finding counterexamples.

Neural Network Verification. Various formal verification techniques have been proposed to verify neural networks including robustness and fairness properties, based on abstract interpretation [18,21,33,40,42,49,50,56,57,59,60,62, 63,65], and constraint solving (e.g., SMT [15,24,28,29,48], LP and MILP [5, 14,34,55,61]). Although these approaches feature theoretical guarantees, they usually suffer limitations in either scalability or efficiency, hence are difficult to be applied to precisely verify large models in practice. To address the issue, different approaches have emerged. A few approaches, such as proof reuse [17], input quantization [26], divide-and-conquer [5], eager falsification [23] and network abstraction [2,16,19,47,52], have been proposed to accelerate the verification while some others were proposed to refine either the estimated output ranges [50,60,63,65] or the abstract network [16,44]. We instead offer an alternative solution by integrating the efficient yet inaccurate testing techniques into the CEGAR-based verification framework. As mentioned before, we did not compare with these approaches, as our main goal is to push the frontier of CEGAR-based verification approaches towards which this work makes a significant step.

Our methodology is general and can leverage any testing methods, iterative abstractions, CEGAR-based schemes and back-end verification engines. As these continue to improve, it is expected that our method will become more scalable.

Combination of Testing and Verification. There also exist techniques in the conventional software verification field combining testing and verification to mitigate the high complexity of verification. For instance, the authors in [11,25] combine both techniques together but the techniques do not assist each other. Instead, they test and verify different subprograms separately by program partitioning or constructing residual programs. The approaches proposed in [43,64] leverage testing techniques to choose a good abstraction for verification, whilst the authors utilize the information from testing to refine the abstraction in the case spurious counterexamples are found [3,22]. Our methodology CLEVEREST presents the first attempt to synergistically combine these two complementary techniques under the neural network setting, specifically, accelerating the de facto CEGAR framework by integrating the abstract-test-refine paradigm.

7   Conclusion

In this paper, we have proposed a new CEGAR-based framework CLEVEREST for DNN verification by synergistically combining testing and CEGAR-based verification techniques, which brings the best of both worlds. We have instantiated and implemented our methodology by leveraging the CEGAR-NN verification approach and the PGD adversarial attack, giving rise to the tool CLEVEREST-NN. Extensive experiments on the ACAS Xu DNN benchmark demonstrated the efficacy of our methodology.

A   Appendix

A.1   PGD Adversarial Attack Algorithm

Algorithm 4 describes the process of the PGD adversarial attack. Given a DNN N, an input $\vec{x} \in X$, the number of restart times n, the number of iteration steps per time m, a step size α, a L_∞ norm distance threshold ϵ, Algorithm 4 returns either an adversarial example $\vec{x}'$ such that $N_c(\vec{x}) \neq N_c(\vec{x}')$ and $\|\vec{x} - \vec{x}'\|_\infty \leq \epsilon$, or NULL indicating that no adversarial example can be found.

In detail, the outer for-loop (lines 1–11) performs up to n times of iterations, each of which has a randomized seed $\vec{x}'$ obtained by adding a Gaussian noise δ onto the input $\vec{x}$ (lines 2–3). During each iteration of the outer for-loop, the inner for-loop (lines 4–10) iteratively computes a seises of new samples (up to m samples) starting from the randomized seed $\vec{x}'$.

During each iteration of the inner for-loop (lines 4–10), Algorithm 4 first computes the classification result $y = N_c(\vec{x}')$ of the DNN N by forward propagating the input $\vec{x}'$ and then compares the result with the ground-truth class $N_c(\vec{x})$. If they are different, $\vec{x}'$ is an adversarial example and Algorithm 4 returns $\vec{x}'$. If they are the same, then $\vec{x}'$ not is an adversarial example. Algorithm 4 performs a backward propagation to get the gradient $\nabla_{\vec{x}}$ (line 9) from which a new sample $\vec{x}'$ is created (line 10).

Algorithm 4: PGD adversarial attack

---

input : a DNN N, an input $\vec{x}$, restart times n, number of steps per time m, step size α, L_∞ norm distance threshold ϵ

output: adversarial example $\vec{x}'$ or NULL

1 **for** $i \leftarrow 1$ **to** n **do**
2 $\quad$ Generate a Gaussian noise $\vec{\delta}$ such that $\|\vec{\delta}\|_\infty \leq \epsilon$;
3 $\quad$ $\vec{x}' \leftarrow \vec{x} + \vec{\delta}$; $\qquad\qquad$ /* Create a randomized seed */
4 $\quad$ **for** $j \leftarrow 1$ **to** m **do**
5 $\quad\quad$ $y \leftarrow N_c(\vec{x}')$; $\qquad\qquad$ /* Get the model output */
6 $\quad\quad$ **if** $y \neq N_c(\vec{x})$ **then**
7 $\quad\quad\quad$ **return** $\vec{x}'$; $\qquad\qquad$ /* Find an adversarial example */
8 $\quad\quad$ **else**
9 $\quad\quad\quad$ $\nabla_{\vec{x}} \leftarrow$ back_propagate($N, J(\vec{x}', N_c(\vec{x}))$); $\qquad$ /* Get gradient */
10 $\quad\quad\quad$ $\vec{x}' \leftarrow$ clip$_{\epsilon, \vec{x}}(\vec{x}' + \alpha \times \text{sign}(\nabla_{\vec{x}}))$; $\qquad$ /* Compute a new sample */
11 **return** NULL;

References

1. Apollo: an open, reliable and secure software platform for autonomous driving systems. http://apollo.auto (2018)
2. Ashok, P., Hashemi, V., Kretínský, J., Mohr, S.: Deepabstract: neural network abstraction for accelerating verification. In: Proceedings of the 18th International Symposium on Automated Technology for Verification and Analysis, pp. 92–107 (2020)

3. Beckman, N.E., Nori, A.V., Rajamani, S.K., Simmons, R.J., Tetali, S.D., Thakur, A.V.: Proofs from tests. IEEE Trans. Softw. Eng. **36**, 495–508 (2010)
4. Bu, L., Zhao, Z., Duan, Y., Song, F.: Taking care of the discretization problem: a comprehensive study of the discretization problem and a black-box adversarial attack in discrete integer domain. IEEE Trans. Dependable Secur. Comput. **19**(5), 3200–3217 (2022)
5. Bunel, R., Lu, J., Turkaslan, I., Torr, P.H.S., Kohli, P., Kumar, M.P.: Branch and bound for piecewise linear neural network verification. J. Mach. Learn. Res. **21**, 1–39 (2020)
6. Carlini, N., Wagner, D.A.: Towards evaluating the robustness of neural networks. In: Proceedings of IEEE Symposium on Security and Privacy, pp. 39–57 (2017)
7. Chen, G., et al.: Who is real Bob? adversarial attacks on speaker recognition systems. In: Proceedings of the 42nd IEEE Symposium on Security and Privacy, pp. 694–711 (2021)
8. Chen, G., Zhao, Z., Song, F., Chen, S., Fan, L., Liu, Y.: AS2T: Arbitrary source-to-target adversarial attack on speaker recognition systems. IEEE Trans. Dependable Secur. Comput., 1–17 (2022)
9. Chen, P., Zhang, H., Sharma, Y., Yi, J., Hsieh, C.: ZOO: zeroth order optimization based black-box attacks to deep neural networks without training substitute models. In: Proceedings of the 10th ACM Workshop on Artificial Intelligence and Security. pp. 15–26 (2017)
10. Clarke, E.M., Grumberg, O., Jha, S., Lu, Y., Veith, H.: Counterexample-guided abstraction refinement for symbolic model checking. J. ACM **50**(5), 752–794 (2003)
11. Czech, M., Jakobs, M.C., Wehrheim, H.: Just test what you cannot verify. In: Proceedings of the 18th International Conference on Fundamental Approaches to Software Engineering, pp. 100–114 (2015)
12. Dimitrov, D.I., Singh, G., Gehr, T., Vechev, M.: Provably robust adversarial examples. In: Proceedings of the International Conference on Learning Representations (2021)
13. Dong, Y., et al.: An empirical study on correlation between coverage and robustness for deep neural networks. In: Proceedings of the 25th International Conference on Engineering of Complex Computer Systems, pp. 73–82 (2020)
14. Dutta, S., Jha, S., Sankaranarayanan, S., Tiwari, A.: Output range analysis for deep feedforward neural networks. In: Proceedings of the 10th International Symposium NASA Formal Methods, pp. 121–138 (2018)
15. Ehlers, R.: Formal verification of piece-wise linear feed-forward neural networks. In: Proceedings of the 15th International Symposium on Automated Technology for Verification and Analysis, pp. 269–286 (2017)
16. Elboher, Y.Y., Gottschlich, J., Katz, G.: An abstraction-based framework for neural network verification. In: Proceedings of the 32nd International Conference on Computer Aided Verification (2020)
17. Fischer, M., Sprecher, C., Dimitrov, D.I., Singh, G., Vechev, M.T.: Shared certificates for neural network verification. In: Proceedings of the 34th International Conference on Computer Aided Verification, pp. 127–148 (2022)
18. Gehr, T., Mirman, M., Drachsler-Cohen, D., Tsankov, P., Chaudhuri, S., Vechev, M.T.: AI2: safety and robustness certification of neural networks with abstract interpretation. In: Proceedings of the 2018 IEEE Symposium on Security and Privacy, pp. 3–18 (2018)
19. Gokulanathan, S., Feldsher, A., Malca, A., Barrett, C.W., Katz, G.: Simplifying neural networks using formal verification. In: Proceedings of the 12th International Symposium NASA Formal Methods, pp. 85–93 (2020)

20. Goodfellow, I., Shlens, J., Szegedy, C.: Explaining and harnessing adversarial examples. In: Proceedings of the 3th International Conference on Learning Representations (2015)

21. Goubault, E., Palumby, S., Putot, S., Rustenholz, L., Sankaranarayanan, S.: Static analysis of ReLU neural networks with tropical polyhedra. In: Proceedings of the 28th International Symposium Static Analysis, pp. 166–190 (2021)

22. Gulavani, B.S., Henzinger, T.A., Kannan, Y., Nori, A.V., Rajamani, S.K.: SYNERGY: a new algorithm for property checking. In: Proceedings of the 14th ACM SIGSOFT International Symposium on Foundations of Software Engineering, pp. 117–127 (2006)

23. Guo, X., Wan, W., Zhang, Z., Zhang, M., Song, F., Wen, X.: Eager falsification for accelerating robustness verification of deep neural networks. In: Proceedings of the 32nd IEEE International Symposium on Software Reliability Engineering, pp. 345–356 (2021)

24. Huang, X., Kwiatkowska, M., Wang, S., Wu, M.: Safety verification of deep neural networks. In: Proceedings of the 29th International Conference on Computer Aided Verification, pp. 3–29 (2017)

25. Jalote, P., Vangala, V., Singh, T., Jain, P.: Program partitioning: a framework for combining static and dynamic analysis. In: Proceedings of the International Workshop on Dynamic Analysis (2006)

26. Jia, K., Rinard, M.C.: Verifying low-dimensional input neural networks via input quantization. In: Proceedings of the 28th International Symposium Static Analysis, pp. 206–214 (2021)

27. Julian, K.D., Lopez, J., Brush, J.S., Owen, M.P., Kochenderfer, M.J.: Policy compression for aircraft collision avoidance systems. In: IEEE/AIAA Digital Avionics Systems Conference (2016)

28. Katz, G., Barrett, C., Dill, D.L., Julian, K., Kochenderfer, M.J.: Reluplex: an efficient smt solver for verifying deep neural networks. In: Majumdar, R., Kunčak, V. (eds.) CAV 2017. LNCS, vol. 10426, pp. 97–117. Springer, Cham (2017). https://doi.org/10.1007/978-3-319-63387-9_5

29. Katz, G., et al.: The marabou framework for verification and analysis of deep neural networks. In: Proceedings of the International Conference on Computer Aided Verification, pp. 443–452 (2019)

30. Kim, J., Feldt, R., Yoo, S.: Guiding deep learning system testing using surprise adequacy. In: Proceedings of the IEEE/ACM 41st International Conference on Software Engineering, pp. 1039–1049 (2019)

31. Krizhevsky, A., Sutskever, I., Hinton, G.E.: ImageNet classification with deep convolutional neural networks. Commun. ACM 60(6), 84–90 (2017)

32. Kurakin, A., Goodfellow, I., Bengio, S.: Adversarial examples in the physical world. In: Proceedings of International Conference on Learning Representations (2017)

33. Li, J., Liu, J., Yang, P., Chen, L., Huang, X., Zhang, L.: Analyzing deep neural networks with symbolic propagation: Towards higher precision and faster verification. In: Proceedings of the 26th International Symposium Static Analysis, pp. 296–319 (2019)

34. Lin, W., Yang, Z., Chen, X., Zhao, Q., Li, X., Liu, Z., He, J.: Robustness verification of classification deep neural networks via linear programming. In: Proceedings of the IEEE Conference on Computer Vision and Pattern Recognition, pp. 11418–11427 (2019)

35. Liu, W., Song, F., Zhang, T., Wang, J.: Verifying ReLU neural networks from a model checking perspective. J. Comput. Sci. Technol. 35(6), 1365–1381 (2020)

36. Ma, L., et al.: DeepGauge: multi-granularity testing criteria for deep learning systems. In: Proceedings of the 33rd ACM/IEEE International Conference on Automated Software Engineering, pp. 120–131 (2018)
37. Ma, L., et al.: DeepMutation: mutation testing of deep learning systems. In: Proceedings of the 29th IEEE International Symposium on Software Reliability Engineering, pp. 100–111 (2018)
38. Madry, A., Makelov, A., Schmidt, L., Tsipras, D., Vladu, A.: Towards deep learning models resistant to adversarial attacks. In: Proceedings of the International Conference on Learning Representations (2018)
39. Mangal, R., Sarangmath, K., Nori, A.V., Orso, A.: Probabilistic Lipschitz analysis of neural networks. In: Proceedings of the 27th International Symposium Static Analysis, pp. 274–309 (2020)
40. Mazzucato, D., Urban, C.: Reduced products of abstract domains for fairness certification of neural networks. In: Proceedings of the 28th International Symposium Static Analysis, pp. 308–322 (2021)
41. Moosavi-Dezfooli, S., Fawzi, A., Frossard, P.: DeepFool: a simple and accurate method to fool deep neural networks. In: Proceedings of 2016 IEEE Conference on Computer Vision and Pattern Recognition, pp. 2574–2582 (2016)
42. Müller, M.N., Makarchuk, G., Singh, G., Püschel, M., Vechev, M.T.: PRIMA: general and precise neural network certification via scalable convex hull approximations. Proc. ACM Program. Lang. 6(POPL), 1–33 (2022)
43. Naik, M., Yang, H., Castelnuovo, G., Sagiv, M.: Abstractions from tests. In: Proceedings of the 39th ACM SIGPLAN-SIGACT Symposium on Principles of Programming Languages, pp. 373–386 (2012)
44. Ostrovsky, M., Barrett, C.W., Katz, G.: An abstraction-refinement approach to verifying convolutional neural networks. CoRR abs/2201.01978 (2022)
45. Papernot, N., McDaniel, P.D., Jha, S., Fredrikson, M., Celik, Z.B., Swami, A.: The limitations of deep learning in adversarial settings. In: Proceedings of IEEE European Symposium on Security and Privacy, pp. 372–387 (2016)
46. Pei, K., Cao, Y., Yang, J., Jana, S.: Deepxplore: automated whitebox testing of deep learning systems. In: Proceedings of the 26th Symposium on Operating Systems Principles, pp. 1–18 (2017)
47. Prabhakar, P., Afzal, Z.R.: Abstraction based output range analysis for neural networks. In: Proceedings of the Annual Conference on Neural Information Processing Systems (2019)
48. Pulina, L., Tacchella, A.: An abstraction-refinement approach to verification of artificial neural networks. In: Proceedings of the 22nd International Conference on Computer Aided Verification (2010)
49. Singh, G., Gehr, T., Mirman, M., Püschel, M., Vechev, M.T.: Fast and effective robustness certification. In: Proceedings of the Annual Conference on Neural Information Processing Systems, pp. 10825–10836 (2018)
50. Singh, G., Gehr, T., Püschel, M., Vechev, M.T.: An abstract domain for certifying neural networks. Proc. ACM Program. Lang. 3(POPL), 41:1–41:30 (2019)
51. Song, F., Lei, Y., Chen, S., Fan, L., Liu, Y.: Advanced evasion attacks and mitigations on practical ml-based phishing website classifiers. Int. J. Intell. Syst. 36(9), 5210–5240 (2021)
52. Sotoudeh, M., Thakur, A.V.: Abstract neural networks. In: Proceedings of the 27th International Symposium Static Analysis, pp. 65–88 (2020)
53. Sun, Y., Wu, M., Ruan, W., Huang, X., Kwiatkowska, M., Kroening, D.: Concolic testing for deep neural networks. In: Proceedings of the 33rd ACM/IEEE International Conference on Automated Software Engineerin, pp. 109–119 (2018)

54. Szegedy, C., et al.: Intriguing properties of neural networks. In: Proceedings of the 2nd International Conference on Learning Representations (2014)

55. Tjeng, V., Xiao, K., Tedrake, R.: Evaluating robustness of neural networks with mixed integer programming. In: Proceedings of the 7th International Conference on Learning Representations (2019)

56. Tran, H., et al.: Star-based reachability analysis of deep neural networks. In: Proceedings of the 3rd World Congress on Formal Methods, pp. 670–686 (2019)

57. Urban, C., Christakis, M., Wüstholz, V., Zhang, F.: Perfectly parallel fairness certification of neural networks. Proc. ACM Program. Lang. 4(OOPSLA), 185:1–185:30 (2020)

58. VNN-COMP: 2nd international verification of neural networks competition. https://sites.google.com/view/vnn2021 (2021)

59. Wang, S., Pei, K., Whitehouse, J., Yang, J., Jana, S.: Efficient formal safety analysis of neural networks. In: Proceedings of Annual Conference on Neural Information Processing Systems (2018)

60. Wang, S., Pei, K., Whitehouse, J., Yang, J., Jana, S.: Formal security analysis of neural networks using symbolic intervals. In: Proceedings of the 27th USENIX Security Symposium on Security, pp. 1599–1614 (2018)

61. Wong, E., Kolter, J.Z.: Provable defenses against adversarial examples via the convex outer adversarial polytope. In: Proceedings of the 35th International Conference on Machine Learning, pp. 5283–5292 (2018)

62. Yang, P., Li, J., Liu, J., Huang, C., Li, R., Chen, L., Huang, X., Zhang, L.: Enhancing robustness verification for deep neural networks via symbolic propagation. Formal Aspects Comput. 33(3), 407–435 (2021)

63. Yang, P., et al.: Improving neural network verification through spurious region guided refinement. In: Proceedings of 27th International Conference on Tools and Algorithms for the Construction and Analysis of Systems, pp. 389–408 (2021)

64. Yorsh, G., Ball, T., Sagiv, M.: Testing, abstraction, theorem proving: better together! In: Proceedings of the International Symposium on Software Testing and Analysis, pp. 145–156 (2006)

65. Zhang, H., Shinn, M., Gupta, A., Gurfinkel, A., Le, N., Narodytska, N.: Verification of recurrent neural networks for cognitive tasks via reachability analysis. In: Proceedings of 24th European Conference on Artificial Intelligence, pp. 1690–1697 (2020)

66. Zhang, H., et al.: Alpha-Beta-CROWN: a fast and scalable neural network verifier with efficient bound propagation (2021). https://github.com/huanzhang12/alpha-beta-CROWN

67. Zhang, Y., Zhao, Z., Chen, G., Song, F., Chen, T.: BDD4BNN: a BDD-based quantitative analysis framework for binarized neural networks. In: Proceedings of the 33rd International Conference on Computer Aided Verification, pp. 175–200 (2021)

68. Zhang, Y., Zhao, Z., Chen, G., Song, F., Zhang, M., Chen, T.: QVIP: an ILP-based formal verification approach for quantized neural networks. In: Proceedings of the 37th IEEE/ACM International Conference on Automated Software Engineering (2022)

69. Zhao, Z., Chen, G., Wang, J., Yang, Y., Song, F., Sun, J.: Attack as defense: characterizing adversarial examples using robustness. In: Proceedings of the 30th ACM SIGSOFT International Symposium on Software Testing and Analysis, pp. 42–55 (2021)

Author Index

Printed in the United States
by Baker & Taylor Publisher Services